IELTS Collected Papers 2

Research in reading and listening assessment

Recent titles in this series include:

Experimenting with Uncertainty: Essays in honour of Alan Davies
Edited by A. Brown, C. Elder, N. Iwashita, E. Grove, K. Hill, T. Lumley, K. O'Loughlin, T. McNamara

An Empirical Investigation of the Componentiality of L2 Reading in English for Academic Purposes
Edited by Cyril J. Weir, Yang Huizhong, Jin Yan

The Equivalence of Direct and Semi-direct Speaking Tests
Kieran O'Loughlin

A Qualitative Approach to the Validation of Oral Language Tests
Anne Lazaraton

Continuity and Innovation: Revising the Cambridge Proficiency in English Examination 1913–2002
Edited by Cyril J. Weir and Michael Milanovic

A Modular Approach to Testing English Language Skills: The development of the Certificates in English Language Skills (CELS) examination
Roger Hawkey

Issues in Testing Business English: The revision of the Cambridge Business English Certificates
Barry O'Sullivan

European Language Testing in a Global Context: Proceedings of the ALTE Barcelona Conference July 2001
Edited by Cyril J. Weir and Michael Milanovic

IELTS Collected Papers: Research in speaking and writing assessment
Edited by Lynda Taylor and Peter Falvey

Testing the Spoken English of Young Norwegians: A study of testing validity and the role of 'smallwords' in contributing to pupils' fluency
Angela Hasselgreen

Changing Language Teaching through Language Testing: A washback study
Liying Cheng

The Impact of High-stakes Examinations on Classroom Teaching: A case study using insights from testing and innovation theory
Dianne Wall

Assessing Academic English: Testing English proficiency 1950–1989 – the IELTS solution
Alan Davies

Impact Theory and Practice: Studies of the IELTS test and *Progetto Lingue 2000*
Roger Hawkey

IELTS Washback in Context: Preparation for academic writing in higher education
Anthony Green

Examining Writing: Research and practice in assessing second language writing
Stuart D. Shaw and Cyril J. Weir

Multilingualism and Assessment: Achieving transparency, assuring quality, sustaining diversity – Proceedings of the ALTE Berlin Conference, May 2005
Edited by Lynda Taylor and Cyril J. Weir

Examining FCE and CAE: Key issues and recurring themes in developing the First Certificate in English and Certificate in Advanced English exams
Roger Hawkey

Examining Reading: Research and practice in assessing second language reading
Hanan Khalifa and Cyril J Weir

Language Testing Matters: Investigating the wider social and educational impact of assessment – Proceedings of the ALTE Cambridge Conference, April 2008
Edited by Lynda Taylor and Cyril J Weir

Components of L2 Reading: Linguistic and processing factors in the reading test performances of Japanese EFL Learners
Toshihiko Shiotsu

Aligning Tests with the CEFR: Reflections on using the Council of Europe's draft Manual
Edited by Waldemar Martyniuk

Examining Speaking: Research and practice in assessing second language speaking
Edited by Lynda Taylor

IELTS Collected Papers 2

Research in reading and listening assessment

Edited by
Lynda Taylor
Consultant to University of Cambridge ESOL Examinations
and
Cyril J Weir
Powdrill Professor in English Language Assessment
University of Bedfordshire

CAMBRIDGE
UNIVERSITY PRESS

CAMBRIDGE UNIVERSITY PRESS
Cambridge, New York, Melbourne, Madrid, Cape Town,
Singapore, São Paulo, Delhi, Tokyo, Mexico City

Cambridge University Press
The Edinburgh Building, Cambridge CB2 8RU, UK

www.cambridge.org
Information on this title: www.cambridge.org/9781107602649

First published 2012

Printed in the United Kingdom at the University Press, Cambridge

A catalogue record for this publication is available from the British Library

Library of Congress Cataloging-in-Publication Data
IELTS collected papers 2: research in reading and listening assessment / edited by
Lynda Taylor and Cyril J Weir.
    p. cm. -- (Studies in language testing ; 34)
 Includes bibliographical references.
 ISBN 978-1-107-60264-9
1. Language and languages--Ability testing. 2. English language--Ability testing.
I. Taylor, Lynda B. II. Weir, Cyril J.

    P53.4.I355 2012
    428.0076--dc23
    2011046099

ISBN 978-1-107-60264-9

In memory of Morgan Terry
1949-2011

Contents

Series Editors' note

The International English Language Testing System (IELTS) has developed over the years in line with theoretical and technical developments in assessment. Lynda Taylor and Cyril Weir's general introduction to this volume is a very useful guide for those who wish to learn about the beginnings of IELTS, its subsequent development and its recent changes, particularly in the Academic Reading and Listening components of the examination.

Since 1995, the IELTS partnership has provided funding for research into various aspects of IELTS. Over the past decade IDP Education Australia and the British Council have jointly published a series of volumes containing reports from the IELTS Joint-funded Research Program and these have recently been made more readily available via the IELTS website.

Many of the grant-funded research studies conducted between 1995 and 2005 focused on the IELTS Speaking and Writing modules. Cambridge ESOL decided to publish an edited selection of these as Volume 19 in the Studies in Language Testing series, entitled *IELTS Collected Papers: Research in speaking and writing assessment* (Eds Taylor and Falvey 2007). At the time of publication it was hoped a companion volume might follow at some point focusing on research into reading and listening assessment. *IELTS Collected Papers 2* fulfils that aspiration by bringing together eight of the joint-funded studies conducted in recent years on the assessment of academic reading and listening in IELTS.

The eight studies published here provide rich insights into issues and concerns that were in the thoughts of those involved in the development and revision of IELTS during the late 1990s and the first decade of the 21st century. All the studies are directly relevant to claims of validity, quality and usefulness made for the IELTS Academic Reading and Listening components. A further important rationale for this volume is to illustrate how applied research into specific issues has contributed to the evolution of IELTS over this period and continues to inform changes to the test in various ways. As such, the reader's attention is drawn to Lynda Taylor's two chapters (5 and 10), which discuss the impact that the particular studies reported in this volume have had on IELTS revisions.

Issues investigated in Part 1 are: the relationship between the academic reading construct as measured by IELTS and the reading experiences of students in the first year of their courses at a British university (Weir, Hawkey, Green, Ünaldi and Devi); the reading requirements in IELTS test items and in university study (Moore, Morton and Price); the cognitive processes underlying the academic reading construct as measured by IELTS (Weir, Hawkey, Green and Devi); and the process of writing test items for the IELTS Academic Reading test (Green and Hawkey).

Part 2 contains four chapters focusing on various issues in listening assessment in IELTS: a cognitive validation of the lecture-listening component (Field); the use of tactics and strategies by Chinese students (Badger and Yan); predictive validity of student coping ability in English-medium undergraduate courses in Spain (Breeze and Miller); and the relationship between test takers' listening proficiency and their performance on the IELTS Speaking test (Nakatsuhara).

Reports of the eight research studies on IELTS combined with the general introduction to this volume and with the chapters on the impact of the studies on IELTS will be, we hope, a valuable contribution to the assessment community, not just to established testing professionals but also to new and recently joining members of the community.

IELTS Collected Papers 2 should be of immediate interest to all those directly involved with IELTS and to anyone concerned more generally with the assessment of reading and listening proficiency, especially as these relate to the demands of academic literacy.

Finally, we are pleased to be able to dedicate this volume to the memory of Morgan Terry. Morgan worked as a freelance consultant on IELTS from the early 1990s, when she and her husband, Steve, were part of a talented and committed team who took on the IELTS 95 Project to revise and re-engineer the test for a long-term and sustainable future. Over a 15-year period, Morgan worked on all the IELTS papers – Reading, Writing, Listening and Speaking. She served as Chair of the Speaking paper for 10 years and was instrumental in the 2001 redevelopment of the assessment criteria, rating scales and examiner training procedures. The growth and success of IELTS is in no small measure due to Morgan's vision and commitment as a faithful and enthusiastic member of the IELTS team. She was a respected colleague and a much-loved friend. Morgan's untimely death is a source of great sadness but we remain grateful for all that she gave us.

Michael Milanovic and Cyril J Weir
Cambridge – August 2011

Acknowledgements

We would like to express our thanks to all the volume contributors for submitting their original research project reports to be considered for publication in this edited volume of *IELTS Collected Papers* and for their willingness to make subsequent revisions in line with our editorial suggestions.

The volume could not have reached publication without the professional, technological and administrative assistance of various staff members based at Cambridge ESOL including: Gad Lim and John Savage in the Research and Validation Group; and Sally Downes in the Stakeholder Relations and Legal Affairs Group. We are grateful to all of them for their support throughout the production process.

Finally, the publishers are grateful to the original copyright holders for permission to use the copyright material reproduced in this book, especially the British Council and IDP:IELTS Australia who funded the research projects and agreed to their publication in an edited *Studies in Language Testing* volume.

Notes on volume contributors

Richard Badger is a senior lecturer in the School of Education at the University of Leeds, Leeds, UK. He co-ordinates the MA TESOL and ICT programme and teaches modules in Teaching and Learning in TESOL and Learning and Teaching Vocabulary. His research interests include authenticity in the teaching of academic writing, argument in academic contexts and academic listening. He has published in *Applied Linguistics, ELT Journal, the Journal of Second Language Writing, the Journal of Pragmatics, System* and *ESP Journal*. He is currently working on projects investigating how listening is taught in China and how IELTS relates to study skills.

Ruth Breeze is Director of the Institute of Modern Languages at the University of Navarra, Spain, where she teaches English for Law, English for Journalism and Academic Writing. She has a PhD in Language Education, and has published widely on discourse analysis and language teaching. She has participated in several research projects, including Transparency in the Acquired Language Competences (Leonardo da Vinci programme) and GRADUN (University of Navarra).

Sarojani Devi is a postgraduate student at the University of Bedfordshire, currently investigating the academic reading of first-year undergraduates at a British university.

John Field is Senior Lecturer in cognitive approaches to language learning at the CRELLA research unit of the University of Bedfordshire, UK. He also teaches at the Faculty of Education, Cambridge University. His main area of expertise is second language listening, on which he has researched and written widely. His recent book *Listening in the Language Classroom* (2008) won the Ben Warren Prize for its contribution to the field. He has written several books on psycholinguistics and is currently engaged in projects that explore the notion of cognitive validity in language testing. Before becoming an academic, he worked in many parts of the world as an ELT advisor, materials writer, curriculum designer and teacher trainer.

Anthony Green is Reader in Language Assessment at the University of Bedfordshire (UK). He is the author of *IELTS Washback in Context* (2007) and *Language Functions Revisited* (2011) and has published widely on language assessment. He is involved in managing funded research projects, supervising research students and carrying out language testing consultancies worldwide. He has extensive experience of all stages of test development and delivery including work as a test designer, item writer and examiner for tests of speaking skills. Current research and consultancy interests include the relationship between assessment and learning, especially in relation to the Common European Framework of Reference (CEFR), the assessment of literacy skills and practical test development.

Roger Hawkey has many years of experience in English language teaching, teacher education, course design, and assessment projects in Africa, Asia and Europe. He is now a consultant on testing with Cambridge ESOL and a Visiting Professor at the Centre for Research in English Language Learning and Assessment (CRELLA), University of Bedfordshire (UK). He has published widely in applied linguistics, language teaching and assessment, including three volumes in Cambridge's *Studies in Language Testing* series – *A Modular Approach to Testing English Language Skills* (2004), *Impact Theory and Practice* (2006) and *Examining FCE and CAE* (2009).

Paul Miller is Deputy Director of the Institute of Modern Languages at the University of Navarra, Spain, and Deputy Director of the University's Master's Degree in Language Teaching. He has a PhD in Applied Linguistics, and his research interests include medical English and computer assisted language learning.

Tim Moore is a senior lecturer in academic literacy at Swinburne University, Australia. He is co-author of *Critical Thinking and Language* (Continuum 2011). Along with research into the IELTS Reading module, he and co-researcher, Janne Morton, have also conducted IELTS-funded research into the Academic Writing module, published in *Studies in Language Testing* 19 (2007).

Janne Morton works in the School of Languages and Linguistics at the University of Melbourne, Australia, as a lecturer in ESL. She is currently completing her PhD in the area of socialisation into disciplinary discourses. Her research interests include academic literacies, spoken genres, and second language testing and assessment.

Fumiyo Nakatsuhara is a lecturer in Language Assessment at the University of Bedfordshire. She has a PhD in Language Testing and an MA in Applied Linguistics from the University of Essex. Her research interests include the nature of co-constructed interaction in various speaking test formats. Her MA dissertation received the IELTS MA Award 2005 from the IELTS partners (University of Cambridge ESOL Examinations, the British Council, and IDP: IELTS Australia). She is the author of the forthcoming book *The Co-construction of Conversation in Group Oral Tests* (Peter Lang). Her recent publications include a book chapter in O'Sullivan, B (ed. 2011) *Language*

Testing: Theories and Practices and research papers in *ELT Journal* (2008) and *Language Testing* (2011).

Steve Price works in the area of academic literacy at Swinburne University. He is currently writing up a PhD on the engagement with legal discourses by international post-graduate law students from non-English-speaking backgrounds. He has research interests in reading, discourse analysis and the discourses of Law.

Lynda Taylor is a Consultant to University of Cambridge ESOL Examinations and formerly Assistant Director of the Research and Validation Group there. She holds an MPhil and PhD in Applied Linguistics and Language Assessment from the University of Cambridge (UK). She has over 25 years' experience of the theoretical and practical issues involved in L2 testing and assessment, and has provided expert assistance for test development projects worldwide. She regularly teaches, writes and presents on language testing matters and has edited, co-edited and contributed to several of the volumes in Cambridge's *Studies in Language Testing* series, including *IELTS Collected Papers* (2007), *Multilingualism and Assessment* (2008), *Language Testing Matters* (2009), *Aligning Tests with the CEFR* (2010) and *Examining Speaking* (2011).

Aylin Ünaldi has a PhD in Applied Linguistics – Language Testing (Bogazici University, Turkey) and an MA in Applied Linguistics (University of Reading, UK). She has experience in foreign language teaching, teacher training, test development and validation. Her research interests include language test validation, academic literacy and reading into writing as an integrated academic skill. She is currently studying academic literacy for second language learners.

Cyril J Weir holds the Powdrill Chair in English Language Acquisition at the University of Bedfordshire (UK) and is Guest Professor at Shanghai Jiao Tong University, PRC. He has taught short courses and carried out consultancies in language testing, evaluation and curriculum renewal in over 50 countries worldwide. He has published many books on language testing, including *Language Testing and Validation: an evidence-based approach (2005)*, *Examining Writing* (2007) and *Examining Reading* (2009). He is also joint Series Editor of *Studies in Language Testing*. Current interests include academic literacy and test validation.

Xiaobiao Yan is a lecturer at Guangdong University of Foreign Studies in Guangzhou, Guangdong, China. He has been engaged in IELTS teaching and research for several years. His research interests are language testing, particularly for listening and writing, and SLA. He has published seven articles on language teaching and testing. He is currently working on a project sponsored by the Natural Science Foundation.

Introduction

Lynda Taylor
Consultant to Cambridge ESOL
Cyril J Weir
University of Bedfordshire

The IELTS Joint-funded Research Program

To support the ongoing development of the International English Language Testing System (IELTS), the IELTS partners co-ordinate an ongoing and wide-ranging research and validation programme. A major component of this programme for the past 15 years has been the grant-funded research.

The origins of this research date back to the mid-1990s when the IELTS Australia Board first set aside grant funding for research purposes associated with the IELTS test and invited external researchers to submit IELTS-related proposals for consideration and selection. The Board believed that such external research would complement internal research and validation activities being conducted by the IELTS partnership to provide valuable additional insights and information on a range of issues relating to the quality and standing of IELTS. Another reason for offering funding grants for external research studies was to help IELTS stakeholders (including English language professionals and teachers) to develop a greater knowledge and understanding of the test, and thus contribute to improved assessment literacy in the public domain. In 1998 the British Council joined IDP: IELTS Australia in setting aside annual funding for research grants and since that time the programme has been jointly funded by these two IELTS partners. Cambridge ESOL, the third IELTS partner, supports the Joint-funded Research Program through the provision of data, materials, advice and various other types of assistance to approved researchers.

The first round of funded studies was conducted in 1995 and selected reports resulting from these projects were edited and published jointly by English Australia English Language Intensive Courses for Overseas Students (ELICOS) and IELTS Australia as *IELTS Research Reports 1998*, Volume 1. Since 1998, 10 more volumes of *IELTS Research Reports* have been published. From 2006 onwards (*IELTS Research Reports 6*), most of the volumes were published jointly with the British Council and they contain a useful introduction by Lynda Taylor discussing and evaluating the impact of findings from the funded studies on the ongoing development of IELTS. In 2011 all the *IELTS Research Reports* were made freely available in electronic format via the IELTS website, in addition to being available for purchase in hard copy.

The annual IELTS Joint-funded Research Program is widely publicised via print and electronic media. The call for proposals is issued in April each year and it aims to reflect current concerns and issues relating to IELTS as a major international English language proficiency test with high-stakes value. A joint research committee, comprising representatives of the three IELTS partners, agrees on the year's research priorities and oversees the tendering process. Research proposals are reviewed and evaluated according to the following criteria:

- relevance and benefit of outcomes to IELTS
- clarity and coherence of the proposal's rationale, objectives and methodology
- feasibility of outcomes, timelines and budget
- qualifications and experience of proposed project staff
- potential of the project to be reported in a form which would be both useful to IELTS and of interest to an international audience.

In determining the quality of the proposals and the research to be carried out, the Committee consults with a panel of external reviewers and with members of Cambridge ESOL's Research and Validation Group, according to their specialist areas of expertise. Research projects are currently funded up to a maximum of £22,000 or AUS$36,000, though from 2012 this figure is expected to be significantly increased. The Committee also oversees the publication and/or presentation of research findings.

Since 1995 the outcomes of the funded research programme have made a significant contribution to the monitoring, evaluation and ongoing development of IELTS, with particular reference to:

- the assessment of speaking in IELTS, e.g. issues of task design, candidate discourse, assessment criteria, test bias, examiner/rater behaviour, examiner/rater training and monitoring
- the assessment of writing in IELTS, e.g. issues of task design, construct validity, features of writing performance, rater training and monitoring, approaches to assessment
- the assessment of reading in IELTS, e.g. issues relating to the construct of academic reading, cognitive processing in reading assessment, approaches to developing reading test materials
- the assessment of listening in IELTS, e.g. issues relating to the construct of academic listening, test-taker strategies, assessing listening-into-speaking ability

- the impact of IELTS in education and society, e.g. stakeholder attitudes, use of test scores, score gains, impact on courses and preparation materials, with key user groups
- computer-based assessment and IELTS.

One of the most valuable outcomes of reports from joint-funded projects is the surveys of recent literature they provide. These help the IELTS test developers stay up to date with theoretical and empirical work in a wide range of fields (including some that are only indirectly linked to language testing) allowing them to take account of these in their work.

Since 1995, more than 90 research studies and over 130 individual researchers have received grants under the IELTS Joint-funded Research Program (up to and including Round 16). Over the years, the funded research programme has become a key component within the larger research and validation agenda in support of IELTS and it reflects the IELTS partners' well-established commitment to the continuing improvement of the test.

The background to this volume

As the body of research from the Joint-funded Research Program steadily increased in the early 2000s, Cambridge ESOL considered publishing a selection of the funded project reports as a single volume, based around a common theme. In this way it was hoped they might become available to a wider audience and illustrate the value of this work within the larger research and validation agenda underpinning IELTS.

Many of the funded research studies conducted between 1995 and 2005 focused specifically on the IELTS Speaking and Writing components, both of which were receiving considerable attention at that time from the test developers. Findings from these external studies complemented internal validation and research studies conducted or commissioned by the IELTS partnership, especially those undertaken by Cambridge ESOL. Taken together, research findings directly informed major revision projects for the productive components of IELTS: the IELTS Speaking Revision Project took place between 1998 and 2001, and the IELTS Writing Revision Project was carried out between 2001 and 2005. Ten studies on IELTS speaking and writing assessment were therefore selected for a volume in the *Studies in Language Testing* series, produced jointly by Cambridge ESOL and Cambridge University Press. The volume was entitled *IELTS Collected Papers: Research in speaking and writing assessment*. It was jointly edited by Lynda Taylor and Peter Falvey and published in 2007. At that time it was hoped that a companion volume might follow at some point with a focus on IELTS reading and listening.

This volume – *IELTS Collected Papers 2: Research in reading and listening assessment*, co-edited by Lynda Taylor and Cyril J Weir – fulfils that aspiration by bringing together eight joint-funded studies on IELTS reading and listening assessment, all of which have been completed in recent years. The eight studies have direct relevance to validation claims made for the Academic Reading and Listening components of IELTS. As such, this title should be of immediate interest to test stakeholders and all who are directly involved with IELTS in some way, e.g. test takers, test score users and teachers preparing students for the test. However, the volume is also likely to be of interest to anyone concerned with the assessment of reading and listening proficiency in English, especially as it relates to language use for academic and professional purposes.

The four studies in Part 1 (Chapters 1–4) focus on the IELTS Academic Reading test. Findings from these studies provided the IELTS partners with valuable insights into the construct validity of the Academic Reading test, as well as into the nature and effectiveness of the test writing process. The four studies in Part 2 (Chapters 6–9) focus on the assessment of listening in IELTS. Findings from these studies offered rich insights into the construct validity of the Listening test, as well as into the nature of test takers' listening performance and the relationship between listening and speaking skills. The findings from the eight studies offer important evidence in support of claims about test usefulness, while at the same time helping to highlight specific aspects needing closer review and possible attention in future test revision projects. In combination with outcomes from other commissioned studies and internal validation investigations, they feed into the ongoing process of development and validation for the IELTS Reading and Listening tests.

The publication of *IELTS Collected Papers 2* is seen by the IELTS partners as part of their continuing contribution to the field of language testing and assessment in a number of ways. It allows more of the IELTS-related funded research conducted in recent years to be shared with a wider audience, not just among IELTS stakeholders but within the broader language testing and assessment community. One rationale for the IELTS Joint-funded Research Program is to promote and support research activity among test stakeholders which not only contributes to the ongoing validation and development of IELTS, but also helps to build greater knowledge and understanding of the strengths and limitations of the test. With this in mind and following the pattern of the earlier *IELTS Collected Papers* in 2007, two additional chapters have been included alongside the eight research reports in this volume. Chapters 5 and 10 review and evaluate the outcomes of the studies presented in this volume in terms of their specific implications for the validation and ongoing development of the IELTS Academic Reading and Listening components. In particular, these sections discuss the value of the research findings and explain why some recommendations made in the studies may not be straightforward to implement.

The development of reading and listening assessment in IELTS

The direct assessment of reading and listening proficiency is a long-established feature of the IELTS test. Its origins can be traced back more than 30 years to the development and introduction of ELTS (English Language Testing Service) – the test which preceded IELTS. To contextualise the more recent developments in the IELTS assessment of reading and listening proficiency, this Introduction will review how L2 reading and listening ability were tested in the past in IELTS and its predecessors. We summarise the history of the Reading and Listening components to provide readers with a brief chronological overview of the steady evolution of the test. For a more detailed and comprehensive account of the development of ELTS/IELTS, and its role within the broader context of English language proficiency assessment for academic purposes over more than half a century, the reader is recommended to consult *Assessing Academic English: Testing English proficiency 1950–1989 – the IELTS solution* by Davies (2008), published as Volume 23 in the *Studies in Language Testing* series.

The English Proficiency Test Battery (1965–80)

From 1965 until 1980 the British Council relied on an English language proficiency measure called the English Proficiency Test Battery (EPTB) as part of its procedures for recruiting overseas students into higher education in Britain. The EPTB was a traditional set of standardised tests in a multiple-choice format, focusing on the receptive skills of reading and listening together with a knowledge of grammar and pronunciation. (Facsimile test material for the original EPTB can be found in Appendices 2.1–2.3 of Davies (2008:120–135).)

Although the EPTB developers readily acknowledged the importance of writing and speaking skills, the practical problems of testing these skills (e.g. the requirement for skilled examiners), combined with the British Council's need for a test which could be taken in a short period of time, meant that tests of speaking and writing could not realistically be included in the EPTB. Thus it was tests of reading and listening comprehension which constituted the primary measures of students' English language proficiency via their implied relationship to students' ability to follow a university course and to pass the associated examinations at the end of the course. Davies (2008) explains the dilemma that faced the original EPTB designers:

> In other words, this was very much a pragmatic approach; could success on an English-medium academic course be predicted on the basis of tests

of reading and listening alone? There was no assumption that speaking or writing were in any way less important than reading and listening, rather, that if the test proved to be satisfactory, then it could be claimed that the language skills relevant to academic success were accessible through reading and listening. They could, of course, be equally accessible through writing and/or speaking if appropriate procedures could be found to test these skills (Davies 2008:14).

Davies records how the Reading component of EPTB included subtests of *grammatical structure, reading speed* and *comprehension* (both science and non-science texts), while the Listening component comprised subtests of *phonemic discrimination* (in isolation and in context), *intonation and stress* (in conversation), and *comprehension* (again, both science and non-science texts) (see Davies 2008:16–20 for more detail on the individual EPTB subtests). With regard to the linguistic features of the Listening subtests, it is interesting to note that the test developers decided to use only a Standard British English dialect, since this was 'the variety most in evidence among the educated', along with modified Received Pronunciation (RP), on the grounds that this was 'the most favoured accent and probably the one best described' (2008:14). The issue of how to address linguistic variation in test development has in recent years become the subject of much debate among applied linguists and test designers (see Taylor 2008, 2009). Though the policy decision made in the 1960s may now appear to us somewhat conservative, and some might see it as 'post-colonial', it is interesting to note that even in the 1960s the test developers clearly saw dialect and accent as a matter for consideration and decision.

In the mid-1970s a project was established to develop a replacement for the EPTB which would address some of the problems the test was facing (e.g. limitations on the number of parallel versions), and which could also take account of the significant changes that took place in the 1960s and 1970s in approaches to language learning and teaching. The new communicative competence paradigm brought with it a much greater emphasis on the use of language skills in context. For the testing of listening and reading this was to mean a move away from assessing linguistic knowledge and comprehension via discrete-point test items derived from the behavioural and structuralist paradigm of the 1960s/1970s, represented in tasks such as cloze-elide, C-test, phonemic or grammatical triplets and conversational adjacency pairs. Instead, there was a shift towards a much more contextualised, language-in-use oriented approach to testing comprehension of spoken and written language (see below). Not surprisingly, the decision to replace EPTB also inspired a fresh discussion of whether the new test could/should now include components to assess writing and speaking skills.

The testing of reading and listening in ELTS (1980–89)

The replacement for EPTB was a brand new test, developed jointly by the University of Cambridge Local Examinations Syndicate (UCLES) and the British Council, entitled the English Language Testing Service (ELTS). It was introduced in 1980 after a four-year period of development. The test's overall design reflected the new paradigm of communicative language teaching and testing, with its emphasis on authenticity and relevance and its concern to assess ability to use language rather than simply test knowledge about language (see Chapter 2 in Davies 2008 for a full account of the development of ELTS).

The new on-demand test also took account of the growing interest at that time in English or Language for Specific Purposes (ESP/LSP). Test tasks in ELTS were based on a careful analysis of the ways in which language was actually used in academic contexts, i.e. as part of study on university courses, and they were intended to reflect the use of language in the 'real world'. A strong emphasis on needs analysis and on communicative language demands in the study/work context meant that, alongside the Reading and Listening components, subtests of writing and speaking ability were now allocated a place within the new test – in the form of the Writing subtest and the Individual Interview.

As far as reading and listening were concerned, there were two 'General Tests' adopting a multiple-choice format: G1 tested reading and G2 tested listening (see summary details of both below). These General Tests were taken by all test takers, regardless of their academic speciality. In addition to G1 and G2, a subject-specific 'Modular Test' (M1) was offered to assess reading comprehension within a specific academic domain: M1 (Study Skills). This Study Skills component was linked to one of six academic 'domains' or areas of study (Life Sciences, Social Studies, Physical Sciences, Technology, Medicine, General Academic; the latter – General Academic – was designed for those whose areas of interest did not fit into any of the preceding domains). In addition to M1 for reading, there was also a writing test (M2) and an oral interview (M3) both of which were available across the six domains (see the Introduction in Taylor and Falvey 2007 for more details of the M2 and M3 modules).

For the three Modular tests – M1, M2 and M3 – each ELTS candidate received a source booklet relevant to their chosen discipline from the six domains available. The source booklet contained extracts from appropriate academic texts, including bibliography and index, and it formed the basis for not only the multiple-choice reading comprehension tasks in M1, but also the writing tasks in M2 and the main discussion in the M3 Interview.

Although undoubtedly innovative in its design and implementation when compared with EPTB and similar tests available at that time (e.g. the Educational Testing Service Test of English as a Foreign Language (TOEFL), the new ELTS test nevertheless presented a number of administrative and practical challenges from the outset. Davies (2008:38–40) reflects that ELTS was a much longer test than EPTB and was more complicated to administer given the multiple and 'tailored' components involved. The direct Writing and Speaking subtests required trained and standardised markers and examiners, thus posing an additional administrative burden on British Council test centres and their staff in terms of recruiting and managing suitably qualified personnel. Furthermore, it was often difficult to match the prospective test candidate to the most appropriate subject domain. Finally, generating sufficient comparable test forms across multiple testing domains posed significant challenges for test production and sustainability. (See also Criper and Davies 1988.)

The assessment of reading and listening in ELTS between 1980 and 1989 can be summarised as follows:

Reading test (G1)

- 40 multiple-choice test items, divided into three sections
- presented in a single question booklet together with the texts on which they are based
- Section 1: sentence-length texts
- Section 2: paragraph-length texts (Multiple Choice Question (MCQ) gap-filling)
- Section 3: three related newspaper articles, with some test items on each text independently and some on the texts as a group
- length = 40 minutes
- assessed on a nine-band scale
- clerically marked according to the MCQ key and using a template.

Listening test (G2)

- a tape and a question booklet with 35 multiple-choice test items in four sections
- Section 1: choosing from diagrams
- Section 2: listening to an interview
- Section 3: replying to questions
- Section 4: listening to a seminar
- length = approx. 35 minutes
- assessed on a nine-band scale
- clerically marked according to the MCQ key and using a template.

Study Skills test (M1)

- linked to one of six academic domains (Life Sciences, Social Studies, Physical Sciences, Technology, Medicine, General Academic)
- based on a source booklet containing 5–6 textual extracts for input – taken from books, articles, reports etc. related to the specific subject area plus additional contents pages, bibliographies, appendices and indices
- an accompanying question booklet with 40 multiple-choice test items
- length = 55 minutes
- clerically marked according to the MCQ key and using a template.

Facsimile Reading and Listening test papers (all versions) for the original ELTS introduced in 1980 can be found in Appendix 6.2 of Davies (2008:203–206).

The ELTS Revision Project (1986–89)

Shortly after its introduction in 1980, the British Council and UCLES commissioned the Institute for Applied Language Studies at the University of Edinburgh to undertake a detailed validation study of the test. The ELTS Validation Project (Criper and Davies 1988) explored aspects of the practicality, validity and reliability of the existing English Language Testing Service (ELTS). Work on the five-year validation project was completed in 1986. In addition, valuable research was conducted by applied linguists elsewhere in the UK during the early 1980s which shed light on the English for Academic Purposes (EAP) language and literacy needs of overseas students at British universities (e.g. Geoghehan 1983, Hawkey 1982, Weir 1983).

By 1986 the producers of ELTS determined that the test was once again due for formal review and possible revision. The report of the ELTS Validation Project provided a convenient starting point for the ELTS Revision Project, a three-year project (1986–89) set up under the direction of Professor Charles Alderson of Lancaster University. British Council management support came from a team headed by Dr Peter Hargreaves, who was at that time with the British Council and from 1988 head of the UCLES EFL Division. An Australian perspective was provided by Professor David Ingram of Griffith University, seconded to the revision project in Lancaster from 1987 with support from the International Development Program (IDP) of Australian Universities and Colleges; IDP later became one of three IELTS partners to produce the test from 1989 onwards.

A large-scale, questionnaire-based consultation exercise was conducted in the mid-1980s with various ELTS user groups (receiving institutions, British Council staff, overseas administrators, EAP teachers, language testers and applied linguists) in order to determine the perceived strengths and weaknesses of the existing test and the desirable characteristics of a revised test (see Alderson and Clapham 1992). User views were also gathered via focus group meetings.

In terms of the practicality and validity of ELTS, those responsible for administering the test at centre level expressed major concerns about the test's length and its logistical complexity, in particular the difficulty of selecting appropriate subject-specific modules for candidates. Specific concerns from test takers about the Reading and Listening components (G1, G2 and M1) touched upon the following issues: the varying ease or difficulty of the reading texts and tasks across and within the General and Modular tests (the M1 subject-specific component was seen as the most difficult); the proximity (or otherwise) of the M1 reading material to the test taker's background knowledge and focus of academic study; the quality of the G2 listening tape and poor acoustics at test venues; and pressure of time in the listening test. An exercise to reconstruct the needs analysis specification by aligning the ELTS Reading and Listening test items to Munby's list of specifications in his *Communicative Syllabus Design* (1978) highlighted the problems inherent in trying to match test items to specified language skills, as well as the challenge of adequate sampling of the relevant reading and listening skills in the tests and comparable coverage of these across the different domain-specific modules (Criper and Davies 1988:89–97).

The ELTS Validation Consultative Conference, held in July 1987, brought together language testing researchers from Britain, Australia, Canada and the USA to review the outcomes of the consultation exercise and to discuss possible options for the future of the test (Hughes, Porter and Weir 1988). It was generally agreed that the test needed shortening, its administration needed simplifying and its reliability needed to be improved.

As far as testing reading skills was concerned, the overlap between the G1 and M1 Reading components was felt to be such that one of these could be dropped without any great loss in order to reduce test length. The consultative committee considered that it made more sense to retain reading in M1 (rather than G1) since this linked reading directly to the M2 Writing component, creating a reading-into-writing proficiency measure which closely reflected academic literacy demands. Reading and writing would remain integrated so that, to some extent at least, candidates' written output depended on the reading input in the Reading subtest, though separate scores would be reported for the two skills.

With regard to testing listening skills, most members of the committee felt that it would be better to convert the Listening test (G2) into an M component, thus making it domain-specific and modular alongside the M1 reading (see Hughes, Porter and Weir 1988:101, Alderson and Clapham 1992:16–17). An integrative test was envisaged, perhaps involving candidates listening to a lecture, making notes and then carrying out a writing task. Unfortunately, practical and logistical constraints were to make such an approach impossible. Most test centres arranged for all candidates to take the existing ELTS G2 Listening test in one room. Offering multiple modular listening tests across different subject domains would require a separate room with appropriate play-back equipment for each version, or for the different Listening test versions to be run at different times. In either scenario, the administrative demands on test centres were deemed unacceptable. Alderson and Clapham comment as follows: 'Until the day when candidates could have individual headphones it looked as if it would be impossible to have Listening in the M component' (1992:17). The assessment of listening skills was therefore to remain 'general' rather than subject-specific. Interestingly, however, the original M3 Interview moved in the opposite direction to be located alongside G2 listening as a non-specific test of oral interaction (G3) (see Alderson and Clapham 1992 on the rationale for this).

ELTS was potentially to be used with 'access' students who needed to take a general proficiency measure but no subject-specific subtests of Reading and Writing. For this reason, it was proposed that a 'general' version of the test should be retained in some form. Listening and oral interaction would be general in nature, and a proposal was made to replace the discarded G1 reading with a lexis and structure component, later renamed 'Grammar' (see Alderson and Clapham 1992:16–17 for further discussion of the rationale for this component).

Finally, it was proposed to reduce the original six subject-specific modules to three to help simplify the module selection process:

- Physical Sciences and Technology (PST)
- Life and Medical Sciences (LMS)
- Arts and Social Sciences (ASS).

These three 'clusters' were believed to offer the best way of broadly categorising the wide range of subject areas represented within the test candidature. A fourth non-academic module was also envisaged to meet the needs of 'access' or vocational students, later referred to as the General Training module. For more details of this first stage of the ELTS Revision Project, see Alderson and Clapham (1992). By 1987 the proposed structure of the new ELTS envisaged:

- a general (G) component containing Grammar (G1) and Listening (G2) subtests, and a 15-minute Speaking subtest (G3)
- an academic (M) component linked to three subject-specific areas (PST, LMS and ASS) containing linked Reading (M1) and Writing (M2) subtests
- a non-academic (general training, i.e. vocationally oriented) component containing linked Reading (M1) and Writing (M2) subtests.

While the Grammar, Reading and Listening subtests would be clerically marked, the new Writing and Speaking subtests would require trained raters.

Information gathered during the early stages of the ELTS Revision Project enabled members of the revision team to redraft the content and format of the test, trial draft tasks and analyse the results with a view to making final decisions based on a combination of expert feedback and empirical evidence. Development and trialling of the revised ELTS test is fully described in Clapham and Alderson (1997), which contains a dedicated chapter on each of the subtests. Foulkes (1997) and Alderson and Clapham (1997) report respectively on the Listening (G2) and the Grammar (G1) subtests; Clapham (1997) discusses the Academic Reading module (M1), in its three domain-related versions; and David Ingram (1997) summarises work on the General Training Reading (M1) subtest.

Charles Alderson and Caroline Clapham provide a useful discussion on the extent to which a test of grammar may also be a test of reading and the implications of this for the work to revise ELTS in the late 1980s. The interested reader is referred directly to their chapter for more information on the G1 (grammar) component since, in the end, this proposed subtest did not go ahead as part of the operational test in 1989. The main reason for this was that trialling results showed such a strong correlation between the G1 subtest and results for the test as a whole that it was considered superfluous to requirements.

John Foulkes highlights a rather more innovative approach to testing listening than had been the case for the 1980 ELTS, both in terms of the stimulus materials and the item types: '. . . a guiding principle was to achieve coherence. There would be no use of discrete-point items, with unpredictable shifts in subject-matter and context . . . [T]he whole test would consist of continuous related speech, either in dialogue or 'mini-talk' form' (1997:4–5). This attempt at coherence and thematic unity across the separate parts of the test was realised through the central person of the storyline, though Foulkes himself acknowledges that this link risked being tenuous and not necessarily obvious to the test taker! Later on, this feature of the test became somewhat demanding and problematic in terms of item writing and test construction; for if one part of the test proved weak following pretesting, then to discard it risked causing thematic disruption across the test as a whole. Attempts at authenticity in the listening input also entailed a measure of compromise and made heavy demands on the test writing team. Foulkes comments: 'Linguistic content was intended to be plausible spoken language. In fact, all the material was scripted, rather than being taken from actual speech, but in the writing and recording an effort was made to incorporate such features of spoken language as hesitations, self-corrections, and – in 'lectures' or mini-talks – shifts of register, asides and digressions, and humour' (1997:5).

Item types to test listening included traditional four-option multiple choice, but also true/false and assorted short constructed response items, e.g. providing short answers to questions or 'guided note-taking' such as completing a form or a grid. Constraints on the marking process (i.e. clerical marking at the test centres in-country, rather than centrally in Cambridge) necessitated a simple and tightly controlled listening mark scheme that could be reliably applied by clerical markers and this inevitably impacted on the scope of test-taker responses. The overall aim in the test tasks was to provide a plausible purpose for listening and an appropriate response to make during listening. Time was to be given to test takers for prior reading and for review of answers afterwards. Though recordings were to be heard once only, stimulus material would contain some naturally occurring internal repetition.

An appendix to Foulkes' chapter contains extracts from the December 1989 Listening test specifications. These provide useful insights in terms of the text types to be sampled, the skills/functions to be covered, the contextual features (including accent variation) and the item types (1997:125–127).

Caroline Clapham (1997) describes the challenge of drafting specifications and test material to produce three comparable reading versions across the three somewhat diverse academic domains – Life and Medical Sciences (LMS), Physical Sciences and Technology (PST) and Arts and Social Sciences (ASS, later renamed BSS – Business Studies and Social Sciences). Decisions had to be agreed on number, length and type of reading texts, likely reading purposes (macro- and micro-) and acceptable item types; these included gapped summary, information transfer, diagram completion, multiple choice and open-ended questions. The Academic Reading module was intended to measure most sensitively at Bands 5, 6 and 7 on the ELTS nine-band scale, but also to function above and below these bands. Clapham describes the overall aim of the drafting, redrafting and trialling process as to:

> . . . make the IELTS reading modules as suitable as possible for students in the three broad areas of BSS, LMS and PST. This was a difficult task because each broad subject area covered two not so perfectly compat-ible narrower ones, so that PST, for example, had to be suitable for both chemists and engineers although the texts required in their two dis-ciplines are different both in subject matter and style. However, this is only a problem when selecting text types and topics; from our content validation study it appears that the academic reading skills required are the same in all three areas, and the test types, although not on the whole typical of the sorts of tasks students would do, are equally appropriate for all three subject areas (1997:66).

An appendix to Clapham's chapter gives extracts from the draft specifica-tions developed for the M1 reading module for LMS (1997:141–145). It pro-vides more detailed insights into how the team conceived the test focus, the stimulus materials and the test tasks.

David Ingram explains how the General Training module (GT) was intended for candidates who were not going on to university-based aca-demic programmes, but rather to undertake workplace experience or training programmes in English-speaking countries. For this purpose, a more general, non-specific test of reading was needed, in the tradition of the so-called Non-Academic module that had existed in the earlier ELTS, capable of measuring most effectively around Bands 4, 5 and 6. An appendix to Ingram's chapter gives extracts from the draft specifications developed for the General Training Reading module for LMS (1997:154–165). Again, it provides more detailed insights into how the team conceived the test focus, the stimulus materials and the test tasks.

A decision was also taken to restrict the highest level for General Training to Band 6 – for two reasons: first, it was considered doubtful whether the GT format would allow reliable rating over the whole nine-band range; and second, there was concern that the possibility of achieving a Band 9 on General Training might attract candidates to take GT rather than Academic for university access.

Draft specifications and tasks were initially developed by dedicated item writing teams for all the above modules, and these were redrafted after input from a range of experts, including applied linguists, pre-sessional and in-sessional English language teachers and tutors in a wide range of different subject areas. Cycles of piloting and main trialling were conducted, with both L2 students and native English speakers, to check the statistical properties of the individual test items and the test components, as well as to confirm the maintenance of standards between the new test and the previous incarnation of ELTS. (See Alderson and Clapham 1997, Clapham 1997, Foulkes 1997 and Ingram 1997 for more detail on the development of test specifications and test versions; see also Griffin and Gillis 1997 for results of the trialling exercises.)

Particular attention during the ELTS Revision Project focused on examining the relationship of test performance to scales and scores and the implications of this for assessing and reporting test performance on ELTS. Band scores had been a feature of the original ELTS from 1980 onwards with scores on the five tests (G1 Reading, G2 Listening, M1 Study Skills, M2 Writing and M3 Interview) reported on a 1–9 scale via a test report form. For G1, G2 and M1, the reported band scores were derived from the raw score on the relevant subtest by means of a conversion grid. The M2 and M3 band scores were derived semi-directly from the rating scale used for assessing writing and speaking performance. In addition, an overall band score was assigned to the test taker by averaging the five band scores. In this way the reporting function of ELTS sought to provide a measure of overall language proficiency and also to fulfil a more diagnostic function at the level of each skill assessed.

A key aim of the Revision Project team had been to enhance the score reporting function of ELTS by generating descriptors that would describe the quality of a test taker's performance on a given skill, thus aiding the process of score interpretation for the benefit of the test user, e.g. admissions officer or study skills co-ordinator. Alderson (1991, 1997) explains how difficult it was to develop such user-oriented descriptors for the Reading and Listening components of ELTS. Although band scale descriptors were initially drafted as part of the Revision Project for both reading and listening, it proved impossible to substantiate the sorts of ambitious and generalised claims made in the draft descriptors given the limited sampling that was possible within the content and length constraints of the actual Reading and Listening subtests. Alderson articulates the question facing the team as follows: 'is it possible to produce meaningful descriptors, for reporting purposes, for those tests where descriptors are not used to judge performance and therefore arrive at a score?' (1997:93). For the testing of writing and speaking, of course, verbal descriptors are typically used to rate performance and these rater-oriented scales can in turn inform the development of user-oriented verbal descriptions to help score users understand the meaning of test scores or grades in numeric form. For reading and listening, however, the situation is different; the indirect testing of reading and listening produces no visible 'performances' that can be described in a comparable manner to the descriptions of directly assessed writing and speaking performances. Alderson explains the conclusion reached by the Revision Project team on their draft reading and listening scales as follows:

> Since the Scales were not, and could not be, used for the purpose of test construction and since the statements they contained were clearly not tenable as descriptions of test performance, it was decided to abandon the attempt to describe performance on the indirect tests of reading and listening for the purpose of score reporting. Instead, reading and listening are reported on an 'overall scale', with general descriptions for each of the nine scale points (1997:94).

The revised ELTS test became operational in 1989 when it was renamed the International English Language Testing System (IELTS) to reflect the involvement from 1987 of the International Development Program of Australian Universities and Colleges (IDP). One important aspect of the new management partnership for IELTS from 1989 was that it ensured a fully international perspective and helped counter any tendency towards a Eurocentric bias. The final formats of the Reading and Listening components introduced for IELTS from 1989 were as follows:

IELTS Academic Reading module
- linked to one of three academic domains (PST, LMS and ASS, later BSS)
- a question booklet containing 3–4 reading passages (a maximum total of 2,500 words), accompanied by around 40 items using multiple choice, multiple matching, true/false/not given and short constructed response formats

- length = 55 minutes
- assessed on a nine-band scale
- clerically marked according to the MCQ key.

IELTS General Training Reading module

- based on a question booklet containing several reading passages (a maximum total of 2,000 words), accompanied by around 40 multiple choice, multiple matching, true/false/not given and short constructed response items
- length = 55 minutes
- assessed on a six-band scale (i.e. no higher than Band 6)
- clerically marked according to the MCQ key.

IELTS Listening test

- tape and question booklet containing around 40 test items, divided across two stages each containing two sections
- Stage 1: language skills needed in social situations, typically involving informal and semi-formal transactional situations e.g. obtaining accommodation, form-filling; one monologue and one dialogue, to include some accent variation
- Stage 2: a test of general listening ability but based within study-related contexts and situations common to the experience of all students, e.g. introduction to library, lecture on a general topic; one conversation with up to four speakers, one monologic lecture – formal and informal styles
- multiple choice, multiple matching, true/false and short constructed response items, including gap filling and summary completion
- length = 30 minutes
- assessed on a nine-band scale
- clerically marked according to the MCQ key.

Facsimile test papers for all IELTS Reading and Listening subtests (and for the Speaking and Writing subtests) can be found in Appendix 12.3 of Davies (2008:381–447). See also Chapter 4 of Davies (2008) for further insightful commentary on the ELTS Revision Project 1987–89.

The testing of reading and listening in IELTS (1989–95)

Following its introduction in 1989, IELTS gained steadily in worldwide rec-ognition and the candidature grew accordingly, from just over 14,000 can-didates for ELTS in 1988 to over 30,000 for ELTS by 1993. By this time, the test was available to candidates in 186 test centres in 105 countries. In the same period, organisational changes within the IELTS partnership (British Council, IDP and UCLES) paved the way for the next review and revision of the test, and developments at UCLES in the early 1990s were particularly significant in this regard.

Developments at UCLES in the early 1990s

By 1990 Dr Peter Hargreaves had moved from the British Council to head up the new English as a Foreign Language (EFL) Division at UCLES in Cambridge. A new Evaluation Unit, headed by Dr Michael Milanovic, had also been created within the EFL Division to focus on matters of validation and research for all the English language proficiency tests produced by Cambridge at that time. Particular attention focused on improving procedures for producing test materials, and on collecting and analysing item-level and task-based responses from candidates taking the Cambridge English tests. This included increased pretesting of materials for item and task calibration and the creation of an electronic item-banking system to enable more effective test construction and equating. More detailed information about the test-taker populations for the Cambridge EFL tests was also needed to achieve an understanding of background factors and test-taker characteristics such as age, gender, first language, level of education, etc.; only by gathering, storing and analysing such data would it be possible to undertake research triangulating test content, candidate background and test performance.

A significant move towards this overarching goal was the development of scannable, Optical Mark Reader (OMR) answer sheets for objectively scored tests such as those for reading, listening and use of English in the Cambridge exams. OMR answer sheets captured test responses directly from candidates – either as a selected response (e.g. candidate shades in a lozenge A, B, C or D), or as a constructed response (e.g. candidate writes in a word or short phrase); in the latter case, the candidate's answers were clerically marked centrally in Cambridge and the clerical marker recorded whether the response was right or wrong by shading the appropriate lozenge. In both cases, the completed answer sheet then passed through a scanning machine to provide electronic datasets of test responses at item level; these in turn could be analysed in a variety of ways – using statistical software packages – to answer questions about test facility, discrimination, and other technical measurement issues. The early 1990s saw extensive exploration by Cambridge into the use of OMR technology for capturing not only candidate responses (to Reading, Listening and Use of English test items), but also examiner assessments (awarded in direct Speaking and Writing tests) as well as key information on candidate background variables via a scannable Candidate Information Sheet (CIS) routinely completed by test takers as part of the test administration. (See Milanovic 1995 for more discussion of the procedures and systems developed at Cambridge during this period.)

Research and development in all the above areas for Cambridge's Main Suite of EFL tests (referred to in this volume as *KET*, *PET*, *FCE*, *CAE*, *CPE*, but recently rebranded as *Cambridge English: Key*; *Preliminary*; *First*; *Advanced*; and *Proficiency*) continued during the period 1990–95 and impacted on the continuing evolution of IELTS, largely because of the central role played in test construction by UCLES as one of the three IELTS partners, especially in relation to the major revision of IELTS undertaken in 1995.

Another emerging area of interest for Cambridge and for other language testers at that time was ethics and professional standards (Kunnan 2000, Saville 2003). In 1990 UCLES began collaborating with other European institutional providers of language examinations within the context of the newly formed Association of Language Testers in Europe (ALTE). Work began to articulate and communicate professional standards for language test providers in the European context. Founder members of the association agreed the importance of a Code of Practice for examination developers and examination users which would help ensure quality and fairness in developing and using assessment procedures. Discussion of what constitutes principles of good practice has continued ever since and reflects a concern for accountability in all areas of assessment. In this respect, it recognises the importance of *test validation* and the role of *research and development* in examination processes. In 1994, ALTE published its first Code of Practice which set out the standards that members of the association aimed to meet in producing their language tests; other testing-related organisations have contributed to an ongoing debate in this area, e.g. *Standards for educational and psychological testing* (AERA/APA/NCME 1999) and the International Language Testing Association's *Code of Ethics* (2000). (See Milanovic and Weir 2004 for more discussion of the development of ALTE.)

There were yet other developments going on in the world of language testing at this time which helped shape assessment theory and practice at Cambridge in the early 1990s and which would inevitably impact on the evolution of IELTS. Davies (2008) highlights the growing role played by technology, suggesting that 'advances in technology were making the development of computerised testing more and more likely and it therefore seemed prudent to build scope for that development into a revised IELTS (2008:92). Furthermore, advances in applied linguistics, language testing and measurement theory, especially recent work on test validity and the consequences of test use (e.g. Bachman 1990, Messick 1989) led to attempts to 'reconcile theoretical developments in applied linguistics and language testing and in measurement theory with a testing organisation's requirements of production and delivery' (Davies 2008:92–93).

The IELTS 95 Revision Project (1992–95)

In the light of the interests and developments outlined above, the IELTS partners turned their attention once again in the early 1990s to the next stage in the evolutionary development of IELTS. This was to include not only a review of test content and format, but also a major 're-engineering' of key aspects of test delivery, administration and processing in order to ensure that IELTS would be able to cope with the increasing demands being placed on it. This was especially urgent given the opening up in the 1990s of opportunities in international education leading to growing numbers of students, especially in the Far East, seeking higher education in English-speaking countries such as Australia, Canada, the USA and the UK.

Results from routine test monitoring and evaluation in the period 1989–94, together with some specially commissioned and independent work conducted on IELTS by external experts (e.g. Clapham 1993) led to the IELTS 95 Revision Project (1992–95) which introduced further modifications to IELTS from April 1995. As in previous projects, the revision process involved successive and iterative cycles of review, consultation, drafting, redrafting and trialling before final decisions were confirmed. This approach was consistent with the model of test development and revision that was emerging at Cambridge ESOL in the early 1990s (see Hawkey 2009, Saville 2003). Significant modifications were made to IELTS in seven key areas (for more details see Charge and Taylor 1997). They included:

- removal of subject-specific subtests and replacement with a single Academic module and a non-academic General Training module (see Clapham 1996 for further discussion of the rationale underlying this); in addition the thematic link between the Reading and Writing components was removed
- the extension of the General Training scales for reading and writing to nine bands to bring them into line with the nine-band scale used for the Academic module
- the extension of the window for the administration of the Speaking component to three days (instead of one) thus allowing greater flexibility in test centres to accommodate rising candidate numbers
- enhancement of the IELTS question paper production methodology for purposes of quality assurance
- enhancement of routine systems for capturing data on test-taker performance and background to improve test processing, validation and research
- improved security measures relating to despatch, management and retirement of IELTS test forms
- a new test centre administration package (ESOLComms) and training for staff at all British Council and IDP test centres.

It will be clear from this brief summary that many of the changes made in the IELTS 95 Revision Project were driven as much by practical concerns, administrative problems and technological developments, as by applied linguistic and measurement issues. This points to the importance of recognising the complex infrastructure which accompanies any large-scale, high-stakes assessment endeavour. The long-term usefulness and sustainability of any test will inevitably depend as much on the successful design of the systems and procedures for producing, delivering and evaluating it in a sustainable way, as on the initial design of test content and format.

Following a period of consultation and a review of the available research, the Revision Project team based in Cambridge drafted revised test specifications for IELTS which were then sent out for external review. The International IELTS Advisory Committee (which included language testing experts from the UK, USA, Australia and New Zealand) gave feedback on the drafts at a two-day meeting in August 1993. A further round of redrafting took place in 1993–94 followed by trialling of test materials, including trialling of individual tasks and full test versions with pre-university, English L1 students in the UK and Australia. (See Chapter 5 in Davies (2008) for more details of the project, the draft specifications, the trialling and the final decisions.)

For the IELTS Reading and Listening components, the major changes in 1995 related to:

- replacement of the three academic subject-specific modules with a single Academic module and a non-academic General Training module
- removal of the thematic link between the Reading and Writing components
- the introduction of computerised item-banking for all reading and listening passages and their accompanying test items so as to enable accurate test equating.

Despite the earlier reduction in 1989 from six to three subject-specific modules, even this simpler, three-way subdivision had continued to cause administrative problems for test centres and receiving institutions between 1989 and 1995. Test candidates and their teachers, along with test centre staff, were sometimes unclear about the appropriate subtests for different courses, and whether to match a candidate to a module based on their previous or intended discipline area. Feedback from IELTS administrators and examiners supported a reduction in the number of subtests. In addition, monitoring of subtest take-up showed that around 75% of IELTS test takers were taking Module C (Business Studies and Social Sciences). Results from Cambridge's internal research into a single-module option, together with results from Clapham's independent investigation into second language reading and ESP testing (Clapham 1996), suggested that one test for all academic candidates did not discriminate for or against candidates of any discipline area.

For this reason, the IELTS 95 Revision Project moved in the direction of one Academic Reading module and one Academic Writing module.

In addition, the strong thematic link between the Reading and Writing components (both Academic and General Training) was removed on the grounds that such a link, though desirable in some respects, increased the potential for confusing the assessment of writing ability with the assessment of reading ability. Monitoring of candidates' writing performance suggested that the extent to which candidates exploited the reading input varied considerably. Some candidates drew heavily on the written content of the reading texts, apparently treating the writing task as a measure of their reading ability; as a result, many risked masking their actual writing ability. Other candidates chose to articulate their own ideas on the topic, either making very little reference to the reading texts or forging artificial connections for the sake of the task. In some cases candidates were confused about whether it would be better to articulate their personal point of view on the topic or to reflect a more 'authoritative' view expressed in the reading text(s). This variation in candidates' treatment of the linked writing task made the achievement of fair assessment at the marking stage a complex process so a more equitable form of task design was sought. Removal of the link also made it easier to control comparability of task difficulty across the multiple test forms that needed to be produced for the IELTS Reading and Writing components each year.

In their 1997 article explaining the changes made to IELTS in 1995, Charge and Taylor comment as follows:

> The revision of IELTS was undertaken in response to four equally important factors: practical concerns, administrative problems, technological developments and theoretical issues. All the changes made in 1995 took account of recent research and development in applied linguistics and language testing, and were only introduced after extensive consultation with the international language testing community (1997:379).

The final format of the Reading and Listening components introduced for IELTS in 1995 was as follows:

IELTS Academic Reading module

- one Academic module only
- no thematic link between the Reading and Writing components
- three sections, each containing one reading passage of 750–1,000 words; total word count = max 2,500
- 40 items across the whole test, approx. 13–14 items per reading passage
- a variety of objectively scored item types: multiple choice, short answer, sentence completion, notes/summary/diagram/table completion, multiple matching (e.g. headings to paragraphs), classification

- reading passages and test items appear together in the question booklet; candidates record their responses on scannable answer sheets
- length of module = 60 minutes
- assessed on a nine-band scale.

IELTS Listening test

- four sections: Stage 1 – Social situations (Section 1 – dialogue, Section 2 – monologue); Stage 2 – Course-related situations (Section 3 – conversation; Section 4 – monologue, e.g. extract from lecture/talk)
- 40 items across the whole test, approx. 10 items per section
- a variety of objectively scored item types: multiple choice, short answer, sentence completion, notes/summary/diagram/table completion, multiple matching (e.g. headings to paragraphs), classification
- test items printed in question booklet
- listening material recorded on cassette and played once
- candidate instructions on cassette and in question booklet
- length = approx. 30 minutes, including time to read questions and write answers in question booklet
- additional 10 minutes to transfer answers from question booklet to answer sheet
- assessed on a nine-band scale.

IELTS General Training Reading module

- no thematic link between the Reading and Writing components
- three sections: 1) social survival (2–4 texts, up to 150 words each); 2) survival in a training context (2–3 texts, 300–500 words each); 3) general reading (1–2 texts, totalling 750–1,000 words)
- 40 items across the whole test, approx. 13–14 items per section
- a variety of objectively scored item types: multiple choice, short answer, sentence completion, notes/summary/diagram/table completion, multiple matching (e.g. headings to paragraphs), classification
- reading passages and test items appear together in the question booklet; candidates record their responses on scannable answer sheets
- length of each module = 60 minutes
- assessed on a nine-band scale.

IELTS research programme from 1995 onwards

Following the introduction of the revised IELTS in 1995, an overarching research framework was established by the IELTS partners to embrace all activities relating to future test research and validation. These included everything, from routine internal test validation and other research studies carried out by Cambridge ESOL, to the externally managed studies which received grant funding from the IELTS Australia Board (from 1995) and from the British Council (from 1998).

The IELTS Impact Study Project (1995–2003)

Growing professional and public concern about the effects of large-scale tests on educational processes, and on society more generally, stimulated Cambridge ESOL to consider how these effects might be investigated in a rigorous and systematic manner, and then to establish a long-term research programme exploring the concepts of test impact and the socio-ethical consequences of test use (Messick 1989). As a high-profile and high-stakes international test, IELTS was considered by Cambridge to be a prime candidate for the investigation of impact. For this reason, as soon as the revised test went live in April 1995, work began in collaboration with a team at Lancaster University to develop suitable research hypotheses, instrumentation, and procedures for monitoring the effect of the test on four key areas:

- the content and nature of classroom activity
- the content and nature of teaching materials
- the views and attitudes of user groups
- the test-taking population and use of test results.

A full account of this work to date is published as Volume 24 in the *Studies in Language Testing* series (Hawkey 2006).

The current approach to assessing reading and listening in IELTS

Although extensive revisions were made to the IELTS Speaking and Writing subtests in 2001 and 2005, relatively few significant changes have been made to the Reading and Listening components since the last major revision of IELTS in 1995. From May 2009, a small but important change was made to the General Training Reading module. Previously, Section 2 of the General Training Reading module focused on the vocational training context, in line with the inherited legacy of the test. From 2009 onwards, Section 2 focused on the workplace context (e.g. applying for jobs, company policies, pay and condition, workplace facilities, staff development etc.). This reflected the fact that the IELTS General Training module was increasingly being taken up by certain employers, professional bodies and immigration authorities who recognised it as meeting their needs for a reliable and secure English language proficiency measure. This change to

Section 2 followed extensive consultation with key stakeholder groups in order to ensure that the module more closely met the needs of candidates taking IELTS for employment or immigration purposes.

Today, a comprehensive and transparent set of test production and validation procedures is in place to support claims about the quality and usefulness of IELTS reading and listening assessment. Information on the technical qualities of these subtests is increasingly available in the public domain, and research studies continue to explore a range of issues in preparation for future test revision and development cycles. Some of these aspects are described in more detail in the following sections.

The production of IELTS Reading and Listening test materials

The IELTS Question Paper Production (QPP) process aims to generate materials for the IELTS test against explicit quality standards. As explained on the IELTS website, the production of IELTS question papers is a lengthy process which includes a number of quality checks. The objective of these checks is to ensure that the material in each test is suitable for the test purpose in terms of topics, focus, level of language, length, style and technical measurement properties. The QPP process employs both qualitative standards for the production of test material involving the judgement of qualified professionals, and quantitative, statistical standards for the selection of suitable test material and the maintenance of consistent levels of test difficulty over time. The stages in the process of producing question papers are shown in Figure 1 below. The first three stages of commissioning, pre-editing and editing involve gathering and choosing appropriate test content that reflects the aims of the Academic and General Training modules. Once the best material has been selected, it is then administered to representative groups of language learners to check that each

Figure 1 The Question Paper Production process for IELTS

question – or item – is at an appropriate difficulty level for IELTS; that candidates will be able to understand the questions and that each question can differentiate between more and less able candidates. This stage is known as pretesting. Approved material is stored in an item bank and can then be introduced to live tests – tests that are used as the basis for awarding official IELTS Test Report Forms – through a process known as standards fixing. Each of these stages is explained in more detail below.

Commissioning

There are one or two commissions each year for each of the item writing teams. These feed material into the QPP process. To reflect the international nature of IELTS, test material is written by trained groups of item writers in the United Kingdom, Australia, New Zealand and the USA and is drawn from publications sourced anywhere in the world. Overall test content is the responsibility of both externally commissioned language testing professionals (the chairs for each of the Listening, Reading, Writing and Speaking subtests) – and of Cambridge ESOL staff.

Item writers work from test specifications. These specifications detail the characteristics of the IELTS subtests, outline the requirements for commissions and guide writers in how to approach the item writing process including selecting appropriate material, developing suitable questions and submitting material for pre-editing and editing.

Pre-editing

Pre-editing is the first stage of the editing process and takes place when commissioned materials are initially submitted in draft form by item writers. A meeting is held involving chairs and Cambridge ESOL staff to review the material.

The purpose of pre-editing is to ensure that test material is appropriate in terms of:

- topic
- topicality
- level of language
- suitability for the task
- length
- focus of the text
- style of writing
- focus of the task
- level of the task.

At this stage, guidance is given to item writers on revising items and texts for resubmission. This is seen as an important element in item writer training and advice is also offered on any rejected texts and unsuitable item types.

Editing

Following pre-editing feedback, material is revised and submitted for editing. Editing takes place at meetings involving Cambridge ESOL staff and chairs. Item writers are encouraged to attend editing meetings dealing with their material. This is seen as another important part of their ongoing training. At the editing stage, texts and selected items are approved for pretesting or are sent back to a writer for further revision. Revised material is then re-edited at a subsequent meeting.

Pretest construction and pretesting

IELTS pretests are very similar to the tests that will be used in live administrations. Listening pretests are professionally recorded to ensure that they are of acceptable quality. Listening and reading pretests are administered to IELTS candidates at selected test centres or to prospective candidates on IELTS preparation courses. The pretests are marked at Cambridge ESOL and statistically analysed.

Pretest review

The Validation Unit at Cambridge ESOL collates and analyses the pretest material. All candidate responses are analysed to establish the technical measurement characteristics of the material, i.e. to find out how difficult the items are, and how they distinguish between stronger and weaker candidates. Both classical item statistics and latent trait models are used in order to evaluate the effectiveness of the material. Classical item statistics are used to identify the performance of a particular pretest in terms of the facility and discrimination of the items in relation to the sample that was used. Rasch analysis is used to locate items on the IELTS common scale of difficulty. In addition, the comments on the material by the staff at pretest centres and the immediate response of the pretest candidates are taken into account.

At a pretest review meeting, the statistics, the feedback from candidates and teachers, and any additional information are reviewed and informed decisions are made on whether texts and items can be accepted for inclusion into potential live versions. Material is then stored in the item bank to await test construction.

Banking of material

Cambridge ESOL has developed its own item banking software for managing the development of new live tests. Each test section or task is banked with statistical information as well as comprehensive content description. This information is used to ensure that the tests that are constructed have the required content coverage and the appropriate level of difficulty.

Standards fixing and grading

Standards fixing ensures that there is a direct link between the standard of established and new test versions before they are released for use at test centres around the world. Different versions of the test report results on the same underlying scale, but band scores do not always correspond to the same percentage of items correct on every test form. Before any test task is used to make important decisions, it is important first to establish how many correct answers on each Listening or Reading test equate to each of the nine IELTS bands. This ensures that band scores on each test indicate the same measure of ability.

Once the test production team is satisfied with the quality of the material, each new test task is introduced as part of a live administration (with limited numbers of candidates and under tightly controlled conditions). Information from this exercise is used to confirm the estimate of how difficult the new task is when compared with the established test material. The task is then ready to be used in combination with other material as part of a fully live test.

Test construction

At regular test construction meetings, Listening and Reading papers are constructed according to established principles. Factors taken into account are:

- the difficulty of complete test versions and the range of individual items
- the balance of topic and genre
- the balance of gender and accent in the Listening subtest
- the balance of item format (i.e. the relative number of multiple choice and other item types across versions)
- the range of listening/reading skills tested.

The item banking software allows the test constructor to model various test construction scenarios in order to determine which tasks should be combined to create tests that meet the requirements.

Marking

All marking of IELTS Listening and Reading subtests takes place at the test centre by trained markers and examiners. Markers of the Reading and Listening subtests are trained to understand the IELTS marking policy and are required to demonstrate that they are marking to standard before they are allowed to mark. Systematic monitoring and double marking of a proportion of answer sheets is carried out at each administration. Markers also undergo a re-certification process every two years to ensure that their marking remains up to standard.

Score processing, reporting and interpretation

Candidates receive scores on a Band Scale from 1 (low) to 9 (high). A profile score is reported for each skill – listening, reading, writing and speaking. The four individual scores are also averaged and rounded to produce an Overall Band Score. Overall Band Scores and scores for each skill-based subtest are reported in whole bands or half bands. Candidates receive a Test Report Form setting out their Overall Band Score and their scores on each of the four subtests: Listening, Reading, Writing and Speaking. Each of these subtest scores is equally weighted. The Overall Band Score is calculated by taking the mean of the total of the four individual subtest scores.

IELTS Listening and Reading papers each contain 40 items and every correct answer is awarded one mark. The maximum raw score a candidate can achieve on a paper is 40. Band scores ranging from Band 1 to Band 9 are awarded to candidates on the basis of their raw scores. Although all IELTS test materials are pretested and trialled before being released as live tests, there are inevitably minor differences in the difficulty level across tests. In order to equate different test forms, the band score boundaries are set so that all candidates' results relate to the same scale of achievement. This means, for example, that the Band 6 boundary may be set at a slightly different raw score across test forms.

The Academic and General Training modules are graded to the same scale. The distinction between the two modules is one of genre or discourse type. Academic papers may contain source texts featuring more difficult vocabulary or greater complexity of style. It is usual that, to secure a given band score, a greater number of questions must be answered correctly on a General Training Reading paper.

Table 1 Reliability estimates for reading and listening forms released in 2010

	Number of test forms	Average alpha
Academic Reading	48	.90
General Training Reading	24	.91
Listening	48	.91

Table 2 Mean, standard deviation and standard error of measurement (SEM) of reading and listening (2010)

	Mean	Standard deviation	Standard error of measurement
Academic Reading	6.04	1.30	0.389
General Training Reading	5.97	1.21	0.382
Listening	5.74	1.37	0.412

Estimating and reporting reliability of IELTS reading and listening assessment

Every year the test producers release multiple forms of the Academic Reading, General Training Reading and Listening components for use by centres testing IELTS candidates worldwide on up to 48 fixed testing dates throughout the year. The reliability of the objectively scored Reading and Listening tests is estimated and reported using Cronbach's alpha which measures the internal consistency of each 40-item test. The reading and listening material released in 2010 had sufficient candidate responses to estimate and report meaningful reliability values as shown in Table 1. The figures obtained for the Listening and Reading components indicate the expected levels of reliability for tests containing 40 items.

Since 2001 the IELTS Annual Review has reported the range of mean band scores for Reading (both Academic and General Training) and Listening test forms released each year, and results show a very consistent pattern across different forms (Table 2).

Information on test quality now appears routinely on the IELTS website as part of annual reporting on test performance. In addition to the routine of test development and validation, the IELTS partners carry out additional academic research to support the tests and sponsor external researchers. Details of this research are given in the IELTS Annual Review, which can also be accessed on the IELTS website: www.ielts.org

Current and future developments

This introductory chapter has attempted to trace the steady development of the Reading and Listening subtests in ELTS and IELTS from the earliest days up to the present moment.

The success of the ELTS and IELTS Reading and Listening modules has always depended upon the close and professional relationship maintained between the three IELTS partners, which reflects a willingness to regularly review the status quo and to embrace change as required, as well as a readiness to share responsibility in matters of test design, production, delivery and processing. At the current time, Cambridge ESOL takes responsibility for matters of test design and production, while the British Council and IDP: IELTS Australia provide the global centre network and manage the worldwide marking and examiner cadre.

Advances in applied linguistics, language pedagogy, psychometrics and technological capabilities constantly challenge test developers to review, refine and reshape their approaches to test design, development, delivery and evaluation. The steady evolution of ELTS and IELTS since the mid-1970s testifies to this reality and demonstrates clearly how such factors shape the life of a large-scale, high-stakes language proficiency measure. The strength of the international IELTS partnership has meant that each new era of challenge has led to creative and innovative responses which seek not only to ensure the intrinsic value of the test in terms of its contemporary relevance and continuing usefulness for immediate test stakeholders, but also to contribute more broadly to our growing understanding of the nature of language proficiency and its place within linguistics and language education.

Conclusion

Twenty-five years ago, in October 1986, an academic conference was held to consider carefully the implications of the *ELTS Validation Project Report*. In their introduction to the published proceedings of that event, Hughes, Porter and Weir (1988) commented as follows:

> The publication of a detailed validation study represents an exercise in public accountability: the question of how far the test does the job it was intended to do is addressed, and is seen to be addressed. The information yielded by such a study is moreover of fundamental importance in the dynamic process of continuing test development. The ELTS test is itself not a static instrument . . . (1988:4).

Hopefully, this introductory chapter has succeeded in demonstrating the extent to which IELTS, like its predecessor ELTS, is not a 'static instrument' but continues to experience a 'dynamic process of continuing test development'. The eight research studies presented in this volume, all of which were funded and supported by the IELTS partners, make an important contribution to that ongoing and dynamic process. As will be apparent from the discussion in Chapters 5 and 10, they complement other IELTS-related research (both internal and externally commissioned) in the ongoing effort to provide a quality measurement instrument for assessing English language proficiency. Like its predecessor, therefore, *IELTS Collected Papers 2* seeks to be 'an exercise in public accountability'.

Lynda Taylor and Cyril J Weir
August 2011

References

AERA/APA/NCME (1999) *Standards for Educational and Psychological Testing*, Washington, DC: American Educational and Research Association/American Psychological Association/National Council for Measurement in Education.

Alderson, J C (1991) Bands and scores, in Alderson, J C and North, B J (Eds) *Language Testing in the 1990s: The Communicative Legacy*, London: Modern English Publications and The British Council, 71–86.

Alderson, J C (1997) Bands and scores, in Clapham, C and Alderson, J C (Eds) *IELTS Research Report 3: Constructing and Trialling the IELTS Test*, Cambridge: The British Council/UCLES/IDP, 87–108.

Alderson, J C and Clapham, C (1992) *IELTS Research Report 2: Examining the ELTS Test – An Account of the First Stage of the ELTS Revision Project*, Cambridge: The British Council/UCLES.

Alderson, J C and Clapham, C (1997) The General Modules: Grammar, in Clapham, C and Alderson, J C (Eds) *IELTS Research Report 3: Constructing and Trialling the IELTS Test*, Cambridge: The British Council/UCLES/IDP, 30–48.

Bachman, L F (1990) *Fundamental Considerations in Language Testing*, Oxford: Oxford University Press.

Charge, N and Taylor, L B (1997) Recent developments in IELTS, *ELT Journal* 51 (4), 374–80.

Clapham, C (1993) Is ESP Justified? in Douglas, D and Chapelle, C (Eds) *A New Decade of Language Testing Research*, Virginia: TESOL, 257–271.

Clapham, C (1996) *The Development of IELTS: A study in the effect of background knowledge on reading comprehension*, Studies in Language Testing volume 4, Cambridge: UCLES/Cambridge University Press.

Clapham, C (1997) The Academic Modules: Reading, in Clapham, C and Alderson, J C (Eds) *IELTS Research Report 3: Constructing and Trialling the IELTS Test*, Cambridge: The British Council/UCLES/IDP, 49–68.

Clapham, C and Alderson, J C (Eds) (1997) *IELTS Research Report 3: Constructing and Trialling the IELTS Test*, Cambridge: The British Council/ UCLES/IDP.

Criper, C and Davies, A (1988) *ELTS Research Report I(i): ELTS Validation Project Report*, Cambridge: The British Council/UCLES.

Davies, A (2008) *Assessing Academic English: Testing English Proficiency 1950–1989 – the IELTS Solution*, Studies in Language Testing volume 23, Cambridge: UCLES/Cambridge University Press.

Foulkes, J (1997) The General Modules: Listening, in Clapham, C and Alderson, J C (Eds) *IELTS Research Report 3: Constructing and Trialling the IELTS Test*, Cambridge: The British Council/UCLES/IDP, 3–13.

Geoghehan, G (1983) *Non-Native Speakers of English at Cambridge University*, Cambridge: Bell Educational Trust.

Griffin, P and Gillis, S (1997) Results of the trials: a cross-national investigation, in Clapham, C and Alderson, J C (Eds) *IELTS Research Report 3: Constructing and Trialling the IELTS Test*, Cambridge: The British Council/ UCLES/IDP, 109–124.

Hawkey, R (1982) *An Investigation of Inter-Relationships between Cognitive/ Affective and Social Factors and Language Learning*, unpublished PhD thesis, University of London.

Hawkey, R (2006) *Impact Theory and Practice: Studies of the IELTS Test and Progetto Lingue 2000*, Studies in Language Testing volume 24, Cambridge: UCLES/Cambridge University Press.

Hawkey, R (2009) *Examining FCE and CAE: Key Issues and Recurring Themes in Developing the First Certificate in English and Certificate in Advanced English Examinations,* Studies in Language Testing volume 28, Cambridge: UCLES/ Cambridge University Press.

Hughes A, Porter, D and Weir C J (1988) *ELTS Research Report I(ii): ELTS Validation Project: proceedings of a conference held to consider the ELTS Validation Project Report,* Cambridge: The British Council/UCLES.

Ingram, D (1997) The General Training Module, in Clapham, C and Alderson, J C (Eds) *IELTS Research Report 3: Constructing and Trialling the IELTS Test,* Cambridge: The British Council/UCLES/IDP, 81–86.

International Language Testing Association (ILTA) (2000) *Code of Ethics,* retrieved March 10, 2011, from: http://www.iltaonline.com/index. php?option=com_content&task=view&id=57&Itemid=47

Kunnan, A J (2000) Fairness and justice for all, in Kunnan, A J (Ed.), *Fairness and Validation in Language Assessment, Selected Papers from the 19th LTRC, Orlando, Florida,* Studies in Language Testing volume 9, Cambridge: UCLES/ Cambridge University Press, 1–14.

Messick, S A (1989) Validity, in Linn, R L (Ed.), *Educational Measurement* (3rd edn), Washington DC: The American Council on Education and the National Council on Measurement in Education, 13–103.

Milanovic, M (1995) Series Editor's note, in Bachman, L F, Davidson, F, Ryan, K and Choi, I C, *An Investigation into the Comparability of Two Tests of English as a Foreign Language: The Cambridge-TOEFL Comparability Study,* Studies in Language Testing volume 1, Cambridge: UCLES/Cambridge University Press, vii–xi.

Milanovic, M and Weir, C J (2004) Series Editors' note, in Milanovic, M and Weir, C J (Eds) *European Language Testing in a Global Context,* Studies in Language Testing volume 18, Cambridge: UCLES/Cambridge University Press, vii–xi.

Munby, J (1978) *Communicative Syllabus Design,* Cambridge: Cambridge University Press.

Saville, N (2003) The process of test development and revision within UCLES EFL, in Weir, C J and Milanovic, M (Eds) *Continuity and Innovation: Revising the Cambridge Proficiency in English Examination 1913–2002,* Studies in Language Testing volume 15, Cambridge: UCLES/Cambridge University Press, 57–120.

Taylor, L (2008) Language varieties and their implications for testing and assessment, in Taylor, L and Weir, C J (Eds) *Multilingualism and Assessment: Achieving Transparency, Assuring Quality, Sustaining Diversity – Proceedings of the ALTE Berlin Conference, May 2005,* Studies in Language Testing volume 27, Cambridge: UCLES/Cambridge University Press, 276–295.

Taylor, L (2009) Setting language standards for teaching and assessment: a matter of principle, politics or prejudice? in Taylor, L and Weir, C J (Eds) *Language Testing Matters: Investigating the Wider Social and Educational Impact of Assessment – Proceedings of the ALTE Cambridge Conference, April 2008,* Studies in Language Testing volume 31, Cambridge: UCLES/Cambridge University Press, 139–157.

Taylor, L and Falvey, P (Eds) (2007) *IELTS Collected Papers: Research in Speaking and Writing Assessment,* Studies in Language Testing volume 19, Cambridge: UCLES/Cambridge University Press.

Weir, C J (1983) *Identifying the Language Problems of Overseas Students in Tertiary Education in the United Kingdom,* unpublished PhD thesis, University of London.

Part One
Academic Reading

1

The relationship between the academic reading construct as measured by IELTS and the reading experiences of students in their first year of study at a British university

*Cyril Weir, Roger Hawkey, Anthony Green,
Aylin Ünaldi and Sarojani Devi*
University of Bedfordshire, UK

Abstract

This study investigates the academic reading activities and problems of students in their first year of study at a British university, and compares the emerging model of academic reading with an analysis of the reading construct as tested in the IELTS Academic Reading module. The contextual parameters of the reading texts of target students are reviewed and a comparison made with those performance conditions obtaining for reading activities in the IELTS test. The extent to which any problems in reading might decrease the higher the IELTS Reading band score obtained before entry is investigated.

1 Introduction

The aims of the project were:

- to establish the nature of academic reading activities performed across a range of courses at a British university with particular reference to contextual parameters and cognitive processing
- to investigate problems experienced by students with respect to these parameters
- to provide initial broad spectrum data on the relationship(s) between the IELTS Reading module and reading in an academic context
- to determine the extent to which any problems in reading might decrease the higher the IELTS Reading band score obtained before entry.

2 Rationale

It is critical that receiving institutions can depend on the results of language tests as valid indicators of the English language proficiency of students with respect to the academic courses they are going to follow. Hawkey (2006:126) finds receiving institutions are concerned with both international students' academic reading problems and with some of the ways in which reading is tested by IELTS.

In the academic context, a high premium is placed on students being able to extend their knowledge beyond what is learned in their university class-room context. To succeed in this, students need to *read to learn* (Maclellan 1997). They must use an appropriate combination of the skills and strategies that are required for the different purposes of reading in tertiary level study. Enright, Grabe, Koda, Mosenthal, Mulcany-Ernt and Schedl (2000) assert that this will involve processing beyond the level of searching *for information* and *basic comprehension of main ideas* in a text and require an understanding of *how information in a text as a whole is connected*, and how to *integrate information from across a variety of texts* for use in written assignments or exam essays. The extent to which these purposes are required in tertiary level study and the extent to which IELTS can predict any problems in fulfilling them are in need of investigation.

A review of the literature indicates that, to date, no serious studies appear to have been undertaken in which the focus is on the contextual parameters and cognitive processing involved in academic reading (see Weir 2005), and the symmetry of these with the IELTS Reading test. In the context of linking students' academic reading activities and problems with the IELTS test, research into reading under the joint British Council–IDP IELTS funded research programme has so far been limited. Only two of the studies since 1995 have had an exclusive focus on the IELTS Reading module. Further research such as the present study is clearly still needed.

The aim of this study is to investigate the academic reading activities and problems of students (both undergraduate and postgraduate) in their first year of study at a British university, then to compare an emerging model of academic reading with our analysis of the reading construct as tested in the IELTS Reading module. This survey of the theoretical and empirical research on reading will thus focus on the nature of reading comprehension, including its cognitive processes, skills and strategies, and then review various models of reading to take account of these elements. Relevant contextual factors such as the reading texts of our target students will then be discussed and a comparison made with those performance conditions obtaining for reading activities in the IELTS test.

3 Reading

The traditional approach to reading adopted by psychologists, language testers and teachers is based on a slow, careful, incremental view of reading for comprehension. In contrast to this orthodoxy, Weir (1983) provided survey data suggesting L2 readers have particular problems in expeditious reading, i.e. quick, selective and efficient reading in the target language. Given the expectation that students need to understand the whole domain of knowledge covered by their degree programme, this entails processing large amounts of text (paper- and web-based) expeditiously (that is quickly, selectively and efficiently) as a precursor to the careful reading which takes place once relevant information has been located (Urquhart and Weir 1998). As Weir (1983) and Weir, Yang and Jin (2000) showed, careful reading ability is not sufficient in itself for academic study.

We advocate a four-cell matrix which distinguishes systematically reading level from reading type, a distinction now significant in many of the reading studies and models in the field. The matrix accounts for key areas in this review of the relevant reading literature. In its distinction between careful and expeditious reading, the issue of the range of purposes, strategies, skills and processes involved in reading is raised. Taking account of recent work in the field we include in the careful reading cell the activities of *careful reading to understand the way ideas are connected in the whole of a text* and the *integration of information across texts* for the purposes of completing written assignments and/or exam essays building on the work of Enright et al (2000). With regard to reading *purpose*, Jordan (1997) similarly makes the connection between academic reading and the writing-based tasks or activities, for assignments, dissertations, projects or reports, for which the reading is often a preparation.

This framework assumes a multi-componential model of reading and its assessment. In the identification of both a global and a local level at which the reading strategies, skills and processes may operate, the question of the place and role of linguistic elements associated with reading performance is raised. The extent to which the test or the reality requires students to comprehend information within and beyond the sentence is a key issue (see Alderson 2000). The themes and elements informing this matrix are pursued below.

3.1 Careful and expeditious reading: processes and problems

Careful reading is characterised as identifying lexis, understanding syntax, seeking an accurate comprehension of explicit meaning and making propositional inferences. These take place at a local or a global level, i.e. within or beyond the sentence right up to the level of the complete text.

Recent research (e.g. Cohen and Upton 2006, Hawkey 2006, Rosenfeld,

Oltman and Sheppard 2004), as well as our initial experience with our project students themselves (see pilot study questionnaire responses in Study 1 below), indicates that careful reading alone is an inadequate construct for the students targeted by our research.

Khalifa and Weir (2009) suggest, in their review of the literature on examining reading, that the significant drawback of many process-based models of reading, as well as many of the earlier componential models of reading (Bernhardt 1991, Coady 1979) is that they are nearly all premised on a careful reading model and do not take sufficient account of the different purposes of reading. They cite Hoover and Tunmer (1993), who observed that their notion of the simple view 'assumes careful comprehension: comprehension that is intended to extract complete meanings from presented material as opposed to comprehension aimed at only extracting main ideas, skimming, or searching for particular details' (1993:8). They also refer to Rayner and Pollatsek (1989:439) who stated that for most of their account of the reading process they are focusing on the skilled, adult reader reading material of the textbook variety. They admit that careful reading models have little to tell us about how skilled readers can cope with other reading behaviours such as skimming for gist (Rayner and Pollatsek 1989:477–478). Most of these reading models therefore fail to describe the processing experience of skilled readers in real-life reading activities.

The actual academic reading demands faced by our target students are likely to involve *expeditious* as well as careful reading (see Weir 1983). Urquhart and Weir (1998) use the term 'expeditious reading' to describe 'how readers process texts quickly and selectively, i.e. expeditiously, to extract important information in line with intended purposes' (1998:101). The construct includes a range of reading types (Urquhart and Weir 1998), abilities (Cohen and Upton 2006, Enright et al 2000), micro-skills (e.g. Munby 1978), skills (e.g. Levine, Ferenz and Reves 2000), and strategies (e.g. Purpura 1998). These overlapping terms exemplify the 'fair amount of confusion' in the literature noted by Urquhart and Weir (1998) in the labelling, and perhaps the conceptualisation, also of elements in the reading activity. Weir et al (2000:19) distinguish between skills defined as text-driven, largely subconscious linguistic processes involved in reading, and those defined as reader-driven, purposeful and conscious aspects of reading.

Expeditious reading would appear likely to include, for new university students, *skimming, search reading,* and *scanning. Skimming* is generally defined (e.g. Levine et al 2000, Munby 1978, Urquhart and Weir 1998, Weir 2005) as reading to obtain the gist, general impression and/or superordinate main idea of a text. The reader asks: 'What is this text as a whole about?', while avoiding anything which looks like detail. For Urquhart and Weir (1998) the defining characteristics of skimming are (a) the reading is selective, with sections of the text either omitted or given very little attention; (b) an attempt is made to build up a macrostructure (the gist) on the basis of as few details from the text as possible. The reader is trying to reach the top-level structure of a text, that is, the discourse topic.

For Urquhart and Weir (1998) *search reading* involves locating information on predetermined topics. The reader wants information to answer set questions or to provide data for example in completing written assignments. It differs from skimming in that the search for information is guided by predetermined topics so the reader does not necessarily have to establish a macro-propositional structure for the whole of the text.

Unlike in careful reading, Urquhart and Weir (1998) argue that in expeditious reading, the linearity of the text is not necessarily followed. The reader is sampling the text, which can be words, topic sentences or important paragraphs, to extract information on a predetermined topic in search reading or to develop a macrostructure of the whole text as in skimming. The process can be top-down when the reader is deciding how to sample the text and which part(s) of the text to be sampled; it can also be bottom-up when the reader's attention is on the sampled part(s) of the text.

Scanning involves reading selectively, to achieve very specific reading goals, e.g. finding the number in a directory, finding a particular author's name. The main feature of scanning is that any part of the text which does not contain the pre-selected symbol(s) is dismissed. It may involve looking for specific words/phrases, figures/percentages, names, dates of particular events or specific items in an index at the local word level. Rosenshine (1980) defines it as involving recognition and matching.

The types of reading summarised in the matrix above will not necessarily be associated with particular types of text. Students may be scanning books, journals (hard copy or online), newspapers or websites, or they may be skimming them or reading them carefully according to their reading purposes, not because of the types of text concerned. Clearly, our collection of data on the nature and the problems of the academic reading activities of the students across their different courses must cover all their reading sources (see Levine et al 2000), not just hard copy.

There is evidence that L1 as well as L2 academic readers have problems (e.g. Urquhart and Weir 1998, Weir 1983). Many universities, including the university at which this study was carried out, offer support programmes for both. But the research in the literature often indicates marked difference between the problems faced by L1 and L2 university students (e.g. Cohen and Upton 2006, Tercanlioglu 2004). Tercanlioglu suggests that L1 students use meta-cognitive strategies more frequently in their academic reading where ESL students may have to spend much of their available processing capacity on decoding information. The *meta-cognitive strategies* referred to here, as in educational psychology, are strategies we exercise consciously involving the active control over the cognitive processes engaged in learning. Livingston

(1997) cites planning how to approach a given learning task, monitoring our comprehension, and evaluating our progress towards the completion of a task as examples of meta-cognitive strategies.

3.2 Models of reading

The relevance to our study of relationships between the academic reading construct as measured by IELTS and the reading experiences of students in the first year of their courses at a British university has already involved us in a consideration of reading types, levels, strategies, skills, sub- or micro-skills, processes, needs and purposes and, now, meta-cognition. This suggests the need to consider models of academic reading in order to frame the study and clarify relationships between the key constructs. The right model would help identify the most appropriate combinations of processes, skills and strategies to be employed for the different types and purposes of reading to achieve effective comprehension of texts from a range of sources.

The models of reading in the literature tend to be categorised under generalised labels. A brief survey of these is helpful in informing the model to be developed in this study even though, as might be expected, the labels and constructs involved overlap and are not used consistently.

Perhaps the most fundamental consideration in the development of a model of the academic reading of new students across fields of study is the *componentiality of reading*. As Weir et al (2000) ask: 'Can reading be broken down into underlying skill or strategy components for the purposes of teaching and testing?' (2000:14). The discussion above already suggests that it can, but the reading research nevertheless includes examples of what Weir and Porter (1994) refer to as 'unitary', 'bi-divisible' and 'multi-divisible' models of the reading construct. They cite empirical studies supporting the single factor hypothesis including Carver (1992), Lunzer, Waite and Dolan (1979) and Rosenshine (1980). Schedl, Gordon, Carey and Tang (1996), in their TOEFL research report on the dimensionality of the TOEFL reading comprehension items, also support the existence of a general reading ability and the essential uni-dimensionality of the TOEFL Reading test, although they accept that there may be a second factor relating to text content or position.

Weir et al (2000) suggest that part of the reason for the uni-componential view of the reading construct is that product-based studies of reading test scores typically use factor analysis. Factor analysis is all about *reduction*, and may be somewhat insensitive to subtle differences such as those across related reading skills and processes. Factor analysis may thus tend to show apparently different reading skills behaving in similar statistical ways. This may be taken to imply that there is one broad ability of reading rather than a range of skills and strategies involved in the activity. However, more process-oriented studies, as already implied above, clearly suggest the reading construct has more than one dimension. Note the bi-divisible views of reading cited in Weir et al (2000), including Carver (1992) and Guthrie and Kirsch (1987), where the two components appear to be reading competence and vocabulary, the latter rather counter-intuitively separated from the essentially uni-dimensional construct of reading competence. The Schedl et al (1996) model of the TOEFL reading test above may also be considered bi-dimensional.

Componential models of reading with two dimensions would also, however, appear less in tune with recent applied linguistic developments than conceptual multi-dimensional models. The current focus is on defining ESOL learner and user communicative needs in the interests of transnational education and employment mobility and the consequent focus on specifying and assessing language proficiency levels foreign language (c.f. the *Common European Framework of Reference for Languages*, Council of Europe 2001).

Nor would models with a small number of broad categories of sub-components be in accordance with current trends. Coady's (1979) three-component (conceptual ability, language proficiency, background knowledge), and Bernhardt's (1991) language, literacy and knowledge model are revealing, process-based and, in the case of Bernhardt, include meta-cognitive strategies such as goal-setting and comprehension monitoring. But in the current era, with its increasing demand for evidence-based validation of *multi-skill* language assessment and proficiency specifications for key stakeholders, reading skills need to be described in comprehensive, multi-componential target language domain terms.

As the matrix in Table 1.1 already suggests, with its careful and expeditious reading cells, each operationalised through a range of skills at both local and global levels, reading is indeed a complex construct. Grabe and Stoller (2002) support this view and classify reading processes into higher and lower-level

Table 1.1 Types of reading

	Global level	Local level
Careful Reading	• Establishing accurate comprehension of explicitly stated main ideas and supporting details across sentences • Making propositional inferences • Establishing how ideas and details relate to each other in a whole text • Establishing how ideas and details relate to each other across texts	• Establishing accurate comprehension of explicitly stated main idea or supporting details within a sentence • Identifying lexis • Understanding syntax
Expeditious Reading	• Skimming quickly to establish: discourse topic and main ideas, or structure of text, or relevance to needs • Search reading to locate quickly and understand information relevant to predetermined needs	• Scanning to locate specific points of information

processes. The lower-level processes include word recognition (lexical access), syntactic parsing, semantic proposition formation and working memory activation. The higher-level processes comprise the formation of a text model of comprehension, a situation model of reader interpretation, background knowledge use and inferencing, and executive control processes, these latter appearing to be similar to meta-cognitive strategies.

The contrasting categories of *bottom-up* and *top-down* in models of reading, with their implications for related approaches, are also worth brief consideration in our development of an appropriate model for university student reading and its assessment. Bottom-up models tend to operate in terms of a hierarchical written text, from grapho-phonic, phonemic, syllabic, morphemic, word, to sentence levels right through to text level. Readers are assumed first to process 'the smallest linguistic unit, gradually compiling the smaller units to decipher and comprehend the higher units (e.g. sentence syntax)' (Dechant 1991). Top-down processing involves the general and domain-specific knowledge that readers can employ to predict text meaning and sentences and words within a text (see Bernhardt 1991).

There are also *hybrid reading models* combining the reasonable insights of both the bottom-up and top-down models. The interactive reading model (e.g. McCormick 1988), developed further by Kintsch (2004) in his construction-integration model of text comprehension, emphasises the reader-driven, purposeful and conscious aspects of reading noted above (and in Weir et al 2000). Further acknowledgement of the reader role in reading is provided in the *interactive-compensatory model* of Stanovich (2000), which suggests that a specific weakness of a reader in a particular skill may be made up for by strengths in others.

Our early pilot questionnaire to some of the student population from which our final samples will be drawn suggests that the students themselves appear to see their own academic reading as multi-dimensional (see Study 1 below). Findings indicate that a key problem is to cope with the heavy reading load, under time pressure. The students accept that the appropriate reading processes, strategies and skills are important, and have interesting ideas about what good academic reading may involve, although there is not much evidence of systematic application of optimal strategies and skills.

From the evidence of theoretical and empirical research involving models of reading, and given the needs of our study, it is likely that the appropriate model developed will be a multi-dimensional dynamic model of reading, taking into account as far as possible the global and local levels of reading as well as the meta-cognitive strategies, the skills and the processes involved in understanding texts from various sources for various purposes.

The model of reading developed will, as suggested above, also have to take account of the model represented by the IELTS Academic Reading module. The IELTS handbook for 2005, although it is, like the latest IELTS website, somewhat short on construct specification, appears to imply a multi-dimensional model of reading even though a single band score is awarded for reading. Under the task types listed as used in the Academic Reading module, are those that require test takers to complete notes, summaries, and a range of iconic presentations (diagrams, flow-charts, tables) using what they have read. They are also expected to identify information in the text, identify writers' views or claims, summarise paragraphs or text sections. A variety of text sources are used in the test including magazines, journals and books. One may infer that, though test users have only a single reading module band score on which to make judgments on candidates' reading proficiency, a range of reading skills have been measured.

Alderson (2000) proposes that part of the problem in actual testing practice is that numerous reading skills probably exist, but are difficult to test separately. Weir and Porter (1994:7) take a different view and state that 'a growing body of literature suggests that it is possible with clear specification of terms and appropriate methodology for testers to reach closer agreement on what skills are being tested'. The body of literature the authors referred to includes Bachman, Kunnan, Vanniarajan and Lynch (1988), Buck and Tatsuoka (1998), Lumley (1993), Teasdale (1989) and Weakley (1993). Khalifa and Weir (2009) point out that in the recent DIALANG project (see Alderson 2005) individual items are now also viewed by Alderson and his colleagues as being associated with identifiable skills.

Alderson's (2000) earlier reservations not withstanding, Koda (2005) feels that the successful identification of specific components that contribute to reading ability is an important paradigm in the current reading research literature. A componential approach based squarely on a sound theory of processing can be useful in that it provides insight into potential components in reading ability which require our attention if we are to approximate to a valid construct of reading in our reading tests.

Oakhill and Garnham (1988:48) query whether, without any theoretical grounding, the tests of these different comprehensions are of any value for diagnostic assessment. They also feel that the problem is that much of the research has focused on product rather than process in reading. Khalifa and Weir (2009) similarly point out that what was largely absent in the componential approach in the past (leaving aside the later process-oriented studies) was any serious attempt to relate components to a model of reading ability. They argue that this may stem from an earlier preference for *a posteriori* statistical analysis of construct in the testing community as against an *a priori* approach concerned with both the theoretical underpinnings of a test's construct before it is administered and its contextual validity.

The main criticism of the product-based, *a posteriori*, statistically driven approach is that it was not usually based on a sound analysis of salient cognitive processes. Furthermore, by its nature, it told us little about what is actually happening when a reader processes text. Further insight may be possible if we attempt to go deeper and examine as far as is possible the actual processing that goes on during reading activities. If we can identify skills and strategies that appear to make an important contribution to the reading process, it should be possible to test these and use the results for reporting on reading proficiency (see Shiotsu 2003, Urquhart and Weir 1998 and Weir et al 2000 for a further discussion of these issues).

In our search for differentiated skills and strategies we need to turn to the theory of what it means to 'comprehend'. Grabe (1991) offers a list of component skills in reading on the basis of reading theories (as against an earlier reliance on armchair intuition):

1. Automatic recognition skills (see Perfetti 1997).
2. Vocabulary and structural knowledge (see Bachman 1990 on grammatical competence, Perfetti 1997 on syntactic parsing, and word representation knowledge).
3. Formal discourse knowledge (see Koda 2005).
4. General and domain knowledge (see Carrell 1983 on formal schemata, Anderson and Pearson 1988 on content schemata, and Kintsch 1998 on domain knowledge).
5. Identifying central ideas of a text (see Baumann 1986 and Oakhill and Garnham 1988).
6. Inferencing skills (Chikalanga 1990, 1992).
7. Meta-cognitive knowledge (Urquhart and Weir 1998 and Weir et al 2000).
8. Skills monitoring (see Carrell, Devine and Eskey 1988).

The work of Enright et al (2000) supports this. Khalifa and Weir (2009) also point to the need to process and integrate information from several texts in a related field for many readers and suggest:

> The cognitive construction of intertextuality offers a useful heuristic for looking at reading into writing at an advanced level and it extends our view of reading beyond the act of comprehension of a single passage (2009:54).

Having accepted in principle the value of a componential approach, empirical enquiry into the reading activities of university students should help us better ground any argument for the cognitive validity of the tasks IELTS employs in its Academic Reading tests. By more closely relating putative skills/strategy components to a cognitive model of academic reading we may be able to better ground what IELTS is testing.

In this recent framework (see Figure 1.1) developed by Khalifa and Weir (2009) there is a synthesis of existing views on cognitive processing that takes

Figure 1.1 A model of reading (Khalifa and Weir 2009:43)

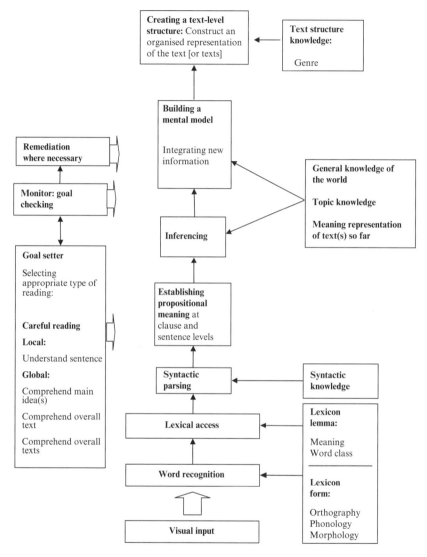

into account the research evidence on componentiality as well as considering the various models that have been proposed to explain reading comprehension (see above for our discussion of these). Khalifa and Weir comment that in the left-hand column they include the meta-cognitive activity of a *goal setter* because, in deciding what type of reading to employ when faced with a text, critical decisions are taken which affect the level(s) of processing to be activated in the central core of the model. The various elements of this processing core in the middle column are thus initiated in accordance with decisions taken in the goal setter. The components of the knowledge base required for text comprehension are included in the right-hand column (2009:43–44).

This literature review of theoretical and empirical research on reading framed our study of relationships between the reading experiences of students in the first year of their courses at the University of Bedfordshire and academic reading as measured by the IELTS Academic Reading test. The view of reading arising from this work is mirrored in the model developed separately by Khalifa and Weir for the Cambridge ESOL constructs volume, (Khalifa and Weir 2009). This model of processing at various levels in L2 together with our literature review and the data from our open-ended pilot questionnaire (see Appendix 1.2 and Section 5 below) proved useful in the development of our main study questionnaire on student reading activities and on the problems students encounter in their academic reading. The questionnaire provides the main database in this study.

3.3 Context validity

A central assumption in Weir's (2005) test validation model is that cognitive processing always occurs within and is significantly affected by a *context*. Weir's context validity relates the features of the task to the language in the text that must be processed if the task is to be completed successfully.

If test task performance is to be used to support inferences about performance in the wider domain of real-world tasks it is essential that both target reading activities and test tasks be described in terms both of cognitive processes and of contextual parameters.

Similarly, Bachman and Palmer (1996) argue that situational and interactional authenticities are essential features of useful test tasks. These factors in judging a test's usefulness (concerning the extent to which test tasks reflect salient contextual parameters and cognitive processes engaged by test takers) are analogous to Weir's contextual and cognitive validities. It is widely accepted that, given the constraints imposed by testing conditions on contextual features (such as the time available to complete a task), full situational authenticity is generally unrealistic for language assessments. However, contextual features of a test ought to reflect as many of the relevant features of the target reading activity as possible. The literature on the textual parameters that are potential sources of text complexity is daunting and we will only scratch the surface of it here before identifying those parameters that appear to be both useful and applicable for our study.

Bachman et al's (1988) and Bachman, Davidson, Ryan and Choi's (1995) test comparison studies involve such textual properties as the *nature of text, length, vocabulary, grammar, cohesion, distribution of new information, type of information, topic of discourse, rhetorical organisation* and *illocutionary acts*. Freedle and Kostin (1993, see also Freedle 1997), in a detailed analysis of reading comprehension item difficulty, take into consideration *vocabulary, concreteness/abstractness, subject matter, coherence* and *length of various segments such as word, sentence, paragraphs* as text-related variables. Fortus, Coriat and Fund (1998) investigated *length, number of negations, number of referential markers, vocabulary, grammatical complexity, abstractness, topic* and *rhetorical structure* as textual variables contributing to the level of difficulty of reading comprehension items. Enright et al (2000) identify two groups of salient textual features to operationalise in test texts: *grammatical/discourse features* and *pragmatic/ rhetorical features*. Alderson, Figueras, Kuijper, Nold, Takala and Tardieu (2004) include *text source, authenticity, discourse type, domain, topic, nature of content, text length, vocabulary* and *grammar* as relevant features for text analysis. Khalifa and Weir (2009) suggest that linguistic demands of task input – reading texts in this case – can be explained in terms of *lexical and structural resources, discourse mode, functional resources, content knowledge* and *writer–reader relationships*.

The text linguistics literature on *complexity* also identifies certain factors as important contributors to the level of difficulty, or ease with which a text can be processed and offers certain methodologies for evaluating this. Readability formulae such as Dale and Chall and Flesch (in Gervasi and Ambriola 2002) involve the calculation of word and sentence length and identification of specific vocabulary. Although in several studies readability formulae are criticised as being inadequate to reveal textual complexity (see, for example, Gervasi and Ambriola 2002 and Masi 2002), they still form the basic aspects in more recent and detailed analyses of textual complexity. Masi (2002) suggests that, together with linguistic and quantitative factors of word and sentence complexity, other semantic and syntactic factors such as *structural embedding, content, background knowledge of the reader* and *the type and genre of text*, should also be taken into account to reveal a more reliable and predictive measure of text complexity. The latter, however, are hardly measurable by automatic procedures such as computerised calculation.

From the picture emerging above, it was possible to identify a group of criterial features that suggested themselves as useful for the analysis of texts for testing purposes. We were careful to select features which facilitated as quick and unambiguous an analysis as possible, i.e. they could be practically used by judges in a short time but with a high consensus. The 'contextual parameters analysis scheme' developed for and used in this project (see Figure 1.2 below) thus involves the parameters listed in this figure, where we draw on contextual parameters most likely to have an impact on Reading test performance.

Figure 1.2 Context validity parameters addressed in this study

CONTEXT VALIDITY	
Task Setting	**Linguistic Demands:** **Task Input & Output**
• Text length	
• Time constraints	• Lexical resources
	• Structural resources
	• Discourse mode
	• Content knowledge
	• Cultural knowledge
	• Reader–writer relationship

Using this framework as our informing source, we will explore salient parameters of context validity in terms of *task setting* and *task linguistic demands* (input and output).

Alderson (1996) and Nuttall (1996) have argued that a *long text* is required for candidates to skim for main ideas, scan for specific information, make relevance judgements and distinguish between main points and subsidiary details. As Alderson et al (2004) have pointed out in relation to the Common European Framework of Reference, distinctions between long and short texts are generally inexplicit, nor is it clear how long a text or what time constraints would need to be imposed to reflect successful skimming, scanning and relevance judgements in academic reading.

It may also be that shorter texts, of the kind used in IELTS, may encourage candidates to engage word-level rather than text-level operations since the memory load involved in processing relatively short texts makes this feasible, although time constraints might serve to offset this effect. This will be investigated in the studies below.

A number of researchers and commentators (Alderson 1996, Nuttall 1996, Perera 1984, Shiotsu 2003, Urquhart 1984, Weir 1993) have identified potential sources of difficulty arising from the *linguistic elements in a text*. They suggest that *structural, lexical, and conceptual difficulty* strongly influence the ease with which a text can be read.

The emergence of computer-assisted analysis of extensive language corpora has facilitated the use of word lists to inform language test development and validation. Of particular value to IELTS are academic word lists that identify words used more commonly in academic than in other contexts, particularly the *sub-technical* vocabulary that occurs across disciplines (Campion and Elley 1971, Coxhead 2000). It would be encouraging to see that IELTS texts reflect the occurrence of such words in academic texts sourced from the university.

Work undertaken by Alderson and Clapham (1992) at the inception of IELTS pointed to a very close relationship between a *test of grammar* and the *IELTS Reading component*. Indeed the relationship was so close that a decision was taken to eliminate the Grammar test from the IELTS battery. Similarly, Shiotsu (2003) explored components likely to affect Reading test performance for Japanese undergraduates and found that syntactic knowledge played a central role. Shiotsu and Weir (2007), using structural equation modelling, demonstrated the relative importance of syntactic over lexical knowledge in accounting for variance in tests of reading with candidates from a variety of language backgrounds.

Texts with less complex grammar tend on the whole to be easier than texts with more complex grammar. Berman (1984) investigated how opacity and heaviness of sentence structures could result in increased difficulty in processing. Again, this suggests that a valid test of academic reading should reflect the syntactic features likely to be encountered in academic texts.

The effect of the use of *cohesive devices* on comprehension is less clearcut. While Alderson (2000) notes that an absence of cohesive devices does not seriously damage comprehension when the topic is relatively familiar to readers, it has been argued that explicit cohesive devices help in establishing textual coherence (Goldman and Rakestraw 2000) and that their lack inhibits the recall of texts, being indicative of a less successful mental representation (Ehrlich 1991).

Urquhart (1984) and Barnett (1989) suggest that *rhetorical features* should be considered together with sentence-level features in estimating text difficulty and this view is supported by available research. Studies investigating the effects of textual organisation on text difficulty (see for example Carrell 1984, Goh 1990, Meyer and Freedle 1984) suggest that differences in rhetorical organisation do affect processing. All three studies found that *problem-solution, comparison*, and *causation structures* resulted in better recall than *classification* or *description structures*. Koda (2005) cites a number of studies reporting the positive effects of improving text structure and the benefits of explicit training in coherence on comprehension and memory. Freedle (1997) finds that texts subjectively judged to be high in coherence yield easier main idea reading comprehension items. Rhetorical features should therefore be a further consideration in the selection of texts for tests of academic reading.

Genre is explained by Weigle (2002:62) as the expected form and communicative function of the written product. Genre is generally understood to encompass 'salient features and conventions which are shaped by communicative purposes' (Hyland 2002:62). It is evident from the literature that specific genres will involve specific conventional features (lexico-grammatical, semantic, and discoursal) which are likely to impinge on the text processing of readers (Bhatia 1997, Hyland 2000). It would seem logical to suggest that if texts to appear in a test are sourced from academic contexts they are likely to share lexical, syntactic and discourse features with texts encountered at a university.

The following genres, identified through the development of the student questionnaire (see Studies 1 and 2 below), are seen as relevant to the present analysis:

- textbook
- magazine and newspaper article
- research/academic journal article
- report.

Rhetorical task refers to 'the primary intent of the author' that guides the reader in understanding the text (Enright et al 2000:20). Enright et al (2000) suggest a three-way classification of rhetorical tasks (which they term 'pragmatic features'):

- *Exposition* informs the reader. It may involve descriptions, comparisons, contrasts, explanations and elaborations.
- *Argumentation/persuasion/evaluation* supports a point of view with reasons, evidence and analysis of an opponent's errors in reasoning. Vocabulary might reflect attitude or perspective and it may be personal in tone. It differs from a balanced, unbiased stance.
- *Historical biographical/ autobiographical narrative* tells a story with a defined setting and episodes.
- *Pattern of exposition* refers to 'subcategories of exposition' (Weigle 2002:62), or a specific pattern a writer employs to communicate. Although a single text may include a number of rhetorical moves, it is the overall theme or main point that is targeted through this feature (Enright et al 2000:23). The following patterns are suggested as being worthy of investigation in the literature:
  - *Definition/description/elaboration* involves providing full definitions of concepts, describing unfamiliar terminology, elaborating on terms specific to the discipline and clarifying specific uses of the terminology.
  - *Illustration* involves providing examples or a short anecdote to fully describe an abstract concept.
  - *Classification* involves grouping several items together according to similar features or principles, showing how discrete items belong to a larger group.
  - *Comparison/contrast* involves designating distinctions among concepts, particularly regarding their similarity and dissimilarity.
  - *Cause and effect* involves analysing causes and effects in relation to an overall point.
  - *Problem/solution* involves describing a problem or a series of problems then proposing a solution, which will have a plausible, salutary effect on a course of action.

- *Justify* as used here is similar to the category of *analysis* used by Enright et al (2000). Texts in this category provide evidence to justify a point of view.
- *Rhetorical organisation* refers to the extent to which there is an explicit pattern of topic progression through the text. Such progression might be signalled by headings, topic sentences and discourse markers.

The contextual parameter of *content knowledge* in the socio-cognitive framework proposed by Weir (2005) and shown in Figure 1.2 above suggests that the relationship between the candidate's pre-existing knowledge and the propositional content of a text will affect the way it is processed. Nuttall (1996) puts forward the widely held view that, all else being equal, the greater a reader's knowledge of the topic of a text, the easier it should be to process. This has been an area of debate for IELTS since its inception as the five academic subject-specific modules inherited from the ELTS test were reduced first, in 1989, to three and finally, in 1995, to one.

The decision to abandon subject-specific modules was taken on the grounds that there was only very limited evidence that it had any effect on text difficulty. Tan (1990) and Clapham (1996) both investigated the effect of content familiarity on candidate performance without finding significant effects on test scores (although Clapham does note an effect for the most specific texts in her corpus). However, Khalifa (1997) made the contrary finding that familiarity with the topic of text can be a good predictor of difficulty. Alderson (2000) also acknowledges the facilitating effect of familiarity with the subject matter and Urquhart and Weir (1998) warn against the danger of using insufficiently specialised texts. It has been suggested that, in order to minimise effects of topic familiarity, test tasks should be based on materials sourced from a variety of academic subject areas (Enright et al 2000).

The concern with the contextual parameter of *nature of information* is with the extent to which the information in a text is concrete (i.e. concerning observable, concrete phenomena) or abstract i.e. (concerning unobservable phenomena such as social institutions) or, at a higher level of abstraction, meta-phenomenal (Moore and Morton 1999) (concerning theoretical treatment of abstract phenomena). Different levels of abstraction may, of course, be found within a single text.

Alderson et al (2004:127) see this as a useful feature to consider in estimating text difficulty in relation to the Common European Framework of Reference. Information that is more abstract may prove to be more difficult to process and so divert cognitive resources from language processing. At the same time abstract information often implies a linguistic complexity that may further stretch the L2 reader's resources.

Studies such as Steffensen, Joag-Dev and Anderson (1979), Chihara,

Sakurai and Oller (1989), Al-Fallay (1994) and Sasaki (2000) have provided evidence that *cultural knowledge* plays an important role in text comprehension. In these studies, certain 'key' words – proper nouns, words describing institutions and words that reflected unfamiliar cultural practices – were changed into words that would be more familiar for the participants. For example, in Chihara et al's (1989) and Sasaki's (2000) studies, which used the same texts, *Joe* was changed to *Hiroshi*, *state* to *prefecture* and a mother *hugged* rather than *kissed* her son because these changes were felt to reflect a Japanese rather than an American cultural context for the narrative. The resulting texts, because they appeared more familiar to the participants, resulted in higher scores on a cloze test based on the passage. In this study the judges were asked to look for words that might be associated with a specific culture, including references to:

- names for specific people, places and products (Harvey; the city of Chicago; Rice Krispies)
- specific historical events or periods (the Norman Conquest; football-related violence in the 1970s)
- local institutions (the probation service; the House of Lords)
- locally familiar objects (breakfast cereals; sharp suits)
- locally situated social practices (window shopping; children in the classroom undertaking problem-solving activities in pairs)
- idiomatic language including culturally specific references (milestone research; professional soap boxes).

The approach currently taken by the IELTS designers is to avoid content that is dependent on knowledge either of specific discipline areas or of particular cultures. Item writers are advised to reject texts that might be too technical for the general reader or that assume knowledge specific to certain cultures.

With regard to the contextual parameter of reader–writer relationship, Nystrand (1989) states that meaning is created between the participants of a discourse and resides in the expectations and assumptions of both the reader and the writer of each other. Writing, rather than being an isolated individual action, involves the endeavours of both the reader and the writer and is shaped through mutual assumptions involved in the understanding of rhetorical situations (Hyland 2002:35). Any act of writing is charged with assumptions about the participant relationships and how these are carried out in culturally and institutionally legitimate ways (Hyland 2002:69). Hyland states that 'managing social relationships, then, is crucial in writing as a text communicates effectively only when the writer has correctly assessed both the readers' resources for interpreting it and likely response to it. This is, in part, achieved through the use of metadiscourse' (2002:72).

Metadiscourse is a term which describes a range of lexical items (words and expressions) whose main function is to enhance communicative efficiency in two main ways: by streamlining the inference process involved in figuring out the relation between parts of the text and the context (including the co-text) and by establishing and managing the rapport between the communicator and the audience.

Discourse relationships are shaped by the writer's choice of specific rhetorical devices. As one important element of reading texts, reader–writer relationship in both undergraduate and IELTS reading texts will be analysed in Section 8 according to the type and frequency of meta-discoursal features listed by Hyland (2005).

Our review of the literature relevant to our research project has covered key insights into reading processes, skills and strategies and reviewed approaches to the modelling of reading to take account of these, in the context of the reading needs, purposes and problems of our target students. The contextual validity of Reading tests has been discussed with reference to task setting and task linguistic demands, with particular reference to linguistic, discoursal and rhetorical features. A key focus of the review has been on the way that the Reading module in the IELTS test addresses the testing of academic reading and we will analyse further the nature of the IELTS reading model in our continuing study of contextual and cognitive parameters below.

The main study questionnaire items we developed for the next stage of our project were principally concerned with investigating the degree to which the students perceived themselves as carrying out the variety of operations in reading suggested by our literature review and a pilot open-ended survey (see Appendix 1.1), and the problems they encountered with these and a variety of contextual parameters.

The main survey is an attempt to establish the components of reading in an academic context and to identify particular operations and performance conditions where students have problems. This data will enable us to examine IELTS to see the extent to which these components are covered and in particular the extent to which attention in IELTS is paid to the problematic operations and conditions.

Our data for this comparison will be firmly rooted in the theoretical literature but also the construct will have been further grounded in relation to the responses of real students studying at one English university.

4 Research methodology

The study employs a mixture of quantitative and qualitative methods as appropriate:

- Critical review of documentation and published literature relating to the nature of reading in an academic context and the problems encountered by overseas students in coping with this.
- Self report by students on:

- – the cognitive processing and performance conditions encountered in academic reading
- – the difficulties occasioned by these.
- • Analysis of level of problems experienced in reading reported by students (i.e. with various activities and performance conditions) in relation to level of IELTS test performance.
- • Investigation of 42 IELTS testlets (14 complete Reading tests in all) through application by expert judges of a descriptive framework of expeditious and careful reading strategies to each item in each testlet.
- • Investigation of 42 IELTS test texts (14 complete Reading tests in all) and 14 extracts from core undergraduate textbooks through application by expert judges of a descriptive framework of textual parameters to each text.

Further details of particular methodologies employed will be provided in respect of each of the studies reported below.

5   Study 1: Open-ended pilot questionnaire on academic reading activities

5.1   Introduction

The pilot questionnaire (see Appendix 1.1) was trialled in several iterations. It asked for biodata, then responses to 13 open-ended questions, and in its final form was administered in April 2006, and elicited 77 responses. The questionnaire data analysed here was intended to inform further data collection approaches and content, in particular the IELTS Academic Reading Project online structured survey administered between 1 June and 31 October 2006.

The sample for the piloting operation was obtained from a range of student types (undergraduate/postgraduate, 1st/2nd/3rd year and home/international students). Despite its opportunistic nature, interesting pilot data emerged on the reading sources, purposes, strategies, experiences and difficulties of University of Bedfordshire students from a range of backgrounds and fields of study. Lessons were learned for the content, design, wording and administration of the Academic Reading Project online structured questionnaire which is the focus of Section 6 of this report.

Given the richness of the responses to the open-ended questionnaire, they were analysed qualitatively using key word and topic counts, with direct quotation indicated appropriately. The summaries are in terms of descriptive statistics.

Key points from the analysis of all pilot questionnaire responses are now summarised.

5.2 Reading source types

Responses confirm that books remain the key source of students' academic reading, but with journals also prominent and a fair number of students doing around half of their academic reading online. The pilot study students offer insightful comparisons between book and online sources of information indicating, for example, that:

- books offer a wider range of sources and more to understand
- print sources may provide deeper information
- print materials tend to be first choice
- online (OL) sources may be for interest but not suitable for assignments
- OL reading complements and follows up print reading
- the Web with its wide range of information can offer explanations, clarifications, of questions raised from reading of books
- useful and convenient to have some journals online, but often limited access
- prefer to print out OL information (2), less comfortable reading from screen
- 'don't use OL so much because can't scribble, highlight, take notes so conveniently'
- online sources less reliable, credible than books, journals.

The pilot questionnaire data provides further evidence that assignment reading is a multi-source task. Of our 65 responses on the item, 34% claimed as many as 10–19 sources for an assignment, fairly evenly divided between books, journal articles and websites, although books were more often the main source of reading than the other two.

It is appreciated, of course, that decisions on what to read are not always the students' own. Table 1.2 summarises responses to the item on how the pilot sample students decide what to read for their courses.

Most of the sample students (77%) did not distinguish between their approaches to reading from different information sources. In the 17 responses which did distinguish, however, the following points were made.

Table 1.2 Student decision influences for their reading

Decision sources	N	%
lecturers, tutors (and peers (3))	19	25%
course, module, lecture reading lists	34	44%
own methods and strategies, i.e.:		
• library searches and book, journal analyses (incl. scanning for relevance, importance etc. (10))	34	44%
• online searches	11	14%

5.3 Reading approaches

Close to the heart of the research question of our project are the students' responses to the question *When you have decided what to read, describe how you read it.* Most responses indicate strategies to identify reading focus according to assignment and the materials needed. A key word count from the 78 responses to this item indicates the following approach focuses:

Table 1.3 Strategies adopted to read assignment information

Reading Approach	n
scan	15
skim	13
notes	19
important, main, relevant (points)	11
highlight, bullets	13
abstract	5
index	2

We note that students do not always appear to distinguish between 'scan', meaning to locate specific information, topic, point, and 'skim' meaning read for gist, general impression, both strategies presumably needed in reading for assignments. Typical sequences of reading action associated with student assignments were:

- 'run through to see if suitable for me, (then) read properly', read cited parts again
- 'read only sub-titles and main issues'
- 'headings, bullet points then, if they are worthy, read the whole article'
- read relevant sections and skim others
- read chosen area, sub-heads, relevant information
- skim and use index.

Note here the students' reference mainly to expeditious rather than careful reading. These responses, central to our research, inform and are pursued in the online questionnaire.

Most of the sample students (77%) did not distinguish between their approaches to reading from different information sources. In the 17 responses which did distinguish, however, the following points were made:

Reading books:

- locate relevant material using title (2), index (2), chapter titles (2), summary.

Reading articles:

- since articles are shorter, browse-reading most relevant sections
- check abstracts, introduction, discussion
- articles are harder
- highlight (2) then go back over (2).

Reading books and articles:

- read books more thoroughly (2), articles selectively
- read whole articles (2), books selectively (2)
- skim books, but articles require more thought, processing
- reading approach depends on prior knowledge rather than materials type.

Again some of these approaches are the focus of further attention in the online questionnaire.

Of the 70 responses to the question on whether students' reading approaches were the same when reading for assignments as for examinations, 34 (48%) said yes. Respondents claiming different approaches suggested the following, many of the strategies and problems specified being relevant to our research focus on reading purposes, strategies and difficulties, and to our focus on IELTS as an exam in its own right. We note reference by the pilot study students here to both expeditious and careful reading.

Reading for exams:

- 'exams require triggers with which you apply theory to questions'
- not everything selected for exams is in books, easy to find most you need on Net
- reading for exams requires more depth (4), more thorough readings (2) critical evidential approach (2), more breadth or topic coverage (6), less detail (2); more specificity, detail (2); more reading to clarify problem topics (2)
- reading for exams is already identified, involves only reading specified chapters and handouts, preparing and memorising (2) for predicted exam questions, essays (4)
- more hard work, tension with exams
- in exams read everything through, then start exam.

Reading for assignments:

- assignment reading takes more time, read twice (2), use more sources (3)
- more variety, less detail (3), more detail (1), more specific (1), more general (3) , more depth so more time to master

- need to read and make notes from selected relevant material (5)
- need to read in order to apply examples
- need to skim.

5.4   Reading problems

The open-ended pilot questionnaire pursued further the question of difficulties experienced by the students in their academic reading. The 58% of the pilot sample responding identified the problems summarised in Table 1.4.

Table 1.4 Reading difficulties

Difficulty area	n
hard text (18) theory, concepts (7)	25
jargon, technical language	12
locating required info	7
time, info overload	6

Very closely related are the *pressures* identified by 61% of the sample with regard to the academic reading, as shown in Table 1.5.

Table 1.5 Reading pressures

Pressure area	n
time, reading load	15
difficulty of understanding	11
searching for required info	5
exam success	4

5.5   Perceptions of successful reading

A revealing and related question was *What do you think a successful reader is at university?* The response data was informative for our focus on perceptions of academic reading. Eighty-one features were identified in the 72 responses, as summarised in Table 1.6.

Interesting *verbatim* responses included these:

- *'someone who understands what's what and achieves most of the reading suggested and completes some off their own bat'*
- *'selective reader using appropriate techniques with the context and time framework'*
- *'has no difficulty reading books, articles, not only course books but other fields, can skim text and know gist, figure out context and meaning without looking up words'*

Table 1.6 Successful reader characteristics

Characteristics	n	%
reading with understanding	28	39
reading all that you need to read	19	26
wide reading	13	18
regular, voluntary reading	9	13
reading and remembering	6	8
reading with other specific micro-skills i.e. selecting (2), 'rooting out', expressing in own words, avoiding over-detailed simplifying	6	8

- *'enjoys and engages in study reading on a regular basis'*
- *'can organise reading, understand, to represent in their minds corresponding to author's'.*

Students' perceptions of what successful readers do are clearly relevant to our analysis of the reading needs of first-year university students and how these are assessed. The leads provided here by the pilot study respondents inform the main questionnaire in Study 2 below.

5.6 Some general conclusions from the open-ended pilot questionnaire

Reading emerges from the pilot study data as indeed a concern for the students, including the English as an L1 majority. Their major problem is coping with the heavy reading load, under time pressure. This being so, appropriate reading processes, strategies and skills are important, and accepted as such. The students have some good ideas about what good academic reading should involve. However, there is not a great deal of evidence of systematic application of optimal strategies and skills by the students themselves.

The rationale for the research is supported by responses to the open-ended pilot questionnaire. In spite of the use of an opportunity sample, the data sought and received usefully informed further stages in the IELTS Academic Reading Project. The responses of the students together with our findings from the literature review informed both the content and the wording of the descriptive categories in the final structured questionnaire (see Study 2 below).

6 Study 2: Main questionnaire survey

Following the analysis of the open-ended pilot questionnaire, and a number of further small-scale piloting stages, the final version of a structured questionnaire was distributed to home and international, undergraduate and postgraduate students at the University of Bedfordshire in May/June 2006 and was also available on the web. When students returned in September 2006, we targeted (electronically through *Blackboard*) former Year 1 students now entering the second year of their courses, especially in those subject areas with low returns so far. For our purposes these were considered students in their first year of study.

The student population was thus sampled opportunistically. The project team had neither the authority nor the resources to design and implement a stratified random sample. Nor, as indicated above, would the purpose of the study have been served by an experimental research design, with its characteristic control of variables and establishment of experimental and control groups, for before and after measurement of isolated variables. In the sections below, however, the nature of the sample will be described, and the responses of student sub-group categories within that sample subjected to descriptive and some inferential statistical analysis to contextualise and justify claims made.

Over the period from the 1 June 2006 launch of the online and paper-and-pencil versions of the questionnaire, until the closing date of 1 October 2006, 434 students responded online and 332 in hard-copy format. This high total respondent figure of 766 students is considered adequate for the purposes for which the questionnaire was designed, and the data elicitation methods used. The total population of the University of Luton at the time (the name of the university changed officially to *University of Bedfordshire* in September 2006) was 16,150, including 6,550 students in their first and 4,400 in their second year.

As noted above and in line with the purpose of the study, the questionnaire was to be administered to students to elicit information and views on their academic reading experiences and the difficulties that they may have encountered in reading for their courses. The focus of the questionnaire was to inform a profile of the students' reading experiences in terms of purposes, strategies and difficulties, so that the relationship between this profile and the academic reading construct measured by the IELTS Academic Reading module might be investigated. The questionnaire is included as Appendix 1.2 of this report.

The survey includes both home and overseas students, undergraduates and postgraduates and students in their second and first year of study at the university across a range of fields of study. Year 2 students were included as a check on whether things altered much in subsequent university study. Responses on key variables are cross-tabulated where such data may inform answers to the main questions this study seeks to answer. Examples of this will be seen in the analyses below, for example, of the reading problems of English as an alternative language (EAL) and English as a first language (EL1) students, or between Year 1 and Year 2 students.

6.1 Gender, age, regional background

Table 1.7 summarises basic information on the Study 2 survey student sample in terms of *gender, age* and *regional background.*

Table 1.7 Gender, age and regional distribution of the questionnaire

M/F	n	%	Age range	n	%	Region	n	%
M	227	29.6	18–22	427	55.7	UK	287	37.6
			23–29	178	23.2	EU	135	17.7
F	537	70.1	30–39	92	12.0	Other	342	44.8
			40+	69	9.0			
N	764			766			764	

There are significantly more female students in the sample than male, with a 70% to 30 % split. The Higher Education Statistics Agency (HESA) statistics for UK universities in the academic year 2003/04 also note a preponderance of female students; approximately 58% of undergraduate students then were women, while 42% were men. In our sample, the gender distribution across the Year 1 and the Year 2 students is similar, the Year 1 group showing a 69.9% to 30.1% distribution, Year 2, 71.2% to 28.8%. The table reveals a good spread of participants across the four *age groups*, with the younger group (age 18–22) predominating, as desired in a study with a focus on first-year students, but with useful sub-samples also in the three broader senior ranges (23–29, 30–39 and 40+). The age ranges for the Year 1 and Year 2 students in the questionnaire sample are almost identical.

The sample population includes British as well as non-British students, in line with the point made in the literature review above, that academic reading problems affect both groups. Of the 62.5% of the questionnaire respondents who are not of British nationality, around 72% are from non-European backgrounds, 28% from Europe. This again compares reasonably well with the HESA figures for non-British UK university students, 64% of whom were from non-European countries, 36.4 from Europe.

6.2 Academic stage

As Table 1.8 indicates, 84.4% of the Study 2 sample are *undergraduates*, across Years 1 to 3 of their studies.

Most (67.7%) of the questionnaire respondents are in Year 1, which is the main focus of our study, but over 30% are in their second year. Comparisons between Year 1 students and their colleagues in Year 2 may provide interesting eventual insights into changes in aspects of their academic reading as time passes, as their experience grows and as the nature of the reading they are called upon to do alters (see further below).

Table 1.8 Level and stage of studies of the questionnaire respondents

Level	n	%	Yr.	n	%
Undergrad	642	84.4	1	513	67.7
Postgrad	119	15.6	2	230	30.3
			3	15	2.0
N	761			758	

6.3 English language status (gender, regional background, academic stage)

The *language background* variable is, as indicated in our project aims and the literature review above, a key focus of this research. In the Study 2 questionnaire sample population, no fewer than 43 languages are represented, English (38.9%) and Chinese (38.4%) being easily the most numerous, with European languages other than English also prominent (14.2%). The first and second year student groups are well matched proportionately across first languages, dominated by EL1 (Year 1 and Year 2 at 36.5% and 44.8% respectively) and Chinese L1 (36.5% and 33.5%).

Of the EAL students, 310 (66.5%) are from outside the UK, 130 (27.9%) from Europe, and 26 (5.6%) from the UK. Among the 298 students in the EL1 group, 261 (87.6%) are UK nationals, five European and 32 (10.7%) from outside the UK and Europe.

We might normally have expected more of the EAL students, most of whom are from overseas, to have come to Britain for *post*graduate studies. But we have already seen that in our sample EAL population a high proportion, 66.2% (n = 310) are between 18 and 22 years old. In fact, a fairly similar proportion of the EAL and the EL1 sub-groups, 81.9% and 88.2% respectively, are studying here at *under*graduate level. Analysis of the year of study category across our EAL and EL1 groups shows high proportions of students (70.1% and 64% respectively) in their *first* year of study at the university. Comparisons between our undergraduate and our postgraduate sub-groups are made below where relevant to our main research questions, especially with regard to academic reading *sources, purposes, strategies* and *difficulties.*

6.4 Subject areas

There is a broad coverage of *subject areas* across the student sample, as may be seen in Table 1.9, which again compares the EAL and EL1 sub-groups. The main

Table 1.9 Subjects studied by the EAL and EL1 questionnaire respondents

Subjects	EAL		EL1		Subjects	EAL		EL1	
	n	%	n	%		n	%	n	%
Advertising, Mktg, PR	94	20.4	12	4.1	Language, Comm., (T)EFL	71	15.4	7	2.4
Art & Design	2	0.4	1	0.3	Law	10	2.2	7	2.4
Biology, Biomed. Sc.	9	2	4	1.4	Leis., Tourism, Sports Mgt.	11	2.4	3	1.0
Business & Finance	137	29.8	18	6.1	Media Arts	24	5.2	10	3.4
CIS	16	3.5	15	5.1	Psychology	16	3.5	28	9.5
Education Studies	5	1.1	66	22.4	Soc. Sciences, Soc. Work	7	1.5	42	14.2
Healthcare, Nursing	7	1.5	40	11.2	Sport & Exercise	3	0.7	31	10.5
Human Resource Mgt.	36	7.8	16	5.4					

subjects of the EAL students are Business and Finance; Advertising, Marketing and Public Relations; and Language, Communication EFL and TEFL, each of these subject areas being pursued by more than 15% of the group. The main subjects of our EL1 students are Education studies, with 22.4% of the sub-group, Social Sciences and Social Work (14.2%) and Sport and Exercise Science (10.5%). Table 1.9 analyses the subject areas represented across our population sample, with particular reference to the EAL and EL1 sub-groups.

The subject areas are fairly evenly shared across the first and second year groups, apart from somewhat larger Year 1 groups in Advertising, Marketing and PR and Human Resources Management (HRM), and slightly more prominent Year 2 groups in Language and Communication (including EFL and TEFL) and Media Arts.

The 766 students in our questionnaire sample are pursuing in the main a similar range of subject areas to those of the overall UK student population as analysed in HESA figures for 2005. These indicate main sub-groups of 22% studying medical and related subjects; 17% education, language and communication; 13% business and administration; 11% maths and the physical and biological sciences; 14% engineering and technology, including computer science (6%).

6.5 IELTS Academic Reading Module scores

Figure 1.3 summarises the scores awarded to the 301 of our sample population who had taken the IELTS Academic Reading test.

The analysis shows that the *mode* band on the IELTS Academic Reading

Figure 1.3 IELTS Academic Reading test scores of the main questionnaire respondents

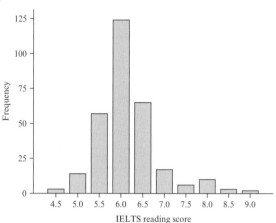

module was 6.0, the band score awarded to 41.2% of our sample. The reported *overall global* average IELTS Academic Reading module band score for 2002 was 5.79. The IELTS *Annual Report* (e.g. 2003) notes a 'minimum of Band 6 in each module' as a common university entrance cut-off band. An IELTS Overall Band Score of 6.0 is, according to the same source, a common English language entrance qualification for undergraduate studies. Note that the IELTS descriptor for Band 6 specifies the following 'Competent User' profile: A 'generally effective command of the language despite some inaccuracies, inappropriacies and misunderstandings. Can use and understand fairly complex language, particularly in familiar situations'. This characterisation of Band 6 English language competence will be borne in mind when we probe further the reading approaches and problems of our student sample population.

The students scoring 5 or 5.5 on IELTS in our sample were in a Foundation programme for overseas students, which prepares them for entry to certificated degree courses.

The next most frequent band score in our sample was 6.5 (21.6% of the IELTS-taking respondents), closely followed by the 5.5 band (18.9%). The 6.5 average band is often cited as appropriate for entrance to *graduate* courses, though there is considerable variation in IELTS cut-off bands across different universities, fields of study and levels (IELTS 2005). Our main questionnaire respondent sample appears to be reasonably near to norm as regards IELTS band scores.

In terms of student year of study, the key central IELTS Reading band scores of our Year 1 and 2 respondents are not significantly different, as Figure 1.4 indicates. Once again, it will be noted, the 6.0 Reading band score predominates, with 6.5 and 5.5 the next most common, respectively.

Figure 1.4 Year 1 and Year 2 IELTS Reading test band scores

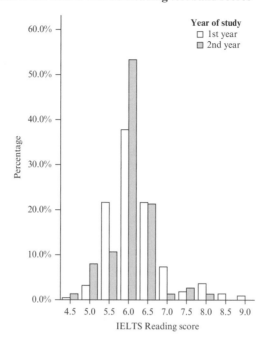

The IELTS Reading score averages of our undergraduate and postgraduate sub-groups were 6.14 and 6.19 respectively.

6.6   The questionnaire Likert scale items

The analyses of our questionnaire from here on are based on responses to Likert scale items, using a five-choice degree of agreement format, including one 'neutral' option. The scale throughout is: *5 – definitely agree, 4 – mostly agree, 3 – neither agree nor disagree, 2 – mostly disagree, 1 – definitely disagree*. Using the *mode* (i.e. the most common selection made by respondents) is the most logical way to indicate the response tendency on each item. Adding the number of *definitely agree* and *mostly agree* selections is also an appropriate way of indicating the strength of respondents' agreement or disagreement with items. Differences between groups are investigated through analysis of variance.

Sources of academic reading information

Section 2 of the questionnaire elicits information from the students on the range of *information sources* on their courses. The responses here are again analysed for the EAL and the EL1 sub-groups. Table 1.10 summarises student responses on the relative importance of *books, journal articles, reports, the*

Table 1.10 Sources of information across EAL and EL1 questionnaire respondent groups

	EAL		EL1	
	D (r/o)	D&M (r/o)	D (r/o)	D&M (r/o)
Books	54.9% (1)	90.0% (1)	77.2% (1)	96.0% (1)
Net	42.9% (2)	78.3% (2)	51.3% (3)	85.5% (2)
Journals	28.4% (3)	65.6% (3)	59.1% (2)	83.3% (3)
Reports	19.5% (4)	56.9% (4)	26.5% (4)	63.4% (4)
Newspapers	10.3% (5)	44.1% (5)	19.5% (5)	58.4% (5)
Magazines	9.0% (6)	35.0% (6)	11.8% (6)	40.5% (6)

internet, newspapers and *magazines* in their academic reading. 'D' in this and subsequent tables, represents the selection of the *definitely agree* category on the Likert scale, 'D&M', the sum of respondents' *definitely agree* and *mainly agree* selections. Rank orders (r/o) of the reading agreement strengths are added in parentheses.

Broadly speaking, and in terms both of measurement of responses by the *definitely agree* choice only, and by the sum of the two positive agreement categories, the order of importance of sources is: *1) books, 2) internet sites, 3) journals, 4) reports, 5) newspapers* and *6) magazines.* Informed by the pilot questionnaire (Study 2 above) a related item on the main questionnaire asks respondents how much reading they actually do online compared with paper print materials. Table 1.11 summarises responses for both EAL and EL1 participants.

Table 1.11 EAL and EL1 group online reading source proportions

	Amount of reading done online				
	0–20%	21–40%	41–60%	61–80%	81–100%
EAL students (n= 458)	16.2%	27.5%	30.3%	17.7%	8.3%
EL1 students (n= 290)	30.7%	28.3%	23.8%	13.1%	4.1%

The message of the table here is that the EAL students appear to do rather more of their reading online than do their EL1 colleagues. The *mode* value for the former group is the 30.3% who do from 41–60% of their reading online, compared with 23.8% of the latter, 30.7% of whom read 0–20% online.

Cross-tabulated reading source data suggests close agreement between first and second year students, except, perhaps, for almost 11% fewer among the Year 2 sub-group definitely agreeing that internet sources are important on their courses. Table 1.12 here summarises the perceptions on reading sources across the two sub-groups.

Table 1.12 Year 1 and Year 2 group online reading source proportions

	Yr 1	Yr 2 %
Books	64.2%	64.9%
Internet sites	49.8%	39.0%
Journals	40.7%	41.7%
Reports	22.0%	22.4%
Newspapers	12.9%	17.1%
Magazines	9.0%	12.7%

The range of academic reading sources and the prominent role played by internet sites in the academic reading of contemporary university students have clear implications for pre-university Reading tests such as IELTS. This is a message to which we return later in this report. In terms of substantive differences of perceptions between our under- and postgraduate sub-samples, it is of interest (as well as intuitively credible) to note that a high 83.5% of our graduate sub-sample *definitely* or *mostly agreed* on the importance of *journal articles* on their course, compared with 70.7% of our undergraduate sub-group. Similar was the substantially higher proportion of the postgraduate group agreeing the importance of *reports* on their courses (75.6% of the graduate sample compared with 56.8% of the undergraduates).

6.7 Students' course reading purposes and how they read for their assignments

We now move into a key area of our research into the reading experiences of students in the first year of their courses at a British university, namely the *purposes* of their reading, in particular how they read for their assignments.

Again, we shall be looking also for potential differences between EAL and EL1 students, this time with regard to their perceived *reading purposes* on their courses. If there are differences in agreement across the two categories of student, the implication could be that EAL and EL1 students, because perhaps of their different levels of target language (TL) reading proficiency, set out with different purposes as they tackle the reading tasks required by their academic studies. If there appears to be no significant difference in perceived reading purposes across the two sub-groups, it may be inferred that students read with similar purposes whether their language status is EAL or EL1. As indicated above, more significant variables across reading purposes may be the field and/or the year of study.

The rubric for Section 3 of the Study 2 questionnaire is: *The following purposes for reading are important on my course.* This is followed by four statements of reading purposes which may be characterised, in the terms emerging from our literature review (above), as *strategic, global* and *expeditious reading* oriented. Table 1.13 summarises student responses to the items, again in terms of the EAL and EL1 sub-groups and using the same analytic categories as Table 1.11 above. The numbering of the reading purposes in the table is that of the original questionnaire (see Appendix 1.2).

Table 1.13 Responses on the importance of reading purposes across EAL and EL1 groups

The following purposes for reading are important on my course:	EAL		EL1	
	D (r/o)	D&M (r/o)	D (r/o)	D&M (r/o)
15. Searching texts to find information for assignments and exams	55.8% (1)	87.7% (1)	77.9% (1)	95.6% (2)
16. Basic comprehension of main ideas	35.5% (4)	79.6% (3)	57.9% (3)	90.1% (4)
17. Understand meaning of text as a whole; how main ideas and details relate to each other and author's purpose	37.4% (3)	80.7% (2)	53.9% (4)	97.5% (1)
18. Integrating information from different texts for use in assignments, exams	40.5% (2)	78.6% (4)	70.4% (2)	91.1% (3)

Analysing the Likert scale responses across the 468 EAL students and the 298 EL1 students, the main inference is that all four purposes are important to the students, in mainly similar rank orders. *Searching texts for required information* appears to be the most important reading purpose on the whole for the students, while the greatest difference between the groups ($p<.01$) appears to be that it is the EL1 group who emphasises more strongly the importance of the reading purpose *basic comprehension of main ideas.* There are clear implications here for the testing of reading, on which light may be shed in the accounts in this report of Study 3 on the cognitive parameters in IELTS and Study 4 on IELTS contextual parameters.

Table 1.14 now presents a re-analysis of the same data on reading purpose, this time to investigate whether there is significant variation across the Year 1 and Year 2 student groups.

Searching texts for required information is again a key reading purpose across the year groups, with the other specified purposes also agreed as important, with no real difference of perception across the Year 1 and Year 2 students. Nor was there substantive difference between our post- and undergraduate sub-samples in terms of the main *purposes* for their academic reading, all of which were again agreed as important by both groups.

Table 1.14 Responses on the importance of reading purposes across Year 1 and Year 2 groups

The following purposes for reading are important on my course:	Year 1		Year 2	
	D (r/o)	D&M (r/o)	D (r/o)	D&M (r/o)
15. Searching texts to find information for assignments and exams	64.1% (1)	91.2% (1)	67.8% (1)	90.7% (1)
16. Basic comprehension of main ideas	42.5% (3)	83.5% (2)	48.7% (3)	84.5% (3)
17. Understand meaning of text as a whole; how main ideas and details relate to each other and author's purpose	42.4% (4)	82.2% (4)	47.1% (4)	82.4% (4)
18. Integrating information from different texts for use in assignments, exams	52.1% (2)	83% (3)	53.3% (2)	85.5% (2)

6.8 Reading for assignments

Section 4 of the questionnaire, under the rubric *How I read for assignments,* includes 16 items, as identified in Table 1.15 on pages 72–73. The table again summarises responses in terms of strength of agreement with each item across the EAL and EL1 groups, average rank orders, with the final two columns making Year 1 : Year 2 comparisons. The table contains a considerable quantity of data which should thus inform the questions our study is asking in order to establish the nature of academic reading activities across a range of courses with particular reference to cognitive processing, contextual parameters and the problems experienced by students with respect to these parameters. There are lessons to be learned here for the valid design of Reading tests for potential university students.

The items in Section 4 are all *strategies* for academic reading. They include conscious actions by the reader taken before the Reading begins (e.g. *I think carefully to ensure that I know exactly what I will be looking for before I start reading),* and while it is taking place (e.g. *While reading I try to relate content to what I know already and judge its value*). Most of the strategies specified would seem to relate to expeditious reading at the global level (e.g. *I quickly look through the whole of the text for a general understanding . . .; I think of key words and quickly look for them or words with similar meanings to check if a text is worth reading; I read critically to establish and evaluate the author's position on a particular topic*). Some of the strategies specified, however, cover *careful reading* approaches at the local level (*ibid.*), e.g. *I read a text slowly all the way through . . .; or* at the global level, e.g. *I try to understand how the text is organised, how the ideas and details connect with each other.*

Evidence from these analyses is that the following reading strategies are the *most strongly agreed* as applied to their academic studies by the questionnaire

Table 1.15 Responses on ways of reading for assignments across EAL and EL1 and Year 1, Year 2 sub-groups

How I read for assignments	EAL		EL1		EAL/L1	Yr 1	Yr 2
	D (r/o)	D&M (r/o)	D (r/o)	D&M (r/o)	x r/o	D&M (r/o)	D&M (r/o)
19. Think carefully to make sure I know exactly what I'll be looking for before I start reading	40.4% (2)	77.4% (2)	38.0% (3=)	80.1% (2=)	2.25	80.5% (2)	76.1% (2)
20. Look quickly through whole text for general understanding before doing anything else	28.4% (6)	72.9% (4)	28.5% (8)	68.8% (10)	7	72.8% (4)	67.3% (8)
21. Gradually understand what a text is about by reading the sentences slowly and carefully in the order they occur	21.6% (10)	56.7% (14)	23.1% (11)	52.9% (15)	12.5	54.8% (14)	56.4% (12)
22. Remember where relevant info is or mark its location for later use in writing my assignment	36.3% (3)	77.1% (3)	47.6% (1)	86% (1)	2	79.2% (3)	85.4% (1)
23. Think carefully of key words and quickly look for them or words with similar meanings to check if text is worth reading more carefully	29.6% (5)	70.6% (5)	38.0% (3=)	81% (2=)	3.75	70.6 (6)	68.0% (7)
24. Look at the titles or headings of a text before deciding to read it quickly	44.2% (1)	82.1% (1)	33.4% (6)	73.3% (9)	4.25	81.1% (1)	73.8% (4)
25. First get overall meaning of text e.g. by reading first paragraph and conclusion and first sentence of other paragraphs	19.2% (13)	57.6% (13)	16.8% (15)	53.4% (14)	13.75	56.4% (13)	55.3% (13)
26. If I do not know the meaning of a word in a text, I try to work out its meaning	27.6% (7)	63.8% (10)	35.5% (5)	77.5% (7)	7.25	69.9% (8)	66.6% (9)
27. I read a text slowly all the way through even if some parts do not seem relevant to my assignment	8.5% (16)	33.4% (16)	10.6% (16)	30.7% (16)	16.0	33.4% (16)	32.6% (16)

Table 1.15 (continued)

28. I read slowly only those sections of a text I have marked as relevant when going through it quickly before	21.4% (11)	67.6% (6)	21.9% (12)	63.7% (11)	10	66.7% (11)	65.7% (11)
29. While reading I try to relate content to what I know already and judge its value	22.8% (8)	67.4% (7)	27.9% (9)	78.9% (5)	7.25	71.2% (5)	75.0% (3)
30. I look back at previous parts of the text to check meaning	18.2% (14)	64.4% (9)	27.8% (10)	75.6% (8)	10.25	69.8% (9)	66.3% (10)
31. I try to understand how the text is organised: how the ideas and details connect with each other	19.4% (12)	61.9% (12)	18.8% (14)	62% (12)	12.5	66.6% (12)	52.0% (15)
32. I make notes on relevant points from the text as I go along	31.0% (4)	66.4% (8)	41.2% (2)	78.7% (6)	5	70.3% (7)	72.3% (5)
33. I integrate information from the text I am reading with information from other texts I have already read	22.6% (9)	62.4% (11)	31.3% (7)	79.1% (4)	7.75	69.3% (10)	69.7% (6)
34. I read critically to establish and evaluate the author's position on a particular topic	12.9% (15)	51.4% (15)	20.1% (13)	59% (13)	14	54.3% (15)	55.3% (13)

respondent sample, with differences between the EAL and the EL1, Year 1 and Year 2 sub-groups as stated:

- The strategy *remembering where relevant information is or marking its location for later use in writing my assignment,* is *definitely* or *mostly agreed* by 77.1% of the EAL group and 86% of the EL1 sub-groups, 85.4% of the Year 2 group and 79.2% of the Year 1 students; this strategy has the highest mean rank order of all the strategies specified, although only just higher than:

- *I think carefully to make sure I know exactly what I'll be looking for before I start reading,* is *definitely* or *mostly agreed* by 77.4% of the EAL group and 80.1% of the EL1 sub-groups, 80.5% and 76.1% of the Year 1 and Year 2 sub-groups respectively.

- *I think carefully of key words and quickly look for them or words with similar meanings to check if text is worth reading more carefully* is *definitely* or *mostly agreed* by 70.6% of the EAL group and 81% of the EL1 sub-groups, 70.6% and 68% of the Year 1 and 2 groups respectively.

- *I look at the titles or headings of a text before deciding to read it quickly* is *definitely* or *mostly agreed* by 82.1% of the EAL group and 73.3% of the EL1 sub-groups. While this strategy receives a strong endorsement from both sub-groups, it is more strongly agreed with by the EAL sub-group [p < .01], who actually rates it their *most* strongly agreed strategy; there also appears to be a difference between the Year 1 group's top ranking of this strategy and the Year 2 students' fourth ranking of the strategy (p < .01).

- *I make notes on relevant points from the text as I go along* is also *a strategy receiving strong endorsement;* as the fifth highest rank-ordered on average, it is *definitely* or *mostly agreed* by 66.4% of the EAL group and 78.7% of the EL1 sub-group [significance of difference p < .01]; both the Year 1 and Year 2 groups also see this strategy as important.

A striking feature of the most strongly agreed academic reading strategies here is that all five are clearly *dual-oriented strategies* in the sense that the reader is pre-specifying or identifying concepts or information for future use as well as current understanding. Such strategies are also, of course, related more closely to expeditious than to careful reading, and are global rather than local in the sense that they appear to involve searching *a whole text* for relevance to an actual assignment task.

If we also consider academic reading strategies which were not particularly strongly endorsed, we find a tendency for these to be rather *less* dual-oriented and expeditious-reading related. The following strategies were given the five weakest agreements, in terms of their rank orders:

- *I read a text slowly all the way through even if some parts do not seem relevant to my assignment.* This clear example of careful reading is the lowest rated and ranked by all groups (EAL, EL1, Year 1 and Year 2) and as measured by all *definitely* and *mainly agree* measures.
- *I read critically to establish and evaluate the author's position on a particular topic.* This strategy is perhaps, more surprisingly, also low-ranked by all groups. Is this an indication of a lack of requirement or inclination to read critically for writer stance?
- *I first get an overall meaning of text e.g. by reading the first paragraph and conclusion and first sentence of other paragraphs.* This strategy is again ranked low (r/o 13–15 across all positive ratings) by both language background and Year sub-groups (although more than 50% of them rate the strategy as *definitely* or *mainly agreed*).
- *I gradually understand what a text is about by reading the sentences slowly and carefully in the order they occur:* this strategy is low-ranked (r/o 10–15, positive rating 56.7% and 52.9% for the EAL and EL1 groups respectively, 54.8% for Year 1 students, 56.4% for Year 2); notice how the strategy is rather less weakly rated than the *read a text slowly all the way through even if some parts do not seem relevant to my assignment* strategy above, both involving slow reading, but the earlier and less agreed strategy not excluding the reading of irrelevant text parts.
- *I try to understand how the text is organised: how the ideas and details connect with each other:* this strategy, similarly ranked to the previous one, may be a semi-unconscious skill rather than a strategy, perhaps therefore under-rated by the students concerned (see below).

The cross-tabulation of the undergraduate : postgraduate sub-groups in terms of assignment reading strategies suggests that the two groups do not differ in many of these. The main exception appears to be *looking quickly through the whole text for a general understanding before doing anything else* (apparently a stronger tendency for the graduates than the undergraduates; 'definitely' and 'mostly agree' percentages 80.7% and 69.7% respectively).

There are certainly interesting issues here in terms of the kinds of reading strategies appropriate for the training and assessment of pre-university students. These are discussed further below.

6.9 Student difficulties encountered when reading for assignments

Now the focus of our questionnaire data moves to the *difficulties* encountered by the target students when reading for their assignments. Overall, as indicated in Table 1.16 below, it is the similarities rather than the differences across the EAL and EL1 sub-groups that strike one. Equally closely matched,

Table 1.16 Responses on difficulties encountered with reading for assignments across EAL and EL1 and Year 1, Year 2 subgroups

Difficulties when reading for assignments	EAL		EL1		Year 1	Year 2
	D (r/o)	D&M (r/o)	D (r/o)	D&M (r/o)	D&M (r/o)	D&M (r/o)
35. the time available to do the necessary reading	24.3% (1)	57.7% (2)	31.3% (2)	59.4% (2)	57.0% (2)	61.9% (2)
36. reading texts where the subject matter is complicated	18.8% (2)	58.5% (1)	32.2% (1)	70.2% (1)	61.0% (1)	67.7% (1)
37. words I do not know	15.6% (3)	44.0% (4)	13.0% (5)	34.6% (6)	41.5% (5)	37.6% (7)
38. sentence structures	11.1% (8)	35.6% (10)	5.8% (13)	21.6% (15)	32.5% (10)	25.0% (16)
39. finding relevant information quickly	14.1% (4)	43.3% (6)	16.3% (4)	42.9% (4)	43.9% (4)	41.3% (4)
40. lengthy texts	13.0% (5)	47.3% (3)	17.1% (3)	47.2% (3)	45.9% (3)	50.9% (3)
41. lack of background knowledge to understand the content	12.1% (7)	41.8% (7)	12.4% (6)	35.5% (5)	39.1% (7)	40.5% (5)
42. making notes on information I will need	8.8% (14)	26.1% (17)	8.6% (10)	19.9% (16)	21.8% (17)	27.8% (13)
43. reading carefully to understand the main ideas	10.9% (9)	31.4% (15)	5.2% (15)	23.5% (14)	28.0% (15)	29.0% (12)
44. summarising ideas from a text in my own words	12.8% (6)	43.5% (5)	11.1% (8)	33.6% (8)	40.9% (6)	38.1% (6)
45. understanding a detailed logical argument	8.0% (16)	37.3% (9)	5.2% (15)	25.3% (11)	32.7% (9)	32.7% (10)
46. reading critically to establish and evaluate the author's position on a particular topic	8.5% (15)	37.9% (8)	8.0% (11)	33.9% (7)	35.6% (8)	36.5% (8)
47. relating the content of a text to my existing knowledge	7.6% (17)	30.7% (16)	4.5% (17)	18.7% (17)	27.3% (16)	24.0% (17)
48. deciding what is important for me and what is not	10.2% (10)	31.7% (13)	11.9% (7)	32.6% (9)	32.2% (11)	32.1% (11)
49. reading a text quickly to decide whether I should study it carefully	9.5% (11)	34.2% (12)	11.0% (9)	30.4% (10)	32.0% (12)	33.1% (9)
50. understanding the text as a whole; how main ideas and details are connected to each other	8.9% (13)	34.6% (11)	5.5% (14)	23.5% (12)	28.9% (13)	26.4% (14)
51. integrating information from text I am reading with info from other texts I have read	9.1% (12)	31.7% (13)	7.6% (12)	23.5% (12)	28.4% (14)	26.4% (14)

as also analysed in Table 1.16, are the reading problems across Year 1 and Year 2 students.

Analysing the Likert scale responses, whether judged in terms of the proportions of *definitely agree* percentages or the combined *definitely* and *mostly agree* categories across the 468 EAL students and the 298 EL1 students, the main difficulties experienced, in rank order, appear to be with:

1. Reading texts where the subject matter is complicated.
2. The time available to do the necessary reading.
3. Reading lengthy texts.
4. Finding relevant information quickly.

The time and reading load problem, it will be recalled, was already signposted by the pilot questionnaire in Study 1. Also connected with the problem of time, is the difficulty of finding relevant information quickly, which is rated fourth across all categories (i.e. EAL, EL1, *definitely agree* selections and *definitely* and *mostly agree* selections combined). A slight difference is with the EAL group percentage on this difficulty, but their *definitely* and *mostly agree* count still ranks it the sixth most prominent difficulty of the 17 problems specified.

The evidence is strong from Table 1.16 here that *time* and *complicated reading subject matter* are the major problems for both EAL and EL1 groups. The two items referring directly to these problems are the highest rated and ranked for difficulty for both EAL and EL1 groups, the EL1 group finding significantly *more* difficulty ($p<.01$) with complicated subject matter suggesting that first language status is not necessarily the major issue when the study subject itself is complicated. Both groups, however, agree that *lack of background knowledge to understand the reading content* is a fairly major problem (41.8% of the EAL group and 35.5% of the EL1 group respectively *definitely* or *mostly* agreeing on this, their seventh and fifth most highly ranked difficulty respectively). Related, most likely, to the problem of time is the need *to find relevant information quickly*, a significant problem for 57% and 59% of the EAL and EL1 groups respectively.

Summarising ideas from a text in my own words, a skill which, of course, integrates reading with writing and speaking, is rated as *definitely* or *mostly* an agreed difficulty by 56.3% and 44.7% of the EAL and EL1 groups respectively, the difference in rating strength significant at p <.05.

Potential reading-related difficulties *not* so highly rated or ranked (though still affecting around 40% of our EAL population) will also inform our analysis below of the appropriateness of IELTS Reading tasks. Table 1.16 suggests the following as among such categories:

• *relating the content of a text to my existing knowledge:* ranked the least or next least of the difficulties of both EAL and EL1 groups.

- *making notes on information I will need:* low-ranked as a reading-related skill by both groups, only 26.1% and 19.9% respectively of the EAL and EL1 groups rating it as a *definitely* or *mostly* agreed difficulty in reading for assignments.
- *understanding the text as a whole; how main ideas and details are connected to each other* and *integrating information from text I am reading with info from other texts I have read:* the next lowest ranked difficulties, both with very similar ratings.

The final two columns in Table 1.16 permit inferences from the Year 1 : Year 2 variable on the matter of student problems in academic reading. Here, as in Table 1.15, Year 1 and Year 2 student responses are compared in terms of percentages of *definitely agree* plus *mostly agree* responses and in terms of rank orders of the 17 reading difficulties concerned, these, of course, derived from the project literature review (see Section 3 above) and the pilot question-naire open-ended data (Section 5). As signalled above, it is the *similarity* of the perceptions of the reading problems of the first and second year students which is notable. This suggests that these problems do not disappear with exposure to a wide range of reading in the first year of study.

Once again, as inferred from the EAL : EL1 group difficulty comparisons above, the same four main problems are identified, in the same rank order by the Year 1 and the Year 2 sub-groups, namely:

1. Reading texts where the subject matter is complicated.
2. The time available to do the necessary reading.
3. Reading lengthy texts.
4. Finding relevant information quickly.

Note that, once more, the evidence is strong that students find their *time* inadequate to handle the problems of finding relevant information quickly from long and complicated texts. The factors and tasks here are closely and explicitly related to the *expeditious reading* construct established in the litera-ture review above, and pursued as a major focus of Study 3 on the cognitive parameters of the IELTS Reading test and Study 4 on the test's contextual parameters.

Next ranked by the Year 1 and 2 sub-groups, both EAL and EL1, is the dif-ficulty of *words I do not know,* though there is an indication (not statistically significant) that this becomes marginally less of a problem in the second year. Such is *not,* apparently, the case with *lack of background knowledge to under-stand reading content,* still a major problem in Year 2, it seems.

There is also evidence in Table 1.16 that reading-related activities *not* so highly rated or ranked are shared across the Year 1 and 2 as well as the EAL and EL1 student groups. The following figure as such less problematic aca-demic reading activities:

- *relating the content of a text to my existing knowledge:* ranked the least or next least of the difficulties by both Year groups as they were by EAL and EL1 groups.
- *making notes on information I will need:* low-ranked as a reading-related skill by both groups, at only 21.8% and 27.8% respectively of the Year 1 and Year 2 groups rating it as a *definitely* or *mostly* agreed difficulty in reading for assignments; the difference between the Year 1 and Year 2 percentages here is significant, however, at $p<.01$, suggesting that this problem is somewhat more severe for students in their second year.
- *understanding the text as a whole; how main ideas and details are connected to each other* and *integrating information from text I am reading with info from other texts I have read* are again, for the Year 1 and Year 2 groups, the next lowest ranked difficulties, both with very similar ratings, but for both first and second year groups only slightly lower rated in terms of difficulty than *reading carefully to understand the main ideas*.

The most substantial difference among the academic reading problems between our undergraduate and postgraduate student sub-samples appears to be with difficulty in finding relevant information quickly, a problem for 45.3% of the former group, 31.7% of the latter.

Our findings on the difficulties encountered by students when reading for their assignments must surely be of interest to the designers of tests such as IELTS, which set out to measure and claim as valid indicators of English language proficiency, the IELTS scores of international students seeking to study at British and other EL1 universities. This message is pursued in the next section of our Study 2 report here.

6.10   IELTS Academic Reading test scores and student reading

Given that this research project is examining the relationship between the academic reading construct as measured by IELTS and the reading experiences of students in their study at a British university, indications from the questionnaire data of relationships between higher and lower scoring IELTS test-taker groups and their reading strategies or problems should certainly be of interest. If, for example, significant differences are found between the lower- and the higher-scoring IELTS groups and their responses on a particular academic reading problem, predictive validity could be inferred for the IELTS Reading test.

Descriptive statistics were run for the 301 IELTS Reading test-taker scores in our questionnaire sample, to establish the extent to which there were significant differences across the highest-scoring group (IELTS Academic Reading band score 6.5 and above) and the mid- and lower-scoring groups (6.0, and 5.5 or less), data and discussion on these band scores in Figure 1.4 and accompanying comment above. Table 1.17 summarises one-way ANOVA results for cases where the differences between high, lower and lowest IELTS-score

Table 1.17 One-way ANOVA statistics indicating student reading problems with a significant (p<.01) difference between students with higher and lower IELTS Academic Reading scores

		Sum of Squares	df	Mean Square	F	Sig.
IELTS Reading score	Between groups	105.299	2	52.649	337.598	.000
Time constraints	Between groups	17.103	2	8.552	7.623	.001
	Within groups	326.438	291	1.122		
	Total	343.541	293			
Words I do not know	Between groups	23.156	2	11.578	9.058	.000
	Within groups	371.936	291	1.278		
	Total	395.092	293			
Make notes on information I will need	Between groups	17.272	2	8.636	6.896	.001
	Within groups	364.429	291	1.252		
	Total	381.701	293			
Reading carefully to understand main ideas	Between groups	30.908	2	15.454	11.773	.000
	Within groups	381.990	291	1.313		
	Total	412.898	293			
Understand a detailed logical argument	Between groups	11.624	2	5.812	5.748	.004
	Within groups	295.237	292	1.011		
	Total	306.861	294			
Relating content to existing knowledge	Between groups	22.065	2	11.032	10.453	.000
	Within groups	306.065	290	1.055		
	Total	328.130	292			
Integrating info from text with other texts	Between groups	16.290	2	8.145	7.211	.001
	Within groups	329.845	292	1.130		
	Total	346.136	294			

groups and particular reading problems as identified on the questionnaire, were found to be significant (p<.01).

Noteworthy in Table 1.17 are the following significant (p<.01) differences, each indicating a relationship between IELTS Academic Reading score and a perceived problem with academic reading at the University of Bedfordshire:

- between the highest (IELTS 6.5+) and lowest (5.5 or less) groups for difficulties:
  - *with the time available to do the necessary reading*
  - *understanding a detailed logical argument*
- between the two higher groups (6.0 and 6.5+) with difficulties:
  - *reading for basic comprehension of the main ideas in a text*
  - *making notes on relevant points from the text 'as I go along'*
  - *lengthy texts*
- between the highest group (6.5+) and both lower groups (6.0 and 5.5−) for difficulties with:
  - *unknown words*
  - *making notes on information I will need*
  - *reading carefully to understand the main ideas*
  - *relating the content of a text to existing knowledge*
  - *integrating information from the text I am reading with information from other texts I have already read*
- and between the lowest (5.5−) and middle group (6.0) on:
  - *gradually understanding what a text is about by reading the sentences slowly and carefully in the order they occur.*

The inference here is that the IELTS test has, for these takers, predicted significant differences in some of the reading problems faced by the students in our sample with their actual academic reading experience at university. If we look more closely at the problems concerned here, we may note that the problems concerned involve both careful reading (e.g. *reading the sentences slowly and carefully in the order they occur*) and expeditious reading (e.g. *relating the content of a text to existing knowledge*), and with both cognitive strategies and contextual factors (e.g. *the time available to do the necessary reading*).

6.11 Overall difficulties of the four skills in university studies

The final item on the main questionnaire attempted to elicit student views on the relative difficulty for them in their studies of the four language skills. Table 1.18 summarises responses for EAL and EL1 sub-groups.

Table 1.18 EAL and EL1 student perceptions of the relative difficulties of the four skills

EAL			EL1		
Macro-skill	Most difficult	2nd most difficult	Macro-skill	Most difficult	2nd most difficult
Listening	23.0% (3)	32.7% (2)	Listening	24.2% (4)	24.6% (4)
Reading	20.9% (4)	33.4% (1)	Reading	24.8% (3)	36.0% (1)
Writing	39.4% (1)	32.6% (3)	Writing	25.9% (2)	29.6% (2)
Speaking	33.4% (2)	29.8% (4)	Speaking	29.6% (1)	27.1% (3)

Of particular interest here is that a *lower* percentage of EAL students see reading as their most *difficult* of the four macro-skills, yet a third of these students regard it as their second most difficult skill. There are implications for the IELTS test, especially in the light of IELTS impact study findings (Hawkey 2006:122) that the 'Reading module is seen as clearly the most difficult of the four IELTS test modules across our candidate and preparation teacher participants'. Is it in fact valid in terms of test construct and content that one of the four test modules should be perceived by test takers as of a different level of difficulty than the others, if the macro-skill it is testing is not the most difficult in the target academic domain? The EL1 sub-group, it will be noted, also does not see academic reading as their most problematic, though again it is rated the second most difficult skill area.

The analysis in Table 1.18 suggests writing as clearly the perceived most difficult academic language skill for our EAL sub-group, speaking for the EL1 students. Perhaps a psycho- and socio-linguistic factor is operating here. The EAL students may well be thinking of language proficiency problems affecting their assignment and other academic writing. The focus of the EL1 students, on the other hand, may be on the stresses of the kind of 'speaking' involved when having to handle an oral presentation.

6.12   Conclusion

In this report of Study 2, we have described our survey sample for the main questionnaire in some detail, with reference across key parameters to the general university population. Data has then been presented and analysed on sources of academic reading information, student course reading purposes and strategies for assignment-related reading, then their perceptions of key academic reading problems. Relationships between the EAL students' IELTS Reading test scores and the cognitive parameters of reading were then explored.

The logic of the study should still be clear. Now that we know more, from

Study 2, of the actual academic reading sources, strategies and problems of our fair cross-section of University of Bedfordshire students, we may investigate, in Study 3, the cognitive parameters tested by the IELTS Academic Reading module and, in Study 4, how the texts used in the IELTS Academic Reading module compare with the kinds of texts that the students actually meet once they are at university.

7 Study 3: Cognitive parameters in IELTS: texts and tasks in the IELTS Academic Reading module

7.1 Approach and instrumentation

Responses to the main project questionnaire to University of Bedfordshire students were helpful in establishing the nature of academic reading activities and problems across a range of courses. The next logical step in the project design was thus to examine IELTS Academic Reading module tests to evaluate the extent to which they may actually cover reading activities and problems revealed by the student questionnaires analysed in Study 2. This was the aim of Study 3.

The instrument for the analysis of IELTS Academic Reading tests was derived from the literature review (above), in particular the reading strategies, skills and processes reported in Section 3.1 above, which discusses the processes and problems of careful and expeditious reading (derived from Urquhart and Weir 1998). Then, in December 2006, all members, staff and students of the CRELLA Project team participated in a standardisation exercise involving the use of a draft matrix specification of expeditious and careful reading strategies, to be matched against actual IELTS Academic Reading test tasks. The matrix, as finalised by the standardisation exercise, appears as Table 1.19 on page 84.

EWS: Explicit within sentence. Establishing basic propositional meaning at sentence level through explicitly stated ideas in the text. Basic comprehension questions are used to assess lexical, syntactic, and semantic abilities and the ability to understand important information presented in sentence-level propositions.

IWS: Implicit within sentence. Inferencing by creating information which is not explicitly stated in a sentence. Understanding information in a sentence may require addressing conceptual gaps by constructing a message from both what is explicitly stated and from our stored knowledge. Such inferences are necessary for a full understanding of the sentence.

EAS: Explicit across sentences. Establishing meaning through explicitly stated ideas across sentences.

IBS: Implicit between sentences. Inferencing meaning which is not explicitly stated between sentences in a text.

TM: A text model. Creating a text model. Constructing an organised representation of the text including main points and supporting details; an integrated understanding of how supporting ideas and factual details of the text form a coherent whole.

SM: A situation model. Answering questions based on a situation model. Addressing conceptual gaps by constructing a message from both what is explicitly stated and from our stored knowledge. Building a situation model involves the reader forming a representation of the content, relating the contextual information of a text to mental models of corresponding real-life situations.

Table 1.19 Finalised reading cognitive parameter matrix and reference key for the analysis of IELTS Academic Reading tests

	Expeditious reading strategies		
	Skimming	Search reading	Scanning
Types of reading strategies and skills	• The reader locates and comprehends information at the overall gist level. • Reading is selective, with sections of the text either omitted or given very little attention. • An attempt is made to build up a macrostructure of the whole text (the gist) based on careful reading of as little of the text as possible.	• The reader locates information quickly and selectively on predetermined topics to answer set questions e.g., by looking for related vocabulary in the semantic field. • The reader is guided by predetermined topics and so does not have to establish a macro propositional structure for the whole of the text. • Once the required information to answer a question has been quickly and selectively located, careful reading will take over.	• The reader reads quickly and selectively to achieve very specific reading goals, e.g., looking for a specific word or phrase, date, figure or word. • Limited careful reading may follow this matching activity.
Types of reading strategies and skills	Careful reading skills					
	EWS	IWS	EAS	IBS	TM	SM

In the standardisation operation project team members used the reading strategy descriptors in Table 1.19 and the draft test task : reading strategy matrix (as in Table 1.20) to describe the strategies they actually used on an authentic IELTS Academic Reading test. This was followed by discussion of the experience by the whole team, suggestions for revisions to the forms, and, finally, approval of the revised reading cognitive parameter matrix and reference key (Table 1.19) and the form in Table 1.20, which was to be used in phase two of Study 3.

Table 1.20 IELTS Reading test task types and the reading strategies to respond to them

Test item format	Reading expeditiously			Reading carefully					
	Skim	Search	Scan	EWS	IWS	EAS	IBS	TM	SM
Matching headings									
Yes/No or True/False/ Not given									
Filling in blanks									
Multiple choice									
Table or other iconic completion									
Short Q + A									

In this, three project members were asked to record independently the reading strategies *they* employed to respond to each task on a selection of 14 IELTS Academic Reading module tests. All the IELTS tests used in the analysis are authentic and now in the public domain. In the account of Study 4 below, the dimensions and other contextual parameters of the IELTS tests are analysed fully, in comparison with typical authentic texts used by students across their main fields of study. We note here merely, from the 14 complete tests selected for our analysis, that:

- most complete IELTS Academic Reading module tests are around 15 A4 pages long
- they contain three separate texts on which candidates must respond to common test tasks of the kind specified in Table 1.20
- there are a total of 40 items in each test
- each test contains an average of 3,458 words to read, including the tasks and rubrics
- the average number of words of *reading text* to read in each test is 2,562 words
- the average test *text* is 854 words long (maximum 1,063 words, minimum 589 words).

As noted in the Table 1.20 matrix, the Reading test tasks included: the *matching* of suggested and actual test content; the categorisation of suggested content as *Yes/No (or True/False) or Not given* in the test text; *gap-filling; multiple-choice; table* or *other iconic completion*, and *short-answer questions*.

The three IELTS Reading test analysts were informed participants. Two, EAL users, responded to all 42 testlets *qua* IELTS-takers, and entered in the matrix in Table 1.20 the cognitive strategies they used in the process, along with any comments they felt relevant to the research purpose. The third team member, an EL1 user, covered the same tests and recorded self-report comments of the process he adopted to complete the Reading test tasks. The research approach to Study 3 thus elicited both qualitative and quantitative data on how the IELTS tests concerned were approached.

7.2   Analysis and findings: qualitative

The *qualitative* comments made by the test-taker-analysts remind us that the very fact that we are reading *as test takers* may affect the strategies and skills applied to our reading tasks, this a matter to be pursued further in Study 4 below, on the contextual parameters of the IELTS test Reading modules. It is appropriate to discuss our qualitative data first here as it provides a general context for the more quantitative analysis of the test taker reading strategies subsequently analysed. The report-backs are presented *verbatim*, with interpretative commentary added as relevant to our research questions.

One EAL team member (test taker A below) added to his quantitative analysis of the reading strategies used to take the tests the following general description of how he approached the IELTS Academic Reading test tasks:

> I usually read the texts carefully from the beginning to the end initially then I go to the questions. I can answer some questions without having to read the text again. If not, I usually remember the place where the info necessary for the answer is located and go there usually by scanning which may be followed by some careful reading. That, I could not make explicit in the analysis.

In revealing that he 'usually read the texts carefully from the beginning to the end initially', the test-taker-analyst makes a point relevant both to our investigation of the cognitive *and* the contextual parameters of reading and its testing. We recall that university student questionnaire data in Studies 1 and 2 above, suggests strongly that, students, in their actual academic reading lives at university, do *not* commonly '*read a text slowly all the way through even if some parts do not seem relevant to my assignment*' (see Table 1.15 above). In fact this strategy was the lowest rated and ranked by all sub-groups (EAL, EL1, Year 1 and Year 2) responding to the main questionnaire. There thus appears to be some conflict between reading as part of student academic studies and the cognitive parameters of the IELTS Reading test. Our reader-analyst here may be exhibiting a tendency for some readers to employ *careful reading strategies* for the test texts *because* this is a Reading test task, with, they can already see, a dozen or more items on it to be answered.

A second Study 3 team member, an EL1 reader, makes the following comments on the approach adopted to the IELTS Reading module, at least partly, it would seem, because it is a test:

> . . . Before reading any questions or, if the "Choose the correct heading for each section from the list of headings below" item is placed before the text, after reading that, I make a decision whether to read through the whole text. But I want to read through *quickly* so I may skip read while trying to keep the gist and main details, predicting likely key question points as well as looking for points we already know we need, to answer the matching question. Then I search for relevant parts of the passage after reading each question, trying to zero in to decide on whether the detail helps me answer the question concerned.

Note here the problem, inherent in the test format, that the reader's decision to read expeditiously appears to be inhibited by only partly knowing in advance what information she is seeking, as she appears to apply a combination of skim, search and scan reading strategies to the text. (We return, in our *quantitative* analysis below, to the issue of partial overlap across the broader expeditious reading strategies.)

The EL1 reader's report-back makes points of interest with regard to relationships between test task types and the cognitive parameters of the strategies used to handle them. Such report-back, like the students' responses to the Study 2 questionnaire items on their actual academic reading, could be helpful in the design and validation of reading tests such as IELTS.

On the IELTS *matching* task type (e.g. *Reading Passage 1 has three sections, A – C. Choose the correct headings for each section from the list of headings below* . . .), the reader-analyst report is tentative but critical. Like most report-backs, it is rather complex, but so, as we have seen in Section 1 of this report, is the process of reading, as are attempts to test it:

> Do candidates deal with this task as skim and then select (someone else's "gist")? The task should involve expeditious reading, *skimming* i.e. *The reader locates and comprehends information at the overall gist level* [Table 1.19]. The reading should be selective, (i.e. looking for info relevant to the heading given) with sections of the text either omitted or given very little attention (i.e. skip over sentences not appearing to refer to the heading given). We should be making an attempt to build up a macrostructure (the gist) based on as few details from the text as possible.
>
> But, in fact, given we're looking for three sets of information, and have also to bear in mind three others (the distractors in the test task),

are we really likely to be that selective in our reading? How much can we really leave out? Especially given the "tricky" questions with their deliberate overlap across the headings. They are probably "designed" to make candidates have to think "Ah, that bit's about disruptive effects of tourism . . . or is it about the expansion of tourism?". So a likelihood of reading more carefully than in the similar real-life situation.

In terms of real-life reading purposes and strategies, we the readers know, for our own real purposes, what overall gist we are trying to skim for; or what topics we are search reading for, (in order THEN to read more carefully about); or what specific info we are scanning for (then, perhaps, to read carefully about). It is possible that we are also aware, as we are searching, skimming or scanning, of what info we do not want (like the distractor headings in the IELTS task that are not the right descriptors of the section . . .). But do we ever *really* read to select, from a surfeit of closely related topics, one rather than others that summarises a part of a text? Does the task not actually force us into careful reading, section by section, in order to be sure of selecting the right summarising heading? Presumably some candidates would:

- read the headings and try to remember their "meaning", then
- read Section A; then compare what they have read with all the headings,
- then select. Then repeat this process two more times. Maybe by Section C, they could expeditiously read a bit because the options by then are narrower?

This report-back is presented in full because it appears to cover several key problem areas in the cognitive parameters of the IELTS Academic Reading test, and to offer an explanation of how a Reading test like IELTS may push test takers towards the careful rather than expeditious forms of reading.

The EL1 reader's further report-back relating the various IELTS *task types* to cognitive parameters are as follows:

Yes/No (or True/False) or Not given:

> I tried not to read closely, but instead to locate key words involved in the task e.g. "cost", "deserts", "hill", "government", then see if the location was right to answer the question. If so write in the Y, N, NG as appropriate. If not, search-read for another cue/key word that I had thought could be "related vocabulary in the semantic field".

Filling in blanks/Table completion:

> Here, we need to scan to locate the people/location context, then find the right word (in the text) for the completion. I read the people/location reference and the clause for completion, then scan the text for the context, then the clause content reference, then write in the word concerned.

Multiple choice

> Here I seemed mainly to end up reading for explicit meaning, or implicit meaning within sentence [EWS or IWS in Table 19 above].

This kind of qualitative report-back data, though complex, can usefully inform our view of reading, as well as our attempts to assess proficiency in it.

7.3 Analysis and findings: quantitative

The *quantitative* analysis for Study 3 is based on the completion, by two informed EAL participants, of the same 14 IELTS tests, including all their 42 texts (at three texts per test), each test with a total of 40 items, and including the seven main task types specified in Table 1.20 above. The two test-taker-analysts thus covered 560 test items, in the solution of each of which they identified the strategy or skill they applied. As the two total numbers in the right-hand columns of Table 1.21 are both just above 560 (at 562 and 585 respectively for test-taker-analysts A and B respectively) the indication is that for a few items the test takers felt that they applied more than one strategy or skill.

Table 1.21 Summary of responses of two EAL test-taker-analysts to the Reading test tasks of 14 authentic IELTS Reading modules

Test-taker/ Analyst	Reading *expeditiously* by:			Reading *carefully* for meaning which is:				Reading		Totals per reader-analyst
	skimming	search reading	scanning	explicit within sentence	implicit within sentence	explicit across sentences	implicit between sentences	to construct a Text Model	for a Situation Model of text and own prior knowledge	
A	0	45	50	277	27	115	45	3	0	562
B	70	6	93	318	12	57	25	4	0	585
Cognitive skill totals	70	51	143	595	39	172	70	7	0	1,154
Sub-totals: *expeditious vs careful reading*	264			883						1,154

As implied by the qualitative analysis and findings above, we would *not* predict that the two EAL test takers would each activate the same cognitive strategies to complete the same tasks. There are several reasons for this, most of these already implied by our review of the reading literature above. Test takers' approaches to taking Reading tests clearly differ. Thus, so do the meta-cognitive strategies employed (see Section 1 above), including the combinations of skills identified by the report-backs above. What is more, as the definitions used in the Study 3 test-completion exercise (see Table 1.19) indicate, the three expeditious reading strategies of *skimming, search reading* and *scanning* involve some overlapping processes and actions (see further below). Add to this the effect of individual differences (also see the literature review above) between the two test-taker-analysts and considerable variations across the tasks and skills are likely.

What we might well expect from the analysis, however, would be similarities in strategy and skill use in terms of the key distinction made throughout this study, namely between *expeditious* (skimming, search reading, scanning) and *careful* reading skills.

Table 1.21 above summarises the responses of the two EAL test-taker-analysts to all the Reading test tasks of the 14 authentic IELTS Reading modules attempted, in terms of the types of reading strategies and skills they perceive that they applied.

Some general conclusions

A number of key points of interest may be inferred from the data in the table. There is indeed a difference of balance between the readers across the expeditious reading strategies of skimming, search reading and scanning. Test-taker-analyst B appears to do significantly more skimming and scanning than test-taker-analyst A, whereas the latter scans and search-reads with similar regularity. But, as our definitions above and their use in the qualitative report-back data both indicate, these expeditious reading strategies do share some elements, for example the aim of locating information quickly, and the likelihood of some consequent careful reading. Some blurring of the edges by readers across the three expeditious strategies is thus possible and acceptable. Furthermore we record above how test-taker-analyst A read through each text carefully before answering the questions and so removed any necessity subsequently for obtaining the overall gist of a passage expeditiously. When he returned to the text scanning and search reading were sufficient to locate information for more careful reading.

The most important finding here in terms of our research questions is the apparent *preponderance of careful reading over expeditious reading strategies* applied by both test-taker-analysts, 77% of the claimed cognitive skills and strategies (883 out of the total of 1,154) apparently belonging to the former category. What is more, 634 of the reading strategies applied by the two readers were apparently *at the sentence level,* compared with 242 strategies applied to items seen as requiring attention *beyond the sentence.* This indicated imbalance is a matter of potential concern given the findings of Studies 2 and 3, that the students at the University of Bedfordshire, when asked about their actual academic reading purposes and problems, saw reading activities of the expeditious kind as more appropriate to their needs than careful reading skills. The data here suggests that the reading skills and strategies tapped by the IELTS Academic Reading module test may need further investigation and possible modification to more closely represent the academic reading constructs of university students through texts and tasks that test more extensively students' expeditious reading skills. The low occurrence of items testing students' ability to process text beyond the sentence level is also a cause for some concern given the nature of the student reading abilities outlined and empirically supported earlier. The almost complete lack of items at the text level, let alone across texts, must similarly be a cause for concern.

Within the two readers' careful reading skill use, there is evidence relevant to the test developers, on the line between information that is *explicit* and information that is *implicit*. Once again, report-back description is revealing, this time from test-taker-analyst B:

> What I understand by explicit is that the answer is directly accessible from the text and may appear in paraphrased form or with synonyms of key words. *I take implicit as [that] the answer is not given directly in the passage but is illustrated by the author thru' examples or style of writing.*

This definition seems reasonable but again reflects a *test-taking* perspective, relating to whether an answer to a test question appears in the text as referenced in the question or in some other form. This is not quite the same as the *implying* defined by the *Webster New World Dictionary*, that is: 'to indicate without saying directly'.

Be that as it may, both test-taker-analysts do find cognitive strategies involving *implicit* meaning at the careful reading level, though in substantially fewer cases (109) than those involving *explicit* meaning (767), as indicated in Table 1.21 above.

8 Study 4: Contextual parameters

8.1 Focus and methodology

As well as generating data on students' reading activities and problems they encounter in academic reading and comparing these with the reading activities required in IELTS, we also carried out an initial investigation of the *contextual* parameters of 14 core undergraduate textbooks at the University of Bedfordshire and compared these parameters with those obtaining in the set of 14 IELTS Reading tests supplied by University of Cambridge ESOL Examinations and investigated in terms of their cognitive parameters in Study 3.

In co-operation with the university library staff we established core first-year undergraduate texts in each of the areas where large numbers (3,000+) of international students are studying in Britain according to the most recent HESA student record data (2004/5). The courses taught at the University of Bedfordshire in these high-density areas were as follows:

Advertising, Marketing and Public Relations
Biology and Biomedical Sciences
Business and Finance
Computing and Information Systems
Criminology
Education Studies
Healthcare (Nursing and Midwifery)
Human Resource Management
Language and Communication (EFL and TEFL)
Law
Leisure, Tourism and Sports Management
Media Arts
Psychology
Social Sciences and Social Work

The selection of the core undergraduate texts in these areas was made on the basis of:

- those books which had had the most reservations made for them in the last three years and in particular the current year
- those books which were taken out the most in the current academic year
- confirmation by course leaders of key books for each area
- books students considered to be the most important (as established through the pilot questionnaire (see above) and direct inquiry).

For Study 4, 42 samples of academic text were collected to match the 42 IELTS texts. These comprised three extracts from each of the 14 different textbooks – sections extracted at random from the opening chapter, the middle and the concluding chapter. These are core texts that undergraduate students are expected to get to grips with during their studies at the University of Bedfordshire. The length of extracts (targeted to be between 500 and 1,500 words) corresponded broadly to the length of the texts included in the IELTS Academic Reading test.

The IELTS texts and the extracts from Bedfordshire academic texts were subjected to a variety of quantitative and qualitative analyses as indicated in Table 1.22 on pages 95–96. Measures of the *quantitative* features listed in Table 1.22 were obtained through the Web VocabProfile available at http://www.lextutor.ca supplemented by analysis through WordSmith Tools (Scott 2006) and text analysis tools packaged with Microsoft Word for Windows.

For the *qualitative* analyses, two expert judges, with doctorates and experience of teaching and test development in the area of academic literacy, employed Likert scales and categorisation tools to evaluate the texts.

Measures of vocabulary include word length (number of characters/word), type-token ratio, lexical density and word frequency levels. Grammatical complexity may be estimated through word/sentence and sentence/paragraph ratios and through the proportion of passive verbs. Summaries of these features are obtained through Web VocabProfiler and text analysis summaries provided through Microsoft Word for Windows. Readability statistics (Flesch reading ease and Flesch-Kincaid grade level) are also calculated using Microsoft Word: both measures being based on the relative numbers of syllables, words and sentences found in a text.

In investigating *discourse mode* here we include genre (or text source), rhetorical task, pattern of exposition and rhetorical organisation.

Each judge independently assigned each text to one of the following genres, identified through the development of the student questionnaire used in Study 1:

- textbook
- magazine and newspaper article
- research/academic journal article
- report.

The judges also identified the subject area with which each text appeared most closely associated, using the HESA classification of courses of study shown above.

Each text was classified by the two judges according to the following discoursal features discussed above:

Rhetorical task

- Exposition
- Argumentation/persuasion/evaluation
- Historical biographical/autobiographical narrative.

Pattern of exposition

- Definition/description/elaboration
- Illustration
- Classification
- Comparison/Contrast
- Cause and effect
- Problem/Solution
- Justify.

The two judges also used five-point Likert scales to make a subjective evaluation of the texts on the following features:

Rhetorical organisation (1 explicit to 5 not explicit). This is intended to reflect the ease or difficulty with which the overall propositional pattern of the text is likely to be understood by the reader.

Grammatical complexity (1 mainly simple sentences to 5 mainly complex sentences).

Cohesion (1 explicit to 5 not explicit). An evaluation of the extent to which relations between the ideas were explicitly marked through reference, conjunctions and connectors.

Content knowledge

Subject specificity (1 general to 5 specific). This involved an evaluation of the frequency of technical vocabulary and the extent to which terms were glossed in the text for the general reader.

Nature of information (1 concrete to 5 abstract). An evaluation of the extent to which the text was concerned with concrete observable phenomena.

Cultural specificity (1 culture neutral to 5 culture specific). This involved an evaluation of the frequency of culture-specific content as set out in the literature review above and the extent to which culturally specific references or examples were explained to the general reader.

Table 1.22 on page 95 specifies contextual parameters for the analysis of IELTS texts and extracts from core undergraduate texts used by students at the University of Bedfordshire.

A guiding principle in this particular study was to develop a set of methodological procedures that can easily be replicated by IELTS test developers in the future. Item writers need to have as clear an idea as possible of the complexity of any texts (across a range of parameters) where there is a *prima facie* case for inclusion in terms of length and appropriateness for testing intended skills and strategies. Study 4 was an initial attempt to establish a set of practical and meaningful procedures which might assist in this process. The point of comparison is the texts actually read by first-year students.

8.2 Quantitative studies

The results of a one-way ANOVA comparing the IELTS and undergraduate texts on the range of contextual parameters are presented in Table 1.23 on page 97. There were significant ($p<.05$) differences between IELTS texts and undergraduate texts for readability measures (Flesch reading ease and Flesch-Kincaid reading level); standardised type-token ratio; proportion of words on the academic word list (AWL); proportion of words appearing on the first 1,000 word frequency and 3,000 word frequency levels and the proportion of infrequent (off list) words. There were no significant differences on any other of the quantitative measures listed in Table 1.22.

Table 1.22 Contextual parameters for the analysis of IELTS texts and extracts from core undergraduate texts

	QUANTITATIVE	QUALITATIVE
GRAMMATICAL FEATURES		
Length	number of words	
Vocabulary	character/word type-token ratio frequency levels K-level evaluation lexical density	
Grammar	words/sentence sentence/paragraph % passive	The sentences in the text are: 1. mainly simple sentences 2. a balance of simple and compound sentences 3. mostly compound sentences 4. a balance of compound and complex sentences 5. mostly complex sentences
Cohesion		Throughout the text, are relations between the ideas explicitly marked through reference, conjunctions and connectors or are such relations not explicit? 1 (explicit)　2　3　4　5 (not explicit)
Readability	Flesch reading ease Flesch-Kincaid grade level	
DISCOURSE FEATURES		
Genre		Identify the most appropriate category. 1. textbook 2. magazine/newspaper article 3. research/academic journal article 4. report
Rhetorical task		Identify the most appropriate category. 1. exposition 2. argumentation/persuasion/evaluation 3. historical biographical/autobiographical narrative
Pattern of exposition		Identify the pattern(s) used in the text. 1. define 2. describe 3. elaborate 4. illustrate 5. compare/contrast 6. classify 7. cause/effect 8. problem/solution 9. justify
Rhetorical organisation		Does the text have an explicit organisational structure? 1 (explicit)　2　3　4　5 (not explicit)

Table 1.22 (continued)

	QUANTITATIVE	QUALITATIVE
READER–WRITER RELATIONSHIP		
	Hyland's (2005) metadiscoursal features	
CONTENT KNOWLEDGE		
Subject area		Mark as it applies. 1. Medicine & dentistry 2. Subjects allied to medicine 3. Biological sciences 4. Veterinary science 5. Agriculture & related subjects 6. Physical sciences 7. Mathematical sciences 8. Computer science 9. Engineering & technology 10. Architecture, building & planning 11. Social studies 12. Law 13. Business & administrative studies 14. Mass communications & documentation 15. Languages 16. Historical & philosophical studies 17. Creative arts & design 18. Education
Subject specificity	% of AWL words % of off-list words	Is the topic of the text of general interest or does it require subject–specific knowledge on the part of the reader? 1 (general) 2 3 4 5 (specific)
Text abstractness		Is the text concrete or abstract? 1 (concrete) 2 3 4 5 (abstract)
CULTURAL SPECIFICITY		
		Is the topic of the text culture-neutral or is it loaded with specific cultural content? 1 (culture neutral) 2 3 4 5 (culture specific)

It is interesting to note that the IELTS texts were estimated both by the Flesch reading ease and Flesch-Kincaid measures to be significantly ($p<.05$) easier to read than the undergraduate texts. The difference between the means for IELTS and for undergraduate texts was 5 points on the 100-point Flesch reading ease scale or one year in terms of the Flesch-Kincaid grade levels. Figure 1.5 on page 98 is a box-and-whisker plot summarising the distribution of Flesch-Kincaid reading levels for IELTS and undergraduate texts. The line in the middle of the boxes represents the median and the upper and lower boundaries of the boxes represent the upper and lower quartiles of the

Table 1.23 Analysis of variance of IELTS and undergraduate text contextual parameters

		Sum of Squares	df	Mean Square	F	Sig.
Flesch reading ease	Between groups	595.73	1	595.734	4.852	0.030
	Within groups	10067.24	82	122.771		
	Total	10662.97	83			
Flesch-Kincaid reading level	Between groups	21.91	1	21.910	5.150	0.026
	Within groups	348.88	82	4.255		
	Total	370.79	83			
Standardised type-token ratio	Between groups	85.124	1	85.124	5.271	0.024
	Within groups	1324.281	82	16.150		
	Total	1409.405	83			
Proportion of words on AWL	Between groups	142.53	1	142.533	16.293	0.000
	Within groups	717.35	82	8.748		
	Total	859.88	83			
Proportion of words within 1,000 word frequency level	Between groups	169.41	1	169.406	4.783	0.032
	Within groups	2904.60	82	35.422		
	Total	3074.01	83			
	Total	695.28	83			
Proportion of words within 3,000 word frequency level	Between groups	8.58	1	8.576	4.519	0.037
	Within groups	155.63	82	1.898		
	Total	164.20	83			
Proportion of words outside 15,000 word frequency level (off list)	Between groups	220.29	1	220.288	34.256	0.000
	Within groups	527.32	82	6.431		
	Total	747.61	83			

distributions. The figure indicates that the IELTS texts were generally of a similar level of readability to the undergraduate texts, falling within the range of undergraduate text readability. However, one text (Test 8, Text 1), appears as an outlier with a reading grade level of 8. This text, which concerns the construction of Hong Kong airport, has the lowest number of words per sentence of any of the texts analysed and is at the lower extreme for the average number of characters per word (4.5). An implication here may be that using readability formulae could assist the test developers in identifying texts that might fall outside the range of readability typically found in university-level texts.

It is also of interest that no IELTS text had an estimated grade level higher than 16, although undergraduate texts ranged as high as 18. This might be taken as a further indication that even the most difficult of the IELTS texts do not reflect the level of the most challenging of the texts that undergraduates might expect to encounter in their first year of study.

The type-token ratio (TTR) is the ratio of different words (types) to the total number of words (tokens). This represents a simple, if rather crude

Figure 1.5 Flesch-Kincaid reading grade levels of IELTS and undergraduate texts

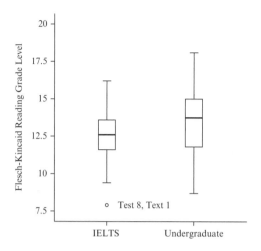

index of the number of different words the reader will need to know to understand a passage. It is generally recommended that a standardised length of text be used as in calculating the TTR as the length of a passage will affect the figure obtained (Scott 2006). Although standardised measures are not provided through the Web VocabProfiler, they can be obtained through another lexical profiling tool: WordSmith Tools. We used WordSmith Tools to find standardised TTRs based on 250 word sections of text and the results are displayed in Figure 1.6 on page 99. It can be seen that the IELTS texts had a significantly higher mean standardised TTR than the undergraduate texts.

The fact that the standardised TTR in the undergraduate texts is noticeably lower than in the IELTS texts could be taken to indicate that candidates in IELTS are exposed to more demanding texts in terms of this ratio. With course books, for example, one is likely to find more repetition of key words so that the reader is able to develop familiarity with these as they progress through the text.

It is also worth noting that the measure of lexical density employed here (the proportion of content words in the text) did not reveal any significant differences between IELTS and the undergraduate texts. This may be taken to suggest that IELTS Reading texts in this respect do reflect a similar range of vocabulary to that appearing in undergraduate textbooks.

IELTS texts included significantly (p<.05) fewer sub-technical academic words (see Figure 1.7 on page 100) and more very frequent words (words at the 1,000 and 3,000 word frequency levels) than the undergraduate texts. The proportion of running words on the academic word list (AWL) in IELTS texts overall was observed to be 7.9%, which is lower than that found in the corpus of academic texts from which the AWL was derived (10.0%), a second corpus

Figure 1.6 Standardised type-token ratio of IELTS and undergraduate texts

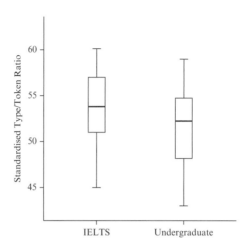

of academic texts investigated by Coxhead (2000) (8.5%) and that for the undergraduate texts investigated here (10.3%). Although the mean proportion of AWL words occurring in IELTS texts was higher than the 4% found by Coxhead (2000) in newspaper texts, the lowest proportion found in an IELTS text (2.2%) was closer to the proportion found in fiction texts (1.4%) and was just over half of the lowest proportion found in any part of an undergraduate text (4.33% for one section of a business studies textbook). This IELTS text was taken from Part 1 of the test and concerned the provision of credit for young people in Zambia. The relatively low proportion of AWL words in the IELTS texts may reflect the high proportion of these texts that are sourced from newspapers and magazines (see the discussion of genre below).

The proportion of AWL words varied by IELTS test part, with Part 1 texts having the lowest (7.65%) and Part 3 texts the highest proportion (8.24%) of AWL words. Even in Part 3 of the test, however, coverage of the AWL was lower than in the undergraduate texts.

The findings in relation to the AWL indicate that IELTS texts typically include a similar, if rather lower proportion of sub-technical academic vocabulary to the undergraduate texts. Again, investigating coverage of the AWL might assist the test developers in identifying texts that lack representative coverage of sub-technical academic vocabulary. This finding appears, like the findings relating to readability, to suggest that IELTS texts may lack some of the features of academic texts that may cause greatest difficulty for students.

The significantly higher proportion of words in IELTS texts at the 1,000 and 3,000 word frequency level may be a corollary of the differences noted in relation to the AWL with a higher proportion of these more 'general' words

Figure 1.7 Comparison between proportion of running words appearing on the AWL in IELTS and undergraduate texts

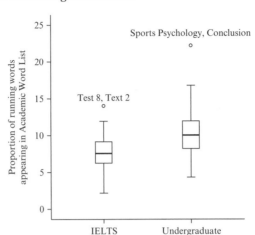

appearing in IELTS texts in place of the sub-technical vocabulary more frequently found in the undergraduate texts.

The undergraduate texts include on average almost four times as many off-list words (words that do not appear on the AWL or on any of the 15,000 word frequency level lists). Items of this nature include proper nouns and acronyms (Marks & Spencer; Charles; Myanmar; the BBC) as well as neologisms and some of the more technical language found in these texts (applet; compurgation; mediastinum; reusability). It is perhaps unsurprising that such words should appear less often in IELTS texts, which are required, as we have noted above, to avoid both cultural and subject specificity.

Although the measures employed here are admittedly crude, it is encouraging for the IELTS Academic Reading test that they appear to reveal few quantifiable differences between the texts that students might expect to encounter in their first year of study and those used in the test. The main areas of concern indicated here are that the IELTS texts generally include a lower proportion of sub-technical academic vocabulary than the undergraduate texts and that IELTS texts may not fully reflect the level of readability found among the more challenging academic texts that first year undergraduates might expect to encounter. Tools such as the Web VocabProfiler used here might prove useful for the test developers in identifying texts with characteristics that are outside the range typically found in academic texts.

8.3 Qualitative data

Following our identification of textual features in the literature review, two judges rated the IELTS texts and undergraduate texts on six criteria:

rhetorical organisation, subject and cultural specificity, abstraction, grammatical complexity and *cohesion.* Rates of agreement between the two judges are shown in Table 1.24. Rates of agreement were highest for the more readily observed textual features of rhetorical organisation, grammatical complexity and cohesion, but were also considered acceptable for the more subjective features of subject and cultural specificity and level of abstraction. Where the two judges disagreed, the average of the two ratings was used in the subsequent analysis.

Table 1.24 Rates of agreement between the two judges on textual features

Criteria	Exact	+/- 1
Rhetorical organisation	52%	93%
Grammar	52%	94%
Cohesion	49%	92%
Subject specificity	31%	87%
Cultural specificity	33%	89%
Abstraction	29%	79%

Table 1.25 below shows the results of the non-parametric tests of difference between IELTS and undergraduate texts. Figure 1.8 on page 102 displays the mean ratings for IELTS and undergraduate texts on each of the six criteria. Results were significant ($p<.05$) for both subject and cultural specificity. Although the undergraduate texts appeared to involve greater levels of abstraction, the results for this variable were not significant. As noted above in relation to the vocabulary measures, the significant difference between the IELTS and undergraduate texts in relation to subject and cultural specificity no doubt reflects the requirement for IELTS to avoid subject specificity and cultural allusion. No significant differences emerged on the measures of rhetorical organisation, grammatical complexity or cohesion.

Table 1.25 Results of non-parametric tests of difference between IELTS and undergraduate texts

	Mann-Whitney U	Wilcoxon W	Z	Asymp. Sig. (2-tailed)
Rhetorical organisation	755.5	1,658.5	−1.203	0.229
Grammar	788.5	1,691.5	−0.914	0.361
Cohesion	716	1,619	−1.601	0.109
Subject specificity	323	1,226	−5.052	0.000
Cultural specificity	473	1,376	−3.706	0.000
Abstraction	686	1,589	−1.781	0.075

Figure 1.8 Mean ratings for IELTS and undergraduate texts on six criteria

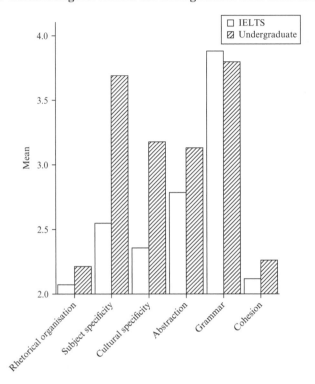

The cultural specificity found in the undergraduate texts (and reflected in the number of non-technical off-list words that occurred therein) could only add to the difficulty of reading them.

This may indicate that *lack of background knowledge to understand the reading content* is not always a matter of knowledge directly related to the subject, but may also arise from writers' assumptions about readers' cultural knowledge. Readers hitherto exposed only to relatively culturally neutral texts of the kind found in IELTS might well find the greater cultural specificity of the undergraduate texts to be a further source of difficulty.

Table 1.26 shows the level of agreement between the two judges in assigning the texts to categories for the features of *genre, rhetorical task, pattern of exposition* and *subject area*.

The categorisation of texts by genre is set out in Table 1.27. The categorisation of the undergraduate texts was straightforward as all were textbooks, but there was some disagreement between the two judges in relation to the IELTS texts. Both agreed that 17 of the texts had been sourced from magazines or newspapers, that seven came from textbooks and that one was a research article. However, the second judge was less likely to identify

Table 1.26 Level of agreement between two judges on features of genre, rhetorical task, pattern of exposition and subject area

Criterion	Agreement
Genre	80%
Rhetorical task	80%
Pattern of exposition	73%
Subject area	85%

magazine or newspaper articles as the source, seeing nine of those so identified by the first judge as coming from textbooks and a further seven from research articles. Discussion following the categorisation exercise indicated that some texts had been more difficult than others to categorise and that it was not always clear to the judges whether an individual text had been sourced from a research article, magazine article or textbook. Although some texts had very obvious journalistic features, such as opening paragraphs that served as 'attention grabbers' and one text had the conventional headings of the research article, distinguishing characteristics were not always so easy to locate. A number of texts had little to indicate whether they had been sourced from a newspaper section, from a popular science magazine, from an introductory textbook or from a more specialised academic publication. It might be of interest to explore how genre is affected by the editing process through which texts are prepared for inclusion on IELTS. It is possible that changes made to texts might have affected the judges' ability to assign them to a genre.

Table 1.27 Categorisation by genre: Results for judge 1 displayed by row, judge 2 by column

Genre		Textbook	Magazine/ newspaper article	Research/ academic journal article	Report
IELTS	Textbook	7			
	Magazine/newspaper article	9	17	7	
	Research/academic journal article			1	
	Report			1	
UG	Textbook	42			

What is clear from the exercise and the subsequent discussion between the judges is that IELTS texts often appear to be somewhat journalistic and that newspaper/magazine texts are well represented in the test. The main study questionnaire responses indicated that newspapers and magazines may feature as sources in first year academic reading, but books, journals, reports and internet sources were all regarded as more important.

As indicated in Table 1.28, both judges agreed that most of the texts were expository in nature – 30 of the IELTS texts and 27 of the undergraduate texts. Both judges also agreed that argumentation and historical/biographical texts were also represented among both sets of texts. In terms of rhetorical task there appears to have been a close match between IELTS and these undergraduate texts.

Table 1.28 Categorisation by rhetorical task: Results for judge 1 displayed by row, judge 2 by column

Rhetorical task		Exposition	Argumentation	Historical/ biographical
IELTS	Exposition	30	2	1
	Argumentation	3	2	
	Historical/biographical	1		3
Undergraduate	Exposition	27		1
	Argumentation	5	2	
	Historical/biographical	3	1	3

With respect to pattern of exposition, as analysed in Table 1.29, the two judges agreed on the classification of 35 of the 42 IELTS texts, but just 26 of the 42 undergraduate texts. Subsequent discussion revealed that IELTS texts were more often felt to reflect one clearly dominant pattern of exposition while the undergraduate texts often involved two or more patterns occurring in sequence. This difficulty may have been caused by the way in which the undergraduate texts were collected; they were extracted from longer texts, often cutting across sections in the textbooks, each of which displayed different patterns.

A further challenge for the judges in identifying patterns of exposition was that the categories are not mutually exclusive – definitions and descriptions often include illustration and a problem–solution text may additionally imply cause–effect. Determining which pattern was dominant in each of the texts investigated did not prove to be straightforward.

The analysis suggested that almost half of the IELTS texts displayed problem–solution or cause–effect patterns while the majority of the undergraduate texts involved elaboration. The selection of texts may have contributed to the difference: the opening chapter of an introductory textbook often being concerned with elaborating the scope of the subject. On the other hand the brevity of IELTS texts and the high occurrence of newspaper/magazine articles may favour problem–solution and cause–effect patterns of exposition. The use of short texts with relatively clear dominant patterns may also bring its own problems; candidates may not be well prepared to encounter lengthier texts and to cope with transitions and relations between sections that follow different organisational principles.

Table 1.29 Categorisation by pattern of exposition: Results for judge 1 displayed by row, judge 2 by column

Pattern of exposition		Define/Describe/Elaborate	Illustrate	Compare	Classify	Cause/effect	Problem/solution	Justify
IELTS	Define/Describe/Elaborate	17						
	Illustrate			1				
	Compare							
	Classify							
	Cause/effect					7		1
	Problem/solution	2				1	11	2
	Justify							
Undergraduate	Define/Describe/Elaborate	25	1			1	4	2
	Illustrate	1	1					
	Compare	1						
	Classify	2						
	Problem/solution	1	1					1
	Justify	1						

In classifying the texts according to subject area (see Table 1.30 on page 106–107) the two judges were in complete agreement in assigning the undergraduate texts to subject area and agreed on 35 of the 42 IELTS texts. A broad range of subject areas were represented among the IELTS texts investigated with social studies, engineering & technology and business & administrative studies emerging as popular topic areas for the test.

8.4   Conclusion

Overall, this study indicates that the kinds of text used in IELTS are those that introduce academic topics to a general audience, often in the form of articles sourced from newspapers or magazines that present research findings to a general audience. These include self-contained reports on developments in science and technology and overviews of academic debates. The IELTS texts often present solutions to problems that are likely to be of interest to the general reader. The advantage of the IELTS approach to text selection is that the texts appearing in the test do, based on the limited corpus explored here,

Table 1.30 Classification of IELTS texts by two judges according to subject area

	1. medicine & dentistry	2. subjects allied to medicine	3. biology	4. veterinary science	5. agriculture	6. physical sciences	7. mathematical sciences	8. computer science	9. engineering & technology	10. architecture, building & planning	11. social studies	12. law	13. business & administrative studies	14. mass comm's & documentation	15. languages	16. historical & philosophical studies	17. creative arts & design	18. education
1. medicine & dentistry	2																	
2. subjects allied to medicine		2																
3. biology			2								1							
4. veterinary science					2													
5. agriculture																		
6. physical sciences						1												
7. mathematical sciences									1									
8. computer science								1										
9. engineering & technology									4		2							
10. architecture, building & planning											1							
11. social studies					1				2		7							
12. law																		
13. business & administrative studies													4					
14. mass comm's & documentation													1					
15. languages	1														1			1
16. historical & philosophical studies															1	1		1
17. creative arts & design																		
18. education																		2

Undergraduate

Subject	Count
1. medicine & dentistry	
2. subjects allied to medicine	6
3. biology	
4. veterinary science	
5. agriculture	
6. physical sciences	
7. mathematical sciences	
8. computer science	3
9. engineering & technology	
10. architecture, building & planning	
11. social studies	6
12. law	6
13. business & administrative studies	12
14. mass comm's & documentation	3
15. languages	3
16. historical & philosophical studies	
17. creative arts & design	
18. education	3

have many of the features of the kinds of text encountered by undergraduates. Although there are minor differences attributable to source (word frequency) and length (TTR), the IELTS texts include a vocabulary and a level of grammatical complexity that would place them within the range of texts encountered in the first year of study.

9 Overall conclusions

This project has attempted to address the relationship between the academic reading construct in terms of what this means for students in their first year of study at one British university and the construct of reading as operationalised by the IELTS Academic Reading test. This has been a huge undertaking, equivalent in many ways to at least three joint-funded IELTS research projects, but nevertheless essential if we are to get to grips in the longer term with this very much under-researched part of the IELTS battery.

However, despite the time and resources we have managed to allocate to it thanks to the collective effort of colleagues and PhD students at the University of Bedfordshire, it is still very much an *initial* attempt to map out the field of academic reading and the relationship with IELTS.

Nevertheless, this project does suggest some valuable conclusions and raises a number of interesting pointers for the future research into, and development of, the IELTS Reading test. These are summarised below:

- It is encouraging to note that, as it stands, IELTS candidates at Bands 6.5 and above, 6 and 5.5 and below can be distinguished in terms of the perceived reading problems our sample appear to have at these levels. There are significant differences in the self-reporting of problems students encounter with a number of important strategies and the higher the band on IELTS Reading the fewer perceived problems there are.

- The major focus of the IELTS test *appears* to be on careful reading whereas the survey data reported here suggests that for university students expeditious skills and strategies are just as critical for academic study and in a number of cases more problematic for both L1 and L2 students.

- A protocol-based study of the cognitive processing of students taking the IELTS Reading test would illuminate further the extent to which this is the case. Research into comparability of performance on items testing careful and expeditious reading skills and strategies by the target population is also necessary. If a clear need is established to distinguish between the two, it may then be necessary for IELTS to be more proactive in trying to test these expeditious strategies in terms of how the test is structured.

- It would also be of interest to explore how texts are shaped and adapted through the item writing process and the implications of this process for the contextual parameters explored here. How might the item writers' conceptions of the skills being tested through the tasks they set compare with the candidates' protocol reports?
- In terms of contextual parameters, the descriptive framework employed in this study has proved useful in identifying individual IELTS texts with idiosyncratic characteristics that do not match those typically identified with academic text. We feel that this project offers a methodology whereby such disparities might be identified at the text selection stage.
- Overall the IELTS texts did generally fall within the parameter ranges exhibited by our small corpus of undergraduate text extracts. However, in relation to a number of contextual parameters there is evidence that the demands imposed by even the most 'difficult' of the IELTS texts may fall some way short of those imposed by the most challenging of the academic texts included here.

Research in reading may, like performance testing more generally (McNamara 1995), be likened to opening Pandora's box. Once it is unlocked a vast array of questions clamour to be answered, some of which will require detailed intensive study on specific areas.

References

Alderson, J C (1996) The testing of reading, in Nuttall, C (Ed.) *Teaching Reading Skills in a Foreign Language*, London: Heinemann, 221–229.

Alderson, J C (2000) *Assessing Reading*, Cambridge: Cambridge University Press.

Alderson, J C (2005) *Diagnosing Foreign Language Proficiency: the Interface between Learning and Assessment*, London: Continuum.

Alderson, J C and Clapham, C M (1992) Applied linguistics and language testing: a case study of the ELTS Test, *Applied Linguistics* 13 (2), 149–167.

Alderson J C, Figueras, N, Kuijper, H, Nold, G, Takala, S and Tardieu, C (2004) *Specification for item development and classification within the CEF: the Dutch CEFR construct project*, paper presented at workshop on research into and with the CEFR, University of Amsterdam, Feb 2004.

Al-Fallay, I (1994) *Limiting bias in the assessment of English as a foreign language: the impact of background knowledge on the proficiency of Saudi Arabian students learning English as a foreign language*, unpublished doctoral dissertation, University of New Mexico, Albuquerque.

Anderson, R and Pearson, P (1988) A schema-theoretic view of basic processes in reading comprehension, in Carrell, P, Devine, J and Eskey, D (Eds) *Interactive Approaches to Second Language Reading*, Cambridge: Cambridge University Press, 37–55.

Bachman, L F (1990) *Fundamental Considerations in Language Testing*, Oxford: Oxford University Press.

Bachman, L F and Palmer, A (1996) *Language Testing in Practice*, Oxford: Oxford University Press.

Bachman, L F, Kunnan, A, Vanniarajan, S and Lynch, B (1988) Task and ability analysis as a basis for examining content and construct comparability in two EFL proficiency test batteries, *Language Testing* 5, 128–159.

Bachman, L F, Davidson, F, Ryan, K and Choi, I (1995) *An Investigation into the Comparability of Two Tests of English as a Foreign Language: The Cambridge-TOEFL Comparability Study*, Studies in Language Testing volume 1, Cambridge: UCLES/Cambridge University Press.

Barnett, M (1989) *More Than Meets the Eye*, Englewood Cliffs, NJ: Prentice Hall Regents.

Baumann, J (Ed.) (1986) *Teaching Main Idea Comprehension*, Newark, Delaware: International Reading Association.

Beard, R (1972) *Teaching and Learning in Higher Education,* Harmondsworth: Penguin Books Ltd.

Berman, R (1984) Syntactic components of the foreign language reading process, in Alderson, J C and Urquhart, A (Eds) *Reading in a Foreign Language*, London: Longman, 139–159.

Bernhardt, E (1991) *Reading Development in Second Language: Theoretical, Empirical and Classroom Perspectives*, New Jersey: Ablex Publishing Corporation.

Bhatia, V (1997) Applied genre analysis and ESP, in Miller, T (Ed.) *Functional Approaches to Written Text: Classroom Applications*, Washington DC: USIA, 134–149.

Buck, G and Tatsuoka, L (1998) Application of the rule-space procedure to language testing: examining attributes of a free response listening test, *Language Testing* 15 (2), 119–157.

Buck, G, Tatsuoka, K and Kostin, I (1997) The sub-skills of reading: Rule-space analysis of a multiple-choice test of second language reading comprehension, *Language Learning* 47 (3) 423–466.

Campion, M and Elley, W (1971) *An Academic Vocabulary List*, NZCER: Wellington.

Carrell, P (1983) Three components of background knowledge in reading comprehension, *Language Learning* 33 (2), 183–207.

Carrell, P (1984) The effects of rhetorical organisation on ESL readers, *TESOL Quarterly* 18 (3), 441–469.

Carrell, P, Devine, J and Eskey, D (Eds) (1988) *Interactive Approaches to Second Language Reading*, Cambridge: Cambridge University Press.

Carver, R (1992) What do standardized tests of reading comprehension measure in terms of efficiency, accuracy and rate?, *Reading Research Quarterly* 27 (4), 347–359.

Carver, R (1997) Reading for one second, one minute, or one year from the perspective of rauding theory, *Scientific Studies of Reading* 1 (1), 3–43.

Chihara, T, Sakurai, T and Oller, J (1989) Background and culture as factors in EFL reading comprehension, *Language Testing* 6 (2), 143–151.

Chikalanga, I (1990) *Inferencing in the Reading Process*, unpublished PhD thesis, University of Reading.

Chikalanga, I (1992) A suggested taxonomy of inferences for the reading teacher, *Reading in a Foreign Language* 8 (2), 697–709.

Clapham, C (1996) *The Development of IELTS: A Study in the Effect of Background Knowledge on Reading Comprehension*, Studies in Language Testing volume 4, Cambridge: UCLES/Cambridge University Press.

Coady, J (1979) A psycholinguistic model of the ESL reader, in Mackay, R, Barkman, B and Jordan, R R (Eds) *Reading in a Second Language*, Rowley, Massachusetts: Newbury House, 5–12.

Cohen, A and Upton, T (2006) *Strategies in Responding to the New TOEFL Reading*, Monograph Series 33, Princeton, NJ: ETS.

Council of Europe (2001) *Common European Framework of Reference for Languages: Learning, Teaching, Assessment,* Cambridge: Cambridge University Press.

Coxhead, A (2000) A new academic word list, *TESOL Quarterly* 34 (2), 213–238.

Dechant, E (1991) *Understanding and Teaching Reading: An Interactive Model,* Hillsdale, NJ: Lawrence Erlbaum.

Ehrlich, M (1991) The processing of cohesion devices in text comprehension, *Psychological Research* 53 (2), 169–174.

Enright, M, Grabe, W, Koda, K, Mosenthal, P, Mulcany-Ernt, P and Schedl, M (2000) *TOEFL 2000 Reading Framework: A Working Paper*, TOEFL Monograph Series 17, Princeton, NJ: ETS.

Fortus, R, Coriat, R and Fund, S (1998) Prediction of item difficulty in the English subtest of Israel's inter-university psychometric entrance test, in Kunnan, A (Ed.) *Validation in Language Assessment: Selected Papers from the 17th Language Research Colloquium, Long Beach,* Mahwah, New Jersey: Lawrence Erlbaum Associates, Inc, 61–87.

Freedle, R (1997) The relevance of multiple-choice reading test data in studying expository passage comprehension: the saga of a 15 year effort towards an experimental/correlational merger, *Discourse Processes* 23, 399–440.

Freedle, R and Kostin, I (1993) *The Prediction of TOEFL Reading Comprehension Item Difficulty for Expository Prose Passages for Three Item Types: Main Idea, Inference, and Supporting Idea Items,* TOEFL Research Reports, No. RR-93–44, Princeton, NJ: Educational Testing Service.

Gervasi, V and Ambriola, V (2002) Quantitative assessment of textual complexity, in Merlini Barbesi, L (Ed.) *Complexity in Language and Text,* Pisa: PLUS-University of Pisa, 197–228.

Goh, S (1990) The Effects of rhetorical organisation in expository prose on ESL readers in Singapore, *RELC Journal* 21 (2), 1–13.

Goldman, S and Rakestraw, J (2000) Structural aspects of constructing meaning from text, in Kamil, M, Rosenthal, P, Pearson, P and Barr, R (Eds) *Handbook of Reading Research,* Mahwah, NJ: Lawrence Erlbaum Associates, 311–335.

Grabe, W (1991) Current developments in second language reading research, *TESOL Quarterly* 25 (3), 375–406.

Grabe, W and Stoller, F (2002) *Teaching and Researching Reading*, London: Longman.

Guthrie, J and Kirsch, I (1987) Distinctions between reading comprehension and locating information in text, *Journal of Educational Psychology* 79, 220–228.

Hawkey, R (2006) *Impact Theory and Practice: Studies of the IELTS test and the Progetto Lingue 2000,* Studies in Language Testing volume 24, Cambridge: UCLES/Cambridge University Press.

Hoover, W and Tunmer, W (1993) The components of reading, in Thompson, G, Tunmer, W and Nicholson, T (Eds) *Reading Acquisition Processes,* Clevedon, England: Multilingual Matters Ltd, 1–19.

Hyland, K (2000) *Disciplinary Discourses: Social Interactions in Academic Writing*, Harlow: Longman.

Hyland, K (2002) *Teaching and Researching Writing*, Applied Linguistics in Action Series, London: Longman.

Hyland, K (2005) *Metadiscourse*, London: Continuum.

IELTS (2005) *IELTS Handbook*, available from http://www.cambridgeesol.org/support/dloads/ielts_downloads.htm

Jordan, R (1997) *English for Academic Purposes: A Guide and Resource Book for Teachers*, Cambridge: Cambridge University Press.

Khalifa, H (1997) *A study in the Construct Validation of the Reading Module of an EAP Proficiency test Battery: Validation from a variety of Perspectives*, unpublished PhD thesis, University of Reading.

Khalifa, H and Weir, C J (2009) *Examining Reading: Research and Practice in Assessing Second Language Reading*, Studies in Language Testing volume 29, Cambridge: UCLES/Cambridge University Press.

Kintsch, W (1998) *Comprehension: A Paradigm for Cognition*, New York: Cambridge University Press.

Kintsch, W (2004) The construction-integration model of text comprehension and its implications for instruction, in Ruddell, R and Unrau, N (Eds) *Theoretical Models and Processes of Reading*, Newark, Delaware: International Reading Association, 1,270–1,328.

Koda, K (2005) *Insights into Second Language Reading: A Cross-Linguistic Approach*, New York: Cambridge University Press.

Levine, A, Ferenz, O and Reves, T (2000) EFL academic reading and modern technology: How can we turn our students into independent critical readers? *TESL EJ* 4 (4), 1–9.

Livingston, J (1997) *Metacognition: An Overview*, available from http://www.gse.buffalo.edu/fas/shuell/cep564/Metacog.htm

Lumley, T (1993) The notion of subskills in reading comprehension tests: An EAP example, *Language Testing* 10 (3), 211–234.

Lunzer, E, Waite, M and Dolan, T (1979) Comprehension tests, in Lunzer, E and Gardner, K (Eds) *The Effective Use of Reading*, London: Heinemann, 37–71.

Maclellan, E (1997) Reading to learn, *Studies in Higher Education* 22, 277–288.

Masi, S (2002) The literature on complexity, in Merlini Barbesi, L (Ed.) *Complexity in Language and Text*, Pisa: PLUS-University of Pisa, 197–228.

McCormick, T (1988) *Theories of Reading in Dialogue: An Interdisciplinary Study*, New York: University Press of America.

McNamara, T (1995) Modelling performance: Opening Pandora's box*, Applied Linguistics* 16 (2), 159–179.

Meyer, B and Freedle, R (1984) Effects of discourse type on recall, *American Educational Research Journal* 21 (1), 121–143.

Moore, T and Morton, J (1999) Authenticity in the IELTS academic module writing test: a comparative study of Task 2 items and university assignments, in Tulloh, R (Ed.) *IELTS Research Reports 1999, Volume 2,* Canberra: IELTS Australia, 64–106.

Munby, J (1978) *Communicative Syllabus Design*, Cambridge: Cambridge University Press.

Nuttall, C (1996) *Teaching Reading Skills in a Foreign Language*, London: Heinemann.

Nystrand, M (1989) A social interactive model of writing, *Written Communication* 6, 66–85.

Oakhill, J and Garnham, A (1988) *Becoming a Skilled Reader*, Oxford: Basil Blackwell.

Perera, K (1984) *Children's Writing and Recording*, Oxford: Basil Blackwell.

Perfetti, C (1997) Sentences, individual differences, and multiple texts: three issues in text comprehension, *Discourse Processes* 23, 337–355.

Purpura, J (1998) Investigating the effects of strategy use and second language test performance with high and low-ability test takers: a structural equation modeling approach, *Language Testing* 15, 339–379.

Rayner, K and Pollatsek, A (1989) *The Psychology of Reading*, Englewood Cliffs, NJ: Prentice Hall.

Rosenfeld, P, Oltman, P and Sheppard, K (2004) *Investigating the Validity of TOEFL: a Feasibility Study using Content and Criterion-related Strategies*, TOEFL Research Report, RR-71, Princeton, NJ: Educational Testing Service.

Rosenshine, B (1980) Skills hierarchies in reading comprehension, in Spiro, R, Bruce, B and Brewer, W (Eds) *Theoretical Issues in Reading Comprehension*, New Jersey: Lawrence Erlbaum Associates.

Sasaki, M (2000) Effects of cultural schemata on students' test-taking processes for cloze tests: a multiple data source approach, *Language Testing* 17, 85–114.

Schedl, M, Gordon, A, Carey, P and Tang, K (1996) *An Analysis of the Dimensionality of TOEFL Reading Comprehension Items*, TOEFL Research Reports No. RR-95-27, Princeton, NJ: Educational Testing Service.

Scott, M (2006) *Oxford WordSmith Tools 4.0*, Retrieved from <http://www.lexically.net/downloads/version4/html/index.html>

Shiotsu, T (2003) *Linguistic knowledge and processing efficiency as predictors of L2 reading ability: a component skills analysis*, unpublished PhD dissertation, University of Reading.

Shiotsu, T and Weir, C J (2007) The relative significance of syntactic knowledge and vocabulary breadth in the prediction of second language reading comprehension test performance, *Language Testing* 23 (4), 99–128.

Stanovich, K (2000) *Progress in Understanding Reading: Scientific Foundations and New Frontiers*, New York: The Guildford Press.

Steffensen, M, Joag-Dev, C and Anderson, R (1979) A cross-cultural perspective on reading comprehension, *Reading Research Quarterly* 15, 10–29.

Tan, S (1990) The role of prior knowledge and language proficiency as predictors of reading comprehension among undergraduates, in de Jong, J and Stevenson, D (Eds) *Individualising the Assessment of Language Abilities*, Clevedon, PA: Multilingual Matters, 214–224.

Teasdale, A (1989) *Introspection and judgmental approaches to content validation: A study using the Test in English for Educational Purposes*, unpublished MAAL dissertation, Department of Linguistics, University of Reading.

Tercanlioglu, L (2004) Postgraduate students' use of strategies in L1 and ESL contexts : links to success, *International Education Journal* 5 (4), 562–570.

Urquhart, A (1984) The effect of rhetorical ordering on readability, in Alderson, J C and Urquhart, A (Eds) *Reading in a Foreign Language*, London: Longman, 160–175.

Urquhart, A and Weir, C J (1998) *Reading in a Second Language: Process, Product and Practice*, Essex, UK: Pearson Education Ltd.

Weakley, S (1993) *Procedures in the content validation of an EAP proficiency test of reading comprehension*, unpublished MATEFL dissertation, CALS, University of Reading.

Weigle, S C (2002) *Assessing Writing*, Cambridge: Cambridge University Press.

Weir, C J (1983) *Identifying the language needs of overseas students in tertiary education in the United Kingdom*, unpublished PhD thesis, Institute of Education, University of London.

Weir, C J (1993) *Understanding and Developing Language Tests*, Englewood Cliffs, NJ: Prentice Hall.

Weir, C J (2005) *Language Testing and Validation: An Evidence-Based Approach*, Basingstoke: Palgrave MacMillan.

Weir, C J and Porter, D (1994) The multi-divisibility or unitary nature of reading: The language tester between Scylla and Charybdis, *Reading in a Foreign Language* 10 (2), 1–19.

Weir, C J, Yang, H and Jin, Y (2000) *An Empirical Investigation of the Componentiality of L2 Reading in English for Academic Purposes*, Studies in Language Testing volume 12, Cambridge: UCLES/Cambridge University Press.

Appendix 1.1
Pilot questionnaire

QUESTIONNAIRE ON ACADEMIC READING ACTIVITIES

Dear Respondent

This study is being conducted by the Centre for Research in English Language Learning and Assessment at the University of Luton. The purpose of this study is to investigate students' reading activities at the university. Your answers will help us to establish where students might need help with Academic Reading.

We intend to use the information you give us to develop on-line, self-access, diagnostic instruments which will be linked to appropriate learning modules on reading skills and strategies. These will help Luton University students improve their reading abilities and make studying here easier and more successful.

All information in this questionnaire is completely confidential and no individuals will be identified. If you do not wish to participate in this study, please do not fill the questionnaire out.

Thank you for your help.

Biodata
1. Age: _____
2. Sex : _____
3. Nationality: _____
4. Undergraduate ▢
   Postgraduate ▢
5. Course: _____
6. Year of Study: _____
7. First language: _____
8. If you are an overseas student, please give your IELTS Reading Band ▢

Reading Research Project Pilot Open-ended Questions

1) Are course books the **most important reading** for your studies? Yes/ No
   If **No**, what are?

2) Do you read **online**? Yes/No
   If **Yes**, how much reading do you do actually **online** as compared to printed materials?

3) Do you read for different **purposes** on your degree course? Yes/ No
   If **Yes**, what are the purposes?

4) How do you decide **what** to read for your course?

5) For an assignment **how many** of each different source (how many books, how many articles, how many internet sites etc) would you normally take information from?

6) When you have decided what to read, describe **how** you read it.

7) Is your approach the same when you read books, articles, etc? Yes/ No
   If **No**, what are the differences in **how** you read?

8) Is your approach the same when you read for **assignments** as against **examinations**? If **No**, what are the differences?

Appendix 1.2
Main survey structured questionnaire

QUESTIONNAIRE ON ACADEMIC READING ACTIVITIES

Dear Respondent

This study is being conducted by the Centre for Research in English Language Learning and Assessment at the University of Luton. The purpose of this study is to investigate students' reading activities at university. Your answers will help us to establish where students might need help with Academic Reading.

We intend to use the information you give us to develop on-line, self-access, diagnostic instruments which will be linked to appropriate learning modules on reading skills and strategies. These will help students improve their reading abilities and make studying here easier and more successful.

All information in this questionnaire is completely confidential and no individuals will be identified. If you do not wish to participate in this study, please do not fill the questionnaire out.

Thank you for your help.

Professor C.J. Weir, Putteridge Bury Room 124 cyril.weir@luton.ac.uk.

Personal details: please tick the appropriate box

1. **Age:** 18–22 ☐
   23–29 ☐
   30–39 ☐
   40+ ☐

2. **Gender:** Male ☐
   Female ☐

9) Do you find anything **difficult** in what you have to read for your course, e.g. in books, articles, etc? Yes/ No
If **Yes**, please give details

10) Do you feel under **pressure** in your academic reading? Yes/ No
If **Yes**, what are the pressures?

11) What do you think a "successful" reader is at university?

12) In this academic year, what was the most important book you read? Please give author and title.

13) In this academic year, what was the most important article you read? Please give author, title and journal.

3. Nationality: UK ☐ EU ☐ International ☐

4. Undergraduate ☐
   Postgraduate ☐

5. Subject area: **Please tick one box**

Advertising, Marketing and Public Relations	
Art and Design	
Biology and Biomedical Sciences	
Business and Finance	
Computing and Information Systems	
Education Studies	
Healthcare (Nursing and Midwifery)	
Human Resource Management	
Language and Communication (EFL and TEFL)	
Law	
Leisure, Tourism and Sports Management	
Media Arts	
Psychology	
Social Sciences and Social Work	
Sport and exercise	

6. **Year of Study** 1st ☐ 2nd ☐ 3rd ☐

7. **First language:** _____

8. If you are an **international** student and have taken IELTS, please tick your **Reading Band score**

9	8.5	8	7.5	7	6.5	6	5.5	5	4.5	4

Academic Reading Research Project

For each statement below, show the extent of your agreement or disagreement:
5 Definitely agree
4 Mostly agree
3 Neither agree nor disagree
2 Mostly disagree
1 Definitely disagree

1) **The following sources of information are important on my course:**

Books	
Journal articles	
Reports	
Internet sites	
Newspapers	
Magazines	

2) **The following purposes for reading are important on my course**

Searching texts to find information I can use in assignments and/or examinations	
Basic comprehension of main idea(s) in a text	
Understanding the meaning of the text as a whole: working out how the main ideas and details in a text relate to each other and to the author's purpose	
Integrating information from different texts for use in assignments and /or examinations	

For each statement below, show the extent of your agreement or disagreement:
5 Definitely agree
4 Mostly agree
3 Neither agree nor disagree
2 Mostly disagree
1 Definitely disagree

3) How I read for assignments:

I think carefully to ensure that I know exactly what I will be looking for before I start reading	
I quickly look through the whole of a text for a general understanding before doing anything else	
I gradually understand what a text is about by reading the sentences slowly and carefully in the order they occur	
I remember where relevant information is or mark its location for later use in writing my assignment	
I think of key words and quickly look for them or words with similar meanings to check if text is worth reading more carefully	
I look at the titles or headings of a text before deciding to read it carefully	
I first get an overall meaning of the text for example by reading the first paragraph and the conclusion, and the first sentence of the other paragraphs	
If I do not know the meaning of a word in a text, I try to work out its meaning	
I read a text slowly all the way through even if some parts do not seem relevant to my assignment	
I read slowly only those sections of a text I have marked as relevant when going through it quickly before	
While reading I try to relate content to what I know already and judge its value	
I look back at previous parts of the text to check meaning	
I try to understand how the text is organised: how the ideas and details connect with each other	
I make notes on relevant points from the text as I go along	
I integrate information from the text I am reading with information from other texts I have already read	
I read critically to establish and evaluate the author's position on a particular topic	

For each statement below, show the extent of your agreement or disagreement:

5 Definitely agree
4 Mostly agree
3 Neither agree nor disagree
2 Mostly disagree
1 Definitely disagree

4) When I read for assignments, I have difficulty with:

the time available to do the necessary reading	
reading texts where the subject matter is complicated	
words I do not know	
sentence structures	
finding relevant information quickly	
lengthy texts	
lack of background knowledge to understand the content	
making notes on information I will need	
reading carefully to understand the main ideas	
summarising ideas from a text in my own words	
understanding a detailed logical argument	
reading critically to establish and evaluate the author's position on a particular topic	
relating the content of a text to my existing knowledge	
deciding what is important for me and what is not	
reading a text quickly to decide whether I should study it carefully	
understanding the text as a whole; how main ideas and details are connected to each other	
integrating information from the text I am reading with information from other texts I have already read	

5) How much reading do you actually do online as compared to reading printed out materials? Please tick one box

Read online	✓
0–20%	
21–40%	
41–60%	
61–80%	
81–100%	

6) Rank the following English language skills in their order of difficulty for you in your university studies (1 = most difficult 2 = second most difficult etc)

Listening	
Reading	
Writing	
Speaking	

2

Construct validity in the IELTS Academic Reading test: A comparison of reading requirements in IELTS test items and in university study

Tim Moore
Swinburne University

Janne Morton
University of Melbourne

Steve Price
Swinburne University

Abstract

The study reported here was concerned with the issue of test development and validation as it relates to the IELTS Academic Reading test. Investigation was made of the suitability of items on the test in relation to the reading and general literacy requirements of university study. This was researched in two ways – through a survey of reading tasks in the two domains, and through interviews with academic staff from a range of disciplines.

Tasks in the two domains were analysed using a taxonomic framework, adapted from Urquhart and Weir (1998), with a focus on two dimensions of difference: *level of engagement*, referring to the level of text with which a reader needs to engage to respond to a task (local vs global); *type of engagement* referring to the way (or ways) a reader needs to engage with texts on the task (literal vs interpretative).

The analysis found evidence of both similarities and differences between the reading requirements in the two domains. The majority of the IELTS tasks were found to have a 'local-literal' configuration, requiring mainly a basic comprehension of relatively small textual units. In the academic corpus, a sizeable proportion of tasks had a similar local-literal orientation, but others involved distinctly different forms of engagement, including tasks that required a critical evaluation of material (i.e. more interpretative), or which stipulated reference to multiple sources (i.e. more global). The study also found a good deal of variation in the reading requirements across the disciplines.

The results of the study are used to suggest possible enhancements to the IELTS Academic Reading test. A useful principle to strengthen the test's validity, we argue, would be to push test tasks, where possible, in the direction of those more 'global-interpretative' reading modes characteristic of academic study.

1   Introduction

Reading has always been a key element of university study. There was a time in fact when the preferred terminology for studying in a subject area at university was 'reading the subject'. Nowadays, many recognise that it is the intelligent engagement with one's sources that more than anything else defines the quality of being academically literate. Taylor (2009), for example, sees most student endeavours in the academy – whether the writing of essays, or engaging with the content of lectures, or the discussing of ideas in tutorials and seminars – as emerging from a 'conversation' with one's readings in a discipline (2009:54). In the domain of language testing, the manifest importance of reading in university study is reflected in the prominence given to this skill area in the various language tests used by universities for the selection of students. Thus, in all the varieties of format found in the more widely used language tests over the last 30 years (e.g. ELTS, IELTS, TOEFL), one single common element has been the use of a dedicated Reading component.

Given the importance of reading within academic study, an issue of continuing interest for researchers and test developers is the validity of tests used to assess students' academic reading abilities. A test is said to be valid if it 'reflects the psychological reality of behaviour in the area being tested' (Hamp-Lyons 1990:71). In the case of a test of academic reading proficiency, this validity relates to a number of different areas, including:

- task stimulus, i.e. the texts that candidates engage with on the test
- task demand, i.e. the test items, which prescribe certain types of interaction between the reader and text
- task processes, i.e. the reader–text interactions that actually take place in the completing of the test (McNamara 1999).

Previous IELTS validation research has seen strong emphasis placed on the first of these areas – the task stimulus component of the Academic Reading test (see, for example, Clapham 1996). Recently commissioned research has also seen some attention given to task processes – in the work of Weir, Hawkey, Green, Ünaldi and Devi (2009) into performance conditions on the test and how these might relate to the subsequent reading experiences of first year university students. To our knowledge, there has been limited validation work done in recent years (one needs to go back to Alderson's (1990a, 1990b) major work on the testing of reading comprehension skills) on the second of these areas – that is, the task 'demands' of the current version of the reading test, and how much these might relate to the types of reading tasks and activities required of students on university programmes.

The study described in this chapter investigated the suitability of test items in the Academic Reading test in relation to the reading and general literacy requirements of university study. Specifically, the research sought answers to the following questions:

1. In what systematic ways can items on the IELTS Academic Reading module be analysed and classified?

2. What does a taxonomic analysis of test items reveal about the construct of reading underlying the IELTS Academic Reading module?

3. What is the degree of correspondence between the reading skills required on the IELTS test and those typically required on a range of undergraduate university programmes?

Two methods were employed in the research: i) a comparative analysis of IELTS test items and assessment tasks from a range of undergraduate courses; and ii) semi-structured interviews with academic staff involved in the teaching of courses covered in i). Findings from the research are used to make suggestions about how the IELTS Academic Reading test could be adapted to make it more closely resemble the modes of reading required in formal academic settings.

2 Review of literature

The literature in the fields of reading research and reading assessment research is vast and complex. In the following section, we review briefly those areas thought to have particular relevance to the current study. These include the idea of construct validity; theoretical models of reading; and inventories of reading skills and strategies. We begin with a brief review of the IELTS Academic Reading test, including an account of some of the changes that have been made to the test over the 20 years of its use.

2.1 The IELTS Academic Reading test

The IELTS system in its current form provides two different Reading tests: a General Training module and an Academic module. The General Training module is designed for a variety of cohorts and assesses 'basic survival skills in a broad social and educational context', while the Academic module is said to 'assess the English language skills required for academic study or professional recognition' (IELTS 2007:iii). The present study is concerned only with the latter of these modules. According to test specifications, the skills tested in IELTS Academic Reading include: following instructions, finding main ideas, identifying the underlying concept, identifying relationships between the main ideas, and drawing logical inferences (cited in Alderson 2000:206, IELTS 1996).

An IELTS Academic Reading test is typically comprised of three sections (or testlets), each organised around a separate reading passage. These passages, which average about 750 words in length, are drawn from a range of sources including magazines, journals, books and newspapers, with topics designed to be of general interest, written for a non-specialist audience. Accompanying the reading passages are a range of tasks (40 in total) used to test students' comprehension of material in the 60 minutes allocated. These tasks or techniques are characterised by IELTS (1999) as follows:

* multiple choice
* short-answer questions
* sentence completion
* notes/summary/diagram/flow chart/table completion
* choosing from a heading bank for identified paragraphs/sections of text
* identification of writer's view/attitudes/claims
* classification
* matching lists
* matching phrases.

Alderson (2000) notes that an 'interesting' feature of the IELTS Reading test is its use of multiple methods to test understanding of any one passage. This is a strength, he suggests, because in real life readers typically respond to reading texts in many different ways (2000:206). The *Official IELTS Practice Materials* (2007) include the following range of tasks used with each reading passage:

* Passage 1: section–summary match; gapped summary; true/false/not given
* Passage 2: true/false/not given; information–category match; multiple choice
* Passage 3: section–summary match; sentence completion.

The IELTS Academic Reading test has been subject to several major changes since its introduction in 1989. The most important of these, the result of extensive monitoring and evaluation work in the early 1990s (e.g. Clapham 1996), saw the removal of subject-specific Reading subtests, and the removal of the thematic link between Reading and Writing tests. The rationale for such changes has been extensively described in the IELTS literature (Charge and Taylor 1997, Taylor 2007). For example, the removal of the discipline-specific component of the Reading test was the outcome of findings that suggested that the range of subject-specific modules was not warranted, and that a single test did not discriminate for or against candidates from various disciplines (e.g. Taylor 2007). The decision to separate the Reading from the Writing test was based on the observation that candidates varied considerably in the extent to which they exploited reading material in the Writing test, with the implications this had for test fairness. It was thought further that having this connection also increased the potential for confusing the assessment of writing ability and reading ability (Charge and Taylor 1997).

As mentioned, the focus of the current study is exclusively on the reading tasks and not on the reading passages that accompany them. It does need to be acknowledged however, that having a separation of these components limits the perspective somewhat. This is for the reason pointed out by Alderson (2000:203) that there may be a relationship between the text type and the sort of task or technique that can be used with it. This idea will be returned to briefly in the concluding section of the report.

2.2   Construct validity

The present study is concerned with investigating the construct validity of the IELTS Academic Reading test. In terms of reading tests, 'construct validity' is a measure of how closely a test reflects the model of reading underlying the test. In other words, the concept of construct validity is related to those abilities it is thought readers need to possess in order to handle the demands of the target language domain. In the case of the IELTS Academic Reading test, this domain is study at university level. Thus, if the ability to scan for specific information is considered an important part of university reading requirements, then the reading construct should include scanning and the test should diagnose the ability to quickly locate specific information (Alderson 2000). Whilst construct validity is often associated with skills, another dimension is task structure. Bachman and Palmer (1996) suggest that a focus on the structure as well as the skills of target language use tasks might lead to the development of more 'authentic' test tasks (1996:147).

The construct validity of a test is particularly important when the test is a large-scale public test, and where there is a close connection between the operations of the test and the conduct of related educational programmes. The construct validity of such tests thus has implications for curriculum and classroom practice through the so-called 'test washback' (Alderson and Wall 1993). As Messick (1996:252) points out:

> . . . [i]f important constructs or aspects of constructs are underrepresented on the test, teachers might come to overemphasise those constructs that are well-represented and downplay those that are not.

Washback is considered harmful then when there is a serious disjunct between a test's construct of reading and the broader demands of real-world or target language tasks.

The IELTS test is an example of a public test that is used to make crucial decisions about large numbers of people – whether they are eligible for English-speaking university entrance or not based on their English language abilities. An increase in the numbers of international students wanting to study at English-speaking universities and a concomitant increase in the number of universities requiring IELTS scores has led to a significant expansion of the IELTS test in recent years. This in turn has resulted in IELTS preparation programmes being an important focus of many English for Academic Purposes (EAP) courses taught in language centres throughout the world (Read and Hayes 2003, Saville and Hawkey 2004). The increased influence of IELTS and possible concerns about test washback suggest the need for, in this case, the reading construct underlying the test to be firmly based on a thorough understanding of the nature of reading demands in university study. It is this issue – the importance for the Reading test to be as authentic as possible given practical and other constraints – that has motivated the present study.

2.3 Dimensions of reading

The current project is framed within broad theories of reading. Central to these are differing views about the nature of textual meanings and the relationships that exist between these meanings and the reader of a text. The more traditional view – the 'transmission model' – sees texts embodying relatively stable, objective meanings, ones that a proficient reader is able to locate and reproduce. Carroll (1964), for example, characterises reading as 'the activity of reconstructing the messages that reside in printed text'. This conception of reading as the finding of pre-existent meanings is arguably the predominant construct in many reading comprehension tests, especially those that rely heavily on multiple-choice formats (Alderson 2000, Hill and Parry 1992).

An alternative view, one that has gained increasing acceptance in many areas of the academy (particularly in education and in some branches of the humanities) is to see texts as having no single definitive meaning, but rather the potential for a range of meanings, meanings that are created through the engagement of individual readers. As Widdowson (1979) states, 'since conceptual worlds do not coincide, there can never be an exact congruence of coder's and encoder's meanings' (1979:32). Despite the growing acceptance of 'receptionist' theories of meaning, there appears to be a reluctance – even on the part of more committed post-modernists – to accept fully the logical consequences of this position – namely, that *any* subjective account of the meaning of a text may ultimately be valid. It is the view of the researchers that both a strong receptionist and a strong transmissionist position represent rather idealised accounts of reading, and are best thought of as end points on a continuum of more reader-oriented and more text-oriented perspectives on meaning.

Related to these broad definitions of reading are differing ideas about what the processes of reading are thought to involve. Traditionally, accounts in this area have tended to aggregate around two broad approaches: bottom-up 'information processing' (with a focus on the processing of more micro-level constituents of texts – letter, words, phrases, sentences etc.); and top-down 'analysis-by-synthesis' (with a focus more on macro-level constituents – genre, text structure, as well as the role of background schematic knowledge etc.). Recently, there has been a move towards a more interactive, hermeneutic approach, one that assumes a degree of bi-directionality in these processes (Hudson 1998). In the current project, research in the area of reading processes was useful as a way of identifying the type(s) of processing that test items appear to be principally concerned with, and also the levels of texts.

2.4   Frameworks used in reading assessment studies

Much of the research into the nature of reading in different domains has relied on taxonomies that seek to divide reading practices into a variety of skills and sub-skills. Particularly influential among these has been Munby's (1978) list of general language skills, used both for the purposes of syllabus and material design, as well as for the design of tests. In a list that he described at the time as 'not exhaustive', Munby distinguished a total of 266 skills – sub-categorised into 54 groups, including such reading specifics as:

- understanding the communicative value (function) of sentences and utterances with explicit indicators
- understanding relations between parts of texts through grammatical cohesion devices of reference, comparison, etc.
- scanning to locate specifically required information: a single point/more than one point involving a simple search.

Amid the complexity of Munby's scheme, it is possible to detect a basic division between reading skills that are involved in the simple comprehension of texts, e.g. *understanding explicitly stated information* (1978:126), and those involving interpretation of some kind, e.g. *interpreting text by going outside it* (1978:128).

In recent years there have been efforts to pare such taxonomies down to a more manageable catalogue of skills (e.g. Carver 1997, Grabe and Stoller 2002). Carver (1997), for example, recognises five basic elements: 'scanning', 'skimming', 'rauding', 'learning' and 'memorising'. Rauding is defined as a 'normal' or 'natural' reading, which occurs when adults are reading something that is relatively easy for them to comprehend (Carver 1997:5–6). For Grabe and Stoller (2002), the activity is best captured under seven headings:

1. Reading to search for simple information.
2. Reading to skim quickly.
3. Reading to learn from texts.
4. Reading to integrate information.
5. Reading to write (or search for information needed for writing).
6. Reading to critique texts.
7. Reading for general comprehension.

One notes that this latter list takes on a slightly simplified form in a recent study conducted for the TOEFL Reading test (Enright, Grabe, Koda, Mosenthal, Mulcany-Ernt and Schedl 2000):

1. Reading to find information (or search reading).
2. Reading for basic comprehension.
3. Reading to learn.
4. Reading to integrate information across multiple texts.

Of the various taxonomies developed, the most useful for the present project was thought to be that proposed by Urquhart and Weir (1998), and used in another recent study into the IELTS Academic Reading test conducted by Weir et al (2009). Rather than compile a list of discrete skills, Urquhart and Weir construct their taxonomy around two dimensions of difference: reading level and reading type. For reading level, a distinction is made between reading processes focused on text at a more global level, and those operating at a more local level. For reading type, the distinction is between what is termed 'careful' reading and 'expeditious' reading, the former involving a close and detailed reading of texts, and the latter 'quick and selective reading . . . to extract important information in line with intended purposes' (Urquhart and Weir 1998:101). The 'componential matrix' formed by Urquhart and Weir's two dimensions has the advantage of being a more dynamic model, one that is capable of generating a range of reading modes.

In the literature on reading taxonomies, one notes a degree of slippage in what construct it is exactly that is being characterised. Most commonly, it is one of reading 'skill' (e.g. Munby), but an assortment of other terms and concepts are typically used, e.g. 'processes' (Carver 1997), 'purposes' (Enright et al 2000, Weir et al 2009), 'strategies' (Purpura 1998). Such terms, which are arguably somewhat inchoate in nature, all refer in some way to the putative abilities or behaviours of readers. In the present project, the construct we are dealing with is not related to any qualities of the readers as such. Rather the focus is on some entity that is external to the reader – the reading task. In this way, the preferred construct for the project is one of 'activity', or rather of 'prescribed activity'.

3 Method

In this section, we outline the analytical framework used in the research, the disciplines investigated and the nature of the data that was collected and analysed in the study.

3.1 Towards an analytical framework

The approach adopted for the development of the analytical framework was a syncretic one, drawing initially on both IELTS tasks and academic tasks to establish broad dimensions of difference between reading tasks and then to refer to relevant theoretical frameworks later to refine the classification scheme. The method followed was similar to the one adopted in a similar validation study of the IELTS Writing test conducted by several members of the research team (Moore and Morton 2007). The framework that was used ultimately was derived in large part from the componential schema of Urquhart and Weir (1998), described in the previous section.

Dimension 1: Level of engagement
The first dimension used was what we term 'level of engagement' with text. For our study of IELTS and academic reading tasks, this dimension refers to how much of a text (or texts) a reader is *required* to engage with in the performing of a prescribed task. It was noted in our preliminary survey of reading tasks that some tasks were focused on quite circumscribed (or 'local') sections of a text (e.g. single sentences or groups of sentences), whilst in others there was a need to appraise larger textual units (e.g. a series of paragraphs or a whole text). The most extensive 'level of engagement' related to those tasks that required engagement with a number of different texts.

For this dimension of reading tasks, the following two broad categories were used after Urquhart and Weir (1998) and Hill and Parry (1992).

As Weir et al (2009) note, different types of reading activities are, of their nature, either more local or more global in their orientation. Thus, for example, the act of 'scanning' (i.e. locating specific information within a text) has a more local focus; on the other hand, the act of 'skimming' (i.e. obtaining an overview of a text) is necessarily a more 'global' form of reading.

Dimension 2: Type of engagement

Our second dimension – 'type of engagement' – involved an adaptation of the Urquhart and Weir (1998) schema. Whereas their categories of 'careful' and 'expeditious' readings refer arguably to the reading 'strategies' (or 'processes') that students may adopt, our focus on academic tasks meant that the interest was more on what was needed to be done with texts, that is to say the prescribed outcomes of the reading. In our preliminary observations of tasks in the two domains (IELTS and academic study), it was clear that different tasks called for different types of readings. Sometimes, for example, the requirement was simply one of understanding the basic content of a text; in other instances, readers needed to bring a more personal response to material.

In developing this dimension, the study drew initially on the distinction traditionally made in linguistics between semantic and pragmatic meaning. The semantic meaning of a text is typically characterised as the sum of the individual propositions contained within it; pragmatic meanings, on the other hand, refer to those meanings that emerge from the relationship between the text and the context of its production (Yule 1996). As Yule (1996:4) explains it, whereas semantics is concerned with the literal meanings of sentences, pragmatics is concerned with probing less tangible qualities, such as 'people's intended meanings, their assumptions, their purposes or goals, and the kind of actions they are performing when they speak [or write]'.

Related to acts of reading, a broad distinction can be made in this way between a focus on what a text *says* (semantic meaning), and what a text *does*, in saying what it says (pragmatic meaning). To illustrate this distinction, Taylor (2009:66) cites the following short text sample from a French History textbook:

> *The winter of 1788–9 was a very harsh one in France, inflicting untold misery on the peasants. The revolution broke out in July 1798.*

These two sentences, as Taylor explains, can be read 'literally', i.e. as a sequence of propositions about events in late 18th century France (a semantic reading); or they can be read more 'interpretatively'; in this case, as an attempt by the author to *explain* events, i.e. to see the first event as a cause for the second (a pragmatic reading). Taylor (2009) suggests that while both types of reading are important in the context of academic study, it is the latter mode – the more interpretative readings – that is often missing in accounts of the types of reading students typically need to do in their studies.

This basic distinction in the way one might engage with a text (or be required to engage) provided the second category of our framework as follows (a similar basic distinction is often drawn in the broader area of learning theory, where engagement with materials is seen to divide between such binaries as surface vs deep learning (Marton and Saljo 1976), higher and lower order skills (Bloom 1956), reproductive vs analytical (Ballard and Clanchy 1991), critical and non-critical approaches to knowledge (Ennis 1987)):

Type of engagement
- literal
- interpretative

Whereas the 'literal' element of our binary refers to the unitary act of comprehending the propositional content of a text, there are arguably many different ways that one might engage with texts 'interpretatively'. These might include, for example, as Alderson (2000:320) suggests:

- identifying the function of a piece of writing
- recognising an author's presuppositions and assumptions
- distinguishing fact from opinion
- recognising an intended audience and point of view.

Wallace (1999:109), working within a more 'critical literacy' paradigm, provides a different list of skills, including:

- understanding the hidden messages in texts
- identifying how texts persuade one to behave or think
- appreciating how texts are written for different audiences
- appreciating how texts might be read in different ways by different audiences.

The present study resisted any effort to draw up a definitive, *a priori* list of these interpretative modes, and indeed to try to establish any hierarchical relationship between them. Instead, the approach employed was to rely on the broad-brush distinction drawn between 'literal' and 'interpretative' forms of reading, and to assess whether reading tasks set for students (either on the IELTS Reading test, or in academic study) seemed, on the face of it, to require more of one form of engagement than the other.

Summary of analytical framework
The two dimensions of the analytical framework – *level of engagement* and *type of engagement* – are represented on the matrix shown in Figure 2.1 below. The *level of engagement* dimension, which describes a continuum from more 'local' to more 'global' engagement, refers to the level of text with which a reader needs to engage to respond to a task. At the extreme left of the axis (most local) would be tasks requiring engagement at the level of 'word'; at the extreme right of the axis (most global) would be tasks requiring engagement with multiple texts.

The *type of engagement* dimension, which describes a continuum from more 'literal' to more 'interpretative' engagement, refers to the way (or ways)

Figure 2.1 Analytical framework used in the study

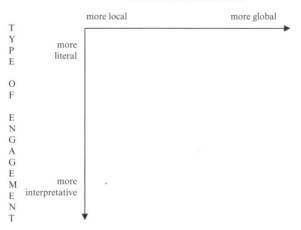

a reader needs to engage with a text to respond to a task. At the top of this axis (most literal) would be tasks requiring a basic comprehension of textual material; at the bottom of the axis (most interpretative) would be tasks requiring a highly critical, and personal engagement with texts.

To demonstrate the use of the analytical framework, a number of reading-related tasks are outlined in Table 2.1 below, with an analysis of each according to the two dimensions of the schema. In Figure 2.2 on page 132 we have shown how such tasks might then be plotted on the two continua of the matrix.

Table 2.1 Analyses of sample reading activities using analytical framework

	SAMPLE READING-RELATED TASK	ANALYSIS
S1	answering a comprehension question relating to a single piece of information	HIGH LOCAL HIGH LITERAL
S2	explaining the connotative meaning of a word in a text	HIGH LOCAL HIGH INTERPRETATIVE
S3	compiling a bibliography of texts related to a specific subject	HIGH GLOBAL HIGH LITERAL
S4	preparing a critical review of the literature on a specific subject	HIGH GLOBAL HIGH INTERPRETATIVE
S5	summarising a single text	MID LOCAL/GLOBAL MID LITERAL/INTERPRETATIVE

Whilst the two dimensions used in the study were conceived of as separate features of reading tasks, it was noted in our preliminary survey of data that

Figure 2.2 Plotting of sample reading tasks on matrix

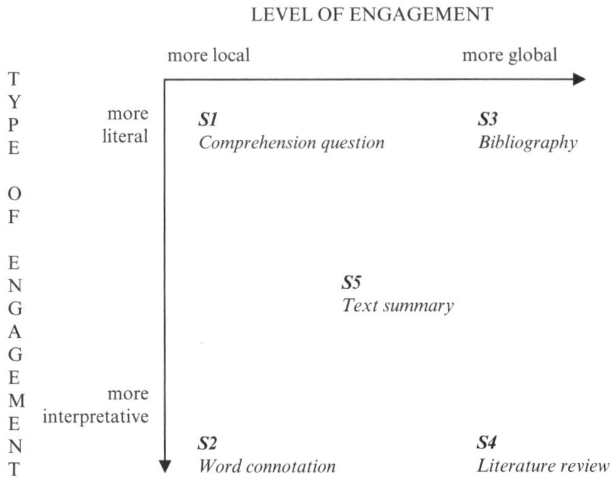

LEVEL OF ENGAGEMENT

	more local	more global
more literal	*S1* *Comprehension question*	*S3* *Bibliography*
	S5 *Text summary*	
more interpretative	*S2* *Word connotation*	*S4* *Literature review*

(TYPE OF ENGAGEMENT)

there was often an inter-relationship between the two. Thus, a general pattern was observed that if tasks were highly 'local' in their focus, it was often the case that a more 'literal' form of engagement was required. Similarly, for those tasks which took in larger more 'global' textual units, the tendency was for the engagement to be pushed more towards the 'interpretative' end of our continuum.

3.2   Disciplines investigated

To obtain a picture of reading requirements across the academy, data was collected from two different universities and from a variety of disciplines. One of the institutions was a long-established Australian university offering programmes of a more traditional nature; the other was what is characterised as a 'new generation' university with a focus on more vocationally oriented programmes. Becher's (1989) matrix of hard-soft/pure-applied disciplines was used to ensure sampling from a cross-section of disciplines. Becher's typology groups academic disciplines on the basis of research methods and attitudes to knowledge. Whilst the disciplines selected in our study fit neatly within the four groupings (see Table 2.2), it is acknowledged that boundaries between groups may not be as clear-cut as a typology such as this suggests (see also Becher 1989).

Within the 12 discipline areas covered, a single subject in each was selected for investigation (Table 2.3). All subjects were offered at first year undergraduate level and were selected partly on the basis of their having relatively high enrolments of students from second language backgrounds. Whilst these subjects were chosen as representative of their discipline area, it is acknowledged that any single subject can only ever cover a portion of the intellectual content and educational practices of the parent discipline as a whole.

Table 2.2 Disciplines investigated in study: Becher (1989) taxonomy

	PURE	APPLIED
HARD	Physics	Engineering
	Biology	Computer Science
	Economics	Architecture
SOFT	Media Studies	Business Studies
	Linguistics	Management
	History	Communications

Table 2.3 List of disciplines and subjects

DISCIPLINE	TITLE OF SUBJECT
Physics	*Life Sciences and Environment*
Biology	*Genetics and the Evolution of Life*
Economics	*Macroeconomics*
Media Studies	*The Media in Australia*
Linguistics	*Intercultural Communication*
History	*Contemporary History*
Engineering	*Engineering Systems Design*
Computer Science	*Informatics – Practical Computing*
Architecture	*Constructing Environments*
Business Studies	*Deriving Business Value*
Management	*Business in the Global Economy*
Communications	*Professional Writing*

3.3   Data and procedure

The study was mainly qualitative in nature involving the use of two research methods: an analysis of tasks (both IELTS and academic tasks) and interviews with academic staff. This combination of methods fits roughly with what Swales (1998) calls 'textography' – described as 'something more than a disembodied textual or discoursal analysis, but something less than a full ethnographic account' (1998:1).

IELTS task survey
A corpus of IELTS Reading test samples was compiled for the study. These were from two sources: i) the official IELTS Practice Test (IELTS 2007); and ii) practice test material published by Cambridge University Press (CUP) (see Appendix 2.1 for list of corpus materials). It is understood that the CUP

materials are made up partly of retired official materials, and so were thought to reflect better than many other commercial materials the actual nature of the official test. No live Reading test materials were available to the study. A total of 13 complete tests were investigated, each made up of a variety of task types.

Reading tasks were analysed by the researchers according to the two dimensions of the study's analytical framework, i.e. the 'level' and 'type' of engagement. Whilst a degree of interpretation invariably enters into any analysis of this kind, some objectivity was achieved on the study by having each researcher analyse tasks independently and then for a consensual analysis to be arrived at through processes of moderation.

Academic task analysis
To compile data for the university component of the study, lecturers from the 12 selected disciplines were contacted and invited to participate in the study. Participation involved initially the passing on of course reading and assessment materials and then later being interviewed about these materials. A provisional analysis was made of the assessment tasks drawing on the same analytical framework used in the IELTS analysis. This analysis was also subject to processes of moderation.

Academic staff survey
As a follow-up to the task analysis, interviews were conducted with the 12 participating staff. Prior to the interviews, a schedule of questions was sent to interviewees (see Appendix 2.2), along with a sample of IELTS Reading test materials. The IELTS materials were selected so as to cover a representative sample of test tasks (see Appendix 2.2).

The interviews were divided into three main phases, covering:

• general reading requirements on courses
• reading requirements on specific assessment tasks
• perceptions regarding the degree of correspondence between the academic reading requirements and those on the IELTS Reading test.

The interviews were semi-structured and followed the procedure known as the 'discourse-based interview' (Odell, Goswami and Herrington 1983). Such a procedure involves discussion with interviewees about specific text samples – in this case, the course materials provided by the lecturers and the sample IELTS Reading test items. The interviews ran for an average of 1 hour. All interviews were audio-recorded, and transcribed. The main themes and ideas to emerge from our informants' commentaries are presented in Section 4.2.

The interview extracts presented throughout the report are in the main verbatim transcriptions of the interviews. In some instances, there has been some minor cleaning up of the text for the purpose of removing any extraneous features – false starts, hesitations, fillers and the like. As in Swales' (1998) study, the intention here was to make some small improvement to the readability of the spoken discourse of informants (1998:26) while at the same time seeking to be faithful to the substance of their talk.

4 Findings

The bulk of the research report is devoted to describing the findings of the study. In the first part of this section, findings from the IELTS task analysis are described. In the second part, we outline the findings from the academic task analysis and interviews.

4.1 IELTS reading tasks

The IELTS corpus compiled for the study consisted of a total of 13 tests, with each of these tests made up, on average, of three Reading testlets (i.e. organised around three separate reading passages). In all, the total number of reading tasks across the corpus was 108, comprising 494 individual items.

A preliminary analysis found a variety of task types, with some featuring regularly in the corpus, and others less so. Table 2.4 lists the different task types identified, along with their relative frequencies. The figures in the left-hand column show the total number of uses of each task type in the corpus, and those in the centre column, the total number of items under each of these types. Thus in the table, we can see for example, that the *True/False/Not given* format was used 23 times in the corpus, which included a total of 130 individual items (an average rate of 5.6 items per use of task type – see right-hand column). Note that the order of frequency of task types in the table is based on the 'total number of items' – see centre column.

Table 2.4 Task type by frequency

Task type	No of occurrences of task type in corpus (% in bracket)		Total no of items under task type (% in brackets)		Average no of items per use of task
1. True/False/Not given	23	(21)	130	(26)	5.6
2. Section–summary match	18	(17)	80	(16)	4.4
3. Gapped summary	14	(13)	78	(16)	5.6
4. Information–category match	12	(11)	61	(12)	5.1
5. Multiple choice	15	(14)	47	(10)	3.1
6. Short answer	8	(7)	33	(7)	4.1
7. Other (e.g. sentence completion, information transfer etc.)	18	(17)	65	(17)	3.6
Total	**108 (100%)**		**494 (100%)**		**4.6**

In what follows, a description is provided for each of the task types identified, along with discussion of how each relates to the 'level of engagement – type of engagement' dimensions used for the analysis. Most space is devoted to describing and analysing the more frequently occurring types. It is noted that in the corpus assembled for the study, the first three task types – *True/False/Not given*, *Section–summary match*, *Gapped summary* – accounted overall for more than half of the total items (57%). The category 'Other' shown at the bottom of the table included a range of additional task types, with each of these constituting less than 5% of items. No individual discussion is provided for these task types.

Type 1: True/False/Not given
The most common task type was *True/False/Not given*, accounting for about a quarter of all items (26% – see Table 2.4 on page 135). In this format, test takers typically needed to evaluate the truth status of summary information derived from the reading passage. In all cases in the corpus, this information was found to be in the form of a single sentence and was normally related to a cognate sentence (or part of a sentence) from the reading passage. In those cases, where the true or false options applied, the sentence was typically constructed either as a synonymous (or near synonymous) paraphrase version of the related information from the passage or was divergent in meaning in some way (e.g. in a contradictory relationship). The exceptional case was the 'Not given' option, where the prompt was a proposition not included in the reading passage.

Sample 1.1 below is an example of the *True/False/Not given* task format, showing several sample items. Included in the sample are extracts from the associated reading passage showing relevant content for each item. Examples of both 'true' and 'false' formats are shown.

An alternative wording for this task type noted in the data was to use *Yes/No/Not given* options rather than *True/False/Not given*. Thus, instead of writing true/false 'if the statement agreed with/contradicted the information', test takers were asked to write yes/no. There would appear to be no substantive difference in these variable rubrics.

True/False/Not given task
Do the following statements agree with the information given in the reading passage?
On your answer sheet write:

TRUE	if the statement agrees with the information
FALSE	if the statement contradicts the information
NOT GIVEN	if there is no information on this

1. It has been suggested that children hold mistaken views about the 'pure' science that they study at school.

Relevant material from reading passage

Many studies have shown that children harbour misconceptions about pure curriculum science . . .

Correct response: TRUE

2. The plight of the rainforest has largely been ignored by the media.

Relevant material from reading passage

Despite the extensive coverage in the popular media of the destruction of the rainforests, little formal information is available about children's idea in this area.

Correct response: FALSE

Sample 1.1: *True/False/Not given* **task** (Sample 1.1 denotes that this is a Type 1 sample (i.e. True/False) and that this is the first sample of this type)

Level of engagement

With respect to text 'level', it is noted that in the design of these tasks, the single sentence proposition contained in the prompt generally matches with a semantic unit of similar length in the passage, as seen in the first item above. This was not always the case however. In the second item above, for example, it is noted that whereas the prompt is a single sentence:

The plight of the rainforest has largely been ignored by the media.

the cognate information in the reading passage is realised in a smaller grammatical unit – a noun phrase:

Despite extensive coverage in the popular media of the destruction of the rainforests . . .

The process was also found to work the other way, where the relevant information in the reading passage stretched over a larger grammatical unit than the prompt. In the following example (Sample 1.2), which shows 'agreement' between prompt statement and text, it can be seen that the relevant components of the prompt statement occur inter-sententially in the passage (shown in bold).

Prompt statement:

The approach to health during the 1970s included the introduction of health awareness programs.

Relevant material from reading passage:

The 1970s was a time of focusing on the prevention of disease and illness by emphasising the importance of lifestyle and behaviour of the individual. Specific behaviours which were seen to increase risk of disease, such as smoking, lack of fitness, and unhealthy eating habits, were targeted. **Creating health meant providing not only medical health care but health promotion programs** and policies which would help people maintain healthy behaviours and lifestyles.

Correct response: TRUE

Sample 1.2: Example of information occurring inter-sententially in *True/False/Not given* format

Overall, however, it was found that most tasks of this type required engagement at or around sentence level. Accordingly in the analysis, such tasks were assigned to the more local end of the local–global continuum.

In performing such an analysis, one also needs to consider the additional component of the task – adjudicating on the 'not given' option. This component suggests engagement at a different textual level. To establish whether certain information is or is not contained within a text requires some appraisal of the content of the whole text and so, for this component, the engagement is judged to be at a more global level.

Type of engagement

The type of engagement required for the completion of *True/False/Not given* tasks is one of establishing the semantic relationship between two discrete units of information (one in the prompt, and a cognate one that needs to be located by the test taker in the passage), and to decide whether the relationship is one of synonymy or non-synonymy (e.g. contradiction). The additional component of the task requires one to establish whether the propositional content of the prompt does in fact occur in some form in the reading passage – consideration of the 'not given' option. Where this option applies, the task is thus one of detecting a lack rather than a presence.

The specific features of this task type – the need to establish the presence of certain propositional content in a text, and then to establish the relationship between this content and a variant version of it – suggest a strongly 'literal' engagement with reading material. Accordingly, this task type was assigned to the higher end of the 'literal–interpretative' continuum.

The preceding analysis gives the configuration shown in Figure 2.3 below (*T1a* refers to the 'True/False' component of the task, and *T1b*, the 'Not given').

Figure 2.3 Analysis of True/False/Not given task type

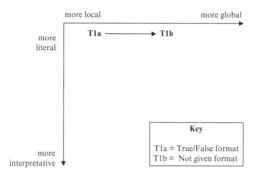

Type 2: Section–summary match

Section–summary match tasks were the second most common format, accounting for 16% of items in the corpus (Table 2.4). In this format, the task for test takers was to match a section of the reading passage (usually a paragraph) with a statement that summarised the principal content of that section. An example of this format is shown below (Sample 2.1).

Section–summary match

Choose the correct heading for sections A–E from the list of headings below. Write the correct number i–x on your answer sheet.

List of Headings

i)   Contrary indications
ii)   Europe's Alpine glaciers
iii) Growing consensus on sea level
iv)   Causes of rising sea levels
v)   Sea level monitoring difficulties
vi)   Group response to alarming predictions
vii) The world 130,000 years ago (etc.)

Relevant section from reading passage:

RISING SEA LEVELS

SECTION A

During the night of 1st February 1953, a deadly combination of winds and tide raised the level of the North Sea, broke through the dykes which protected the Netherlands and inundated farmland and villages as far as 64 km from the coast killing thousands. For people around the world who inhabit low-lying areas, variations in sea levels are of crucial importance and the scientific study of oceans has attracted increasing attention. Towards the end of the 1970s, some scientists began suggesting that global warming could cause the world's oceans to rise by several metres. The warming, they claimed, was an inevitable consequence of increasing carbon dioxide in the atmosphere, which acted like a greenhouse to trap heat in the air. The greenhouse warming was predicted to lead to rises in sea level in a variety of ways. Firstly heating the ocean water would cause it to expand. Such expansion might be sufficient to raise the sea level by 300mm in the next 100 years. Then there was the observation that in Europe's alpine valleys, glaciers had been shrinking for the past century. Meltwater from the mountain glaciers might have raised the oceans 50mm over the last 100 years and the rate is likely to increase in the future. A third threat is that global warming might cause a store of frozen water in Antarctica to melt, which would lead to a calamitous rise in sea level of up to five metres.

Correct response: iv) Causes of rising sea levels

Sample 2.1: Section–summary match item

It is noted that in this particular sample, the summary information is given as a 'List of headings' (i.e. *Contrary indications*; *Europe's Alpine glaciers*; *Growing consensus on sea level*, etc.), with the correct heading in this case being option iv) – *Causes of rising sea levels*.

A variation on this theme noted in the corpus was for the 'headings' category not to be used for the summary text, but instead for this material to be constructed in a more extended form. In these instances, prompts were designated 'information', as shown in Sample 2.2 below (emphasis added). Note that the relevant option for the reading passage extract is ii) *Predictions regarding the availability of the synthetic silk*.

Section–summary match 2

Reading passage 1 has nine paragraphs, A–I

Which paragraph contains the following **information**?

    i)   A comparison of the ways two materials are used to replace silk-producing glands

    ii)   Predictions regarding the availability of the synthetic silk

    iii)   Ongoing research into other synthetic materials

    iv)   The research into the part of the spider that manufactures silk

    v)   The possible application of the silk in civil engineering

---

SPIDER SILK CUTS WEIGHT OF BRIDGES

SECTION H

At Du Pont's laboratories, Dorsch is excited by the prospect of new super-strong biosilk materials, but he warns they are many years away. "We are at an early stage but theoretical estimates are that we will wind up with a very strong, tough material, with an ability to absorb shock, which is stronger and tougher than man made materials that are conventionally available to us", he says.

Sample 2.2: Section–summary match item, using 'information' rubric

The two samples provided above point to an additional variation in the *section–summary match* format. This relates to the relative number of summary prompts and sections. Thus, for example, in Sample 2.1 above the number of summary prompts exceeds the number of sections, whilst in Sample 2.2, the ratios are reversed, with sections outnumbering prompts. This variation has implications for the process by which section and summary are matched up. In the former case (greater number of prompts), the process requires consideration of the text sections first, followed by identification of the appropriate summary prompt from the list given. In the latter case (greater number of sections), the sequence is reversed, with test takers needing to begin with the summary prompt and then to match each of these up with the appropriate section of the text.

Level of engagement

As the designated name of this task type indicates (i.e. *section–summary match*), the level of engagement in this format is clearly at a supra-sentential level. In almost all cases in the corpus, the unit of text to be negotiated in the completion of tasks was the paragraph. Some variation was noted regarding the length of these paragraphs. In Sample 2.1 above, for example, the relevant paragraph is 10 sentences long (240 words); in Sample 2.2 it is considerably shorter, running to only two sentences (67 words). In the whole corpus, the average paragraph length was five sentences. Overall for this task type, we can say that the level of engagement is on a more 'global' scale than for the *True/ False* format analysed in the previous section (see Figure 2.4 on page 144).

Type of engagement

To complete *section–summary match* tasks, test takers need to be able to match up a putative summary of a section of text with the propositional content of this section. A feature of these summaries is their tendency to draw on a number of broad rhetorical categories, e.g. cause and effect, comparison, prediction, etc. (Trimble 1985). Thus, in Sample 2.1, we saw that the relevant rhetorical category for the section of text in question was 'causality' (*Causes of rising sea levels*); in Sample 2.2, this category was 'prediction' (*Predictions regarding the availability of the synthetic silk*).

The task for test takers then, in many instances, is to be able to recognise the connection between the content of the designated section of text, and this broader rhetorical unit around which the summary prompt is structured. In the case of Sample 2.1, this requires drawing a semantic link between the category of 'causation' in the prompt, and various 'causal' elements in the text – for example, i) certain key lexis (e.g. *cause, consequence, threat*) and ii) key structures (e.g. *Y would lead to a calamitous rise in sea level*). Similarly, in Sample 2.2, the task is to be able to recognise how key lexical items such as *prospect, warning*, as well as future time constructions – e.g. *we will wind up with a very strong, tough material* – equate to the rhetorical category of 'prediction'. We note in passing the wide range of rhetorical functions used in the constructing of the summary prompts. The more prominent of these identified in the corpus are shown in Table 2.5, along with prompt samples for each category.

For this type of engagement, the moving between propositional content and summary, or what van Dijk and Kintsch (1983) call a mediating of 'micro- and macro-processes', is analysed as an 'interpretative' form of reading, or at least a more interpretative one than was seen in the *True/False/ Not given* format discussed previously. The task for test takers in the *Section– summary match* format does not involve identifying a one-to-one correspondence between propositions as we saw in Task Type 1, but instead requires a 'pragmatic' understanding of material of the type identified by Taylor (2009 – see Section 3.1). On the 'literal-interpretative' continuum on our grid, the

Table 2.5 Rhetorical categories used in summary prompts

Rhetorical category	Sample prompt
Definition	*Definition of health in medical terms*
Role	*The role of the state in health care*
	The role of video violence
Importance/significance	*Relative significance of trade and service industry*
	The importance of taking notes on body language
Comparison	*A comparison of the ways two materials are used to replace silk-producing glands*
Causes/reasons	*Causes of volcanic eruptions*
	Reasons for the increased rate of bullying
Impacts/effects	*The impact of the car on city development*
	The effects of bullying on children
Changes	*Changes to concepts of health in Western society*
Problems/difficulties/failures	*Sea level monitoring difficulties*
	The failure of government policy
Merits/benefits	*The relative merits of cars and public transport*
	The benefits of an easier existence
Reactions/responses	*Group response to alarming predictions*
	Reaction of Inuit communities to climate change
Methods/approaches	*Holistic approach to health*
Predictions	*Predictions regarding the availability of the synthetic silk*
Views/consensus	*The views of the medical establishment*
	Growing consensus on sea level
Suggestions/recommendations	*A suggestion for improving trade in the future*

generic *Section–summary match* task is therefore placed somewhat below the first task type (see Figure 2.4).

Regarding the degree of 'interpretative-ness', a variation in the design of *Section–summary match* tasks deserves brief comment here. Whereas most summary prompts were typically realised in a neutral, academic style, it was observed that in some instances a more idiomatic, 'journalistic' style of heading was used. Examples of this latter style are shown in Sample 2.3 below. (In this case the prompts relate to a reading passage describing the function of different types of security devices.)

These more journalistic-style headings are notable in the first instance for their lack of reference to the larger rhetorical units evident in many of the other prompt samples (e.g. *cause, prediction,* etc.). Other distinguishing linguistic features include the use of:

- a range of syntactic structures, i.e. noun phrases (e.g. *Fighting fraud, Common objectives*); full sentences (e.g. *This type sells best in the shops*); question forms (e.g. *How does it work?*)
- more idiomatic phrasing or 'prefabs' (e.g. *The figures say it all, Accepting the inevitable*)
- inexplicit pronominal reference (e.g. *They can't get in without these*).

List of headings

i)   Common objectives
ii)   Who's planning what
iii) This type sells best in the shops
iv)   The figures say it all
v)   Early trials
vi)   They can't get in without these
vii) How does it work?
viii) Fighting fraud
ix)   Systems to avoid
x)   Accepting the inevitable

Sample 2.3: Journalistic-style headings used in Section–summary match task

A number of writers have commented on the challenges generally involved in interpreting journalistic language (Myers 2003, Nwogu 1991). It seems reasonable to suppose that dealing with less systematic categories of the type shown in Sample 2.3 is likely to require a greater interpretative stretch for the test taker. In the grid shown in Figure 2.4 below, an attempt has been made to account for this task variety (see T2b).

Figure 2.4 Analysis of Section–summary match task type

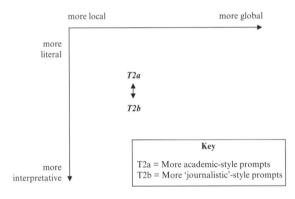

Type 3: Gapped summary

The next most common format, by number of items in the corpus (16% of total items), was the *Gapped summary*. These tasks involved a different type of summary activity from that noted in the previous section. Here test takers are presented with a continuous prose summary of a section of the reading passage from which key information/lexis has been removed. The task for test takers is to draw on the reading passage to restore the omitted information.

We noted two alternative formats used for this task type: i) tasks where there was a bank of word/phrase options to choose from; and ii) where no options were provided. In the 'no options' format, test takers are instructed to limit their responses to a maximum of two or three words from the passage. Examples of the two formats are shown in Sample 3.1 and 3.2. Relevant sections of the reading passage are provided for each sample.

Level of engagement

Each item in the gapped summary tasks, it was noted, was focused on the locating of quite specific information. For example, in responding to items in Sample 3.1 below, candidates need to identify the various 'protective' measures that have been employed in the airport project discussed (sea walls, island, geotextile). On this basis, we would say that the level of engagement with the text is fairly local.

Gapped summary 1

Complete the summary below.

Choose your answers from the box below the summary and write them in boxes 10–13 on your answer sheet.

There are more words than spaces, so you will not use them all.

The island will be partially protected from storms by . . .(10). . . and also by . . .(11). . . Further settlement caused by . . .(12). . . will be prevented by the use of . . .(13). . .

construction workers	coastline	dump-trucks
geotextile	Lantau Island	motorway
rainfall	rock and sand	rock voids
sea walls	typhoons	

Relevant section of reading passage:

AIRPORTS ON WATER

The airport, though, is here to stay. To protect it, the new coastline is being bolstered with a formidable twelve kilometers of sea defences. The brunt of the typhoon will be deflected by the neighbouring island of Lantau; the sea walls should guard against the rest. Gentler but more persistent bad weather – the downpours of the summer monsoon – is also being taken into account. A mat-like material called geotextile is being laid across the island to separate the rock and sand particles from being washed into the rock voids, and so causing further resettlement. This island is being built never to be sunk.

Correct responses:

10 = sea walls	(either order possible)
11= Lantau Island	(either order possible)
12= rainfall	
13 = geotextile	

Sample 3.1: Gapped summary sample, with options bank

Gapped summary 2

Complete the summary of Paragraph G below. Choose NO MORE THAN THREE WORDS from the passage for each answer.

Write your answers in boxes 37–40 on your answer sheet.

A linguist can use a corpus to comment objectively on **37**............... . Some corpora include a variety of language while others are focused on a **38**............... . The length of time the process takes will affect the **39**............... of the corpus. No corpus can ever cover the whole language and so linguists often find themselves relying on the additional information that can be gained from the **40**............... of those who speak the language concerned.

Relevant section of reading passage:

OBTAINING LINGUISTIC DATA

A representative sample of language, complied for the purpose of linguistic analysis, is known as a *corpus*. A corpus enables the linguist to make unbiased statements about the frequency of usage, and it provides accessible data for the use of different researchers. Its range and size are variable. Some corpora attempt to cover the language as a whole, taking extracts from many kinds of texts; others are extremely selective, providing a collection of material that deals only with a particular linguistic feature. The size of the corpus depends on practical factors, such as the time available to collect, process and store the data: it can take up to several hours to provide an accurate transcription of a few minutes of speech. Sometimes a small sample of data will be enough to decide a linguistic hypothesis; by contrast corpora in major research projects can total millions of words. An important principle is that all corpora, whatever their size, are inevitably limited in their coverage, and always need to be supplemented by data derived from the intuitions of native speakers of the language, through either introspection or experimentation.

Correct responses:
  37 = frequency of usage
  38 = particular linguistic feature
  39 = size
  40 = intuitions

Sample 3.2: Gapped summary sample – without options bank

However, it was noted that in some Gapped summary tasks individual items could not be treated entirely in isolation, but instead needed to be considered in relation to the whole summary text, as well as to the relevant section of the reading passage. Thus, for example, in completing items 12 and 13 below (from Sample 3.1), one is not able to confirm the answer to 12 without looking further on in the reading passage to establish the likely response to 13.

> Further settlement caused by . . .(12 **rainfall**) . . . will be prevented by the use of . . .(13 **geotextile**). . .

> Gentler but more persistent bad weather – the downpours of the summer monsoon – is also being taken into account. A mat-like material called geotextile is being laid across the island to separate the rock and sand particles from being washed into the rock voids, and so causing further resettlement.

We would say then that the 'level of engagement' for this task type relates to the span of text in the reading passage that is the subject of the summary. Some variation was noted in the length of these sections, ranging from summaries of a single paragraph from the original passage, to coverage of up to three or four paragraphs. This variation in engagement level is captured on the 'local–global' scale in Figure 2.5 on page 148.

Type of engagement
Whilst the level of engagement in the *Gapped summary* extends beyond the single proposition, the way in which test takers need to engage with material is arguably a fairly literal one. As was the case with the *Yes/No/Not given* format, the task for test takers involves, in essence, the matching of information from the reading passage with a paraphrased version of this information in the summary. Thus, the following items (taken from Sample 3.2) are completed by juxtaposing information in the item with corresponding information in the original passage.

Sample item 1

Some corpora include a variety of language while others are focused on
a __38__.

**Correct response = ** particular linguistic feature

Relevant section from reading passage

Some corpora attempt to cover the language as whole, taking extracts from
many kinds of texts; others are extremely selective, providing a collection
of material that deals only with a particular linguistic feature.

Sample item 2

The length of time the process takes will affect the __39__ of the corpus.

**Correct response = ** size

Relevant section from reading passage

The size of the corpus depends on practical factors, such as the time available to collect, process and store the data: it can take up to several hours to
provide an accurate transcription of a few minutes of speech.

The relatively 'literal' form of engagement suggested by *Gapped summary*
tasks is indicated in our analytical matrix shown in Figure 2.5.

Figure 2.5 Analysis of Gapped summary task type

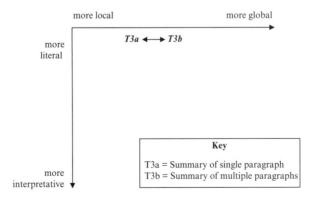

We note in passing that *Gapped summary* items can suffer from the
problem of having items which it may be possible to complete (or partially

complete) without referring to the original reading passage (Alderson 2000). This is a characteristic however, only of the 'options provided' variant of this task type. In the sample items below, for example, we can see that certain items among the provided options are semantically implausible within the information structure of the summary sentence, and so can be immediately discounted as possible answers (e.g. rainfall, typhoons).

The island will be partially protected from storms by . . .(10). . . and also by . . .(11). . .

construction workers	coastline	dump-trucks
geotextile	Lantau Island	motorway
rainfall	rock and sand	rock voids
sea walls	typhoons	

An additional dimension to this aspect were those cases where the provided options come in a variety of grammatical forms, and where some options could be automatically discounted on the grounds that they were syntactically anomalous in the summary sentence.

Alderson (2000) suggests that the problem with formats such as this is that they may be involved in testing constructs other than those that the instrument purports to test. Thus, with some of the *Gapped summary* tasks shown above, we might conclude that engagement with material is involved as much with grammatical competence or with principles of logical analysis, as with reading comprehension processes *per se*.

Type 4: Information–category match

Information–category match tasks were one of the less frequently occurring tasks accounting for 12% of items (Table 2.4 on page 135). Under this format, test takers need to match information from the reading passage with a specific information category to be selected from a range of category options. The category type used in the design of these tasks was found to be salient in some way in the reading passage, and which could be used as a basis for differentiating key information contained within it. Thus, in Sample 4.1 below, a task based on a reading comparing the design of different airports, the category of 'airport location' is used as the distinguishing element. Other category types noted in the corpus of these tasks were places (e.g. cities); people (e.g. types of employees); time periods (e.g. decades).

A specific type of *information–category match* task noted in the corpus was that which used individual scholars/writers as the category type. These were often used in tasks that accompanied reading passages consisting mainly of the attributed ideas or research findings of various individuals. The task for test takers in this particular format then was to match a summary statement of a specific idea (or finding) described in the text with an individual scholar.

Questions 1–5.
Classify the following statements as applying to:
A   *Chek Lap Kok airport only*
B   *Kansai airport only*
C   *Both airports*
Write the appropriate letter A–C in boxes 1–5 on the answer sheet.
Sample statements:
1.   *having an area of over 1,000 hectares*
2.   *built in a river delta*

Sample 4.1: Information–category match item

Sample 4.2, based on a reading passage about endangered languages, is illustrative of this format.

Questions 5–9.
Look at the following statements (Questions 5–9), and the list of people in the box below.
Match each statement with the correct person.
Write the appropriate letter A–E in boxes 5–9 on the answer sheet. NB You may use any letter more than once.

A   Michael Kraus
B   Salikoko Mufwene
C   Nicholas Ostler
D   Mark Pagel
E   Doug Whalen

Sample statements:
1. Endangered languages cannot be saved unless people learn to speak more than one language.
2. The way we think may be determined by our language.

Sample 4.2: Information–category match – scholar as category

Level of engagement
Information–category match items were generally found to be concerned with the locating of fairly specific information in the reading passage

(e.g. size of airport in Sample 4.1). A feature of these tasks however, was that information often had to be retrieved from several different places in the text. Thus, for example, in the following item taken from the airport sample (Sample 4.1), test takers need to identify whether the following statement concerning size of airport pertains to just one of the locations or both:

(Which airport) has an area of over 1,000 hectares

Completion of such an item thus necessitates engagement with several separate sections of the passage, as follows:

> An island six kilometres long and with a total area of 1248 hectares is being created there. The new island of Chek Lap Kok, the site of Hong Kong's new airport, is 83% complete.

> As Chek Lap Kok rises however, another new Asian island is sinking back into the sea. This is a 520 hectare island built in Osaka Bay, Japan that serves as a platform for the new Kansai airport.

Correct response = Chek Lap Kok airport only **(Option A)**

This particular characteristic of *Information–category match* tasks means that whilst engagement is generally at a local level, it is not as narrowly local as we have seen for other 'specific information' task types e.g. *True/False/Not given* (see Figure 2.6 on page 152).

Type of engagement
The airport example above suggests a highly literal engagement with reading material. In this case, the task for test takers is to identify specific information concerning the total area occupied by each airport site. A slightly less literal engagement is required arguably for the 'scholar as category' tasks (shown in Sample 4.2). In such tasks, the relevant ideas/findings of the scholar cited in the text are summarised in a relatively condensed form. The task for test takers is to be able to link this condensed summary to the more extended version of the idea cited in the passage, as shown in the following example below.

Statement:

The way we think may be determined by our language.

Relevant section in reading passage:

> There is mounting evidence that learning a language produces physiological changes in the brain. "Your brain and mine are different from the brain of someone who speaks French for instance", Pagel says, and this could affect our thoughts and perceptions. "The patterns and connections we make among various conceptions may be structured by the linguistic habits of our communities".

Correct response = Mark Pagel **(Option D)**

Overall, the engagement with material in *Information–category match* tasks was concluded to be quite literal, but with some variation noted around the 'scholar as category' examples. An attempt has been made to capture this variation in Figure 2.6 below.

Figure 2.6 Analysis of information–category match task type

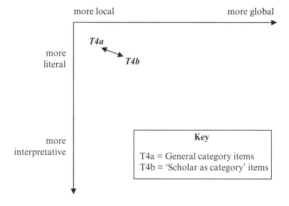

Type 5: Multiple choice
About 10% of items in the corpus used a standard multiple-choice format, with almost all relying on a 4-option structure. For all items, test takers were required to select a single 'correct' option. Sample 5.1 shows a range of multiple-choice items related to a passage about the development of cinema.

Level of engagement
The *Multiple choice* task format in the IELTS corpus was found to be distinctive for implying no particular level of engagement with text. This is in contrast with the other task types considered so far. Thus, we saw for example that the *True/False/Not given* format was linked to engagement at a mainly sentential level; similarly the principal unit of analysis in *Section–summary match* was

Questions 10–13

Choose the correct letter A, B, C, D.

Write the correct letter in boxes 10–13 on your answer sheet.

10 When cinema first began, people thought that
   A it would always tell stories
   B it should be used in fairgrounds
   C its audiences were unappreciative
   D its future was uncertain

11 The writer refers to the film of the train in order to demonstrate
   A the simplicity of early films
   B the impact of early films
   C how short early films were
   D how imaginative early films were

12 What is the best title for this passage?
   A The rise of the cinema star
   B Cinema and novels compared
   C The domination of Hollywood
   D The power of the big screen

Sample 5.1: Multiple choice sample

seen to be the paragraph. No such generalisation could be made however, for the multiple-choice tasks in the corpus, with different items probing quite different levels of text. This is evident in the sample items above. In Item 10, for example, shown with the relevant section from the associated reading passage, the required engagement is at a more 'local', propositional level (Correct response = D).

10. When cinema first began, people thought that
   A it would always tell stories
   B it should be used in fairgrounds
   C its audiences were unappreciative
   D its future was uncertain

Relevant section from reading passage:

When the Lumiere Brothers and other pioneers began showing off this new invention, it was by no means obvious how it would be used.

In contrast, Item 11 requires engagement with a more extended section of text – what in the passage is a full paragraph, as seen below (Correct response = B).

11. The writer refers to the film of the train in order to demonstrate

    A the simplicity of early films

    B the impact of early films

    C how short early films were

    D how imaginative early films were

Relevant section from reading passage:

One of the Lumiere Brothers' earliest films was a 30-second piece which showed a section of a railway platform flooded with sunshine. A train appears and heads straight for the camera. And that is all that happens. Yet the Russian film director Andrei Tarkovsky, one of the greatest of all film artists, described the film as a 'work of genius'. 'As the train approaches', wrote Tarkovsky, 'panic started in the theatre; people jumped and ran away. That was the moment when cinema was born. The frightened audience could not accept that they were watching a mere picture. Pictures are still, only reality moved; this must therefore be reality. In their confusion, they feared that a real train was about to catch them.'

Finally, the last question in this sample, Item 12, requires consideration of the whole reading passage – a text consisting of 10 paragraphs (Correct response = D).

12. What is the best title for this passage?

    A The rise of the cinema star

    B Cinema and novels compared

    C The domination of Hollywood

    D The power of the big screen

Significantly, items of this latter kind – requiring test takers to decide between different possible titles for a reading passage – were the only tasks found in the corpus that called for engagement at this whole text level. A total of five instances of this item type, all in a multiple-choice format, were noted in the overall corpus, accounting for 1% of items.

From the examples above we can see that multiple-choice items in the IELTS Reading test probe a variety of textual units, ranging from the very local to the very global, as shown in Figure 2.7.

Type of engagement

As was the case with the level of engagement, IELTS multiple-choice tasks in our corpus resisted any simple generalisation regarding the way test takers needed to engage with material. The sample items above suggest a variety of modes. Thus, Item 10, requiring identification of quite specific information (i.e. the perceived future of cinema), is clearly of a more literal type. In contrast, Item 12, which asks test takers to consider how the contents of the whole text can be encapsulated in a single noun phrase title (i.e. 'The power of the big screen'), involves a more 'interpretative' engagement.

Between these two examples is the third sample item (Item 11), requiring test takers to consider what point is made in the text through the citing of particular information (i.e. reference to the film of the train).

11. The writer refers to the film of the train in order to demonstrate

    A the simplicity of early films

    B the impact of early films, etc.

Such an item, with its focus on the underlying rhetorical purpose of a span of text, was analysed as requiring a less literal form of engagement. The variety in the required form of engagement in these items is captured in Figure 2.7.

Figure 2.7 Analysis of Multiple choice task type

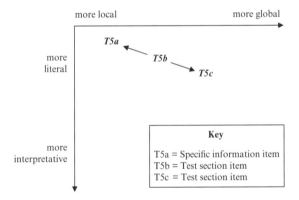

Type 6: Short answer

In *Short answer* tasks in the corpus (7% of total items), test takers needed to locate quite specific information from the reading passage in response to basic wh-questions. A stipulation of responses in this format was that answers needed to be limited to no more than two or three words (or numbers), and that answers were composed only of lexis drawn from the reading passage. An example of this type, referred to by Bachman and Palmer (1996) as 'limited production response', is shown in Sample 6.1 below. The questions in this sample relate to a passage describing methods used to enhance the performance of athletes.

Questions 11 and 12

Answer the questions below.

*Choose **NO MORE THAN THREE WORDS AND/OR A NUMBER** from the passage for each answer.*

Write your answers in boxes 11 and 12 on your answer sheet.

11 What is produced to help an athlete plan their performance in an event?

12 By how much did some cyclists' performance improve at the 1996 Olympic Games?

Sample 6.1: Short answer sample

Level of engagement

Like a number of other 'specific information' task types we have seen previously (e.g. *True/False/Not given*; *Gapped summary*), engagement with the passage in *Short answer* tasks is at a local level, as shown in the examples below.

Question 11:

What is produced to help an athlete plan their performance in an event?

Relevant section from reading passage:

> Well before a championship, sports scientists and coaches start to prepare the athlete by developing a 'competition model', based on what they expect will be the winning times.

Correct response = 'competition model'

Question 12:

By how much did some cyclists' performance improve at the 1996 Olympic Games?

Relevant section from reading passage:

> At the Atlanta Olympic Games in 1996, these [coolant jackets] sliced as much as two percent off cyclists' and rowers' times.

Correct response = two percent

The requirement of these tasks – that is, to use a minimal number of words in relation to quite specific items of information – makes these tasks particularly 'local' in their orientation, as indicated in Figure 2.8.

Type of engagement

The *Short answer* format in IELTS Reading, as we have seen, has a focus on quite specific items of information (e.g. the name of a specific performance-enhancement tool; the rate of improvement in a sports performance). We would say then that this involves a very basic form of text comprehension, and so this task type is located very much towards the literal end of our 'literal–interpretative' continuum. The allocated position of this task type on the matrix below suggests in fact that the short answer format constitutes the most 'literal' and most 'local' of all the task types considered so far.

Figure 2.8 Analysis of Short answer task type

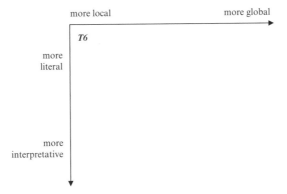

Type 7: Other

A number of other, infrequently occurring task types were identified in the corpus, as follows:

- sentence completion (4%)
- information transfer (completion of table, diagram, flow chart etc.) (4%)
- information–paragraph match (2%)
- information identification (0.8%).

All of these formats had a minimal presence in the corpus (<5%), and so were not analysed on an individual basis. It is noted that none appear to involve engagement of a distinctly different order from the patterns already identified in the previous task types.

Summary of analysis of IELTS reading task types

In summary, the analysis found that a majority of tasks in the IELTS corpus were of a distinctly 'local–literal' configuration, requiring mainly a basic comprehension of relatively small textual units (sentences, inter-sentences, paragraphs). It was noted that for a number of the more common task types, the required engagement was in fact of a highly 'local' and highly 'literal' kind (i.e. *True/False/Not given*; *Short answer*). Other task types were found to be slightly less 'local and literal' in their orienta-tion (i.e. *Section–summary match*), but were thought nevertheless to mainly inhabit the 'local–literal' region of our analytical matrix. The only items in our corpus that clearly traversed the 'local–literal' domain were certain multiple-choice items that required an appraisal of the reading passage as a whole (e.g. items requiring the selection of a title for a reading passage). It was noted that the *Not given* option in *True/False* questions also required a more global engagement (i.e. in order to establish whether information is in fact present in a text). As was discussed however, items of this type arguably constitute a special case.

For the analysis overall, it does need to be acknowledged that the results are based on a limited sample of test tasks, and also one not deriving from actual live test materials. Assuming, however, that the data used represent some approximation of current item-design practices at IELTS, we would argue that the analysis provides at least a broad picture of the tests' overall construct– that is, a distinct orientation towards reading of a 'local' and 'literal' nature.

4.2   Academic reading tasks

In the second part of the study, investigation was made of the types of reading tasks required of students in undergraduate study in a range of disci-plines. As discussed, a total of 12 discipline areas were investigated. This part of the study was informed by two different research methods: interviews with academic staff, and an independent analysis of reading-based tasks provided by these academics.

In what follows, we provide first of all a summary of the findings from the interviews, covering such issues as the quantity and type of reading pre-scribed on undergraduate courses, along with discussion of the way students are expected to engage with the material prescribed. This is followed by the analysis of the academic tasks. For this latter section, we draw on the frame-work used in the analysis of the IELTS tasks; that is to say, a consideration of the two key dimensions of the study – 'level' and 'type' of engagement with reading material.

Findings from interviews

The importance of reading in university study

The first substantive finding from the interviews was that reading in some form was a requirement in all the subjects investigated. Some informants were at pains, in fact, to stress that it was the activity of reading more than anything else that underlay the educational processes in their subject area. Thus, the lecturer in Media Studies saw reading as providing the common thread for all the various activities on his course:

> MEDIA STUDIES: *The reading is just so essential, and it's just integral to the whole structure of my course. We set weekly readings which are of course what the lectures are based on, and then we use these readings as the basis for our discussions in tutes . . . And then later on hopefully [this material] will reappear in a different form when it comes to [students] writing their essays and assignments.*

For the Linguistics lecturer, the development of key skills in reading was one of the more important objectives on her course:

> LINGUISTICS: *I am trying to encourage students to be critical thinkers and readers and reflect on the material that they have . . . not just having an approach to learning where we transmit some knowledge and they absorb it. So being able to critically engage with texts is very much a primary generic skill on the course.*

A number of other informants spoke of the effort they put in at the beginning of semester to persuade students to commit to doing the prescribed reading on their courses. For many, any adequate participation on academic programmes (whether it be related to attending lectures, discussion in tutorials, participation in lab sessions) was contingent on students coming along to classes having read the relevant material. The lecturer from Communications, for example, drew attention in interview to the following 'firm instruction' to students contained in the course manual:

> COMMUNICATIONS: *I really hammer the following home to students at the beginning of the course* (Referring to course outline document)*: "Please make sure you have done the reading before each lecture. The lectures and workshops will be based on the assumption that you have done this reading, and you will be expected to demonstrate some familiarity with the content".*

Whilst not emphasising reading to quite the same extent, some lecturers in the more technical ('hard') areas also affirmed the importance of this activity on their courses. The Architecture lecturer, for example, saw the development of good habits of reading as a key part of students' professional training:

> ARCHITECTURE: *Even though we are a more technical subject, students need to appreciate that it is principally through reading that they will acquire key knowledge in the discipline. We're aware of this not only for their university study, but for their ongoing development as professionals too . . . I say to my students that good habits of reading will make them good professionals.*

The overwhelming importance of reading in academic study was perhaps stated most emphatically by the informant from History:

> HISTORY: *What is very clear is that those students who do a lot of reading do better at whatever they are called upon to do than students who don't do very much, and this seems to be the case with virtually all the academic work we set.*

As we shall see later in the discussion of the interview findings, a number of staff reported a not-always-felicitous relationship between the expectations they had of reading, and the actual reading behaviours and attitudes that students brought to their studies.

Quantity and type of reading prescribed on courses
Whilst there was general agreement among informants about the importance of reading, a fair amount of variation was noted regarding the amount and types of reading prescribed in specific subject areas. The differences observed here were mainly disciplinary ones and, perhaps not surprisingly, were found to divide mainly along the hard–soft distinction we have drawn between the disciplines investigated in the study.

Such differences were quite noticeable, for example, in the quantity of reading expected of students. In the 'softer' disciplines, informants spoke of the need for students to do 'substantial' reading on their courses, and generally to go beyond the set readings:

> MEDIA STUDIES: *There is a standard textbook. Every week there are particular pages of references they need to read, but then there are other important books, journals, magazine articles as well. To be properly informed in this subject, students also need to get into the habit of reading newspapers every day, and to be monitoring articles on media developments.*

For the History lecturer, seeking out a range of sources and a variety of interpretations on a topic was an indispensable part of engaging with the discipline:

HISTORY: *To properly engage with the subject is very much dependent on having a certain level of knowledge which . . . is why we say to students you must do adequate reading otherwise you cannot respond to the questions [that we pose]. You might find a perfectly reasonable answer in a single book on this topic, but you're in no position to evaluate that unless you've read alternatives.*

Other informants in the softer disciplines said they were quite precise to students about the quantity of materials that needed to be read each week, and the time that should be put in. The Linguistics lecturer, for example, said she advised students they should be reading the prescribed material from the textbook each week and at least two relevant journal articles. The lecturer in Communications insisted to her students that they should devote at least 3–4 hours per week to reading in her subject.

In general, whereas the softer humanities disciplines required extensive reading and from a range of different sources and genres, in the harder more technical areas reading was found to be less extensive and mainly confined to the reading of the prescribed textbook in a subject:

COMPUTER SCIENCE: *There is a textbook. Students are expected to read a chapter a week, but not every week, just for the first eight weeks or so. That's the first half of the textbook – which amounts to only about 150 pages for the course.*

It was explained that in these harder disciplines the main purpose of weekly readings was to support the content of lectures:

PHYSICS: *The textbook would be the main form of reading that students would do. We like students to be prepared for lectures and so we ask them to read the sections of the textbook that are relevant for a particular lecture.*

Whilst in this case, the textbook material was intended to be read in advance of lectures, in other subjects the purpose of textbook reading was mainly for review:

ENGINEERING: *We have a textbook in the subject and after every lecture we put up the relevant pages of the textbook that they should read. So the idea is for them to read the PowerPoint slides, read the textbook and then write up their notes.*

Several lecturers from other hard fields went on to explain that it was the nature of their discipline that the reading of texts was not always the only means of engaging with disciplinary knowledge:

ARCHITECTURE: *Reading is important in this subject, though because of the nature of the discipline there are other literacies that come into play – visual literacy, kinesthetic literacy – to the extent that students are actually building things. Numeracy is also very important.*

COMPUTER SCIENCE: *We have a specialist type of reading in this subject which is related to the programming component. Students have to spend a bit of time reading other people's code, and this is a new type of reading for most.*

The nature of reading on courses

Along with variation in the quantity and type of reading material prescribed on courses were perceived differences in the ways that students needed to engage with this material. Early piloting of the research suggested to us that it would not necessarily be a straightforward task for academic staff to expound at length on different types of required reading skills, nor indeed for them to be able to distinguish these skills in any substantive way. This was partly because the characterisation of such skills constitutes arguably an 'insider' educational discourse, one related to the study of academic literacy *per se*, and a discourse not necessarily readily accessible to academics working within their own disciplinary specialisations. As a way of facilitating discussion around this point in the interviews, it was decided to provide a list of possible reading skills ('abilities') drawn from the literature (Alderson 2000, Grabe 1999) and to ask informants to comment on which of these they thought were relevant to study in their subject area (see below). This list seeks to capture some of the distinctions we have used in our analytical framework (i.e. type and level of engagement).

Ability to

1. Have a **basic comprehension** of key information in a text (LOCAL + / LITERAL +).
2. **Summarise** the main ideas in a text in one's own words (GLOBAL + / LITERAL +).
3. Understand an idea for the purpose of **applying** it to a particular situation or context (LOCAL +/ INTERPRETATIVE +).
4. Understand the **purpose** for why a text may have been written (GLOBAL +/ INTERPRETATIVE +).
5. **Critically evaluate** the ideas in a text (GLOBAL +/ INTERPRETATIVE +).
6. Identify **a range of texts** relevant to a topic (GLOBAL +/ LITERAL +).
7. Draw on ideas from a range of texts to **support** one's own argument (GLOBAL +/ INTERPRETATIVE +).

Given the relatively small sample size in interviews, the results are reported qualitatively (rather than quantitatively), with a focus on the key skill areas commented on by informants. Again, basic differences were observed in the perceptions of academics across the disciplines. It was noted, for example, that those in the 'harder' disciplines thought skills towards the top of the list had the most obvious relevance to study in their subject area. The following are a sample of the responses from the more technical areas:

ENGINEERING: *In Engineering I think we're mainly concerned with basic comprehension* (item 1 in the list above) *and summary skills* (item 2). *My sense of summary is students being able to convey the ideas back to us. So they need to understand the ideas and concepts, and report them back.*

PHYSICS: *I would be emphasising those skills more towards the top of the list. So we don't really ask students to identify a range of texts relevant to a topic* (item 6) *nor draw on ideas from a range of texts to support one's own argument* (item 7). *This is because students are not really making arguments at a first-year level. There are not so many things that are contestable at this level.*

BIOLOGY: *Well certainly basic comprehension and summarising of ideas* (items 1 and 2), *but understanding the purpose of why text is written is not important* (item 4) *Critically evaluate ideas* (item 5), *well only to a very limited extent – in most of first-year biology we don't really challenge the ideas – we sort of present them as these are the ideas you need to know, and the last two are not important for us.*

ARCHITECTURE: *I think all have some importance, but apart from the first one (i.e. having a basic comprehension of key information in a text), they are not as important in this subject, as they might be in other subjects.*

The main picture to emerge from these commentaries was that the important type of reading in these more technical disciplines was that related to basic comprehension of material. From these informants, it was generally felt that what was crucial in the first year of study in their disciplines was for students to come away with a good working knowledge of foundational ideas and concepts – and not to be spending too much time deciding whether such ideas were valid or not. A number pointed out that whilst more 'interpretative' forms of reading were clearly important in students' overall academic development, they had less obvious relevance in the early stages of training in the discipline. Among these more interpretative forms included in the list of skills, the least relevant, they thought, were those that involved 'critical evaluation' of material. As one informant explained it: 'In the first year, we want students to accept certain things more-or-less as read, and to hold off with too much critical scrutiny of them at this stage.'

However, several informants explained that such a profile of reading skills was a specific feature of the first years of undergraduate programmes and that at more advanced levels in these disciplines, the other more interpretative types of reading had a much greater role to play:

> BIOLOGY: *As students move through the discipline I guess some of the things that were previously taken for granted start to become a bit more contentious – and we see these other skills like critically evaluating texts* (item 5) *coming more into play. Certainly students need to have a critical eye out when they read research articles, and the sorts of claims that are made in these.*

The view expressed from the more humanities-oriented areas represented a clear contrast. For informants in these areas, all items on the list were thought to be important and particularly those at the lower end. A common theme here was that in one's teaching, the more 'literal'-based skill areas were taken for granted to some extent, and that much of what students were expected to do simply assumed an understanding of basic concepts in the field.

> LINGUISTICS: *I think I make certain assumptions about those items further up the list, like being able to understand the ideas we present* (item 1). *That is, that students come to my course able to do these things.*

> MANAGEMENT: *Having a basic comprehension* (item 1), *well obviously that's really important. If [the students] can't do that, the rest [of the skills] become a bit redundant.*

For these academics, the focus was squarely on the more interpretative reading skills. Among those on the list, the idea of being critical of texts (item 5), and of being able to draw on multiple sources to support an argument (item 7) had particular resonance:

> LINGUISTICS: *The really important [skills] on the course are definitely critically evaluate* (item 5) *and drawing on ideas from range of texts to support argumentation* (item 7). *They are all important but those are the important formative skills for this subject. That's really the point that I try to get students to by the end of semester.*

> MEDIA STUDIES: *All of the skills are important – having a basic comprehension, summarizing* (item 1) *is obviously important. On my course, however, students being critical in their reading is absolutely essential* (item 5). *Students need to assess arguments, and part of this is identifying where arguments and ideas have been left out.*

> MANAGEMENT: *The aim [on my course] is for [students] to develop an awareness of multiple types of sources, multiple viewpoints and to build confidence in their writing to draw on these different viewpoints in advancing their own view* (item 7).

Among the more humanities-oriented areas, additional distinctions were observed at the individual discipline level. Our History informant, for example, attached special significance to students being able to 'understand the purpose for why a text may have been written' (item 4). For him, such an ability related to a crucial part of the training students needed to undergo as novitiate historians – namely the ability to read and interpret primary source material:

> HISTORY: *Working with primary source material is, I suppose, a specialist kind of reading in history, and we spend a lot of time on that. Students need to be able to see what's surrounding a document, why it was created, what the author of the document is trying to achieve through it.*

Additional variation was also found in the more applied disciplines. For informants in these areas a key skill emphasised was the ability to draw on concepts in one's reading for 'the purpose of applying them to a particular situation or context' (item 3). Thus, the informant from the new applied Business discipline of *E-commerce* was keen to stress the essentially utilitarian nature of reading in the field:

> BUSINESS STUDIES: *The focus of E-commerce is very much about finding solutions to practical problems, and to develop electronic means to advance existing ways of doing things. Our sense of students learning is really about them grasping a concept and then being able to apply it. Later on they might want to be critical of the concept, but in the first instance we just want them to focus on using it in some practical way.*

In another of the applied disciplines, Communications, a similarly utilitarian conception of reading was emphasised. In this case, the focus was not so much on students being able to draw on conceptual resources for the purpose of solving real-world problems; but instead to draw on *linguistic* resources within texts for a different practical purpose – namely, the development of their writing. The lecturer in the subject explained this particular type of reading thus:

> COMMUNICATIONS: *Students need to write in a variety of genres, say, for example, the book review, and we get them to look at samples of these genres as a resource for their own writing.*
>
> INTERVIEWER: *So how would you describe the nature of the reading that students have to do in this situation?*
>
> COMMUNICATIONS: *Well, I tell them in the beginning that they are not reading so much as consumers anymore, but that they are reading it like a carpenter might look at a chair – not so much to sit in it, but to see how it is put together.*

Perceived changes in students' reading practices

A final area covered in this summary of interview findings is informants' perceptions of students' reading practices on their courses. Interestingly, this was an issue not directly probed in the interviews. As has been stressed, the primary construct that informed the research was the notion of 'task demand', and so it was not an imperative of the study to investigate issues of actual student behaviour and performance. We found, however, that these were key issues for informants and ones that many were keen to air in the course of our discussions. In short, concern was expressed by a number of informants – and indeed a degree of disdain by some of these – about the lack of commitment shown nowadays by students towards reading on their courses. The following are some representative comments on this issue:

> LINGUISTICS: *It is a constant struggle to get students to do the reading these days. So for example in the tutorial that I had earlier this week, I asked what I thought was a really self-evident question, and the answer was very clearly in the second reading from the week. Nobody got it. Literally nobody had even read the article.*

> COMPUTER SCIENCE: *At the end of this semester we asked for a show of hands of how many of the students actually had a copy of the textbook and it was a slightly depressingly low proportion. So I think quite a lot of students [aren't] actually doing the reading.*

> MEDIA STUDIES: *I've told you about what we expect, but one can't avoid mentioning what actually happens. So reading in fact has become a major problem. Students are just doing less reading than they've ever done before, and that would be local students as much as international . . . Many complain that the standard of textbook is just too difficult . . . We feel, though, that we have to resist dumbing these things down. It's a university textbook we prescribe; we can't go looking at something fit for secondary level.*

Whilst the last informant, from Media Studies, thought vigilance was necessary to avoid any 'dumbing down' of requirements, others thought the pressures to scale things down – both the quantity and level of reading – difficult to resist at times. The Management lecturer, for example, described how the subject he taught had been forced in recent years to take a less rigorous, less 'literary' turn in response to changing student cohorts and preferences:

> MANAGEMENT: *I've taught the course for about five years. I took the course over from two of the older academics here who are probably well . . . more literary in their take on the world. One was a trained historian; the other was an economic historian. But I've had to tone down the volume of reading and that's in response to the changing student mix and changing*

student behaviour. I have probably shifted it more to use of business press material, less academic material.

More ominously, another lecturer thought that on some programmes, the reading load had had to be reduced partly in response to certain pressures felt through formal processes of student review and feedback:

ENGINEERING: *Students only have to read the textbook and the PowerPoint slides to be successful in this subject nowadays. And this is a lot to do with student expectations, because we have found that they are very reluctant to do extra reading. And again this has to do with quality of teaching. If you give them a lot of reading, you are going to get really knocked back on quality of teaching scores.*

Mention was made in interviews of some of the possible factors underlying this apparent decline in reading, including a general sense of students disengaging from study, financial pressures, time spent in employment and so on. Another clear factor identified – one related to actual literacy practices – was students' increasing use and reliance on digital resources, and the effect this seemed to be having on the way they engage with textual material. The view generally was that a lot of online working with material was not encouraging of good reading practices:

MEDIA STUDIES: *There is a lot of material now that students access that they just typically browse. It's a kind of trawling for information. They just don't read this stuff in any serious and sustained way.*

Concern was expressed too that access to the limitless resources available on the web has resulted in some students being less-than-judicious in their use of materials:

COMMUNICATIONS: *Research is showing that the evaluation and management of material that's coming out over the internet is the biggest issue. And some students do not have particularly well-developed evaluation skills.*

Some thought however, that the considerable changes in the way that information is now accessed had major implications for teaching and that there was a need to address these issues positively with students. Several, for example, spoke of the importance of developing students' 'information literacy' and 'media literacy' skills:

HISTORY: *The web has been a boon to the study of history. But we have to help students to be a bit discerning about their use of websites . . . We actually have discussions in tutorials. How can we tell whether this is a reliable site or not? So it's evaluation of who is producing this, in what context, and for what purpose.*

MEDIA STUDIES: *What I try to teach [students] is to get them to be selective in their reading of the media . . . so, I want them to understand the context of what [they] are reading, and also the legitimacy of what they are reading.*

For at least one informant, the lecturer from Linguistics, to resist such developments was really a futile pursuit and the onus was very much on the universities to adapt to emerging literacy practices. For her, the shift from a print-based academic culture to a more digitally based one posed a much greater challenge for many academics than for students:

LINGUISTICS: *So I think we in the university have to learn more about students' reading habits and practices and to rethink our assumptions. And we are probably going to have to make big adjustments about what it is that students do these days when they study.*

Findings from task analysis

Along with the conducting of interviews with staff about reading requirements, the research also collected samples of the various academic tasks set by these staff on their courses. Each of the tasks compiled in the corpus involved a reading component of some kind and included the following formats:

1. Weekly exercises and questions, set principally for the purpose of lecture and tutorial preparation/review.
2. Questions and tasks set in examinations, tests, etc.
3. Assignment tasks, set as part of the major assessment requirements on courses.

In the analysis that follows, we draw on the same framework used to analyse the IELTS reading task types, involving an allocation of each task to a category in the schema. This was done both through processes of moderation between members of the research group and also through reference to informants' descriptions of these tasks in interview. The findings of this section are organised around the four analytical categories, *viz*:

- local–literal
- global–literal
- local–interpretative
- global–interpretative.

LOCAL–LITERAL

In our corpus, we could find many examples of tasks that required a mainly 'local–literal' form of engagement with reading material. It is significant to note also that such examples were present in *all* the discipline areas covered in the study. The following two items are presented as samples from the corpus fitting this 'local–literal' configuration:

Read Chapter 8 of *The Gecko's Foot – Bio-inspiration: Engineered from Nature,* and take notes around the following questions.

1. What is meant by the concept of 'ordered crumpling'? Why, according to the author, is this concept useful?

Sample A1: Weekly exercise task – *Architecture*
(A1 denotes that this is an Academic task, and this is the first task.)

---

2. Postmodernists basically believe that:

a) All texts are closed   b) Most texts are closed
c) All texts are open   d) Most texts are open
e) All of these depending on the circumstances

Sample A2: Exam question – *Media Studies*

The first example, Sample A1, is from a set of exercise questions, pre-scribed as part of the weekly readings in the *Architecture* subject. This task, as the rubric states, requires students to produce a short summary ('notes') of a specific concept from the readings ('ordered crumpling'), along with an account of its 'usefulness' – as described by the passage's author. This focus on explication of a single concept clearly fits with a more 'local and literal' engagement with material. Such interpretation was confirmed by the lecturer, who described the purpose of 'basic comprehension-style' tasks like this as being 'to help students come to grips with material and to get a grasp of key concepts in the subject'. The lecturer went on to explain that in her subject such concepts were then typically drawn on in some practical way – in this case, it was to explore in tutorial discussion the issue of 'how certain patterns in nature can be applied to design'.

The second sample, Sample A2, is a multiple-choice question set in an exam context. The lecturer in this subject (*Media Studies*) explained in interview that this particular question related to 'quite specific informa-tion' contained in the textbook (and also covered in lectures), and that it would involve students, as he explained, recalling 'basically factual information about one of the core beliefs of this intellectual movement' (Correct response: C). Other multiple-choice questions on the exam in this subject, the lecturer explained, followed a similar format, requiring the same literal recall of key content covered on the course. It was noted, however, that the exam paper in *Media Studies* also included other question types (e.g. short essays), the specifications of which, as we shall see, fit with other configurations on our matrix.

The sample tasks we have described cover two of the task formats noted above, namely:

1. Weekly exercises and questions, set principally for the purpose of lecture and tutorial preparation/review.
2. Questions and tasks set in formal examinations.

It is interesting to note that virtually all the 'local–literal' examples in our corpus relate to these two formats; that is to say, tasks set principally for the purposes of either *inputting* key concepts and knowledge during a course of study or else for the *testing* of students' acquisition of these concepts and knowledge at the end of a course (or course segment). We discuss each of these two formats briefly below.

Weekly exercises and questions
A number of lecturers stressed the importance of weekly exercise tasks as a way for students to acquire (or to have reinforced) key content in their subject area:

> COMPUTER SCIENCE: *We set questions each week which are generic technical questions, and involve encyclopedia-style retrieval of the relevant information from the textbook and lecture.*

As explained by some, such questions do not usually need to be answered formally, but often involve the taking of notes (or 'scribblings') from the set readings, that students would then bring to class to discuss:

> MANAGEMENT: *In terms of reading for the tutorials, there is definitely a set of study questions each week . . . where the students can scribble things down and that will form part of the discussions of the tutorials. So those questions are guiding them through the reading, comprehension questions to make sure they have understood the reading.*

As suggested in the discussion of Sample A1 above, a focus of these comprehension-style questions is often on key *concepts* in the discipline. This was a point taken up by a number of informants:

BIOLOGY: *Students have a handbook of tutorial questions that they get at the start of semester. Their purpose very much is to filter out what is most important about a specific concept. So in their reading they have to be able to look for the concepts and fish out the most crucial points.*

The lecturer in *Physics* explained that part of this 'conceptual' understanding involved students recognising how terms within a discipline often carry with them quite distinctive meanings, ones that differ from a term's everyday usage:

PHYSICS: *In physics [like other disciplines], there are particular conceptual challenges that students have, in part related to the fact that we do use some words which have a very precise meaning in physics that is different from how they are used in normal everyday usage.*

This lecturer went on to explain that often the study questions she set were intended to draw out these distinctive meanings. Examples she gave were the terms 'heat' and 'temperature':

PHYSICS: *If we actually unpack a word like 'heat' and use it in the precise way it is intended then we are actually thinking about some energy being transferred from one object to another because their temperatures are different. That's not normally how one would use the word, and there are lots of words like that. So words like 'heat', 'temperature' have really precise meanings and we try to bring this out in the questions we set for students.*

Samples A3–6 show questions from a variety of disciplines, all which have this focus on facilitating students' understanding of specific discipline-based concepts. It was noted, interestingly, that in the format of many such questions, the relevant concept with which students need to engage is often signalled through the use of inverted commas or italics.

Read Section X of the textbook on *thermal energy*:
Which has the greater amount of *thermal energy*, an iceberg or a cup of coffee? If the coffee and the iceberg were placed in contact, what would happen? Use this context to explain clearly the terms *temperature*, *heating* and *thermal energy*.

Sample A3: Weekly exercise question – *Physics*

> What is 'currency risk'? Why does international business inevitably involve this type of risk? How can firms reduce these risks?

Sample A4: Weekly exercise question – *Management*

> What is the difference between the 'Lossy' and 'Lossless' types of media compression?

Sample A5: Weekly exercise question – *Computer Science*

> Explain what a 'speech act' is, and give several examples.

Sample A6: Weekly exercise question – *Linguistics*

Exam and test questions
Exams and tests were set in almost all of the subjects investigated, the only exception being Communications. The reading requirements for exams, as explained by a number of informants, mainly involved reviewing the content of lecture and textbook material:

> ENGINEERING: *The exam is basically about testing students' under-standing of key ideas and terms. As preparation for the exam [students] would need to look at the PowerPoint slides of the lectures and reread the relevant sections of the textbook.*

Among the items set on the exam/test papers was a sizeable proportion requiring a mainly 'local–literal' engagement with material. These included 'Short answer' questions, very much in the vein of the 'study'-type questions discussed in the previous section – that is, questions requiring short summaries of key concepts and ideas. Samples of such question types are shown below (A7–10):

> What assumption about 'savings behaviour' is made by the Solow Swan model?

Sample A7: Short answer exam question – *Economics*

Briefly explain Fukuyama's *End of History* thesis.

Sample A8: Short answer exam question – *History*

What is meant by the concept of 'value configuration'?

Sample A9: Short answer exam question – *Business Studies*

What is the hypodermic model of media effects?

Sample A10: Short answer exam question – *Media Studies*

Also used in the exam/test samples collected were a range of more objective, 'closed' formats. The most common of these was *Multiple Choice*; *True/False*, and *Gap fill* formats were also noted. Examples from the corpus of each of these formats are shown below:

An etic description of a cultural practice:

A. reflects the culture member's own understanding
B. focuses on sound differences
C. takes an outsider's perspective
D. requires a prolonged engagement and "going native"

Sample A11: Multiple choice question – *Linguistics*

The statements A–D are either correct or incorrect. Record whether the statement is Correct by entering 11 or Incorrect by entering 12.

A. The binomial name of a species is by convention printed in italics
B. Phylogeny is the study of the life cycle of an organism
C. Slime moulds get their name from the mucilage trains they leave behind
D. Diatoms and dinoflagellates are important photosynthetic plankton contributing greatly to the productivity of the oceans.

Sample A12: True/False question – *Biology*

In a Keynesian short-run model of a two sector economy, suppose that savings are greater than planned investment. This will result in _____ in inventories.

a) unplanned, increases   b) unplanned, decreases
c) planned, increases   d) planned, decreases

Sample A13: Gap fill question – *Economics*

Such formats, on the face of it, bear a close resemblance to some of the IELTS reading task types we have seen. One needs to be mindful, however, of an important difference in the processes involved in completing tasks in these two contexts. On the IELTS test, test takers have access to the information required to complete tasks, i.e. as information contained in the reading passage. This is not normally the case in subject-based examinations, where students are not usually permitted access to reading materials during the exam. Thus the two contexts rely arguably on different cognitive processes – in the IELTS test, these mainly involve the locating and comprehending of specific information to be found in the reading materials; in the examination format there is a distinctive 'memory and recall' component to the required form of engagement.

Such differences relate very much to the very different purposes of reading in the two domains. In a Reading test such as IELTS, the focus is more on assessing the extant skill level of test takers; in university exam items, such as in the examples we have seen above, the focus is less on skill and more on the extent to which students have acquired key knowledge in the discipline area. In short, in the university context, content is salient; in a language testing context, it is largely incidental. The implications of this difference for test design are discussed in more detail in Section 5 of this report.

GLOBAL–LITERAL

According to the study's analytical schema, tasks of a 'global–literal' configuration are those that require primarily basic comprehension of textual material (literal) in relation to larger textual units – i.e. whole texts as well as multiple texts (global). It was noted that almost all tasks in our corpus fitting these patterns were *assignment tasks* (i.e. out of class tasks, set as part of the major assessment requirements on courses). Most, but not all, came from the 'softer' humanities disciplines. Examples of such task types are presented and discussed below.

Summary tasks – single text

We saw in the previous section ('local–literal'), a number of tasks requiring the summary of a single concept (e.g. 'thermal energy' in Physics, 'speech acts' in Linguistics). Tasks requiring the summary of a single *whole* text were relatively uncommon in the corpus. The following from the *History* subject, involving here the summary of a book chapter, was a rare example:

> **Secondary source summary**
>
> One of the most important skills in conducting research in history is the ability to comprehend a particular text, and then to summarise its major arguments and conclusions in your own words.
>
> For this exercise, you need to read chapter X of *The path to genocide* by Christopher Browning, and then write a 500 word summary.

Sample A14: Assignment task – *History*

In setting this task, the History lecturer explained that it was important for students not just to give 'some simple blow-by-blow recapitulation of the text':

> HISTORY: *What I stress to students is that they need to read chiefly with the purpose of identifying the author's main argument. And the other part is then to identify the evidence the author presents to support this argument. All this needs to come out in their summaries.*

Summaries of arguments – multiple texts

A more common type of summary task was that requiring the summary of a number of texts, as in the following two samples from *Management* and *Media Studies*. As in the History example above, the main focus of these tasks was for students to give an account of *arguments* contained within texts. In both the sample tasks below, a key component is for these arguments to be seen as part of a larger debate – in the *Management* task (A15), it is one about how much globalisation has progressed as a phenomenon; in the *Media Studies* task (A16), it is a debate about different policy approaches to media ownership.

Both lecturers were keen to stress that such tasks were really focused on developing the skill of accurately representing the views of various writers on an issue. As the Management lecturer explained it:

> **The globalisation debate**
>
> In no more than 800 words, address the following question:
>
> **What are the arguments for and against the idea that 'the world has become flat' in recent years?**
>
> Please base your discussion on readings for Week 3 and further research. You must meet the referencing requirements listed below.
>
> *Business in the global economy*

Sample A15: Assignment task – *Management*

> **Media ownership**
> What are some of the basic for and against arguments in the debate about abolishing the cross media ownership AND foreign ownership laws in Australia? Refer to at least 4 primary sources in your response.

Sample A16: Assignment task – *Media Studies*

> MANAGEMENT: *Students often struggle in just seeing what the main points of a piece of writing are, to have the confidence to say: "Yes, this is what this person is saying, this is what they're arguing".*

This lecturer went on to explain that in such tasks, students were sometimes under the misapprehension that they should also be expressing their own view in the debate. For this lecturer, the ability to provide a clear summary of 'the arguments of others' in the field was a basic foundational skill, one which was then built on later in the course:

> MANAGEMENT: *One thing [students] struggle with is that it's actually a summary task. I'm after a set of arguments. I'm not after [their own] opinions which can throw them a little. We tell them that comes in later.*

Summaries of research findings
A different version of the summary task was one that focused not on the identification of the arguments contained within expository texts, but rather on the purposes and findings contained within empirical research studies. In

Sample A17 below, an essay set in the *Biology* subject, a major component of the work for students is to 'summarise a range of recent studies' concerned with the search for a cure for malaria.

Malaria

Why do botanists study the malarial parasite (Plasmodium) and how do they hope to find a cure for this disease? In your response, you should summarise a range of recent studies, focusing on the kinds of drugs currently being tested, and why.

Sample A17: Essay task – *Biology*

Another example of a task requiring students to document a series of research findings is the following from the *Linguistics* subject (Sample A18). In this instance, students need to conduct their own research, but first of all to place their study in the context of previous work done in the area, involving 'a summary of earlier studies in the subject'.

Speech act research

The purpose of this assignment is for you to collect and analyse speech act data. You will be expected to design a brief Discourse Completion Task (DCT) which elicits apologies or requests.

Write your paper with the following sections (including inter alia):

Introduction (about 400 words): Talk about the speech act you're investigating, and the role of politeness for realising it. Define your terms, **and summarise some of the earlier studies on the subject** (you may use your reader and lecture notes for this).

Sample A18: Research project task (extract) – *Linguistics*

LOCAL–INTERPRETATIVE
Our category of 'interpretation' is a broad one and, as explained earlier, has been defined for the purposes of the study as 'those forms of engagement with reading material that go beyond a literal comprehension of a text's propositional content'. In this sense, as we pointed out, it is a more reader-focused than text-focused form of engagement.

Under the 'local–literal' category discussed earlier, we saw a range of tasks that were focused on students showing their understanding of key *concepts* in the discipline (e.g. 'thermal energy' in Physics, 'speech acts' in Linguistics, 'value configuration' in Business Studies). Tasks falling under this new category, 'local–interpretative', had a similar focus on key disciplinary *concepts*, but were distinguishable from these largely comprehension-based tasks in their requirement that students engage in some reflective way with this material. Such a distinction is well-illustrated in the following quotation from one informant:

> ARCHITECTURE: *Some of the texts in the subject are difficult so we typically set some guide questions to help [students] pick out what we see as the key points in the reading. But we also want them to reflect on what they have read and always relate it somehow to their design work.*

In the analysis of our corpus, we observed two main types of interpretative tasks around this more local material: i) tasks requiring students to show how a concept or idea in their reading could be utilised in their work in the discipline (application), and ii) tasks requiring some assessment of the validity, worth and so on of an idea, or concept (evaluation).

Application tasks
The first of these task types, the 'application type', was the more common in the corpus, with instances identified in a range of discipline areas. In the following task, taken from the *Architecture* subject, we see exemplification of the principle enunciated above by the lecturer in this subject (Sample A19). As outlined in the task rubric, students here need first of all to consider certain concepts presented in their course reader (in this case 'efficient structures found in nature'), and then to reflect on how these concepts might be applied in their 'future design work'.

Structures in nature
The chapter *Introduction to Building Structures* gives a good overview of the structural systems you have been learning about. The author also looks at how *efficient structures* found in nature are good case studies in which to examine structural principles.

Make some notes from your reading on several of these structures, and suggest how you think the concepts discussed could be **useful** to you in your future design work.

Sample A19: Exercise task – *Architecture*

The following are additional tasks that have this focus on the *application* of key disciplinary concepts (Samples A20 and A21). In the Economics task (A20), students need to draw on a particular economic model ('Solow-Swan model') as a basis for analysing a particular economic state-of-affairs (or rather a state-of-affairs imputed by a particular economic commentator). A similar configuration is evident in the Physics task (A21), where students need to draw on a concept in the literature ('gel electophoresis'), as a basis for assessing the 'accuracy' of an example constructed by themselves.

> Consider the following statement made by a leading Australian economic commentator:
> *Where once our economic growth was determined solely by the number of machines, today it is determined by our ability to generate new ideas and develop new ways of producing output.*
>
> Using the Solow-Swan model, assess this statement.

Sample A20: Exercise task – *Economics*

> **Extended written answer**
>
> a) From a physics perspective, and using the simple model (F= CAv), discuss how gel electrophoresis allows fragments of different mass and/ or electric charge to be separated over time.
>
> b) Using an example constructed by you (i.e. you decide the mass, size, and charge of each fragment), demonstrate that two different fragments will separate over time.
>
> c) **consult the literature on gel electrophoresis** and briefly discuss one aspect of your initial analysis that is idealised or inaccurate.

Sample A21: Exercise task – *Physics*

In their commentaries on these more interpretative tasks, informants emphasised the need for students to be operating beyond any 'simple factual' understanding of knowledge, where answers fall neatly into correct and incorrect responses. Interestingly, such a view was also enunciated by some from the hard technical disciplines, including the Physics lecturer who was keen to disavow students of the idea that studies in her subject involved a simple quest for the right answer:

PHYSICS: *People think traditionally that Physics is really just about the mathematical solving of problems, and coming up with the right answer. In fact there's a lot in it that's just not that. A lot is about being able to understand concepts and working out how and when to apply them.*

A similar view was expressed by the Architecture lecturer who also stressed the 'open-ended' nature of reading tasks in her discipline area. She pondered whether this in fact was a conception that was at odds somehow with those held by students from certain educational backgrounds:

ARCHITECTURE: *In terms of tasks we set around reading, we have many open-ended tasks with no right or wrong answer. If students are coming from a different culture where there is an expectation that they need to get something right, then there are difficulties there I suppose.*

Evaluation tasks

Less prominent among the tasks fitting a 'local–interpretative' pattern were those that required explicit *evaluation* of material, involving the assessment of the value, worth, benefit, etc. of some entity. Consistent with the finding from the interviews, it was noted that such tasks in the corpus were confined to the softer 'humanities' disciplines, as seen in the following examples. We note in passing that a range of different types of entities are presented here as the objects of evaluation: in Sample A22 it is a 'policy', in A23 it is a 'thesis', and in A24 it is a 'concept'.

Explain what a 'polycentric' staffing policy is. What are the positives and negatives of a firm adopting such a policy?

Sample A22: Exam question – *Management*

What is Samuel Huntington's 'Clash of civilizations'? How convincing is his thesis?

Sample A23: Exercise task – *History*

What is 'liquid modernity'? How useful do you find this concept? Discuss in relation to the phenomenon of reality television.

Sample A24: Exercise task – *Media Studies*

In such tasks, one sees clear expression of the 'critical' approach to knowledge advocated by a number of informants, as seen in the following remarks made by the lecturers from Media Studies and History:

> MEDIA STUDIES: *On my course . . . students being critical in their reading is absolutely essential. Students need to assess arguments, and part of this is identifying where arguments and ideas have been left out.*

> HISTORY: *I stress to students the need for a critical approach. The way I get at this is to say to them: "Well just because this guy writes it in a book, it's not something you have to accept".*

GLOBAL–INTERPRETATIVE

The category 'global–interpretative' refers to those tasks requiring students to bring a broadly interpretative approach to their reading in relation to whole texts or multiple texts. Most tasks in the corpus fitting this configuration were assignment tasks, taking in a range of genres: essays, reports and the like. The most prominent of these genres identified in the data are discussed below.

Essays

The assignment-type task most clearly requiring a 'global–interpretative' approach to reading material was found to be the expository essay. In the study, the essay genre was set for students in about half the subjects investigated – with the majority of these prescribed in the 'soft' disciplines. Below are two such samples, from *Management* (Sample A25) and *History* (Sample A26). In the rubric of these tasks we can see the need for students to engage with a variety of materials ('a range of views'; 'available evidence' etc.) and to bring a critical approach to these materials ('to examine', 'to assess', 'to come to your own judgment').

Globalisation and cultural risk

"Globalisation is reducing cultural differences between countries and thus cultural risk. International firms can now pursue global strategies without fear of failure". Please assess the merits of this advice. Can firms ignore cultural risks?

In your essay you will need to consider a range of views on this issue before coming to your own final judgment.

Sample A25: Essay task – *Management*

> **Kennedy's Vietnam policies**
>
> In retrospect, JFK can be seen to have increased the American commitment in Vietnam. Many argue, however, that Kennedy would have resiled from extending the War. Examine the available evidence, including the views of Kennedy's contemporaries and the historians who have studied his presidency to assess the nature and impact of JFK's Vietnam policies.

Sample A26: Essay task – *History*

This 'global–interpretative' approach was also outlined by informants in interview:

> HISTORY: *We require our students to read widely – both primary and secondary material. I stress to them that they need to do adequate reading otherwise they cannot respond to the questions that we pose. I say "You might find a perfectly reasonable answer in a single book on this topic, but you're in no position to evaluate that unless you've read alternatives".*

Accompanying such essay tasks in the subject manuals was a good deal of material covering issues of appropriate use of sources and plagiarism, including the following from the History manual:

> Essay writing is an essential part of the learning process and a vital medium through which we can assess your understanding of the subject. The essay must therefore be your own work. This does not mean you should not make extensive use of the work of others. However when you quote or paraphrase the explanations of others, you must acknowledge your sources in full.

Figure 2.9 Advice concerning plagiarism – History course manual

In relation to essay writing, a number of informants spoke of the challenges of imparting to students how they should go about using reading material legitimately in their writing:

> MANAGEMENT: *Using sources appropriately is a tertiary skill, and in teaching that we try to inculcate some of the ideas of what plagiarism is . . . but we do often face issues with students on that score.*

Reports

Another assignment-type requiring a 'global–interpretative' engagement was the report. In the following example, a section of a linguistics research report task (cited earlier – Sample A18), students needed to interpret the results of their study against the findings of a range of studies described earlier in the report.

> **Speech act research**
> *Discussion & Conclusion* (400–500 words). Analyse and interpret your findings: Why did it turn out like this? What is the reason for the differences you found? **How do these results stand with respect to some of the studies you reported in the introduction?** End with a brief example for you to focus your analysis . . . Drawing on key concepts

Sample A27: Research project task (extract) – *Linguistics*

In the following case study report from *Business Studies,* students needed to draw on certain discipline-related concepts ('value configuration', 'business structure') as a basis for analysing the effectiveness ('value') of a specific business organisation.

> **Value proposition analysis**
> This assessment task requires you to analyse how the environment, value configuration and business structure affect the nature of a value proposition.
>
> **Task:** Your tutor will assign you with a small to medium business (SME) example for you to focus your analysis . . . . Drawing on key concepts from the course, you need to analyse various aspects of the business to explain and evaluate where and how an organisation delivers value to their customers.

Sample A28: Report task – *Business Studies*

Text analysis

One final type of 'global–interpretative' reading task involved forms of text analysis. This type of task is arguably a more recent task type set for students in the academy, and reflects the growing influence of notions of 'genre' and 'academic literacy' on teaching in university programmes. In such tasks in our corpus, students were typically encouraged to see particular texts as 'generic resources' from which they could draw for their own writing, as seen in Sample A29 below. In this task, from the *Communications* subject, students

> **Writing an Op Ed piece**
>
> For this task you need to research and write an opinion piece on a timely topic. You need to express an opinion and then to make an argument to support that opinion. This type of article is called in the industry an 'op-ed' piece. No ESSAYS please. Note that the op-ed is an entirely different genre from the academic essay.
>
> To prepare for the writing of this piece, you should locate several examples of op-ed pieces written on a similar topic from a major newspaper (eg *The Age*). These examples of the genre can serve as a model for your own writing. In consulting the piece, you should consider what is said about the topic in question, but also – and very importantly – how the piece is put together (the language used, structure etc).

Sample A29: Assignment task – *Communications*

need to investigate a range of Opinion pieces from a newspaper (Op-Ed articles) as a basis for writing their own pieces.

This genre-based reading was elaborated on by the Communications lecturer, who saw such training as essential to the development of students' writing abilities:

> COMMUNICATIONS: *Because they have to write in this subject, if they don't read, then they will be completely' 'off genre'. They'll just be writing stuff that they would have written at high school. So I get them to analyse texts. I actually get them to do things like count the words in the sentences, get the sentence range, what style of language it is. Is it elaborate or is it plain? And then they need to emulate that.*

Whilst the setting of tasks such as this is quite understandable in the context of a course explicitly aimed at developing writing skills in students, we noted similar genre-based activities set on courses without the same focus on writing *per se*. Thus, in Sample A30 below from the *Management* subject, students are instructed to study a sample answer based on 'The Globalisation Debate' task discussed earlier (Sample A15), and to use this as an 'indicative guide' for completion of the 'debate' task set for students.

A different type of text analysis task was one where students needed to adopt a 'critical' approach to language use. Examples of such tasks were confined to the *Media Studies* subject, such as the following 'Media Watch' task (Sample A31), requiring students to analyse different media representations of a particular story or issue.

> **Sample review**
> The following text is a sample review in the manner of the debate review exercise (see sample X).
>
> Study the text carefully. It should be used as an indicative guide to the sort of tone, analysis and structure expected of such a review. The references and quotations used are fictional and solely for illustrative purposes.

Sample A30: Exercise – *Management*

> **Media Watch**
> Groups of 4–5 students will choose to look at one contemporary issue currently represented on media outlets – eg issues to do with politics, economics, religious affairs, sport, music, celebrity or even the media itself. You should consult a variety of media outlets eg print media (including online sites), television news and current affairs.
>
> The main purpose of this assignment is to analyse the similarities and differences in the coverage of the one story or issue that the different media organisations put out. Pay special attention to the language used and how this might involve distortion, bias, plagiarism or unethical reporting.

Sample A31: Assignment task – *Media Studies*

The focus of such a task, as the rubric indicates, is very much on the way that language is used to construct particular representations of events. The lecturer in the subject described the approach thus:

> MEDIA STUDIES: *In the course we're interested in students becoming deconstructive readers. The emphasis is not so much on what the meanings of the texts are, and whether I agree with them, but rather how meaning is being created. I want them to focus on how the words used in a text can carry particular nuances of meaning, or how images are used to create certain effects.*

Such readings, which operate arguably at the most 'interpretative' end of our literal–interpretative continuum fit very much with recent developments in language analysis including critical discourse analysis (Fairclough 1998) and critical literacy (Gee 2008).

Summary of academic task analysis

The analysis of the reading tasks showed a wide variety of reading requirements across the disciplines investigated. As we saw, instances of tasks fitting all four configurations in our matrix were identified (i.e. local–literal; global–interpretative etc.). Because of the largely qualitative nature of the study, it is not possible to make any definitive statements about which of these four reading modes was the most prominent overall. There are however, a number of broad generalisations that can be made:

1. Most reading tasks in the corpus fitting a *local–literal* configuration tended to be in the form of short weekly exercise tasks or examination questions, and were set principally for the purpose of either inputting or testing a student's understanding of key foundational knowledge in the discipline. Such tasks were linked very much to readings from prescribed textbooks in subjects.

2. Most reading tasks that fitted the other configurations from the matrix (*global–literal, local–interpretative, global–interpretative*) tended to be related to more extended written assignment tasks, and often involved readings from a variety of genres: monographs (or sections of monographs), research articles, newspapers and magazines, internet sites, etc.

3. The variety of assessment requirements across the disciplines pointed to some discipline-based differences in reading modes, with *local–literal* patterns more prominent in the harder technical disciplines, and *global–interpretative* more so in the softer humanities disciplines.

4.3 Findings from interviews – Comments on IELTS reading tasks

In this final results section, we turn again to the responses from informants in the interviews. As described earlier, the interview was divided into three phases, covering discussion of: i) general reading requirements on courses; ii) reading requirements on specific assessment tasks; and, in the final phase iii) perceptions regarding the correspondence between reading requirements on courses and those on the IELTS Reading test. To facilitate discussion in this final part of the interview, informants were provided with samples of IELTS reading tasks and asked to comment on perceived similarities and differences in reading requirements in the two domains (Appendix 2.2). They were also asked to speculate on how useful they thought these sample IELTS tasks were likely to be as preparation for the reading demands of their courses. Responses to these questions were of three broad types:

1. An overall positive view of the relationship between reading in the two domains.
2. A more qualified view of the relationship.
3. A critical view of the relationship.

As has been the case in previous parts of the study, there was an identifiable disciplinary bias in the responses of informants, with those more positive about the relationship generally coming from the more technical areas, and those having a more critical view from the humanities disciplines.

Those who commented most favourably on the relationship between the IELTS test and study on their courses were the lecturers from Computer Science, Engineering, Biology, Business Studies, and Communications, comprising almost half the study's informants (five out of 12). In general, these informants saw a clear connection between some of the IELTS task types and the types of tasks set on their courses, as seen in the following comments:

> BIOLOGY: *I think the skills required here [on the IELTS test] would be very closely aligned to what I would expect a student in first-year biology to come to terms with. There's a fair bit of reading there and a fair bit of basic comprehension, and that is certainly what our students need.*

> COMPUTER SCIENCE: *Our exam questions are not dissimilar to some of the questions [on IELTS]. [This is] certainly true of the multiple-choice format, not so much true or false. One of the questions in our exam also involves the students rearranging lines of code in order to create a logical program, and that looks like at least one of the items in this material.*

Several informants in this group expressed surprise at what one described as the test's 'unexpected complexity'. The view here was that the reading demands on the IELTS Reading test appeared to them to be higher than those in their particular subject area – though it does need to be acknowledged that in such comments a clear distinction was not always drawn between the demands of the test items and those of the reading passage on which the items were based:

> COMPUTER SCIENCE: *If anything, we're expecting less of students in terms of reading. The test is definitely relevant and having it at a higher level than what we're asking for in the course is a good thing. So it seems to be an appropriate sort of thing to be testing them on.*

> COMMUNICATIONS: *I think [the IELTS Reading test] would be good preparation actually. I found the science-based articles and items quite complicated actually. If I had to answer questions about the science, I'd have to go back and read it twice.*

For informants in this 'more positively disposed' group, the sense of correspondence between reading demands in the two domains, as well as the test's perceived difficulty led them to believe that IELTS would be an unequivocally useful form of preparation for tertiary study:

> ENGINEERING: *These sorts of skills [tested in IELTS] would definitely be useful in a generic sense . . . and I can see that it would be good preparation for what we require on our course.*

> BIOLOGY: *I think looking at [these samples], I would be happy if a student was coming to me with those skills.*

> COMMUNICATIONS: *I think [the IELTS Reading test] would be good preparation actually . . . I think if the students scored well on this then they would probably be OK.*

Another group of informants had a generally positive view of the test – or at least of the sample materials provided in the interview – while at the same time expressing some reservations about its overall usefulness. A similar number of informants fell into this group as the previous (five out of 12), and consisted of the lecturers from Physics, Architecture, Economics, History, and Management. The main reservation expressed was a sense of a limited degree of correspondence between the test and reading requirements in their particular disciplinary domain, as suggested in the following remarks:

> ECONOMICS: *I think [the IELTS material] is fine. It's just comprehension really . . . I've got no problems with that whatsoever. Where economics is slightly different from this is that we use a combination of mathematical techniques, diagrammatic techniques and texts . . . It's a very abstract mathematical way of thinking about the real world.*

> HISTORY: *I'd see this as all useful. The test is very focused on reading comprehension . . . that is a basic pre-requisite for our courses. It doesn't cover the quite discipline-specific methods of reading we're concerned with . . . for example the way students need to be able to handle the reading of primary source material.*

> ARCHITECTURE: *The topic area of the test – bridges – is spot on for our area. I think the type of questioning is also ideal for the level of language skill required in [our subject]. It's not clear though whether you just have to match words, or whether you have to read between the lines a bit – students certainly need to do some [of the latter] on the course.*

In asserting these distinctions, a common theme among this group related to the importance of students reading to understand certain key concepts in the discipline and to be able to show their understanding of these. This was felt by some to be a quite basic difference between the two formats:

ARCHITECTURE: *I think a difference is that we want students to pull out key concepts from paragraphs. In IELTS it seems they are given the concepts and just need to match these up.*

PHYSICS: *In Physics, the majority of material in the text is trying to explain concepts and also explain problem-solving strategies, and this is what we want [students] to get from their reading. The IELTS tasks seem more arbitrary in what they pick out from the text . . . and seem to be mainly about pattern recognition.*

One other gap commented on was the lack of connection with processes of writing on the IELTS Reading test. Several informants discussed the considerable challenges on their courses in getting students to understand and also adopt acceptable use of reading material in their written work. The view here was that this was perhaps an aspect of academic reading that could somehow be given explicit coverage in the test:

MANAGEMENT: *[To use sources appropriately] students need to see concrete examples to know what is acceptable and what's not . . . I can't see much evidence in the test of this aspect of academic study, and this would certainly be helpful.*

Whilst identifying certain differences in the skills in the two domains, informants in this second group acknowledged that it would be most difficult to create a generic reading test that could accommodate in any systematic way the various discipline-bound forms of reading identified. One informant also thought it necessary to be realistic about the extant reading skills that students bring to their courses and was sure that the responsibility for the teaching of any discipline-specific skills lay squarely with academics on their particular programmes.

HISTORY: *We just can't make too many assumptions nowadays about our students and their capacities. And this is irrespective of their background. . . . the onus is clearly on us to develop these capacities within our courses.*

A final group – a considerably smaller one than the previous two – had a more critical view of the test and its likely usefulness. This group was confined to just two informants – those from the humanities disciplines of *Media Studies* and *Linguistics*. The general view expressed by these two was that the construct of reading in the test was somehow at odds with that which operated in each of their discipline areas, and that, as a result, the test risked giving students a misleading impression of the nature of academic reading. Their takes on this disjuncture were slightly different ones. For the *Media Studies* lecturer the problem was at heart an epistemological one:

MEDIA STUDIES: *In the tasks on the test, it seems to me that students are really just dealing with information. That's the way these texts are presented. And then it's mainly about regurgitating the information. This author is saying this. But it doesn't allow students options to engage with the material. Whether they think what is being said in the text is valid or not. I see it as pretty low level.*

This lecturer went on to explain that from the outset on his course, he did not want students to see texts fundamentally as 'repositories of information and facts', but rather as the expression of particular ways of seeing and constructing the world:

MEDIA STUDIES: *There's a need for students to have an argumentative, conceptual, even ideological understanding of material. [I tell them that when] they come to university they need to learn how to critique . . . well everything . . . You question all that you read, and all that your lecturer gives you, and I can't see much evidence of this in the test.*

The concerns of the Linguistics lecturer related more to what she saw as the non-contextual nature of reading on the IELTS test. What was notable about reading at university, she thought, was that it always operates within a context, one which is shaped by the discipline itself and also by the particular task with which students are engaged. This, she thought, was a feature strongly lacking in the IELTS test:

LINGUISTICS: *There is a broader context for interpreting the reading which university students have because they have a purpose for assignments, and the discipline serves to make it clear what is important and what is not. . . . so [in the IELTS test], this is quite strange and difficult to relate to because the tasks are completely out of context. What is missing is the purpose for knowing this information.*

This lecturer thought that a way to improve the test in this regard would be to construct tasks around particular contexts of study (or 'scenarios'), which could serve to provide this sense of purpose:

LINGUISTICS: *I think a good way to go would be if students had some background information like: "You are a student. You are studying blah blah blah, you need to know X, Y and Z in order to complete a certain assignment. This is the context for your reading. Now try and answer some specific questions. How would this information be useful to you and why?" Because that is the sort of expectations we have of students.*

5 Summary and discussion of findings

A range of findings have been presented so far, drawn from the two methodologies employed in the study; namely, the analysis of the IELTS and academic tasks and the interviews with academic staff. In what follows we provide a summary of these findings focusing on:

1. Main findings, which are those patterns to emerge from the data as a whole.
2. More specific findings, which relate to particular areas of the data.

5.1 Main findings

IELTS reading vs academic reading
A feature of the study's design was the development of an analytical framework that would allow systematic comparison to be made between reading requirements in the two domains – IELTS and academic study. As discussed, this framework took in two dimensions:

i) the 'level' of engagement with text, which distinguished between a more 'local' and a more 'global' engagement with material, and

ii) the 'type' of engagement, where the distinction was one between more 'literal' and more 'interpretative' readings of this material.

Drawing on this analysis, we can say there is evidence in the study of some correspondence between the reading requirements in the two domains, but also evidence of a fair degree of difference.

The main similarity is to be found in those forms of reading that required mainly a local and literal engagement with material. As was noted previously, this configuration was true for the vast majority of items in the IELTS corpus, with many tasks requiring mainly a basic comprehension of relatively small textual units (sentences, inter-sentences, paragraphs). In a similar vein, a sizeable proportion of tasks in the academic corpus were also found to have the same 'local–literal' orientation. Such tasks within the academic data, it was noted, tended to be set as weekly class exercises or on exams and tests, and had as their focus the need for students to understand certain discipline-based concepts.

But while this particular similarity was evident, the study also noted a good deal of divergence between the two domains. This was mainly found to arise from the considerable variety of reading tasks identified in the academic corpus, especially in those that related to more extended assignment tasks (e.g. essays, reports). Thus, whereas the IELTS corpus saw virtually all task types fall within the 'local–literal' area of our analytical matrix, the academic corpus was notable for incorporating tasks that covered all four areas. Amid this diversity were tasks which seemed, on the face of it, to be quite remote from the IELTS profile of tasks, including, for example, those which required a critical engagement with material, or which stipulated engagement with 'a multiplicity of sources and viewpoints'.

These patterns – both of similarity and of difference – were largely confirmed in the interview commentaries of staff. Thus, some of our informants saw a basic congruence between the type of reading they expected their students to do on their courses and what they perceived to be the demands of the IELTS test. Others, by contrast, were keen to point out what for them were clear differences.

Disciplinary variation in reading requirements
The similarities and differences observed between the IELTS Reading test and academic study can be accounted for in part by the variety in the types of reading required across the disciplines considered in the study. Much of this variety, as we have noted, related to the broad division in the disciplines investigated; that is between the 'harder' technical disciplines on the one hand, and 'softer' more humanities-oriented disciplines on the other. Thus, it was noted that in the more technical disciplines (e.g. Engineering, Architecture, Physics, Biology), less reading overall was required of students, and that much of this had the clear purpose of having students assimilate certain foundational concepts in the discipline. Such a view of reading was affirmed in the interviews, where it was suggested that the contents of reading materials on such courses were presented to students as essentially 'the ideas they needed to know'.

In the more humanities disciplines, by contrast, reading was found to take on many different guises. While students on these courses (including Media Studies, Linguistics, History, Management) were also required to learn basic 'concepts and viewpoints' in their field, there were many additional ways they were expected to interact with material. In some contexts, for example, the task for students was one of comparing different ideas and viewpoints on an issue; in other contexts, it was to evaluate these ideas; in others again, students needed to synthesise a range of material as a basis for developing their own viewpoints. In contrast to the mainly 'assimilationist' approach to reading described by informants in the technical disciplines, the view from these latter fields was that students needed always to bring their own perspective to bear on material – an approach characterised by one informant as 'the need to question everything'.

The findings from this part of the study suggest then, that in the first year of undergraduate study at least the types of materials students need to read on their courses and the ways they need to go about reading this material are subject to a good deal of variation. This feature of academic study points to the difficulties inherent in trying to conceive of some generalist construct of academic reading, one that has clear relevance to all disciplinary contexts. The implications of this situation are discussed in the final sections of the report.

5.2   Specific findings

Along with these general findings were a number of more specific findings that emerged from the data, ones that provide greater detail about some of the differences observed between the two domains.

Epistemic entities
It was noticed in the two task corpora (IELTS and academic) that the types of entities that students/test takers needed to focus on in their reading were generally of a different order. In the IELTS test samples, for example, these entities were typically characterised as 'information', as exemplified in the following sample rubrics (our emphasis):

> Do the following statements agree with the *information* given in the Reading Passage?   (Sample 1.1)
> Which paragraph contains the following *information?*   (Sample 2.2)

In the academic tasks, by contrast, this knowledge tended to be characterised in a variety of ways. Firstly it was noticed that it was quite rare in fact for students to be asked to engage with 'information' *per se*; instead they needed to contend with a range of different entities. Most prominent among these was a characterisation of knowledge as 'concept' (or related entities – 'model', 'definition' and the like), as seen in a number of tasks in the academic corpus. Among the more humanities disciplines, we also saw an emphasis on entities associated with the ideas of particular scholars – including 'arguments', 'viewpoints', 'theses', 'perspectives', etc. Other entity-types were those related to the outcomes of empirical research, e.g. 'studies' and 'findings'.

This contrast in the epistemic entities in the two domains points to a more 'constructivist view' of knowledge in the case of the academic tasks, where knowledge is typically seen to arise from the thinking and researching of individual scholars in a field, or from the collective disciplinary community as a whole (Myers 1992). The contrasting focus in IELTS on reading content as 'information' suggests instead a more positivist view of knowledge, where, as Hill and Parry (1992) suggest, 'authorship is essentially anonymous' (1992:439).

Interpretative readings
These different ways of conceiving of academic knowledge were found to have implications for the way that this knowledge needed to be engaged with in the two domains. Thus, we saw that the essential task for students in many of the IELTS items was to demonstrate a basic comprehension of the propositional content of reading material. By contrast, the focus of many of the academic tasks was not only to arrive at a basic understanding of material,

but also to 'work' with this material in order to proffer some interpretation of it. This basic requirement of academic study was well summarised by one informant thus:

> *... we typically [want students] to pick out ... the key points in the reading. But we also want them to reflect on what they have read and always relate it to their ... work somehow.*

In the academic corpus, it was noted that two types of interpretative reading tasks predominated – what we have termed *application* and *evaluation*. In application-related tasks, students were typically required to show how a concept or idea in their reading could be utilised in their work in the discipline; in evaluative tasks, the focus was more on making some explicit assessment of these concepts (e.g. with respect to their validity, worth, etc.). Of these two interpretative modes, the application-related tasks were found to be the more common.

We note in passing that interpretations such as these tend to be very much discipline-based (McPeck 1992), evident not only in the specific concepts and ideas that students need to engage with, but also in the types of 'interpretations' they need to make of these concepts along the way. Indeed for some scholars, the process of being trained in a discipline is often characterised in these precise terms; that is, to learn the particular ways in which certain concepts are 'applied' and 'evaluated' within a field (Lave and Wenger 1991). As Bourdieu (1990) points out, such practices are not only cognitive in nature, but are effective when assimilated into habituated dispositions. The strong discipline-base of these more interpretative forms of reading may provide some explanation for the apparent absence of these modes among the various IELTS tasks collected for the study. We can also recognise in this situation the challenges that would be involved in incorporating such modes into any possible adapted version of the test.

Readings of multiple texts
Another difference noted between the two domains was the quantity of reading required to complete some tasks. As we saw, all tasks in the IELTS corpus were focused on engagement with a single text (the relevant reading passage), and in the case of some task types, a focus on relatively small components of the text. In contrast, a feature of some of the academic tasks, especially in the more humanities areas, was the need for students to engage with a range of texts. Examples of such tasks were: i) summary tasks which required students to give an account of a variety of sources in relation to a particular topic; and ii) essay tasks requiring the exploration of a range of views as a prelude to students presenting their own views on the topic.

Some of the academic tasks, as we saw, alluded again to a particular conception of knowledge, one that sees knowledge in a discipline being advanced through processes of debate and dialogue between scholars, as opposed to the furnishing of single, definitive answers to issues and problems. Several informants were sure that it was only through the engagement with multiple sources that students could develop a suitably critical frame in their studies. As one informant explained it, students might feel they have come across 'a perfectly reasonable answer' to a question, but that they are in fact only in a position to presume this if they've had the opportunity to 'measure this answer against alternatives'.

The contextual nature of reading
Reading in the two domains was also seen to differ around the notion of context. One observation made about the IELTS samples provided to informants was the apparent lack of an underlying intellectual purpose for the particular questions posed in tasks; that is to say that, in many tasks, the particular items of information needing to be focused on appeared, on the face of it, to be rather arbitrary. In contrast, it was suggested that it is the nature of university study that there is usually a clear purpose and context for the type of reading that students need to do. As one informant explained it, such a context – which is created at once by the broader knowledge base of a discipline and also by the immediate demands of tasks and assignments set within courses – 'serves to make it clear to students what [information] is important and what is not'.

This disparity between reading in the testing and academic domains has been commented on in the literature. Alderson (2000) notes after Barton (1994) that it is rarely the case in academic study that reading as an activity is performed *in vacuo*; that is, without being related in some way to other academic activities. A concept invoked to capture this idea is 'literacy event', described by Barton and Hamilton (1998:9) as a series of observable activities mediated by text. As Alderson explains it:

> Often literacy events – TLU [Target Language Use] reading tasks – are not undertaken in isolation . . . A coursework reading assignment leads to note-taking, which leads to further reading, to drafting a written paper, re-reading the draft critically (Alderson 2000:148).

To accommodate this feature of academic study within the IELTS test is undoubtedly a challenge; as Weir et al (2009) suggest, full contextual authenticity 'is generally unrealistic for language assessments (2009:12). The suggestion from one of the study's informants was to construct tasks around specific study 'scenarios', ones that would seek to place the reading of test passages into some real-world context for students.

The reading–writing nexus

Arguably one of the more significant literacy events in academic study is that which involves the integrating of one's reading on a topic into some related writing activity (Horowitz 1986, Moore and Morton 2007). This was evident in many of the academic tasks analysed in the study, with virtually all of the assignment-style tasks in the corpus having a substantive reading component attached to them. A number of informants commented on the importance of this reading–writing nexus, seeing it as an area of particular challenge to students. Concern was expressed here about students' abilities to use and document sources appropriately, along with perceptions about the growing incidence of plagiarism on courses. Several informants noted the absence of these reading–writing connections in the sample IELTS materials provided, and wondered whether this dimension of academic reading could be incorporated into the test somehow.

Information literacy

Another area thought to have limited coverage in the test related to the skills involved in locating, selecting and evaluating information sources. In their discussions of the reading practices of students, a number of informants noted the opportunities, but also the considerable challenges created for students by the increasing online environment of academic study. As we saw, concern was expressed that students did not always bring a particularly 'discerning' attitude to the vast textual resources now available to them. The response of some of our informants to this situation was increasingly to adopt an 'information literacy' approach in their teaching, with students called upon to appraise texts in some broader social context, and to develop an awareness of such matters as the context of their production, their authorship, communicative purpose, and ultimately their 'reliability' as sources.

It was noted by some informants that the increasingly important skills related to the searching and selecting of sources appeared to have little or no coverage in the IELTS Reading test. Indeed, the tendency of IELTS tasks to focus on quite specific items of information in reading passages would seem to limit the possibilities of appraising texts in the broader social and contextual terms of an 'information literacies' approach (Shapiro and Hughes 1996).

Genre readings of texts

A final type of reading evident in the academic corpus is what we have called 'genre readings of texts'. As noted, a number of reading tasks in the corpus required a focus not so much on the contents of texts, but rather on the ways in which 'texts are put together'. (The focus of such tasks was on such textual features as rhetorical organisation, sentence structures, lexical choices, etc.). In some of these tasks, it was noted, the main purpose was a more utilitarian one; that is, for students to 'get a feel for the genre', as one informant described it, so that they might emulate the particular written style in their own work. In other tasks, the purpose was more a critical or 'deconstructive' one, with students needing to identify how language operates in texts to create certain meanings – including 'ideological meanings'.

As was mentioned, these types of 'genre readings', which take in both more 'pragmatic' approaches (Allison 1996, Johns 1997, Swales 1990) and more critical approaches (Shor 1999, Street 2003), reflect the increasing role of textual analysis activities in academic study. It is fair to say that readings such as this were not really apparent in the IELTS corpus compiled for the study.

An explanation for differences

The study has identified a number of differences between reading demands in the two domains, even if they are ones that can be readily accounted for. Arguably, the purpose of a test of reading is to assess students' abilities to process written text. In this context, as we have seen, the actual contents of the reading tend to be somewhat incidental. In university study, by contrast, such content – which relates to study in a discipline – is of paramount importance. Thus, in university study, there is not the same interest in the skills of reading *per se*; instead acts of reading, as we have seen, are tied intimately to the acquisition, application and ultimately to the advancement of disciplinary knowledge. This contrast in the role of knowledge in the two domains necessarily entails some quite basic differences in the nature of the texts students need to read and what it is students need to do when they read them.

6 Implications of findings for future development of the IELTS Academic Reading test

In considering the implications of the study, there are arguably two key questions that need to be addressed:

1. Is there a case for making some modification to the IELTS Academic Reading test?
2. If so, how could the test be modified?

6.1 Should the IELTS Academic Reading test be modified?

In relation to the first question, the general push in language assessment to maximise a test's 'authenticity' would suggest that some modification to the IELTS Academic Reading test is at least worth considering. Bachman and Palmer (1996) define inauthenticity as that situation where the link between the TLU task and the test task is weak. Whilst the findings of the task analysis do not suggest overall a 'weak' link between tasks in the two domains, they do suggest that it is one that could at least be strengthened. Such a view was also reflected in the responses of some of the academic informants in our study, where it was felt that the demands of the test might be brought more into line with the type of reading required on their courses. The ever-expanding influence of IELTS – and especially its curriculum effects on programmes of English for Academic Purposes – provide additional impetus for modification of some form.

Clearly, however, there are important practical considerations in any push to institute changes to a well-established test such as IELTS. One can point to a number of caveats. The first of these relates to the broad issue of achieving the right balance between the validity of a test and its reliability (Wigglesworth and Elder 1996). For the IELTS Academic Reading test, this would include, among other things, ensuring that any modified version of the test fits with the overall structure of the current IELTS battery, e.g. for the Academic Reading test to remain as a separate test of reading without significant overlap with other modules such as Writing (Charge and Taylor 1997); and for it to be retained as a clerically markable module within the battery. A second caveat relates to the difficulty of accommodating the many different versions of academic reading we have seen in the study all within the one test. Much of this variety, as was noted, arose from the quite different reading demands evident in different disciplines and programmes. This suggests a need to be prudent in selecting the type of reading tasks on the test, so as to avoid having items which may be pertinent in one disciplinary area, but have little relevance to others.

A final consideration is the matter of what one can reasonably expect an objective test of reading to cover. On this point, Taylor (2007) suggests we need to recognise the limits to which a test such as IELTS can simulate (and indeed should be expected to simulate) language use in the target situation. Thus, she notes that 'IELTS is designed principally *to test readiness to enter* the world of university-level study in the English language' and does not assume that test takers have already mastered the skills they are likely to need (original emphasis, 2007:482). Taylor goes on to explain that students will often 'need to develop many of these skills during their course of study', including those 'skills . . . specific to their academic domain'. Such an understanding was voiced, as we saw, by at least one of the study's informants who suggested that the onus was clearly on academic staff to develop discipline-specific capacities 'within courses'.

6.2   How could the IELTS Reading test be modified?

If any modifications were to be made to the Academic Reading test, one useful principle to employ, we believe, would be to seek to push test tasks, or at least a proportion of them, in the direction of the more global/more interpretative regions of the analytical matrix used in the study, as shown in Figure 2.10.

Figure 2.10 Suggested principle for modification to Reading test

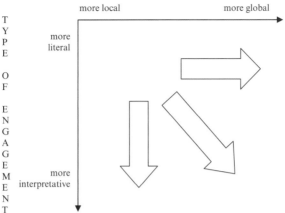

In what follows we provide a number of sample tasks, where the intention is to indicate how we think some of these less-covered areas of the matrix could have some coverage in the test. The samples have been divided up into three areas of 'extension', each relating to the three under-represented quadrants of our matrix *viz*:

1. Extension 1: Local–interpretative
2. Extension 2: Global–literal
3. Extension 3: Global–interpretative

Several samples are provided for each extension; some additional samples are shown in Appendix 2.3. In the construction of these tasks, we have attempted to incorporate some of the specific differences noted between reading in the two domains (see Section 5.2) with a focus on such dimensions as: authorial stance; specific academic entities (e.g. arguments); reading–writing connections; information literacy skills; genre readings of texts; text evaluation; and so on. In some of these tasks, there has also been an effort to structure tasks around the idea of relating tasks to specific study scenarios (see Section 5.2).

It will be noted that all of the sample tasks provided follow a multiple-choice format. This is for the reason noted earlier – namely that the multiple-choice tasks by nature appear to have a greater versatility than some of the other task types currently used in the test, and, on the face of it, seem better able to incorporate these more 'global' and 'interpretative' engagements with material. This is not to suggest, however, that one would necessarily want to see a greater use of multiple-choice items on the test. Following Alderson (2000:211–214), we recognise that multiple-choice tasks have a number of limitations, including the potential effect of candidates guessing the correct response. We would argue in fact that it is a major challenge for the test's designers to develop certain conventionalised techniques that are able to test some of the more 'interpretative' and more 'global' dimensions of reading we have identified.

EXTENSION 1 → LOCAL/INTERPRETATIVE

In Passage A, the writer states that . . . . . PROPOSITION (Line B)

The **implication** of this sentence is that the writer thinks:

a) X is a good thing and should be encouraged
b) X is a bad thing and should be discouraged
c) not enough is known about X, and it should be investigated further
d) sufficient research has been conducted into X

Sample 1.1: Focus on inferential readings of sentences

A student referred to information in Paragraph B of Passage A in an essay. Which sentence is a reasonable interpretation of the writer's view?:

a) Smith (2000) argues that X is a Y
b) Smith (2000) argues that X is not a Y
c) Smith (2000) argues that X is a Z
d) Smith (2000) argues that X is not a Z

Sample 1.2: Focus on reading–writing connections (scenario format)

EXTENSION 2 → GLOBAL/LITERAL

> The author of Passage A claims that (Proposition Y). The main evidence presented in the text for this claim is:
>
> a) Findings from a study she conducted
> b) Findings from a study conducted by B
> c) Findings from a study conducted by her, and by B
> d) Findings from several different studies conducted by B and C

Sample 2.1: Focus on macro-content of text (Epistemic entities= claim/ evidence)

> Imagine you are writing an essay on the following topic (State topic X). Which paragraph from Reading Passage A do you think would be the **most useful** to draw information from?:
>
> a) Paragraph 1
> b) Paragraph 2
> c) Paragraph 3
> d) Paragraph 4

Sample 2.2: Focus on use of sources – information literacy (scenario format)

EXTENSION 3 → GLOBAL/INTERPRETATIVE

> Which of the following do you think best describes the main purpose of Reading Passage A?:
>
> a) to advise on the best ways to do X
> b) to criticise the current ways of doing X
> c) to provide background information on X
> d) to predict what will happen to X

Sample 3.1: Focus on overall rhetorical purpose of text

The following are some possible criticisms that could be made of Passage A. Which particular criticism seems the most **relevant** to this text?:

a) The writer states his support for X, but does not consider the other side
b) The writer claims that X is Y, but provides no evidence for this claim
c) The writer presents contradictory views about X
d) The writer gives practical information about X, but doesn't indicate how it can be used

---

Sample 3.2: Focus on evaluation of text

It will be clear from the samples above that the use of certain item techniques is very much dependent on having to hand reading passages which are relevant to the particular focus of the technique. For instance, an item that was focused on the relationship between claims and evidence in a reading passage would clearly only be able to be used in relation to text samples that were structured around these particular rhetorical characteristics. The study deliberately confined itself to a study only of reading tasks without consideration of the texts upon which they are based. It may be however, that any proposed shift in focus towards more global and/or interpretative modes on items would have major implications for reading passage design and selection on the test. The broad principle of the inseparability of reading technique and task has been commented on by Alderson (2000). Any modification to the test may indeed require substantial investigation into this aspect of reading assessment.

6.3 Further research

McNamara (1999), as noted earlier, has identified three areas of focus in appraising the validity of a reading proficiency test:

- *task stimulus,* i.e. the texts that candidates engage with on the test
- *task processes,* i.e. the reader–text interactions that actually take place in the completing of the test
- *task demand,* i.e. the test items, which prescribe certain types of interaction between the reader and text.

This list provides a useful framework for thinking about further study into the IELTS Academic Reading test. In relation to 'task stimulus', the issue of text selection on tests has already been identified as an area of priority. Such an investigation would also be well complemented by additional research into the nature of texts typically used in studies in the disciplines in the contemporary university (Green, Ünaldi and Weir 2010). Whilst the present study observed the continuing importance of traditional texts such as textbooks and journal articles, the ever-increasing role played by various electronic media was also noted. Any efforts to enhance the validity of the text component of the test ('task stimulus') would need to be based on a thorough and up-to-date understanding of these developments, along with the dynamic effects they appear to be having on literacy practices in the academy.

Another area of interest is the way that students actually read and interact with reading materials when engaged with specific academic tasks ('task processes'). Whilst the analysis used in the present study allowed us to make some estimate of what was required to complete certain tasks, it was not possible to know definitively from the data what the 'psychological reality' would be for students actually engaged in such tasks. Indeed research in the field of activity theory (Lantolf and Thorne 2006) has shown that one must be wary about assuming any straightforward correspondence between the 'task-assigned' and the 'task-performed' (Coughlan and Duff 1994). Weir et al's (2009) study provides useful general information about student performance on the Reading test and the TLU situation. Additional research could also be conducted to find out about how these processes compare between performance on specific test items and on larger 'literacy events' in academic study (Barton and Hamilton 1998).

Finally, in the area of 'task demand', the present study was relatively small-scale in its design, investigating the assessment requirements in only a limited number of subject areas. The largely qualitative findings obtained could be complemented by larger-scale survey research which looked into reading requirements across a wider range of disciplines and institutions. To have a fuller picture of university reading would not only help in processes of test validation, but also assist us in a broader educational aim – to be able to prepare our students as best we can for the challenges and demands they will face in their studies.

Acknowledgements

The researchers wish to thank the following for their assistance with this project:

- staff from the two site universities who participated in the research
- Professor Tim McNamara, and Associate Professor Catherine Elder (University of Melbourne) who provided advice as members of the project's reference group.

The researchers also wish to thank IELTS for their support of the project.

References

Alderson, J C (1990a) Testing reading comprehension skills (Part One), *Journal of Reading in a Foreign Language* 6 (2), 425–38.

Alderson, J C (1990b) Testing reading comprehension skills (Part Two), *Journal of Reading in a Foreign Language* 7 (1), 465–504.

Alderson, J C (2000) *Assessing Reading*, Cambridge: Cambridge University Press.

Alderson, J C and Wall, D (1993) Does washback exist?, *Applied Linguistics* 14 (2), 115–29.

Allison, D (1996) Pragmatist discourse and English for academic purposes, *English for Specific Purposes* 15 (2), 85–103.

Bachman, L F and Palmer, A (1996) *Language Testing in Practice*, Oxford: Oxford University Press.

Ballard, B and Clanchy, J (1991) Assessment by misconception, in Hamp-Lyons, L (Ed.) *Assessing Second Language Writing in Academic Contexts,* Norwood, NJ: Ablex, 19–36.

Barton, D (1994) *Literacy: An Introduction to the Ecology of Written Language*, Oxford: Basil Blackwell.

Barton, D and Hamilton, M (1998) *Local Literacies: Reading and Writing in One Community*, London: Routledge.

Becher, T (1989) *Academic Tribes and Territories: Intellectual Enquiry and the Cultures of Disciplines,* Buckingham: Open University Press.

Bloom, B S (1956) *Taxonomy of Educational Objectives*: *The Classification of Educational Goals*, New York: Longman.

Bourdieu, P (1990) *The Logic of Practice*, Stanford: Stanford University Press.

Carroll, J B (1964) *Language and Thought*, Engelwood Cliffs NJ: Prentice-Hall.

Carver, R (1997) Reading for one second, one minute, or one year from the perspective of rauding theory, *Scientific Studies of Reading* 1 (1), 3–43.

Charge, N and Taylor, L (1997) Recent developments in IELTS, *ELT Journal* 51 (4), 374–380.

Clapham, C (1996) *The Development of IELTS: A Study in the Effect of Background Knowledge on Reading Comprehension*, Studies in Language Testing volume 4, Cambridge: UCLES/Cambridge University Press.

Coughlan, P and Duff, P (1994) Same task, different activities: analysis of a second language acquisition task from an activity theory perspective, in Lantolf, J P and Appel, G (Eds) *Vygotskian Approaches to Second Language Research,* Norwood, NJ: Ablex Pub Corp, 173–191.

Ennis, R (1987) A taxonomy of critical thinking abilities and dispositions, in Baron, J and Sternberg, R (Eds) *Teaching Thinking Skills*, New York: WH Freeman, 9–26.

Enright, M, Grabe, W, Koda, K, Mosenthal, P, Mulcany-Ernt, P and Schedl, M (2000) *TOEFL 2000 Reading Framework: A working paper*, TOEFL Monograph Series 17, Princeton: ETS.

Fairclough, N (1998) *Critical Language Awareness,* Harlow: Longman.

Gee, J P (2008) *Social Linguistics and Literacies: Ideology in Discourses*, London: Routledge.

Grabe, W (1999) Developments in reading research and their implications for computer-adaptive reading assessment, in Chaloub-Deville, M (Ed.) *Issues in Computer-adaptive Testing of Reading Proficiency,* Studies in Language Testing volume 10, Cambridge: UCLES/Cambridge University Press, 11–47.

Grabe, W and Stoller, F L (2002) *Teaching and Researching Reading*, London: Longman.

Green, A, Ünaldi, A, and Weir, C (2010) Empiricism versus connoisseurship: Establishing the appropriacy of texts in tests of academic reading, *Language Testing* 27 (2), 191–211.

Hamp-Lyons, L (1990) Second language writing: assessment issues, in Kroll, B (Ed.) *Second Language Writing: Research Insights for the Classroom*, Cambridge: Cambridge University Press, 69–87.

Hill, C and Parry, K (1992) The test at the gate: Models of literacy in reading assessment, *TESOL Quarterly* 26 (3), 433–461.

Horowitz, D (1986) What professors actually require of students: Academic tasks for the ESL classroom, *TESOL Quarterly* 20, 445–462.

Hudson, T (1998) Theoretical perspectives on reading, *Annual Review of Applied Linguistics* 18, 124–141.

IELTS (1996) *The IELTS Handbook,* UCLES/British Council, IDP Education Australia, Cambridge.

IELTS (1999) *The IELTS Handbook*, Cambridge: UCLES/Cambridge University Press.

IELTS (2007) *IELTS Official Practice Materials*, Cambridge: Cambridge University Press.

Johns, A (1997) *Text, Role and Context: Developing Academic Literacies*, Cambridge: Cambridge University Press.

Lantolf, J P and Thorne, S L (2006) *Sociocultural Theory and the Genesis of Second Language Development*, Oxford: Oxford University Press.

Lave, J and Wenger, E (1991) *Situated Learning: Legitimate Peripheral Participation*, Cambridge: Cambridge University Press.

Marton, F and Saljo, R (1976) On qualitative differences in learning I: outcome and process, *British Journal of Educational Psychology* 46, 4–11.

McNamara, T F (1999) Computer-adaptive testing: A view from outside, in Chaloub-Deville, M (Ed.) *Issues in Computer-adaptive Testing of Reading Proficiency*, Studies in Language Testing volume 10, Cambridge: UCLES/Cambridge University Press, 136–149.

McPeck, J (1992) Thoughts on subject specificity, in Norris, S (Ed.) *The Generalizability of Critical Thinking: Multiple perspectives on an educational ideal*, New York: Teachers' College Press, 198–205.

Messick, S (1996) Validity and washback in language testing, *Language Testing* 13 (3), 241–256.

Moore, T and Morton, J (2007) Authenticity in the IELTS Academic Module Writing Test: A comparative study of Task 2 items and university assignments, in Taylor, L and Falvey, P (Eds) *IELTS collected papers: Research in speaking and writing assessment*, Studies in Language Testing volume 19, Cambridge: UCLES/Cambridge University Press, 197–248.

Munby, J (1978) *Communicative Syllabus Design,* Cambridge: Cambridge University Press.

Myers, G (1992) Textbooks and the sociology of scientific knowledge, *English for Specific Purposes* 11, 3–17.

Myers, G (2003) Discourse studies of scientific popularisation: questioning the boundaries, *Discourse Studies* 5, 265–279.

Nwogu, K (1991) Structure of science popularisations: A genre-analysis approach to the schema of popularised medical texts, *English for Specific Purposes* 10 (2), 111–123.

Odell, L, Goswami, D and Herrington, A (1983) The discourse-based interview: A procedure for exploring the tacit knowledge of writers in nonacademic settings, in Mosenthal, P, Tamor, L and Walmsley, S (Eds) *Research on Writing: Principles and Methods,* New York: Longman, 221–236.

Purpura, J E (1998) Investigating the effects of strategy use and second language test performance with high and low-ability test takers: A structural equation modeling approach, *Language Testing* 15, 333–379.

Read, J and Hayes, B (2003) The impact of IELTS on preparation for academic study in New Zealand, *IELTS Research Reports volume 4*, Canberra: IELTS Australia, 153–206.

Saville, N, and Hawkey, R (2004) A study of the impact of the International English Language Testing System with special reference to its washback on classroom materials, in Cheng, R L, Watanabe, Y and Curtis, A (Eds) *Washback in Language Testing: Research Contexts and Methods*, Mahwah, NJ: Lawrence Erlbaum and Associates, 97–112.

Shapiro, J and Hughes, S (1996) Information literacy as a liberal art, *Educom Review* 31 (2), 31–35.

Shor, I (1999) What is critical literacy?, in Shor, I and Pari, C (Eds) *Critical Literacy in Action,* Portsmouth NH: Boynton/Cook, 1–30.

Street, B (2003) What's new in 'New Literacy' Studies: Critical approaches to literacy in theory and practice, *Current Issues in Comparative Education* 5 (2), 77–91.

Swales, J (1990) *Genre Analysis: English in Academic and Research Settings,* Cambridge: Cambridge University Press.

Swales, J (1998) *Other Floors, Other Voices: a Textography of a Small University Building,* Mahwah, NJ: Lawrence Erlbaum Associates.

Taylor, G (2009) *A Student's Writing Guide*, Cambridge: Cambridge University Press.

Taylor, L (2007) The impact of the joint-funded research studies on the IELTS writing test, in Taylor, L and Falvey, P (Eds) *IELTS Collected Papers: Research in speaking and writing assessment*, Studies in Language Testing volume 19, Cambridge: Cambridge University Press, 479–492.

Trimble, L (1985) *English for Science and Technology: A discourse approach*, Cambridge: Cambridge University Press,

Urquhart, A H and Weir, C J (1998) *Reading in a Second Language: Process, product and practice*, New York: Longman.

Van Dijk, T A and Kintsch, W (1983) *Strategies of Discourse Comprehension*, New York: Academic Press.

Wallace, C (1999) Critical language awareness: Key principles for a course of critical reading, *Language Awareness* 8 (2), 98–110.

Weir, C J, Hawkey, R, Green, A, Ünaldi, A and Devi, S (2009) The relationship between the Academic Reading construct as measured by IELTS and the reading experiences of students in the first year of their courses at a British University, in Thompson, P (Ed.) *IELTS Research Reports volume 9*, London: British Council, 97–156.

Widdowson, H (1979) *Explorations in Applied Linguistics*, Oxford: Oxford University Press.

Wigglesworth, J and Elder, C (1996) Perspectives on the testing cycle: Setting the scene, *Australian Review of Applied Linguistics Series* S, No. 13, 13–32.

Yule, G (1996) *Pragmatics*, Oxford: Oxford University Press.

Appendix 2.1
List of materials used in IELTS task corpus

Official IELTS practice materials, University of Cambridge; British Council; IDP, IELTS Australia, 2007 (1 x Academic Reading test)

Cambridge IELTS 2: Examination papers from University of Cambridge ESOL Examinations, Cambridge University Press, Cambridge, 2000 (4 × Academic Reading tests)

Cambridge IELTS 4: Examination papers from University of Cambridge ESOL Examinations, Cambridge University Press, Cambridge, 2005 (4 × Academic Reading tests)

Cambridge IELTS 6: Examination papers from University of Cambridge ESOL Examinations, Cambridge University Press, Cambridge, 2007 (4 × Academic Reading tests)

Appendix 2.2
Schedule used in interviews with academic staff

Interview schedule

The following questions will form the basis of the interview.

PART 1 Introduction (content, skills, general reading requirements)

1. How would you describe the main content of the course you teach on?

2. What do you see as the course's main objectives regarding the skills/ attributes to be developed in students?

3. How would you describe the general reading requirements for students on the course?
   i) How much reading do students need to do?
   ii) Are there weekly reading requirements?
   iii) What sorts of texts do students need to read?
   iv) Are there any activities they need to complete when doing the weekly readings?
   v) What purposes do you have for setting weekly readings for students?
   vi) Have the reading requirements on your course changed over the years?
   vii) What challenges generally do students face in handling reading requirements on the course? What about students from second language backgrounds?

PART 2 Reading and Assessment tasks

4. What are the main assessment tasks/activities you set for students on the subject?
   Taking **each of these tasks** at a time:
   i) What do students need to do to successfully complete the task?
   ii) How much reading is required to complete the task? How many texts? What types of texts?
   iii) How would you describe the nature of the reading they need to do to successfully complete the task? (e.g. basic comprehension of material? Some form of interpretation?)

iv) What type of material from the reading would students need to include in the written assignment?

v) What challenges do students face in drawing on reading material for this assignment? Are there particular difficulties for students from second language backgrounds?

5. The following is a list of specific reading skills required of students in their academic study. All are important in some way – which ones would you see as being **particularly important** on your course? Explain? Are there any other important skills not included on the list?

Be able to
– have **a basic comprehension** of key information in a text
– summarise the main ideas in a text in one's own words
– understand an idea for the purpose of **applying it to a particular situation**
– **understand** the purpose for why a text may have been written
– critically evaluate the ideas in a text
– **identify a** range of texts relevant to a topic
– draw on ideas from a range of texts to **support** one's own argument
OTHER

PART 3 IELTS reading tasks

Questions in this section concern comparisons between the assignment tasks you provided and the attached sample IELTS reading tasks.

6. What do you see as the main similarities and/or differences between the type of reading set on the IELTS test, and the type of reading you require of your students on the course?

7. On the evidence of these IELTS tasks, to what extent do you think training for the IELTS reading test would be useful preparation for the reading demands on your course? Explain.

Sample IELTS Reading test material distributed to interviewees for comment:

Official IELTS practice materials, University of Cambridge; British Council; IDP, IELTS Australia, 2007

READING PASSAGE 1

You should spend about 20 minutes on Questions 1–14, which are based on

Spider silk cuts weight of bridges

A strong, light bio-material made by genes from spiders could transform construction and industry

A Scientists have succeeded in copying the silk-producing genes of the *Golden Orb Weaver* spider and are using them to create a synthetic material which they believe is the model for a new generation of advanced bio-materials. The new material, biosilk, which has been spun for the first time by researchers at DuPont, has an enormous range of potential uses in construction and manufacturing.

B The attraction of the silk spun by the spider is a combination of great strength and enormous elasticity, which man-made fibbers have been unable to replicate. On an equal-weightbasis, spider silk is far stronger than steel and it is estimated that if a single strand could be made about 10m in diameter, it would be strong enough to stop a jumbo jet in flight. A third important factor is that it is extremely light. Army scientists are already looking at the possibilities of using it for lightweight, bullet-proof vests and parachutes.

C For some time, biochemists have been trying to synthesise the drag-line silk of the *Golden Orb Weaver*. The drag-line silk, which forms the radial arms of the web, is stronger than the other parts of the web and some biochemists believe a synthetic version could prove to be as important a material as nylon, which has been around for 50 years, since the discoveries of the Wallace Carothers and his team ushered in the age of polymers.

D To recreate the material, scientists, including Randolph Lewis at the University of Wyoming, first examined the silk-producing gland of the spider. 'We took out the glands that produce the silk and looked at the coding for the protein material they make, which is spun into a web. We then went looking for clones with the right DNA,' he says.

E At DuPont, researchers have used both yeast and bacteria as hosts to grow the raw material, which they have spun into fibers. Robert Dorsch, DuPont's director of biochemical development, says the globules of protein, comparable with marbles in an egg, are harvested and processed. 'We break open the bacteria, separate out the globules of protein and use them as the raw starting material. With yeast, the gene system can be designed so that the material excretes the protein outside the yeast for better access,' he says.

F 'The bacteria and the yeast produce the same protein, equivalent to that which the spider uses in the drag lines of the web. The spider mixes the protein into a water-based solution and then spins it into a solid fiber in one go. Since we are not as clever as the spider and we are not using such sophisticated organisms, we substituted man-made approaches and dissolved the protein in chemical solvents, which are then spun to push the material through small holes to form the solid fiber.'

G Researchers at DuPont say they envisage many possible uses for a new biosilk material. They say that earthquake-resistant suspension bridges hung from cables of synthetic spider silk fibbers may become a reality. Stronger ropes, safer seat belts, shoe soles that do not wear out so quickly and tough new clothing are among the other applications. Biochemists such as Lewis see the potential range of uses of biosilk as almost limitless. 'It is very strong and retains elasticity; there are no man-made materials that can mimic both these properties. It is also a biological material with all the advantages that has over petrochemicals,' he says.

H At DuPont's laboratories, Dorsch is excited by the prospect of new super-strong materials but he warns they are many years away. 'We are at an early stage but theoretical predictions are that we will wind up with a very strong, tough material, with an ability to absorb shock, which is stronger and tougher than the man-made materials that are conventionally available to us,' he says.

I The spider is not only the creature that has aroused the interest of material scientists. They have also become envious of the natural adhesive secreted by the sea mussel. It produces a protein adhesive to attach itself to rocks. It is tedious and expensive to extract the protein from the mussel, so researchers have already produced a synthetic gene for use in surrogate bacteria.

Questions 1–5

Reading Passage (1) has nine paragraphs, A–I.
Which paragraph contains the following information?
Write the correct letter, A–I, in boxes 1–5 on your answer sheet.

1 a comparison of the ways two materials are used to replace silk-producing glands

2 predictions regarding the availability of the synthetic silk

3 ongoing research into other synthetic materials

4 the research into the part of the spider that manufactures silk

5 the possible application of the silk in civil engineering

Questions 6–11

Complete the flow-chart below.
Choose NO MORE THAN THREE WORDS from the passage for each answer.
Write your answers in boxes 6–11 on your answer sheet.

Synthetic gene grown in 6 .... or 7 ....
→
globules of 8 ....
→
dissolved in 9 ....
→
passed through 10 ....
→

Questions 12–14

Do the following statements agree with the information given in Reading Passage 1?
In boxes 12–14 on your answer sheet, write

TRUE   if the statement agrees with the information
FALSE   if the statements contradicts the information
NOT GIVEN   if there is no information on this

12 Biosilk has already replaced nylon in parachute manufacture.

13 The spider produces silk of varying strengths.

14 Lewis and Dorsch co-operated in the synthetic production of silk.

Appendix 2.3
Additional sample items showing more global and/or interpretative engagements

1 EXTENSION 1 → LOCAL/INTERPRETATIVE

1.1 Focus on connotative meanings of words

In Passage A, the author refers to X as a "Y" (Line B). This use of the term "Y" suggests that the writer sees X as:

a) eg a positive development
b) eg a negative development
c) eg an expected development
d) eg an unexpected development

1.2 Focus on author purpose

The writer of Passage A refers to X in Paragraph B, in order to demonstrate:

a) X is a good thing and should be encouraged
b) X is a bad thing and should be discouraged
c) not enough is known about X, and it should be investigated further
d) sufficient research has been conducted into X

2 EXTENSION 2 → GLOBAL/LITERAL

2.1 Focus on macro-content of text (Epistemic entity = argument)

Which of the following statements best summarises the author's main argument in Reading Passage A?:

a) that X is a good thing, and should be encouraged
b) that X is not a good thing, and should be discouraged
c) that X is neither a good thing nor a bad thing
d) that X is a good thing for some, but not for others.

2.2 Focus on macro-content of text (Epistemic entity = study)

Reading Passage A describes a study conducted into X. Which of the following statements best summarises the study's main outcomes?:

a) that X is a Y
b) that X is not a Y
c) that X is neither an X or Y
d) no clear outcomes were obtained

2.3 Focus on macro-content of text (Scenario format)

Four different students wrote a one sentence summary of Passage A. Which one most accurately reflects the content of the passage?:

a) The writer discusses the main difficulties of X and describes some of the solutions that have been proposed
b) The writer discusses the main difficulties of X, and recommends a range of solutions
c) The writer discusses the main difficulties of X, and suggests that the problems are too difficult to solve
d) The writer discusses the main difficulties of X, without recommending any solutions

2.4 Focus on multiple texts

Consider Reading Passage A and Reading Passage B. The main content difference between these two passages is best summarised as:

a) Reading Passage A is about X and Reading Passage B is about Y
b) Reading Passage A is about Y and Reading Passage B is about X
c) etc

3 EXTENSION 3 → GLOBAL/INTERPRETATIVE

3.1 Focus on authorial stance in text

In Passage A, the writer discusses the issue of X. Which of the following statements best characterises the writer's view of this issue?:

a) The writer appears to be a supporter of X
b) The writer appears to be an opponent of X
c) The writer recognizes both the advantages and disadvantages of X
d) The writer expresses no personal view about X

3.2 Focus on genre/source of material

Reading Passage A is concerned with X. Which of the following do you think best describes the type of text it is?:

a) a research article
b) a magazine article
c) a textbook extract
d) a newspaper report

3.3 Focus on author purpose/audience

Passage A provides information about X (eg higher education). Which type of reader do you think the author had in mind when writing this text?:

a) a student wanting to improve their grades
b) a student wanting to choose which course they will do
c) a lecturer wanting to develop their teaching methods
d) a lecturer wanting to advise students on course options

3 The cognitive processes underlying the academic reading construct as measured by IELTS

Cyril Weir, Roger Hawkey, Anthony Green and Sarojani Devi

University of Bedfordshire, UK

Abstract

This study, building on CRELLA's (Centre for Research in Language Learning and Assessment) 2006/07 IELTS grant-funded research (Weir, Hawkey, Green, Ünaldi and Devi 2009, and also this volume), clarifies further the links between what is measured by the IELTS Academic Reading test and the construct of academic reading as practised by students in a UK university by eliciting from IELTS candidates, by means of a retrospective protocol, the reading processes they engage in when tackling IELTS Academic Reading tasks. The study provides grounded insight into the congruence between the construct measured by IELTS and that of academic reading in the target domain.

1 Rationale

If they are to provide a useful service to receiving institutions, language tests that address the English language proficiency of overseas students must reflect the demands of the academic courses these students are going to follow. Providers of international examinations have a responsibility to provide valid information for stakeholders and to demonstrate the qualities of their offerings. This two-part project explores the basis for the validity of the IELTS Academic Reading test in terms of its relationship to the academic reading practices of students at a British university.

Little research is available on the relationship between the IELTS Academic Reading module and academic reading *in situ*. This study, building on CRELLA's 2006/07 IELTS-funded research (Weir, Hawkey, Green, Ünaldi and Devi 2009, and also this volume), clarifies further the links between what is measured by IELTS and the construct of academic reading by students in a UK university by eliciting from IELTS candidates, by means of a retrospective protocol, the reading processes they engage in when tackling IELTS reading tasks.

Considerable attention in IELTS-funded research has been given to the skills of writing and speaking (see projects reported in previous volumes in this series), but, as Hawkey (2006) argues in the concluding chapter of his book in the Studies in Language Testing series on IELTS impact: '. . . there were certain focus areas in the original long-term research design which are still to be covered . . . there is a need for further investigation of the validity of IELTS reading . . .' (2006:163).

Weir et al (this volume) carried out a survey-based IELTS research study which sought to:

• establish the nature of academic reading activities performed across a range of courses with particular reference to contextual parameters and cognitive processing, and provide initial data on the relationship(s) between the IELTS Academic Reading module and reading in an academic context

• investigate problems experienced by students with respect to these parameters and determine the extent to which any problems might decrease the higher the IELTS band score obtained before entry.

This first-phase study focused on the cognitive processing involved in academic reading, specified under a variety of contextual parameters in the target domain. This was considered a logical first step, providing the necessary empirical basis for a subsequent investigation of the cognitive processes involved in taking the IELTS Academic Reading module. Not least, it would help establish the categories of description that we might ask candidates to apply to their IELTS test-taking experience.

The current study thus constitutes the second phase of our linked research agenda for the validation of the IELTS Academic Reading component. We identify through participant retrospection the range of cognitive processes students employ when they are performing the various tasks in the IELTS Academic Reading test. This will provide grounded insight into the congruence between the construct measured by IELTS and academic reading practices in the target domain.

2 Literature review

In earlier frameworks of reading, especially in those that take into account the purposeful and strategic activities of readers, several types of reading are specified (see Khalifa and Weir 2009 and Weir et al, this volume, for a full description of these). In general terms, the reading types covered are *expeditious reading*, i.e. quick, selective and efficient reading to access desired information in a text (scanning, skimming and search reading), and *careful reading*, i.e. processing a text thoroughly with the intention to extract complete meanings from presented material. The multiple reading models that are now acknowledged in the second language literature suggest that reading for different purposes may engage quite different cognitive processes or constellations of processes on the part of the reader.

Khalifa and Weir (2009) capture the elements deemed important in earlier frameworks and account for the interactions between reader purpose, cognitive processes and knowledge stored in long-term memory (see Figure 3.1 on page 215). They hypothesise that difficulty in reading is a function of both the level of processing required by reading purpose and complexity of text. In its present form, following Urquhart and Weir (1998), the Khalifa and Weir framework is a conceptualisation of reading skills on multiple dimensions; both *expeditious* versus *careful* and *local* versus *global*.

In developing reading tests, as well as ensuring the contextual appropriateness of the test tasks, we advocate a cognitive processing approach designed to model what readers actually do when they engage in different types of reading. The principal concern in this study is a comparison between participants' processing of IELTS Reading test items and the mental processes readers employ in comprehending texts when engaging in different types of real-life reading.

Khalifa and Weir (2009) outline the cognitive processes contributing to reading according to purpose and their model is summarised in Figure 3.1 below. The left-hand column specifies the metacognitive activity of a goal setter because, in deciding what type of reading to employ when faced with a text, critical decisions are taken on the level(s) of processing to be activated in the central core of the model. The various elements of this processing core are listed in the middle column. Processing at a variety of levels might be initiated by decisions taken at the goal setter stage. Reading is divided into four levels including careful local within sentences, and careful global across sentences (the mental model), text (the text model) and multiple texts levels (the documents model).

It is argued that the goal setter in the left-hand column is critical because decisions taken about the purpose for reading will determine the relative importance of these levels (mental model, text, documents) in the central processing core when carrying out a reading activity.

The various exponents of these two dimensions are listed in the model below and then described briefly. A full description is available in Khalifa and Weir (2009), but we offer here a brief outline of key elements in the model to contextualise the design of our retrospective protocol form.

Urquhart and Weir's (1998) distinctions between global/local and careful/expeditious are of particular importance to the design of the form used in this study and we will briefly describe them here. Global comprehension refers to

Figure 3.1 Cognitive processing in reading (Khalifa and Weir 2009:43)

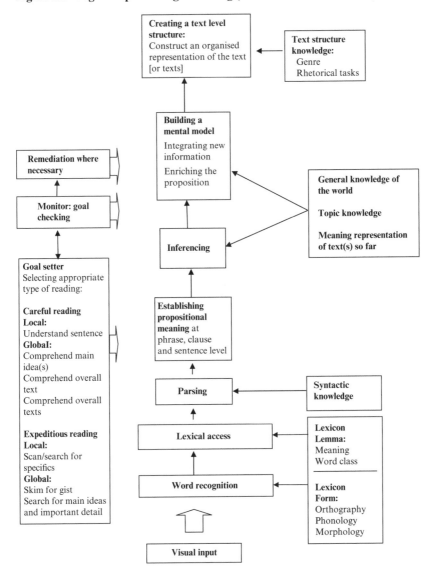

the understanding of information beyond the sentence, including main ideas, the links between ideas in the text and the way in which these are elaborated. Local comprehension concerns the understanding of propositions within the sentence (individual phrases, clauses and sentences). In the model above, local comprehension involves word recognition, lexical access and syntactic parsing and establishing explicit propositional meaning at the phrase, clause and sentence level. Careful reading involves extracting complete meanings from text, whether at the global or local level. As noted above, this is based on slow, careful, linear, incremental reading for comprehension. Expeditious reading, in contrast, involves quick, selective and efficient reading to access relevant information in a text. In careful global reading the reader may try to identify the main idea(s) by reconstructing the macro-structure of a text. Logical or rhetorical relationships between ideas are represented in complexes of propositions (see Vipond 1980), often represented by the writer by means of paragraphing; global reading involves attempting to reconstruct these complexes.

The distinction across types of careful reading reflects the real-life reading processes in academic settings generally. Readers find themselves having to read and learn from a whole text as well as integrating information from various texts especially for the preparation of assignments. It is clear from the brief definition of the frameworks above that careful reading as an umbrella term encompasses processing at sentence, multi-sentence, text and multi-text levels.

In the past, models of reading have usually been developed with only careful reading in mind (see, for example, Hoover and Tunmer 1993, Rayner and Pollatsek 1989). However, careful reading models have little to tell us about how skilled readers cope with other reading behaviours such as skimming for gist (Rayner and Pollatsek 1989:477–478). Carver (1992) and Khalifa and Weir (2009) suggest that the speed of reading is important as well as comprehension. In relation to reading for university study, Weir et al (this volume), found that 'for many readers reading quickly, selectively and efficiently posed greater problems than reading carefully and efficiently'.

Three types of expeditious reading are distinguished in the model: scanning, skimming and search reading. Scanning is a form of expeditious reading that occurs at the local level. It involves reading highly selectively to find specific words, figures or phrases in a text. Skimming is generally defined (Urquhart and Weir 1998, Weir 2005) as reading quickly by sampling text to abstract the gist, general impression and/or superordinate idea: skimming relates exclusively to global reading. In academic study contexts, readers may try to establish the macro-structure of a text and the discourse topic (see Kong 1996) by skimming, using careful global reading to determine how the ideas in the whole text relate to each other and to the author's purpose.

Unlike skimming, search reading involves predetermined topics. The reader does not necessarily have to establish a macro-propositional structure for the whole of the text, but is, rather, seeking information that matches their requirements. However, unlike scanning (where exact word matches are sought) the search is not for exact word matches, but for words in the same semantic field as the target information. Search reading can involve both local and global-level reading. Where the desired information can be found within a single sentence the search reading would be classified as local and where information has to be constructed across sentences it would be seen as global.

The different types of reading that readers might choose to carry out (the left-hand column of the model), the different levels of processing that might be activated (the central column), and the knowledge base necessary to successfully complete an assigned reading task (the right-hand column) provide us with the theoretical framework on which our retrospection protocol form is based. The form is thus intended to elicit from participants taking the IELTS Academic Reading test how their approach to reading the texts and responses to the tasks presented to them reflects the model of cognitive processing in Figure 3.1 above.

We will briefly review the case for the use of protocol analysis in establishing test validity and examine its history before describing in more detail the instrument developed for our study.

2.1 A processing approach to defining reading

It is common for language testers to adopt what has been called a *subskills* approach, based on the assumption that it is possible to target particular types of item or test task to specific types of reading so that one item might target the ability to understand the meaning of an individual word in a text and another might target the ability to extract the overall meaning of a text within a very limited time frame (skimming). Alderson and Lukmani (1989) have questioned the feasibility of classifying reading test items in this way on the grounds that 'expert' judges were unable to reach agreement on which subskills individual items were addressing. However, Weir and Porter (1994:7) responded that 'a growing body of literature suggests that it is possible with clear specification of terms and appropriate methodology for testers to reach closer agreement on what skills are being tested'. The body of literature the authors referred to includes Bachman, Kunnan, Vanniarajan and Lynch (1988), Lumley (1993), Teasdale (1989) and Weakley (1993). Alderson also now appears to have revised his earlier position, adopting an approach for the DIALANG project in which individual items are said to test identifiable skills (Alderson 2005:125–137).

The debate over subskills centred on the ability of expert judges to arrive at a consensus about what was being tested and the essential role of the candidate was largely overlooked. The majority of studies paid surprisingly little attention to the cognitive processing required for candidates to carry out test tasks. Alderson (2000:97) argues that:

> The validity of a test relates to the interpretation of the correct responses to items, so what matters is not what the test constructors believe an item to be testing, but which responses are considered correct, and what process underlies them.

In other words, to clearly establish the trait that has been measured we need to investigate the processing necessary for task completion.

2.2 Protocol analysis

A process-oriented approach to defining reading activity in language tests seeks an experimental method which permits comment on the actual reading process itself. Verbal report is a widely used experimental procedure where participants describe the linguistic process in which they are engaged and the results are often known as protocols. The approach is not new. Thorndike (1917) in looking at 'reading as reasoning' investigated what students were thinking whilst answering comprehension questions in a test. More recently Anderson, Bachman, Perkins and Cohen (1991), Block (1986), Crain-Thoreson, Lippman and McClendon-Magnuson (1997), Nevo (1989), Perkins (1992), Phakiti (2003), and Weir, Yang and Jin (2000) provide descriptions of protocol-based studies in reading. Such studies can cast illuminative light on whether the different types of reading that have been proposed do in fact instigate the different processing activities that have been shown to occur in normal processing in reading outside of tests.

Methodological advances in language testing in the 1980s saw researchers such as Alderson (1990a and 1990b) advocating the importance of gathering information on test-taking processes as part of construct validation and the use of introspective data to throw light on the nature of the trait under consideration.

For discussion of the methodology of protocol studies see: Cohen (1984 and 2007) on verbal reports for investigating test taking; Gass and Mackey (2000) for a useful theoretical and practical account of verbal protocol analysis; Ericsson and Simon (1993) on the use of protocol analysis to investigate cognitive processing; Green (1998) on verbal protocol analysis in language testing research; Pressley and Afflerbach (1995) on verbal protocols for reading; and Stratman and Hamp-Lyons (1994) on concurrent think-aloud protocols.

With respect to using students' introspective data as a method of investigation in reading research, most of the studies carried out in testing reading research using introspection techniques imply the existence of subskills: Anderson, Bachman, Perkins and Cohen (1991), Cohen (1984), Feldmann and Stemmer (1987), Grotjahn (1987), Hosenfeld (1977) and Nevo (1989) to name but a few.

However, a note of caution is sounded by a number of researchers including Afflerbach and Johnston (1984) and Cordon and Day (1996). The latter found that the process of immediate retrospection may interfere with the ability under investigation: '... thinking aloud was found to have a significant detrimental effect on students' ability to identify the passage's main ideas'

(288). The very act of reporting may distort the process of reading. Field (2004:318) also notes that '. . . students tend to describe processes as rather more systematic than they actually are; while some subjects lack the necessary *metalanguage* to analyse their experience accurately'. Such tendencies point to the importance of careful design and piloting to ensure that participants are confident that they are able to carry out the verbal protocol task.

A further concern is that, because of the intensive nature of verbal protocol research, which requires participant training and may generate a very large quantity of data for each individual, studies typically involve no more than a handful of participants. In the current study we set out to triangulate the detailed protocol data we had obtained in the Weir et al study (this volume) with less nuanced data elicited from a much more extensive group of participants.

3 Methodology

3.1 Research instruments

In the previous IELTS-funded study in this project, Weir et al (this volume) established that a typical sequence of reading activities associated with student assignments often involved expeditious reading followed by selective and intensive careful reading with information then being integrated into the students' developing understanding of the focal topic.

In the current study we set out to learn which activities and sequences typified reading for the purpose of taking an IELTS Academic Reading test. Initially, we drew on an element of the earlier study (Weir et al this volume) involving the elicitation of both qualitative and quantitative data from a small group of four participants on how the IELTS Academic Reading test might be approached. One (EAL – Englishas an alternative language) respondent provided the following general description of how he combined careful and expeditious reading types in approaching the IELTS Reading test tasks:

> I usually read the texts carefully from the beginning to the end initially then I go to the questions. I can answer some questions without having to read the text again. If not, I usually remember the place where the info necessary for the answer is located and go there usually by scanning which may be followed by some careful reading.

This careful-expeditious-selective strategy pattern contrasts with the expeditious-selective-careful strategy suggested as a common response to academic assignments by the responses to the questionnaire on academic reading outlined above. This may point to important differences in how candidates approach IELTS texts and how students approach reading for study purposes.

Weir et al (this volume) identified potential limitations of the IELTS Reading test as a reflection of academic reading skills in four areas. There was said to be a lack of items requiring:

- expeditious reading skills
- integration of information beyond the sentence level
- information at the level of the whole text
- information accessed across texts.

In the current study we sought data on whether the strategies reported by the earlier small focus group were reflected in the wider IELTS test-taking population. Participants were given one part of an IELTS Academic Reading test and responded to a brief retrospective protocol form concerning the types of reading they had employed.

We selected two tests from the Weir et al (this volume) study for this purpose. These comprised two Academic Reading tests taken from *Cambridge Practice Tests for IELTS: Volume 2* (Cambridge University Press 2000). The IELTS partners do not release retired IELTS forms for research purposes, but the material appearing in these books is developed by Cambridge ESOL, the IELTS partner responsible for test production, using their standard IELTS test production procedures. It conforms to the IELTS specifications and is therefore representative of genuine IELTS test material. The selected tests appear as Tests E and F in the Weir et al (this volume) study and were selected on the basis that they:

- included only question types still used in the current IELTS Reading test format (www.ielts.org), but provided a variety of these
- included a range of items that had been identified in the Weir et al (this volume) study as requiring both explicitly stated and implicit information located across sentences as well as within sentences
- included items that had been identified by Weir et al (this volume) as motivating expeditious as well as careful reading types
- had not been identified in the previous study as having any characteristics that would make them atypical of IELTS texts (see Weir et al this volume for the range of textual measures used).

Each IELTS Academic Reading test may involve a different combination of item types. The 10 broad categories of item type used on the test are listed on the IELTS website (www.ielts.org) with links to further information about each. The list is reproduced below (the seven item types found in the two tests included in this study are marked ✓). Each item type is glossed with a brief explanation of the skills being targeted, based on information found on the IELTS website:

    ✓ Type 1 – Multiple Choice
       – *Multiple choice items are used to test a wide range of reading skills. They may require the candidate to have a detailed understanding of*

specific points or an overall understanding of the main points of the text.

✗ Type 2 – Short-answer Questions

✓ Type 3 – Sentence Completion

- *Candidates are asked to complete the sentence in a given number of words taken from the passage or from a list of possible options.*

✓ Type 4 – Notes, Summary or Table/Flow-chart Completion

- *This task type often relates to precise factual information, and so is often used with descriptive texts.*

✗ Type 5 – Labelling a Diagram

✓ Type 6 – Choosing Headings for Paragraphs or Sections of a Text

- *This task type is used with passages that contain paragraphs or sections with clearly defined themes.*

✓ Type 7 – Locating Information

- *This task type may test a wide range of reading skills, from locating detail to recognising a summary or definition etc.*

✓ Type 8 – Identification of Writer's Views/Claims or of Information in a Text

- *Tests the candidate's ability to recognise particular points of information conveyed in the passage. It can thus be used with more factual texts.*

✗ Type 9 – Classification

✓ Type 10 – Matching

- *This task type is designed to test the candidates' ability to recognise opinions or theories.*

The full IELTS Academic Reading test has three parts. Each test part has one input text and may include up to four sections or sets of items of the same format. For example, Part 1 of Test E has three sections made up of 'Yes/No/Not Given' items, multiple choice items and summary completion items. The full test has 40 items (with 13 in each of the first two parts and 14 in the last) and takes a total of 1 hour to administer. For the purposes of this study each test part was administered separately with a time limit of 20 minutes. Participants were then given a further 10 minutes (or longer if required) to complete the retrospective questionnaire. The test was administered in this way to allow time for participants to complete the retrospection form and review their answers within a typical 40-minute class and to avoid overburdening them with having to complete the questionnaire in addition to the demands of a full three-part IELTS test.

A breakdown of the item types found in these two tests is given in Table 3.1. Both tests included here involve mainly selected response items with

Table 3.1 Test parts and item types included in this study

Test part	Topic	Section 1	Section 2	Section 3	Section 4
E.1	Green consum- erism	6 items Type 8 – Identification of Writer's Views/ Claims or of Information in a Text – Yes/No/ Not Given	3 items Type 1 – 4-Option Multiple Choice	4 items Type 4 – Summary Completion – select from a list of answers	—
E.2	Child literacy	4 items Type 1 – 4- Option Multiple Choice	4 items Type 8 – Identification of Writer's Views/ Claims or of Information in a Text – Yes/No/Not Given	4 items Type 7 – Locating Information	1 item Type 6 – Choosing a Heading – for the whole text
E.3	Human genome project	6 items *Constructed response* Type 3 – Sentence Completion – select words from the passage	8 items Type 10 – Matching	—	—
F.1	Nurse absenteeism	7 items Type 8 – Identification of Writer's Views/ Claims or of Information in a Text – Yes/No/ Not Given	6 items *Constructed response* Type 4 – Summary Completion – select words from the passage	—	—
F.2	Dependence on motor vehicles	6 items Type 7 – Locating Information	7 items Type 8 – Identification of Writer's Views/ Claims or of Information in a Text – Yes/No/Not Given	—	—
F.3	Biometric security systems	7 items Type 6 – Choosing Headings for Paragraphs or Sections of a Text	7 items Type 10 – Matching	—	—

Type 8: Identification of Information in a Text and *Type 1: 4-Option Multiple Choice* items making up between them the majority of items on Test E (10 and 15 respectively of the 40 items) and *Type 8: Identification of Information in a Text* and various forms of text-to-list matching (*Type 7: Locating Information, Type 6: Choosing Headings* and *Type 10: Matching*) making up the majority on Test F (14 and 20 of 40). Six items on Test E (short answer questions) and six on Test F (summary completion) involve a constructed response format, although the participants are able to choose words found in the passages to complete both of these tasks.

To investigate the reading types employed by participants responding to the tests, we developed a questionnaire form modelled on the earlier (Weir et al this volume) survey of students engaging in academic reading at the University of Bedfordshire. This form was intended to be used by participants as a retrospective protocol immediately following administration of a part of an IELTS Academic Reading test.

The retrospection form (see the example in Appendix 3.3) was designed to address the choices between reading types (see above) made by participants as they encountered the reading texts and items in IELTS. Questions about the participants' background and previous experience of IELTS (age, gender, first language, nationality, date of most recent IELTS test, IELTS Academic Reading score, and intended university subject) were included on the answer paper (see Appendix 3.2).

The three sections of the retrospection form were as follows:

1) Sequence of reading activities

Each IELTS text is accompanied by 13 or 14 items and these are usually divided into between two and four item sets (groups of items, each with a different question format such as multiple choice or gap-filling). This section of the questionnaire sought information on whether participants were reading the text before looking at each item set and whether they were using expeditious or careful reading when doing so.

The three choices given for each test section were: a) read the text or part of it slowly and carefully (careful reading); b) read the text or part of it quickly and selectively to get a general idea of what it was about (expeditious reading – skimming); c) did not read the text.

2) Strategies for responding

This section sought information on how participants read to find the answers to each item. Here the focus was on establishing the processes that participants engaged in to locate the correct answer to each individual item. These processes might include lexical matching between words in the question and words in the text, using knowledge of discourse conventions to select the relevant part of the text or integrating information from the text with prior knowledge about the topic. The 12 items were as follows:

1. Match words that appeared in the question with exactly the same words in the text (local–scan reading based on word recognition).
2. Quickly match words that appeared in the question with similar or related words in the text (local – search reading based on lexical access).
3. Look for parts of the text that the writer indicates to be important (global, text level).
4. Read key parts of the text such as the introduction and conclusion (global, selective reading at text level).
5. Work out the meaning of a difficult word in the question (local, word recognition).
6. Work out the meaning of a difficult word in the text (local, word recognition).
7. Use my knowledge of vocabulary (lexical knowledge).
8. Use my knowledge of grammar (syntactic knowledge).
9. Read the text or part of it slowly and carefully (careful reading, establishing propositional meaning – global or local).
10. Read relevant parts of the text again (careful reading – global or local).
11. Use my knowledge of how texts like this are organised (text structure knowledge).
12. Connect information from the text with knowledge I already have (general/topic knowledge).

3) Information base for the response

This section sought information on where participants felt they had found the necessary information to enable them to answer each question. They were asked to indicate whether they had found the necessary information:

- within a single sentence (propositional level)
- by putting information together across sentences (mental model level)
- by understanding how information in the whole text fits together (text level)
- without reading the text (general/topic knowledge)

  or, alternatively, whether they 'could not answer the question'.

The instructions explained that all items allowed for the selection of more than one of the response options. This provision was made so that complex and recursive response strategies could be at least partially captured by the questionnaire.

After passing through several iterations within the research team, the form underwent trialling with a small focus group of three IELTS participants who reported back to the researchers on their experience. Revisions were made to the content and format to make the retrospection form more accessible to language learners before it was used with larger numbers of participants (see the discussion of changes relating to the operationalisation of inferencing below). To reflect the different numbers of items and of item sets associated with each of the texts, a separate form was prepared for each of the six IELTS test parts used in the study. An example is provided as Appendix 3.3.

3.2 Participants and settings

Participants included some 352 learners on IELTS preparation, university pre-sessional and advanced general English classes in the UK and Taiwan over the period July to October 2007. Although we would not claim that these learners are a stratified random sample of the global IELTS test-taking population, the groups were, as well as being accessible to our research team, the kinds of learner for whom the IELTS Academic modules are intended (they were mostly preparing for higher academic study).

Learners were each given one of the six IELTS test parts we had identified for the purposes of the study and these were administered in class by their teachers. The teachers explained what the students had to do and an instruction sheet was provided for each participant (Appendix 3.1). Immediately following the administration of the questionnaire and collection of answer papers, the teachers were free to review the answers and to discuss reading approaches with their students on the basis of their questionnaire responses. Table 3.2 here describes the participants by number and institution.

Table 3.2 Participants by institution

Institution	N	Form 1 (E1)	Form 2 (E2)	Form 3 (E3)	Form 4 (F1)	Form 5 (F2)	Form 6 (F3)
Anglia Ruskin U					4	7	
U of Bedfordshire		36	20	16	23	29	31
Birmingham U					3	8	
Coventry U			13				14
LTTC Taiwan		6	5	5	4	7	14
U of Southampton		32	27	35			
Warwick U					6	7	
Total		74	65	56	40	58	59

4 Analysis

In our data analysis, we generated descriptive statistics for preview reading, response strategy and location of necessary information by test section and compared the patterns of response across these both by participant reading ability and by item type. We also compared the findings of the current study with the outcomes from Weir et al (this volume).

For the purpose of comparing the approaches to reading adopted by higher and lower-ability participants, we divided the participants into three groups according to their total scores as a measure of reading ability. IELTS test parts vary only a little in overall difficulty across forms. As a result, we felt that using the same score ranges across test parts as a basis for categorisation would provide a crude but adequate indication of overall reading ability for the purposes of this study.

In dividing the participants by level, we employed three broad categories: 0 to 5, 6 to 8, and 9 and above points. These categories are (based on the equivalences published at www.ielts.org) roughly indicative of IELTS band scores of 5.5 and below, and 6.0 and 6.5 and above, respectively.

Using these score categories, we carried out chi-square analysis and analysis of variance as appropriate to explore whether reading ability had any significant ($p<.05$) effect on preview reading, response strategy use or locating necessary information.

5 Results

Figure 3.2 on page 227 shows the distribution of scores on each test part. Mean scores ranged from 6.99 on Test Part E2 to 8.14 on Test Part F2. This places the majority of participants on all test parts at around the equivalent of a Band 6.0 level for IELTS Academic Reading. The mean score for participants worldwide is 6.04 for females and 5.90 for males (www.ielts.org).

Table 3.3 on page 228 displays the numbers of participants by first language and gender. 78.9% of the participants were L1 speakers of Chinese with 4.3% Arabic and 4.0% Thai speakers making up the next largest L1 groups. 4.8% of participants did not respond to this question. IELTS no longer publishes information on the proportion of speakers of specific L1s among the worldwide candidature, but we would assume that the study population includes a relatively high proportion of Chinese speakers. The majority of our participants (58.8%) were women. This compares with 51.3% of the IELTS Academic module candidates worldwide (www.ielts.org). Participant ages ranged from 14 to 57 with a median age of 22 years.

In the following sections we describe the responses to the three sections of the reading protocol form in turn looking both at overall response patterns and at responses to each test section. We also examine differences between higher-scoring and lower-scoring participants.

Figure 3.2 Participants and score distributions – total scores by test part

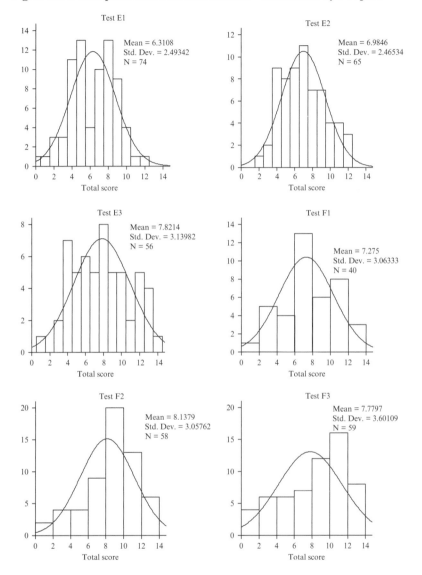

5.1 Text preview

The first section of the protocol form asked participants about whether they read the text before looking at the tendencies:

- read the text or part of it slowly and carefully

Table 3.3 Participants by first language and gender

L1	N	%
No response	17	4.8
Arabic	15	4.3
Chinese	278	78.9
English	1	0.3
French	2	0.6
German	2	0.6
Greek	2	0.6
Hungarian	1	0.3
Italian	2	0.6
Japanese	2	0.6
Korean	6	1.7
Portuguese	1	0.3
Russian	3	0.9
Spanish	2	0.6
Tamil	1	0.3
Thai	14	4.0
Turkish	3	0.9

Gender		
Male	145	41.2%
Female	207	58.8%

Age	
Median	22
Max	14
Min	57
St Dev	5.31

- read the text or part of it quickly and selectively to get a general idea of what it was about
- did not read the text.

Each test has three parts, each with its own text. Sets of questions associated with each text may follow different formats. Each part includes at least two sets of questions, referred to here as sections. Participants were asked to indicate whether or not they read the text before looking at the questions in each of these sections. The results are summarised in Figure 3.3 on page 229. Note that only one Test Part (E2) included more than three sections. As E2.4 is made up of a single item, it is not included in Figure 3.3.

An analysis of participant responses to the first section of the protocol form revealed the following (Figure 3.3):

1. A majority of participants chose (b) *read the text through quickly and selectively* before reading each of the questions for each section; skimming

the text without specific questions in mind: 61% did this before reading the questions in the first section, 55% before reading the questions in the second section and 46% before reading the questions in the third section.

2. 22%, 26% and 36% chose (a) *reading slowly and carefully*.

3. 17%, 19% and 18% chose (c) *not reading the text before attempting the questions*.

Figure 3.3 Text preview by test section

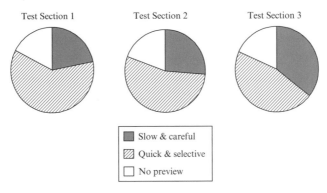

Although, as we see from this data, a majority of participants read quickly and selectively before approaching the questions, on the third section of Test E Part 1, more participants read slowly and carefully before looking at the questions (a – 40%) than quickly and selectively (b – 35%) with 25% not previewing the text (c) before reading the questions for this section. The increase in the number of participants who did not preview this section probably reflects the position of the task – the last of three tasks relating to the same text. Participants may either have felt they did not need to read the text again before addressing the questions or perhaps may have felt under time pressure as they approached the end of the time available. Conversely, a large proportion of participants may have found they had enough time available to read through the text again carefully before attempting Section 3.

When the protocol data was compared with IELTS test part scores, participants who did not preview the text tended to have higher scores than the quick and selective pre-readers, who in turn tended to have higher scores than the slow and careful pre-readers. Chi-square tests comparing the pre-reading choices of low (5 and below), mid (6 to 8) and high (9 and above) scorers on the tests confirmed that these differences were significant (p<.01) across all sections within the test parts.

Figure 3.4 refers to the three sections (sets of questions of the same format) within the test parts. Pre-read 1, 2 and 3 refer to whether and how participants read the relevant text before reading the questions in each section.

Figure 3.4 Total scores by test preview

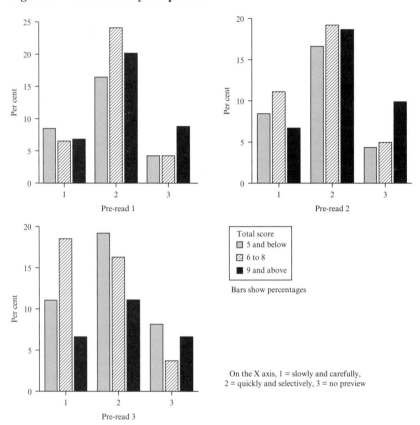

The figure provides a comparison between participants at the three levels of total score: those scoring 5 or below, 6 to 8, or 9 and above on the relevant part of the test. The charts indicate that participants at the highest level were less likely than lower-scoring participants to read the text before the questions (although a majority even of these higher-level participants did preview the text quickly and selectively). It may be that the higher-scoring participants did not need to spend as much time on previewing the text in order to respond successfully. Certainly a strategy involving reading the questions first before turning to the text is closer to the expeditious reading behaviour reported by most undergraduates in the Weir et al (this volume) study.

5.2 Test response strategies

Figure 3.5 on page 231 indicates that strategies 1, 2, 3, 4, 9 and 10 were all relatively popular, being selected at least once by over 60% of participants.

Strategies 5, 6, 7, 8, 11 and 12 were less so, each being selected by less than 40% of participants.

Figure 3.5 Response strategy use by score level

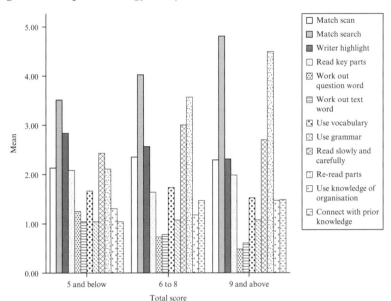

Across test parts the most popular test strategy was 2 – *quickly match words that appeared in the question with similar or related words in the text.* This emerged as the most frequently endorsed item on 10 of the 15 test sections with 83% of participants reporting using this strategy at least once. 10 – *read relevant parts of the text again* was also popular, appearing as the most popular choice on two test sections and being selected at least once by 77% of participants. 3 – *look for parts of the text that the writer indicates to be important* was the most popular strategy on another two test sections and was selected at least once by 76% of participants. 4 – *read key parts of the text such as the introduction and the conclusion* and 12 – *connect information from the text with knowledge I already have* were equally the most popular on one section. The least popular strategy was 8 – *use my knowledge of grammar* which was chosen for one or more items by 26% of participants.

One-way analysis of variance (Table 3.4 on page 232) comparing the three groups of test takers on strategy use (including all test sections) indicated significant differences (p<.05) by level on three strategies: strategy 2, strategy 5 and strategy 10. The significant differences on strategies 2 and 10 suggest that higher-scoring participants were more likely to use an approach combining search reading with careful re-reading of relevant sections of text. Such an approach parallels the most widely adopted approach to academic reading taken by participants in Weir et al (this volume) and may suggest that the more successful participants are approaching the IELTS tasks in a similar way to students reading for an assignment. The significant difference for strategy 5 presumably reflects the greater difficulty that low-scoring participants have with word recognition.

Table 3.4 Analysis of variance: Response strategy use, all participants

Strategy	F	P (<.05)
ST2 Search reading	3.343	0.036
ST5 Work out question word*	5.384	0.005
ST10 Re-read parts	10.545	0.000

* *The effect for ST5 was negative i.e. greater use of ST5 was associated with lower scores*

The picture of reading in response to IELTS test items that emerges is consistent with the general approach to academic reading reported by student readers in the Weir et al (this volume) protocol study: quick and selective search reading followed by intensive careful reading of relevant text parts.

5.3   Test response strategy use by test section

To explore the implications of task type for response strategy use, we compared the responses by test section.

Table 3.5 on page 233 shows patterns of text preview, response strategy use and locating information across sections. Where mean scores for a strategy use in a test section are above a threshold value (see Table 3.5), these are identified in the table. Graphs displaying this data in more detail are provided in Appendix 3.4 below.

Comparing strategy use by test section reveals some clear differences between the sections (see Table 3.5 and Appendix 3.4), while patterns of strategy use were loosely associated with item type. Two sections (E1.2 and E2.1) included items of Type 1 (Multiple Choice). E1.2 and E2.1 yielded mutually consistent patterns of strategy use with the five most popular strategies occurring in the same order of preference on both: 2 (*match related words*), 1 (*match exact words*), 3 (*look for parts of the text that the writer indicates to be important*), 10 (*read relevant parts of the text again*) and 9 (*read slowly and carefully*). It is notable that this item type, together with sentence and summary completion, was particularly associated with the direct word matching strategy (1). However, there were also differences in how participants responded to the multiple choice tasks. On E1.2 the information required was most often reported within the sentence while in E2.1 it was found across sentences.

Table 3.5 Text preview, response strategy and locating information by test section

Task type	Section	Text prev. + mean >.2			Response strategy + mean > .15													Locating information + mean > .3				
		PR1	PR2	PR3	ST1	ST2	ST3	ST4	ST5	ST6	ST7	ST8	ST9	ST10	ST11	ST12	LI1	LI2	LI3	LI4	LI5
MCQ	E1.2	+	+		+	+	+						+	+			+				
	E2.1	+	+		+	+	+						+	+				+			
Sent Comp	E3.1	+	+		+	+					+			+			+				
Summ Comp	E1.3	+	+	+	+	+	+						+	+	+	+		+	+		
	F1.2		+		+	+							+	+				+	+		
Heading	F3.1	+	+			+	+	+					+	+				+	+		
	E2.4		+	+				+							+	+			+		
Locate Info	E2.3	+	+			+	+						+	+				+	+		
	F2.1	+	+			+	+	+					+	+				+	+		
Y/N/NG	E1.1		+		+	+	+						+	+				+	+		
	E2.2		+			+	+				+		+	+			+	+	+		
	F1.1		+			+	+	+					+	+				+	+		
	F2.2	+	+			+							+	+				+	+		
Match	E3.2	+	+			+	+						+	+				+			
	F3.2		+	+	+	+							+	+			+	+			

PR1 read the text or part of it slowly and carefully
PR2 read the text or part of it quickly and selectively to get a general idea of what it was about
PR3 did not read the text

ST1 match words that appeared in the question with exactly the same words in the text
ST2 quickly match words that appeared in the question with similar or related words in the text
ST3 look for parts of the text that the writer indicates to be important
ST4 read key parts of the text such as the introduction and conclusion
ST5 work out the meaning of a difficult word in the question
ST6 work out the meaning of a difficult word in the text
ST7 use my knowledge of vocabulary
ST8 use my knowledge of grammar
ST9 read the text or part of it slowly and carefully
ST10 read relevant parts of the text again
ST11 use my knowledge of how texts like this are organised
ST12 connect information from the text with knowledge I already have
----
LI1 within a single sentence
LI2 by putting information together across sentences
LI3 by understanding how information in the whole text fits together
LI4 without reading the text
LI5 could not answer the question

Test E, Part 1, Section 1 (E1.1); E2.2, Test F1.1 and Test F2.2 all involved IELTS item Type 8, Identification of Writer's Views/Claims or of Information in a Text, with a selected response, the True/False/Not Given format. All involved widespread use of strategies 2 (*match related words*), 9 (*read slowly and carefully*) and 10 (*read relevant parts of the text again*) and participants most often reported locating the necessary information across sentences followed by across the text as a whole (see Table 3.5 and Appendix 3.4).

Response strategy 3 (*look for parts of the text that the writer indicates to be important*) was the most popular selection on F1.1 (see Appendix 3.4). This strategy seems particularly well-suited to Text F1 as it includes subheadings that might have helped to signpost where relevant information was to be found (the other section in which response strategy 3 was the most popular – F3.1 – involved matching subheadings to paragraphs).

The two test sections involving partially constructed responses – the selection of a word or words from the passage to complete sentences or summaries of the text (E3.1 and F1.2) – both involved a high proportion of strategies 2 (*match related words*) and 1 (*match exact words*) followed in popularity by 10 (*read relevant parts of the text again*) and 7 (*knowledge of vocabulary*). Necessary information was located within a single sentence. A third section involving summary completion (E1.3), but with a selected response format, was identified with the use of information distributed throughout the text and with strategies 2 (*match related words*), 10 (*read relevant parts of the text again*) and 9 (*read slowly and carefully*).

Both E3.2 and F3.2 involved Type 10 (Matching) items and also produced a broadly similar pattern of strategy use. On section E3.2 strategy 10 (*read relevant parts of the text again*) was most popular, followed by 2 (*match related words*), 9 (*read slowly and carefully*), 3 (*look for parts of the text that the writer indicates to be important*) and 7 (*knowledge of vocabulary*). On F3.2, strategy 2 was the most popular, with 10 second and 9 third. Strategy 1 (*match exact words*) was in fourth place and 3 in fifth.

Necessary information was most often reported as being found across sentences in E3.2, but within sentences in F3.2. This reflects differences between the items in the two sections. E3.2 provides paraphrases of facts and opinions expressed by the writer and these cannot be answered through exact word matching. F3.2 on the other hand requires matching of the names of systems described in the text (fingerprint scanner, voiceprint etc.) to groups of people (sports students, welfare claimants). The necessary information is explicitly stated in one or two sentences of the text. For example, the sentence 'In some California housing estates, a key alone is insufficient to get someone in the door; his or her voiceprint must also be verified' allows the participant to match item 39 '*home owner*' to option D, '*voiceprint*'.

5.4   Analysis of variance

Having found indications of a relationship between strategy use and item type, we explored whether strategy use had an impact on participants' scores on each test section. Using one-way analysis of variance we compared the three student groups' use of strategies on each test section. Significant (p<.05) results were found for one or more strategies on the following test sections (Table 3.6).

Strategy 2 (*match similar words*), the most popular strategy overall, was associated with success on E2.1 (4-option Multiple Choice) and F3.2 (Matching). The answers to F3.2, which also yielded a significant effect for strategy 1 (*exact word match*) as we have seen above, involved explicitly stated information at the sentence level with cues provided by exact or near-exact matches between answer options and words in the text. E2.1 also yielded a significant effect for strategy 9 (*slow careful reading*) suggesting that similar word matches (perhaps between the phrase *the youngest readers* in item E17 and *beginner readers* in the text for example) might have served as a precursor to more careful and intensive reading in identifying the correct answers, which were mainly said to be found across sentences.

It is interesting that strategies 3 and 4 emerged as significant (p<.05) on sections F1.1 and F3.1, both sections on which strategy 3 (*look for parts of the text that the writer indicated to be important*) was the most popular strategy and strategy 4 (*read key parts of the text such as the introduction and conclusion*) also ranked among the five most selected strategies. This suggests that the more successful participants on these sections were able to make use of information at the text level in arriving at a correct response.

Table 3.6   Analysis of variance: Test response strategy by test section

Test section	Strategy	F	p(<.05)
E2.1	ST2	7.995	0.007
	ST9	2.313	0.136
E2.2	ST11	5.277	0.027
E2.3	ST8	4.372	0.043
E3.2	ST7*	8.338	0.007
	ST8	8.596	0.006
F1.1	ST3	5.643	0.023
	ST4	11.783	0.001
	ST12	4.123	0.049
F3.1	ST3	6.571	0.014
	ST4	14.871	0.000
F3.2	ST1	5.101	0.030
	ST2	4.334	0.045

* *The effect for ST7 was negative i.e. greater use of ST7 was associated with lower section scores*

General topic knowledge appears to have been beneficial in responding to F1.1. Further investigation indicated that it was the results on items 3 and 4 that were particularly affected by background knowledge. These two items were 3 *Just over half the nurses in the 1986 study believed that management understood the effects of shift work on them* and 4 *The Canadian study found that 'illness in the family' was a greater cause of absenteeism than 'work to do at home'*. It may be that participants with some experience of a working environment were better able to predict the answers (*No* and *Yes* respectively). This would appear to indicate a potential vulnerability in these two items that is highlighted by this retrospection exercise.

Strategy 8 was associated with higher scores on both E2.3 and E3.2. Although the formats were different, both of these test sections involved matching summaries to information or views given in the text. In E3.2 a four-way choice is offered between hopes expressed by the writer, fears expressed by the writer, fears expressed by others and facts reported by the writer. Grammatical knowledge may have proved useful in helping the participants to recognise that all of the hopes are expressed through 'will' constructions, the fears through 'may' and the facts through 'is + to be'.

5.5 Location of necessary information

Participants most often reported finding the information necessary to respond to the tasks *by putting information together across sentences* (2). This was selected most frequently on nine of the 15 test sections and was chosen at least once by 89% of participants. 1 (*within a single sentence*) was the most popular selection on four test sections and was chosen at least once by 76%. 3 (*by understanding how information in the whole text fits together*) was the most frequent selection on one section and was the second most popular choice overall, being chosen at least once by 82% of participants. The fourth and fifth options, 4 (*without reading the text*) and 5 (*could not answer the question*) were not often selected on any test section, but were selected for one or more items in total by 26% and 27% of participants respectively. Of the 234 answers reportedly given without reference to the text, 92 (39.3%) were correct. Nineteen of these occurred on Section F2.2 (against 13 incorrect guesses) and a further nine (against five incorrect guesses) on another section with Type 8 items (Identification of writer's views/claims or of information in a text – Yes/No/Not Given): E2.2. This suggests that Type 8 items may be particularly vulnerable to guessing – a point underlined by the discovery that the researchers were also able, without reading the texts, to give the correct answer to those items that had yielded more correct than incorrect test taker guesses.

Only a handful of items involved more than five participants reporting that they were unable to find an answer: Test E, items 11 (7 participants unable to find an answer, item facility [p =.35]), 12 (6 participants, p=.28), 32 (6 participants, p =.48) and 38 (6 participants, p =.46) and Test F item 13 (9 participants, p=.30). As the low item facility values above suggest, these were all among the more difficult items in their sections and most occurred towards the end, suggesting the effects of time pressure. The exception, item E32, occurred in section E3.1 (Sentence Completion) and required participants to find a second success of genetic research in finding the cause of disease (*cystic fibrosis*). The level of confusion that is suggested by the high number of participants unable to find an answer may be attributable both to the constructed response nature of the item (participants needed to refer to the passage for an answer, not to a list of given options) and to a lack of independence in the item, which seems to require that participants should identify the first success – *muscular dystrophy* (the answer to Item 31) – before being able to recognise the second.

In 11 of the 15 sections, the results of the current study were broadly consistent with the small-scale protocol study on the same test materials conducted by Weir et al (this volume) (see Table 3.7 below), although the participants in the earlier study were generally more likely to report finding information within sentences and, unlike many of those in the current study, did

Table 3.7 Location of necessary information: comparison with findings reported in Weir et al (this volume)

	Weir et al (this volume)			Current study		
Test section	Within sentence	Across sentences	Whole text	Within sentence	Across sentences	Whole text
E1.1		+			+	
E1.2	+			+		
E1.3	x					x
E2.1	x				x	
E2.2	x	+*			+	
E2.3		+			+	
E2.4			+			+
E3.1	+			+		
E3.2	x				x	
F1.1	+			+		
F1.2	x				x	
F2.1		+			+	
F2.2	x	+*			+	
F3.1		+			+	
F3.2	+			+		

* *In these two cases the participants found answers to near equal numbers of items in a section from information located within the sentence and from information distributed across sentences* not find information to answer questions by drawing on the text as a whole (except in responding to item E26 (Section E2.4) – choose a heading for the text).

This tendency for the participants in the current study to report drawing on more of the text than those in the earlier research, using information across sentences and across the whole text in responding, is also reflected in the four sections where the results were discrepant: E1.3, E2.1, E3.2 and F1.2. The differences may be explained at least in part by proficiency level, the Weir et al (this volume) participants being native speakers of English or language learners with a higher level of proficiency than most of the current participants.

These discrepancies may also have been an artefact of the research method as participants in the earlier study were asked not only to decide whether an answer was to be found within or across sentences, but also whether the information was explicitly stated or implicit. The explicit : implicit distinction was dropped in the current study because of the impracticality, revealed through piloting, of operationalising it sufficiently clearly for participants to use at a distance. The distinction between implicit and explicit information may have led the earlier (Weir et al this volume) participants to report finding the necessary information within the sentence even where this required bridging inferences based on other parts of the text.

This may be illustrated by item F1.1–2. The item requires participants to identify (Yes/No/Not Given) whether the following proposition is supported in the text: *Nurses in the Prince William Hospital study believed that there were benefits in taking as little sick leave as possible.* To answer, participants would need to relate information about the study (given in the statement, *The study reported here was conducted in the Prince William Hospital in Brisbane, Australia*) to the reported attitudes concerning sick pay (given in the two sentences, *A prevalent attitude amongst many nurses in the group selected for study was that there was no reward or recognition for not utilising the paid sick leave entitlement allowed them in their employment conditions. Therefore, they believed they may as well take the days off – sick or otherwise.*). Participants in the earlier study agreed that they had found the necessary information within the sentence. The theme of the study at the Prince William hospital, which had also appeared in item 1, could, for these participants, now be treated as 'given information' and could perhaps be inferred in responding to item 2. The key sentence presenting new information was, *they believed they may as well take the days off – sick or otherwise* and this may have provided enough to support a correct response to item 2. Without the distinction between implicit and explicit information, the largest group of current study participants (48%) reported finding the necessary information across rather than within the sentence (selected by 30%).

The clear discrepancy between the findings relating to E1.3 may point to alternative approaches to this item type (Type 4 summary completion with selected response). As this section involves completing a summary of the text, it is unsurprising that the participants in the current study tended to find answers by drawing on the text as a whole. However, the answer options are generally identical to or closely related to words in the text (e.g. question option – *honesty and openness* / text – *honest and open*; question option – *social record* / text – *social record.*) This implies that a direct word matching strategy starting from the answer options and focusing on sentence level propositions might, together with a degree of inferencing, have supported success on this section for the Weir et al (this volume) participants, although strategy 1 (*exact word matching*) was not a particularly popular choice on this section for participants in the current study.

6 Conclusion

Weir et al (this volume) reported that: the ' . . . major focus of the IELTS Academic Reading test appears to be on careful reading whereas the survey data reported here suggest that for university students expeditious skills and strategies are just as critical for academic study and in a number of cases more problematic for both L1 and L2 students.'

This was followed by a call for an extensive protocol-based study of the cognitive processing of students taking the IELTS Academic Reading test to illuminate whether this was the case. The current study provides clear evidence that, for most participants across the different task types, expeditious reading in fact plays an important role in the way they seek to answer the questions. We found that, consistently across test sections, the majority of participants chose to read the text through quickly and selectively before reading the question. The most popular test strategy was 2 – *quickly match words that appeared in the question with similar or related words in the text.* This emerged as the most popular selection on 10 of the 15 test sections with 83% of participants reporting using this strategy at least once.

However, this does not imply that expeditious reading is tested separately from careful reading in IELTS, but rather that the two appear to be integrated. Two key strategies that were noted in the earlier study were also prominent in participant self-reported behaviour in this. 10 – *read relevant parts of the text again* appears as the most popular choice on two test sections and was selected at least once by 77% of participants. 3 – *look for parts of the text that the writer indicates to be important* was the most popular strategy on another two test sections and was selected at least once by 76% of participants.

The picture of reading in response to IELTS test items that emerges is consistent with the general approach to academic reading reported by student readers in the Weir et al (this volume) protocol study: quick and selective search reading followed by intensive careful reading of relevant text parts.

It is also clear from the protocol data that IELTS participants have extensive scope for careful reading. Because IELTS includes 13 or 14 questions relating to each short text, there are opportunities to read the text or parts of it several times in finding the information necessary to respond. The longest text here (E3) has 1,034 words (including the title and glossary) and the shortest (E2) has 586. If a participant were to spend about one third of the available time reading the questions and writing the responses, they would still only need to read at the very slow rate of around 50 to 75 words per minute in order to read through each text once. IELTS allows for very intensive careful reading of material that we have already seen is probably of only modest difficulty when compared with the introductory undergraduate readings described in Weir et al (this volume).

Earlier concerns by native speaker informants in Weir et al (this volume) relating to the number of items that seemed to focus on the sentence level were lessened. Participants most often reported finding the information necessary to respond to the tasks by putting information together across sentences (2). This was selected most frequently on nine of the 15 test sections and was chosen at least once by 89% of participants. There is some evidence that there may nonetheless be a high proportion of test items where the answer can be found within one sentence. 1 (within a single sentence) was the most popular selection on four test sections and was chosen at least once by 76% of participants.

Fears that IELTS was not addressing understanding at the whole text level also appear to be ill grounded. 3 (by understanding how information in the whole text fits together) was the most frequent selection on one section and was the second most popular choice overall, being chosen at least once by 82% of participants. This points to the value and necessity, in addition to expert judgement, of using protocol studies as a means of establishing what participants themselves perceive they are doing when they respond to the tasks.

The demonstrated relationship between the adoption of certain strategies and success on various items indicates the critical importance of ensuring that there is a clear match between the strategies that are being elicited by items in a test and the construct that is being measured. Most formats in IELTS emerge from this study in a positive light in this respect but there must be some concern about Type 8 items (Identification of Writer's Views/Claims or of Information in a Text – Yes/No/Not Given): E2.2, which may be particularly vulnerable to guessing.

Unfortunately for the test developer, it is also apparent that the relationship between item type and response strategy may not be straightforward. Certain item types do appear to provoke the use of certain strategies; multiple choice and summary completion are associated with direct word matching, for example. On the other hand, task type is not a very reliable predictor of patterns of strategy use. Some test sections employing Yes/No/Not Given items encouraged the use of expeditious reading strategies such as looking for parts of the text the writer indicates to be important or reading key parts (F1.1), while others do not (F2.2). Some response strategies were common across test sections, particularly the lexical relatedness strategy 2 (*quickly match words that appeared in the question with similar or related words in the text*) and careful reading strategies 9 (*read the text slowly and carefully*) and 10 (*read relevant parts of the text again*). While this suggests that IELTS does involve the use of expeditious reading strategies on the part of participants, this is almost invariably associated with careful reading of relevant passages. Perhaps the only means of testing expeditious reading is to enforce time constraints; Section E2.4 is the only section that appears to encourage expeditious reading without careful reading. This section includes a single item and occurs at the end of a test section, suggesting that time constraints were likely to have played a part in determining participant response strategies.

In brief, the researchers recommend that the IELTS partners should consider the following:

- as part of the pretesting process, make routine use of response protocols to investigate how test takers respond to test tasks – response strategies cannot be assumed from item type
- ensure that each test form includes a variety of task types that are likely to require both expeditious and careful reading and that involve both global and local information processing
- give close attention, in trialling, to the possibility of guessing correct answers, particularly to Yes/No/Not Given items
- impose time constraints on part of the test to encourage the use of the expeditious reading strategies necessary for university study.

References

Afflerbach, P and Johnston, P (1984) On the use of verbal reports in reading research, *Journal of Reading Behaviour* 16 (4), 307–321.

Alderson, J C (1990a) Testing reading comprehension skills (Part One), *Reading in a Foreign Language* 6 (2), 425–438.

Alderson, J C (1990b) Testing reading comprehension skills: getting students to talk about taking a reading test (Part Two), *Reading in a Foreign Language* 7 (1), 465–503.

Alderson, J C (2000) *Assessing Reading*, Cambridge: Cambridge University Press.

Alderson, J C (2005) *Diagnosing Foreign Language Proficiency: the Interface between Learning and Assessment*, London: Continuum.

Alderson, J C and Lukmani, Y (1989) Cognition and Reading: cognitive levels as embodied in test questions, *Reading in a Foreign Language* 5 (2), 253–270.

Anderson, N, Bachman, L F, Perkins, K and Cohen, A (1991) An exploratory study into the construct validity of a reading comprehension test: triangulation of data sources, *Language Testing* 8 (1), 41–66.

Bachman, L F, Kunnan, A, Vanniarajan, S and Lynch, B (1988) Task and ability analysis as a basis for examining content and construct comparability in two EFL proficiency test batteries, *Language Testing* 5, 128–159.

Block, E (1986) The comprehension strategies of second language readers, *TESOL Quarterly* 20 (3), 463–94.

Carver, R (1992) Reading Rate: theory, research and practical implications, *Journal of Reading* 36 (2), 84–95.

Cohen, A (1984) On taking language tests: What the students report, *Language Testing* 1, 70–81.

Cohen, A (2006/7) The coming of age of research on test-taking strategies, *Language Assessment Quarterly* 3 (4), 307–331.

Cordon, L, and Day, J (1996) Strategy use on standardized reading comprehension tests, *Journal of Educational Psychology* 88, 288–95.

Crain-Thoreson, C, Lippman, M and McClendon-Magnuson, D (1997) Windows on comprehension: reading comprehension processes as revealed by two think-aloud procedures, *Journal of Educational Psychology* 89 (4), 579–591.

Ericsson, K and Simon, H (1993) *Protocol Analysis: verbal report as data,* Cambridge, MA: MIT Press.

Faerch, C and Kasper, G (Eds) (1987) *Introspection in Second Language Research,* Clevedon: Multilingual Matters.

Feldmann, U, and Stemmer, B (1987) Thin____ Aloud A____ Retrospective Da___ in C-Te___ Taking: Diffe____ Languages Diffe____ Learners- Sa_____ Approaches?, in (Eds) Faerch, C and Kasper, G, *Introspection in Second Language Research,* Clevedon: Multilingual Matters, 251–267.

Field, J (2004) *Psycholinguistics: the Key Concepts,* London: Routledge.

Gass, S M and Mackey, A (2000) *Simulated Recall Methodology in Second Language Research,* Mahwah, N J: Lawrence Erlbaum.

Green, A (1998) *Verbal Protocol Analysis in Language Testing Research,* Studies in Language Testing volume 5, Cambridge: Cambridge University Press.

Grotjahn, R (1987) On the methodological basis of introspective methods, in Faerch, C and Kasper, G (Eds) *Introspection in Second Language Research,* Clevedon: Multilingual Matters, 54–81.

Hawkey, R (2006) *Impact Theory and Practice: Studies of the IELTS Test and Progetto Lingue 2000,* Studies in Language Testing volume 24, Cambridge: Cambridge University Press.

Hoover, W A, and Tunmer, W E (1993) The components of reading, in Thompson, G B, Tunmer, W E and Nicholson, T (Eds) *Reading Acquisition Processes,* Great Britain: WBC Print Ltd, 1–19.

Hosenfeld, C (1977) A preliminary investigation of the reading strategies of successful and nonsuccessful second language learners, *System* 5 (2), 110–123.

Khalifa, H and Weir, C J (2009) *Examining Reading: Research and Practice in Assessing Second Language Reading,* Studies in Language Testing volume 29, Cambridge: UCLES/Cambridge University Press.

Kong, D (1996) *An empirical study of the strategies adopted by EFL readers while reading EAP materials for main ideas – implications for teaching and testing reading,* unpublished MA TEFL dissertation, CALS, University of Reading.

Lumley, T (1993) The notion of sub-skills in reading comprehension tests: An EAP example, *Language Testing* 10, 211–234.

Nevo, N (1989) Test-taking strategies on a multiple-choice test of reading comprehension, *Language Testing* 6 (2), 199–215.

Perkins, K (1992) The effect of passage and topical structure types on ESL reading comprehension difficulty, *Language Testing* 9 (2), 163–172.

Phakiti, A (2003) A closer look at the relationship of cognitive and metacognitive strategy use to EFL reading achievement test performance, *Language Testing* 20 (1), 26–56.

Pressley, M and Afflerbach, P (1995) *Verbal Protocols of Reading: the Nature of Constructively Responsive Reading,* Hillsdale, NJ: Lawrence Erlbaum.

Rayner, K and Pollatsek, A (1989) *The Psychology of Reading,* Englewood Cliffs, NJ: Prentice Hall.

Stratman, J and Hamp-Lyons, L (1994) Reactivity in concurrent think-aloud protocols, in Smagorinsky, P (Ed.) *Speaking about Writing: Reflections on Research Methodology,* CA: Sage, 89–111.

Teasdale, A (1989) *Introspection and judgemental approaches to content validation: a study using the test in English for educational purposes,* unpublished MA dissertation, University of Reading.

Thorndike, E L (1917) Reading as reasoning, *Journal of Educational Psychology* 8, 323–332.

Urquhart, A and Weir, C J (1998) *Reading in a Second Language: Process, Product and Practice,* London: Longman.

Vipond, D (1980) Micro- and macro-processes in text comprehension, *Journal of Verbal Learning and Verbal Behaviour* 19, 276–296.

Weakley, S (1993) *Procedures in the content validation of an EAP proficiency test of reading comprehension,* unpublished MA TEFL dissertation, CALS, University of Reading.

Weir, C J (2005) *Language Testing and Validation: an Evidence Based Approach,* Basingstoke: Palgrave Macmillan.

Weir, C J and Porter, D (1994) The multi-divisibility or unitary nature of reading: the language tester between Scylla and Charybdis, *Reading in a Foreign Language* 10 (2), 1–19.

Weir, C J, Hawkey, R, Green, A, Ünaldi, A and Devi, S (2009) The relationship between the academic reading construct as measured by IELTS and the reading experiences of students in the first year of their courses at a British university, in Thompson, P (Ed.) *IELTS Research Reports Volume 9*, British Council/IELTS Australia, 97–156.

Weir, C J, Yang, H and Jin, Y (2000) *An Empirical Investigation of the Componentiality of L2 Reading in English for Academic Purposes,* Studies in Language Testing volume 12, Cambridge: UCLES/Cambridge University Press.

Appendix 3.1
Instructions to participants

Instructions

You will have **30 minutes** to do the test and fill out the questionnaire.

Please answer the test questions on the ANSWER sheet provided. After answering each question, please fill out the QUESTIONNAIRE for that question.

Questionnaire Section 1

In this section of the questionnaire, please describe what you did before you read the test questions.

For example, if you read the text or part of it slowly and carefully before reading questions 1 to 6 of the test, you should tick the box on the right like this:

Before reading questions 1 to 6, I ...		
a	read the text or part of it slowly and carefully.	☑
b	read the text or part of it quickly and selectively to get a general idea of what it was about.	☐
c	did not read the text.	☐

Questionnaire Section 2

After answering each question on the test, please turn immediately to the questionnaire and tick the sentences (1 to 12) that describe what you did when you answered the test question. Then go on to the next test question, and repeat the same procedure until you have answered all the questions.

For example, immediately after answering question 1 if you *matched words that appeared in the question with exactly the same words in the text*, you would tick sentence 1 under Q1. If you also *worked out the meaning of a difficult word in the text*, you would also tick sentence 6:

		Q1	Q2
1	match words that appeared in the question with exactly the same words in the text	✓	☐
2	quickly match words that appeared in the question with similar or related words in the text	☐	☐
3	look for parts of the text that the writer indicates to be important	☐	☐
4	read key parts of the text such as the introduction and conclusion	☐	☐
5	work out the meaning of a difficult word in the question	☐	☐
6	work out the meaning of a difficult word in the text	✓	☐
7	use my knowledge of vocabulary	☐	☐
8	use my knowledge of grammar	☐	☐
9	read the text or part of it slowly and carefully	☐	☐
10	read relevant parts of the text again	☐	☐
11	use my knowledge of how texts like this are organised	☐	☐
12	connect information from the text with knowledge I already have	☐	☐

Sentences 13 to 17 are about how you found the answer to each question. If you found the answer within a single sentence, you would tick sentence 13.

	Q 1	Q 2
13 within a single sentence	☑	☐
14 by putting information together across sentences	☐	☐
15 by understanding how information in the whole text fits together	☐	☐
16 I knew the answer without reading the text	☐	☐
17 I could not answer the question	☐	☐

Thank you very much for your cooperation.

Appendix 3.2
Example answer paper

Name:

Age: Gender: Male / Female

First Language:

Date of most recent IELTS test:

IELTS Reading score:

Subject you intend to study at university:

Question number	IELTS Reading Test Answers	
1		
2		
3		
4		
5		
6		
7		
8		
9		
10		
11		
12		
13		

Appendix 3.3
Example participant retrospection form

Name: _____

Section 1: Tick(✓) the sentence that best describes what you did.

Before reading questions 14 to 19, I ...

a   read the text or part of it slowly and carefully. ☐

     read the text or part of it quickly and ☐

b   selectively to get a general idea of what it was about. ☐

c   did not read the text. ☐

Before reading questions 20 to 26, I ...

a   read the text or part of it slowly and carefully. ☐

     read the text or part of it quickly and ☐

b   selectively to get a general idea of what it was about. ☐

c   did not read the text. ☐

Section 2: Tick (✓) any sentences that describe what you did when you answered each question on the test. You may tick more than one sentence for each question on the test.

To find the answer to the question, I tried to...

		Q14	Q15	Q16	Q17	Q18	Q19	Q20	Q21	Q22	Q23	Q24	Q25	Q26
1	match words that appeared in the question with exactly the same words in the text	☐	☐	☐	☐	☐	☐	☐	☐	☐	☐	☐	☐	☐
2	quickly match words that appeared in the question with similar or related words in the text	☐	☐	☐	☐	☐	☐	☐	☐	☐	☐	☐	☐	☐
3	look for parts of the text that the writer indicates to be important	☐	☐	☐	☐	☐	☐	☐	☐	☐	☐	☐	☐	☐
4	read key parts of the text such as the introduction and conclusion	☐	☐	☐	☐	☐	☐	☐	☐	☐	☐	☐	☐	☐
5	work out the meaning of a difficult word in the question	☐	☐	☐	☐	☐	☐	☐	☐	☐	☐	☐	☐	☐
6	work out the meaning of a difficult word in the text	☐	☐	☐	☐	☐	☐	☐	☐	☐	☐	☐	☐	☐
7	use my knowledge of vocabulary	☐	☐	☐	☐	☐	☐	☐	☐	☐	☐	☐	☐	☐
8	use my knowledge of grammar	☐	☐	☐	☐	☐	☐	☐	☐	☐	☐	☐	☐	☐
9	read the text or part of it slowly and carefully	☐	☐	☐	☐	☐	☐	☐	☐	☐	☐	☐	☐	☐
10	read relevant parts of the text again	☐	☐	☐	☐	☐	☐	☐	☐	☐	☐	☐	☐	☐
11	use my knowledge of how texts like this are organised	☐	☐	☐	☐	☐	☐	☐	☐	☐	☐	☐	☐	☐
12	connect information from the text with knowledge I already have	☐	☐	☐	☐	☐	☐	☐	☐	☐	☐	☐	☐	☐

I found the answer...

		Q14	Q15	Q16	Q17	Q18	Q19	Q20	Q21	Q22	Q23	Q24	Q25	Q26
13	within a single sentence	☐	☐	☐	☐	☐	☐	☐	☐	☐	☐	☐	☐	☐
14	by putting information together across sentences	☐	☐	☐	☐	☐	☐	☐	☐	☐	☐	☐	☐	☐
15	by understanding how information in the whole text fits together	☐	☐	☐	☐	☐	☐	☐	☐	☐	☐	☐	☐	☐
16	I knew the answer without reading the text	☐	☐	☐	☐	☐	☐	☐	☐	☐	☐	☐	☐	☐
17	I could not answer the question	☐	☐	☐	☐	☐	☐	☐	☐	☐	☐	☐	☐	☐

Appendix 3.4 Text preview, test response strategy use and locating information by test section

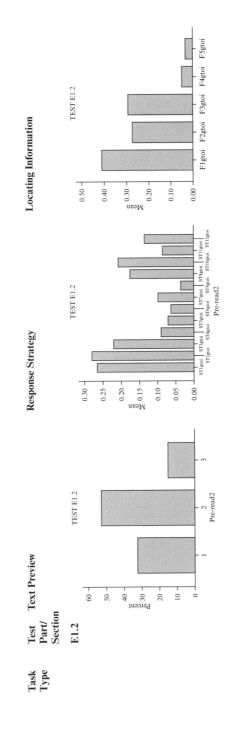

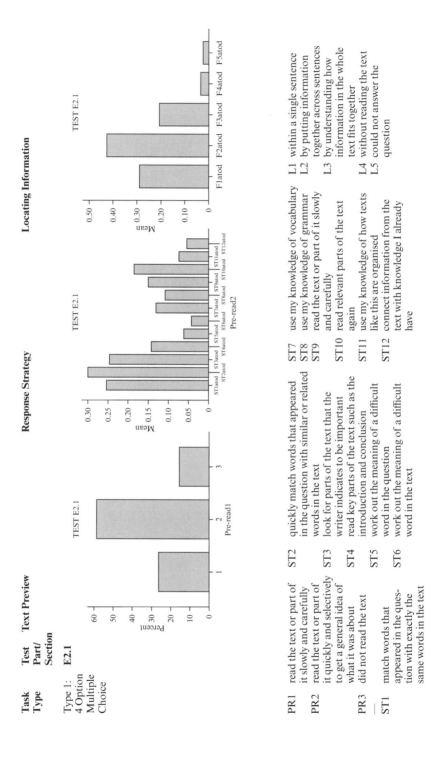

Task Type | **Test Part/Section** | **Text Preview** | **Response Strategy** | **Locating Information**

Test Part/Section: **E2.1**

Type 1: 4 Option Multiple Choice

PR1 read the text or part of it slowly and carefully
PR2 read the text or part of it quickly and selectively to get a general idea of what it was about
PR3 did not read the text

ST1 match words that appeared in the question with exactly the same words in the text
ST2 quickly match words that appeared in the question with similar or related words in the text
ST3 look for parts of the text that the writer indicates to be important
ST4 read key parts of the text such as the introduction and conclusion
ST5 work out the meaning of a difficult word in the question
ST6 work out the meaning of a difficult word in the text
ST7 use my knowledge of vocabulary
ST8 use my knowledge of grammar
ST9 read the text or part of it slowly and carefully
ST10 read relevant parts of the text again
ST11 use my knowledge of how texts like this are organised
ST12 connect information from the text with knowledge I already have

L1 within a single sentence
L2 by putting information together across sentences
L3 by understanding how information in the whole text fits together
L4 without reading the text
L5 could not answer the question

Task Type	Test Part/Section	Text Preview	Response Strategy	Locating Information

Type 6: **F3.1**
Choosing
Headings
(for Para-
graphs or
Sections
of a Text)

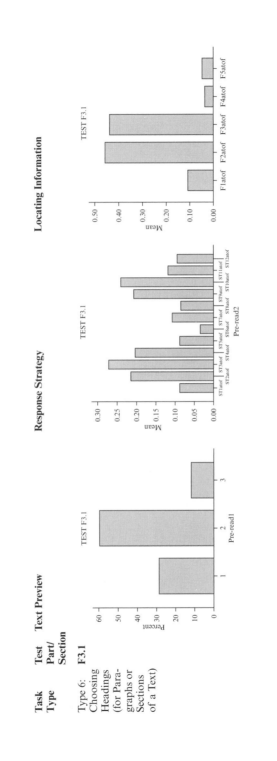

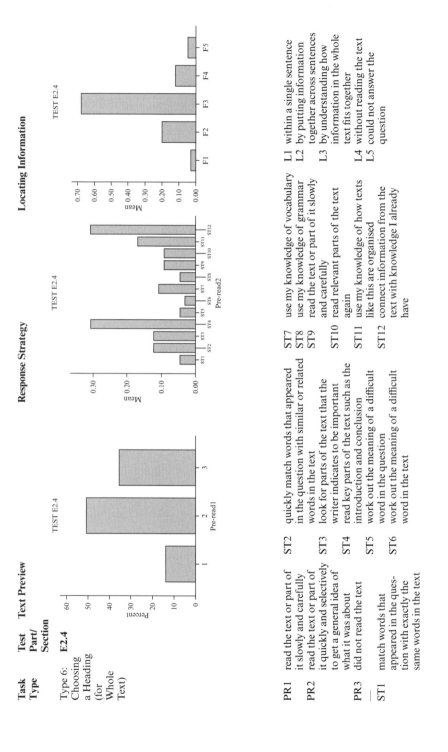

Task Type | Test Part/Section | Text Preview | Response Strategy | Locating Information

Type 6: Choosing a Heading (for Whole Text)

Test Part/Section: **E2.4**

PR1 read the text or part of it slowly and carefully
PR2 read the text or part of it quickly and selectively to get a general idea of what it was about
PR3 did not read the text

ST1 match words that appeared in the question with exactly the same words in the text
ST2 quickly match words that appeared in the question with similar or related words in the text
ST3 look for parts of the text that the writer indicates to be important
ST4 read key parts of the text such as the introduction and conclusion
ST5 work out the meaning of a difficult word in the question
ST6 work out the meaning of a difficult word in the text
ST7 use my knowledge of vocabulary
ST8 use my knowledge of grammar
ST9 read the text or part of it slowly and carefully
ST10 read relevant parts of the text again
ST11 use my knowledge of how texts like this are organised
ST12 connect information from the text with knowledge I already have

L1 within a single sentence
L2 by putting information together across sentences
L3 by understanding how information in the whole text fits together
L4 without reading the text
L5 could not answer the question

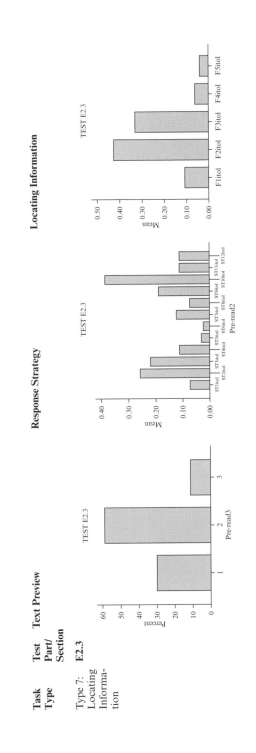

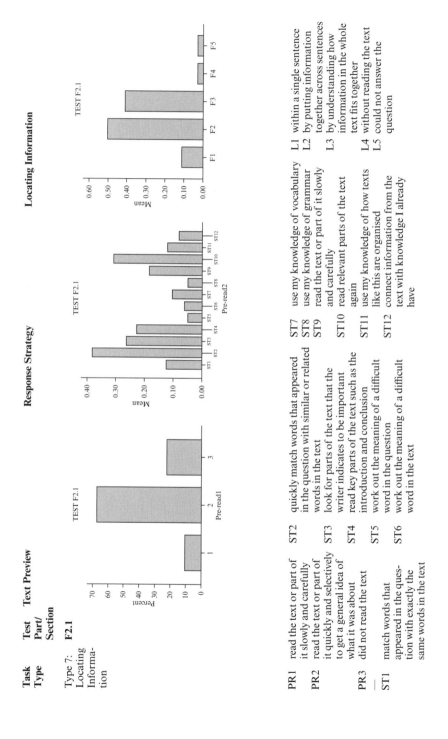

Task Type | **Test Part/Section** | **Text Preview** | **Response Strategy** | **Locating Information**

Type 7: Locating Information | F2.1

TEST F2.1 — Pre-read1 (Percent)

TEST F2.1 — Pre-read2 (Mean)

TEST F2.1 — Locating Information (Mean)

PR1 read the text or part of it slowly and carefully

PR2 read the text or part of it quickly and selectively to get a general idea of what it was about

PR3 did not read the text

ST1 match words that appeared in the question with exactly the same words in the text

ST2 quickly match words that appeared in the question with similar or related words in the text

ST3 look for parts of the text that the writer indicates to be important

ST4 read key parts of the text such as the introduction and conclusion

ST5 work out the meaning of a difficult word in the question

ST6 work out the meaning of a difficult word in the text

ST7 use my knowledge of vocabulary

ST8 use my knowledge of grammar

ST9 read the text or part of it slowly and carefully

ST10 read relevant parts of the text again

ST11 use my knowledge of how texts like this are organised

ST12 connect information from the text with knowledge I already have

L1 within a single sentence

L2 by putting information together across sentences

L3 by understanding how information in the whole text fits together

L4 without reading the text

L5 could not answer the question

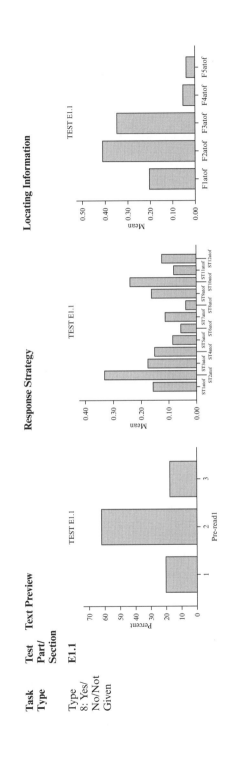

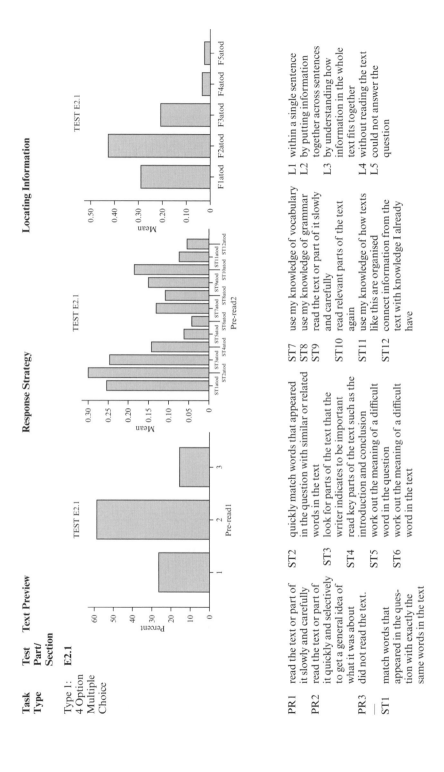

Task Type	Test Part/ Section	Text Preview
Type 3: Sentence Comple-tion	E3.1	

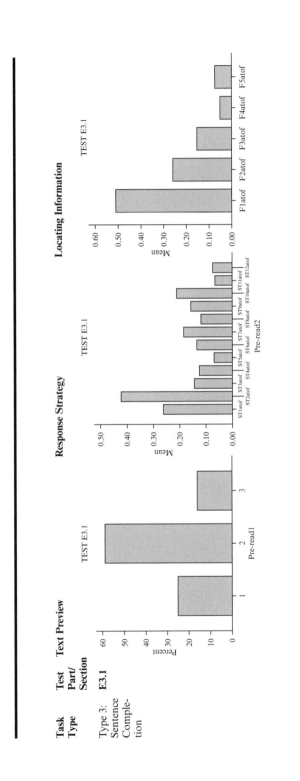

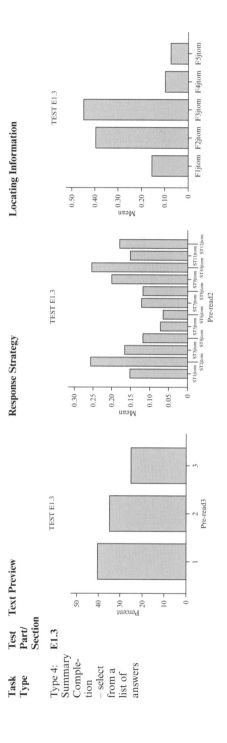

Task Type	Test	Test Part/Section	Text Preview	Response Strategy	Locating Information

Type 4: Summary Completion – select from a list of answers

E1.3

TEST E1.3

TEST E1.3

TEST E1.3

PR1 read the text or part of it slowly and carefully
PR2 read the text or part of it quickly and selectively to get a general idea of what it was about
PR3 did not read the text

ST1 match words that appeared in the question with exactly the same words in the text
ST2 quickly match words that appeared in the question with similar or related words in the text
ST3 look for parts of the text that the writer indicates to be important
ST4 read key parts of the text such as the introduction and conclusion
ST5 work out the meaning of a difficult word in the question
ST6 work out the meaning of a difficult word in the text

ST7 use my knowledge of vocabulary
ST8 use my knowledge of grammar
ST9 read the text or part of it slowly and carefully
ST10 read relevant parts of the text again
ST11 use my knowledge of how texts like this are organised
ST12 connect information from the text with knowledge I already have

L1 within a single sentence
L2 by putting information together across sentences
L3 by understanding how information in the whole text fits together
L4 without reading the text
L5 could not answer the question

Task Type	Test Part/Section	Text Preview
Type 4: Summary Completion – select words from the passage	**F1.2**	

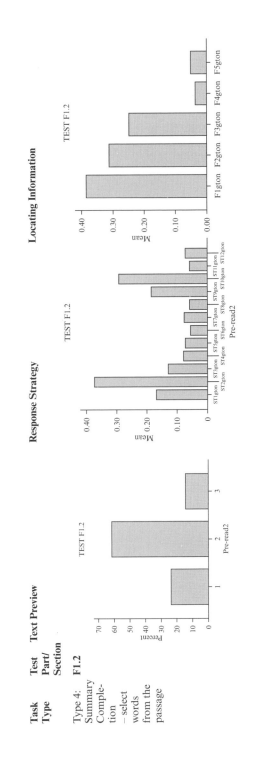

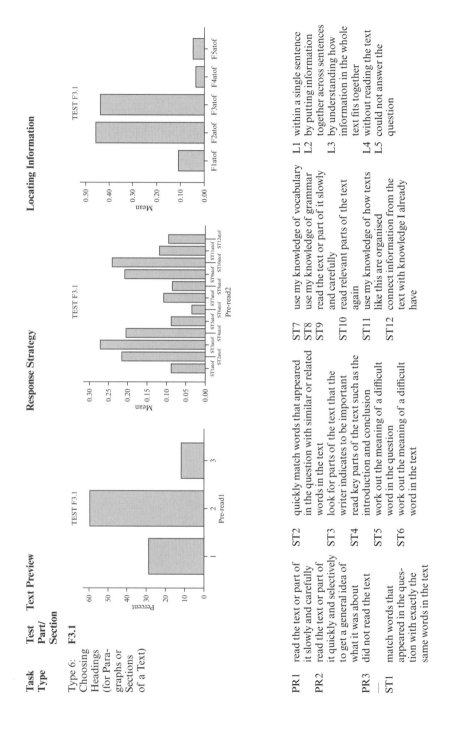

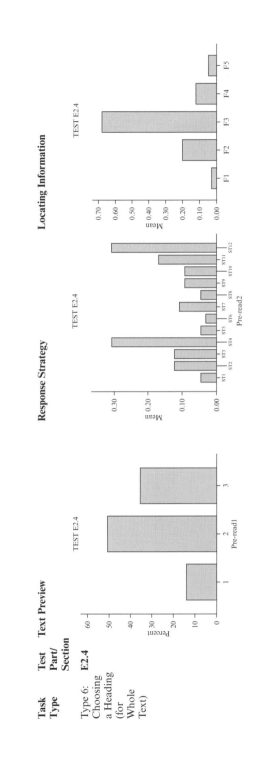

Task Type	Test Part/ Section	Text Preview	Response Strategy	Locating Information
Type 6: Choosing a Heading (for Whole Text)	E2.4			

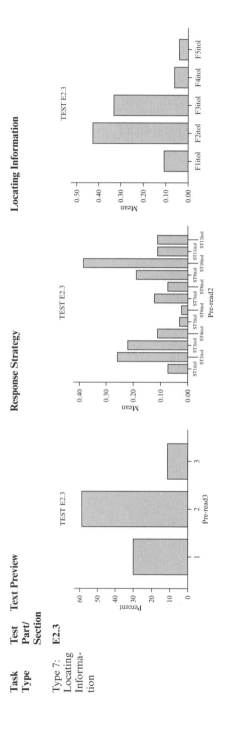

Task Type	Test Part/Section	Text Preview	Response Strategy	Locating Information
Type 7: Locating Information	E2.3			

PR1 read the text or part of it slowly and carefully
PR2 read the text or part of it quickly and selectively to get a general idea of what it was about
PR3 did not read the text

ST1 match words that appeared in the question with exactly the same words in the text
ST2 quickly match words that appeared in the question with similar or related words in the text
ST3 look for parts of the text that the writer indicates to be important
ST4 read key parts of the text such as the introduction and conclusion
ST5 work out the meaning of a difficult word in the question
ST6 work out the meaning of a difficult word in the text

ST7 use my knowledge of vocabulary
ST8 use my knowledge of grammar
ST9 read the text or part of it slowly and carefully
ST10 read relevant parts of the text again
ST11 use my knowledge of how texts like this are organised
ST12 connect information from the text with knowledge I already have

L1 within a single sentence
L2 by putting information together across sentences
L3 by understanding how information in the whole text fits together
L4 without reading the text
L5 could not answer the question

Task Type	Test Part/ Section	Text Preview

Type 7: Locating Information

F2.1

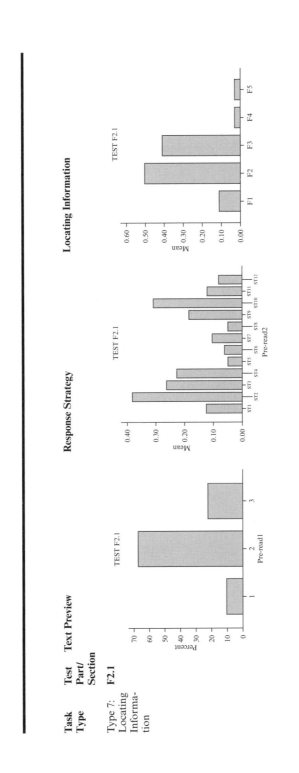

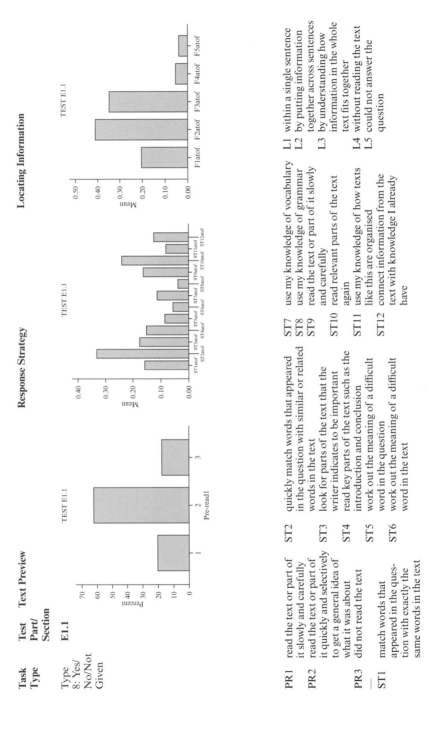

Task Type | **Test Part/Section** | **Text Preview** | **Response Strategy** | **Locating Information**

Type 8: Yes/No/Not Given | E1.1

PR1 read the text or part of it slowly and carefully
PR2 read the text or part of it quickly and selectively to get a general idea of what it was about
PR3 did not read the text
—
ST1 match words that appeared in the question with exactly the same words in the text

ST2 quickly match words that appeared in the question with similar or related words in the text
ST3 look for parts of the text that the writer indicates to be important
ST4 read key parts of the text such as the introduction and conclusion
ST5 work out the meaning of a difficult word in the question
ST6 work out the meaning of a difficult word in the text

ST7 use my knowledge of vocabulary
ST8 use my knowledge of grammar
ST9 read the text or part of it slowly and carefully
ST10 read relevant parts of the text again
ST11 use my knowledge of how texts like this are organised
ST12 connect information from the text with knowledge I already have

L1 within a single sentence
L2 by putting information together across sentences
L3 by understanding how information in the whole text fits together
L4 without reading the text
L5 could not answer the question

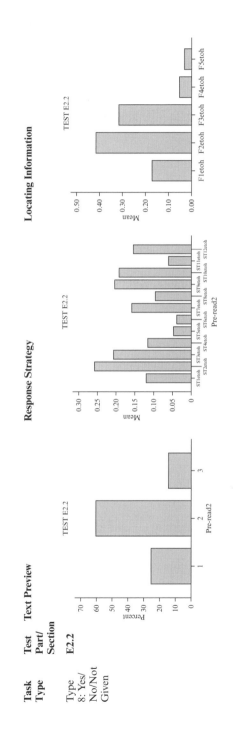

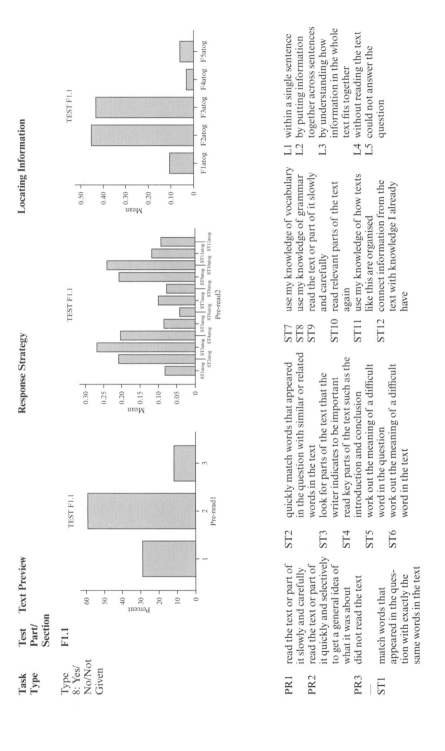

Task Type: Type 8: Yes/No/Not Given

Test Part/Section: F1.1

Text Preview — TEST F1.1 — Pre-read1 (Percent)

Response Strategy — TEST F1.1 — Pre-read2 (Mean)

Locating Information — TEST F1.1 (Mean)

PR1 read the text or part of it slowly and carefully
PR2 read the text or part of it quickly and selectively to get a general idea of what it was about
PR3 did not read the text

ST1 match words that appeared in the question with exactly the same words in the text
ST2 quickly match words that appeared in the question with similar or related words in the text
ST3 look for parts of the text that the writer indicates to be important
ST4 read key parts of the text such as the introduction and conclusion
ST5 work out the meaning of a difficult word in the question
ST6 work out the meaning of a difficult word in the text
ST7 use my knowledge of vocabulary
ST8 use my knowledge of grammar
ST9 read the text or part of it slowly and carefully
ST10 read relevant parts of the text again
ST11 use my knowledge of how texts like this are organised
ST12 connect information from the text with knowledge I already have

L1 within a single sentence
L2 by putting information together across sentences
L3 by understanding how information in the whole text fits together
L4 without reading the text
L5 could not answer the question

Task Type	Test Part/Section	Text Preview
Type 8: Yes/No/Not Given	**F2.2**	

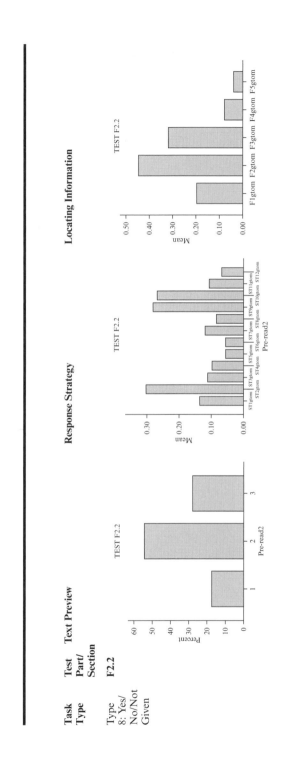

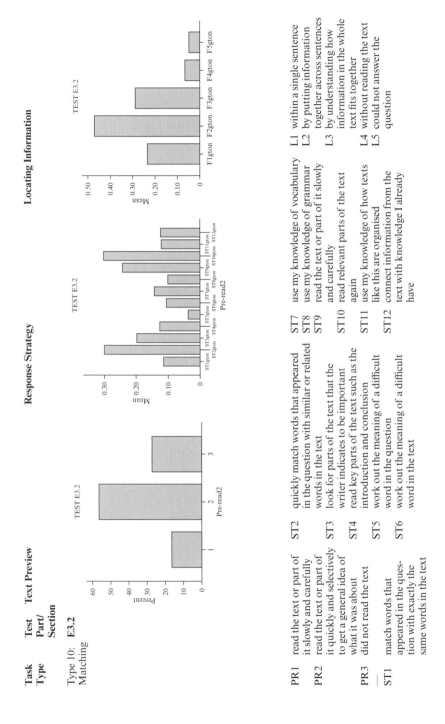

Task Type **Test** **Text Preview**

Test Part/ Section

Type 10: **E3.2**
Matching

TEST E3.2

Percent: 60, 50, 40, 30, 20, 10, 0

Pre-read2: 1, 2, 3

Response Strategy

TEST E3.2

Mean: 0.30, 0.20, 0.10, 0

Pre-read2: ST1gton ST3gton ST5gton ST7gton ST9gton ST11gton
ST2gton ST4gton ST6gton ST8gton ST10gton ST12gton

Locating Information

TEST E3.2

Mean: 0.50, 0.40, 0.30, 0.20, 0.10, 0

F1gton F2gton F3gton F4gton F5gton

PR1 read the text or part of it slowly and carefully
PR2 read the text or part of it quickly and selectively to get a general idea of what it was about
PR3 did not read the text
—
ST1 match words that appeared in the question with exactly the same words in the text

ST2 quickly match words that appeared in the question with similar or related words in the text
ST3 look for parts of the text that the writer indicates to be important
ST4 read key parts of the text such as the introduction and conclusion
ST5 work out the meaning of a difficult word in the question
ST6 work out the meaning of a difficult word in the text

ST7 use my knowledge of vocabulary
ST8 use my knowledge of grammar
ST9 read the text or part of it slowly and carefully
ST10 read relevant parts of the text again
ST11 use my knowledge of how texts like this are organised
ST12 connect information from the text with knowledge I already have

L1 within a single sentence
L2 by putting information together across sentences
L3 by understanding how information in the whole text fits together
L4 without reading the text
L5 could not answer the question

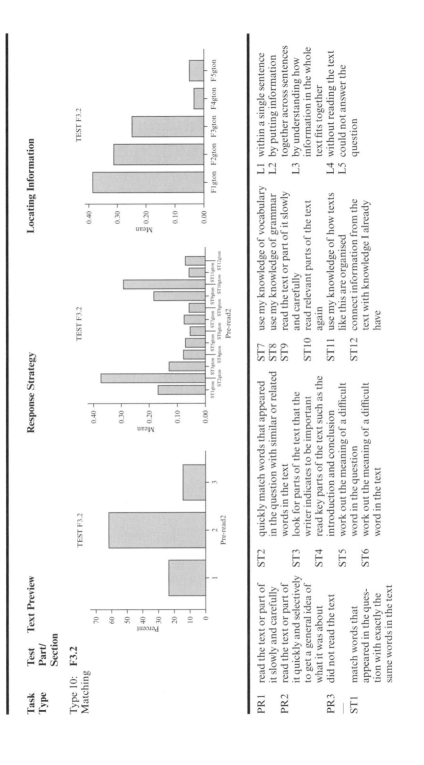

Task Type   **Test Part/Section**   **Text Preview**   **Response Strategy**   **Locating Information**

Type 10: Matching   **F3.2**

PR1 read the text or part of it slowly and carefully

PR2 read the text or part of it quickly and selectively to get a general idea of what it was about

PR3 did not read the text

ST1 match words that appeared in the question with exactly the same words in the text

ST2 quickly match words that appeared in the question with similar or related words in the text

ST3 look for parts of the text that the writer indicates to be important

ST4 read key parts of the text such as the introduction and conclusion

ST5 work out the meaning of a difficult word in the question

ST6 work out the meaning of a difficult word in the text

ST7 use my knowledge of vocabulary

ST8 use my knowledge of grammar

ST9 read the text or part of it slowly and carefully

ST10 read relevant parts of the text again

ST11 use my knowledge of how texts like this are organised

ST12 connect information from the text with knowledge I already have

L1 within a single sentence

L2 by putting information together across sentences

L3 by understanding how information in the whole text fits together

L4 without reading the text

L5 could not answer the question

4

An empirical investigation of the process of writing Academic Reading test items for the International English Language Testing System

Anthony Green and Roger Hawkey
University of Bedfordshire, UK

Abstract

This report describes a study of reading test text selection, item writing and editing processes, with particular reference to these areas of test production for the IELTS Academic Reading test. Based on retrospective reports and direct observation, the report compares how trained and untrained item writers select and edit reading texts to make them suitable for a task-based test of reading and how they generate the accompanying items. Both individual and collective test editing processes are investigated.

For Phase 1 of the study, item writers were invited to respond to a questionnaire on their academic and language teaching and testing background, experience of IELTS and comments on its Reading module (see Appendix 4.2). Two groups of participants were selected: four officially trained IELTS item writers (the experienced group) and three teachers of English for academic purposes who had prepared students to take IELTS, but had no previous experience of item writing for the IELTS Academic Reading module (the non-experienced group). In Phase 2 of the project both groups were asked to select and prepare texts and accompanying items for an IELTS Academic Reading test, and to bring their texts and items to separate interview and focus group sessions. In the first of these sessions, participants were interviewed on how they had selected and edited their texts and how they had generated the items. In a second session, the item writers worked in their two groups to further refine the texts and items to make them more suitable for the test (as the trained item writers would normally do in a test editing meeting).

The analyses of the texts and accompanying items produced by each group, and of the discussions at all the Phase 2 sessions have produced valuable insights into the processes of text selection, adaptation and item writing. The differences observed between the experienced and non-experienced groups help to highlight the skills required for effective item writing for the IELTS Academic Reading test, while at the same time suggesting improvements that could be made to the item production process so that it might more fully operationalise the IELTS reading construct.

1 Aims

This research report describes a study of reading, test text selection, item writing and editing processes, areas of test production that have rarely been transparent to those outside testing organisations. Based on retrospective reports, direct observation and analyses of the texts produced, the report compares how trained and untrained item writers select and edit reading texts to make them suitable for a task-based test of reading and how they generate the accompanying items. Both individual and collective editing processes are investigated. The analyses in the study are expected to inform future high-stakes reading test setting and assessment procedures, in particular for examination providers.

2 Background and related research

2.1 A socio-cognitive test validation framework

The research is informed by the socio-cognitive test validation framework (Weir 2005), which underpins test design at Cambridge ESOL (Khalifa and ffrench 2008). The framework, further developed at the Centre for Research in Language Learning and Assessment (CRELLA) at the University of Bedfordshire, is so named because it gives attention both to context and to cognition in relating language test tasks to the target language use domain. As outlined in Khalifa and Weir (2009), Weir, Hawkey, Green, Ünaldi and Devi (Chapter 1 of this volume) and Weir, Hawkey, Green and Devi (Chapter 3 of this volume) and, in the socio-cognitive approach, difficulty in reading is seen to be a function of i) the complexity of text and ii) the level of processing required to fulfil the reading purpose.

In Weir et al (Chapter 1 of this volume) IELTS texts were analysed against 12 criteria derived from the L2 reading comprehension literature (Alderson, Figueras, Kuijper, Nold, Takala and Tardieu 2004, Bachman, Davidson, Ryan and Choi 1995, Enright, Grabe, Koda, Mosenthal, Mulcahy-Ernt and Schedl 2000, Fortus, Coriat and Ford 1998, Freedle and Kostin 1993 and Khalifa and Weir 2009). These criteria included: *vocabulary, grammar, readability, cohesion, rhetorical organisation, genre, rhetorical task, pattern of exposition, subject area, subject specificity, cultural specificity and text abstractness.* In the current study, we again employ such criteria to consider the texts produced by item writers and to analyse the decisions they made in shaping their texts.

In Weir et al (2009b) the cognitive processes employed by test takers in responding to IELTS reading tasks are analysed, with a particular focus on how test takers might select between expeditious and careful reading and between local and global reading in tackling test tasks.

Local reading involves decoding (word recognition, lexical access and syntactic parsing) and establishing explicit propositional meaning at the phrase, clause and sentence levels. Global reading involves the identification of the main idea(s) in a text through reconstruction of its macro-structure in the mind of the reader.

Careful reading involves extracting complete meanings from text, whether at the local or global level. This is based on slow, deliberate, incremental reading for comprehension. Expeditious reading, in contrast, involves quick, selective and efficient reading to access relevant information in a text.

The current study was expected to throw light on how the item writers might take account of the processes engaged by the reader/test taker in responding to the test tasks and how item writers' conceptions of these processes might relate to reading for academic study.

2.2 Item writing

Item writing has long been seen as a creative art (Ebel 1951, Wesman 1971) requiring mentoring and the flexible interpretation of guidelines. This has been a source of frustration to psychometricians, who would prefer to exert tighter control and to achieve a clearer relationship between item design characteristics and measurement properties. Bormuth (1970) called for scientifically grounded, algorithmic laws of item writing to counter traditional guidelines that allowed for variation in interpretation. Attempts at standardisation have continued with empirical research into the validity of item writing rules (Haladyna and Downing 1989a and 1989b); the development of item shells – generic items with elements that can be substituted with new facts, concepts or principles to create large numbers of additional items (Haladyna 1999); and efforts to automate item generation (Irvine and Kyllonen 2002). Numerous studies have addressed the effects of item format on difficulty and discrimination (see Haladyna and Downing 1989a, Haladyna, Downing and Rodriguez 2002) and guidelines have been developed to steer test design and to help item writers and editors to identify common pitfalls (Haladyna and Downing, 1989a, Haladyna 1999). For all this, Haladyna, Downing and Rodriguez (2002) conclude that item writing remains essentially creative as many of the guidelines they describe remain tentative, partial or both.

Yet stakeholder expectations of evidence-based, transparently shared validation for high-stakes language exams are increasingly the order of the era (see Bachman 2005, and Chalhoub-Deville, Chapelle, and Duff 2006), often specified through codes of practice (e.g. ALTE 1994). Rigour is increasingly expected of item-writer guidelines in the communicative language skills testing sector. The new Pearson Test of English (PTE), introduced in 2009, aims, like IELTS, to provide language proficiency scores, including reading measures, for colleges, universities, professional and government bodies requiring academic-level English. De Jong (2008) proposes an analysis, for PTE item writer training purposes, of item types (14 potentially applicable to the testing of reading) and a schema for item writer training structured around a general guide, item-specific instructions, reference materials, codes of practice, an item writer literature review and the Common European Framework of Reference (CEFR). Cambridge ESOL's own framework for the training and development of item writers is referenced in some detail below.

A number of handbooks include guidance on item design and quality assurance issues in language tests (e.g. Carroll and Hall 1985, Davidson and Lynch 2002, Heaton 1990, Hughes 2003, Norris, Brown, Hudson and Yoshioka 1998, Valette 1967, Weir 1993). These provide advice on the strengths and weaknesses of various item formats and stress the need for item review and piloting. It is generally taken as axiomatic that trained test item writers are superior to the untrained (Downing and Haladyna 1997).

While the focus of research has been on the characteristics of items, very little attention has been given to the processes that item writers go through in creating test items and the contributions that these may make to the quality of test material. In a rare piece of research focusing on this area, Salisbury (2005) uses verbal protocol methodology and a framework drawn from the study of expertise to explore how text-based tests of listening comprehension are produced by item writers. Salisbury (2005:75) describes three phases in the work of the item writer:

- Exploratory Phase: 'searching through possible texts, or, possibly, contexts'
- Concerted Phase: 'working in an intensive and concentrated way to prepare text and items for first submission'
- Refining Phase: 'after either self-, peer- or editor-review, polishing/ improving the test paper in an effort to make it conform more closely to domain requirements'.

She found that in comparison to novices, more expert item writers, i.e. those producing more positively evaluated texts and items that met the requirements of the test developers (UK examining boards offering tests of English as a Foreign Language):

- are more aware of the test specifications and are quickly able to recognise texts that show potential as test material; where novices tended to devise a listening script from a source text first and then to write the questions, experts were more inclined to start from the required item types and then to build a script to fit with these

- are more aware of the needs of candidates for clear contextual information and are better able to provide accessible contextualising information in the form of short, accessible rubrics and co-text
- explore a range of possible task ideas rather than committing immediately to one that might later prove to be unworkable
- use many more learned rules or 'ruses' than non-experts including, for example, exchanging words in the text and in the question so that the hypernym appears in the text
- adding additional text to the script to introduce distraction and reduce the susceptibility of the questions to guessing strategies.

Although more experienced item writers tended to outperform the recently trained, expertise was not simply a function of experience. One writer with no previous experience of test item writing performed better in the judgement of a review panel than two item writers with extensive experience (Salisbury 2005). Salisbury also concludes that expertise in Listening test item writing is collective in nature. Individual writers rarely have sufficient capability to meet institutional requirements at the first attempt and need the feedback they receive from their colleagues to achieve a successful outcome. It might be added that item writer expertise itself is not sufficient to guarantee test quality. Even where items are subject to rigorous review, piloting usually reveals further deficiencies of measurement.

The Cambridge ESOL approach to test development is described in detail by Saville (2003) and by Khalifa and Weir (2009). The IELTS test production process for the Reading and Listening papers is outlined in a document available from the IELTS website, www.ielts.org. The goal of this test production process is that 'each test [will be] suitable for the test purpose in terms of topics, focus, level of language, length, style and technical measurement properties' (IELTS 2007:1).

IELTS test material is written by freelance item writers externally commissioned by Cambridge ESOL in a process centrally managed from Cambridge and carried out according to confidential test specifications or item writer guidelines laid down by the test developers (although see Clapham 1996, 1997 for an account of the role of externally commissioned item writing teams in developing the IELTS Academic Reading module). These guidelines, periodically modified to reflect feedback from item writers and other stakeholders, detail the characteristics of the IELTS modules (Speaking, Listening and Academic or General Training Reading and Writing), set out the requirements for commissions and guide writers in how to approach the item writing process. The guidelines cover the steps of selecting appropriate material, developing suitable items and submitting material. However, a good deal of the responsibility for test content is devolved to the externally commissioned workers including the item writers and their Team Leaders or chairs for each of the modules. Khalifa and Weir (2009) describe the chair as having responsibility for the technical aspects of item writing and for ensuring that item writers on their team are fully equipped to generate material of the highest quality.

According to the Cambridge ESOL website (www.CambridgeESOL.org) the overall network of Cambridge item writers working across the Cambridge ESOL product range includes 30 chairs and 115 item writers. Reflecting the international nature of the examination, Cambridge ESOL employs teams of IELTS item writers in the United Kingdom, Australia, New Zealand and the USA.

There are one or two commissions each year for each item writing team (IELTS 2007). The writers are commissioned to locate and adapt suitable texts 'from publications sourced anywhere in the world' (IELTS 2007:1). This work is carried out individually by item writers who may adapt their sources to meet the requirements of the test. Khalifa and Weir (2009) list a number of reasons for an item writer to adapt an original text. These are drawn from the Item Writer Guidelines 2006 for general English examinations (*KET*, *PET*, *FCE*, *CAE* and *CPE*) produced by Cambridge ESOL (the organisation that is also responsible for producing IELTS) and include:

- cutting to make the text an appropriate length
- removing unsuitable content to make the text inoffensive
- cutting or amending the text to avoid candidates being able to get the correct answer simply by word matching, rather than by understanding the text
- glossing or removing cultural references if appropriate, especially where cultural assumptions might impede understanding
- deleting confusing or redundant references to other parts of the source text
- glossing, amending or removing parts of the text which require experience or detailed understanding of a specific topic.

Item writers submit their material in draft form for review at a preliminary pre-editing meeting. This meeting involves the chairs of the item writer teams, experienced item writers and Cambridge ESOL exam managers – members of staff with overall responsibility for the production, delivery and scoring of specific question papers. Green and Jay (2005:5) describe how 'at this stage, guidance is given to item writers on revising items and altering texts, and feedback is provided on rejected texts and/or unsuitable item types'. This step is identified by the IELTS partners as an important element in item writer training because advice is given by the pre-editing team on reasons for rejecting or refining texts and on the suitability of proposed item types (IELTS 2007).

Pre-edited material is returned to the item writer together with comments from the pre-editing panel. If the text has been evaluated as potentially acceptable for test use, the item writer then prepares an adapted version with accompanying items ready for inclusion in a test form. The modified material is submitted to an editing meeting, which takes place centrally and, in addition to the writer concerned, involves Cambridge ESOL staff and the chair. According to the IELTS partners (IELTS 2007:2) 'item writers are encouraged to participate in editing meetings dealing with their material' because this further contributes to their professional development as writers. Khalifa and Weir (2009:272) describe the aims of editing as follows:

- to check or re-check the quality of material against specifications and item writer guidelines
- to make any changes necessary to submitted materials so that they are of an acceptable standard
- to ensure that the answer key and rubrics are appropriate and comprehensive
- to further develop the skills of item writers in order to improve the quality of materials submitted and the input of item writers to future editing sessions.

Following editing, material either passes into the IELTS test bank for inclusion in pretests to be trialled with groups of test takers, or is returned to the item writer for further revision and another round of editing. Pretests are administered to groups of students at selected IELTS centres and data is obtained indicating the measurement characteristics of the test items. A further meeting – the pretest review meeting – is held to consider the item statistics and feedback from candidates and their teachers. Texts are submitted for pretesting with more questions than will appear in the final version and those items that fall outside target difficulty ranges or that have weak discrimination are eliminated. Again at this point unsatisfactory material may be rejected.

All IELTS item writers are said to receive extensive training. Ingham (2008:5) describes the standard processes of recruitment and training offered to item writers. This takes place within 'a framework for the training and development of the externals with whom [Cambridge ESOL] works in partnership. The framework has the acronym RITCME: Recruitment; Induction; Training; Co-ordination; Monitoring and Evaluation'. To be recruited as item writers, individuals must have a university degree, a suitable qualification in English language teaching and five years' teaching experience together with some familiarity with materials production and involvement in preparing students for Cambridge ESOL examinations (Ingham 2008). After completing a screening exercise and preparatory tasks (induction), successful applicants are invited to complete a 'training weekend' (Ingham 2008:5) with

Cambridge staff and external consultants. The Cambridge item writer trainers work with between 12 and 16 trainees, introducing them, *inter alia*, to item writing techniques, issues specific to the testing of different skills and the technical vocabulary used in the Cambridge ESOL context.

After joining the item writing team for a specific paper such as the IELTS Academic Reading paper, writers 'receive team-specific training before they start to write' (Ingham 2008:6). They are invited to further training sessions with their team, led by the chair, on an annual basis. In time, successful item writers gain work on additional tests to those for which they were originally recruited and may progress in the hierarchy to become chairs themselves. Writers who fail to generate sufficient acceptable material are offered support, but according to Salisbury (2005:75) may 'gradually lose commissions and eventually drop from the commissioning register'.

Salisbury (2005) points out that the role of the item writer appears, superficially, to be limited to delivering material in line with predetermined requirements. However, it is also widely recognised that formal written specifications can never be fully comprehensive and are always open to interpretation (Clapham 1996, Fulcher and Davidson 2007). Perhaps inevitably, what Salisbury (2005:176) describes as 'non-formalised specifications', representing the values and experience of the item writing team and exam managers, emerge to complement the formal set provided by the test developers. These non-formal specifications are less explicit, but more dynamic and open to change than the item writer guidelines. We have already noted that in the Cambridge ESOL model, elements of these non-formal specifications can become formalised as regular feedback from item writers informs revisions to the guidelines. Item writers are therefore central to the operational IELTS reading construct.

Khalifa and Weir (2009) point to the critical importance of professional cultures or communities of practice (Lave and Wenger 1991) within a testing body such as Cambridge ESOL. They suggest that question paper production perhaps depends as much on the shared expertise and values of the item production team as on the procedures set out in item writer guidelines. All members of this team, whether they be internal Cambridge ESOL staff or external consultants, bring their own expertise and experience to the process and shape its outcomes at the same time as their own practices are shaped by the norms of the established community that they are joining.

While a number of language test development handbooks offer advice on suitable item types for testing reading and suggest criteria for judging test items (Alderson 2000, Hughes 2003, Weir 1993) the work of the item writer remains under-researched. Studies have been undertaken to investigate the thought processes involved on the part of candidates in responding to IELTS test tasks (Mickan and Slater 2000, Weir et al 2009a and 2009b) and on the part of examiners in scoring IELTS performance (Brown 2003, 2006,

Furneaux and Rignall 2007, O'Sullivan and Rignall 2007), but no research is yet available on how IELTS item writers go about constructing test items and translating test specifications into test tasks.

3 Research methodology and design

3.1 Deduction and induction

The review of previous research and current theory and practice related to high-stakes test item writing underlines the complexity of the process. Its investigation is likely to involve qualitative as well as quantitative data collection and analyses, inductive as well as deductive approaches. In the analysis of the reading texts selected and adapted by our participants, for example, models already established are used deductively to produce theory-based quantitative measures of difficulty, word frequency and readability – for example the Academic Word List (AWL) (Coxhead 2000), word frequency levels based on the British National Corpus (BNC) (Cobb 2003) and indices of readability (Crossley, Greenfield and McNamara 2008).

However, for the participant discussions relating to text search, selection, adaptation, item writing and item editing (audio-recorded with the permission of the participants) a generally inductive approach to data analysis is used. In this process observations are made with the expectation of contributing qualitative insights to a developing theory, seeking processes and patterns that may explain our 'how' and 'why' questions. Patton (1990:390) sees such inductive qualitative analysis as permitting patterns, themes, and categories of analysis to 'emerge out of the data rather than being imposed on them prior to data collection and analysis'. Dey (1993:99) finds that induction allows a natural creation of categories to occur with 'the process of finding a focus for the analysis, and reading and annotating the data'. As our description of the project's discussion sessions in Section 6 below will indicate, the analysis 'moves back and forth between the logical construction and the actual data in a search for meaningful patterns' (Patton 1990:411). The meaning of a category is 'bound up on the one hand with the bits of data to which it is assigned, and on the other hand with the ideas it expresses' (Dey 1993:102).

3.2 Design

The research was undertaken in two phases. In the first, an open-ended questionnaire (see Appendix 4.2) was distributed to the item writers accepting our invitation to participate. Questionnaire respondents included all seven Phase 2 participants and three other experienced item writers from the UK, Australia and New Zealand. The instrument elicited data relating to their background and experience, served to contextualise the second, in-depth focus group phase of the study and informed the analyses of the item writer interview and focus group sessions described below.

Two groups of item writers were involved in these sessions. One group consisted of four trained IELTS item writers. This required the co-operation of Cambridge ESOL in facilitating contact with item writers able to participate in the research, permitting their involvement and in providing the researchers with access to the item writer guidelines for the Academic Reading paper. As the guidelines are confidential we were asked not to discuss them in detail or to quote from them in this report.

The second group included three teachers of English for academic purposes with a range of experience of the IELTS test and of IELTS preparation but no previous experience of writing Reading test items for an examinations board. These teachers were familiar with the appearance of the test, but not with its underlying design.

Data collection took place over two sessions. On the basis of Salisbury's (2005) division of the item writing process into *exploratory*, *concerted* and *refining* phases, the first session concentrated retrospectively on the exploratory phase and prospectively and concurrently on the concerted phase (see above). In the second session the item writers worked as a group to further refine their texts and items to make them more suitable for the test (as the trained item writers would normally do in an actual test editing meeting). In Salisbury's terms, this session may be said to have been concerned retrospectively with the concerted phase and prospectively and concurrently with the refining phase.

In preparation for Phase 2, each participating item writer was sent a commissioning letter (see Appendix 4.1), based on a model provided by Cambridge ESOL, inviting them to choose a text that would be suitable for use in IELTS, to edit this text as appropriate and to write 16 or 17 test questions to accompany the text.

In the first session of Phase 2, we sought insights into the strategies that item writers use in selecting and preparing texts and the role that the test specifications, experience and other sources of knowledge might play in this process for experienced and inexperienced writers. Writers were interviewed about their selection of texts for item writing purposes. Key questions for this session included how item writers select texts, how they adapt the texts to shape them for the purposes of the test and how they generate items. The focus was on the specific text selected by the item writer for this exercise, the features that made it attractive for the purpose of writing IELTS items and the edits that might have been required to shape the text to meet the requirements of the test.

The second session of Phase 2 was similar to an IELTS editing meeting (see above). Item writers brought their texts and items to the focus group to discuss whether these did, as intended, meet the requirements of the test. Again, observation of differences between the experienced and inexperienced writers was intended to provide insights into the practices of those item writers working within the IELTS system for test production. Here the researchers sought to understand the kinds of issues that item writers attend to in texts prepared by others, the changes that they suggest and features of texts and test questions that are given approval or attract criticism. Once again, the analyses of the deliberations linked themes and categories emerging from the recordings and transcripts to the insights provided by the socio-cognitive framework (Khalifa and Weir 2009, Weir 2005, Weir et al 2009a). It was expected that differences between the experienced and non-experienced groups would highlight the practices of item writers working within the IELTS system for test production and the nature of their expertise. As will be seen below, the study provides insights into how item writers prepare texts and items, and their focus of attention in texts prepared by others; also into the features of texts and test questions that attract approval or criticism in editing.

4 Analysis and findings from interviews and focus group discussions

4.1 Non-experienced IELTS item writer group

Session 1: participant discussion of their experience with their commission to select an appropriate IELTS Academic Reading text, edit and adapt for testing purposes and generate test items

This first information collection exercise was organised as a researcher-led discussion session. Here participants discussed their experience with their commission to select an appropriate IELTS Academic Reading text, edit and adapt it for testing purposes and generate test items. Each of the participants in turn (see Table 4.10 in Appendix 4.2 for CV and other information on them) was first invited to describe the processes through which an 'IELTS text' was selected and adapted, then Reading test items created. The intended ethos was participant-centred and informal, with discussion welcomed of each participant's initial account of the experience concerned. Both researchers were present but played a low-key role, intervening infrequently and informally. All proceedings were recorded (see above).

4.1.1 IELTS text search, selection and characterisation

The experiential information provided orally by the three participants on the selection of potential reading texts for IELTS use during the first discussion session of the day is summarised in Table 4.1, which analyses responses by the three participants according to criteria emerging from the analysis of the transcripts made by the researchers.

Table 4.1 Non-experienced participants: sources of and influences on IELTS Academic Reading module text selection

Source/Influence?	Item Writer		
	Victoria	Mathilda	Mary
Own interest	✓	✓	
Others' interest		✓	
Web	✓	✓	✓
IELTS website	✓	✓	
Published IELTS papers	✓	✓	✓
Magazines, journals	✓	✓	
Newspapers			✓
Bookshops			✓
Environment topics		✓	

Table 4.1 may be read, for example, as indicating that, in their accounts of IELTS text selection, both Victoria and Mathilda (all participant names used throughout this report are pseudonyms) referred in the discussion to using, among other sources, magazines and journals in their selection of suitable texts. For all three participants, it will be noted from the table (and the three non-experienced item writers' own flow charts of their whole item writing process, from text search to adapted text and accompanying items in Table 4.3 on pages 283–6) that topic interest and web searches are key initiating steps. So is public domain IELTS information accessed via the IELTS website and IELTS test preparation material.

Table 4.2 below summarises the characteristics of target IELTS-type texts as interpreted by the three participants and the number of mentions of each as counted from the transcript of the discussion. It will be noted from the table that IELTS texts tend to be perceived as likely to be on subjects of popular interest presented in a formal, report-like format, academic in tone, but not so technical that non-specialist readers would be handicapped in understanding them. The three participants differ interestingly across the text criterial characteristics used in Table 4.2 as potentially significant in this part of the discussion. Mary, for example, is apparently more concerned with the characteristics of IELTS texts from an assessment point of view. Victoria, perhaps influenced by her experience as an IELTS Writing paper Assistant Principal Examiner, appears more confident in her interpretation of what IELTS texts are like than the other two non-experienced item writers (see her generally higher criterion counts).

Table 4.2 Non-experienced participants: perceived characteristics of IELTS Academic Reading module texts

Perceived IELTS text characteristics	Item Writer		
	Victoria	Mathilda	Mary
Academic	7	2	
Report	1		
Descriptive/conceptual	2	1	3
Impersonal, hedging	2		1
Pop-scientific/current	1	2	1
Not too specialist	1	2	
Technical but not too	2	1	
Literary	1	2	
Not journalistic/news item	1		1
Avoidance of bias, offence	4		2
Of an assumed difficulty			3
Length			3
Grammar			
Cohesion	1		1
Range/complexity			2

4.1.2 Participant text search treatment and item development: flowcharts and discussions

We now analyse more qualitatively the non-experienced item writers' discussion session of their item writing processes. These deliberations had been recorded, transcribed and coded by topic before the quantitative summary analysis as presented in Tables 4.1 and 4.2 above. Table 4.3 below summarises the more qualitative inductive description here, allowing further inferences to be drawn on the processes involved in efforts by the three non-experienced item writers to locate and select potential IELTS Academic Reading texts. The submitted materials – texts and accompanying items – are provided in Appendix 4.3.

The three were asked to sketch flowcharts of the ways they had located, edited and prepared items for their IELTS Reading tests, after which they were invited in turn to explain their flowcharts (see Table 4.3). It was intended in the design of the study that this activity would provide internal triangulation for the findings of the previous discussion by the participants of their experience in selecting and characterising an appropriate IELTS Academic Reading text, editing and adapting for testing purposes. This proved indeed to be the case. The main points made by the three participants in their discussions of their flowchart are summarised in Table 4.3 under the headings: text search, editing and item writing, with a final question on their preferred

Table 4.3 Non-experienced participants: descriptions of the item writing process

Text search		
Victoria	Mathilda	Mary
5–6-step flowchart (Victoria thinks now there are more steps than in her flowchart)	5 main steps in flowchart	6-step flowchart:
1. task familiarisation 2. topic selection (based on knowledge from past papers, website, course books) 3. begin task to determine suitability 4. research topic to test credibility and usefulness of text 5. satisfied with text 6. editing text for cohesion and text type	1. looking at sample IELTS texts 2. browsing for a suitable text 3. selection of text from shortlist 4. text adaptation 5. selecting parts of text to target and writing questions / tasks based on the example of the sample tests	1. task assessment 2. background research 3. text search and rejection 4. text decision and editing 5. text review 6. item writing and text adjusting
	Used practice IELTS tests (and her own experience as a candidate)	Used *IELTS Express*, *Impact IELTS*, past papers, old IELTS copies (Internet)
Googled neuro-linguistic programming (NLP) and other potential topics > decided on topic of content of dreams > refining down topic > sub-topics within dreams > other articles > also possible choices? > so settled on the dreams text > tried items out on her EL1 partner; 'apparently native speakers do really badly on IELTS reading'	Googled scientific magazines first 'then within the magazines I looked for specific things' … 'you get articles related to it then do a search on words related to it'	searched under variety of topics, 'try to refine, refine, refine' e.g. *science and nature*, down to *robots*, 'using more and more refined words in order to be able to find an article that would be suitable' tested text and items on friend

Text editing		
Victoria	*Mathilda*	*Mary*
Believes in significant 'fixing up process' on text	Mathilda made hardly any changes: about 3 words	Text editing can mean: 'changing text structure, paragraphing, cohesion'
Did various things to make the text more academic: took out by-line, added more research-type 'rigour' (e.g. evidence-based), more hedging		

Table 4.3 (continued)

			Mary
			Didn't want to change text too much but one person's 'changing a lot' is not another's?
			Different texts need different amount of changing; editing is relative
			Is text editing for the sake of the tasks, changing text to fit a task type . . . a validity issue?

Item writing			
Victoria	**Mathilda**		**Mary**
Knew the 10 task types, returned to IELTS website handout re format and stylistic aspects of task types	Looked at task types (IELTS website says 10 different types) checked which would suit the text		Matching task (paras with researcher names) selected to test summary of main text topics
Her 'fixing up' of the text 'summons up the kind of task types there are'; so she could see e.g. MCQ (multiple-choice questions), wanted to do a Y?N?NG (not given) (students 'have a hard time with NG'); ended up doing another type as well; she 'forgot to stop'	Deciding which bits of info in text or which passages to summarise, making decisions on that in parallel; back and forth at same time		Summary completion task suited density of description of an experiment
Text very 'driven by definitions', which lend themselves to 'confusing test takers'; so a lot of her MCQ definitional; test takers can be led astray by MCQ text bits adjacent to the term	Decided to use matching paras with short summaries task as . . . 'more suitable' for this type of text		Short paraphrasal text with candidates to use words from text in new context, to check their understanding
MCQ items testing whether Cs 'have kept up with the order'	Used true / false / not given task . . . 'put in a few correct ones, made up a few others' e.g. collapsing info 'that did not really go together . . .' to reveal lack of understanding		Didn't just want to test vocab. meaning; tried to elicit specific answers
Linked items with reading purposes e.g. careful reading where you have to 'go back to text and work hard to understand it'	Tested vocab. e.g. 'if you don't know that adjacent means next then you don't know whether that info is correct or not . . .'		Favoured the control offered by multiple choice (MCQ) but now felt she should have been more careful in designing distractors

Item writing		
Victoria	Mathilda	Mary
MCQ distractors of similar lengths but not necessarily the same style?	MCQ suitable task for text as it has lots of straightforward info relatively easy finding distractors: easy to find similar info which could be selected 'if you don't look properly or if you understood it half way'	Often had difficulty finding the 4th alternative
Tried to keep the items in the order of the text as with IELTS		Should there be distractors not actually in the text but from test designer's mind?
Wished there were only 3 alternatives; 4th just an 'add on', 'just rubbish', easy for test taker to spot	Found a fine line between good and bad distractors, and also between distractors 'which could also be correct . . . because the text might suggest it and also because . . . you could actually accept it as a correct answer'	Should we actually add to text to get distractors? Mary thinks no as it impairs authenticity
Asks 'can you use words that you know, not in the text'; Must it be in the text? What's the rule?	Marked up text suitable for items i.e. that seemed important for overall understanding and 'for local, smaller bits of info where I thought I would be able to ask questions'; then made up items, vocab, others asking for longer stretches as text 'sort of like offered itself'	Never threw any questions away, but did dispense with 'a couple of distractors'
Victoria not much practice in SAQs (short answer questions); too many alternative responses; hard to generate all possible answers	Adjusting if she felt that they were either too easy (distractors obviously wrong, didn't really test anything or item wording did not make clear what I mean)	IELTS items do not have to be in the order the item topic appears in the text?
	Regrets not testing items with someone; 'if you . . . word them and reword them and go over them again you . . . lose touch with it and don't really understand it yourself anymore'	

Table 4.3 (continued)

Threw away only one or two items but modified about half or her original items		
Thought the website said all the items are in the order they are in the text		
Short answer questions (SAQs) may be good for definitions, too		

Which of your sections are you happiest with?		
Victoria	**Mathilda**	**Mary**
Likes her T/F NG – it works	MCQ strongest, not a native speaker so can 'imagine what it's like' so easier to 'make up the wrong ones'!	Matching (sentences to researcher names) the best
Stylistically her MCQ wrong because the items are of uneven length, though the questions are 'sort of OK'	Task type 7, summary info to match paras, too vague, so her worst	Summary completion task the easiest to write so perhaps the worst!
In her SAQs she is not convinced the answers are the only ones possible		MCQ task actually the worst because of her difficulty finding the final distractors
		Summary completion the easiest – so the worst is her first section (the matchings)

items. The table should be read both for the similarities and for the differences in the processes engaged in across the three participants.

Item writer Victoria had begun by visiting the official IELTS website for information and samples of Academic Reading module topics and task types. She then, like all the three untrained participants, carried out an internet search for potential topics which she had already identified (there were six of these) and selected the one of most interest to her, i.e. neuro-linguistic programming. The text on this, however, she rejected as *'too technical, too specialist'*, as she did her next text, on the Japanese tea ceremony, which though *'a really pretty text'*, she found too *'instructional'*, and – a common theme in text selection – biased in favour of particular candidate groups. Victoria's final choice she rated immediately as the kind of *'really studious topic that IELTS uses'*, namely: How the Brain Turns Reality into Dreams (see Appendix 4.3 for the text concerned). For Victoria, the search was about *'choosing a text, looking at it, deciding what I can do with it'*.

Victoria, as we shall see emphasised in the next section, was from the outset viewing prospective texts in terms of what she could do with them to make them suitable as IELTS texts with appropriate tasks to go with them. The Dreams text she found right because it was *'pseudo-scientific'*, a view shared by all three in the group as characterising IELTS texts (see below) and, significant for our discussions of test text adaptation in the section below, because it *'lent itself to being fixed up'* (Victoria's frequent term for adapting texts).

Mathilda confessed to being initially unsure of the level of difficulty and complexity of IELTS reading texts. Her visit to the IELTS website suggested to her *'sort of'* scientific texts but not too specific, specialist; *'a bit more populist, kind of thing'*. She then carried out a search, guided by topics fitting this construct, and which were *'very up to date'* and which *'nowadays should interest most people'*. She thus used search terms such as *'environment'* and *'future'* but rejected several texts as too specialist, too material-intensive given the IELTS reading time limit. Mathilda saved four possible texts and made her final choice, of the one on environmentally friendly cities of the future, which she found engaging, information rich and apparently suitable for test questions.

Mary found the text search time-consuming and quite difficult. She had started by checking with IELTS tests in the *Cambridge Practice Tests for IELTS* series, focusing in particular on their subject matter. She had then searched in magazines such as the *New Statesman*, *The Economist* and the *New Scientist*, as well as newspaper magazine sections. Articles from these sections she rejected because of their length (Mary *'would have struggled to edit down'*), complexity or cultural bias. Mary pursued the topic of robots online after reading a newspaper article on the subject, although this had been much too short for IELTS purposes. She then searched the BBC website without finding texts she felt she would not have to edit too heavily – something (see below) she expressed particular antipathy towards doing. Finally, through *Google News*, Mary found an article on robots which she considered at the right level of difficulty, grammar and range: expressing opinions, yet with an appropriate descriptive element. The piece Mary said *'would have been something I would have read at uni. had I studied anything like this!'*.

4.1.3 Participant focus group discussions

The non-experienced group participated next in a focus group discussion structured around a set of nine semantic differential continua (Osgood, Suci and Tannenbaum 1957) using the unlabelled scale format (compared with other formats by Garland 1990) and as seen in Table 4.4 on pages 289–90. In the table, summaries of the comments made by the participants in their 25 minutes of unmediated discussion are placed in their approximate location on the continua for the nine scales. The adjectives for the continua were selected by the researchers.

The points made by the three participants in the focus group discussion certainly served as triangulation for the views they had expressed in the preceding IELTS text search and treatment and item development: flowcharts and discussions already reported. Once again we see strong evidence of time-consuming searching for suitable texts but uncertainty of the target level(s) of such texts and, to some extent, the topic range; major problems with the design of tasks, in particular multiple choice (MCQ) items and, as might be expected of this non-experienced item writer group, frustration caused by lack of item writing guidance.

The research team pursued with the participants certain emerging issues immediately after the end of the participant-led semantic differential discussion, in particular the issue of *'the level of English language proficiency associated with IELTS'*, about which the three participants admitted to being uncertain. Mathilda had learned from her own experience as an IELTS test taker but still felt that the IELTS website and other guidance on proficiency levels was *'vague'*. Victoria felt that she had had to develop her own proficiency level criteria while selecting her text and making items. She noted how the text *'comprehensibility factor'* seemed to dominate her decisions on text and item difficulty. Mathilda felt that her text would not be *'that easy'* for candidates whose English was *'not so developed'* as her own. Participants were aware that an IELTS Band of 6 or 6.5 was conventionally seen as a cut-off point for students entering BA courses. Mary and Victoria were also informed by the levels of their own IELTS students (IELTS Bands 5.0–7.5, and 8.0 respectively). This for Mary meant that her test might not discriminate effectively at the higher end as she felt that she might not have enough experience of the highest scoring candidates to be able to target items at this group.

The discussion was now focusing on the actual reading construct espoused by IELTS. Victoria and Mary had heard that EL1 users had difficulty with

Table 4.4 Summary of non-experienced participant focus group comments and ratings on semantic differential scales

clear	choosing texts (Victoria, Mary)	IELTS reading texts supposed to be at three different levels (Victoria) balancing general vs specific items (Mary)	getting texts the right level (Mathilda) whether items should be in order of the text (Mary) guidelines on the target reading construct?	designing 4 good MCQ distractors (Mary, Victoria, Mathilda) lack of guidelines on how tasks are made and assessed (Mathilda, Mary, Victoria)	**confusing**
interesting	achieving good text and items (Victoria, Mary) writing items (Mary) literary, fiction texts would be (Mathilda) but might not be appropriate (Mary, Victoria)	trying to drive the process, not letting the text drive it (Victoria)	finding the text (Mary) informative texts (Mathilda) finding items (Mathilda)		**dull**
time-consuming	everything! (Mary) looking for texts (Mathilda)	developing items (Mary) editing (Mary, Victoria)	editing (Mathilda)		**quick**
rewarding	finally finding the right text (Victoria, Mary) finishing everything (Victoria, Mary, Mathilda)	driven by possibility it will be used as a 'real' test (Victoria)	unsure whether doing it right (Mathilda, Mary)	no-one's going to answer the items (Mary, Victoria) no feedback, no knowledge underneath the task they're doing (Mary, Victoria, Mathilda)	**unrewarding**
worrying	not knowing if they are doing it right (Mathilda, Mary)	worrying about the right level (Mary) not being privy to the process of editing, trialling (Victoria)			**pleasing**

Table 4.4 (continued)

	creative			programmatic	
	whole process of creating items, driving the process oneself (Mary); making up credible distractors (Mathilda)		straightforward informational text (Mathilda); forcing in distractors (Mary)		programmatic
The creative is constrained by the programmatic (Mathilda, Mary, Victoria)					
challenging	creating a viable 4th distractor in MCQ (Victoria, Mary)	forcing text into particular task types (Victoria); how much to edit (Mary); matching text and task types (Mathilda)	choosing task types (Mary)		**straightforward**
frustrating	finding the right text (Mary)	making items for the matching tasks (Mary)	completing the matching task (Mary); perfecting answer keys for SAQ task (Victoria)	finishing preparation and editing of a good, cohesive text (Victoria)	**satisfying**
supported	feedback of friend useful (Mary); topic checks with friends (Victoria); IELTS materials vital (Mary, Mathilda)		didn't know she could seek help; too little help on level of difficulty (Mathilda); needed more samples and guidelines for texts (Mathilda)	item writer guidelines confidential (Victoria)	**unsupported**

the IELTS Academic Reading module, and that test performance on this module tended anyway to be weaker than on the other IELTS modules, even for stronger candidates. This is a common perception of IELTS (see Hawkey 2006), although test results published on the IELTS website show that overall mean scores for Reading are higher than for the Writing and Speaking papers. Mathilda wondered whether the IELTS Academic Reading module was perhaps testing concentration rather than 'reading proficiency'. Victoria recalled that IELTS was described as testing skimming and scanning, but thought that skimming and scanning would also involve careful reading once the information necessary for the response had been located. But Mary was sure that reading and trying to understand every word in an IELTS text would mean not finishing the test. Mary felt that a candidate could not go into an IELTS exam *'not having been taught how to take an IELTS exam'* and that a test taker might not do well on the test just as a *'good reader'*. Mary also claimed that she had never, even as a university student, read anything else as she reads an IELTS reading text. When reading a chapter in a book at university, one generally wants one thing, which one skims to locate, then *'goes off'* to do the required reading-related task (although, conversely, Mathilda claimed often to *'read the whole thing'*).

The participants were then asked what other activities the IELTS text selection, editing and item writing processes reminded them of. Victoria recalled her experience working for a publisher and editing other people's reading comprehension passages for the *Certificate of Proficiency in English* (*CPE*) examination, which included literary texts (see Appendix 4.2).

Mary had worked on online language courses, where editing other people's work had helped her thinking about the question-setting process (as well as surprising her with how inadequate some people's item writing could be). The experience had reminded Mary how much easier it was to write grammatical rather than skills-based items. Victoria agreed, based on her own (admittedly rather unrewarding) experience composing objective-format usage of English items which she had prepared during her experience in publishing.

The participants were then asked whether their experience with the research project commission had changed their opinions of the IELTS Reading paper. Victoria had found herself asking more about the actual process of reading, her answers to this question underlining why IELTS Academic Reading was such *'a tough exam'* for candidates. Mathilda had become more curious about how the test was used actually to measure proficiency, something she feels must be difficult to *'pin down'*. Mary feels more tolerant of IELTS texts that may appear boring, given the difficulty she experienced finding her own text for the project. All three participants would welcome further experience with IELTS Academic Reading item writing, especially the training for it.

4.2 Procedures with and findings from the experienced IELTS item writer group

Session 1: experienced item writer participant discussion of their experience with their commission to select an appropriate IELTS Academic Reading text, edit and adapt for testing purposes and generate test items

As with the non-experienced group, the four experienced participants discussed this commission to select an appropriate IELTS Academic Reading text, edit and adapt it for testing purposes and generate test items, but this group was also, of course, able to discuss the regular experience of carrying out IELTS item writing commissions. Again this was organised as a researcher-led discussion session. Each participant (see Table 4.11 in Appendix 4.2 for background information) was invited to describe the processes through which an 'IELTS' text was selected and adapted, and then Reading test items created. Again, both researchers were present, but intervened only infrequently and informally. All proceedings were recorded (see above).

4.2.1 Participant text search treatment and item development: flowcharts and discussions

The experiential information provided orally by the four participants is summarised in Table 4.5, which analyses responses on the issue of text sources.

Unlike the non-experienced writers, this group did not mention the IELTS website or published IELTS material as a source of information on text selection. All reported that they referred to the item writer guidelines and to specific recommendations on topics made in the IELTS commissioning process.

Table 4.5 Experienced participants: sources and influences re IELTS Academic Reading module text selection

Source/Influence?	Item Writer			
	Jane	Anne	William	Elizabeth
IELTS Guidelines or Commission	✓	✓	✓	✓
Own interest			✓	
Web	✓	✓	✓	✓
Magazines, journals		✓		✓
Newspapers	✓			
Bookshops		✓		

Table 4.6 summarises the characteristics of target IELTS-type texts as interpreted by the four participants. The experienced writers seemed to share with the non-experienced group the perception of IELTS texts: subjects of

Table 4.6 Experienced participants: perceived characteristics of IELTS Academic Reading module texts

Perceived IELTS text characteristics	Item Writer			
	Jane	Anne	William	Elizabeth
Academic	1	2	2	3
Including a number of ideas/opinions		2	1	1
Factual		1	1	
Not too specialist	1	1		1
Accessible to the general reader	1	2		2
Not too technical (for item writer to understand)	1		2	
Avoidance of bias, offence	1	2	5	1
Small and specific rather than big and general				1
Cohesion	1	1	1	1
Range/complexity		1		
Suitability for (multiple) task types	3	1	1	2

popular interest presented in a formal, report-like format, academic in tone but not so technical that non-specialist readers would be handicapped in understanding them. As with the non-experienced group, there were differences between participants in the attention given to different text features. William was particularly concerned with issues of bias and cultural sensitivity while Jane seemed to pay most attention initially to the suitability of a text for supporting certain item types.

As with their non-experienced counterparts, the four experienced item writers were asked to sketch flowcharts of the ways they had located, edited and prepared items for their IELTS Academic Reading tests, after which they were invited in turn to explain their flowcharts. In the following section we analyse the four experienced item writers' discussions. As above, these were transcribed and coded for topic before the semi-quantitative summary analysis as presented in Tables 4.5 and 4.6. The discussion is summarised in Table 4.7 (see pages 295–300).

Three of the four item writers involved were able to use texts that they already had on file, although in William's case, this was because his initial effort to find a new text had failed. Anne reported that in between commissions she would regularly retain texts which seemed promising for IELTS and that in this case she had found a suitable text on the topic of laughter (although actually finding that she had a suitable IELTS text on file was rare for her). From the outset, the potential for the text to generate items was a key concern. An ongoing challenge for Anne was to locate texts that included enough discrete points of information or opinions to support enough items to fulfil an IELTS commission: '*with a lot of articles, the problem is they say the same thing in different ways*'.

The propositional 'complexity' of the text seemed to be of central concern so that a suitable text '*may not be for the academic reader, it may be for the interested layperson . . . if the complexity is right*'. On the other hand there was a danger with more clearly academic texts of what Anne called '*over-complexity*': '*over-complexity is when the research itself or the topic itself needs so much specialist language*'. A good IELTS text would be propositionally dense, but not overly technical. Occasionally Anne might add information from a second source to supplement a text – Elizabeth and William (and Victoria of the non-experienced group) had also done this for IELTS, but not Jane.

Initially Anne would carry out '*a form of triage*' on the text, forming an impression of which sections she might use as '*often the texts are longer than we might need*' and considering '*which tasks would be suitable*'. Once she had settled on a text, she would type it up and it would be at this point that she could arrive at a firmer conclusion concerning its suitability. On occasion she would now find that she needed to take the decision – '*one of the hardest decisions to take*' – that '*in fact those tasks aren't going to fit*' and so have to reject the text. Anne saw personal interest in a text as being potentially a disadvantage when it came to judging its quality: '*it blinds you the fact that it isn't going to work*'.

Elizabeth reported that she asked herself a number of questions in selecting a text: '*is the content appropriate for the candidature? Is the text suitable for a test, rather than for a text book? Will it support a sufficient number of items?*' She considered that an ideal IELTS text would include, '*a main idea with a variety of examples rather than just one argument repeated*'. Elizabeth reported that she usually selected texts that were considerably longer than required. As she worked with a text, she would highlight points to test and make notes about each paragraph, using these to identify repetitions and to decide on which item type to employ. Passages which were not highlighted as a source for an item could then be cut.

Like Anne, Elizabeth also reported looking for texts between commissions: '*you sort of live searching for texts the whole time*'. On this occasion, she too had a suitable text on file. In approaching a text she reported that she considers the candidature for the test (an issue we return to later), the number of items that could be generated and the '*range of ideas*'. Although she did not type up the text as Anne did, she made notes on it '*per paragraph*' because this '*helps to see if it's the same ideas* [being repeated in the text] *or different ideas*'. An '*ideal* [IELTS] *text*' would '*have a point to it, but then illustrate it by looking at a number of different things; a main idea with examples or experiments or*

Table 4.7 Experienced participants: descriptions of the item writing process

Overview of the item writing process			
Jane	**Anne**	**William**	**Elizabeth**
6-step flowchart:	11-step flowchart:	11-step flowchart:	10-step flowchart:
1. Refer to commissioning letter to identify topics to avoid, read sections needed (10 mins)	1. Text sourcing: check in files, investigate previously fruitful websites, Google a topic suggested in commission or that seems promising (30 mins–1 day)	1. Think of subject – look at own books and articles for inspiration	1. Keep eyes open for texts
		2. Google possible topics	2. Choose from available texts
		3. Locate a text and check suitability – how much needs glossing, any taboo subjects?	3. Evaluate selected text
2. Finding possible sources, read quickly to decide whether possible (1hr–2hrs)	2. Careful reading (30 mins)	4. Consider whether text will work with task types	4. Summarise main points and edit out redundant/inappropriate material
	3. Typing up with amendments (1 hr)	5. Scan or download text	5. Identify possible task types
3. Collect likely sources and read again – topic suitability, suitable for task types, enough testable material (1hr)	4. Length adjustment (to target plus 100–200 words) (15 mins)	6. Edit text to roughly required length (or slightly longer), modifying to keep coherence	6. Write items
			7. Cut text to required length
	5. Work on first (most obvious) task type (30 mins–2hrs [for MCQ]	7. Choose and draft first task, modifying text to fit (abandon task if necessary)	8. Tidy up text and items checking keys
	6. Mark up further areas of text for suitable items (30 mins)	8. Prepare other tasks	9. Leave for a day, print out and amend as needed
4. Start cutting to appropriate length, identifying information to test and which parts go with which item types (1hr–2hrs)	7. Work on further tasks – amending text as necessary (1hr–2hrs)	9. Revise text for coherence, length, to fit tasks, adapting tasks at the same time as needed	10. Send off
	8. Print off and attempt tasks (30 mins–1hr)	10. Have a break	No timings given
	9. Write answer key (10 mins)	11. Check and revise text and tasks	
		Timings	
		Steps 1 and 2: 10 mins–2 hrs; Steps 3 to 9: 1hr–2 hrs; Step 9: 20 mins; Step 10: 10 minutes to 1 week; Step 11: 20 mins	

Table 4.7 (continued)

Overview of the item writing process

Jane	Anne	William	Elizabeth
5. Work on tasks, amending and cutting text as needed to fit tasks (1–2hrs per task type)	10. Check length and prune if necessary (10 mins–1hr)		
6. First draft – check that tasks work, check for overlap between items, cut to word limit (1hr)	11. Review and proof read (10mins–30mins)		
	Found text already in her file (keeps an eye on potential sources) – looking for a Section 1 (relatively easy) task		

Text search

Jane	Anne	William	Elizabeth
'I don't normally have texts waiting'	Sometimes has to reject texts at her typing stage 'one of the hardest decisions to take'	Subject matter is the first thing.	'You're looking for texts the whole time'
'I have certain sources that I go to regularly''	'I think sometimes being interested in a text is a positive disadvantage'	'It's finding the text that takes longest'	Asks the following questions about the text:
'There were quite a few texts and I made a decision'	It is a challenge to find articles that have enough discrete information or opinions: 'A lot of articles,	For this commission 'I decided I would like to write about a particular topic and wasted over two hours on the internet: I couldn't come up with anything that was long enough or varied enough so I gave up'	'Is the content appropriate for the candidature*?' 'Will the text support the items? 'Does it have a range of ideas?'
'Texts are nearly always nearly three or four times the length we will need'		'You get nervous about IELTS in particular because there are so many rules [restricting topic areas] that arise, sometimes unexpectedly' as a result 'I try to play safe'	A suitable text, 'has a point to it but then illustrates it by looking at lots of different things'

	Jane	Anne		Elizabeth
	'If I can't understand a text, I wouldn't use it' 'Opinion texts are more difficult to find' 'You can't assume that the candidates are specialists'	'the problem is they say the same thing in different ways' 'It may not be for the academic reader, it may be for the interested layperson . . . if the complexity is right' 'The over complexity is when the research itself or the topic itself needs so much specialist language'		*The candidature 'I think about places I have worked and people I have know and try and look at it through their eyes' 'You can't assume they are particularly interested in the UK' 'We are going for the academic reader, but it's got to be understood by anyone'

Text editing

Jane	Anne	William	Elizabeth
'I have a split screen working on items and text at the same time'.	'Sometimes we might add a bit from other sources' 'I cut out the first paragraph from my text because it was journalistic'	This text was long therefore . . . 'I ended up not only cutting it a lot and moving things around more than I would aim to do usually' Journalistic texts tend to begin from a hook – an example or 'attractive little anecdote' – more academic texts start from the general and move to the specific examples. IELTS texts should reflect the latter and have an academic tone. 'Adapt the text to fit the tasks', don't see the text as 'sacrosanct'	Articles that are not written by a specialist, but by a journalist can misrepresent a subject. To check this, 'I quite often Google stuff or ask people [about the topic]' Need to edit out references to 'amazing', 'surprising' or 'incredible' information in journalistic text

Table 4.7 (continued)

Jane	Anne	William	Elizabeth
		'Rewriting the text and trying out a task, then rewriting the text again and so on' 'Make a task loosely based on the text then make sure the text can fit the task'	
		Expressing a number of ideas and opinions, which would make it a Section 3	
		If it's fairly factual more Section 1	
		Genuine academic texts are unsuitable because they assume too much knowledge and would require too much explanation	
		'I try and make sure that I understand it and can make it comprehensible'	

Item writing

Jane	Anne	William	Elizabeth
I think I make a decision fairly early on about which task type I will use	Headings are difficult True–false is usually quite easy	My first main thing is how well the tasks fit that text Chooses tasks that 'leap out from the text'	I think multiple choice can work across a range of texts including at a more basic factual level

I decided this particular text was suitable for certain task types	Not something that could be answered by someone who knows the subject	A diagram or even a flowchart can be more personal than you realise. I made a diagram from one text that failed because it was my idea and it didn't reflect other people's ideas
'I don't like doing the diagram type ones or flowcharts'	Considers which tasks pay more, which are worth the effort and so avoids MCQ if possible.	I often write notes on texts before deciding which one to use
'Quite often in articles you get a little diagram, but it's too complex or guessable'	Factual information you can test with true false not given	
'I read a lot of texts and cut them down before I decide which one to use'.	We need to cover the whole text – every paragraph is tested	
In other papers you choose a text with one task type – IELTS needs a text that will work with three: sometimes this is quite difficult: it doesn't work as easily with the third task	A text ought to lend itself to having a topic in each paragraph that can be captured in a heading	
With discrete information you can make it work with that	I think the paragraphs overlapped in this case MCQ: coming up with four plausible opinions which are wrong is difficult: the danger is that you are pushed into testing something that is trivial . . . they should all be important pieces of information or opinions or functions	
Multiple choice questions fit best with an opinion text	Flowcharts are either a sequence that can be guessable or it's a false way of presenting the information – it's not really a flowchart	
	I work on items at an early stage and will dump a text after 10 minutes if I feel it will not work	

Table 4.7 (continued)

Which of your sections are you happiest with?			
Jane	Anne	William	Elizabeth
		Unusually, I wrote all three tasks simultaneously	The need to scan the whole text three times for different information seems unfair: 'you wouldn't usually scan [a text] three times for different sorts of information' – we have had advice to cut down on that now
		There were problems of overlap with other tasks. Questions 1 and 16 were all about Blake and Wordsworth: a bit problematic and other people might feel they are not independent of each other	
		Paragraphs F and H each only have one item, which is not ideal	I usually try to focus two of my tasks on specific information and have a third one that is more of an overview
		Something like a summary of one paragraph can be too easy because the answers are all together	This text does have one basic idea and really the whole text is saying that. I was testing the support for the idea
		Identifying the paragraph containing information where it's in random order and could be anywhere in the text requires you to scan the whole text for each individual item which seems to me to be far more difficult for candidates	There is a stage when I think 'this is going to work and I'm not going to dump this
			I thought there were enough discrete words that would make a key to support multiple choice
			I am very conscious of how much of a text I am exploiting

that sort of thing rather than one argument'. On the basis of these notes she would then begin to associate sections of text with task types so that, for example, *'paragraphs one to three might support multiple choice questions . . . there might be a summary in paragraph five, there's probably a whole text activity like matching paragraphs or identifying paragraph topics'*.

At this point Elizabeth would begin cutting the text, initially removing material that could obviously not be used including *'taboo topics, repetitions, that sort of thing'* but would still expect to have a longer text than would be required. With the text and the developing items displayed together on a split screen she would then highlight sections of text and produce related items. After completing the items, she might then remove sections of text that had not been highlighted, *'fairly stringently'* to end up with a text of the right length.

William had decided to write about a *'particular topic'*, but *'wasted over two hours'* looking for a suitable text on this topic on the internet. He was unable to *'come up with anything that was long enough or varied enough'*. Instead he turned to a text that he had previously considered using for a commission, but had not submitted partly because of doubts about the perceived suitability of the topic (*'too culturally bound to Britain'*) and the need to explain the names being discussed (Blake, Wordsworth). The text was somewhat problematic because of its length so that William *'ended up not only cutting it a lot, but rewriting parts of it and moving things around more than* [he] *would aim to do'*. As a result of this rewriting *'there was a risk that it might end up not being as coherent as it ought to be'*; a risk that might, in a regular IELTS commission, have led him to reject the text. William reported feeling *'nervous about IELTS in particular because there are so many rules that arise, sometimes unexpectedly'* and so he usually sought to *'play safe'* with the topics he chose.

William scanned the text from the source book and worked with it on his PC. He reported that he would usually shorten the text by cutting it at this point to *'a little over the maximum'*. He would then work on the items and text together with a split screen, adapting the text *'to make sure it fits the tasks'*. In choosing the tasks, he would ask himself which tasks *'fit the specifications'* and, ideally, *'leap out from the text'*. William would ensure that the tasks *'work'* and would change the text *'to fit'* as necessary. The text was not *'sacrosanct'*, but could be adapted as required.

Jane reported that she did not *'normally'* store texts on file, but went to certain sources regularly on receiving a commission. On this occasion she looked for a new source. As *'case studies'* had been requested in a recent IELTS commission, she took this as a starting point and searched for this phrase on the internet. There were *'quite a few texts'* that she looked at before taking a decision on which to use. Typically, Jane takes an early decision on the task types that would best suit a text: *'something like multiple choice requires a completely different text to True/False'*. As she first scanned it, she identified the text she eventually chose as being suitable for '*certain task types, not really suitable for others*'. She also noticed that it contained too much technical detail, which she would need to cut. She claimed that texts are '*nearly always three times, if not four times the length that we need*'. There was then a process of '*just cutting it and cutting it and cutting it, deciding which information you can target and which bits of the text will be suitable for particular task types*'. Like the others she used a split screen to work on the items and text simultaneously.

4.2.2 Participant focus group discussions

The experienced group, like the non-experienced group (above) participated next, in a focus group discussion structured around a set of nine semantic differential continua (Osgood et al 1957) as seen in Table 4.8 on pages 304–306. In the table, summaries of the comments made by the participants in their 20 minutes of unmediated discussion are placed in their approximate location on the continua for the nine scales. As before, the adjectives for the continua were selected by the researchers.

Again, points made by participants in the focus group discussion served to triangulate views expressed in the preceding interview activity concerning IELTS text search and treatment and item development: flowcharts and discussions already reported. Following discussion of the semantic differentials, the research team pursued emerging issues with the group.

The experienced group, like the non-experienced, expressed uncertainty about candidates' level of English language proficiency. The four discussed the need to keep the candidates in mind when writing items, but agreed that it was challenging to do this, given '*the variety of the situation and [the candidates'] levels of English*'. All the participants had their own points of reference for these. Anne also worked as an examiner for the Speaking paper and so met many candidates while both William and Elizabeth had experience of preparing students for the test. However, Elizabeth reminded the group that the candidates they met in the UK would not be representative of the full range of candidates taking the test – especially those from relatively underprivileged backgrounds.

Item writers also received information about candidates from IELTS. An annual report on demographic data is provided by Cambridge ESOL and 'common wrong answers' to open response items are discussed at pretest review meetings. What Anne described as the '*off the wall*' nature of some of these wrong answers and the observation that '*some people have been accepted at universities, where I thought their English was totally inadequate*' led William to the conclusion that '*you can do reasonably well on IELTS, I think. And still have what seems to be a low level of English*'. Elizabeth also questioned whether IELTS candidates would need to arrive at a full understanding of the text in order to succeed on the questions, suspecting that in

IELTS *'half the time the candidates don't read the text from beginning to end because they don't have to'* as local details in the text were being tested by the items rather than the overall meaning. However, Anne wondered whether William's concern could be justified as success on the test would require adequate levels of performance on the direct Speaking and Writing papers as well as Reading and Listening.

There was discussion of how the participants had developed their item writing expertise. For Jane this was not easy to explain: *'It's difficult to say sometimes exactly what you're doing and how you're doing it'*. Anne agreed, observing that *'the processes you go through aren't necessarily conscious'*.

However, there were item writing skills that could be learned. Anne had come to appreciate the importance of *'working the task'*: attempting it as a candidate would. Jane agreed that this was helpful, but admitted she rarely did this prior to submission because of the pressure of deadlines. Elizabeth had found very helpful the advice given to her at her initial training session to focus on what she felt to be the key points of the text, finding that this could help her when she was *'stuck on something'*.

Anne felt that her items had improved *'over years of seeing other people's and having to mend your own'*. William pointed to the value of attending editing meetings to obtain insights and Elizabeth felt that feedback at editing meetings had been one of her main sources of learning about item writing especially where the chair of the meeting, as an experienced and successful item writer, had been effective at showing how a text or item could be improved.

William spoke of having learned how to devise plausible distractors for multiple choice items. However, there were limits to how far this could be learned as an item writing skill and he wondered about the role of background knowledge in eliminating incorrect options: *'I think there's a risk with IELTS because if it's a scientific text, I may not know nearly enough to know what would be a plausible distractor. What seems plausible to me could be instantly rejected by somebody who knows a little more about the subject.'*

Testing implicit information was seen to be problematic. There were cases of disagreement between the item writers and their colleagues carrying out pre-editing reviews about *'whether [a point] is implicit, but strongly enough there to be tested or not'* (William). For Jane, testing the writer's interpretation against others' was a further argument in favour of the pre-editing and editing processes: *'fresh eyes are invaluable when it comes to evaluating a task'*.

Although Jane reported that she tried to keep the level of language in mind as she wrote, the group agreed that the difficulty of items was not easy to predict. None of the writers seemed to have a clear sense of the proportion of items associated with a text that a successful IELTS candidate at Band 6.0 or 6.5 might be expected to answer correctly. Pretesting results often revealed items to be easier or more difficult than expected.

Table 4.8 Summary of experienced participant focus group comments and ratings on semantic differential scales

clear				confusing
The guidelines are clear (Anne)				Finding texts can be confusing (Anne) Trying to read pre-editing teams' minds can be confusing (William) Texts can be confusing (Elizabeth) Some tasks confusing for candidates (William) 'We used to fill in a form identifying what each item was testing – it was confusing but also really useful in focussing the mind on what items are actually doing' (Elizabeth)
interesting				**dull**
The topic and the texts – I have learned a lot (William) You get to grips with texts that you might not otherwise read (Anne) Texts must be engaging to keep you interested for a day (Jane)	Final stages of item writing – proof reading (Elizabeth) MCQ can be quite interesting and creative (Anne) Making sure that everything fits together (William)	More interesting than business English texts (Anne)		Proof reading (Jane)
time-consuming				**quick**
Finding the texts (All)	Editing can be 'deathly' when you are working with others' text that is problematic (William) Sometimes rewriting is easier alone than by committee (William)	Depends on time of day (Anne) and team (Elizabeth)		If it's the right text, it can be quick (Anne, Jane)

rewarding	Making it work (William) Pretest review acceptance (William)	Improving the quality of the source text (Anne) Often we are in effect creating a new text – fit for a different purpose (William)	Getting the task to work (Jane)	un-rewarding
worrying	When you can't find a text (Anne)	You can easily spend half a day and come up with nothing (Elizabeth)		pleasing
creative	All the writing is creative, even though we are starting with something – rather like putting on a play (William)	Editing problem solving can be creative, but not satisfactory when you seem to be doing another item writer's work for them (William)	Proof reading Techniques for writing enough items – 'in summaries you've got to go for the nouns, which you didn't know when you first started' (Anne)	program-matic
challenging	Finding the texts and shaping them (Anne) Understanding a subject you may not be familiar with (William)	Creating the items once a suitable text has been chosen (Elizabeth)		straight-forward
frustrating	Feedback that you don't agree with (William) 'There are times when you have to have a quick walk round the garden' (Anne)	Losing a submission altogether (rejection)	Disagreement about issues of bias – William finds Business papers less sensitive; others find Cambridge Main Suite papers more sensitive	satisfying

Table 4.8 (continued)

supported			unsupported
Editing and pre-editing is supportive on the whole (Anne)	You can ask for elaboration of pre-editing feedback. (Elizabeth)	Some texts accepted when I could answer on basis of topic knowledge, others rejected when answers did not seem guessable to me (William)	Looking for a text is unsupported (Anne)
Colleagues are generally helpful and supportive.	I don't think I have ever disagreed with pre-editing feedback (Jane)	The whole issue of how guessable items are is difficult (Anne)	
Rejection of tasks comes when topic not checked in advance (William)		A collocation can be guessable to a native speaker, but not to NNS (William) but part of reading is the ability to predict (Elizabeth)	

5 Analysis and findings on the texts

The analysis here is applied to the texts as they were submitted by the seven participants, before any changes made during the public editing process reported below. The texts and items submitted by the item writers (in their adapted, but unedited state) are presented in Appendix 4.3. This analysis shows how the texts were shaped by the writers and so serves to contextualise the comments made in the interview and focus group sessions.

In this section, we again begin with the texts submitted by the non-experienced group. Following Weir et al (2009a) we employed automated indices of word frequency and readability to inform and supplement our qualitative text analyses. Outcomes of these procedures are given in Figures 4.1 to 4.3 below and are discussed in relation to each submission in the following section.

N.B. lower scores on Flesch-Kincaid and higher scores on Coh-Metrix represent greater reading ease.

Figure 4.1 Results of word frequency analyses for original source texts and adapted IELTS text: percentage of very frequent words at the BNC 1,000, 2,000 and 3,000 word frequency levels

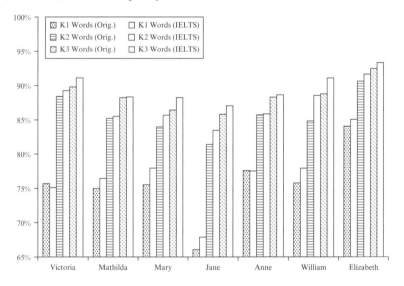

Figure 4.2 Results of word frequency analyses for original source texts and adapted IELTS text: percentage of sub-technical academic (AWL) and very infrequent words

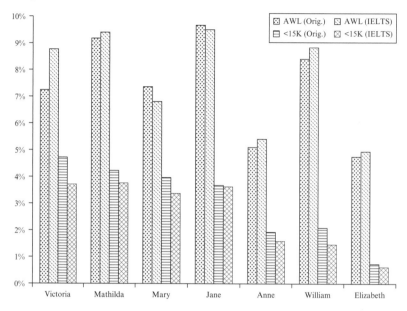

Figure 4.3 Results for Flesch-Kincaid grade level and Coh-Metrix readability estimates for original source texts and adapted IELTS texts
N.B. lower scores on Flesch-Kincaid and higher scores on Coh-Metrix represent greater reading ease.

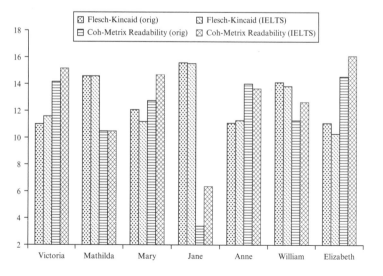

5.1 The non-experienced group

Victoria's text

> *How the brain turns reality into dreams: Tests involving Tetris point to the role played by 'implicit memories'* Kathleen Wren
>
> MSNBC: http://www.msnbc.msn.com published online 12 October 2001

Victoria's text was a science feature published on the website of online news service MSNBC. It describes research into the nature of dreams recently reported in the journal *Science*. The text is organised around a problem–solution pattern. The problem is that of accounting for how dreams relate to memory. The solution is provided by new research, based on the dreams of amnesiacs, identifying dreams with implicit rather than declarative memories.

Victoria made the most extensive changes of all the untrained writers, making revisions to all but one of the paragraphs in her text with a total of 77 edits. Uniquely among writers in both groups, her adapted text was longer (by 44 words) than her source. It also involved an increase in AWL words and a reduction in the most frequent words (BNC 1,000 word level) in the text (Figure 4.1 and Figure 4.2 above). However, in common with all the writers in the study except Mathilda, the effect of Victoria's adaptations was to increase the proportion of words with a frequency in the BNC of one in 3,000 or higher.

Victoria reported that in editing the text she wanted to make it more academic in register and therefore better suited to the context of university study. She had achieved this, she said, by increasing the complexity of sentences, using passive forms and hedges to create academic distance and by adding a methodology section to the article.

There are a number of changes that would seem to be directed at making the text appear less journalistic. A reference to 'Friday's issue of *Science*' in the opening paragraph, which reflects the news value of the article, is removed (although this is the only reference in the article to another text).

These changes include reframing the relationship between writer and reader. The original text addresses the reader as 'you', while the revised version instead employs 'we', passive constructions or, in one case, 'subjects' (in the sense of research subjects). Contractions are replaced with full forms or alternative constructions, as in, 'the hippocampus is not active during REM sleep' or the substitution of 'people with amnesia shouldn't dream' by 'individuals suffering with amnesia should not be capable of dreaming'.

Further changes to the text seem to reflect the intention to achieve a more formal, academic register. These include the use of less frequent vocabulary – 'different parts of the brain' becomes 'a region of the brain'; nominalisation – 'But they can still affect your behavior' becomes 'But they still have the potential to affect behaviour' (note that Victoria changes behavior to behaviour to reflect British spelling conventions); use of reporting verbs – 'said' becomes 'states', 'believes' becomes 'upholds'; references to research procedures – 'therefore' becomes 'from these results', 'the people in the study . . .' becomes 'The methodology designed for Stickgold's study had two groups of subjects . . .'; and hedging – 'Much of the fodder for our dreams comes from recent experiences' in the original text is prefixed in the adapted version with 'Such research suggests that . . .'.

Pronoun references are made more explicit: 'That's called episodic memory' becomes 'To differentiate this information from declarative memory, this particular [form] of recollection is referred to by scientists as episodic memory' and '. . . the procedural memory system, which stores information . . .' is expanded to give '. . . the procedural memory system. This particular system stores information . . .'.

Victoria does not generally choose to replace technical vocabulary with more frequent alternatives, but in one case does add a gloss that does not occur in the source: 'amnesia, *or memory loss*'. She replaces one instance of 'amnesiacs' with 'people suffering from memory loss', but in three other instances she chooses to use 'amnesiacs' directly as it appears in the source text and in a fourth replaces it with 'the amnesiac group'. She also follows the source text in glossing such terms such as 'neocortex', 'hippocampus' and 'hypnogagia', but (again following the source) chooses not to gloss 'REM sleep'. Victoria's changes make the text more difficult to read by the Flesch-Kincaid grade level estimate, which is based on word and sentence length, but easier according to the Coh-Metrix readability formula (Crossley et al 2008), which reflects vocabulary frequency, similarity of syntax across sentences and referential cohesion (see Figure 4.3 on page 308).

Mathilda's text

How – and Where – Will We Live in 2015? The future is now for sustainable cities in the U.K., China, and U.A.E. by Andrew Grant, Julianne Pepitone, Stephen Cass

Discover magazine: http://discovermagazine.com, published online 8 October 2008

Mathilda made the fewest changes of any writer to her source text, which came from *Discover*, a Canadian magazine concerned with developments in science, technology and medicine. This text also has a problem–solution structure, although it is more factual and descriptive and less evaluative than Victoria's. The article portrays three new city developments in diverse locations that are all intended to address ecological problems. The majority of the text is devoted to describing the innovative features of each city in turn: transport, power and irrigation systems.

Mathilda reported that she too had found her text on the internet after looking at examples of IELTS material from the IELTS website. Although she would have preferred a more emotionally engaging literary text, she looked for such popular science topics as *'the environment'*, *'dreams'* and *'the future'* in the belief that these were closer to the topics of the IELTS texts she had seen. After briefly scanning a large number of possible texts, she saved four to her computer for more detailed consideration. She had considered using a text concerning the evolution of the human skeleton, but rejected this as being too technical: *'pure biology'*. She made her choice because she felt it was *'easy to read'* and had sufficient information to support a large number of questions. In common with both Mary and Victoria, she found choosing the text the most time-consuming element in the process.

In editing the text Mathilda cut the attribution and removed the pictures, but left the text itself largely untouched. All four of the textual edits that she made involved replacing relatively infrequent words with more frequent alternatives: 'gas-guzzling cars', which she felt was too idiomatic, became 'gas-consuming cars'. Relatively technical terms were replaced with more frequent words; 'photovoltaic panels' was replaced with 'solar technology'; 'potable water' with 'drinking water' and 'irrigate' with 'water'. These changes somewhat increased the proportion of very frequent and AWL words (panels, technology), and reduced the proportion of very infrequent words, but did not affect the length of the text (748 words) or the readability estimates.

Mary's text

The Rise of the Emotional Robot by Paul Marks

From issue 2650 of *New Scientist* magazine, pages 24–25, published 5 April 2008

As noted in Section 5 above, Mary eventually chose a source text from *New Scientist*, the science and technology magazine noted by Weir et al (2009b) as a popular source for IELTS texts. Unlike both Mathilda and Victoria, Mary chose a source text that, at 1,094 words needed to be pruned to bring it within the maximum IELTS word limit of 950 words. This text, like Victoria's, reports on recent research. The writer reports two studies in some detail and cites the views of other researchers. The situation of human emotional engagement with robots is described and solutions involving making robots appear more human-like are explored. As in Victoria's text, there is an element of evaluation and different points of view are quoted.

Mary was concerned with the authenticity of her text and sought to make as few changes as possible in adapting it for IELTS. Like Mathilda, Mary, who made 30 edits in all, made a number of changes to the vocabulary of her text. These included changing 'careering' to 'moving'; 'resplendent in' to 'wearing'; 'myriad' to 'a multitude of'; 'don' to 'put on' and two instances of 'doppelgänger' to 'computerised double' and 'robotic twin'. As in Mathilda's text, these changes all involved replacing relatively infrequent words with more frequent alternatives, although, reflecting the nature of the text, none of these appear particularly technical to the field of robotics. Mary's changes reduced the proportion of both AWL and infrequent words while increasing the proportion of very frequent words (Figure 4.1 and Figure 4.2 on pages 307–308).

Mary explained that the need to reduce the length of the text led her to remove contextualising points of detail such as the identity of a researcher's university ('. . . who research human–computer interaction at the Georgia Institute of Technology in Atlanta'), reporting '. . . presented at the Human–Robot Interaction conference earlier this month in Amsterdam, the Netherlands', or the location of a research facility ('in Germany') and references to other texts '(*New Scientist*, 12 October 2006, p. 42)'.

Mary also chose to summarise stretches of text. For example, she reduced 'But Hiroshi Ishiguro of Osaka University in Japan thinks that the sophistication of our interactions with robots will have few constraints. He has built a remote-controlled doppelgänger, which fidgets, blinks, breathes, talks, moves its eyes and looks eerily like him. Recently he has used it to hold classes . . .' to 'Scientist Hiroshi Ishiguro has used a robotic twin of himself to hold classes . . .'. However, she chose to introduce this section of the text with three sentences of her own composition: 'Whether robots can really form relationships with humans and what these can be is much disputed. Only time will really tell. However, despite the negative criticism there is one scientist with strong evidence for his view.' This would seem to reflect the focus of her tasks on the identification of views expressed by different experts mentioned in the text.

There is evidence that Mary was aware of the need to avoid potentially sensitive topics in IELTS when choosing her cuts as well as in the initial text selection. Three of the four sentences in a paragraph concerning the emotional attachment formed by American soldiers to robots employed in the Iraq war were deleted from the IELTS text.

Although expressing the most concern for authenticity and favouring a light editorial touch, of all the writers, Mary was the only one to substantially reorder her text. She reported that she had found the original text poorly organised. She wanted to focus in her questions on opinions expressed by different researchers, but found that these were distributed across paragraphs and felt that her questions would be more effective if the paragraphing was addressed.

The first four sentences of the fifth paragraph in her source text, which quotes the views of a named researcher, are cut, and appended to the sixth paragraph. The final sentence is removed altogether. The change, which brings together two quotations from the same expert, reflects Mary's concern for the influence of the task type (matching views to protagonists) and the need to avoid diffusing the views of the experts across the text. Taken together, Mary's changes had the effect of making the text easier to read according to both the Flesch-Kincaid grade level estimate and the Coh-Metrix readability formula (Figure 4.3 on page 308).

We now turn our attention to the texts submitted by the experienced item writers.

5.2 The experienced group

<u>Jane's text</u>

> *Wildlife-Spotting Robots* by Christine Connolly
>
> *Sensor Review*: Volume 27 Number 4 pages 282–287, published in 2007

Uniquely among the writers in this study, Jane chose a text originating in a peer reviewed journal, albeit one directed more towards an industrial than an academic audience (*Sensor Review: The international journal of sensing for industry*). The text concerned the use of remote robotic sensors in wildlife photography exemplified by a secondary report on an application of this technology to capture evidence of a rare bird. The text describes the role of robotic cameras in wildlife observation with examples of the equipment used. There is an extended description of the use of an autonomous robotic camera system in a search for a rare bird, and of a further development of the technology which allows for remote control of the camera over the internet.

Ranging from 1,592 to 2,518 words, the source texts used by the experienced writers were all very much longer than those of the non-experienced group (748 to 1,094 words). At 1,870 words the length of Jane's source text was typical for the experienced group. She cut it by 50%, making 45 edits, to give an IELTS text of 937 words.

This was the most technical of all the texts and like other writers Jane cut a number of technical terms. These related both to wildlife and animal behaviour ('hawks', 'herons', 'double knock drummings') and to the technology being used to record it ('RECONYX cameras', 'XBAT software', 'auto-iris'). However, she also retained many such words in her IELTS text including, 'ornithology', 'geese', 'fieldwork', 'vocalisations', 'actuators', 'teleoperation' and 'infrared'. In spite of the changes, Jane's final text included the lowest proportion of high frequency words of any writer. The most frequent 3,000 words of the BNC accounted for just 88.6% of her IELTS text while the 95% coverage said to be required for fluent reading (Laufer 1989) came only at the 8,000 word frequency level of the BNC.

Some of Jane's edits appear to be directed at clarification or at improvement of the quality of the writing. Compare the original and edited versions of the following:

> *Original text*: 'More than 20 trained field biologists were recruited to the USFWS/CLO search team, and volunteers also took part.'
> *IELTS text*: 'The project started in 2005 with over 20 trained field biologists taking part in the search team, and volunteers also being recruited.'

> *Original text*: 'The search also made use of . . . cameras . . . for monitoring likely sites without the disturbance unavoidable by human observers.'

> *IELTS text*: 'The search also made use of . . . cameras . . . for monitoring likely sites. This method was ideal since it did not lead to the disturbance that is unavoidable with human observers.'

Jane expanded some abbreviations ('50m to 50 metres', '8h per day' to '8 hours per day'), but not others ('10m to 40mm' is retained to describe a camera lens focal range, and sound is 'sampled at 20kHz for up to 4h per day'). 'UC Berkeley' is expanded to 'University of California, Berkeley' on its first occurrence, but not on its second. Three occurrences of 'Texas A&M' are retained unchanged.

The deletion of the abstract, subheadings and the two citations had the effect of making the final text appear less like a journal article. The removal of a block of 653 words in five paragraphs that described the technical attributes of robotic cameras, together with the cutting of photographs of the equipment and examples of the images captured, had the effect of foregrounding the application to wildlife research (problem–solution) and diminishing the attention given to the attributes of the equipment (description/elaboration): the central concern of the journal. One paragraph within this block explained why the equipment qualified as 'robotic' and its deletion modifies and diminishes the relationship between the title (Wildlife-spotting robots) and the adapted text. In IELTS the 'robotic' nature of the cameras is not explicitly explained, although three uses of the term do remain. This became a source of some confusion for the editing team (see Section 7).

Jane's edits had little effect on the Flesch-Kincaid grade level of the original text, but did make it easier to read according to the Coh-Metrix readability formula. However, by both measures her IELTS text was the most difficult of all the edited texts in this study.

Anne's text

> *The Funny Business of Laughter* by Emma Bayley
>
> *BBC Focus*: May 2008, pages 61 to 65

Anne's text was taken from *BBC Focus*, a monthly magazine dedicated to science and technology. This expository text, which draws on a range of research from different disciplines, describes and elaborates the functions and origins of laughter and their implications for our understanding of the human mind. Anne reported that she had found this text in a file she kept for the purpose of item writing, storing suitable texts between item writing commissions.

Like all the experienced writers, Anne took a relatively lengthy source (1,606 words) and cut it extensively (her edited text was 946 words long), making 54 edits altogether. She discarded 15 of the 31 words in the source text that fell outside the 15K frequency level and 31 of 82 from the AWL. This results in a slightly higher proportion of academic words and a lower proportion of very infrequent words in the edited text than in the source (Figure 4.2 on page 308).

In common with all the other writers Anne chose to cut a number of technical terms including 'neurological' and 'thorax' (replaced with 'chest') although she retained 'bipedal' and 'quadrupedal' as well as other technical words such as 'neuroscientist', 'primate' and 'stimulus'. She also excised a number of infrequent words including synonyms for laughter (the topic of the text) such as 'chortle', 'yelping' and 'exhalations', replacing this latter word with another infrequent (though more transparent) word borrowed from the deleted opening section of the original: 'outbreath'.

One means of reducing the length of the text that Anne exploits is to cut redundancy in word pairs such as 'rough and tumble play' or restatements such as 'laboured breathing or panting'. Some changes seem to reflect an editor's desire to improve the linguistic quality and accuracy of the text: she inserts the conjunction 'that' in the sentence 'It is clear now *that* it evolved prior to humankind' and replaces 'most apes' with 'great apes', presumably because the text has cited only orang-utan and chimpanzee behaviour.

Anne eliminated references to a 'news' aspect of her story by deleting the first and last paragraphs: the original article opened and closed with references to the forthcoming 'world laughter day'. Another change that makes the text less journalistic, in line with Anne's stated desire to reduce *'journalese',* is the increase in formality. The idiomatic 'having a good giggle' is replaced by 'laughing'; some abbreviations and contractions are exchanged for full forms so that 'lab' becomes 'laboratory', 'you've' becomes 'you have' and 'don't' is replaced with 'do not'. However, unlike Victoria, Anne chooses to retain contractions such as 'that's' and 'it's' and even modifies one occurrence of 'it is' in the original to 'it's'. In her final IELTS text, 'it's' occurs three times and 'it is' four times. Whimsical, informal and perhaps culturally specific references to aliens landing on earth and to the 'world's worst sitcom' are also removed.

Through her deletions Anne relegates one of the central themes of her original text – the role of laughter in the evolution of socialisation and the sense of self. As a result, the IELTS text relative to the source, although less journalistic, seems more tightly focused on laughter as a phenomenon *per se* than on its wider significance for psychology or, as expressed in a sentence that Anne deletes, *'such lofty questions as the perception of self and the evolution of speech, language and social behaviour'.* However, elaboration is the primary rhetorical function of the IELTS text as it is for the source. The effect of Anne's changes on the readability of the text is to make it somewhat more difficult according to both the Flesch-Kincaid and Coh-Metrix estimates.

William's text

> *Introduction* from *Poor Monkey: The Child in Literature* by Peter Coveney
>
> Published in 1957 by Rockliff

William's source text, the only one taken from a book, was an essay by Peter Coveney (1957). This was the longest chosen by any writer and William cut around 60% of the original, making 60 edits in developing his 909 word IELTS text. The third and eighth paragraphs of the original text are almost entirely discarded, as are lengthy stretches (50 words or more) of every paragraph except the first and fourth.

Much in the rejected passages concerns the original author's informing theory of the relationship between literature and social change. In the third paragraph, he anticipates criticism and defends his approach: 'To suggest a relation between literature and society might seem to imply that too much, perhaps, is to be explained too easily by too little'. This is eliminated from the IELTS text, while in other cases William offers summaries of parts of the original, of varying length. The first two sentences of the original text – 'Until the last decades of the eighteenth century, the child did not exist as an important and continuous theme in English literature. Childhood as a major theme came with the generation of Blake and Wordsworth.' – is replaced by a single sentence in the edited text – 'Childhood as an important theme of English literature did not exist before the last decades of the eighteenth century and the poetry of Blake and Wordsworth.', saving nine words. The sentence 'Art was on the run; the ivory tower had become the substitute for the wished-for public arena' substitutes for 169 words on this theme in the original.

References to specific works of literature (*The Chimney Sweeper*, *Ode on Intimations of Immortality*, *The Prelude*, *Hard Times*, *Dombey and Son*, *David Copperfield*, *Huckleberry Finn*, *Essay on Infantile Sexuality*, *Way of All Flesh*, *Peter Pan*) and to a number of writers (Addison, Butler, Carroll, Dryden, James, Johnson, Pope, Prior, Rousseau, Shakespeare, Shaw, Twain) are removed, together with references to other critics (Empson), although the names of Blake, Dickens, Darwin, Freud, Marx and Wordsworth are retained. Some technical literary vocabulary such as 'Augustan', 'ode', 'Romantics' and 'Shakespearian' is cut (although 'lyrics', 'poetry' and 'sensibility' are retained), as are relatively infrequent words such as 'cosmology', 'esoteric', 'moribund', 'congenial' and 'introversion'. As a result, in common with most other writers, the proportion of frequent words is higher and the proportion of very infrequent words lower in the edited text than in the source (Figure 4.1 and Figure 4.2 on pages 307–308).

As was the case for Anne and Jane, one effect of William's changes is to narrow the scope of the essay. The edited version is focused more closely on the theme of the treatment of childhood at the expense of discussion of specific works and of arguments supporting the thesis of literature as an expression of social change and crisis. As a result, the adapted text takes on more of the characteristics of an historical narrative with a cause/effect structure and loses elements of persuasion and argumentation. The changes to the text had little effect on the Flesch-Kincaid grade level estimate (Figure 4.3), but made it easier to read according to the Coh-Metrix readability formula.

Elizabeth's text

> *Time to Wake Up to the Facts about Sleep* by Jim Horne
>
> *New Scientist*: published on 16 October 2008, pages 36 to 38

In common with Mary, Elizabeth chose a source text from the *New Scientist*. As was the case for Anne, this was a text that Elizabeth already held on file. The text questioned popular myths about people's need for more sleep. Resembling the texts chosen by Victoria, Mary, Jane and Anne, this article reports on recent research, although in this case the author of the text is one of the researchers and refers to a study carried out by 'My team' (the IELTS text retains this). The author argues against perceptions that people living in modern societies are deprived of sleep and draws on a range of research evidence, including his own study, to support his view. Like William's, this is a text that involves argumentation and is organised around justifying a point of view. Reflecting the personal tone of the original, Elizabeth retains the attribution by incorporating it into a brief contextualising introduction following the title: 'Claims that we are chronically sleep-deprived are unfounded and irresponsible, says sleep researcher Jim Horne'.

Elizabeth cut the 1,592 word source text by 60% to 664 words, making 48 edits. Like Mary, Elizabeth cuts references to other texts – '(Biology Letters, vol 4, p 402)' – and removes a number of technical terms: she removes the technical 'metabolic syndrome', but retains 'metabolism'. She also chooses to keep 'obesity', 'insomnia', 'precursor', 'glucose' and the very infrequent 'eke'. Elizabeth's source text included relatively few academic and very low-frequency words and more high-frequency words than the texts chosen by any other writer (Figure 4.1 and Figure 4.2).

Like Anne and Victoria, Elizabeth replaces informal journalistic touches with more formal alternatives – 'shut eye' becomes 'sleep' (although 'snooze' is retained), 'overcooked' becomes 'exaggerated' (but 'trotted out' is retained).

The most intensively edited section of the text is an extended quotation from a researcher. As was the case for Anne and Jane, clarity and style seem to be important. Compare the following:

> *Original text*: We did this by asking when they usually went to sleep and at what time they woke up, followed by, 'How much sleep do you feel you need each night?'

> *IELTS text*: We asked respondents the times when they usually went to bed and woke up, and the amount of sleep they felt they needed each night.

Another change may reflect the need for sensitivity to cultural diversity in IELTS mentioned by Elizabeth in relation to her awareness of candidate background. The author's assumption about the identity of his readers seems to be reflected in one phrase that he uses: 'we in the west'. In the IELTS text this becomes the less positioned 'most people in the west'. Rhetorically, Elizabeth retains the function of the text as an opinion piece organised around justification of a point of view.

The changes made in editing had the effect of making the text easier to read according to both the Flesch-Kincaid grade level estimate and the Coh-Metrix readability formula (Figure 4.3).

6   Analysis and findings on the editing process

The participants were mainly left to organise and implement the joint editing session without intervention from the research team. The summary here seeks to identify and quantify the occurrences of key points raised, as informing the investigation of IELTS Academic Reading test item writing processes.

The analysis of the texts as originally submitted by the three non-experienced participants appears in Section 5 above. This section describes the changes made to the texts and items in the process of joint test editing. We begin with the non-experienced group.

6.1   The non-experienced group

Victoria text editing

As noted in the text analysis below, Victoria's text, How the Brain Turns Reality into Dreams, was taken from the online news website MSNBC, describing research into dreams reported in the journal *Science*. Victoria, who, it will be recalled, often referred to her process of 'fixing up' her text, made 77 edits, revised all her paragraphs and actually increased the length of the original text from 897 to 941 words.

At the beginning of the editing session on her text and items, it was suggested by her colleagues, who had just read her text, that Victoria should make the following additional changes to her text:

- the deletion of one or two hedging phrases she had added to give the text a more academic tone
- the shortening of two clauses for compactness.

Victoria item editing

Victoria had chosen True/False/Not Given (T/F/NG), Multiple Choice (MCQ) and Short Answer Questions (using not more than three words from the passage) (SAQ) as her task types.

The following were the main issues raised over the tasks and items proposed by Victoria:

- the possibility, especially in the T/F/NG task, that test takers may infer differently from the item writer, but plausibly, yet be penalised even when their understanding of the point concerned is not wrong
- the question whether, in actual IELTS item writing, there were conventions on the distribution of the T/F and NG categories in a set
- the colleagues themselves found Victoria's multiple choice items difficult
- that having two incorrect alternatives which mean the same (though in different words) was in a way increasing the test taker's chance of selecting the right alternative
- that the SAQ task should be a test of content rather than grammatical structure.

Mathilda text editing

As noted above and confirmed in the text analysis below, Mathilda made the fewest changes, only four, of any writer to her source text, How – and Where – will we Live in 2015? The text came from *Discover*, a Canadian science and technology magazine. It was relatively short at 748 words.

At the beginning of the editing session on her text and items, Mathilda wondered whether her text was perhaps too easy, being straightforward and factual, with no complex argument and a sequential key point structure. Mathilda was reminded by her colleagues that a straightforward text might well be accompanied by difficult questions. In fact, this would not be in accordance with IELTS practice.

Mathilda item editing

The following matters were raised in discussions of the tasks and items proposed by Mathilda:

- whether it was legitimate test practice to include, for example in the multiple choice distractors, information which is not actually in the text

- the 'give-away' factor when a distractor is included that clearly comes from a part of the text distant from the one on which the question set is focusing
- the possible bias of items concerning a project in countries from which some candidates and not others, actually came, and who might know more from personal experience.

In the editing discussion of items here, as for all three texts, colleagues were able to point out one or two items which were flawed because of a falsifying point in the text unnoticed by the actual item writer.

Mary text editing

Mary's text, The Rise of the Emotional Robot, had been taken from the *New Scientist*. She had herself reduced the original by 15% to meet the 950 word maximum for an IELTS text. Mary was found (see next section) to have made 30 edits in all, including vocabulary changes – (more changes in fact than Mary herself had indicated, feeling, as she claimed, that texts should not, in the interests of authenticity, be changed too much – see Table 4.3 above).

At the beginning of the editing session on her text and items, Mary made the following additional points regarding changes to her original text:

- modifications to render the text more academic, 'cohesive' (and 'IELTS-like') through order change
- changes to the final paragraph to add strength and self-containedness to the end of the text
- one deletion from the original was made both to shorten the text to within IELTS limits (950 words) and because the experiment concerned was not one she intended to ask questions about.

After discussion with Victoria and Mathilda, who had just read her text, three further modifications were made to Mary's text:

- one sentence was deleted from the text, as repetitive
- reference to the theory of mind was reinstated from the original text
- the order of sentences in the final paragraph was modified for stylistic reasons.

Mary item editing

In the context of the research, the discussions of the tasks and items drafted by Mary, Mathilda and Victoria should be informative with regard to both the item writing and editing processes. The following were the main issues raised over the tasks and items proposed by Mary:

On the matching task:

- potential overlap was identified across the source statements leading to some ambiguity in the pairings; modifications were suggested accordingly
- use in the items of the same word(s) as in the text could give away some answers; IELTS-oriented textbooks tend to teach for parallel meanings.

On the summary completion task:

- there was some confusion over the difference, if any, between 'passage' and 'text'
- it was clarified that the (not more than three) completing words had to actually appear in the original text but some doubt remained over whether a different form of the same word was eligible for use
- the summary completion passage was modified to allow for this.

On the multiple choice task:

- instances of more than one item choice being acceptable because of semantic overlap (e.g. 'respect' and 'love'), were discussed
- the discussion here raised a multiple choice task issue of whether all alternatives should be similar in function, e.g. all four about facts or all four inferences, or whether alternatives can be mixed in terms of function, presence or absence in the text (as in a true / false / not given item) etc.?; do candidates know such IELTS rules or conventions? – in such cases, the test designer has the option of changing the item or changing the distractors
- the test item writing and editing process here is described by Mary as '*finding the area and going over it with a fine-tooth comb*'.

It emerged during the editing session that as a part of the editing process both Mary and Victoria had asked friends to take their tests as a check on whether these were successful. Both writers had found this helpful in guiding further improvements.

This part of the session ended after 40 minutes' discussion of the items.

6.1.1 Choosing the text for the exam

The initial choices among the three non-experienced item writers were as follows:

Mary favoured Mathilda's *Sustainable Cities* text, finding:

- the robot text (her own) lacked '*meat*'
- the dreams text was '*too hard*' (for her)
- the cities text, being descriptive, was more easily exploited for items and distractors.

Mathilda favoured Mary's *Robots* text, finding:

* it contained enough meat in the opinions expressed, the tensions described, the hurdles presented
* it was at an appropriate level of difficulty, yet was reader-friendly.

Mathilda now considered her own sustainable cities text:

* too fact-based and argument free
* lacking the challenge or need for deeper understanding of an argumentative text.

6.1.2 Change of view caused by the editing process?

Victoria still liked her *Dreams* text but was now less confident about her tasks. She considered it necessary to do far more analysis of potential texts and tasks. The three in the group still did not know the optimum processes but were, rather, acting on the basis of common sense and their experience as teachers. Mathilda felt the need for a whole range of IELTS tests and tasks to analyse to increase her awareness of suitable texts, tasks and what they are supposed to be testing. Mary agreed, not having been trained as an IELTS item writer, it was difficult to know which words you can use in a text, how much you can test inferences.

Victoria would like to know about technical testing matters such as evenness of distractor and response lengths, Mathilda wanted more official information on IELTS to know more about IELTS level of difficulty, mark allocation and analysis. All three participants felt that the '*rules*' of IELTS are '*pretty well hidden*'. Their own help to their IELTS students in how to deal with IELTS Reading test items was common sense rather than officially informed.

Victoria, who was aware of IELTS Writing paper pretesting and other validation procedures, wondered whether the Reading paper was subject to similar procedures. As will be apparent from our review above, IELTS does publish information on these issues on its website and through other sources such as Cambridge ESOL's *Research Notes*. The response of this group therefore may indicate lack of awareness rather than lack of availability.

In response to the final question, what the three participants felt they had learned from their day:

* Victoria, assuming that reading for an IELTS Reading test was different from other reading and in spite of having looked at information on task types on the IELTS website, still wished to know how test takers should read in the test
* Mary, on the issue of what we are meant to be testing and how do we test it, wondered when it is appropriate to be testing vocabulary and when it is not

- Mathilda wished to know, relatedly, how questions towards the broader and narrower understanding of a text should be balanced.

Learning from the activities of the day, the participants noted the following things that they would do differently in future:

- Mary would, in advance, chart her intended items in terms of their intended difficulty and scope, to ensure evenness of coverage
- Mathilda would like to challenge herself using a fictional, more literary text (for example a short story) for her item writing; she still wondered why IELTS reading seemed not to use such texts; her impression was that the range of topics covered by IELTS Academic Reading modules was somewhat narrow
- Victoria would do a close analysis of more IELTS Reading papers before she began setting her own; she was seeking a match between text type and task type – this could mean a change of direction from choosing text and topic first; as an item writer, she might prefer to feel more responsible for the kinds of task she was going to set
- Victoria did not feel that the experience of the day had clarified why test takers often found the IELTS Reading module more difficult than the other modules (although, as noted above, Reading scores are generally higher than for Writing and Speaking); perhaps it was less clear with the Reading module than with the others what test takers were supposed to be doing.

6.2   The experienced group

With Anne taking the role of chair, the participants were asked to organise and implement the joint editing session as they would a routine IELTS editing meeting (without further intervention from the research team). The intention was to prepare at least one text and set of items for the next stage in the test production process: pretesting.

Given the constraints on time, it was anticipated that it might not prove possible to go through the full process with all of the texts. In the event, the group was able to carry out the full editing process with Jane's text and looked closely at the text and one of the three item sets for both William's and Elizabeth's submissions. The group spent an intensive 85 minutes on Jane's text and items – the majority of the time (66 minutes) being devoted to the items. This seemed to the participants to be quite typical of the degree of attention that might usually be given to a submission in an editing meeting, although the point was made that a number of the issues might have been identified in a pre-editing session: a step that was not included in this project.

The 85 minutes spent on Jane's submission compares with a total of 68 minutes spent on the other two submissions considered at the meeting (29 minutes on William's and 39 minutes on Elizabeth's). Because of the time constraints and because it is not usual for the chair of an editing meeting to lead the evaluation of her own submission, Anne's was not addressed at the meeting, although her text is considered in Section 6 above. As with the non-experienced writers, the following summary focuses, qualitatively and inductively on key points raised.

In each case, the group began by commenting on a text, suggesting changes which were noted by the chair. They then looked in detail at the related items, agreeing on and noting changes before passing on to the second writer's work.

Jane text editing

There was some discussion about the meaning of the text and the nature of the automated systems described. For example, the use of 'scheduled', 'selective' and 'sift' in the first paragraph caused some confusion with discussion about whether it was the machines or human experts selecting and sifting material. Elizabeth asked whether others shared her understanding that the 'CONE' system was partly and 'ACONE' entirely autonomous. William sought to clarify the roles of the university partners in the study and this question was discussed at some length. Anne queried the ordering of the units used in describing the camera's focal range in the fifth paragraph: 10m to 40mm. William also questioned whether this was accurate as 40mm seemed very short. It was agreed that the figures should be checked.

A number of proof reading errors were identified. For example, William found an intrusive comma in line 3. Problems were also noted with the formatting of the text and the appearance of abbreviations for measures. It was agreed that the names of the universities involved in the research and the order of their listing should be standardised.

Some issues were identified concerning technical vocabulary: Anne suggested glossing 'GPS' in the third paragraph and this was agreed.

A number of changes were intended to improve the coherence of the text:

- There were questions relating to the paragraphing. Elizabeth suggested having the first sentence as a subheading as it seemed not to relate closely to what followed. This was agreed and the change was made. She also questioned whether the last sentence of the second paragraph should be moved to the third paragraph. This was not agreed.
- Elizabeth suggested removing the sentence 'They also use ultra-light aircraft to conduct aerial surveys' in the third paragraph as it seemed to contradict statements about the entirely automated nature of the ACONE system. This was agreed.
- The first sentence of the fourth paragraph was reworded. The original wording was: 'In February 2007, the University of California, Berkeley

announced the installation of a high resolution intelligent robotic video system . . .'.

This was revised to give, 'In February 2007 a further stage of the project began when the University of California, Berkeley announced the installation of a high resolution intelligent robotic video system . . .'. This was felt to clarify the relationship between the installation of the video system described in the fourth paragraph and the research described in the third paragraph.

- Elizabeth suggested that, as the acronym had already appeared, CONE in the final paragraph did not need to be expanded again here. This was agreed.

<u>Jane item editing</u>

On the *True/False/Not Given* items:

Item 1   Anne questioned whether the first item was sufficiently precise as it could be taken to refer to all wildlife experiments. Elizabeth pointed out that the whole task covered the use of equipment in wildlife experiments and that the necessary information might therefore be difficult to locate. Suggested rewordings were not satisfactory and, following discussion, the item was rejected. As a result, a new item needed to be written.

Item 2   Elizabeth suggested that 'only a few occasions' might better reflect the sense of the text than the more negative 'little chance' in the item. Jane wanted to replace 'chance' as this repeated a word in the text. The word 'record' was preferred to 'capture' which seemed ambiguous when discussing wildlife.

Item 3   William objected that the text implied that this 'Not Given' statement was true. Elizabeth queried the meaning of 'examine the different species': in the text it was recordings that were being examined. These two objections were dealt with by rewording the item as, 'Those examining the data on target species would benefit from further training' which was felt to be more clearly 'Not Given' in the text.

Item 5   Anne queried the order of items 4 and 5. Jane confirmed that these should be reversed. The tense of 'will activate' was changed to 'activates' and 'some' was replaced by 'certain'.

Item 4   This was accepted with little discussion.

Additional item   The group agreed that a new item could be generated from the untested material at the end of the second paragraph. The distinction that had been discussed earlier between CONE and ACONE was identified as important information. The group arrived at 'CONE relies entirely on input from non-human sources'. William suggested that the word 'entirely' could be a trigger to test-wise candidates, but this objection was overridden. Nonetheless the group was unable to arrive at an agreed wording. After 4 minutes of discussion, the group failed to arrive at a satisfactory conclusion and decided to move on. Returning to this section after editing the other items and following discussion of a number of alternative suggestions, finally they settled on:

'CONE uses data from robotic devices instead of input from scientists'.

On the Notes Completion items:

Item 6   The item wording was ambiguous: 'in' could refer to time (1940, the intended key) or place (North America). Adding 'year when' at the beginning was felt to be unnatural for a set of notes. The compromise arrived at involved changing the text provided to the candidate to read:

'when bird was last seen'.

Item 7   This was accepted.

Item 8   'involves' was replaced by 'causes'. In the following line, 'old recordings' was felt to be ambiguous and 'of target species' was added to clarify this.

Item 9   The item was seen to depend on syntax: 'a' in the item cued 'match' in the text. It could be unclear what the 'match' referred to. The item was revised to give: 'results analysed to identify any [matches] with original recordings'. The text was also edited so that 'a match' became 'matches'.

Item 10   This was accepted.

Item 11   This was accepted following discussion.

Item 12   The use of 'already' was questioned. This was replaced with 'have'. William pointed out that 'birds' would also be correct here. The agreed item read: 'birds that cameras have taken pictures of'.

On the short answer questions:

Item 13   Anne had not been able to find the correct answer and suggested replacing 'professional group' with 'professionals'. This was accepted.

Item 14   This was accepted without changes.

Item 15   William felt this was ambiguous as 'from' could be associated with the events or the monitoring: 'events from the field' or 'monitoring events from the laboratory'. It was decided that 'from' should be replaced with 'in' in the text. The agreed item read 'Where are the biologists in the CONE study located when they are monitoring events': the key was '(in) (their) laboratories'.

Item 16   The word 'feature' was replaced with 'function'.

William text editing

The reference to the doctrine of 'original sin' in the second and seventh paragraphs was queried on the grounds that this might be confusing to students from a non-Christian background. 'Christian tradition' was replaced with 'long held belief'. William argued that the term 'sinful' should be acceptable without glossing, but the religious implications were seen to make the text questionable. Alternatives such as 'wickedness' and 'guilt' were considered, but rejected. Anne felt that 'it would be very difficult to get round this, quite frankly' because religion was considered a 'taboo' subject for IELTS. William observed that 'most history seems to be impossible' because of the cultural element. Words such as 'church' or 'mosque' could not, he felt, be used in IELTS. The question of how to eliminate the religious element in the text was put to one side so that editing could proceed.

Elizabeth and Jane both questioned the use of 'ivory tower'. After a number of attempts at rewording, the sentence 'Art was on the run; the ivory tower had become the substitute for the wished for public arena' was eliminated on the grounds that the idea had appeared in the previous sentence.

The 'dense' nature of the text was seen to be a potential shortcoming and there was some confusion over the temporal progression of ideas. Elizabeth asked for clarification of 'late' C19th in Paragraph 7.

William item editing

The group looked closely at William's second set of questions (matching) and identified certain issues:

* Potential guessability: Jane had been able to guess items 8 and 10, but wondered whether these would be guessable for certain candidates. How far might candidates be expected to know about the history of English literature?
* The stems for items 7 and 11 ('Authors working prior to the late 18th century' and 'In the harsh society of the 19th century, some authors') did not seem to fit well with the stems for items 8, 9 and 10.

The conclusion of this session was that the text would probably have been returned to the writer at the pre-editing stage with comments on the cultural elements. The issues identified and communicated to the writer would need to have been resolved before the text could have progressed to editing.

Elizabeth's text editing

All three other writers queried the inclusion, in paragraph 3, of 'eke out the very last quantum of sleepiness', but Anne decided to delay revising this until the group came to address item 2, to which it related. They also questioned 'trotted out' as being too colloquial. The latter was replaced with 'frequently put forward'. These were the only issues raised in relation to Elizabeth's text.

Elizabeth item editing

Item 1   Anne had failed to find the correct answer, although William believed it was 'strongly there'. The use of 'accurately reported' in option C was questioned as it might refer to the original reporting of the Stanford study by the researchers rather than to subsequent misrepresentations of it. The use of 'misunderstood' seemed to address this. Anne suggested replacing 'with' in the question stem with 'in'.

Item 2   William felt that option B could also be true. The use of 'unrealistic' was identified as problematic and was replaced with Elizabeth's suggestion of 'stressful'. Here the focus moved to finding an appropriate rewording of the problematic element in the text identified earlier. After discussion, 'they are able to eke out the very last quantum of sleepiness' was replaced with 'participants are able to exploit their opportunity to sleep to the full'. As a result of the change, 'unnoticeable' at the end of the sentence became problematic. This had modified 'sleepiness'. The issue was resolved by substituting 'unattainable' for 'unnoticeable'. Elizabeth then suggested reversing the order of options C and D so that the key (originally D) would not come last in the set. This was agreed.

Item 3   No suggestions were made and the item was accepted.

Item 4   No suggestions were made and the item was accepted.

Item 5   All distractors dealt with the issue of the relationship between sleep and obesity and were felt to be acceptable.

Item 6   William suggested that confusion that might be caused by using the negatively worded 'underestimating how little sleep'. The alternative 'overestimated the amount of sleep' was preferred.

Item 7   The use of the vague 'a particular type of question' in the stem was queried. This was replaced with 'a question like "would you like more sleep?"' which had the advantage of being both more explicit and matching exactly the relevant section of the text (the eighth paragraph). However, the implications of making the relationship between item and text so much more explicit were not discussed. Option B was then felt not to work with the revised stem. This was replaced with 'may give rise to answers on other topics'. The options were then reordered to make D the key, balancing the number of each option that appeared as the key.

Conclusions from the day's activities and discussions
Reflecting at the end of the day, the group felt that the meeting had represented a typical editing meeting, working at what Anne described as a '*realistic pace*', at least on Jane's material. However, the point was made that the pre-editing stage would probably have helped to eliminate some of the textual issues that had emerged.

William's submission had highlighted the difficulties of exploiting arts texts, answering, in a sense, the question raised by Mathilda during the inexperienced item writers' deliberations. Arts texts often included a number of culture-specific elements. Elizabeth suggested that it was also an issue that such texts assumed background knowledge: '*they always assume you have read the work or seen the picture*'. William was reminded that the editing meeting would always throw up problems that he had failed to find when reviewing the text: '*I always find things at editing that I hadn't noticed before*'.

Aspects of Elizabeth's text such as 'trotted out' had highlighted the need to remove journalistic touches from the text to achieve a more neutral academic style. Magazine articles often began with an attention-grabbing anecdote or example before moving to a more general point, while, William suggested, academic texts more often started from a generalisation. Anne had cut the first paragraph from her source text for this reason.

There was a contrast between the length of IELTS texts and the length of the texts that students would need to read: '*900 words versus a book*' as Elizabeth put it. Elizabeth defended the use of relatively short tests in IELTS, stating that '*we are not testing what they may be able to do after a few months at university; we are testing whether they will be able to cope, I think*'. William pointed to the great variety of texts that could be encountered at university, some of which would be more straightforward for students than IELTS texts. He suggested that '*somebody who struggles with texts like these might be able to cope perfectly well with physics texts*' which might contain more technical vocabulary, but less subordination.

Anne felt that IELTS, by moving between topics and by moving from fact-based to more discursive texts might '*reflect in miniature what [students] have*' *to do . . . look at a variety of sources, get key ideas, get attitudes, get opinions'* while Elizabeth countered that, given the practical restrictions on what could be covered in a 1-hour test *'there is a huge amount we don't do of course: dealing with contents, dealing with indexes, dealing with chapters and all that sort of macro stuff. We can't do it.'*

Preparation courses were considered to be helpful in improving reading skills and in building exam technique. Elizabeth reported that students she had taught had found learning for IELTS useful in preparing them to read longer texts. Elizabeth believed that there was a *'core vocabulary'* for the test that could be taught and there was general agreement that the strategies used in IELTS would transfer to reading texts for academic purposes.

6.2.1 Analysis and findings on the items

As with the texts in Section 6, the analysis here is applied to the items as they were submitted by the seven participants, before any changes made during the public editing process. Again, links are made with the comments from the participants and the edits made during the meetings.

Table 4.9 on page 331 shows the task types selected by the three writers for their commissioned items. No writers chose Types 3 (Sentence Completion), 5 (Labelling a Diagram), 6 (Choosing Headings for Paragraphs or Sections of a Text) or 9 (Classification). This may reflect the difficulty, discussed by the experienced writers, of finding or creating suitable diagrams. It is also of interest, given the reservations expressed by Jane, that all three non-experienced writers attempted these, but only one of the four experienced writers did so. However, this might also reflect the relative familiarity of this item type for the non-experienced group.

The most popular task type, chosen by six of the eight writers, was Identification of Writer's Views/Claims or of Information in a Text or True/False/Not Given (T/F/NG). It is clear from the focus group discussions that this is seen by the experienced writers as a flexible and relatively straightforward task type to work with. In the following section we analyse the writers' items in some detail, drawing on Macmillan's (2007) typology of lexical relationships between texts and items, to explore how items are used and how the two groups interpreted the requirements. In this case, we begin with the experienced writers' items.

Jane was the only one of the experienced writers whose T/F/NG items were edited at the meeting. The comments and revisions made provide insight into the experienced writers' conception of this item type.

Jane's only False item (item 1) relies on antonymy. The location of the necessary information is clearly signalled by the repetition of 'programmed' and 'data' in the item while 'random intervals' in the stem is contrasted with 'scheduled intervals' in the text. However, the editing team objected to the open-ended reference of 'wildlife experiments' and were unable to find a

Table 4.9 Task types (based on list given at www.ielts.org) selected by each item writer

Task types		Victoria	Mathilda	Mary	Jane	Anne	William	Elizabeth
Type 1	Multiple Choice	✓	✓	✓				✓
Type 2	Short Answer Questions	✓			✓			
Type 3	Sentence Completion							
Type 4	Notes, Summary or Table/ Flow chart Completion			✓	✓	✓		✓
Type 5	Labelling a Diagram							
Type 6	Choosing Headings for Paragraphs or Sections of a Text							
Type 7	Locating Information		✓			✓	✓	✓
Type 8	Identification of Writer's Views/ Claims or of Information in a Text	✓	✓		✓	✓	✓	
Type 9	Classification							
Type 10	Matching			✓			✓	

satisfactory alternative. As a result they chose to reject the item. A replacement item was written and added to the end of the set during the editing meeting and is discussed below.

Item 2 (True) is also clearly signalled (through the repetition of 'chance' and 'species') and involves lexical repetition: 'the chances are very low' (item): 'there is little chance' (text); 'the target species' (item): 'the species being investigated' (text); and synonymy: 'the equipment used will capture': 'recording an occurrence'. The phrase 'some cameras' in item 5 (True) matches 'some wildlife cameras' in the text and the item paraphrases a single sentence from the text.

In item 3 (Not Given), the location of the necessary information might seem to be most clearly cued by the similarity between 'field studies' in the stem and 'fieldwork' in the text, although this is probably not the intended location as 'fieldwork' occurs in the opening line and items of this type usually follow the sequence of the text. The word 'experts' in the stem repeats 'expert' in the first paragraph, although this word occurs twice more in the text. The repetition of 'species' might serve to limit the search, but also cues the previous item and so might be thought to jeopardise item independence.

Assuming that it is the occurrence of 'expert' in the first paragraph that is intended, the successful test taker would need to recognise either that there is no mention of either experts or cameras examining 'the different species' or that the 'insufficient' number of 'experts' mentioned in the stem is not suggested as a reason for sifting the field data. It may be, however, that this is a plausible inference. For this reason, this does not appear to be a very satisfactory item. The item writers recognised the plausibility of the inference and rewrote the item. The revised item 'Those examining the data on target species would benefit from further training' includes direct repetition of the phrase 'target species' and 'examining' matches 'examination' in the following line. There is a reference to 'trained biologists' in paragraph 3, which might serve to distract the test taker, but there is no other reference to training. There is no relationship between 'would benefit from further training' and the information given in the text so the new item appears to be unambiguously Not Given.

The location of the necessary information for item 4 (also Not Given) is more clearly signposted: 'cameras for wildlife filming' and 'surveillance cameras' in the stem co-refer with (and repeat words from) the phrases 'wildlife cameras' and 'surveillance systems' in the text. The text compares the operation of the two systems, but does not make any statement about the organisations that manufacture them. Here both the noun phrase 'organisations' and the verb phrases 'produce' and 'make' relate to information that is also entirely absent from the text. This item was accepted by the group without changes.

The task types used by Anne include Type 8: Identification of Writer's Views/Claims or of Information in a Text (True/False/Not Given), Type 4: Summary Completion and Type 7: Locating Information. Information required to respond to the first section was located in the first, second, fifth, sixth and seventh paragraphs (of nine). Information required to respond to the second section could be found in paragraphs four and five and that for the final section in paragraphs eight and nine.

The information required to respond to Anne's T/F/NG items can be found in sequence in the first seven paragraphs of her text. Each question consists of a paraphrase of information given in the text. Identifying whether the answer is correct rests on the ability to identify co-reference and hence to map words or phrases in the question on to words in the text. Generally there is a clue to the location of the information provided by use of words or phrases in the question that precisely match words in the text ('six million years ago' in item 3, 'tickling machine' in item 8), are different forms of the same words ('humour' in item 4 matches 'humorous' in the text), or that are close synonyms ('wrote down' in item 1 matches 'noting' in the text; in item 7 'research into tickling' can be matched to 'studies of tickling' in the text).

Inference is also important to finding the correct answers, despite the potential risk of personal differences of interpretation (see above). In item 1, the correct response (False) requires the understanding that 'students' are not equivalent to 'people' in 'public places' while in item 6 'nearly' implies development later than six million years ago, not 'before' as in the item. Antonymy is also used: in item 7 (False) a 'considerable amount' contrasts with 'thin on the ground'.

In Anne's first Not Given item (item 3), there seems to be no clear signal of where the necessary information occurs in the text. There are a number of plausible lexical links to the text: the word 'episode(s)' comes at the beginning of the second paragraph, followed by the division ('sorted') according to the characteristics of research subjects, but this information is targeted by the previous item and there is the identification of three 'facts about laughter' in the following sentence. In either case, the test taker might recognise that the division mentioned is not connected to 'kinds of laughter', as in the stem. Further, there is no mention here of options that Provine (the key researcher in the text) may have 'considered' for his data analysis. Recognising that such information is not available is likely to require reading both more of the text and more careful reading than Jane's item 4 or revised item 3.

Compared with Anne, William includes more direct phrasal matches – lexical repetition – in his items with the relevant information in the text. His items also involve more direct word matches than Jane's. Item 1 has 'Blake and Wordsworth' and 'expressing'; item 2 has 'industrial revolution' ('Industrial Revolutions' in the text) and 'social problems' matching 'social, political and especially intellectual problems' in the text. Item 6 (False) has the most extensive cues with almost half of the words also occurring in the text including 'the 19th century' and 'the concept of the innocence of children', which repeat elements of their co-referents in the text: 'the nineteenth century' and 'the concept of the child as a symbol of innocence'. As in Anne's items, William's questions make extensive use of paraphrase, synonymy and antonymy. Item 1 (False), for example, would seem to require understanding the contrast between 'adapted a tradition' in the item stem and 'an essentially new phenomenon' in the text.

Perhaps because so many phrases recur in the text, a number of William's items might appear to a candidate plausibly to relate to several locations. Item 6 contrasts 'retained its power' with 'deterioration', although this proposition is echoed in the following sentence: 'only a residue', 'retaining little or nothing'. Similarly, there are several clues to the answer to item 4 (True): the proposition that serious writers were marginalised by the growth of mass literature is effectively repeated three times: 'mature voice . . . diminished', 'art was on the run' and 'ivory tower . . . arena' – a fact exploited in the editing meeting when the team decided to eliminate the reference to 'ivory towers'. Item 5 (True) seems to paraphrase a sequence of three related sentences which repeat the idea that nineteenth century authors used the image of the child to express their alienation from industrial society.

William's two Not Given items both repeat lexis from the text to point to the location of the necessary information. In each case one phrase in the text is inaccurately paraphrased in the item stem so that in both cases, substitution of one phrase would yield a True item. For item 2, in the text, it is the author of the text, rather than 'a number of writers' who identifies the industrial revolution as a 'cause of social problems' while in item 3 the phrase 'was proportionally diminished' – paraphrased in the item by 'featured less often' – relates to the 'creative voice' of the serious writer rather than 'children'.

The variation in the relationship between the items and the text found among these writers is consistent with and so perhaps might help to explain the variation found in the strategies used by test takers responding to four T/F/ NG test sections by Weir et al (2009b). In that study, test takers made greater use of word-matching strategies and knowledge of vocabulary in some T/F/ NG sections of the tests they took than in others. There were also differences in whether the information necessary to answer the question was most often reported as being found within sentences or across sentences. Thus different interpretations of the guidelines appear to lead writers to produce items that target different types of reading on the part of test takers. We note that there was no discussion among the item writers of how changes in the items might affect the reading skills being used by test takers or of the implications of variation in T/F/NG items for the nature of the test.

Of the three non-experienced writers, Victoria and Mathilda employed T/F/NG items. Victoria's T/F/NG items are closer to the experienced item writers' than are Mathilda's in their use of paraphrase and synonymy. She prefers to reorder or rephrase constituents from the text in her items so that in item 1 (False) 'dreams seem to make perfect sense to people . . .' is rephrased as 'people tend to make the most sense of their dreams . . .'; in item 4 (True), 'loss of memory' becomes 'memory loss'; in item 6 (True), 'much like [a], [b]' is replaced with 'both [a] and [b]'. There are lexical repetitions between text and item – 'experiences' (Item 3), declarative' (Item 4), 'the hippocampus' (Item 5), but these are usually individual words rather than phrases. Arriving at correct responses to Victoria's items generally involves relating phrases in the items to co-referents in the text. Sometimes, as in the case of item 1 (False), this also involves resolution of referencing within the text – recognising that 'some answers' refers to the question of 'their origins', which in turn refers to 'dreams'.

In comparison to the trained item writers and to Victoria, Mathilda's T/F/ NG items make less use of synonymy and paraphrase; instead her strategy involves repeating extensively from sections of the text, paraphrasing only the necessary information. The sequencing of information within the sentence in the text is retained in the item – item 2 (True) reads: 'More than a quarter of carbon emissions in the USA result from burning oil for transportation'. This closely reflects the relevant passage in the text: '28 percent of carbon emissions in the United States result from the burning of 14 million barrels of oil a day for transportation'. Similarly in item 1 (True) the item closely reflects the text and matching the paraphrase 'being built next to' with 'under construction adjacent to' gives the answer. Item 3 (False) is equally explicit, but the paraphrase ends with 2013 (which occurs in the preceding clause) in place of 'next year' from the text. Mathilda's two Not Given items represent rather different approaches to the item type. In the first (item 4), she paraphrases a sentence from the text, here replacing one constituent, 'residential sources' with another, 'motor traffic'. Item 5, in contrast, is inadequate as a paraphrase because it incorporates details from the following clause into the definition of the 'green roof'.

7 Comparisons between groups

The approach adopted for this study involved asking both experienced and inexperienced writers about their practices based around Salisbury's (2005) phases of the item construction process. The study collected both written (flowchart) and oral (interview and focus group) data on item writer processes and products (draft and edited texts and items) and incorporated both deductive and inductive approaches to analysis.

This approach has proved useful in identifying differences across the item writer groups and between individuals within the groups. These differences highlight both the importance of item writer training and guidelines and suggest changes that might be advisable. In the context of recent research undertaken by the University of Bedfordshire into the IELTS Academic Reading test, the current study can help to explain some of the characteristics of IELTS texts identified by Weir et al (2009a) and the types of reading employed by IELTS test takers (Weir et al 2009b).

7.1 Item writing processes

Both the experienced and non-experienced item writers seem to pass through similar steps in constructing their items. They typically begin from a topic, locate texts related to the topic, identify and evaluate potential IELTS texts before selecting one that seems appropriate – this is clearly Salisbury's (2005) exploratory phase. Both groups reported that they found this the most time-consuming stage in the item writing process.

With the exception of Jane, the experienced writers all included more steps in their item writing flow charts than their non-experienced counterparts. The flowcharts include similar attention to text editing in both groups, but there is greater attention to task development among the experienced group: this being broken down into a number of steps including revision and re-editing of the text following or in conjunction with item writing.

In the next phase – recognisable as Salisbury's (2005) concerted phase – all of the writers carried out an iterative process of editing the text and developing the items. Unlike the writers in Salisbury's (2005) study, who were devising scripts for tests of listening comprehension, these writers could not be said to have started from their items in writing their texts. However, as observed by Salisbury (2005) in her study, the experienced writers seemed to have a repertoire of gambits for efficiently exploiting their source texts and paid attention to task type in text selection. They also paid attention to potential items during the initial exploratory phase – highlighting or making notes on testable material. While the untrained writers selected material that was already close to the appropriate length, trained writer texts chose much longer pieces then progressively cut out passages that seemed to repeat information or that included elements that would not be tested. The extent of editing and the desire to avoid repetition perhaps explain why the texts analysed in Weir et al (2009a) displayed relatively high type:token ratios in comparison with undergraduate textbooks (indicative of a wide range of vocabulary use and rapid progression of ideas).

As a first step in what Salisbury (2005) calls the refining phase, the experienced group favoured attempting the task themselves after an intervening period (although deadlines sometimes limited the opportunities for this). The non-experienced writers also reported attempting their own tasks, but Mary and Victoria additionally asked friends to respond to their tasks and so were able to obtain some further feedback on how well the items were working before coming to the editing session.

7.2 The texts

The non-experienced writers drew on very similar sources to their experienced counterparts. Both Mary and Elizabeth chose articles from *New Scientist* articles while both Mary and Jane selected texts concerning robot technology. Victoria's text was an article from a popular science magazine concerning dreams while Anne's was an article from a popular science magazine concerning sleep. Readability statistics for the two groups were also very similar. The easiest and most difficult texts according to the Flesch-Kincaid and Coh-Metrix measures were both produced by experienced writers (Jane and Elizabeth respectively).

Both groups expressed a concern that the selection of topics in the test may be rather narrow. Where the non-experienced group saw this as a constraint imposed by the need to produce IELTS-like texts, the experienced group saw it as a by-product of the need for accessibility and cultural neutrality: arts texts tend to assume or require background knowledge in a way that popular psychology or technology-based texts do not.

Members of both groups edited their (magazine) texts to make them more 'academic' in style and tone and less journalistic. All of the texts involved plausibly academic topics presented for the general reader. All writers in both groups edited to eliminate (some) vocabulary on the grounds that it was either too technical for the general reader, too colloquial to be appropriate in an academic text or too infrequent and so difficult for IELTS candidates. Both groups included factual texts (Mathilda's text on cities and Jane's wild-life cameras text) and opinion texts (William's essay on literature, Elizabeth's sleep text, Anne's laughter text from the experienced group; Mary's robots text and Victoria's dreams text from the untrained group).

Members of both groups also sought to avoid potentially divisive or offensive issues and to eliminate culturally specific knowledge from their texts. Mary removed a paragraph from her text concerning war. The experienced group was concerned to avoid religious issues in William's text.

The trained writers seemed more ready to edit their texts; reshaping them if necessary to meet the requirements of the items. Of the untrained writers Mary seemed to have the strongest objections to revising her text, but in fact made the most substantial changes of this group. These changes included moving material between paragraphs to square her text with the items she wanted to use.

In sum, the effect of editing for both groups, apparent in the analysis of the submitted texts and from the discussions in the editing meetings, was to increase the coherence and information density of the texts and to make them more accessible to readers from non-English-speaking backgrounds. The changes also served to reduce technical and cultural specificity, colloquialism, journalistic touches (such as sensationalism, personal engagement of writer etc.) and, particularly in the case of the experienced group's texts, to reduce the repetition of ideas.

In devising their items, both groups made use of a range of item types. The True/False/Not Given (T/F/NG) item type was chosen most often across groups, but no clear differences in item type selection could be seen from the small sample submitted.

As was to be expected, the experienced item writers submitted items of better quality – clearly more likely to be accepted for use in a test – and were better able to correct the problems that they found. A greater number of shortcomings that would breach the IELTS item writer guidelines could be identified in the untrained writers' submissions. For some untrained writers, items within sets did not consistently follow the order of information in the text where this would usually be expected (as in Mary's MCQ items: 15 and 17 concern the first paragraph, 16 is associated with the sixth paragraph and the necessary information for item 18 is distributed throughout the text). Items within a set were sometimes isolated from each other: Mathilda's item 17, for example, relates to her ninth paragraph while the rest of her T/F/NG items are associated with the first four paragraphs of her text.

The items submitted by the untrained writers sometimes addressed the same parts of the text more than once. Victoria, for example, has three pairs of items that seem to address the same sentences in her text (items 2 and 3; 4 and 5; and 8 and 13). Untrained item writers' texts included stretches of untested material: five of Victoria's 16 paragraphs did not include information required to respond to any of her items.

The non-experienced writers felt that their lack of guidance about the test inhibited their ability to produce adequate items. They felt that they would have benefited from information on devising MCQ distractors and on the skills being targeted by items of different types. It should be noted that these writers had been directed to the Teaching Resources section of the IELTS website, which provides some guidance on this question under the heading of 'What skills are tested in this task type?' However, the information is inexplicit. For Task Type 8 – Identification of Writer's Views/Claims or of Information in a Text, the explanation is as follows:

> The first variation of this task type aims to test the candidate's ability to recognise opinions or ideas and is thus often used with discursive or argumentative texts.

This is not clear enough to guide an item writer. The intended relationship between the items and the text is not made plain and so the type of reading required is not explicit. The lack of guidance is reflected in the very different ways in which Mathilda and Victoria interpreted this task type.

In the editing meeting, the non-experienced group was relatively less critical of each other's work (although it should also be noted that, unlike the experienced group, they had not met each other before the day of the editing meeting). The experienced writers appeared more efficient in their approach to the editing meeting and worked intensively on improving the texts and items. Each writer contributed numerous suggestions and the chair sought consensus on the proposed changes.

The experienced group was pleased with the guidance they had received from the item writer guidelines and from the experience of training and editing meetings and felt that this had contributed to their expertise. Nonetheless there were clear inconsistencies in the interpretation of task requirements between the experienced writers. The group seemed to share a conception that IELTS tasks should target key, salient facts or opinions expressed in a text and appeared less concerned with the reading skills involved.

The group had discussed at some length the nature of the information that could be targeted using Type 1 MCQ items and the extent to which inferences might be tested using Type 8 T/F/NG items. These discussions left open the possibility that different writers might be targeting different reading skills when using the same item type – as observed in Section 8, each set of T/F/NG items bore a somewhat different relationship to its partner text. This has implications for the comparability of different forms of the test as it makes it more challenging to ensure that every form reflects the required range of reading skills. These issues had not been resolved by the end of the session.

When reviewing and revising items, the writers identified ambiguities and suggested clarifications, but did not generally discuss the implications of changes of wording on the nature of the reading skills that might be required in arriving at a correct response or to the balance of skills being tested in a passage. The three task types in Anne's submission, for example, all appear to involve careful local reading. The items include eight Type 8 T/F/NG items, which involve paraphrase of information in the text, and two Type 7 Locating Information items which are also based on recognising paraphrases of information in the text – in this case distinguishing between the two sentences that paraphrase the information in the text (similar to True items) and the three that do not (similar to False and Not Given items). The item below illustrates how similar this is to a T/F/NG item. There are similar lexical relationships involving repetition (speech), synonymy (develop: evolve) and co-reference (early man: our ancestors).

> In the item: Human speech began to develop when early man ceased walking on four legs.

> In the text: When our ancestors stood up on two feet, the chest was freed of these mechanical demands making it possible for speech to evolve.

The third item set – Type 4 Summary Completion – involves selecting two-word expressions from the text to complete a summary of paragraphs 3, 4 and 5, and also seems to require understanding at a local level.

8 Conclusions and recommendations

The researchers were favourably impressed by the conscientiousness and professionalism of the IELTS item writers that we interviewed and observed and the quality of the texts and items that they produced. Nonetheless, we would suggest that there are a number of recommendations that could be made on the basis of our study to refine the IELTS Academic Reading item production process. The inter- and intra-group differences revealed by our research have implications for test preparation that could be addressed through information provided to teachers of IELTS candidates and implications for the consistency of test material that could be addressed through the guidelines and training given to item writers and the process of text and test review.

Firstly, consideration should be given to better informing teachers about the test by increasing the amount of guidance offered concerning the reading skills being targeted and the intentions behind using the variety of item types on the test. The information currently offered on the IELTS website does not seem to be sufficient to inform teachers about the construct of the test. The non-experienced writers felt that, based on the examples they had seen, they had a clear sense of the kinds of texts being used in IELTS, but were less clear on why such texts were being used. This impression was largely borne out by the texts they produced, which resembled the texts produced by the experienced group and those analysed by Weir et al (2009a). However, the untrained writers did not feel well equipped to produce items that would test the same skills as the IELTS Academic Reading test. Although all were familiar with the Academic Reading test, they did not feel well informed about the function of the different items types or the implications of these for the types of reading being tested. More information on these aspects of the test could be communicated through the IELTS handbook, website and other communication channels than is at present the case.

From the testimony of both groups, there seems little doubt that observing the processes of editing and refinement that we report in this study is of great help to item writers in developing their own skills. Indeed, we would suggest that this research could be of use in training new item writers by providing insights into how texts and items are reshaped for the test and might also serve to inform a wider audience about the extent of the work that goes into producing each IELTS item. However, there would seem to be a need for an additional strand of training and guidance that pays greater attention to the construct of academic reading intended to be operationalised through the IELTS Academic Reading module.

In an earlier study (Weir et al 2009a) we recommended that objective text analysis tools could play a valuable role in assisting the evaluation of texts (and perhaps items) as part of the review process. We repeat this recommendation here because, as exemplified in our analyses, such tools can help in the identification of infrequent or technical vocabulary, help to highlight inconsistencies between the texts used across versions of the test and assist in identifying differences in textual genre that might be helpful in better defining the requirements for texts suited to the purposes of the test.

The participant interview and focus groups raised a number of questions that should be addressed in the item writer guidelines or related training packages:

- What are the reading skills that the test as a whole is intended to address? And in what proportion?

- Why these reading skills? And how do they relate to the available task types?
- Within each task, what kinds of linguistic relationships should T/F/NG (and other types of items) have to the text and in what proportion? What are the implications of these for the reading skills being targeted?
- What range of skills should be addressed in each section of the test and what item types should be used to target them?

The experienced item writers speculated on a number of issues including the kinds of information that could legitimately be targeted by MCQ and the extent to which inference could legitimately be targeted: there appeared to be room for individual interpretation in these areas. It is perhaps inevitable that individual writers (and separate teams of writers) will interpret specifications differently (and that there will be some misinterpretation), but questions of this kind should be answerable through the item writer guidelines. To the extent that they are, there should be greater attention to the guidelines during editing. To the extent they are not, the guidelines should be updated to address them.

The test providers should keep item writers informed about relevant assessment issues including current theoretical perspectives on the reading process, the nature of the reading demands made on beginning university students and the implications of these for IELTS. Such meetings, by raising issues of concern to writers, could also serve to direct further research into these questions that will inform the design of the test.

Elizabeth made reference to the discontinued practice of asking item writers to identify the skills being tested by each of their items. Elizabeth had found this difficult, but useful and consideration might be given to re-introducing such a practice as a training exercise if not as a routine requirement. It might also be advisable to introduce clearer controls on the range of task types and the range of skills to be targeted for each text.

Item writers reported that from their perspective some decisions made about test content could appear inconsistent. The fairness review element of the pre-editing and editing process was one area of concern. Items based on factual details in a text might inevitably advantage candidates who are familiar with the subject matter, but the question of which facts should be considered to be widely known and which not was a grey area for our participants. Similarly, these writers, who all worked on other Cambridge ESOL papers as well as IELTS, felt that there might be inconsistencies in the definition of potentially 'offensive' or 'sensitive' material across examinations. It may be that there is a rationale for such differences based in the nature of the candidatures for these different tests, but the implications for test content were not sufficiently clear to the item writing team. If this view is shared more generally by item writers, mechanisms should be found to create greater consistency in the interpretation of the rules, or to better articulate to item writers justified differences across testing programmes within Cambridge ESOL.

Finally, we believe that this study points towards a number of interesting avenues for future research. A comparison between the item writer practices investigated here and test taker strategies of the kind investigated by Weir et al (2009b) would provide insights into the extent to which candidate reading behaviours conform to item writer expectations. Similarly, it would be interesting to obtain candidate views on the kinds of editing changes made by item writers or to compare candidate judgements of what constitutes 'key' information in a text with item writer judgements. It would be useful, as a form of evaluation, to carry out a follow-up study after changes to item writer training and guidance have been implemented.

References

Alderson, J C (2000) *Assessing Reading*, Cambridge: Cambridge University Press.

Alderson, J C, Figueras, N, Kuijper, H, Nold, G, Takala, S and Tardieu, C (2004) *The development of specifications for item development and classification within the Common European Framework of Reference for Languages: learning, teaching, assessment. Reading and listening*, final report of the Dutch CEF construct project, retrieved from http://eprints.lancs. ac.uk/44/1/final_report.pdf 15 August 2008

Association of Language Testers in Europe (ALTE) (1994) *Code of Practice*, Cambridge: University of Cambridge Local Examinations Syndicate.

Babbie, E (1992) *The Practice of Social Research*, 6th ed, Belmont, CA: Wadsworth Publishing Company.

Bachman, L F (2005) Building and supporting a case for test use, *Language Assessment Quarterly* 2 (1), 1–34.

Bachman, L F, Davidson, F, Ryan, K and Choi, I (1995) *An Investigation into the Comparability of Two Tests of English as a Foreign Language: The Cambridge-TOEFL Comparability Study*, Studies in Language Testing volume 1, Cambridge: UCLES/Cambridge University Press.

Baranowski, R A (2006) Item editing and editorial review, in Downing, S M and Haladyna, T M (Eds) *Handbook of Test Development*, New York: Lawrence Erlbaum Associates, 349–358.

Bauman, J (2005) *The item writing process for access to ELLS: outline involvement by ESL teachers*, presentation to the Illinois 28th Annual Statewide Conference for Teachers serving Linguistically and Culturally Diverse Students, 24–27 January, Centre for Applied Linguistics, Washington DC.

Bormuth, J R (1970) *On the Theory of Achievement Test Items*, Chicago: University of Chicago Press.

Brown, A (2000) An investigation of raters' orientation in awarding scores in the IELTS oral interview, in Tulloh, R (Ed.) *IELTS Research Reports Volume 3*, Canberra: IELTS Australia, 131–152.

Brown, A (2003) Legibility and the rating of second language writing: An investigation of the rating of handwritten and word-processed IELTS Task Two essays, in Tulloh, R (Ed.), *IELTS Research Reports Volume 4*, Canberra: IELTS Australia.

Brown, A (2006) An examination of the rating process in the revised IELTS Speaking Test, in McGovern, P and Walsh, S (Eds) *IELTS Research Reports Volume 3*, London: IELTS Australia and British Council, 41–70.

Cambridge ESOL, n.d., *Cambridge ESOL exams and the CEFR: Familiarisation with the CEFR – making it work for us*, retrieved 20 June 2008 from http://www.cambridgeesol.org/what-we-do/research/cefr/cef-familiarisation.html

Carroll, B J and Hall, P J (1985) *Make Your Own Language Tests: A Practical Guide to Writing Language Performance Tests*, Oxford: Pergamon.

Chalhoub-Deville, M, Chapelle, C and Duff, P (Eds) (2006) *Inference and Generalizability in Applied Linguistics: Multiple Perspectives*, Amsterdam: Benjamins.

Clapham, C (1996) *The Development of IELTS: A Study of the Effect of Background Knowledge on Reading Comprehension*, Studies in Language Testing volume 4, Cambridge: UCLES/Cambridge University Press.

Clapham, C (1997) The Academic Modules: Reading, in Clapham, C and Alderson, J C (Eds) *IELTS Research Report 3: Constructing and Trialling the IELTS Test*, Cambridge: The British Council/UCLES/IDP, 49–68.

Cobb, T (2003) *VocabProfile, The Compleat Lexical Tutor*, retrieved 5 December 2008 from http://www.lextutor.ca

Coxhead, A (2000) A new academic word list, *TESOL Quarterly* 34 (2), 213–238.

Crossley, J, Greenfield, J and McNamara, D S (2008) Assessing text readability using cognitively based indices, *TESOL Quarterly* 42 (3), 475–493.

Davidson, F and Lynch, B K (2002) *Testcraft: A Teacher's Guide to Writing and Using Language Test Specifications*, New Haven, CT: Yale University.

De Jong, J (2008) *Procedures for training item writers and human raters*, presentation, 5 May 2008, http://www.ealta.eu.org/conference/2008/docs/friday/deJong.pdf

Dey, I (1993) *Qualitative Data Analysis: A User-friendly Guide for Social Scientists*, London: Routledge.

Downing, S M and Haladyna, T M (1997) Test item development: validity evidence from quality assurance procedures, *Applied Measurement in Education* 10 (1), 61–82.

Downs, P E (1978) Testing the upgraded semantic differential, *Journal of the Market Research Society* 20, 99–103.

Ebel, R L (1951) Writing the test item, in Lindquist, E F (Ed.) *Educational Measurement*, Washington, DC: American Council on Education, 185–249.

Enright, M K, Grabe, W, Koda, K, Mosenthal, P, Mulcahy-Ernt, P and Schedl, M (2000) TOEFL 2000 Reading Framework: A working paper, *TOEFL Monograph MS-17*, Princeton, NJ: Educational Testing Service.

Fortus, R, Coriat, R and Ford, S (1998) Prediction of item difficulty in the English section of the Israeli Psychometric Entrance Test, in Kunnan, A (Ed.) *Validation in Language Assessment*, London: Routledge, 61–87.

Freedle, R and Kostin, I (1993) The prediction of TOEFL reading comprehension item difficulty for expository prose passages for three item types: Main idea, inference, and supporting idea items, *TOEFL Research Reports RR-93-44*, Princeton, NJ: Educational Testing Service.

Friedman, H H, Friedman, L W and Gluck, B (1988) The effects of scale-checking styles on responses to a semantic differential scale, *Journal of the Market Research Society* 30, 477–482.

Fulcher, G and Davidson, F (2007) *Language Testing and Assessment*, London: Routledge.

Furneaux, C and Rignall, M (2007) The effect of standardisation-training on rater judgements for the IELTS Writing Module, in Taylor, L and Falvey, P (Eds) *IELTS Collected Papers: Research in speaking and writing assessment*, Studies in Language Testing volume 19, Cambridge: UCLES/Cambridge University Press, 422–444.

Garland, R (1990) A Comparison of Three Forms of the Semantic Differential, *Marketing Bulletin* 1, 19–24, Article 4, Page 1 of 7 http://marketing-bulletin. massey.ac.nz

Green, A and Jay, D (2005) Quality assurance and quality control: Reviewing and pretesting examination material at Cambridge ESOL, *Research Notes* 21, 5–7.

Haladyna, T M (1999) *Developing and Validating Multiple Choice Test Items*, Mahwah, NJ: Lawrence Erlbaum Associates.

Haladyna, T M and Downing, S M (1989a) A taxonomy of multiple-choice item-writing rules, *Applied Measurement in Education* 2 (1), 37–50.

Haladyna, T M and Downing, S M (1989b) Validity of a taxonomy of multiple-choice item-writing rules, *Applied Measurement in Education* 2 (1), 51–78.

Haladyna, T M, Downing, S M and Rodriguez, M C (2002) A review of multiple-choice item-writing guidelines for classroom assessment, *Applied Measurement in Education* 15 (3), 309–334.

Hawkey, R (2006) *Impact Theory and Practice: studies of the IELTS test and Progetto Lingue 2000*, Studies in Language Testing volume 24, Cambridge: UCLES/Cambridge University Press.

Hawkins, D L, Albaum, G and Best, R (1974) Stapel Scale or semantic differential in marketing research?, *Journal of the Market Research Society* 11, 318–322.

Heaton, J B (1990) *Classroom Testing*, London: Longman.

Holmes, C (1974) A statistical evaluation of rating scales, *Journal of the Market Research Society* 16, 87–107.

Hughes, A (1989) *Testing for Language Teachers*, Cambridge: Cambridge University Press.

Hughes, A (2003) *Testing for Language Teachers* (2nd Ed), Cambridge: Cambridge University Press.

Hughes, G D (1975) Upgrading the semantic differential, *Journal of the Market Research Society* 17, 41–44.

IELTS (2007) *The IELTS Question Paper Production Process*, retrieved 21 March 2008 from http://www.ielts.org

Ingham, K (2008) The Cambridge ESOL approach to Item Writer training: the case of ICFE Listening, *Research Notes* 32, 5–9.

Irvine, S H and Kyllonen, P C (2002) *Item Generation for Test Development*, New York: Lawrence Erlbaum Associates.

Khalifa, H and ffrench, A (2008) *Aligning Cambridge ESOL Examinations to the CEFR: Issues and Practice*, paper presented at the 34th Annual Conference of the International Association for Educational Assessment, Cambridge, UK, 7–12 September 2008.

Khalifa, H and Weir, C J (2009) *Examining Reading: Research and Practice in Assessing Second Language Reading,* Studies in Language Testing volume 29, Cambridge: UCLES/Cambridge University Press.

Laufer, B (1989) What percentage of text-lexis is essential for comprehension? in Lauren, C and Nordman, M (Eds) *Special Language: From Humans Thinking to Thinking Machines*, Clevedon: Multilingual Matters, 316–323.

Lave, J and Wenger, E (1991) *Situated Learning: Legitimate Peripheral Participation*, Cambridge: Cambridge University Press.

Macmillan, F (2007) The role of lexical cohesion in the assessment of EFL reading proficiency, *Arizona Working Papers in Second Language Acquisition and Teaching* 14, 75–94.

Menezies, D and Elbert, N F (1979) Alternative semantic scaling formats for measuring store image: an evaluation, *Journal of Marketing Research* 16, 80–87.

Mickan, P and Slater, S (2000) Text analysis and the assessment of academic writing, in Tulloh, R (Ed.) *IELTS Research Reports Volume 4,* Canberra: IELTS Australia, 59–88.

Norris, J M, Brown, J D, Hudson, T and Yoshioka, J (1998) *Designing Second Language Performance Assessments*, Honolulu, HI: University of Hawaii.

O'Sullivan, B and Rignall, M (2007) Assessing the value of bias analysis feedback to raters for the IELTS Writing Module, in Taylor, L and Falvey, P (Eds) *IELTS Collected Papers: Research in Speaking and Writing Assessment,* Studies in Language Testing volume 19, Cambridge: UCLES/Cambridge University Press, 446–476.

Osgood, E C, Suci, G J and Tannenbaum, P H (1957) *The Measurement of Meaning*, Urbana-Champaign: University of Illinois Press.

Patton, M Q (1990) *Qualitative Evaluation and Research Methods,* Newbury Park, CA: Sage.

Rodriguez, M C (2005) Three options are optimal for multiple-choice items: A meta-analysis of 80 years of research, *Educational Measurement: Issues and Practice* 24 (2), 3–13.

Salisbury, K (2005) *The edge of expertise: towards an understanding of listening test item writing as professional practice*, unpublished doctoral thesis, King's College London.

Saville, N (2003) The process of test development and revision within UCLES EFL, in Weir, C J and Milanovic, M (Eds) *Continuity and Innovation: Revising the Cambridge Proficiency in English Examination 1913–2002*, Studies in Language Testing volume 15, Cambridge: UCLES/Cambridge University Press, 57–120.

Schertzer, C B and Keman, J S (1985) More on the robustness of response scales, *Journal of the Market Research Society* 27, 261–282.

Valette, R M (1967) *Modern Language Testing: A Handbook*, New York: Harcourt, Brace and World.

Weir, C J (1993) *Understanding and Developing Language Tests*, Hemel Hempstead: Prentice Hall.

Weir, C J (2005) *Language Testing and Validation: An Evidence-Based Approach*, New York: Palgrave Macmillan.

Weir, C J, Hawkey, R, Green, A, Ünaldi, A and Devi, S (2009a) The relationship between the academic reading construct as measured by IELTS and the reading experiences of students in their first year of study at a

British university, in Thompson, P (Ed.) *Research Reports Volume 9*, British Council/IDP Australia, 97–156.

Weir, C J, Hawkey, R, Green, A and Devi, S (2009b) The cognitive processes underlying the academic reading construct as measured by IELTS, in Thompson, P (Ed.) *Research Reports Volume 9*, British Council/IDP Australia, 157–189.

Wesman, A G (1971) Writing the test item, in Thorndike, R L (Ed.) *Educational Measurement*, Washington, DC: American Council on Education, 99–111.

Wildt, A R and Mazis, W (1978) Determinants of scale response: label versus position, *Journal of Marketing Research* 15, 261–267.

Appendix 4.1
Commissioning letter (based on a model letter used in IELTS commissioning supplied by Cambridge ESOL)

Date

Address

Dear XXX

IELTS Academic Reading Commission (Item Writer Research Study), September 2008

Thank you for agreeing to produce material for our Item Writer Research Study. I am now writing to confirm that we would like you to produce the following as indicated:

- One IELTS Academic Reading section with 16 or 17 items.
- The text should be of between 750 and 950 words in length.
- Suitable sources include magazines, newspapers, books, academic papers and journals.
- The text may be cut and edited as you see fit to make it more suitable for IELTS.
- You may use 2 or 3 different item types for your questions.
- The items should be arranged in sections according to type – e.g. 6 multiple choice items followed by 6 matching questions followed by 5 short answer questions.
- Each item will carry 1 mark.
- The tasks may focus on understanding gist, main ideas/ themes, specific information, making inferences or recognizing opinions/ attitudes.
- The item types used should be based on the list and guidance provided by Cambridge ESOL at http://www.cambridgeesol.org/teach/ielts/academic_reading/index.htm

Appendix 4.2
Background questionnaires

Table 4.10 Non-experienced item writers

	Victoria	Mathilda	Mary
Qualif-ications	BA English and Linguistics Postgraduate Diploma in Education/MA TESOL	BA Communication and English Language/MA Pragmatics	BA Politics Certificate in English Language Teaching to Adults (CELTA) Diploma in English Language Teaching to Adults (DELTA)
Experience in EL	18 years teaching, 5 years as an examiner, 2 years in publishing	As advanced learner	6 years teaching
Experience of IELTS	IELTS examiner (Writing and Speaking), IELTS preparation teacher	As test taker and preparation course student	2 years teaching IELTS preparation
Comments on IELTS	Through working as an examiner I have noticed that I sometimes get repeat candidates who score very well: band 8+ on the other three tests and then perform poorly in comparison on reading. Unfortunately for these candidates they have to score well on all four tests. One candidate I have been examining for the last two years. She is a pharmacist originally from Lebanon who in order to practise in the UK needs Band 7 or more for all four tests. My current employer used to run its own internal IELTS test for placement purposes. The tests used were past papers. Here too candidates/ students consistently performed badly on reading in relation to the other three tests. Interestingly, native speakers are reputed to not score well on IELTS Reading.	My impression is that factual texts by far outweigh literary texts (if any). The latter might be more suitable for people intending to study/work with the literary or similar genre rather than in a technical field.	I find the Reading test to be very dense which does help the student concentrate on the skills needed for reading, instead of just the reading. I think this is a really positive thing. However, I think some of these skills are quite specific and need to be taught (which could be seen as quite a negative thing. I think the True False and Not Given questions are not always presented well in practice materials. I find the reading topics to be questionable sometimes.

Table 4.11 Experienced item writers

	Jane	Anne	William	Elizabeth	UK1	AUS1	NZ1
Qualifications	BA (Hons) RSA Diploma in Teaching English as a Foreign Language to Adults (Dip TEFLA)	MA Modern Languages RSA Dip. TEFLA	BA (Hons) in English Language and Literature MA in Modern English Language RSA Dip TEFLA	BA/MA	Cert Ed B Ed Adv Dip Ed M Ed RSA Cert in TEFLA	BA (Hons) MA RSA Dip in TEFLA	MA, Dip Tchg... Dip TESL
Experience in EL	12 years teaching EFL 12 years item writing for Cambridge ESOL papers 8 years chairing Cambridge ESOL papers Co-author of preparation book for another Cambridge ESOL exam	20 years teaching EFL In-house teacher training, course design, materials preparation and testing Item writing for other Cambridge ESOL examinations Examiner for IELTS Speaking and Writing tests Published author of IELTS and other exam preparation books	16 years teaching EFL Writing and marking written university exams, conducting oral university exams Examiner for BEC Vantage and Higher Writing Translation from a number of languages into English	34 years teaching EFL 23 years teacher training 30 years course design 32 years materials preparation 32 years testing/ examining Published author of IELTS preparation books	13 years teaching EFL EAP course design 4 years as Cambridge ESOL subject manager 14 years as freelance item writer for other IELTS papers and Cambridge ESOL tests Principal Examiner for IELTS Published author of IELTS and other exam preparation material	21 years teaching EFL Designed courses and materials for IELTS preparation 9 years as IELTS examiner	3 years teaching EFL and 7 years as Director of Studies at University English Language Centre 8 years as IELTS Examiner Trainer 13 years as IELTS Examiner

Table 4.11 (continued)

	Jane	Anne	William	Elizabeth	UK1	AUS1	NZ1
Experience of IELTS	7 commissions	Can't remember – 4 or 5 years	15+ commissions Published IELTS preparation book	Item writer – 27+ commissions	So many I can't remember	I can't recall – 6 years	10–12 commissions
Training as item writer	Editing meetings Formal training session at Cambridge ESOL	–	Training sessions plus informal training through participation in editing meetings	As provided by Cambridge ESOL	'I have trained many item writer teams for IELTS and wrote most versions of the item writer guidelines'	1 day training session Regular update sessions, and visits from Cambridge ESOL staff	One formal 2-day course with a Principal Examiner A couple of informal sessions with Team Leader
Background and training you feel have most helped you in your item writing for the Academic Reading test (Please explain how this	Teaching and experience on writing for other papers Approaches to finding a suitable text, and the editing of texts are similar across papers. Also,	Item writer training days and editing meetings plus pretest review meetings Seeing what other writers do e.g. the texts they choose and the way they craft	Work on BEC Higher Reading (the first Reading paper I was involved in) provided excellent groundwork and under-	Ten years' experience of teaching/ materials/test writing and course design for courses for medical and science	Training I have received for other CESOL papers has helped me with IELTS; e.g. production of MCQs and gap-fill questions	I don't know how to answer this – all the training we have had has been helpful. The best thing is probably	Everything in my back-ground has been useful

training has helped you)	IELTS shares many types of task with other papers and experience of having written these helps considerably.	the items is one of the best ways of learning. Attending pretest review meetings shows you what kind of items work out too hard or too easy and what sort of texts prove too complex for candidates.	standing of the demands of item-writing, e.g. giving awareness of potential pitfalls My academic background has been helpful for selecting and understanding texts	undergraduates overseas provided confidence and interest in science and technology and awareness of approaches to the testing of reading skills	– / editing meetings.	–
Do you feel that your item writing for the Academic Reading test has improved with experience?	I hope so. It is always helpful to see the kinds of texts other writers are using and how they approach the task types.	Definitely. It takes a while to learn how to write for different papers and also where to source appropriate texts from.	Yes – I think I work faster than I used to	Not necessarily just due to experience – guidelines have become more precise	Yes – writing well for any paper is an ongoing, developmental experience	Sometimes I wonder – I still end up with a lot of work to do on my items	Yes, definitely
Has the proportion of successful reading commissions increased in that time?	This has remained fairly constant	Most have been accepted	Most have been accepted	Most have been accepted	Yes	Most have been accepted	Yes, somewhat, though has always been fairly high

Table 4.11 (continued)

	Jane	Anne	William	Elizabeth	UK1	AUS1	NZ1
IELTS support materials (e.g. item writer guidelines) you consult before or while you select texts and write test items	When I am writing the items, I sometimes refer to the item writer guidelines Commissioning letter from Cambridge ESOL	–	Item writer guidelines Commissioning letter from Cambridge ESOL Item writer feedback forms from pre-editing review	Item writer guidelines I might use Google to check up on details of input text content where this seems unclear I may also use a thesaurus to provide synonyms e.g. in multiple choice questions	I always refer to the guidelines when I am writing The Specimen materials are dated so I don't use these	What materials are there apart from the guidelines?	Item writer guidelines
What additional support materials might assist you with text selection, editing and item writing?	I'm not sure. There is considerable support in the item writer guidelines – especially for writing the items. Text selection is probably one of the hardest aspects and more guidance with this is always welcome.	Samples of good practice i.e. texts and tasks that have worked well	None	Access to appropriate published materials on the internet e.g. if I had access to undergraduate/ postgraduate sites	It might be useful to have more good 'models', particularly for some of the trickier task types A better insight into how candidates take the test might be helpful	–	–

Do you see your IELTS Academic Reading material in the meetings below? If so, how much of your material do you see at each? (e.g. If you see all your material edited at editing meetings, you should put 100%)

pre-editing meetings:	Writers don't always attend these	–	No	Item writers do not normally see their own material at pre-editing for IELTS or other Cambridge ESOL examinations	None	Nil	100%
editing meetings:	I have attended one pre-editing meeting since I started	100%	No	Usually 100%	Most, say 85%	100%	100%
pretest review meetings:	Every commission	It depends – sometimes quite a lot. On other occasions none of your material may come up at a pretest review meeting	Yes – generally 100%, occasionally 66% or 75%	Variable	Ditto	100%	No
How would you describe the experience of attending these IELTS meetings?	I have attended a few PTR meetings – perhaps once a year	Helpful	It depends very much on the other people involved. IELTS Academic Reading is positive.	Productive	I am usually chairing these meetings. From that perspective, they run smoothly, writers are very experienced and make very useful contributions.	A tremendous struggle, but great. We have a really terrific team.	Very positive and useful

Table 4.11 (continued)

	Jane	Anne	William	Elizabeth	UK1	AUS1	NZ1
What do you think are the key characteristics of more/less successful IELTS Academic Reading items?	PTR meetings are always informative. As a writer, it helps to see which items candidates have found too difficult and to think about the reasons for this.	Successful items require candidates to process the text carefully Less successful items are: – too easy (e.g. numbers that stand out) – answerable without understanding surrounding text – convoluted – based on complex extracts which candidates cannot process	More successful: – clear focus on a specific piece of text (fact, opinion, etc.), clearly distinguishable from text tested by surrounding items – unambiguous phrasing	Successful items focus on key points of the text and involve the strategies that would be used by a good reader of that text	Clear keys; appropriate level; well-sequenced (if appropriate); targeting salient information, well cued without giving the answer away; written according to item specific guidelines; independent; well-written surrounding text (when appropriate)	Successful items are ones that don't need to have a lot of work done on them after they have been submitted	–
What do you think are the characteristics of more/less successful IELTS	A range of things including: – giving candidates support for where to look in the text	Successful item writers find appropriate texts which suit the item types and which do	More successful: – eye for detail – ability to identify ambiguity	Ability to identify and evaluate texts from a variety of academic subject areas	More successful writers follow the guidelines, ensure that their texts will yield sufficient items before they	Having the knack of choosing the right parts of the text to	–

Academic Reading item Writers?	clarity in phrasing of items/awareness of language level of candidates	not need to be altered very much	– being pedantic – being intelligent enough to understand not only the text but interrelations between items, and options in different items – having a wide enough general knowledge to understand a range of texts – understanding how different types of items work and how they can go wrong	and to exploit texts using the specified item types	begin, have time to do the job, pay meticulous attention to detail, repeatedly proof their work, are good writers of English themselves, listen well at meetings and have clear heads Less successful writers do not satisfy some of the criteria above and may have their own agenda about what IELTS should test	test; being helpful to other writers; knowing a good text when they see one	–
What do you enjoy/dislike about IELTS Academic Reading item writing work?	Experience of writing other test material and attention to detail	I like writing for IELTS because you can use texts which are challenging and interesting. I often find that I learn a lot while I am working with the texts.	Enjoy: selecting texts on a variety of subjects, intellectual satisfaction of adapting text to suit the constraints and creating successful items	I enjoy most aspects of this work, particularly the variety of content	The texts are generally more interesting than other EL texts, which makes it more enjoyable looking for them. The task types are more varied and there is some choice; writing	I enjoy editing texts; attending meetings; finding a good fit between text and items. I dislike the fact that	I enjoy the challenge of finding a suitable text, editing or adapting it, writing the best items possible,

Table 4.11 (continued)

	Jane	Anne	William	Elizabeth	UK1	AUS1	NZ1
	–	I like writing for IELTS because you can use texts which are challenging and interesting. I often find that I learn a lot while I am working with the texts.	Dislike: what can sometimes seem like oversensitivity to candidates' sensibilities	–	questions is less mechanical than it is for other papers. There isn't much I dislike about this paper!	I am not as good at writing items as I would like to be.	and working with a small and committed team of like-minded professionals who are very good at what they do.
Which aspects do you find easiest/most challenging?	The source material that I read through to find suitable texts is different from other papers that I work on and is sometimes interesting	–	Easiest: finding interesting texts Most challenging: making text fit certain task types, e.g. flow-chart, 5-option multiple choice that isn't too easy	Finding the texts is most challenging. The rest is relatively straightforward though teamwork is necessary to produce good working items.	Some task types are more difficult to write than others; namely: summary completion, paragraph headings and sentence completion with a box. Other task types are more straightforward to write.	Finding and editing texts is the easy part	After the creative part is over it always feels tedious when the feedback comes back after a considerable time lapse, to have to

In what respects do you think the IELTS Academic Reading test reflects (or fails to reflect) the reading skills needed by students entering English-medium higher education?						
Finding suitable texts is usually easier than for general English papers	I think it does reflect the skills required quite well – above all the ability to read a quite complex text at quite a fast pace and get the main points from it without being thrown by items of vocabulary that are completely unfamiliar.	Reflects: requirement for speed; distinguishing between main points and detail; interpreting texts that include unfamiliar vocabulary; need for a broad vocabulary and understanding of a wide range of structures; need for intellectual curiosity	My students found preparation for IELTS useful in developing awareness of text type and structure as well as academic vocabulary and reading skills such as understanding main idea and detail. The relatively heavy reading load also encouraged them to increase their reading speed. The exam does not test reference skills (e.g. use of contents/index or reading at chapter/whole	IELTS differs from other Reading papers in that there is a wider range of task types to reflect the range of skills that students might need at university; e.g. reading for detail, main idea, gist, etc. It is possible to match certain tasks to skills and to feel assured that the test covers the main ones. The texts are selected for inclusion according to the density of ideas, vocabulary level and text type (descriptive, argument-based, etc.)	I think the texts are often far away from the level of difficulty encountered in real academic texts. Things (e.g. lexical items) which are in the least challenging are glossed or removed. Many of the students who enter our higher education institutions should not be doing so anyway	re-visit the commission and input all the recommended changes

I think it's a good reflection. |

Table 4.11 (continued)

Jane	Anne	William	Elizabeth	UK1	AUS1	NZ1
–	–	–	book level) or text evaluation skills. Appropriate humanities texts (e.g. English literature) are hard to find due to cultural and stylistic reasons. When looking for a well-written text at the target level, it is much easier to find texts on science and technology than on the humanities.	There may be other requisite reading skills for academic study that are subject specific or task specific but these may not be 'assessable' in a global language test of this kind. (Candidates may attempt every question using strategies that evade 'real' reading but this is not to say that they will get the answers correct and/or get the band score they are capable of getting had they used more appropriate skills.)	– IELTS 6 is in no way adequate to allow someone to undertake an English-medium degree.	–

What changes, if any, would you like to see in the IELTS Academic Reading test and why?	—	As far as I know, the test reflects the reading skills needed by students reasonably well. //I think the test is different, however, from independent reading. The texts are short and most of the less significant information has already been cut by the item writer. Also, many of the items, for example note-taking or tables, provide the reader with a framework.	None	It would be interesting to look at the possibility of varying text length – e.g. one much shorter text with items focusing on detail and one much longer one, to test outlining/ summary skills. However, given the size and nature of the candidature, any changes of this nature would need to be very well researched before implementation.	—	Perhaps a greater variety of text types and fewer potential short cuts for candidates. (The latter is really an editing issue.)	—
Other comments on IELTS Academic Reading module item writing	—	It's certainly a challenge at times but enjoyable on the whole	None	—	—	I have faith in the ACR paper and believe that candidates get a good deal. It is rigorously produced and meets many of the pedagogical/ theoretical requirements of an EAP reading test.	—

Appendix 4.3
Item writer submissions

Non-experienced group: Victoria
Text

How the Brain Turns Reality into Dreams

Dreams seem to make perfect sense as we are having them. Yet, on awakening they typically leave us feeling befuddled; without any clear idea about their origins. Research, however, investigating the dreams of individuals with amnesia may provide some answers.

Such research suggests that much of the fodder for our dreams comes from recent experiences. For this reason, scientists have tentatively supposed that the dreaming brain draws from its "declarative memory" system. This system stores newly learned information.

The declarative memory stores the type of information that can be "declared" to be known by subjects; the name of one's dog, for example. Often, subjects can even remember when or where they learned something – for example, the day you discovered the harsh truth about Santa Claus. To differentiate this information from declarative memory this particular of recollection is referred to by scientists as episodic memory.

It seems subjects who permanently suffer from amnesia or loss of memory are unable to add new declarative or episodic memories. The part of the brain involved in storing this type of information, a region called the hippocampus, has been damaged. Although, subjects who suffer from memory loss are able to retain new information temporarily, they are unable to permanently retain it. Studies have shown that new information for such individuals is lost sometimes within minutes.

If such is the case, that dreams originate from declarative memories, then individuals suffering with amnesia should not be capable of dreaming at all. Current research directed by Robert Stickgold of Harvard Medical School, however, suggests quite the opposite.

Stickgold's study shows that, much like individuals with normal memory, amnesiacs also replay recent experiences whilst asleep. The only difference seems to be that the amnesiacs are unable to recognize what they are dreaming about.

The methodology designed for Stickgold's study had two groups of subjects playing several hours of the computer game Tetris, which requires users to direct falling blocks into the correct positions as they reach the bottom of the screen. At night, the amnesiac group did not remember playing the game but, they did describe seeing falling, rotating blocks while they were falling asleep.

A second group of players with normal memories reported seeing the same images.

From these results, Stickgold's research team felt reassured in making the claim that dreams come from the types of memory amnesiacs do have, defined as implicit memories. Such memories can be measured even when individuals have no conscious awareness of them. One class of implicit memories is found in the procedural memory system. This particular system stores information that is used, but is somehow beyond the individuals' ability to state how they know, to perform actions. A pertinent example being, when one rides a bicycle for the first time in years, a reliance on procedural memory has come into play.

Another type of implicit memory uses semantic knowledge, and resides in a region of the brain called the neocortex. One aspect of semantic knowledge involves general, abstract concepts. Both groups of Tetris players, for example, only described seeing blocks, falling and rotating, and evidently did not see a desk, room, or computer screen, or feel their fingers on the keyboard.

Without help from the hippocampus, new semantic memories are too weak to be intentionally recalled. But they still have the potential to affect behaviour. In contrast, the information in episodic memories is associated with specific times, places or events thus providing "anchors" to reality. In contrast, implicit memories based on semantic knowledge do not possess such grounding and it is for this reason the study's authors say that dreams are so illogical and full of discontinuity.

We have to enquire as to the benefit to the individual of being able to dream. Stickgold upholds that dreams serve a purpose for the brain, allowing it to make necessary emotional connections among new pieces of information.

Dreams let us consolidate and integrate . . . experiences, without conflict with other input from real life. Dreaming is like saying, 'I'm going home, disconnecting the phone, and nobody talk to me. I have to do work Stickgold.

Because the hippocampus seems to be inaccessible for this "off-line" memory processing, the brain may use the abstract information in the neocortex instead.

According to Stickgold's theory, dreaming is like choosing an outfit by reaching into bins labelled 'shirts, trousers' and so on. You'll happen upon something to wear, but it won't be a perfectly matching ensemble.

The period of sleep that Stickgold's team studied is called hypnagogia: an in-between state between being fully awake and fully asleep. Many people who have just had an intense new experience of some kind, either mental or physical, often report replays of that experience during this stage.

In his poem, 'After Apple Picking', for example, Robert Frost describes seeing the apples and apple blossoms, and feeling the ladder sway as he nods off to sleep. Stickgold's first encounter with this phenomenon occurred after a day of mountain climbing, when he felt the sensation of rocks under his fingertips as he fell asleep.

Hypnagogic sleep is different from REM sleep, the period marked by rapid eye movement, when standard dreams most often occur. According to Stickgold, other studies suggest that the hippocampus is not active during REM sleep either. Therefore, he proposes, the brain activity responsible for the Tetris images is probably similar to the dreaming that occurs in REM sleep.

Interpreting REM sleep dreams, however, is a highly subjective process. Stickgold states, 'what is so nice about the images in our experiments is that they are so accurately re-creating the Tetris experience – no interpretation is necessary.'

(941 words)

Non-experienced group: Victoria

Items

Type 8 – True, False, Not Given

Do the following statements agree with the information given in the Reading Passage?

True	if the statement agrees with the information
False	if the statement contradicts the information
Not Given	if there is no information on this

1 People tend to make the most sense of their dreams while waking up.
2 Dream research may one day help people with memory loss.
3 The content informing dreams comes from experiences had by an individual in the last few days.
4 Permanent memory loss is associated with the declarative memory storing section of the brain.
5 One way in which to restore memory of amnesiacs is to repair the hippocampus.
6 Both amnesia sufferers and people with normal memory function go over recent activities during sleep.

Type 1 – Multiple Choice

Choose the correct letter, A, B, C or D.

7 Declarative memory can be best understood as
A a memory that is similar to episodic memory.
B memory that entails episodic memory.
C memory that is distinct from episodic memory.
D memory that is identical to episodic memory.

8 The research team used the following evidence to state that dreams come from implicit memories because
A the normal group could both recall playing Tetris and dreaming about it.
B the amnesiac group could both recall playing Tetris and dreaming about it.
C the normal group could not recall playing Tetris but could describe having dreamt about tumbling shapes.

D the amnesiac group could not recall playing Tetris but could describe having dreamt about tumbling shapes.

9 Implicit memory differs from episodic memory in that

A it does not relate to definite events.

B it only applies to non specific events.

C it only applies to semantic memories.

D it is completely distinct from episodic memory.

Type 2 – Short-Answer Questions

Choose **NO MORE THAN THREE WORDS** from the passage for each answer.

10 The writer describes several different types of memory. The type of information stored by declarative memory *can be known/ declared.*

11 The writer describe the kind of condition during the hypnagogia stage of sleep *an in-between state.*

12 The writer uses the Frost poem as an example of *intense physical experience.*

13 The research benefit the Tetris experience provides is that it *makes interpretation unnecessary/ redundant.*

Words in italics are the answers

Non-experienced group: Mathilda

Text

How-and Where-Will We Live in 2015?

The future is now for sustainable cities in the U.K., China, and U.A.E.

Future City Madsar

No cars in the land of oil.

In an ironic twist, the first city to fully turn its back on petroleum is likely to spring up in the United Arab Emirates, the oil-producing giant in the Middle East. Madsar, a carbon-neutral, zero-waste, walled metropolis now under construction adjacent to the Abu Dhabi airport, will have many innovative green technologies, but it may be most noteworthy for one thing it won't have: gas-consuming cars.

Nearly all of the world's motor vehicles run on petroleum, and the environmental consequences are obvious. For example, 28 percent of carbon emissions in the United States result from the burning of 14 million barrels of oil a day for transportation, primarily in cars and small trucks. Madsar will do away with this problem. Urbanites will walk along shaded sidewalks, and if the sweltering desert heat gets to them, they will never be more than 500 feet from a public transportation network that puts traditional buses and subways to shame. Small electric vehicles, guided in part by magnets embedded in the road, will act as driverless taxicabs serving 83 stations situated throughout the roughly 2.5-square-mile city. Meanwhile, two electric rail systems will connect Madsar to the outside, carbon-polluting world.

The Madsar project was announced in 2006, and development is already in full swing; much of the financing is coming from the emirate of Abu Dhabi, which committed $15 billion. Developers have set a goal of sustaining 55,000 residents and visitors by 2013, with the first section of the city scheduled to open next year.

Future City London

An old industrial site gets a green makeover

A. In 2006 London produced eight percent of the United Kingdom's 560.6 million tons of carbon emissions, 70 percent of it from residential sources. In response, the city has developed an ambitious long-term plan known as the Mayor's Energy Strategy, which calls for, among other things, the establishment of one zero-carbon community in each of the city's 32 boroughs by 2010.

B. A prototype is planned for a three-acre area on the Royal Albert Dock. Called Gallions Park, it will be a sustainable community with at least 200 residential units. What makes this site important for other cities attempting to shrink their carbon footprint is that the dock area is land that was previously used by industry. Many upcoming eco-cities are being built on virgin land; success at Gallions Park would open other abandoned industrial sites to similar development possibilities.

C. While the Gallions Park development includes several earth-friendly features, such as community greenhouses, a key element of the zero-carbon strategy will be a combined heat and power (CHP) plant to generate electricity and provide hot water. The CHP plant will use biomass, such as wood, for fuel. The community's buildings will also create renewable energy through roof-mounted wind turbines and solar technology that converts light into electricity.

D. A budget has not yet been released by the developer, but the planning application for Gallions Park was filed in July, and construction is expected to begin by early 2009.

Future City Dongtan

China watches over every drop of water

E. On a small, thinly populated island about 14 miles off the coast of Shanghai, a city is rising that could spell salvation for the 1 billion people expected to live in China's urban areas by 2045. Like several other planned cities, Dongtan will showcase an array of eco-friendly technologies such as wind power and zero-emission vehicles, but its most important innovation may be that it is designed to consume 43 percent less water than a conventional city. If Dongtan succeeds, many of its technologies will be employed in other cities in China.

F. Access to water has become a critical issue for much of the world. The United Nations estimates that by 2025, 1.8 billion people will live in regions where drinking water is scarce. The problem is particularly urgent in China, where major rivers (including the Yangtze, which feeds into Shanghai) are heavily polluted. Dongtan aims to reduce its water needs by using technologies such as green roofs-buildings tops covered with plants-to capture and filter rainwater and by recycling sewage and other waste to fertilize and water nearby farms.

Although Dongtan is in the earliest stages of construction, Arup, the U.K. design and engineering firm hired by the Chinese government to oversee its

development, says that as many as 5,000 people will be living there by 2010. There have been delays and setbacks-originally Arup anticipated up to 10,000 settlers by 2010-but the firm says the city is still on track to have as many as 500,000 residents by 2050.

(748 words)

Non-experienced group: Mathilda

Items

Task Type 1 – Multiple Choice

1. *Choose the correct letter, A, B, C or D.*
What is going to be the most special feature of the future city Madsar?
   A It is going to play a major role in oil production.
   B There will be no cars that run on petrol.
   C The city will pioneer in carbon waste recycling.
   D There will be no airport in the city's vicinity.

2. *Choose the correct letter, A, B, C or D.*
Madsar will do away with the problem of
   A overcrowding on traditional buses and subways.
   B oil consumption of cars and small trucks in the United States.
   C vehicles causing environmental damage due to carbon emissions.
   D people walking along the sidewalks.

3. *Choose the correct letter, A, B, C or D.*
Which country is contributing considerably to the financing of the Madsar project?
   A Emirate of Abu Dhabi.
   B China.
   C USA.
   D United Kingdom.

4. *Choose the correct letter, A, B, C or D.*
What makes Gallions Park a particularly important example for other environmental projects?
   A It will have residential units.
   B It is a three-acre area.
   C It is not clear yet what the budget for the project is going to be.
   D It was previously used by industry and is not built on virgin land.

5. *Choose the correct letter, A, B, C or D.*
The CHP plant will generate electricity and hot water by using
   A wind turbines.
   B solar technology.
   C biomass.
   D fossil fuel.

6. *Choose the correct letter, A, B, C or D.*
Who has the job of overseeing the development of the city Dongtan?
   A The Chinese government.
   B The future residents of the city.
   C The United Nations.
   D A design and engineering firm from the UK.

Answers:

1. B
2. C
3. A
4. D
5. C
6. D

Task Type 7 – Locating Information

Questions 7–11

The reading passage has 6 paragraphs, A–F

Which paragraph contains the following information?

Write the correct letter A–F in boxes 7–11 on your answer sheet.
NB You may use any letter more than once.

7 Information about the planning stages of the London project

8 A description of the technologies employed in environmentally-friendly developments in order to minimise water use

9 An example of an area that is being developed into a zero-carbon community

10 Mention of a lack of drinking water caused by polluted rivers

11 The introduction of a future city that will use less water than a conventional citywww

Answers:

7. D
8. F
9. B
10. F
11. E

Task Type 8 – Identification of Information in a Text

Questions 12–17

Do the following statements agree with the information given in Reading Passage 1?

In boxes 12–17 on your answer sheet write

TRUE	if the statement agrees with the information
FALSE	if the statement contradicts the information
NOT GIVEN	if there is no information on this.

12 The city of Madsar is being built next to the Abu Dhabi airport.

13 More than a quarter of carbon emissions in the USA result from burning oil for transportation.

14 The first section of the city of Madsar is going to open in 2013.

15 In London, a large part of carbon emissions is caused by motor traffic.

16 The long term plan for London is to develop 32 zero-carbon communities by 2010.

17 A green roof is a building top covered with plants used to fertilize crops.

Answers:

12. TRUE
13. TRUE
14. FALSE
15. NOT GIVEN
16. TRUE
17. FALSE

Non-experienced group: Mary

Text

The rise of the emotional robot

- 05 April 2008
- From *New Scientist* Print Edition.
- Paul Marks

Duke is moving noisily across a living room floor wearing the dark blue and white colours of Duke University in Durham, North Carolina. He's no student but a disc-shaped robotic vacuum cleaner called the Roomba. Not only have his owners dressed him up, they have also given him a name and gender. Duke is not alone. Such behaviour is common, and takes a multitude of forms according to a survey of almost 400 Roomba owners, conducted by Ja-Young Sung and Rebecca Grinter. "Dressing up Roomba happens in many ways," Sung says "and people also often gave their robots a name and gender". Kathy Morgan, an engineer based in Atlanta, said that her robot wore a sticker saying "Our Baby", indicating that she viewed it almost as part of the family.

Until recently, robots have been designed for what the robotics industry dubs "dull, dirty and dangerous" jobs, like welding cars, defusing bombs or mowing lawns. Even the name robot comes from robota, the Czech word for drudgery. But Sung's observations suggest that we have moved on. "I have not seen a single family who treats Roomba like a machine if they clothe it," she says. "With skins or costumes on, people tend to treat Roomba with more respect." Sung believes that the notion of humans relating to their robots almost as if they were family members or friends is more than just a curiosity. "People want their Roomba to look unique because it has evolved into something that's much more than a gadget," she says.

These changing relationships with robots are something which is particularly in the minds of roboticists at present. Figuring out just how far humans are willing to go in shifting the boundaries towards accepting robots as partners rather than mere machines will help designers decide what tasks and functions are appropriate for robots. Meanwhile, working out whether it's the robot or the person who determines the boundary shift might mean designers can deliberately create robots that elicit more feeling from humans. "Engineers will need to identify the positive robot design factors that yield good emotions and not bad ones – and try to design robots that promote them," says Sung.

To work out which kinds of robots are more likely to coax social responses from humans, researchers led by Frank Heger at Bielefeld University are scanning the brains of people as they interact with robots. The team starts by getting humans to "meet" four different "opponents": a computer program running on a laptop, a pair of robotic arms that tap the keys of a laptop, a robot with a human-shaped body and rubbery human-like head, which also taps at a laptop, and a human. Then the volunteers put on video goggles and enter an MRI machine. While inside the machine, a picture of the opponent they must play against flashes up inside their goggles. The volunteers then must choose between cooperating with their opponent or betraying them. As they can't tell what their opponent will do, it requires them to predict what their opponent is thinking. The volunteers then indicate their choice from inside the scanner.

Heger's team have carried out the experiment on 32 volunteers, who each played all four opponents. Then they compared the brain scans for each opponent, paying particular attention to the parts of the brain associated with assessing someone else's mental state. This ability is considered a vital part of successful social interactions. Unsurprisingly, the team found that this part of the volunteers' brains were active to some extent when playing all opponents. However, it was more active the more human-like their opponent was, with the human triggering the most activity in this region, followed by the robot with the human-like body and head. Heger says that this shows that the way a robot looks affects the sophistication of an interaction.

Not surprisingly, though there are similarities between the way people view robots and other human beings, there are also differences. Daniel Levin and colleagues at Vanderbilt University showed people videos of robots in action and then interviewed them. He says that people are unwilling to attribute intentions to robots, no matter how sophisticated they appear to be. Further complicating the matter, researchers have also shown that the degree to which someone socialises with and trusts a robot depends on their gender and nationality.

These uncertainties haven't stopped some researchers from forming strong opinions. Herbert Clark, a psychologist at Stanford University in California, is sceptical about humans ever having sophisticated relationships with robots. "Roboticists should admit that robots will never approach human-like interaction levels – and the sooner they do the sooner we'll get a realistic idea of what people can expect from robots." He says that robots' lack of desire and free will is always going to limit the way humans view them.

Whether robots can really form relationships with humans and what these can be is much disputed. Only time will really tell. However, despite the negative criticism there is one scientist with strong evidence for his view. Scientist Hiroshi Ishiguro has used a robotic twin of himself to hold classes at his university while he controls it remotely. He says that people's reactions to his computerised double suggest that they are engaging with the robot emotionally. "People treat my copy completely naturally and say hello to it as they walk past," he says. "Robots can be people's partners and they will be."

(920 words)

Non–experienced group: Mary

Items

Questions 1–5: Matching

Look at the following list of statements based on research into robots and their emotional relationships to humans.

Match each statement (1–5) with the correct person A–E.

1. People are reluctant to think that robots can have intentions.
2. People's opinion of robots will always be limited.
3. People have moved on from thinking of robots as only useful for risky and repetitive tasks.
4. People react more to robots that are physically similar to humans.
5. People can and will interact with humans in a completely natural way.

Researchers:
A: Herbert Clarke
B: Hiroshi Ishiguro
C: Ja-Young Sung
D: Daniel Levin
E: Frank Heger

Questions 6–13: Summary Completion

Complete the summary below.

Choose NO MORE THAN TWO WORDS from the passage for each answer.

A recent study by Frank Heger concluded that how a robot 6. _____ it can have with humans. In his experiment, volunteers had to assess four opponents ranging from very machine-like equipment to real 8. _____. Volunteers were put in a MRI scanner, which measured the activity of their 9. _____, wearing 10. _____ showing images of their opponents. They then had to decide whether to work with or 11. _____ the opponent. Their scans showed that their assessment of their opponents' 12. _____ was more active when their opponent appeared more 13. _____.

Questions 14–17: Multiple Choice

Choose the correct letter (A, B, C or D)

14. People dress up their Roombas and give them names because . . .
   A. . . . they want their robots to be different from all the others.
   B. . . . they love their robots.
   C. . . . they give their robots names and genders.
   D. . . . their robots are respected.

15. Daniel Levin indicated that levels of social interaction with robots can depend on . . .
   A. . . . the age of the human.
   B. . . . their intentions.
   C. . . . the sex and nationality of the human.
   D. . . . the way they view humans.

16. Roomba is . . .
   A. . . . a baby
   B. . . . a cleaning device.
   C. . . . a robot in human form.
   D. . . . a student.

17. Experts' views on the extent that robots can be humanised.
   A. . . . are varied.
   B. . . . are critical.
   C. . . . are positive.
   D. . . . are consistent.

Answer Key

Questions 1–5: Matching

1. People are reluctant to think that robots can have intentions. **D Daniel Levin**
2. People's opinion of robots will always be limited. **A Herbert Clarke**
3. People have moved on from thinking of robots as only useful for risky and repetitive tasks. **C Ja Young Sung**
4. People react more to robots that are physically similar to humans. **E Frank Heger**
5. People can and will interact with humans in a completely natural way. **B Hiroshi Ishiguro**

Questions 6–13: Summary Completion

A recent study by Frank Heger concluded that how a robot 6. **looks** is essential in determining the 7. **(social) interaction** it can have with humans. In his experiment, volunteers had to assess four opponents ranging from very machine-like equipment to real 8. **humans.** Volunteers were put in a MRI scanner, which measured the activity of their 9. **brains,** wearing 10. **video** goggles showing images of their opponents. They then had to decide whether to work with or **11. betray** the opponent. Their scans showed that their assessment of **12. mental state** was more active when their opponent appeared more **13. human-like.**

Questions 14–17: Multiple Choice

Choose the correct letter (A, B, C or D).

14. People dress up their Roombas and give them names because . . .
   A. . . . they want their robots to be different from all the others. **Correct**

15. Daniel Levin indicated that levels of social interaction with robots can depend on. . . .
   C. . . . the sex and nationality of the human. **Correct**

16. Roomba is . . .
   B. . . . a cleaning device **Correct**

17. Experts views on the extent that robots can be humanised . . .
   A. . . . are varied. **Correct**

Experienced group: Jane

Text

Wildlife-spotting robots

Conservationists are using robotic cameras to help search for rare wildlife. Biology fieldwork is very labour intensive, so there is increasing use of technology to collect data in an unobtrusive way. Autonomous sound recording units and video imaging equipment can be programmed to collect data at scheduled times in remote areas, and it is often possible, via long-range wireless communications, to access the data from a distant location. However, the chances of recording an occurrence of the target species are very low, so it is important that the equipment should be selective in what it records, or have the ability to sift the data and pick out likely candidates for expert examination.

Some wildlife cameras are controlled by passive infrared motion sensors which detect a nearby animal, point the camera towards it and trigger an image-capture sequence. Some are directly controlled by remote observers, in a similar way to web cameras or surveillance systems. A project, led by University of California, Berkeley and Texas A & M aims to integrate signals from both sensors and humans in the control of a hybrid teleoperated/autonomous robotic device called the collaborative observatory for natural environments (CONE). The developers are building an "observatory" that will enable scientists to study animals in their natural habitat via the Internet. A purely automatic version of this, the ACONE, is aiding researchers at Cornell University in their systematic search for the North American ivory-billed woodpecker.

The ivory-billed woodpecker is a large, vividly coloured bird that was widely thought to be extinct. There has been no officially confirmed sighting of it since 1940, but a spate of recently reported glimpses inspired a determined search effort by the United States Fish and Wildlife Service and Cornell Lab of Ornithology (CLO). The project started in 2005 with over 20 trained field biologists taking part in the search team, and volunteers also being recruited. They had to become familiar with the use of GPS, digital video cameras and microphones, and cell phone technologies. The search also made use of time-lapse video recording cameras for monitoring likely sites. This method was ideal since it did not lead to the disturbance that is unavoidable with human observers. They played back a 1935 recording of the ivory-billed woodpecker to try to attract the bird. They also used ultra-light aircraft to conduct aerial surveys. Autonomous sound-recording units recorded the ambient sounds at selected sites, and sampled at 20 kHz for up to 47h per day, and the results were analysed at CLO to pick out any new recordings that were a match to the known vocalisations of the ivory-billed woodpecker. Despite the 6,347 field-hours of the Cornell-coordinated search, no definitive sighting was made in the 2005–2006 season.

In February 2007, the University of California, Berkeley announced the installation of a high-resolution intelligent robotic video system developed in collaboration with Texas A&M University. Mounted on an electrical transformer and positioned to view the birds flying through the narrow corridor surrounding an existing power line, two cameras collect video images, and software examines them in real time, discarding any images that have no relevance. The software looks for a large bird flying at 20 to 40 mph. The images saved are then examined by human experts.

The camera lens has a focal range of 10 m to 40 mm, giving a horizontal field of view varying from 32° to 8°. The cameras are positioned so that they look along the corridor in opposite directions. They are mounted 3 metres in the water in the marsh, and angled upwards to observe birds flying between the tree-tops through the 50 metre corridor. With a 20° horizontal field of view, each camera observes the full width of the corridor at a point 366 metres away, and can switch to a wider field of view as the bird approaches. Each camera captures 20 frames per second, and the software continually examines the images, carrying out statistical background subtraction to allow for changing weather conditions, and looking for large connected foreground components on every seventh image. In its first 120 days, operating for 8 hours per day, it captured a total of 76 million images, but the software selected only 5,825 of these for storage. This autonomous system has already demonstrated its success in capturing images of large birds, and its powerful selectivity avoids wasting experts' time.

A more general project to develop "Collaborative Observatories for Natural Environments" (CONE) is underway at the Universities of Texas A & M and UC Berkeley, with input from natural scientists and documentary filmmakers, funded by the National Science Foundation. The observatories are located in the field and are run on solar energy. They incorporate sensors and actuators and software to carry out a periodic systematic observation of the surrounding scene, or automatically point the camera in the direction of a sensed event, and also respond to the signals of biologists who are making observations and inputting instructions from their laboratories. This combination of teleoperation and autonomy builds upon years of work by Professor Ken Goldberg, an engineering professor, and Dr Dehzen Song, assistant professor of computer science. Song's work involved the development of a system that allows multiple users to share simultaneous live control of a camera via the internet. The system collects the requests from users and calculates, for example, which zoom setting would best satisfy them all. This advance in intelligent software has helped CONE biologists to improve the selectivity of images captured and stored, and improved the responsiveness of remote systems to their live imaging needs.

(937 words)

Experienced group: Jane

Items

Questions 1–5

Do the following statements agree with the information in Reading Passage 1?

In boxes 1–5 on your answer sheet, write

TRUE   if the statement agrees with the information

FALSE   if the statement contradicts the information

NOT GIVEN   if there is no information on this

1   The equipment in wildlife experiments is programmed to obtain data at random intervals.

2   There is little chance that the equipment used will capture the species being investigated.

3   There are insufficient experts to examine the different species that are recorded in field studies.

4   The organisations that produce surveillance cameras also make cameras for wildlife filming.

5   The movement of animals through an area will activate some cameras.

Questions 6–12

Complete the notes below.

Choose NO MORE THAN ONE WORD AND l OR A NUMBER from the passage for each answer.

Write your answers in boxes 6–12 on your answer sheet.

A CONE study of the ivory-billed woodpecker

background to the study

• bird last seen in: 6 ....

• most people believed the bird to be: 7 ....

2005–2006 season

• camera study preferable since observation by people involves: 8 ....

• old recordings played to attract the bird

• results analysed to identify sounds that were a: 9 ....

• no definitive sighting

• cameras positioned to view birds flying through narrow corridor

• images analysed to assess their: 10 ....

• cameras fixed at a height of: 11 ....

• cameras already taken pictures of: 12 ....

Questions 13–16

Answer the questions below. Choose NO MORE THAN TWO WORDS ANDl OR A NUMBER from the passage below for each answer.

Write your answer in boxes 13–16 on your answer sheet.

13   Which professional group is working with scientists on the CONE study?

14   What are the CONE observatories powered by?

15   Where are biologists in the CONE study monitoring events from?

16   Which camera feature can be controlled by the software developed by Dehzen Song?

Key

1   F
2   T
3   NG
4   NG
5   T
6   1940
7   extinct
8   disruption
9   match
10 relevance
11 3 metres
12 geese
13 (documentary) filmmakers
14 solar energy
15 (their) laboratories
16 zoom (setting)

Experienced group: Anne

Text

What makes us laugh?

If we ask ourselves what triggers a good laugh, the obvious answer is that it is a response to something we find funny. But one scientist, Robert Provine, who has spent nearly two decades studying laughter, says that humour has surprisingly little to do with it. Provine, a neuroscientist at the University of Maryland in the US and author of Laughter: A Scientific Investigation, realised early on in his research that you cannot capture real-life laughter in the laboratory because as soon as you place it under scrutiny, it vanishes. So, instead, he gathered his data by standing around in public places, eavesdropping on people's conversations, secretly noting when they laughed.

Over the course of a year he collected 1200 laugh episodes – an episode being defined as the comment immediately preceding the laughter and the laughter itself – which he sorted by speaker (the person talking), audience (the person being addressed), gender and pre-laugh comment. His analysis of this data revealed three important facts about laughter. Firstly, that it is all about relationships. Secondly, that it occurs during phrase breaks in speech. And thirdly, that it is not consciously controlled. 'It's a message we send to other people – it practically disappears when we are by ourselves,' he says. Perhaps most surprising of all is Provine's finding that only 15–20 per cent of everyday comments preceding laughter are remotely humorous. 'Laughter usually follows comments like "I've got to go now" or "Here's John."'

The fact that we don't have control over when we laugh suggests that it must be deeply embedded in our nature. Indeed, studies of the play behaviour of great apes suggest that laughing has been around a lot longer than we have. Chimpanzees laugh while they are having play fights although the sound is quite different to that made by humans due to their different vocal apparatus. Instead of chopping a single outbreath into the 'ha-ha' sound that characterises our laughter, chimps' laughter sounds like panting.

A recent study of orangutans reveals a deeper similarity with humans. A team of researchers watched the play behaviour of 25 individuals aged between two and twelve at four primate centres. 'In particular we analysed the facial expressions that they produce during social play,' says Dr Marina Davila-Ross of the University of Portsmouth. 'It's a relaxed expression where they open their mouth and show their upper teeth. It's very similar to the human expression of laughter.'

The team discovered that when one orangutan displayed this expression, its playmate would often produce the same expression less than half a second later. The speed with which this mimicry occurred indicated that the orangutan had not had time to decide on the response – in other words the laughter was contagious. 'In humans, mimicking is a mechanism that enables us to understand our social partner better, and this helps us to cooperate and form social bonds. It is clear now that it evolved prior to humankind,' says Davila-Ross.

The fact that we share laughter with great apes suggests that it emerged in our ancestors sometime before the split with chimpanzees six million years ago. But it may have evolved even earlier than that. Research conducted at Bowling Green State University in Ohio, US, found that even rats produce chirping sounds comparable to laughter when playing or when tickled and the common ancestor of rats and humans lived 75 million years ago. The fact that laughter is triggered by tickling suggests a strong link to humans, because, as Provine puts it, 'tickle is the most ancient and reliable stimulus of laughter.' One of the earliest games parents and children play is when the parent tickles the baby on the stomach or under the arms until it laughs.

Studies of tickling, although thin on the ground, should therefore be able to tell us a lot more about laughter. For example, we all know that we cannot make ourselves laugh by tickling ourselves. But could a machine tickle us? One team of researchers at the University of California at San Diego built a mechanical tickling machine to look at this very question. They discovered that their subjects laughed just as much in response to the machine as to the experimenter. This tells us that a successful tickle does not depend on another person, but merely on another entity, something that's not you.

Discovering that laughter can be used as a tool to explore other aspects of our behaviour has, for Provine, been one of the most rewarding aspects of his research. Perhaps his most important insight concerns the evolution of speech.

Provine believes that the evolution of speech and bipedal locomotion are causally related. He came to this conclusion after analysing the difference between chimp and human laughter. 'It occurred to me that basically the human 'ha-ha' came about as a result of the evolution of breath control that chimps lack,' he explains. We hold our breath as we lift heavy objects and quadrupedal animals must do the same when moving in order to support their body when their four limbs hit the ground. When our ancestors stood up on two feet, the chest was freed of these mechanical demands making it possible for speech to evolve.

By breaking away from traditional models of laughter and discovering its links to deep elements of human nature such as speech and sociality, Provine has reinforced just how ancient laughter is. It has been around for as long as rough play, an activity that you see in mammals, from rats and squirrels to chimpanzees and humans, and has most likely evolved from the laboured breathing that accompanies such play.

(946 words)

Experienced group: Anne

Items

Questions 1–8

Do the following statements agree with the information given in Reading Passage X?

In boxes 1–8 on your answer sheet, write

> **TRUE** if the statement agrees with the information
>
> **FALSE** if the statement contradicts the information
>
> **NOT GIVEN** if there is no information on this

1 Provine wrote down more than a thousand examples of what made some of his students laugh.

2 Provine classified his research material into male and female subjects.

3 Provine considered dividing the laugh episodes into the kind of laughter generated.

4 Provine observed that laughter is mostly stimulated by remarks that are without humour.

5 Copying another person's gestures or behaviour is believed to assist in the creation of communal attachments.

6 It is clear that laughter developed in man nearly six million years ago.

7 There has been a considerable amount of research into tickling.

8 The tickling machine is to be tried out on a range of different mammals.

Questions 9–14

Complete the summary below.

Choose **TWO WORDS ONLY** from the passage for each answer.

Write your answers in boxes 9–14 on your answer sheet.

Laughter in Great Apes

When observing chimpanzees, researchers have noted that laughter occurs when the animals are involved in 9............ The chimpanzees make a noise similar to 10............ and this is because their internal 11............ is not the same as that of humans.

Other researchers have studied orangutans in captivity and focused on the common 12............ that they exhibit when relaxing together. The researchers were especially interested in the fact that the top **13**.............. of the orangutans were visible when they were 'laughing'. When observing one animal 'laughing', researchers frequently noted that another orangutan immediately copied this behaviour, suggesting that the laughter could be described as **14**...............

Questions 15 and 16

Choose TWO letters, A–E.

Write the correct letters in boxes 15 and 16 on your answer sheet.

Which **TWO** of the following statements are mentioned in the passage?

A It is thought that laughter in apes is related to their ability to stand upright at times.

B Laughter in chimpanzees probably originated when they learned to hold their breath.

C Human speech began to develop when early man ceased walking on four legs.

D All mammals demonstrate some kind of laughter when playing.

E Laughter may originate in the physical response to the exertion of play.

Key

1	False
2	True
3	Not Given
4	True
5	True
6	False
7	False
8	Not Given
9	play fights
10	panting
11	vocal apparatus
12	facial expressions
13	teeth
14	contagious
15 /16	C/E (in either order)

Experienced group: William

Text

The changing image of childhood in English literature

A Childhood as an important theme of English literature did not exist before the last decades of the eighteenth century and the poetry of Blake and Wordsworth. There were of course children in English literature before then, as the subject of lyrics and complimentary verses. But in drama, the main body of poetry and the novel, the child is virtually or entirely absent.

B With Blake and Wordsworth we are confronted with an essentially new phenomenon, that of major poets expressing something they considered of great significance through the image of the child. In time, the child became the central figure of an increasingly significant proportion of English literature. The concept of the child's nature which informed the work of Blake and Wordsworth was that children were naturally innocent, and were slowly corrupted by the society in which they lived – in contradiction to the long Christian tradition that everyone, child and adult alike, is sinful.

C The nineteenth century saw the beginnings of a spiritual crisis. The securities of the eighteenth-century peace dissolved in the era of revolution, leading to social and political ferment. The social, political, and, more especially, the intellectual problems arising from the French and Industrial Revolutions found no resolution. In a rapidly dissolving culture, the nineteenth-century artist faced alienation. The concern of the modern European intellect has been, in part, the maintenance of individual integrity within the search for the security of universal order. At no time has that maintenance and search been so pressing in its demand as in the nineteenth century, when long-accepted ideas were challenged not only by the upheavals mentioned above, but also by the revolutionary thinking of Darwin, Marx and Freud.

D The society created by the industrial developments of the late eighteenth and nineteenth centuries was increasingly unconcerned with and often hostile to art. The novelist Charles Dickens was the last major English writer to have a really successful public voice, in the mid 1800s. By the end of the century, there was a new literate public who were unresponsive to the best creative work. A new mass literature supplied the demands of uninformed literacy; and the relative influence of the mature creative voice was proportionally diminished. Art was on the run; the ivory tower had become the substitute for the wished-for public arena.

E In this context of isolation, alienation, doubt and intellectual conflict, it is not difficult to see the attraction of the child as a literary theme. The child could serve as a symbol of the artist's dissatisfaction with the society which was in process of such harsh development about him or her. In a world given increasingly to utilitarian values and the machine, the child could become the symbol of imagination and sensibility, of nature set against the forces in society actively de-naturing humanity. Through the child the artist could express awareness of the conflict between human innocence and the cumulative pressures of social experience, and protest against the horrors of that experience.

F If the central problem of the artist was in fact one of adjustment to the realities of society, one can see the possibilities for identification between the artist and the consciousness of the child, whose difficulty and chief source of pain often lie in adjustment and accommodation to his or her environment. In childhood lay the perfect image of insecurity and isolation, of fear and bewilderment, of vulnerability and potential violation. Some authors took the identification to an extreme, turning to this image as a means of escape, a way of withdrawal from spiritual and emotional confusion in a tired culture. They could be said to have taken refuge in a world of fantasy and nostalgia for childhood.

G The nineteenth century saw the deterioration of the concept of the child as a symbol of strength and richness in life. The symbol which had such strength and richness in the poetry of Blake and Wordsworth and some later novels became in time the static and sentimentalised child-figure of the popular nineteenth-century imagination; only a residue of a literary theme, retaining little or nothing of the significance it had earlier borne. It was against this conventionally innocent child that a revolution was effected at the turn of the nineteenth century. Just as the eighteenth century had turned from the Christian doctrine of original sin to the cult of original virtue in the child, so the nineteenth century turned from the assumption of original innocence to the scientific investigation of the infant and child consciousness and its importance to the development of the adult mind.

H A distinction can be made between those late eighteenth- and nineteenth-century authors who went to the child to express their involvement with life, and those who approached the symbol as a retreat from 'life's decay'. In writing of childhood, we find that in a very exact and significant sense the modern author is writing of life. In the literature of the child in the nineteenth and twentieth centuries we have a reflection of the situation of certain artists in modern times; their response, at a deep and significant level, to the condition in which they found themselves; and, if their feelings could achieve the projection, the condition in which they found humanity. Considering the nature of that condition, it is perhaps not remarkable that through writing of childhood there should be those who wanted to go back to the beginning to begin again, and others who wanted just to go back.

Experienced group: William

Items

Questions 1–6

Do the following statements agree with the information given in Reading Passage 0?

In boxes 1–6 on your answer sheet, write

    TRUE   if the statement agrees with the information

    FALSE   if the statement contradicts the information

    NOT GIVEN   if there is no information on this

1 Blake and Wordsworth adapted a tradition of expressing ideas through children.

2 A number of writers identified the industrial revolution as a major cause of social problems.

3 Children featured less often in 19th century literature for the masses than in serious literature.

4 During the 19th century, serious writers found themselves increasingly marginalised by the popularity of mass literature.

5 Some 19th century authors saw in childhood a reflection of their own difficulties in adjusting to society.

6 The concept of the innocence of children retained its power as a symbol throughout the 19th century.

Questions 7–11

Complete each sentence with the correct ending, A–G below.

Write the correct letter, A–G in boxes 7–11 on your answer sheet.

7 Authors working prior to the late 18th century

8 Blake and Wordsworth

9 Darwin, Marx and Freud

10 Dickens

11 In the harsh society of the 19th century, some authors

A wrote about the relationship between children and their parents.

B added to the difficulty of reconciling individual needs with those of society.

C recognised the damage that children could inflict on each other.

D used children as a vehicle for protest.

E rarely included children in any significant role.

F researched the effects of revolution on children.

G used children as symbols of innocence.

H gained a degree of popularity that later 19th century writers failed to equal.

Questions 12–17

Reading Passage 0 has eight paragraphs, A–H.
Which paragraph contains the following information?

Write the correct letter, A–H, in boxes 12–17 on your answer sheet.

12 a comparison between changes in concepts of children in two distinct periods

13 a reference to the impact of new ideas during the 19th century

14 a contrast between two psychological motives for writing about children

15 a reference to an increase in the number of people able to read

16 how Blake's and Wordsworth's view of the child differed from the prevailing concept

17 a contrast between qualities symbolised by children and the realities of society

Key

1	False	10	H
2	Not given	11	D
3	Not given	12	G
4	True	13	C
5	True	14	H
6	False	15	D
7	E	16	B
8	G	17	E
9	B		

Experienced group: Elizabeth

Text

Time to wake up to the facts about sleep

Claims that we are chronically sleep-deprived are unfounded and irresponsible, says sleep researcher Jim Horne

A

Ask people whether they would like more sleep, and most will say yes. Does that mean they are not sleeping enough? The apparent desire for more sleep, together with oft-repeated assertions that our grandparents slept longer, all too easily leads to the conclusion that most people in the west are chronically sleep-deprived. It has also been claimed that inadequate sleep causes obesity and related disorders such as diabetes.

Claims of widespread sleep deprivation in western society are nothing new – in 1894, the British Medical Journal warned that the 'hurry and excitement' of modern life was leading to an epidemic of insomnia. But even then it probably wasn't true. The fact is that most adults get enough sleep, and our sleep debt, if it exists at all, has not worsened in recent times.

B

The well-known 'fact' that people used to sleep around 9 hours a night is a myth. The figure originates from a 1913 study by researchers at Stanford University, which did find that average daily sleep was 9 hours – but this applied to children aged 8 to 17, not adults. Even today, children continue to average this amount. Over the past 40 years, there have been several large studies of how much sleep people actually get, and the findings have consistently shown that healthy adults sleep 7 to 7½ hours a night.

More support for today's epidemic of sleep debt supposedly comes from laboratory studies using very sensitive tests of sleepiness, such as the multiple sleep latency test, in which participants are sent to a quiet, dimly lit bedroom and instructed to 'relax, close your eyes and try to go to sleep'. These tests claim to reveal high levels of sleepiness in the general population, but as they are performed under relaxing conditions they are able to eke out the very last quantum of sleepiness which, under everyday conditions, is largely unnoticeable.

Another line of evidence trotted out for chronic sleep deprivation is that we typically sleep longer on vacation and at weekends, often up to 9 or 10 hours a night. It is often assumed that we do this to pay off a sleep debt built up during the week. However, just because we can easily sleep beyond our usual daily norm – the Saturday morning lie-in, the Sunday afternoon snooze – it

doesn't follow that we really need the extra sleep. Why shouldn't we be able to sleep to excess, for indulgence? After all, we enthusiastically eat and drink well beyond our biological needs.

C

What of the risk of a sleep shortage causing obesity? Several studies have found a link, including the Nurses' Health Study, which tracked 68,000 women for 16 years. The hazard, though real, is hardly anything to worry about. It only becomes apparent when habitual sleep is below 5 hours a day, which applies to only 5 per cent of the population, and even then the problem is minimal. Somebody sleeping 5 hours every night would only gain a kilogram of fat per year.

The link between short sleep and diabetes has also been exaggerated. It's true that healthy young adults who are restricted to 4 hours' sleep a night for several nights show the beginnings of glucose intolerance, which can be a precursor to type 2 diabetes. However, that doesn't mean it happens in the real world. For one thing, the effect quickly reverses after one night of recovery sleep. Moreover, 4 hours' sleep is highly artificial and the vast majority of people cannot sustain it for more than a few days. Our very lowest natural limit seems to be 5 hours, yet the researchers did not test the effect of 5 hours' sleep on metabolism, and many have just assumed that what is found with 4 hours' sleep applies to short sleep in general.

D

Not only have chronic sleep deprivation and its consequences been overstated, I also believe that our apparent desire for more sleep isn't all it seems. Do we really mean it when we say 'yes' to the question, 'Would you like more sleep?' It's a leading question that invites a positive response, in the same way as asking whether you would like more money, a bigger house or more holiday. Who, in all honesty, would say no? The real test of inadequate sleep is whether people feel excessively sleepy during the daytime.

E

My team recently investigated sleep deprivation by giving around 11,000 adults a questionnaire asking about it in an indirect way. We asked respondents the times when they usually went to bed and woke up, and the amount of sleep they felt they needed each night. The responses to these two questions allowed us to get an estimate of the shortfall. They also completed another questionnaire to assess daytime sleepiness. Half the respondents turned out to have a sleep shortfall and around 20 per cent had daytime sleepiness.

We then asked, 'If you had an extra hour a day, how would you prefer to spend it?' The alternatives were exercising, socialising, reading or relaxing, working or sleeping. Few people opted to use their extra hour for sleep. It seems that people may want more sleep, but they may not actually need it, and they will happily forego extra sleep in favour of other leisure activities.

F

Does any of this matter? I believe it does. Propagating the myth of a sleep-deprived society adds to the anxieties of people who wrongly believe they are not getting enough sleep, leading to a greater demand for sleeping pills. Rather than attempting to increase our sleep, maybe we should spend those 'extra' hours of wakefulness doing something more productive.

(937 words)

New Scientist 18 October 2008

Experienced group: Elizabeth

Items

Questions 1–6

Choose the correct letter, *A, B, C or D.*

Write the correct letter in boxes 1–6 on your answer sheet.

1 What problem does the writer identify with the study done at Stanford University in 1913?

  A The research was based on a false assumption.

  B The findings conflict with those of later studies.

  C The conclusion has not been accurately reported.

  D The researchers did not clearly identify age groups.

2 The writer claims tests such as the multiple sleep latency test may not have valid results because

  A they do not use a representative sample of the population.

  B they require the subjects to try to sleep in unrealistic conditions.

  C they do not make precise enough measurements of the time slept.

  D they encourage the subjects to sleep more than they would normally.

3 The writer mentions the 'Saturday morning lie-in' as an example of

  A a treat that may actually be harmful to health.

  B something unnecessary that is done for pleasure.

  C a time when we can catch up on the sleep we need.

  D something that may not actually lead to extra sleep.

4 What is the writer's conclusion about the link between sleep and obesity?

  A A good way to lose weight is to sleep less.

  B The risk of lack of sleep causing obesity is insignificant.

  C Too much sleep leads to obesity in only 5% of cases.

  D There is no relationship between lack of sleep and obesity.

5 The writer criticises a study linking lack of sleep with diabetes because

  A it was not based on a natural situation.

  B it underestimated how little sleep people really need.

  C it only concentrated on recovery sleep.

  D it did not test the effect of lack of sleep on metabolism.

6 The writer suggests that when researchers use a particular type of question, this

   A may provide data that is inaccurate.

   B may show how materialistic people are.

   C may elicit information that is surprising.

   D may make people afraid of answering honestly.

Questions 7–12

Complete the summary below.

Choose NO MORE THAN TWO WORDS from the passage for each answer.

Write your answers in boxes 7–12 on your answer sheet.

The writer's team carried out a study on 11,000 adults. Perceptions of sleep deprivation were estimated by comparing the answers to two **7**.......................... questions, and the team found that half the respondents had sleep deprivation. **8**.......................... was also assessed, and found to be less common. The team also found that if they were given an extra hour a day, few people would use this for sleeping.

The writer concludes that people do not **9**.......................... more sleep. He says his findings are important because false beliefs about sleep deprivation are creating **10**.......................... which have no basis in reality, and encouraging people to ask for **11**.......................... People should therefore not try to **12**.......................... the number of hours they sleep.

Questions 13–17

Reading passage x has six sections A–F.

Which paragraph contains the following information?

Write the correct letter, A–F, in boxes 13–17 on your answer sheet.

NB You may use any letter more than once.

13 a mention of a medical condition which may precede a more serious illness

14 a reference to sleep deprivation in a specific academic publication

15 some examples of things people could do instead of sleeping

16 a statement of the amount of sleep the writer believes is needed by an adult

17 a summary of the reasons why sleep deprivation is seen as a problem today

Answer key

1 C
2 D
3 B
4 B
5 A
6 A
7 indirect
8 Daytime sleepiness
9 need
10 anxieties
11 sleeping pills
12 increase
13 C
14 A
15 F
16 B
17 A

378

5 The impact of the funded research studies on the IELTS Academic Reading test

Lynda Taylor
Consultant to Cambridge ESOL

The four funded research studies reported in Part One of this volume all focused on the IELTS Academic Reading test and were conducted between 2005 and 2010 (under Rounds 11–13 of the IELTS Joint-funded Research Program). The studies provided the IELTS partners with valuable insights into the construct validity of the Academic Reading test, as well as into the nature and effectiveness of the test-writing process. Research findings offered useful evidence in support of claims about test usefulness, while at the same time helping to highlight specific aspects needing closer review and possible future revision. In combination with outcomes from other commissioned studies and internal validation investigations, they feed into the ongoing process of IELTS Reading test development and validation. The specific contribution of each of the four studies is reviewed and evaluated in the sections that follow.

Chapter 1: The relationship between the academic reading construct as measured by IELTS and the reading experiences of students in their first year of study at a British university (Weir, Hawkey, Green, Ünaldi and Devi)

The study by **Cyril Weir**, **Roger Hawkey**, **Anthony Green**, **Aylin Ünaldi** and **Sarojani Devi**, which appears as Chapter 1, is the first of three studies in this volume to explore the construct validity of the IELTS Academic Reading test. The researchers set out to investigate the academic reading activities and problems encountered by students in their first year of study at a British university. They went on to compare the emerging model of academic reading with an analysis of the reading construct as tested in the IELTS Academic Reading test. Employing a mixture of qualitative and quantitative methodologies, they gathered and analysed various types of data, including student self-report data, via a questionnaire on background variables, cognitive processing and performance conditions encountered in academic reading, and data resulting from an investigation of IELTS test materials and core undergraduate textbook extracts.

Overall, the study found evidence that the IELTS Academic Reading texts fall generally within the parameter ranges exhibited by the undergraduate text corpus that they assembled and analysed. For example, the IELTS texts reflected a similar range of vocabulary to that which appeared in undergraduate textbooks. Comparability was also detected on the measures of rhetorical organisation, grammatical complexity and cohesion. This is encouraging news for the IELTS test developers and it supports claims made about the validity and usefulness of the test. The researchers suggest, however, that the reading texts used in IELTS can sometimes lack certain features of academic reading texts that cause students significant difficulty in their studies. One such feature is cultural specificity, and Weir et al speculate that readers exposed only to relatively culturally neutral texts of the kind typically found in IELTS (and perhaps in most large-scale, international proficiency tests) might find the greater cultural specificity of undergraduate texts more demanding when they encounter these in their academic studies. They comment that the kinds of text used in IELTS are those that tend to introduce academic topics to a general audience, often in the form of articles sourced from newspapers or magazines presenting research findings to the general public. The study found that even the most difficult of the IELTS texts did not appear to reach the difficulty level of the most challenging undergraduate texts, suggesting perhaps some sort of ceiling effect for the reading material that is selected for inclusion in the IELTS Academic Reading test.

In their conclusions, Weir et al suggest that the Band 6.5 threshold appears to mark a significant boundary between those students who report experiencing few reading problems and those who encounter greater difficulties. This finding seems to support the widespread use of Band 6.5 or above for Academic Reading (and perhaps also for the other skills tested by IELTS) as an appropriate cut-off for entry to university courses, especially those courses that entail heavy reading loads.

The researchers also observe that the IELTS Academic Reading test focuses heavily on testing *careful reading* skills, possibly at the expense of *expeditious reading*, which is the type of reading that university students tend to find more challenging during their studies. This point is well-taken (though see below the findings from a follow-up study to this one by Weir, Hawkey, Green and Devi). In the future, the IELTS test developers would be well-advised to explore how a greater proportion of the Academic Reading test might be targeted at testing expeditious as well as careful reading skills, perhaps by exploiting computer-based technology for reading assessment of reading, since this mode may offer the control of timing and text presentation that is needed to provoke expeditious reading.

Finally, the research team highlights some interesting applications of their methodology to the process of selecting texts for use in reading tests, especially in relation to certain contextual parameters (see below and Chapter 4 in this volume for more discussion of the test-writing process for the IELTS Academic Reading test). Such findings can feed directly into the item writing process for IELTS Reading tests helping to identify texts that conform to typical academic texts and those which are idiosyncratic in some way and therefore potentially less suitable.

Chapter 2: Construct validity in the IELTS Academic Reading test: a comparison of reading requirements in IELTS test items and in university study (Moore, Morton and Price)

Tim Moore, **Janne Morton** and **Steve Price** set out to investigate the suitability of IELTS Academic Reading test items in relation to the reading and general literacy requirements of university study in an Australian context. Their study is therefore complementary to the one by Weir, Hawkey, Green, Ünaldi and Devi described above (Chapter 1 in this volume).

The researchers conducted a survey of reading tasks in the two domains of the IELTS Academic Reading test and university study, as well as interviews with academic staff across a range of academic disciplines. A taxonomic framework was then constructed to analyse the IELTS and university-based reading tasks, with a focus on two dimensions of potential difference: *level of engagement*, referring to the level of text with which a reader needs to engage to respond to a task (local versus global); and *type of engagement*, referring to the way (or ways) a reader needs to engage with texts on the task (literal versus interpretative). The study sought to make explicit the task demands of reading items in the IELTS Academic Reading test so as to understand the types of interaction being provoked between text and reader, and the extent to which these reflect the types of reading tasks and activities required of students on university programmes. This study therefore has a strong construct validity focus, complementing similar research undertaken in the UK on academic reading and IELTS by Professor Cyril Weir and his colleagues at the University of Bedfordshire (see Chapters 1 and 3 in this volume).

The findings of the study are once again encouraging for the IELTS test producers inasmuch as they provide further empirical evidence of a clear correspondence between the reading requirements of the IELTS Academic Reading test and some of the skills needed for academic study in the world beyond the test. Similarity was observed in those types of reading requiring a mainly local and literal engagement with material, i.e. a basic comprehension of relatively small textual units (and perhaps analogous to the careful reading phenomenon discussed by Weir et al). Most of the IELTS Academic Reading test items were observed to reflect features of reading tasks found in the corpus of academic texts gathered for the study, texts which had as their focus the need for students to understand certain discipline-based concepts. At the same time, however, there was evidence of some divergence between the two domains, with a variety of reading tasks in the academic corpus appearing to require a more critical engagement with material or interaction with multiple sources and viewpoints. These task types and demands were noticeably less evident in the IELTS task corpus under scrutiny.

The patterns of similarity and difference between the IELTS Academic Reading tasks and the academic task corpus were confirmed in the interviews with academic staff, though it is interesting that perceptions varied among subject staff from differing disciplines about the degree of congruence between the type of reading they expected their students to do on courses and the apparent demands of the IELTS test. Moore, Morton and Price reported a broad division between the 'harder' technical disciplines on the one hand (e.g. Engineering, Architecture, Physics, Biology), where reading expectations seem to be characterised more narrowly, e.g. as requiring the assimilation of information, and the 'softer' humanities-oriented disciplines on the other hand (e.g. Media Studies, Linguistics, History, Management), where academic reading requirements seem to be more complex, often comparative or evaluative in nature. This would suggest that in the first year of undergraduate study – at least in the Australian context – the types of materials students need to read on their courses, and the ways they need to go about reading these, can vary markedly depending upon the disciplinary field.

In discussing their research findings the researchers offer us some valuable insights into key features that appear to differentiate the reading demands of IELTS from the demands of academic reading in the university study context, including specific features relating to epistemic entities, interpretative readings, readings of multiple texts, the contextual nature of reading, the reading–writing nexus, information literacy and genre readings of texts. The researchers' discussion touches upon the central issue in language assessment of *construct under-representation*, i.e. the extent to which a test does, or does not, sample adequately from the universe of tasks and activities linked to the construct of interest, in this case the construct of academic reading. Moore, Morton and Price advocate strengthening the link between the two domains (of the IELTS test and the world of undergraduate study) by including more test items requiring global/interpretative rather than just local/literal reading. This, they suggest, would help bring the cognitive demands of the test more into line with the type of reading required on students' courses. Their comments echo the recommendations of Weir et al on the value of having in the test more texts and tasks that require fast and efficient high-level processing.

It is encouraging to see that the researchers are not at all naïve about the practical considerations involved in test production and they readily acknowledge the challenges associated with modifying the IELTS test in order to improve construct representation along the lines proposed. We clearly need to recognise the limits to which a test such as IELTS can (or should be expected to) fully simulate language use in the target use situation in its entirety. The testing of reading in IELTS is premised upon a generalist construct of academic reading and the researchers are right to highlight the inevitable challenge that disciplinary variation in reading requirements at university raises for a test such as IELTS. Furthermore, as previously mentioned, IELTS is designed principally to test *readiness to enter* the world of university-level study in the English language and does not assume test takers have already mastered the high-level academic literacy skills they are likely to require for their future studies. Such skills may well need to be developed during their studies, perhaps even during the early months of their first academic year, and within a specific disciplinary context which will have its own specialist discourse and approach to academic literacy.

Despite these caveats, the IELTS test producers are committed to maintaining a cycle of systematic monitoring and continuous improvement of the test and they recognise their responsibility to enhance test content and delivery in the light of ongoing research and as conditions and circumstances allow. Thus the researchers' practical suggestions for how IELTS reading tasks might be extended to reflect a greater degree of global and interpretative reading are immediately relevant to the test-writing process. The sample tasks offered at the end of the report should offer valuable input to the IELTS item writing teams currently working on material for the Academic Reading module. It may be that closer attention can be given by the test writers to ensuring a larger proportion of Reading test items that function at the global and interpretative levels. As mentioned earlier, in the longer term it is interesting to speculate whether future computer-based development of IELTS might permit a greater inclusion in the Reading test of some of the features that characterise academic reading, and thus a broader representation of the construct of interest. Innovative computer-based testing techniques, for example, might enable the test taker to do one or more of the following: engage with larger quantities of text; interact with multiple texts; exercise skills related to the searching and selecting of sources, including electronic media; and even undertake more sophisticated reading-into-writing tasks.

Recent theoretical and empirical work discussed in the field of L2 reading and reading assessment (see *Examining Reading* by Khalifa and Weir 2009) highlights the critical parameters that appear to characterise the higher levels of second language reading ability: in particular, the ability to go beyond simply establishing propositional meaning at the clause, sentence and paragraph level in order to build complex mental models, creating a text level representation based on a single text and an inter-textual representation drawing upon multiple textual sources. This is the sort of reading, it is argued, that characterises the C1 and C2 levels of the Common European Framework of Reference (CEFR); and it is the type of high-level academic reading that students typically need to undertake in their university courses. Although full contextual authenticity is generally unrealistic for language assessments, our growing understanding of the nature of high-level L2 reading proficiency, combined with the evidence from empirical studies such as those by Moore, Morton and Price in the Australian context, and by Weir and his colleagues in the UK, undoubtedly have important implications for the future development of the IELTS Academic Reading test.

Chapter 3: The cognitive processes underlying the academic reading construct as measured by IELTS (Weir, Hawkey, Green and Devi)

The study by **Cyril Weir**, **Roger Hawkey**, **Anthony Green** and **Sarojani Devi** built upon the earlier Weir et al study (see above and Chapter 1 in this volume) and set out to investigate in greater depth the cognitive processes underlying the construct of academic reading. The rationale for the project highlights the responsibility of test providers to supply appropriate evidence showing how a language proficiency test adequately reflects the demands of academic courses. This study thus constituted the second phase of a larger research agenda for the validation of the IELTS Academic Reading test. It used participant retrospection to identify the range of cognitive processes that students employ when they are performing the various tasks in an IELTS Academic Reading test.

Over 350 pre-university-level students undertaking English courses across the UK and in Taiwan were given one of six IELTS Academic Reading tasks. They were asked to complete the task in class and then fill in a retrospective questionnaire that captured reading types and response strategies apparently used to answer the test questions. The resulting data was quantitatively analysed to produce both descriptive and inferential statistics. The picture of reading that emerged was consistent with the general approach to academic reading reported by student readers in the earlier Weir et al protocol study (see above and Chapter 1 in this volume). Quick and selective search reading was followed by intensive careful reading of relevant text parts. The earlier study had raised concerns that the approach in testing IELTS Academic Reading focused strongly on careful, intensive reading but allowed little opportunity for expeditious reading, a skill much needed by students in academic study. This follow-up study, however, provided evidence that expeditious reading did in fact play an important role in the way participants sought to answer the test items. Thus, rather than expeditious reading being tested separately from careful reading in IELTS, the two may be integrated. The researchers also found evidence of reader understanding at the whole text level rather than at sentence level only.

The study demonstrates that the relationship between item type and response strategy in a Reading test is not straightforward, and this finding is in line with other research outcomes. While certain item types do appear to provoke certain strategies (e.g. multiple choice items encourage close reading and direct word matching), item type is not a very reliable predictor of patterns of strategy use. This relatively unpredictable relationship between item type and cognitive processing underpins the rigorous test development process for IELTS, which combines the expertise and judgement of item writers with a system of pretesting and item calibration to ensure that items are appropriately targeted in terms of their level of difficulty. A subsequent joint-funded project (see below and Chapter 4 in this volume) investigated the process of Writing test items for the IELTS Academic Reading test, exploring in depth the intuitions and decisions of IELTS test writers with regard to text and task type selection and offering useful insights for enhancing test writer training in the future.

Weir et al's observations suggest that forcing expeditious reading strategies in the context of a Reading test remains a challenge for test developers and that this may only be achieved by enforcing time constraints on the test taker's reading activity. Work continues to identify ways of testing expeditious reading more systematically and effectively in IELTS.

Chapter 4: An empirical investigation of the process of writing Academic Reading test items for the International English Language Testing System (Green and Hawkey)

Anthony Green and **Roger Hawkey** explored an aspect of the IELTS Academic Reading test that has so far received relatively little attention under the Joint-funded Research Program. While a few previous studies have focused on the characteristics of texts and test items, there has been little investigation of the actual processes that item writers go through when selecting texts and creating items, and the way these contribute to the overall quality of the test material. This study thus breaks new ground for IELTS and is a welcome addition to the growing body of research relating to the Academic Reading test, complementing previous funded research studies that have explored test content and design. Furthermore, this study helps to explain some of the characteristics of the IELTS texts and the types of reading identified by the Weir et al studies (Chapters 1 and 3 in this volume).

Green and Hawkey investigated the text selection, item writing and editing processes involved in the development and production of material for the IELTS Academic Reading test. Using the methodology of retrospective reports and direct observation, they set out to compare how trained and untrained item writers, both individually and collectively, select and edit reading texts in order to make them suitable for a task-based test of reading and how they generate the accompanying items. Both written (flowchart) and oral (interview and focus group) data were gathered on item writer processes and products (draft and edited reading texts and items), and both deductive and inductive approaches to analysis were employed.

The investigation was useful in identifying differences across the item writer groups and also between individuals within the groups. Both the experienced and non-experienced writers seemed to pass through similar stages when selecting texts and constructing items, though the researchers noted that those in the experienced group were able to articulate their experience more explicitly and in greater detail, and also generated higher-quality test material. The latter group also manifested a repertoire of gambits for efficiently exploiting source texts and task types, including the willingness to confidently edit texts for reasons of accessibility or cultural neutrality, reshaping them as necessary to meet the requirements of the test items. The expertise of the experienced test writing group appears to have been significantly influenced by their item writer training, by the item writer guidelines which guided their activity and by their collaborative approach during editing, which involved not only being able to freely critique each other's material but also make constructive proposals for improving another's work.

This study provides the field with some valuable insights into the processes of text selection, adaptation and item writing for a test of reading comprehension ability, as well as more generally into the nature of expertise. The differences observed between the experienced and non-experienced groups help to highlight the skills that are required for effective item writing. Overall, the researchers report being favourably impressed by the conscientiousness and professionalism of the trained IELTS item writers that they interviewed and observed, and by the quality of the texts and the items that they produced. This should be a source of encouragement for the IELTS test producers who have undertaken extensive investment since the mid-1990s to develop rigorous policy and procedures for item writer selection, training and monitoring. It also strengthens the view that such expertise is collective in nature, rather than residing in individuals, and it supports the IELTS partners' decision to have IELTS item writing teams based in different parts of the English-speaking world.

The researchers make some useful recommendations for refining and strengthening the current approach and procedures for IELTS test material production. One recommendation suggests making the principles and processes of test production more transparent and accessible to external stakeholders such as teachers and test preparation material publishers, particularly concerning the types of reading skill being targeted and the intention behind use of certain task types. This could be done relatively easily by enhancing the public information already available on the IELTS website or through other communication channels, such as stakeholder seminars. Such an initiative would be consistent with the now well-established policy of the IELTS partners to communicate as much useful information as possible to test stakeholders and it would assist those who prepare candidates for IELTS in ensuring the match, in terms of construct validity, between test preparation activities and what candidates actually encounter in the test.

Perhaps more important for the IELTS test developers is the recommendation offered in this study to extend and deepen the training of the item writing teams. The insights gained through this study have undoubted application in the initial training of new item writers when they first join the team, helping them to understand how texts and items can be reshaped for the test and to develop their own skills in this regard. They also have relevance for more experienced item writers who may benefit from additional training and guidance on the detailed nature of the academic reading construct and how this is best operationalised through the IELTS Academic Reading module. The suggestion of using electronic tools for objective text analysis is certainly worthy of consideration by the IELTS item writing teams. Software such as Compleat Lexical Tutor or Coh-Metrix could prove valuable practical tools for identifying or confirming key features of academic text genres and helping to ensure comparability across test versions.

The point is also well made that test providers should keep item writers informed about relevant assessment issues, including current theoretical perspectives on the reading process, the nature of the reading demands on beginning university students and the implications of these for assessment. Articulating the ability construct and approaches to operationalising it for assessment, especially across different proficiency levels and domains, is the underlying rationale for the series of skills-related volumes currently being published by Cambridge ESOL and Cambridge University Press in the *Studies in Language Testing* series. Khalifa and Weir's *Examining Reading* (2009), for example, focuses on the assessment of second language reading ability, including the nature of reading at higher proficiency levels in academic and professional contexts. The hope is that volumes such as these will increasingly be used in practical ways to develop item writers' understanding of the constructs that are the focus of assessment, thus enabling them to more fully operationalise the academic reading construct in IELTS and other tests.

References

Khalifa, H and Weir, C J (2009) *Examining Reading: Research and Practice in Second Language Reading*, Studies in Language Testing volume 29, Cambridge: UCLES/Cambridge University Press.

Part Two
Listening

6 The cognitive validity of the lecture-based question in the IELTS Listening paper

Dr John Field
CRELLA, University of Bedfordshire, UK

Abstract

This study investigates the cognitive validity of two samples of IELTS lecture-listening material taken from past papers. In one condition, participants were asked to undertake the original test and to provide a retrospective verbal report explaining why they had chosen the answers that they had favoured. In a second condition, they were asked to take notes under the less constrained circumstances that obtain during a lecture and then to report on them. The material was distributed on an AB–BA principle so that the possible effects of recording and test method could be compared.

The scores obtained by individuals under 'test' conditions were compared with the extent to which the same individuals showed themselves capable of accurately reporting units of information in the freer 'lecture' condition. No clear correlation was demonstrated.

The verbal reports were then examined for evidence of the cognitive processes adopted by participants under test conditions, and were matched against conventional psycholinguistic accounts of first-language listening (see, for example, Brown 1995, Field 2008a). A distinction was made between: *normal processes* which might equally well be adopted by a native academic listener; *strategic behaviour* which aimed to compensate for problems of understanding; and *test-specific behaviour* representing the user's response to characteristics of the test. Evidence of the last raised concerns about cognitive validity. The protocols showed participants adopting specific routines that were tailored to the test method. They also provided considerable evidence of participants favouring test-wise strategies and attempting to exploit loopholes in the format of the test, such as the availability of questions in a written form.

A third line of enquiry investigated participants' responses to listening under the two conditions in order to establish which they had found the more demanding. An unexpected result was the number of participants who found lecture listening less demanding than undertaking the test. Possible reasons are explored.

1 Background

1.1 Need for the study

Cambridge ESOL takes pains, in designing the specifications of the IELTS Listening paper, to ensure that the test achieves content validity (cf. Clapham 1996:65–72, on content validation for the parallel Reading paper). The criteria ensure that the four listening passages are closely linked to an academic context by specifying the situations and text genres that candidates are likely to encounter, either socially or in the course of study. In this way, the designers ensure that the test achieves validity in relation to linguistic factors such as the lexical, discoursal and pragmatic content of the target field.

However, IELTS is first and foremost a test of language *skills*. It serves as a predictor of performance, on the assumption that its results correlate with a candidate's ability to handle the real-world demands of an academic programme. It thus has to be evaluated in terms of a second type of construct validity, namely cognitive validity (Glaser 1991, Weir 2005). In Weir's (2005) evidence-based validity framework, the term refers to the extent to which the cognitive demands of the test reflect those of the target context. In relation to the IELTS Listening paper, this entails establishing that the types of listening behaviour which the test elicits correspond to those which an academic environment requires.

Traditionally, this type of validation is conducted in a *post hoc* fashion, with statistical methods such as factor analysis applied to test results in order to establish the nature of the construct which has been tested. Weir expresses concerns over this approach, raising the issue of whether the data under examination might not to some extent be compromised by the form and content of the test and by the assumptions underlying its design. In effect, he draws attention to the dangers of relying exclusively on an approach that attempts to track back from a product to the process that gave rise to it. He argues instead for what he terms *theory-based validity* (or, more recently, *cognitive validity*): a complementary approach to test validation which takes account, before the test is designed, of external empirical evidence concerning the nature of the construct that is to be assessed. Weir makes his point powerfully:

> There is a need for validation at the *a priori* stage of test development. The more fully we are able to describe the construct we are attempting to measure at the *a priori* stage, the more meaningful might be the statistical procedures contributing to construct validation that can subsequently be applied to the results of the test. Statistical data do not in themselves generate conceptual labels. We can never escape from the need to define what is being measured, just as we are obliged to investigate how adequate a test is in operation (Weir 2005:18).

This additional strand of construct validation requires that, alongside benefiting from feedback from piloting and past administrations, test design also draws in a principled way upon external evidence concerning the nature of the expertise which is to be targeted.

As noted, insights into the processes applied by candidates are especially important in the case of tests which are used to predict later performance. It is precisely these predictive tests which are worst served by a product-based approach. A researcher might indeed employ factor analysis to indicate the aspects of the target construct that have been tested; or might compare the rankings achieved in the test to other measures of the candidates' current competence. But neither result demonstrates the candidate's ability to perform on arrival in the target setting. The obvious way such a finding can be achieved is longitudinally – by measuring achievement once the academic programme has begun – but here the researcher faces a potential confound. If one uses overall measures of achievement during the course of the programme, it becomes difficult to separate the candidate's flair for the chosen subject of study from their L2 study skills. Similarly, one can trace broad correlations between overall IELTS scores and overall academic success; but it is difficult to single out performance in specific skills areas.

One possible line of enquiry for cognitive validation is to seek evidence in other disciplines – in the case of language skills, from the detailed models of L1 processes which cognitive psychology has been able to build on the strength of long-term empirical findings (see Shaw and Weir 2007 and Field 2011 for applications of this approach to the cognitive validation of L2 skills tests). An alternative course is to seek evidence not *a priori* as Weir proposes, but on-line, while a task is being carried out. Comparisons can be made between the observed or reported behaviour of the candidate when performing the task under test conditions and the candidate's parallel behaviour when the task is performed under conditions which more closely resemble those of the real life context for which they are preparing. Such evidence meets Weir's strictures in that it is not tied narrowly to test outcomes but directs enquiry to the processes which give rise to those outcomes.

The present study adopts the second approach. It investigates the cognitive validity of the IELTS Listening test by comparing the performance of participants during sample IELTS tasks with their performance during a task which more closely replicates the demands of an actual academic context. By 'performance' is to be understood both evidence of successful comprehension and evidence of the processes that are employed by the candidate to achieve that goal. The process evidence will be considered in relation to established models of listening drawn from cognitive psychology and underpinned by extensive empirical evidence. In this way, Weir's plea for the greater use of external, scientifically validated information will be met.

The IELTS Listening test falls into four sections. The first two sections contain recorded content that relates to what are termed 'social needs'; the third tests ability to understand a conversation with details of course content and assignments; the fourth tests lecture listening. Of these, it is the last which affords the most compelling case for cognitive validation. Its predictive validity rests heavily upon the extent to which it can be shown to model performance in a one-way lecture-listening situation (admittedly, with some limitations such as lack of visual support). It is thus from this section that the present study selects its material.

1.2   Cognitive validity and L2 listening

Weir (2005) stresses the importance of applying criteria that are based upon an understanding of the processes underlying the L2 skill to be tested. However, he leaves the precise nature of those criteria to some extent open to discussion. Reflection suggests that one might establish the benchmark for cognitive validation in two different ways:

a. by treating predictive validity as a primary criterion; and comparing the processes in which non-native listeners (NNLs) engage when performing a particular task under test conditions with those which they employ under non-test conditions

b. by treating native-like performance as a primary criterion; and comparing the processes in which NNLs engage when performing a particular task under test conditions with the processes adopted by native listeners (NLs) in real-life conditions.

Given the important predictive role of IELTS, the focus of the present study is upon the first.

When one considers the question of cognitive validity with specific reference to L2 skills (and within them L2 academic skills), it is important to differentiate between three different types of behaviour. They will be referred to generally as 'processes', but a distinction needs to be made between:

- Behaviour which is part of the *normal processing* – in the present case, behaviour which might equally well be adopted by a native academic listener.

- *Strategic behaviour* which aims to prepare for a task, to maximise the amount that is retained or to compensate for problems of understanding. In listening, much of this behaviour will be specific to the L2 listener in that it anticipates or deals with problems of understanding that are due to individual perceptual or linguistic limitations. (Note that the term *strategy* is used rather more narrowly than, for example, in Buck 2001:103–4.)

- *Test-specific behaviour* representing the user's response to features of the test. It would seem to take two distinct forms. The candidate might adopt specific routines which assist in the achievement of the particular task set in the test, but which would not normally play a part in the corresponding real-life activity (in the present case, lecture listening). Or the candidate might adopt certain test-wise strategies in an attempt to second-guess the intentions of the setter or to exploit loopholes in the format of the test such as (in listening) the availability of questions in a written form. Clearly, either of these constitutes a negative factor when attempting to establish cognitive validity.

The present study aims to keep these three performance components as separate as possible. One needs:

a. to seek parallels between the language processes involved when taking the test and those involved in listening to the same material when unconstrained by test conditions

b. to seek parallels between the compensatory strategies applied to problematic areas of the input when a participant is under test and under non-test conditions

c. to identify strategies specifically related to test taking, which raise possible concerns about cognitive validity.

1.3   Choice of method

The most appropriate method for the study was verbal report (Ericsson and Simon 1993). It has a number of disadvantages, which are acknowledged below. However, it is widely employed as a means of investigating various forms of expertise (including mathematical thinking and chess playing) and of identifying the operations which underlie them. Clearly, there are differences between the type of cognitive process which can be elaborated heuristically in terms of a set of consciously formulated stages and the type which entails a much less structured process such as deriving meaning from a text. However, both types of performance might be characterised as goal-oriented, and in both cases the goal (here in the form of the listener's answers) can be used as a means of tracking back to the thinking which gave rise to it.

Verbal report has been used successfully to investigate the processes of second language learners, who have proved capable of recording the thought processes which led them to particular interpretations of texts (Faerch and Kasper 1987). It has even been used (Cohen 1998) to research speech production and reception. Clearly, in the latter case, report has to be retrospective – which means that it is important to avoid memory effects. In fact, the circumstances of a Listening test support retrospection well in that the participant has to provide a set of answers, which provide triggers to assist recall of the thought processes that led to them. In non-test conditions, the participant can be asked to write concurrent notes, which similarly support recall.

An important constraint of verbal report as a method should be mentioned at this point. Gathering and transcribing protocols is costly in terms of time, and consequently imposes limitations upon the size of the population that can be studied. Whereas it is possible to administer a test such as the IELTS Listening paper over a very large population for the purposes of, for example, *post-hoc* factor analysis, a study that investigates individual on-line processing must inevitably draw upon a smaller group of respondents. The present project should be regarded in much the same way as a case study, though it reports on a larger number of respondents than do most. The numerical and statistical results recorded here must be regarded as broadly indicative rather than conclusive. That said, what is lost in generalisability will, it is hoped, be compensated for in the depth of the information that is obtained.

1.4   Theoretical framework

The present study bases its analysis upon a data-driven approach in which the researcher seeks patterns of similarity and difference in the responses recorded by participants with no *a priori* assumptions. However, any study of this kind also ideally requires a wider framework against which its findings can be measured.

Two possible theoretical areas suggest themselves within the literature on second language listening; but neither is extensive enough or well enough supported by rigorous empirical research. Firstly, there have been a number of proposals for taxonomies of listening sub-skills, of which the most notable are perhaps Buck (2001:57–59), Richards (1983), Rost (1990:150–158), and (specifically related to assessment) Dunkel, Henning and Chaudron (1993). But all of them contain categories with a degree of overlap, a lack of supporting research evidence based on listening in a natural context and no criteria to mark out certain characteristics as carrying more weight than others. A second possible source is the considerable work that has taken place in recent years on L2 listening strategies. It suffers from a number of theoretical problems – not least, the rather miscellaneous taxonomy adopted by many researchers and based upon Oxford (1990). As Alderson (2000:309) commented in relation to L2 reading, 'Much of the research into, and teaching of, reading strategies remains fairly crude . . . and frequently fails to distinguish between strategies as defined more generally in the strategy literature and "skills" as often used in the reading literature'. Much of the research (see e.g. Vandergrift 2005, Vandergrift, Goh, Mareschal and Tafaghodatari 2006) has been dependent upon the use of questionnaires – a method which can at best only provide information about the strategies that learners *believe* they employ and is very much open to challenge in that it invites learners to provide information on processes that may not be accessible to report. Most importantly, an approach based solely on strategy use provides useful insights into the techniques employed by the listener in order to resolve local problems of understanding, but does not capture what is of equal concern in a study of cognitive validity, namely, the processes which a listener employs in decoding input and analysing meaning under circumstances that are unproblematic.

A more reliable theoretical framework is therefore found in the models of listening and of meaning construction which have been developed by psycholinguists investigating first language speech processing (see, for example, in Gaskell 2007, papers by McQueen, Pisoni and Levi, Singer, Tannenhaus, van Gompl and Pickering). They are elaborated in considerable detail, soundly based upon current thinking in cognitive psychology and underpinned by solid research findings. Granted, these are accounts of L1, not L2, language processing, but one can argue that, in identifying the traits of the skilled L1 listener, they provide a yardstick for assessing the performance of the L2 listener at any level, and a goal towards which the EAP listener in particular might be expected to strive. Reference will be made to cognitive models of this type during the discussion. Particularly germane will be the ways in which they represent the cognitive demands that a given task places upon a language user.

1.5   Research questions

The present study investigates the extent to which the fourth section of the IELTS Listening test achieves cognitive validity by:

- replicating the processes in which candidates would engage when listening to a lecture in a non-test context
- measuring the ability of candidates to engage in the processes entailed in listening to a lecture in a non-test context.

The specific research questions are as follows:

1. To what extent can the fourth section of the IELTS Listening test be said to achieve construct validity in terms of the cognitive processes which it requires of the candidate?
2. How great is the role played in the fourth section of the IELTS Listening test by processes which are specific to the text context?
3. What are the perceptions of candidates as to the demands of the test when compared with those of listening to an academic lecture in non-test conditions?

The study first compares results achieved by means of the test with those achieved in a less constrained lecture-listening situation. Using verbal report, it then seeks evidence of the extent to which candidates taking Section 4 of the test employ test-wise strategies and other techniques specific to the test-taking context. It also examines the comments of participants on whether the test situation adds to or reduces the difficulty of academic listening.

2 Research design

2.1 General outline

- A group of participants (N=29) were studied, all of whom were preparing for university entrance.
- There were two conditions: test and non-test. The test condition entailed listening once to a passage from Section 4 of an IELTS Listening test and supplying the answers required by the test setters. The non-test condition entailed listening to a Section 4 recording from another IELTS test, making notes during listening and writing a short summary.
- Validity would be compromised if participants were to hear the same listening passage twice. Two passages were therefore employed, and an AB–BA design was adopted. Fifteen participants reported on Passage A in the test condition and Passage B in the non-test; and the remaining 14 reported on Passage B in the test condition and Passage A in the non-test. So far as possible, each AB participant was paired with a BA one who shared the same first language.
- After each task, participants were invited to describe:
    - the processes involved in achieving answers under test conditions
    - the processes involved in extracting information and building meaning under non-test conditions.

2.2 Methods

2.2.1 Verbal report

Verbal report is widely used in research into expertise generally (Ericsson and Simon 1993) and into cognitive validity specifically (Baxter and Glaser 1998). It has a number of drawbacks as a method of researching language skills performance (see Brown and Rodgers 2002:53–78; McDonough and McDonough 1997:191–200) especially in relation to the receptive skills and to non-native participants. They include the following:

a. Thinking does not proceed on a step-by-step basis as it might in the resolution of a problem in (e.g.) mathematics or chess playing that involves logic.

b. The reading and listening skills can only be investigated indirectly; and some of the processes involved may not be readily accessible to report.

c. The process of reporting can interfere with the ecological validity of the task. In the case of listening, it is clearly impossible for participants to engage in concurrent verbal report. The use of retrospective report, however, carries possible memory effects.

d. Language limitations may prevent non-native participants from reporting as fully as they might.

e. The level of reporting may vary considerably from one participant to another – with implications for reliability.

One way of overcoming the memory effects associated with retrospective report is to provide 'stimulated recall' in the form, for example, of a video replay of the activity to be reported on (Gass and Mackey 2000). The importance of retrieval cues is well attested in memory research findings within cognitive psychology (for a non-specialist review, see Chapter 5 in Kellogg 1995). Tulving's influential *encoding specificity hypothesis* (Tulving 1983) states that accurate recall is critically dependent upon activating the same cues in retrieval as those originally encoded with the event to be recalled. In the test condition, such a trigger was available in the answers chosen by the participant. In an interview setting, the participant was asked to report their answers and then to explain the process by which the answer had been derived. In the non-test condition, the content of the participant's notes and written summary served similarly to provide a set of retrieval cues.

The approach adopted also attempted to reduce possible memory effects by ensuring a minimal time lapse between the process to be reported and the report itself (Brown and Rodgers 2002:55). The target listening passages were divided into three, providing pauses in which the test taker could record from three to four answers and report their thought processes after a relatively short listening period. The aim was to ensure greater detail and greater accuracy. The practice did not materially change the conditions under which the IELTS Listening test is undertaken, since takers are allowed only one listening and thus have to record their answers in an on-line fashion.

Pausing the recording at appropriate intervals where there was a change of sub-topic was felt to be more ecologically valid than pausing it as each answer was achieved. The latter procedure would have been disruptive of the process of meaning building at a global level. It would also have meant that the researcher would need to signal the point at which the answer was identified, thus eliminating the uncertainty about matching a question to a possible answer that is an important feature of the experience of taking an L2 Listening test.

So far as the non-test condition was concerned, the recording was paused only once and briefly, to ensure that the participant did not feel too challenged by the demands of note-taking.

Clearly in any research into listening and speaking, the verbal reports obtained need to be retrospective. Here, they were of two kinds.

a. *In the test condition*, participants reported each answer they chose and then explained their reasons for choosing it.

b. *In the non-test condition*, participants were interviewed after writing a summary of the passage; and asked to report as much as possible of what they had heard in the recording (assisted by the notes they had taken and the summary they had written). They were allowed to decide for themselves the relative importance of what they reported and the discourse-level relationships between the different points.

A particular concern was that limitations of linguistic ability might be an obstacle to informative reporting. The two tasks, together with the reporting phase, were therefore piloted with six participants who shared the same background as the target group but had slightly lower overall IELTS scores. They proved to be capable of reporting clearly and accurately their reasons for choosing particular answers and ignoring others. Their comments also provided indications of the types of strategic decision that they had made.

2.2.2 Note-taking and summary

The original research design included a second source of data in the form of a written summary of what participants had heard in the non-test condition. Participants were to take notes while listening to the mini-lecture, and were then to write them up as comprehensively as possible. The purpose was to achieve hard evidence of how accurately and extensively each individual was able to report the mini-lecture on the basis of their notes. This would enable experienced judges to rate the participant's lecture-listening skills. The study would then seek possible correlations between the summary rating and the marks obtained in the IELTS test format.

Summary is a very informative method of testing listening comprehension skills, though it obviously poses practical difficulties of reliability and ease of marking in international tests (Alderson 2000:232–3). Unlike more formal test methods, it provides evidence of ability to identify main points and speaker's purpose, to assess the relative importance of information and to show propositional links. It also requires the summariser to draw entirely upon information supplied by him/herself rather than using test items as a basis. Finally, it has some ecological validity in relation to a lecture-listening task, since clearly the content of real-life lectures may ultimately find its way into a student's assignment.

However, the piloting phase raised questions about the value of using summaries in this particular project. Participants were told that they could take as long as they liked to write their summary, but in practice they often wrote very little. Two factors seemed to constrain them. The first was the face-to-face situation: they seemed to feel that their inevitably slow writing as L2 users was holding up the proceedings. The second was the instinct to express themselves with care in the L2 so as to avoid grammar errors and imprecise lexis. Participants were told that language errors were not a concern of the researcher, but they clearly found it difficult to set aside the prescriptions of their L2 instructors.

The brevity of what was written did not appear to be the consequence of a failure of auditory understanding. Indeed, during the retrospective verbal reporting that followed, participants tended to recall considerably more than they had covered in their writing, even without prompting by the researcher. They also tended to report coherently and logically, and the interview situation enabled the researcher to follow up the points made so as to establish whether the main propositions and the connections between them had been fully grasped. It became clear that writing imposed greater constraints than oral reporting, and that the summary task might even be seen as imposing heavier cognitive demands and additional skills such as the ability to précis.

On the evidence obtained, it seemed unlikely that the summaries would be informative enough to enable raters to form reliable judgements as to the lecture-listening skills of the writer. The conclusion was that verbal report was likely to prove a more valuable source than summary.

The research design was therefore revised. In the Non-Test condition, participants were still asked to take notes and to write them up, but these components of the task were used simply as prompts to assist the verbal report. Note-taking served an important role in reducing dependence upon memory and in simulating the real-life lecture situation, but it was also felt to be worthwhile to retain the summary-writing stage, since it enabled the participant to structure the information that had been obtained before presenting it orally to the researcher.

The proposal to assess lecture-listening skills by means of subjective ratings of written summaries was replaced by a more objective system of quantification based upon the number of macro- and micro-propositions accurately identified by the participant during the course of the verbal report. Further details are provided in Section 2.4.

2.3   Task conditions

Each participant was asked to undertake two tasks:

1. *Test-based.* They undertook an IELTS test from Section 4 of a past Listening test, the section which aims to assess the candidate's ability to follow lecture-style material. Conditions were exactly as in the test: participants were given a brief period before listening to look through the questions, and were only allowed one hearing of the passage. The only difference was that the test was interrupted at certain points, when the researcher asked participants to report their answers and to attempt to give reasons for choosing them. All participants proved capable of reflecting and reporting on their own behaviour. The researcher followed

up many of the explanations with requests for clarification or for further information; throughout, his attitude to the responses given was entirely neutral. At the end of the task, he asked respondents two general questions:

- *What was the main point or the main points of this talk?*
- *Were there any parts of this talk that you found difficult to understand? At the beginning? In the middle? At the end?*

2. *Lecture-based.* In the second task, participants listened to a second Section 4 paper as if they were listening to a live lecture, and took notes with a view to writing a summary of what they had heard. They were allowed as much time as they wished to write the summary. They were then asked to report orally to the researcher on what they had understood of the interview. Like those in piloting, most summaries proved to be shorter than expected, and not as informative as the oral responses. However, this part of the task was retained because:

a. it assisted recall for the oral report

b. it gave participants the opportunity of representing the logical links between the various ideas in the talk and of assembling the information they had obtained before expressing it orally

c. it had some ecological validity in that it modelled what a university student might well be required to do when incorporating the content of a lecture into an assignment.

At the end of this task, the researcher asked the participant three questions:

- *What was the main point or the main points of this talk?*
- *Were there any parts of this talk that you found difficult to understand? At the beginning? In the middle? At the end?*
- *Which of the two exercises did you find easier: the first or the second? Can you explain why?*

These last questions were followed up where necessary by a sub-question to establish more clearly if the perceived difficulty derived from the recording or from the task.

2.4   Materials and procedure

The two papers chosen for the study were taken from a recent collection of past papers (Cambridge ESOL 2005). They were Section 4 of Paper 1 in the collection (on the urban landscape) and Section 4 of Paper 4 (on the meshing of sharks in Australia). They were chosen because both had a similar relatively short running time and a similar density of informational content, and both featured a concrete but non-specialist topic. Question types were rather different; but it was felt to be important to control principally for listening content. The first recording is referred to as Text A and the second as Text B. The transcripts of the recordings appear as Appendix 6.1 at the end of this report and the task sheets for completion appear as Appendix 6.2.

The participants were divided into two groups. One group performed the first (test-based) task using Text A and the second (lecture-based task) using Text B. This is referred to as Condition A–B. With the other group, the order of texts was reversed; this is referred to as Condition B–A.

The two mini-lectures were transferred from CD to an iPod Nano for the purposes of the research. They were played to the participants through high-quality Bose Companion 2 speakers designed for iPod reproduction. The participants' verbal reports were recorded to computer using a Røde NT1-A studio microphone and digitised by a Roland Edirol USB UA25 interface. They were subsequently transferred to master CDs and then to cassettes to assist the transcriber.

Participants were explicitly told in the first task that they would be under-taking an IELTS test, but that the test would be paused from time to time for them to report, if they could, the reasons for choosing their answers. The pauses took place consistently after Questions 35 and 38 for Text A and after Questions 34 and 38 for Text B. Before the second task, participants were told that they should imagine that they were listening to a lecture in a UK univer-sity and taking notes in order to write up a summary of the lecture.

All the ethical requirements of the University of Reading were met. The project was given approval by a departmental ethics committee, and each participant was asked to sign a statement of compliance before testing took place. Participants were paid £10 for their time.

The verbal reports were transcribed by a professional transcriber, using a format which numbers the lines of each report to ensure ease of reference. The transcription included not only the words of the participant but also any interventions by the researcher. To ensure confidentiality, participants were allocated letters in the order in which they were interviewed (from A to Z, then from AA to AC). As they appear in the transcription, each protocol has been coded according to the participant – the task – the text. For example, D2b refers to the protocol of Participant D when performing the second (lecture) task in relation to Text B.

Samples of two transcripts are included in Appendices 6.3 and 6.4, one in the A–B condition and one in the B–A. The two samples are from Participants R and V. They were chosen partly because these participants proved to be good at reporting on the processes they had employed and partly because the processes recorded were representative of those mentioned by the group as a whole. The participants counterbalance each other in that R was one of the Chinese sub-group, while V was European. Despite the differences in cultural background, there were certain similarities in their strategic behaviour. With

V, this behaviour proved productive while with R it did not. R achieved one of the lower scores on Text A while V achieved the highest test score on Text B.

2.5 Population

The starting date of this research exercise was delayed until August 2006 to ensure the availability of suitable respondents. The project required naïve listeners – i.e. those without extended experience of residence or study in the UK. This was necessary in order to control for level of listening development: given that, once immersed in an L2 environment, different listeners develop at markedly different rates and in different ways. Furthermore, the experimental task entailed verbal report and thus required respondents to possess a level of English which enabled them to comment on aspects of their own listening behaviour. Of those available earlier in the year, a number were considered by their teachers to fall below such a level.

The population chosen for study was drawn from a group of students recently arrived to attend a pre-sessional course at the University of Reading. Intake in Reading is staggered, with the students possessing weakest proficiency scores arriving earliest. Participants were therefore chiefly drawn from the third (August) intake, on the grounds that they were not the highest fliers but that their speaking skills were likely to be equal to the task demanded of them.

All students in the August intake were circulated with a request for volunteers for the research study. The response was encouraging and sufficient to permit relatively careful controls to be applied in selecting participants. Volunteers were eliminated who had been previously resident in the UK for two months or more. In terms of first language, there was a heavy preponderance of students from the Far East. A decision was therefore taken to restrict to 12 the number of respondents whose L1 was declared to be Mandarin Chinese, of whom eight were citizens of the PR of China and four were from Taiwan. In addition, to ensure a wider spread of first languages, a small number of students of European origin from the fourth intake were invited to participate.

Participants were chiefly limited to those whose listening scores on the university's own entry test ranged from 14 to 15 out of a maximum of 20 (IELTS 5.5 to 6 for those who had taken the exam). Speaking scores averaged 5.5 (IELTS also 5.5) out of a maximum of 10; they did not always correlate with Listening scores. However, three participants were admitted whose scores showed them to be weaker listeners (10–12 on the Reading scale/5 in IELTS) though their speaking scores suggested that they were adequate for the task.

The original proposal had been to base the study upon 20 students. However, student responses proved to be briefer than had been anticipated, with a typical session lasting around 50 minutes and the verbal report amounting to about 15 minutes per respondent. Data was therefore collected from 29 students in all. The wish to study greater numbers was prompted by emerging evidence of personal listening styles and processes. It also derived from the researcher's wish to ensure, so far as possible, that respondents were paired within first language groups, with one member of a pair performing in Condition A–B and one in Condition B–A. Clearly, L1 can be expected to affect the difficulty which a candidate encounters in a Listening test – not simply in cases where L1 bears a phonological similarity to L2, but also in cases where the two languages share a substantial number of cognates. Hence the wish to test speakers from a wide spread of first languages and the need to distribute first languages evenly across the two conditions.

Table 6.1 below lists the first languages of the respondents and shows how they were paired across the two conditions. By extending the numbers studied, it proved possible to group participants systematically, with only three anomalies (one Italian speaker grouped with one Portuguese, one Japanese speaker grouped with three Thai speakers; one Lithuanian speaker with extensive exposure to Russian grouped with three Russian speakers). The table also shows the balance that the study attempted to strike between respondents of Far Eastern origin and those of European origin. It had been the intention to feature speakers of Arabic and possibly Persian; but unfortunately those who were available had had previous periods of residence in the UK and had to be excluded from the study.

Of the 29 participants, 19 were female and eight were male.

Table 6.1 Paired participants showing first language

Condition A–B		Condition B–A	
Student	**First language**	**Student**	**First language**
A	French	V	French
G	Portuguese (Braz.)	B	Italian
AA	Italian	AB	Italian
W	Greek	X	Greek
D	Thai	C	Thai
S	Thai	F	Japanese
I	Chinese (Taiwan)	K	Chinese (Taiwan)
L	Chinese (Taiwan)	M	Chinese (Taiwan)
N	Chinese	O	Chinese
P	Chinese	Q	Chinese
R	Chinese	U	Chinese
T	Chinese	Z	Chinese
AC	Russian / Turkmen	J	Russian / Turkmen
Y	Russian		
E	Lithuanian		
		H	Nepali

The results for the one unmatched speaker (of Nepali) are omitted when comparing performance across the two conditions (and particularly when comparing them numerically). The results are also omitted for Participants E and Y (the Lithuanian–Russian pair) as they both fell into Condition A–B. This leaves 13 pairs, which include a block of six pairs of native speakers of Mandarin. Within this block, it was felt to be important to distinguish between those originating in Taiwan and those originating in mainland China because of their different educational backgrounds and traditions.

3 Data analysis

The data analysis adopts three main lines of enquiry:

a. It compares the marks achieved in the formal IELTS test with a quantification of the extent to which participants were successful in extracting information from a mini-lecture in non-test conditions.

b. It examines evidence from verbal report of the means by which answers were achieved in the simulated IELTS test; and distinguishes between processes specific to the test condition and those which might also occur in a less constrained experience of lecture listening.

a. It examines verbal reports by participants comparing the test and the non-test conditions, to establish how different they perceive the underlying processes to be.

3.1 IELTS score

The tests were first marked by reference to the answers specified by the setters. To ensure maximum reliability, the exam board's regulations require strict adherence to these forms, in terms of both wording and spelling. However, this stipulation would have disqualified a disturbingly large number of the participants' responses (19 in total) which strongly indicated that full understanding had been achieved. The items in question were as follows:

Text A

Q 35 less *dangerous*
  1 instance of *danger*

Q38 *considerably reduce / decrease / filter* (the wind force)
  5 instances of *break* 1 instance of *reduce*

Text B

Q34 (Sharks locate food by using their) *sense of smell*
  10 instances of *smell* 2 instances of *nose*

A limited range of answers is provided to markers in these tests; but it is curious that variants like those evidenced here did not occur during piloting by Cambridge ESOL. *Smell* is clearly not as elegant as *sense of smell*, but is surely acceptable given that candidates' written expression is not at issue. As for *nose*, it fits the context perfectly adequately. The entire chunk *break the wind force* actually appears in the recording in a slightly different form (*break the force of the wind*); given this, it seems unfair to rule it out as a possibility. A check of the verbal protocols showed that in all of the cases cited the respondent had achieved a full understanding both of the tenor of the question and of the relevant information from the recording. On these grounds, the variant responses were accepted for the purposes of this study.

With this adjustment, the results recorded for the two tests ranged from 6 to 10 for Text A (N = 15) and from 5 to 9 for Text B (N = 14). The respective means were 8.2 (SD 1.37) and 7.07 (SD 1.07). The spread of marks was unexpectedly wide, given that all respondents except three had achieved very similar scores in the IELTS Listening test and in the Reading one.

3.2 Lecture-listening competence

In the lecture-based task, the protocols obtained from participants consisted of free recall of as much as possible of the mini-lecture that had been heard, prompted by the notes and summary that had been written. An objective means was sought of establishing what proportion of the available information was reported by each participant. To this end, it was necessary to identify the different points that were made by the speaker – but to do so in a way that was sensitive to the relative value of those points and to their contribution to the overall discourse structure.

The two target texts were rather different in structure. Whereas the first featured one overriding topic (the role of trees in urban planning), the second embraced two (the characteristics of the shark and the use of netting to protect bathers). Within those topics, a series of macro-propositions were identified in Text A, based upon the paragraphing which the setter had used when transcribing the lectures. Within the paragraphs, a set of micro-propositions was then identified. Text B was treated simply as a series of micro-propositions

The topics and propositions for each recording were listed with no indication as to perceived importance. They were submitted to five judges with extensive experience of ELT (and particularly of the teaching of discourse for EAP), who were asked to grade them in relation to the texts as 'macro-', 'micro-' or 'peripheral' (i.e. at a low level of importance to the text as a whole). Their feedback was then compared and collated to form profiles of the content and discourse structure of the two recordings used in the study. The profiles appear in the two panels on pages 408 and 409.

RECORDING 1: *Trees and the urban environment*

MACRO-PROPOSITIONS
1. Trees change climate
2. Trees regulate own temperature
3. Trees reduce the strength of winds
4. Trees reduce traffic noise
5. Problem: trees need space

MICRO-PROPOSITIONS
1a. less windy
1b. cooler
1c. more humid
1d. less dangerous

2a. water through leaves
2b. trees cooler than buildings [buildings 20% more than human temp]
2c. trees humidify the air

3a. high buildings produce winds at ground level
3b. trees filter the wind

4a. BUT much vehicle noise goes through trees
4b. BUT low frequency noise goes through trees

5a. roots and branches
5b. difficult to plant in a narrow street
5c. water, sunlight, space

The procedure thus in many ways adhered to the 'macro' / 'micro' principles of Van Dijk and Kintsch (1983), but with added validation obtained from:

a. external judgements as to the relative importance of the propositional information

b. the neutral decisions made by the IELTS transcriber when dividing up the content of the mini-lectures into paragraphs.

At one point, an attempt was made to represent the complex hierarchical relationships between propositions along the lines of Gernsbacher's (1990) Structure Building model. However, the exercise proved too complicated for practical purposes. It was also recognised that in the informal conditions of

RECORDING 2: *Shark meshing*

TOPIC 1 Characteristics of the shark

MICRO-PROPOSITIONS
1a. Large: length [10–16 metres]
1b. Large: weight [795 kg]
1c. Flexible skeleton
1d. Barbs not scales
1e. Quick swimmers
1f. Fins and tail
1g. Keep swimming unlike other fish
1h. Bottom of ocean
1i. Food on ocean floor
1j. Sense of smell

TOPIC 2 Shark meshing

MICRO-PROPOSITIONS
1a. Large nets parallel to shore
1b. Set one day, taken out to sea the next

2a. Began 1939, only Sydney
2b. 1949 extended [beaches to south]
2c. 1970 Queensland

3a. NZ and Tahiti – no
3b. South Africa – yes

4a. 1,500 first years
4b. 150 per year now
4c. caught in warmest months [active when air/ocean at max temp] [Nov–Feb]

5a. NOT sharks unafraid
5b. NOT sharks biting holes
5c. waves and currents
5d. sand moving, can't hold nets

---

verbal report (the main source of data), participants could not be expected to mark inter-propositional relationships as unambiguously as they might in a written summary.

The protocols for the lecture-based task were then analysed to establish how many propositions each participant had reported. The number of relevant propositions identified was taken to constitute evidence of how much information an individual listener had succeeded in extracting from the text. For Text A, the count included those identified as both macro-propositions and as micro-propositions. For Text B, micro-propositions only were counted. Also calculated were the number of propositions incorrectly reported and the number of peripheral items of information included (an indication that the main argument had not been followed).

The results were tabulated alongside the scores obtained by participants in the earlier administration of the IELTS test. They appear in Tables 6.2 and 6.3 below. Participants are ranked by their scores in the test-based task, shown in the first column of figures.

Table 6.2 Test scores (Text A) versus evidence of successful lecture listening (Text B)

Participant (N = 13)	Test score (A)	Correct propns (B) (Tot = 24)	Incorrect propns (B)	Peripheral info (B)
A	6	1		
P	6	5	4	2
D	7	8		
R	7	4	4	1
T	7	7	2	
S	8	7	1	
W	8	5	1	
AA	8	16		
G	9	8		3
I	9	3	1	3
N	9	4	5	
L	10	11	3	
AC	10	14	1	
Mean	8.0 (1.35)	7.15 (4.34)		

As part of the cognitive validation exercise, evidence was sought of a statistical correlation between the figures for correct answers in the test and the figures for number of propositions reported. The two conditions (A–B and B–A) were treated separately. For A–B (test based on Text A and propositions reported from Text B), the Spearman rho correlation was $r_s = 0.43$, $N = 13$, n.s. For the B–A condition (test based on Text B and propositions reported from Text A) the correlation was $r_s = 0.53$, $N = 13$, n.s. In neither case did the statistic indicate a significant relationship between the score obtained on the lecture-based section in the IELTS paper and the ability to report propositional information from a recording of a lecture heard under

Table 6.3 Test scores (Text B) versus evidence of successful lecture listening (Text A)

Participant (N = 13)	Test score (B)	Correct propns (A) (tot: 19)	Incorrect propns (A)	Peripheral info (A)
Z	5	7	1	
C	6	6		
F	6	8		
AB	6	12		
B	7	11		
J	7	7	1	
K	7	10		
M	7	6		
O	8	13		
Q	8	15	1	
U	8	13		
X	8	11		
V	9	8		
Mean	7.08 (1.11)	9.77 (2.98)		

non-test conditions. The lack of correlation between the two measures is confirmed by the scattergrams in Figures 6.1 and 6.2.

Figure 6.1 Scattergram: score Text A vs proposition Text B

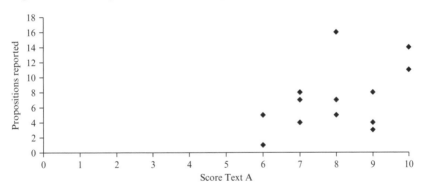

In considering this evidence, the cautionary note sounded earlier needs to be repeated: the sample was a relatively small one (inevitably, given the method employed). A normal distribution cannot be ensured, and these results should be treated as broadly indicative rather than conclusive.

In these circumstances, it is worthwhile examining individual cases. The two participants who scored lowest in the IELTS test based on Text A also showed signs of difficulty in unconstrained lecture listening. Participant A only succeeded in reporting one proposition, and, while P reported 5, she also

Figure 6.2 Scattergram: score Text B vs proposition Text A

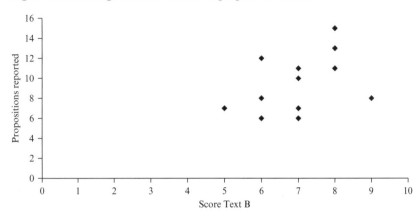

misreported 4 and included information that was not central to the topic. Similarly, Participants L and AC who achieved scores of 10 in the test were also among the three highest in terms of the number of micro-propositions reported. These cases do indeed suggest some relationship between the aspects of the listening construct tested in the IELTS section and the skills demanded by a more ecological lecture-listening experience.

Of course, the possibility remains that what is tested in the IELTS paper is a general listening construct which has relevance to all listening tasks, rather than any trait specific to lecture listening. Furthermore, the examples cited are not entirely supported by the results from the B–A condition, where the participant with the highest test score only succeeded in identifying the same number of propositions as a participant with the second lowest. The participant who was most successful in the lecture task only achieved a score of 8 in the test. Perhaps the most interesting anomaly lies in Participant AA from the first group. She achieved a score close to the mean on the test and had a low IELTS Listening score of 5 from earlier testing; but she produced an impeccably detailed and accurate account of the lecture.

Results for the subset of eight participants from mainland China were examined separately and compared with those for the participants as a whole. The mean scores for both Test A and Test B were 7.25, close to the overall means. Curiously, members of this group showed themselves markedly less able than others to extract propositional information from Text B (mean number of propositions = 5, as compared to 7.15) but markedly more able to do so from Text A (mean number of propositions = 12.5, as compared to 9.77). Given the small numbers, too much should not be made of this finding.

Clearly, limitations of linguistic knowledge and listening competence restricted the information that the participants were able to derive from the text. A further possible explanation can be found in the additional cognitive demands associated with processing input in a second language. The need to focus greater attention upon word recognition and syntactic parsing potentially imposes restrictions upon the amount of information that can be processed, stored and/or recalled. It is entirely understandable therefore that relatively few micro-propositions were recorded by some listeners. That said, their ability to identify larger topics in a text like Text A (at least at the stage where the mini-lecture was summarised) seemed to be relatively unaffected by processing difficulties or demands at local level.

3.3   Test-specific behaviour

A second line of enquiry examined the protocols relating to the test-based task, for evidence of how participants had arrived at the answers they had given. Each participant had been asked not only to report each of their 10 answers orally but also to provide a rationale for having chosen it. The purpose of studying these rationales in detail was to identify to what extent the processes employed by test takers conformed to those that might be applied in real-life lecture-listening situations and to what extent they took advantage of the additional information available in a test and/or explored strategic routes that were specific to the testing context.

3.3.1   Cognitive validity of the tasks

It is worthwhile at the outset to take note of the differences between the information available to a candidate taking the two IELTS Listening sections that formed the basis of the study and the information that might be available to a participant in a typical academic context. It is also worthwhile to draw some general comparisons between the requirements imposed by the test methods and those that language processing research tells us obtain in real-life listening contexts.

The task sheets for completion by candidates form Appendix 6.2 of this report. The task for Text A consisted of a note-completion exercise that is much favoured by IELTS setters in the Listening test – presumably on the grounds that it achieves face validity by resembling the type of note-taking that might take place in an authentic context. The first part of the task for Text B consisted of a similar note-completion exercise. It was followed by four multiple-choice items of four options and a further one in which two options had to be chosen out of seven.

The note-completion task for Text A provides a strategically minded candidate with the following *gratis* information before even hearing the recording:

- an outline of what the lecture covers, with some lexical gaps
- a set of gaps to be filled that closely follow the sequence adopted by the lecturer (some even forming part of a list)
- key words by means of which to locate information in the mini-lecture

- one constituent of two relatively frequent collocations: *ground level, low frequency*
- two sequences which reproduce the oral text word for word, with one word omitted.

Interest here attached to the test-wiseness of the participants in the study and the extent to which the protocols showed that their answers were influenced by this externally provided information rather than by the evidence of their ears.

The gapped notes for Test A are quite detailed – raising issues of whether validity is compromised by a task that taps into the reading skill to such a degree. In process terms, the level of detail and the organisational structure of the notes mean that the candidate is not required to undertake certain critical meaning building operations which would normally play a central part in lecture listening. These include (Brown 1995, Field 2004a:163–5, Field 2008a:241–265):

- distinguishing main points from subsidiary ones (though admittedly this function may be provided by a handout in a real-life lecture context)
- distinguishing new propositions from instances of rephrasing and exemplification
- recognising the argument relationships that link propositions
- integrating incoming information into an ongoing discourse representation.

The focus of the testing, in other words, is very much 'bottom-up' in that what the candidate has to contribute chiefly takes the form of lexical matching. In this respect, it is difficult to see that it replicates the range of EAP processes for which the test aims to serve as a predictor.

The similar task for Test B was in a much more abbreviated form, imposing a lighter reading load. The answers were to some extent predictable using topic knowledge, though similar strategic behaviour might well be employed by a listener in a non-test context. The multiple-choice options were mainly brief and some required the candidate to assess the status of two or more pieces of propositional information rather than simply performing lexical matches (for example, recognising the negative attached to *Tahiti* and *New Zealand*). The exception lay in questions 39 and 40, where key words (*strong waves and currents, moving sands*) closely echo the recording. On this analysis, one might say that the tasks set for Text B appear to achieve greater cognitive validity than those for Text A, and that one might expect less evidence of test-specific strategies.

3.3.2 Evidence from protocols

Two lines of enquiry were adopted. A distinction was made between responses which indicated that the participant had relied upon the written words in the task items in arriving at an answer (in other words, a listening process driven by reading) and those which suggested a primary reliance upon the spoken signal.

Use of written information

There was extensive evidence of participants adopting a procedure of matching information from the written task sheet against what was heard in the recording. The cues that were used seemed very often to be at word level rather than at propositional level. The listening process was partly shaped by a strategy of scanning the recording for words which resembled those in the items or were paraphrases. This attention to word level was sometimes at the expense of wider meaning. One participant, who scored the mean of 8 in Test A, was candid about the way he focused his attentional resources:

> (1) *[the main point was] preserve tree but I'm not quite sure because +
> every every time I use + I mean my my method to + listen to to do the
> IELTS listening + yeah I just look at the words not focus what it is about*
> (S1:145)

Here and throughout, quotations from protocols are referenced by the participant's code (here S) followed by the figure 1 or 2 (indicating first or second task) plus a reference to the line in the protocol where the extract begins. To separate citation from main text, the participant's turns are italicised, while the researcher's interventions are shown in a non-italic font. The reverse is true in the database.

The scanning strategy was supported by the convention that items follow the same sequence as the text and a widely shared expectation that items would not occur too closely together. The latter feature is entirely reasonable in that the candidate needs time to record an answer; but participants showed themselves aware of the strategic possibilities afforded by the feature of the test:

> (2) *so when I was reading the answering the first one + she was maybe she
> had already finished the list no? + the other case is even if the words maybe
> were I made some mistakes in other parts I mean + but you have time to
> write to listen because when you were + when I was writing er + she was
> speaking about something else not important for the test.* (AA1:148)

There was evidence from the protocols that some participants used the spaces between pieces of targeted information to switch their attention back to the written task sheet in search of possible cues to the next item to come. This became apparent when several of them admitted missing information in the recording because of excessive attention to the written material.

> (3) *I missed it because I didn't I didn't + I didn't realise the 'frequency' has
> came so quickly* (P1: 99)

(4) *er when I try to get this answer um + he he is already talking about the make cities cooler yes + so I missed the answer* (T1:19)

The text-to-recording strategies varied from participant to participant and from question to question, but were classified as falling into four main types. As already noted, they seemed to operate principally at lexical level, with single words, lexical phrases or potential collocations used as cues.

    a. The respondent used a word or words from the written text as a means of locating information in the spoken text. [Q loc]

(5) *and maybe also for the wind force when I hear two er + two thing er+ two different level + ground and high+ and so it's um + I don't know which one is good because er + with just looking about something before 'level' + and if we have two + twice 'level' it's + it's confusing a bit* (A1:39)

    b. The respondent listened for words in the spoken text that formed a one-to-one match with those in the written. [Q match]

(6) *yes because she introduced the um + er wind effect on buildings so er + when I heard this word 'buildings' + 'wind effect' 'wind force on buildings' + so I concentrate um + she perhaps she followed the the question written* (AA1:85)

    c. The respondent sought a paraphrase in the spoken text of a proposition expressed in the written one. [Q para]

(7) *yes I because 'coastline', 'beach' er + is + are very similar so um + I don't know + the meaning is quite the same . . .* (B1:37)

    d. The respondent chose an answer according to its position in a list or in a sequence of propositions in the written test. [Q seq]

(8) *and her er + some the recording give some some interrupt er + because er + he she said she 'water' before 'the sunlight' + but at end is the room* (R1:107)

Table 6.4 shows the strategies reported by participants in respect of the two tests. The most common strategies were widely generalised across participants, with only two out of 13 failing to record a Q loc for Text A and two out of 13 for Text B. No participant recorded more than four occurrences of the same strategy across the 10 items – suggesting that their use reflects the form and demands of the item.

Table 6.4 Test-wise strategies employing visual cues

	Q match	Q loc	Q para	Q seq
Test A (N = 13)		26 (18.98%)	2 (1.46%)	15 (10.95%)
Test B (N = 13)	30 (22.56%)	25 (18.80%)	2 (1.50%)	3 (2.56%)

Percentages are based upon a total of 137 instances for Test A and 132 for Text B. The totals exceed the number of items answered (130 in each) as two processes were sometimes cited as having contributed to a single answer.

The finding that candidates make use of test item wording in achieving their answers will cause no surprise – though it raises concerns for construct validity since the cue employed engages a different modality from the construct that the test aims to measure. But it is striking here how many of the participants' answers were achieved by these means. The table shows that strategies generated by written input in the form of test items were cited as instrumental in achieving around 40% of the answers given in Test B and 30% in Test A. It is also apparent (despite the initial impression recorded above that Test B was more cognitively valid) that the multiple-choice format employed in B promoted a greater level of test-wise strategy use. Several of the participants attested to the way in which the multiple-choice (MCQ) options had led them to seek the spoken forms, associates or synonyms of key words which they had seen in written form. In cognitive terms, the MCQ format could be said to promote a process of checking information against pre-established cues rather than the more ecological one of receiving, interpreting and organising it.

The issue so far as cognitive validity is concerned is that these channels for establishing meaning would not be available to the participant in a natural lecture setting. Admittedly, their role might to some extent be paralleled in the provision of a handout; but the process of matching handout propositions to those in the presentation is a somewhat different one. Handout material is unequivocal (as against the multiple options offered by MCQ), is fully formed (as against gapped notes) and constitutes, in effect, an abbreviated paraphrase of the spoken text. The process in which the auditor engages entails tracking from proposition to proposition rather than from key word to proposition.

Auditory word matching
A second group of processes seemed to be more reliant upon the auditory signal. In distinguishing these instances from those in Table 6.4 (identification on the basis of a written cue), it was not easy to determine what role, if any, the wording of the test items might have played. One must assume that, at the very least, the identification process was assisted by an awareness of the word class and lexical field to which the target item belonged.

Here again, the focus of attention seemed to be very strongly at lexical level. The rationale supplied for an answer was very frequently 'I heard the word'. Figures indicating the extent to which lexically based techniques were employed appear in Table 6.5.

Table 6.5 Reported lexically based strategies employed by participants

	Lexical recognition	Cognate in L1	Collocation recognised	Phonological transcription
Text A	60 (43.80%)	3 (2.19%)	5 (3.65%)	10 (7.30%)
Text B	31 (23.31%)	0	2 (1.50%)	0

Four processes were identified: matching to a known word, matching to a cognate in L1, identifying a two-word collocation and attempting the transcription of an unknown word using phoneme-grapheme correspondence rules. It sometimes proved difficult to establish if the lexical matches entailed a full grasp of the surrounding context; but in some cases it was made clear by the participant that it did not. Here are some examples where understanding above the lexical level was not achieved, but was sufficient to achieve a correct answer:

> (9) What does low frequency mean?
> *++ it means er + the trees can reduce the noise er + because I think the noise goes through the trees . . .*
> but what does 'low frequency' mean?
> *low frequency mean ++ not er frequently* (T1a:141)

> (10) *. . . answer number 36 is 'leaves' and er + I don't know its exact spelling + um but OK was clear because er + it's the last word of the sentence . . .*
> OK + what did they say about leaves?
> *er I don't remember + I was concerning to wait for the the next point . . . I was actually paying paying attention to the building* (AA1:64)

> (11) *humid yeah + probably um + what's the nature of tree like er + um + how how are how do trees er grow and um + something like that* (S1:169)

The much greater incidence of lexical targeting in relation to Text A would seem to indicate that test method was an important factor, with the gap-filling exercise encouraging candidates to direct attention at word level. As for Text B, 13 of the 31 instances recorded (9.8%) were cases where either the gap or the MCQ option demanded a number, and participants admitted to simply scanning the upcoming section of the text for numbers.

Here, conclusions on cognitive validity need to be hedged. On the one hand, lexically based lines of attack appear to be very common among L2 listeners whose understanding of a listening passage is less than complete (Field 2004b, 2008b). They would certainly be employed in the circumstances of listening to an actual lecture. On the other hand, the 'bottom-up' nature of the gap-filling testing method must surely play some part in directing additional attention to local, word-level processing. Because human attention is a limited resource, a processor needs to be selective in the information it retrieves (Styles 2006). This may explain why some of the participants reported having located a correct word without understanding its significance to the lecture as a whole. The problem was not one of general comprehension, but one of having directed attention in 'spotlight' fashion to the word or phrase which supplied the necessary answer, leaving insufficient capacity for wider considerations.

Other processes

Table 6.6 provides a summary of the remaining processes reported by participants. With the exception of the use of world knowledge, they featured in the reported behaviour of only one to three participants.

Table 6.6 Additional processes reported by participants

	Miss	Random guess	World knowledge	Prom.	Discourse	Elim.
Text A	10 (7.30%)	1 (0.73%)	4 (2.92%)	1 (0.73%)		
Text B	5 (3.76%)	6 (4.51%)	18 (13.53%)	0	2 (1.50%)	9 (6.75%)

Some of these processes do indeed play a part in successful useful lecture-listening skills. For example, many participants used world or topic knowledge with Text B. It quite often led them to wrong conclusions in the test condition – though interestingly it did so considerably more often in the non-test condition where they had to construct a meaning representation from scratch:

> *[they] try to suggest how do we + er how do they er + preserve the shark* (S2:32–33)
> *how about they attack humans + on the beach, swimming beach* (P2:27–28)
> *and the shark only live in the warm water um* (R2:22)
> *he said that sharks were not so dangerous* (Y2:29)

Much is made in the literature of the value of topic knowledge in supporting comprehension (Long 1990, Schmidt-Rinehart 1994); but this data indicates that its effect can also be counter-productive, and lead to second-guessing.

Curiously, two techniques for lecture listening which are much discussed in EAP listening materials (such as Lynch 2004) – namely, paying heed to prominent items ('Prom' in Table 6.6) and to discourse markers ('Discourse') – were little reported.

Other processes appear to be test-specific. 'Miss' records instances where participants missed the information because their attention was directed elsewhere. The cause was often explicitly related to the demands of the test: the need to spell correctly and check previous answers or (as already noted) a strategy of closely following the order in which test items occurred. 'Elim' indicates cases where the participant reached a conclusion as to the most likely MCQ option by rational consideration of the evidence. The types of cue used were: most likely option, the option on which most was said and the option mentioned last by the speaker (on the reasoning that speakers often reject several points before accepting one). Again, here the participant's behaviour seems to be chiefly driven by the format and demands of the test.

The processes used by the L1 Mandarin group to achieve answers were examined separately. There was extensive use of lexical identification and of the strategy of using item wording to locate information in the text. While these patterns of behaviour were not dissimilar to those of some other participants, what was striking was how consistent they were across all members of the subset. These participants appeared to be more consistently strategic as a group – or possibly had been trained to be so.

3.3.3 Ability to identify 'main points'

The apparent bias towards processing at word level that had been evidenced in the protocols for the test-based condition was investigated by studying participants' responses to the question: *What do you think the text was about?* Four participants were not asked the question directly, but their responses indicated quite unambiguously whether they had or had not grasped the main points.

The responses were analysed using very narrow criteria. Participants were credited with having understood the 'main points' of the two tests if they specifically mentioned:

For Text A: *cities / urban environment* and *trees*

For Text B: *description of sharks* and *protecting beaches from sharks*

A score was given for each point mentioned.

One hypothesis was that listening to the text under test conditions might have diverted attention from the main points. An alternative hypothesis was that listening under non-test conditions without the support of the task sheet might have made it much more difficult for learners to identify the main points.

Results were totalled for 26 participants, of whom 13 had heard Text A under test conditions and 13 had heard Text B. Means were calculated (out of a maximum of two per text) and appear in Table 6.7 below.

Table 6.7 Main points identified: means across participants

	Text A Test	Text A Non-test	Text B Test	Text B Non-test
Mean (max 2)	1.54	1.77	1.15	1.38

With the usual rider about the smallness of the sample, it would seem that this population was more likely to identify the main points of the lecture in a natural situation than in a test one. The test method may have served to distract attention from the main points – despite the fact that test takers held evidence of the speaker's intentions in the form of a worksheet and that many of them reported paying close attention to this information. One conclusion is that the participants' attention was quite closely directed to the wording of the worksheet as part of a test-wise strategy of key word matching, at the expense of wider meaning.

4 Reported experience of participants

4.1 Relative cognitive demands

A third and final line of enquiry examined participants' perceptions of the relative difficulty of the two tasks, and the reasons they gave for their views. As reported above, all participants were asked *Which of the two exercises did you find easier: the first or the second?* They were also asked to explain their choice.

A working hypothesis was that most of them would respond that the non-test condition (note-taking and oral report) had proved more demanding than the test condition. The reasons for adopting this assumption were as follows:

a. As discussed in Section 3.3.1, a test candidate benefits from supportive information in the wording of the test items. The information was not available in the note-taking condition.

b. The non-test condition was more complex in that it required the participant to engage in three processes: note-taking, summary writing and oral report. It also demanded a longer attention span in that the recording was only paused once and very briefly. On these grounds, it was assumed that the task was considerably more cognitively demanding than the test items and would be reported as such by the participants.

If this hypothesis were true, one might expect participants to respond consistently that the first task was easier than the second. In other words, in the A–B condition, they would report their experience of processing Text A to have been easier than that of processing Text B (A < B). They would report the converse in the B–A condition (B < A). This finding would raise issues of cognitive validity in that it would suggest that the processes elicited by the test were less cognitively demanding than the real-life ones for which the test is intended to serve as a predictor.

Participants' responses to the 'Which was easier?' question are shown in Table 6.8 below. No response is recorded for Participant A as she was not asked the question. It is evident that the hypothesis was not supported in any consistent way. Especially striking is the extent to which the responses varied according to which test had been taken. The majority of respondents indicated that their experience of taking Test A was less demanding than the subsequent note-taking task. Even here, two participants (S and AA) dissented, while one respondent (E) indicated that she found the two tasks equally demanding. By contrast, when the material presented under test conditions was B, the majority of the responses (by nine to five) indicated that the respondents *had found the note-taking task easier than undergoing the test.*

Table 6.8 Participants' reports of relative task difficulty

Text A in test condition		Text B in test condition	
D	A < B	B	A < B
E	A = B	C	A < B
G	A < B	F	B < A
I	A < B	H	A < B
L	A < B	J	B < A
N	A < B	K	B < A
P	A < B	M	B < A
R	A < B	O	A < B
S	B < A	Q	A < B
T	A < B	U	A < B
W	A < B	V	A < B
Y	A < B	X	B < A
AA	B < A	Z	A < B
AC	A < B	AB	A < B

Two important differences distinguish the two IELTS tests that were chosen for this study. Firstly, the recorded material in A is less detailed and less propositionally complex than the material in B (see panel in Section 3.2). Secondly, while the test method in A consists entirely of gap filling, in B it is a combination of gap filling and multiple choice.

The researcher was at pains to ask participants to consider the difficulty of the task separately from that of the recording (indeed, two participants, Q and X, actually gave different answers for task and recording). Even so, one has to recognise that some participants may have found it difficult to separate the two when reporting on the cognitive demands of the exercise. But an alternative conclusion is that at least some participants who reported A < B were influenced by the heavy attentional demands made by the multiple-choice format. In other words, it was not so much that note-taking was easy as that the demands imposed by the test were hard.

4.2 Protocol evidence

4.2.1 Views on note-taking

Further insights were obtained by examining in some detail the comments of participants on the two tasks. Here, an entirely unexpected finding was that eight of the 28 participants questioned (28.5%) categorically asserted that they found the process of note-taking easier than operating under test conditions. Some extracts follow to illustrate the points that were made in support of this argument.

> (12) did you find it more difficult to take notes or to answer the questions?
>
> *I think sharks + um sharks is more difficult to answer the question + because the question is is + how do you say that? um + um in the sharks there are some questions I can't catch it exactly.*
>
> so the questions make you listen for things?
>
> *yes.*
>
> and sometimes you don't hear them?
>
> *yes + so I can guess it.*
>
> so when you're taking notes you don't have to listen for anything.
>
> *yeah.*
>
> you can just write down what the lecturer was saying?
>
> *yes and I can er + from the stress I can know which is much important.*
>
> right from + from what the lecturer says?
>
> *yeah.*
>
> so it's easier to do it when you don't know what you are going to hear . . .
>
> *yeah yeah. (Q2:40)*

> (13) OK + what about writing the notes and everything? + was that difficult?
>
> *um yeah + difficult to write to find what is main point about.*
>
> right.
>
> *but I think it's not difficult if we we try to get information + but + er + I don't know if it necessary or not.*
>
> right + OK + but the notes that you wrote . . .
>
> *yeah.*
>
> . . . were they more difficult than filling in the um + answers for the urban landscape?
>
> *yeah, they're easier.*
>
> you think it was easier to write notes?
>
> *easier to write notes. (S2:55)*

> (14) well the last question is + did you find this more difficult than the last one with the sharks or not?
>
> *I think er why do the question is more nervous + and*

the questions make you nervous, do they?

yes make me nervous and er + maybe I have read the questions + sometimes maybe questions can give some information about the + what they will say + but the questions it's they er + more interesting in some numbers or some words er + maybe I can I am not understand the words and

and that worries you?

yes that worries me.

so did you find the shark one more difficult to do than writing notes?

yes because I have + I have to read some questions and + that does use a lot of my account attention + and I cannot put so many attention on the context it said + such as the questions + OK this questions ask for something + and I just wait for the question and do not listen to others. (U2:54)

(15) Which did you find more difficult?

the first one + definitely.

why?

because um with this + this tests it it is um + how can I? + it's + I have I have a lot of more stress with this sort of test because you um + you don't want to miss any answer + but with this technique it's + it is different + um even if you miss something er + you you you will understand the the general idea what is talking about + but in this test sort of test um + you when you miss miss the point + then you get you get stress and then for er+ for the following questions it's harder + and so it's quite difficult.

do you think you were behaving differently as a listener in the second one? Were you doing things that were different from the first one to the second?

if if what? + I'm sorry.

were you behaving differently as a listener when you did the first test + to the way you behaved in the second + were you listening in a different way?

um yes definitely + there's not the same way + yeah + because in the first part I'm just focusing on words not the general meaning + but in the second I focus on the the the general ideas + the most interesting points. (V2:26)

(16) why did you find [the second task] easier?

um maybe I can focus on the um + the the the the lecture + um she said um + what really is important + and can summarise + but I if I heard the the + and deal with some question sometimes I feel nervous + and just focus out or + catch the catch the word.

so the questions make you nervous?

yes.

but you don't feel nervous when you're listening

yes lecture.

to a lecture.

yes + yes.

OK + didn't you find it difficult to take notes + and to understand what the person was saying?

no + I think er taking notes it's better.

taking notes is easier for you.

yeah is easier for me.

do you think you understood more?

yes + understood more. (Z2:62)

(17) um you've done an exercise on the urban landscape and one on the sharks + which did you find easier?

um + maybe this one.

the one on the sharks?

yeah.

why?

because er + when I take my notes I can + I don't pay attention to my er spelling + I use abbreviations symbols something + that after if I have the time I can recognise a symbol or something + in that case I have + I think that I will + I would have been marked also for the spelling.

oh you mean with the + with the urban landscape?

that one + yes + so er and um + I don't know + I think it's easier because you you + there you have something ready filled + already filled out.

yeah, I see + this is the urban landscape?

something you know you have also to check out + before what's filled out what's not + and er + here er was my job + I mean I know what I'm going to write + I recognised the the key key words and whatever +, what else er + he said + I these key words make me remember all the rest.

yeah.

or +

which one do you think you understood better?

this.

the shark one.

yeah I didn't really + I didn't care + when I if I have to fill out only some particular sentence + a word in a sentence + I pick actually that sentence + and I wait to listen on some words that are OK. (AA2:51)

(18) which did you find harder to do + answering the questions or taking notes?

er ++ hard to do + to take notes or answer the question?

yeah.

(laughs) It is + it is different strategies because er + I I'm + my + generally I take notes so for me perhaps it's more simple + but other people perhaps er + it's better to read the the question + the . . .

what did you find?

me fine to take note because I usually take note + but perhaps if you er + know that the IELTS test is based on the question + you can er + learn to read quickly the question + and then these are different strategies I think but +

so you found it difficult because you had to read the questions and so on yeah?

sometime to read the question is better because you can er + predict of you have to listen + but er I I don't either pref + for example if I have to do the IELTS test + I I can improve my excuse to read the question then to answer + in my example er for me it's more simple to take note because er + I'm just usually take notes during a lecture not to read the question + but er if you have only to take a test er + perhaps it's better to have the question then + as well to answer the question + OK. (AB2:46)

These protocols have been quoted at length because they serve to highlight two important findings:

a. Some participants (Q, U, V) appear to feel that, under test conditions, the process of storing questions in the mind and scanning the recording for appropriate answers imposes considerable task demands. Indeed some (U, V, Z) claim that it causes stress. AA mentions the additional demand (irrelevant to the listening construct) of ensuring accurate spelling.

b. Some participants (V, Z, AA, AB) report that they listen very locally and at a level of minor detail under test conditions but much more globally when note-taking.

On these grounds and contrary to expectations, the participants quoted found note-taking *less* cognitively demanding than operating under test conditions.

4.2.2   Support provided by the task sheet

Quite a large number of respondents took the opposite view: that working under test conditions is easier. As predicted, a number of them represented note-taking as imposing greater cognitive demands. Participant M put it as follows:

> (19) *er this was more difficult I think because it's er + ser yeah a lot of serious speech in this detail + and she didn't stop in each part + and we have to er + summarise in our mind every part of his speech and to organise again + because some some of her idea is the + jump + this is for + this part is problem.*
>
> so you think she + her ideas moved very quickly?
>
> *quickly.*
>
> from one point to another one?
>
> *and she the point + yes where we have to summarise in my mind and try to write down the summaries + they more difficult + and we + direct questions I don't have to + the the end the question yeah + so I can follow the question to find some details.* (M2:47)

What M is drawing attention to in her first turn is a major difference between the test taker and the note-taker: the latter has to establish the relative importance of the points that are made by the speaker and to construct an overall discourse representation (see Gernsbacher 1990 on the complex demands of building argument structures). In the circumstances of a test, either the setters tend to target a series of points regardless of their relative importance, or the task sheet provides the candidate in advance with an argument framework for interpreting the recording. A similar point is made by S in the quotations in the previous section, though he still maintains that note-taking is easier.

The support provided by the test paper is mentioned by many of those who felt that note-taking was more demanding. A point frequently made concerned the fact, explored in Section 3, that a test provides additional cues in written form which materially assist the decoding of the recording.

> (20) *++ when I um + because I have no um no um + text, I cannot follow + so I don't know when I have er + a paper + I can trace and and focus on the key word what the + what the exam want me to do + um + even though I don't I can't get the main idea but + um that's the text er require + you just fill in the key words + but when I do the second test*

um + you have to follow the speaker line by line + and you don't know um + what will the key words come. (L2:68)

(21) why did you find it more difficult?

because er because I I have no paper + I have er some some main ideas from the paper + I read it + er + before I I read the answer I listened the the the cassette yeah + and I can focus my eyes on some + some er special + some some gap yeah + I can sometimes I can guess + I can guess all what's + what they will talk about yeah + and but this + this one the second one I think er + there is no no some background of my + yeah and no some some information to survey before I listen to this yeah + this this lecture + yeah + maybe if you give some papers like this + I can I can finish these very well. (N2: 48)

(22) why did you find it more difficult?

um + if + er if I have this something like this to ask me to do some + do some test er + maybe I can do it, but

so if you have a sheet or an answer sheet it helps you.

yeah yeah + er they can help me to um + to get some key words + and I use the key word to find the answer + but just listen and do some write + I I find I think is more difficult. (R2:45)

Of course, there may be a gap between the respondents' faith in the assistance provided by these cues and what actually occurs in practice. There was evidence in the verbal reports that reliance upon the wording of the task sheet sometimes leads to inefficient strategies which handicap the candidates' ability to extract meaning from the recording. One recurrent problem took the form of a respondent switching attention from the recording to the written text and missing mention of the point that provided the correct answer. Examples of this have already been given in protocol extracts (3) and (4) while (5) shows an instance of a simple match at word level throwing up two alternatives, with no criterion for distinguishing between them if wider context is missing. Problems also arise when candidates lose their way – either overlooking an item on the task sheet (looking for a match for item 35 when the speaker is still covering point 34) or failing to notice a relevant point in the recording (looking for a match for item 35 when the speaker has already moved on to 36).

(23) *um ++ I don't + I don't have that that answer sorry.*

is that because you didn't understand everything or you didn't recognise a word or what?

yeah.

what what was the problem there?

er I can't understand er the recording + it it still talk about air + but the record is about air.

you were looking at the wrong sentences?

yeah yeah.

when the recording was talking about something else.

yeah.

OK + what about number 35?

I just haven't found it. (laughs)

so that was the same thing?

yeah.

looking at sentences at the beginning when you hadn't realised it had + it had moved on?

mhm. (R1:35)

There is also, as ever, the issue of the limits to the attention capacity which a listener/reader has available. At times, it seemed likely that the participant had lost track of the recording as a result of lending too much attention to possible written cues.

(24) why was that difficult?

um because er + mhm + I I haven't prepared + I haven't warm up to listen + not really ready to listen.

right + you weren't ready + but was that because you were looking at the paper? + or because you don't know the voice of the person who was speaking?

er no.

or you don't know the topic + or what?

um I think I I don't know the + I just look at the paper sometimes.

so you were looking at the paper?

yeah the paper.

So you weren't really listening.

yeah just focus on the the word + probably the speaker might might not say that word er + so I missed it. (S1: 176)

5 Discussion

The study provided a number of useful insights into the way in which candidates respond to two types of test method (gap filling and MCQ) that are quite widely used in IELTS Listening Section 4. The insights enable us to gauge the extent to which the cognitive processes adopted resemble those that candidates would employ in a real-life lecture-listening situation.

5.1 The use of test-wise strategies

It was apparent from the protocols that the participants had adopted a number of strategies which reflected the nature of the test rather than the demands of lecture listening or the kinds of gap in understanding that are caused by limited knowledge of L2. The extent and form of these strategies varied quite considerably from one participant to another. In some cases (especially the group from mainland China), there was evidence of test strategy training, as shown by their use of terms like 'key word'. The training was by no means always beneficial; indeed, it quite often led to a dependence on the written text (itself a challenge for the Chinese learner) which reduced the amount of attention given to the spoken signal.

Firstly, many participants made use of cues provided by the wording of the items.

- Participants reported using a word from the task sheet in order to locate the relevant information in the listening text. Here, they particularly took advantage of collocates (listening for *level* and *frequency* in Text A so as to target the word which preceded them). The location of the correct items was not always accompanied by an understanding of what had been said (witness the two participants who interpreted *low frequency* in terms of infrequency).
- Participants used a classic 'key word' strategy, listening out for content words from the task sheet that appeared to be important to the topic or listening out for associates and synonyms of those words.
- Participants made use of lists and sequences of words. Where, for example, the gap-filling task showed a gap at the end of a list, they listened out for the last word.

Secondly, they used the ordering of items on the worksheet as a kind of checklist with which to approach the recording. Here, they relied on the convention that the order of the questions closely follows the order in which the information occurs in the recording. Several of them also recognised the constraints upon a test setter when designing a gap-filling exercise where a test only permits one hearing of the recording. The information targeted needs to be quite widely spaced to allow participants to tune out partially in order to focus attention on the missing word (and pay due heed to its spelling) before tuning in again to anticipate the next piece of information.

It became evident that using test items in this way to direct the listening process involved a great deal of switching of attention between task sheet and recording. It was also sometimes counter-productive in that it led to participants missing a piece of information when they were consulting written text (see extracts (3) and (4)).

For the test to achieve cognitive validity as a predictor of real-life behaviour, the methods and material used need to replicate at least some of the processes which apply in the special circumstances of academic listening. As we have already noted, a learner in an academic context can certainly expect written input that supports the spoken. It might take two forms: a handout giving an overview of the lecture and/or PowerPoint slides providing visual support for individual points. The critical consideration for cognitive validity lies not in the availability of that input but in how the listener uses it.

The protocols in this study made it clear that much of the use of the written input was at the level of the word or lexical phrase rather than the level of the idea. Instead of extracting a proposition from the test item and then matching it against a proposition expressed by the speaker, the candidate seems typically to use the lexical content of the items to provide cues with which to locate information in the text. The candidate's thinking operates in the direction: *written lexical input > spoken lexical input*.

Compare that with the visual support in a real lecture-listening context. Second language listeners might use the headings in a handout as 'signposts' in order to impose a structure on what is being heard; here there are perhaps parallels with the convention that test items follow the order of information in the recording. They might even attempt some matching at the level of word or lexical phrase like that observed in this study, though without the strategic goals of a test taker. But much of the processing would proceed in the opposite direction: with the listener first picking up a string of words or an idea in the spoken input and then checking it against the handout to confirm that the point in question had been fully understood. A good handout would also be transparent: there would be none of the ambivalence of the multiple-choice item.

As for PowerPoint slides, in a good presentation aimed at a native speaker audience, they tend to operate at propositional level. Whether or not they contain the actual words the lecturer uses, they serve to identify discrete points of information which anticipate or accompany those conveyed by the oral signal. Except in the case of a listener with extremely limited knowledge of L2, they thus provide cues at the level of the idea, not the word.

To be sure, the gap-filling exercise could be said to achieve some simple ecological validity in that it simulates the kinds of notes that a lecture listener might take. The argument is not entirely convincing when the items employed consist of a series of micro-propositions of varying importance without an argument structure to hold them together. But, from a cognitive angle, it is not so much the notes as the gaps which are an issue. Their effect is to fix the candidate's attention at the level of the word or short phrase, giving rise to precisely the types of word-based strategy that have been commented on.

To summarise, while written input is indeed available to support the type of listening that takes place in an academic context, it is unlikely that it would be used in the same way as it is in the test conditions studied. The evidence of these test-wise strategies therefore raises a first set of concerns about the cognitive validity of the methods that were featured.

5.2 Shallow processing in the test condition

A second area of concern follows directly from the first. The protocols suggested that much of the processing was at a very local level. A number of participants who had scored quite well in the test condition were unable to report the two main topics of the lecture in question, to expand upon what the lecturer had said or to trace links between the points that were made. Some showed that they were quite aware of having focused their attention on lexical matches rather than on wider meaning:

> (24) *if they um ++ how to say? + what I have to do I have to fill words + so I don't er + listen for the meaning of the whole test text + I am choosing these words + if I have to understand meaning and then write an essay it will be another* (Y1:40)

Strikingly, participants showed themselves more able to identify main points for both recordings in the non-test condition, which had been hypothesised to be the more demanding task.

There would appear to be at least three reasons for this finding:

- the extent to which the test methods and items were dependent upon word matching
- the targeting by the test of certain points which were not central to the main argument (e.g. the fact that low frequency noise does not pass through trees, the weight of a large shark)
- the cognitive load imposed by the test methods (to be discussed in due course).

An earlier brief characterisation of the meaning construction process in academic listening suggested that it included the important processes of distinguishing main points from subsidiary ones and of recognising the argument relationships that link propositions. It may indeed be difficult to ensure that these processes feature in any test of L2 listening (important though they are to lecture-listening expertise). All one can say here is that they did not seem to have played a significant part when participants in the test condition were asked to report at a global level.

5.3 Distinctive processes in the test and lecture-listening conditions

There was evidence on three counts suggesting a degree of mismatch between the processes demanded by the test and those demanded by a 'free' lecture-listening situation. Firstly, no correlation was found between the scores achieved by participants in the administration of the test and the number of micro-propositions reported by them when note-taking and not required to answer specific questions. Secondly, most participants reported differently on the two tasks – expressing the view that one or the other was less demanding. Thirdly, a number of respondents with IELTS Reading and Listening scores at the lower end of the target range performed badly in the test condition but well (in one case extremely well) in the note-taking condition.

The researcher's working hypothesis was that respondents would tend to report the note-taking task as harder than the test-based one, on the grounds that the written items in the test supply the candidate with a schematic frame-work for the passage that is to be heard. This indeed was what a number of them reported. However, entirely contrary to expectations, nearly a third of participants reported that they found the note-taking task easier than the test. They included both those of European origin and those of Far Eastern origin; both respondents with higher previous test scores and those with lower. Some of them averred that tracking questions made them nervous (extracts (14) to (16)). They specifically mentioned the need to focus on detail in the test, with the accompanying danger that a word or phrase would be overlooked (extracts (15) and (16)).

These reactions would seem to be a consequence in particular of the time-constrained nature of the exercise. Candidates are only allowed to hear the recording once, increasing their fear that they may overlook a low-level detail. They are also sensitive to a phenomenon, for which there is evidence in the protocols, where a listener fails to match an item to the relevant piece of information in the text and goes on listening for it long after it is past – thus missing the answers to subsequent items as well.

The researcher had assumed that the note-taking task would be more cognitively demanding than the test with its accompanying written support. But he had overlooked the important factor of *the additional demands imposed by handling two different sources of information in two different modalities.* They are hinted at in the comments in extract (17) where Participant AA2 expresses concern about monitoring his spelling at the same time as attending to the listening passage. But they emerge most clearly in the following extracts:

(25) *if I don't write now also I don't know if it is correct + and um it is hard to write to read all the tasks before listening + it is better because I when I am filling the first part I don't remember what is following +*

and when we listen for the next part I have while I'm listening + I have to read and to know what do they want to do. (Y1:122)

(26) do you um + do you manage to read and write and listen OK when you . . .
no no + this time I'm not manage this good.
mhm.
and
is that usual?
Yes + that's usual.
. . . but when you're doing note-taking you're writing and listening.
yes + I think er writing um + quickly we would be happy to er + memorise the lecture.
Mhm + so you think that it's OK to write and listen
yes yes.
but you find it difficult to read and write and listen?
yes yes. (Z2:110)

What the researcher had not allowed for – and what emerged in these and some of the other protocols – was the complexity of the tasks demanded by the two test methods represented here. Gap-filling might appear to be an activity that closely approximates to the type of note-taking that takes place in a lecture. But it does not really do so, because the notes have not been generated by the candidate and therefore represent an unseen text that has to be mastered. The test format demands a combination of reading, listening and writing. Attention needs to be switched between the three skills (with the added complication of Cambridge ESOL's accurate spelling requirement) and even at times divided between them. As already noted, human attention is limited in capacity and attention-dividing activities make complex demands upon the processor. Something similar can be said of MCQ. It has often been remarked that MCQs load heavily on to the reading skill because of their complexity. But the issue here is not so much the part played by reading as, once again, the requirement upon the candidate to manipulate two skills, both demanding high levels of attention. Wickens' multiple resource theory (1984) suggests there may be particular tensions when two sources of information share a single channel, as some commentators would claim the two receptive skills do at comprehension level.

In this respect then, the test methods used in connection with Section 4 appear to make considerably *heavier cognitive demands* upon the candidate than would a real-life situation.

5.4   Additional cognitive demands of note-taking

That said, there was incidental evidence that in certain other areas the note-taking task was more demanding for participants than undertaking the test. Participants showed themselves to be vulnerable in three areas in particular when performing in lecture conditions.

a. Constructing meaning representations
Without the support of the kind of outline that is provided by a set of test items, participants were much more prone to construct their own hypotheses as to the main direction of the speaker's argument or the main themes of the lecture. These hypotheses could be close to the truth but they could also lead the listener into establishing meaning representations which did not accurately represent what was in the recording. In forming their assumptions, participants were assisted or misled by their knowledge of the topic (particularly so with the shark text) and sometimes by their intuition as to what might be a current angle on the topic (protecting trees, protecting sharks).

It has to be said, though, that mistaken hypotheses were by no means restricted to the note-taking condition; they were also observed in the test condition despite the availability of supportive written text. What seemed to be more prevalent among note-takers was a tendency to construct an elaborate meaning representation on the basis of a single word – sometimes a word that had not been correctly recognised. Thus, three participants reported on shark *machines* (= 'meshing') while one misheard the word *beach* as *breed* and interpreted the entire lecture as being about the propagation of shark species.

b. Propositional density and complexity
Without targeted questions, participants seemed prone to lose their way when confronted with sequences which were particularly dense propositionally or complex in terms of the relationships between the propositions. An example of the first was that several of them commented on the heavy factual load of the shark lecture. An example of the second was that very few of them managed to make sense of the exposition of how high buildings created wind tunnels.

c. Lack of selectivity
Some participants had difficulty in distinguishing central facts from peripheral ones when reporting orally on Text B (see 'peripheral' in Tables 6.2 and 6.3 on pages 410–11).

In these three areas, the note-taking task was arguably more demanding. The point at issue is that, here again, there would appear to be a lack of fit between the demands of the test formats and those of the target behaviour. A key to handling the types of issue that have been identified lies in the listener's ability to *self-monitor*, checking the relevance and reliability of incoming information in the light of the meaning representation built up so far. This aspect of lecture listening is sidelined when the listeners have detailed written prompts that help build a representation for them, regardless of what they have extracted from the recording.

6   Recommendations

6.1   Some tentative suggestions for IELTS testing in this area

It should be stressed at this point that the view of cognitive validity presented in the report is a somewhat idealised one. It is clearly not possible for any test to replicate all the processes that a real-life listening event demands. In addition, exam boards have to observe a number of important considerations – not least, the need to achieve marker reliability. Any proposals that are made in this section must therefore remain tentative and subject to the usual constraints associated with efficient test administration.

Nevertheless, the study has served to highlight several ways in which current test formats are either more cognitively demanding than a lecture-listening task or fail to embrace some of its more important aspects (selecting relevant information, linking points made by the speaker, building a macro-/ micro-comprehension structure, self-monitoring). It should not be impossible to adjust or replace the methods that are used in IELTS Listening Section 4 in order to make this test a more sensitive detector of the ability to perform in real-life academic listening contexts. Some suggestions follow.

6.1.1   Test method

The gap-filling and MCQ formats as they are currently employed may need reconsidering. They appear to make cognitive demands upon the candidate which exceed those of normal lecture listening. The former has the unfortunate effect of focusing candidate attention at word level and providing *gratis* a great deal of the structure of the lecture which it should be the listener's responsibility to construct. The latter imposes heavy reading demands. Both foster a practice of switching attention away from the recording to the written modality (seen by learners as easier to process because it can be consulted over and over again).

Ways of refining the gap-filling format might be:

* to focus more strictly upon points which are central to the main argument
* to target propositions at macro- as well as at micro-level – perhaps by featuring two short sets of notes of which one provides an overview of the lecture
* to rely more heavily upon paraphrase than at present so as to avoid word-matching strategies

- to provide a skeleton outline of the lecture rather than simulated notes, with macro- as well as micro-elements to be filled in
- (given the number of correct answers in the data which would have been disallowed by the strict marking scheme) to allow more latitude both on acceptable responses and on spelling.

In many ways, however, it would be advisable to abandon this format, given its heavy cognitive demands and the way it fosters test-wise strategies. More valid alternatives would require the candidate to write a summary of the lecture or to insert notes under various headings (not necessarily following the order of the text). However, these methods would certainly create problems of marker reliability.

More practical alternatives might include:

- jumbled propositions (paraphrased from the recording) for the candidate to number in order to form a skeleton outline of the lecture
- a coherent paraphrased summary of the text where candidates have to complete sentences using two or three words
- (to test structure building) a paraphrased summary of the text with gaps for candidates to insert connectives chosen from a limited set.

The first two of these would need to be carefully controlled to ensure that they did not load too heavily on to reading.

Ways of adapting the MCQ format would be:

- to focus more strictly upon points which are central to the main argument
- to provide shorter options and options which are less finely differentiated so as to reduce the reading load.

A rather threadbare argument in favour of MCQ is that it replicates what is in the mind of a listener, who approaches a lecture with expectations that need to be tested. This does not hold up from a process perspective in that accessing those expectations requires a complex reading operation. A more viable alternative along these lines might be to expand the use of the traditional 'true/false/not mentioned' format in Section 4. Even better would be to ask a candidate to read a complete and coherent (but concise) summary of the lecture which was incorrect in some respects and to underline the propositions which were wrong.

The most ambitious but also the most cognitively valid alternative would be to ask candidates to listen to not one but two lectures on the same topic and to collate the information from them into a table.

6.1.2 Double play

There are a number of reasons for the present policy of only allowing one hearing of the text (for a rationale, see Geranpayeh and Taylor 2008:4). One is historical: the single-play stipulation has always set IELTS apart from the exams of the main Cambridge suite. One is practical: double play extends the length of listening time and thus potentially restricts the length, number and variety of the recordings that can be employed within the time frame of the test. However, it would appear that the convention has a number of unfortunate side effects. As evidenced in this study, it creates tension in the candidate who is afraid of missing a point (often a point of detail) and it fosters test-wise strategies at the expense of overall meaning. In other words, it exercises an effect upon the cognitive processing that takes place in the course of the test.

An 'ecological' argument is sometimes put forward that in real life lecture listeners only hear a point once and have to grasp it or lose it; but it is not entirely convincing in the context of a test and moreover one that is based upon audio input. Firstly, a real-life lecture has far greater redundancy than the type of brief recording that, for obvious practical reasons, features in an international exam. The lecture mode relies quite heavily upon rephrasing and repetition to underline critical points; it also has a distinctive discourse structure in which the lecturer provides an outline at the outset and a summary at the end. Candidates hearing a short IELTS recording do not have the benefit of these features; small wonder that the one-off opportunity to grasp a point sometimes contributes to the kind of stress mentioned in the protocols. In addition, the candidate who hears an audio recording of a lecture cannot be said to be in a situation that resembles a real-life one in cognitive terms. Processing demands are affected by the fact that the candidate has no access to PowerPoint support of the kind that would normally be available or to the paralinguistic cues that would normally be provided by the lecturer.

Also persuasive is the evidence of what listeners do when they know that they will hear an audio recording twice. As Buck (1990) testifies, they tend to listen at a rather local level during the first play; during the second, they engage in structure building, assembling the points they have identified into a coherent whole and recognising the logical connections between them. It was precisely this element that was found to be absent in the accounts of many of the participants in the test-taking condition. They proved capable of scoring IELTS points by providing the locally based information that the tests required; but they were not able to achieve what successful lecture attendance would normally demand – a coherent account of the main points of the lecture and the ways in which they were linked. The convention of only allowing a single play would thus seem to be implicated in the low level of processing in which candidates engaged. It also contributed importantly to the heavy cognitive demands imposed by the gap-filling task in that it required candidates not only to operate in three different ways (reading, listening and writing) but to do so under extreme pressures of time and attention allocation, given that they were unable to listen again to check their impressions.

Whatever the ecological arguments (and it has been suggested that they are not strong), the present study seems to show that the single play stipulation detracts from cognitive validity. The IELTS partners might perhaps consider the benefits of a double play.

6.1.3 Propositional density and complexity

The comments of a number of participants about the texts they heard (as against the tasks they performed) indicate a level of concern with parts of the recording that were dense in terms of the amount of detail they contained or complex in terms of the links between propositions. These considerations should perhaps be accorded greater weight by test setters. A transcript that suggests that a recording is rich in details that can be tested may seem to be an attractive proposition but may make unfair cognitive demands of the candidate – not least because of the point made in the previous section that candidates only hear a short presentation and cannot benefit from the more elaborate discourse structure and the level of redundancy that counterbalance informationally dense sections in a normal lecture context.

6.1.4 Greater authenticity

Finally, it is worth recording that a real-life lecture is a multi-modal event to which a number of sources of information contribute. Many of them are absent in the current format, reshaping the cognitive operations that are required of the listener. They include:

- handout material
- PowerPoint slides
- facial expression and gestures of the lecturer
- the tendency of the lecture mode towards redundancy in the form of repetition and rephrasing.

Long term, it would be desirable to ensure that the IELTS test (and particularly the lecture-listening component) approximates more closely to these real-life conditions. That would entail taking advantage of current technology to ensure that the input to the candidate has visual as well as auditory components and that the components replicate as closely as possible those available to the academic listener. Clearly, full account would need to be taken of the limited technological resources in some parts of the world where the test is taken; this might well delay the use of DVD or downloadable materials. But innovation is likely to prove necessary at some stage if the test is to increase its validity as a predictor of actual lecture-listening behaviour.

6.2 Limitations of the study and further research

The most suitable way of obtaining the evidence needed for this study was felt to be by retrospective verbal report. The method is demanding in terms of time and the type of analysis involved; and only permits the study of a relatively small sample population. Its findings therefore need to be accompanied by the rider that they can only be indicative. It would certainly be of value to extend the study by examining the test-taking and lecture-listening behaviour of a further group of participants.

It would also be valuable to extend it by using the same methodology but employing other past IELTS papers. This might enable one to establish the extent to which characteristics of the recording or of the test method are factors in the types of process that candidates are likely to adopt.

Attempts were made to balance the population studied across first languages. Nevertheless, the size of the study did not permit of any detailed investigation of the possible effects upon cognitive processes of a) first language, b) cultural and educational background, or c) preparation in the home country for IELTS. All of these factors merit further exploration – possibly in a limited set of country-by-country studies.

The issue of cognitive validity seems likely to gain in importance as a consideration in test design. What will surely be needed long term are longitudinal studies which attempt to evaluate the predictive power of an IELTS Listening score. These might track former IELTS candidates during their first year at an English-medium university. Ideally, one could video-record live lectures within their discipline and re-run them to the participants in order to assess at intervals their developing ability to process the content. A study of this kind should certainly make use of the type of verbal report that has been employed here; it would be instructive to see if participants' strategies changed as they gained more experience of lecture listening and better knowledge of L2.

That said, listening development is a complex area to which many different factors contribute. Quite apart from the very varied ways in which individuals respond to the challenge of L2 listening, there are considerations such as distance of L2 from L1, familiarity with western patterns of logic, extent of integration into the host community, motivation, grasp of the discipline being studied and the communicative imperative felt by the listener. All this suggests that any longitudinal research will need to rely upon a whole series of case studies. There seems to be scope for a great deal of investigation in this area in years to come.

Acknowledgements

I am extremely grateful to Ros Richards, Director of the Centre for Applied Language Studies at Reading University for allowing me access to students and facilities at the centre. I am also very grateful to the unfailingly supportive staff of CALS (especially Colin Campbell, Jonathan Smith and John Slaght) who allowed me to contact their students and assisted with evidence on the students' backgrounds. Particular mention should be made of the technical advice I received from Pete Cox of Reading University and from Mark Huckvale of University College London. I am indebted to Sheila Thorn for her truly impressive transcription skills.

Special thanks are owed to the students from many parts of the world who participated in the data collection: for their interest in the project and for the engaged and helpful way in which they reported on their experience of undertaking the tasks.

Many thanks to Professor Cyril Weir of the University of Bedfordshire for some stimulating conversations on the topic of cognitive validity.

Finally, I express my appreciation to the British Council for funding what I believe to be much-needed research into the extent to which the processes underlying test performance replicate the processes that would be applied in a non-test context. I trust that it will be of assistance to future test design.

References

Alderson, J C (2000) *Assessing Reading*, Cambridge: Cambridge University Press.

Bachman, L F (1990) *Fundamental Considerations in Language Testing*, Oxford: Oxford University Press.

Baxter, G P and Glaser, R (1998) Investigating the cognitive complexity of science assessments, *Educational Measurement: Issues and Practice* 17 (3), 37–45.

Brown, G (1995) *Listeners, Speakers and Communication*, Cambridge: Cambridge University Press.

Brown, J D and Rodgers, T (2002) *Doing Second Language Research*, Oxford: Oxford University Press.

Buck, G (1990) *The testing of second language listening comprehension*, unpublished PhD thesis, University of Lancaster, UK.

Buck, G (2001) *Assessing Listening*, Cambridge: Cambridge University Press.

Cambridge ESOL (2005) *Cambridge IELTS 4*, Cambridge: Cambridge University Press.

Clapham, C (1996) *The Development of IELTS: A Study of the Effect of Background Knowledge on Reading Comprehension,* Studies in Language Testing volume 4, Cambridge: UCLES/Cambridge University Press.

Cohen, A (1998) *Strategies in Learning and Using a Second Language*, Harlow: Longman.

Dunkel, P, Henning, G and Chaudron, C (1993) The assessment of an L2 listening comprehension construct: A tentative model for test specification and development, *Modern Language Journal* 77, 180–191.

Ericsson, K A and Simon, H A (1993) *Protocol Analysis: Verbal Reports on Data*, 2nd ed, Cambridge MA: MIT Press.

Faerch, C and Kasper, G (1987) *Introspection in Second Language Acquisition Research,* Clevedon: Multilingual Matters.

Field, J (2004a) *Psycholinguistics: the Key Concepts*, London: Routledge.

Field, J (2004b) An insight into listeners' problems: too much bottom-up or too much top-down? *System* 32, 363–377.

Field, J (2008a) *Listening in the Language Classroom*, Cambridge: Cambridge University Press.

Field, J (2008b) The L2 listener: type or individual?' *RCEAL Working Papers in English and Applied Linguistics* 12, 13–32.

Field, J (2011) Cognitive validity, in Taylor, L (Ed.) *Examining Speaking: Research and practice in assessing second language speaking*, Studies in Language Testing volume 30, Cambridge: UCLES/Cambridge University Press, 65–111.

Gaskell, G (Ed.) (2007) *The Oxford Handbook of Psycholinguistics*, Oxford: Oxford University Press.

Gass, S M and Mackey, A (2000) *Stimulated Recall Methodology in Second Language Research*, Mahwah, NJ: Erlbaum.

Geranpayeh, A and Taylor, L (2008) Examining listening developments and issues in assessing second language listening, *Research Notes* 32, 2–5.

Gernsbacher, M A (1990) *Language Comprehension as Structure Building*, Hillsdale, NJ: Erlbaum.

Glaser, R (1991) Expertise and assessment, in Wittrock, M C and Baker, E L (Eds) *Testing and Cognition*, Englewood Cliffs: Prentice Hall, 17–30.

Kellogg, R (1995) *Cognitive Psychology*, London: Sage.

Long, D R (1990) What you don't know can't help you, *Studies in Second Language Acquisition* 12, 65–80.

Lynch, T (1994) Training lecturers for international audiences, in Flowerdew, J (Ed.) *Academic Listening: Research Perspectives*, Cambridge: Cambridge University Press, 269–289.

Lynch, T (2004) *Study Listening*, Cambridge: Cambridge University Press.

McDonough, J and McDonough, S (1997) *Research Methods for English Language Teachers,* London: Arnold.

Oxford, R (1990) *Language Learning Strategies: What Every Teacher Should Know*, Rowley, MA: Newbury House.

Richards, J C (1983) Listening comprehension: Approach, design, procedure, *TESOL Quarterly* 17 (2), 219–239.

Rost, M (1990) *Listening in Language Learning*, Harlow: Longman.

Schmidt-Rinehart, B (1994) The effects of topic familiarity on second language listening comprehension, *Modern Language Journal* 78 (2), 179–189.

Shaw, S D and Weir, C J (2007) *Examining Writing: Research and practice in assessing second language writing*, Studies in Language Testing volume 26, Cambridge: UCLES/Cambridge University Press.

Styles, E (2006) *The Psychology of Attention*, 2nd ed, Hove: Psychology Press.

Tulving, E (1983) *Elements of Episodic Memory*, New York: Oxford University Press.

Van Dijk, T A and Kintsch, W (1983) *Strategies of Discourse Comprehension*, New York: Academic Press.

Vandergrift, L (2005) Relationships among motivation orientations, metacognitive awareness and proficiency in L2 listening, *Applied Linguistics* 26, 70–89.

Vandergrift, L, Goh, C, Mareschal, C and Tafaghodatari, M H (2006) The Metacognitive Awareness Listening Questionnaire (MALQ): Development and validation, *Language Learning* 56, 431–462.

Weir, C J (2005) *Language Testing and Validation: an evidence-based approach,* Basingstoke: Palgrave Macmillan.

Wickens, C (1984) Processing resources in attention, in Parsuraman, R and Davies, D R (Eds) *Varieties of Attention*, Orlando, FL: Academic Press, 63–102.

Appendix 6.1
Recorded texts used in the study

TEXT A

[Test 1, Section 4, *Cambridge IELTS with Answers*, 4, 2005:134-5]

Good day, ladies and gentlemen. I have been asked today to talk to you about the urban landscape. There are two major areas that I will focus on in my talk: how vegetation can have a significant effect on urban climate, and how we can better plan our cities using trees to provide a more comfortable environment for us to live in.

Trees can have a significant impact on our cities. They can make a city, as a whole, a bit less windy or a bit more windy, if that's what you want. They can make it a bit cooler if it's a hot summer day in an Australian city or they can make it a bit more humid if it's a dry inland city. On the local scale – that is, in particular areas within the city – trees can make the local area more shady, cooler, more humid and much less windy. In fact trees and planting of various kinds can be used to make city streets actually less dangerous in particular areas. How do trees do all that you ask?

PAUSE INSERTED

Well, the main difference between a tree and a building is a tree has got an internal mechanism to keep the temperature regulated. It evaporates water through its leaves and that means that the temperature of the leaves is never very far from our own body temperature. The temperature of a building surface on a hot sunny day can easily be twenty degrees more than our temperature. Trees, on the other hand, remain cooler than buildings because they sweat. This means that they can humidify the air and cool it – a property which can be exploited to improve the local climate.

Trees can also help to break the force of winds. The reason that high buildings make it windier at ground level is that, as the wind gets higher and higher, it goes faster and faster. When the wind hits the building, it has to go somewhere. Some of it goes over the top and some goes around the sides of the building, forcing those high level winds down to ground level. That doesn't happen when you have trees. Trees filter the wind and considerably reduce it, preventing those very large strong gusts that you so often find around tall buildings.

PAUSE INSERTED

Another problem in built-up areas is that traffic noise is intensified by tall buildings. By planting a belt of trees at the side of the road, you can make things a little quieter, but much of the vehicle noise still goes through the trees. Trees can also help reduce the amount of noise in the surroundings, although the effect is not as large as people like to think. Low frequency noise, in particular, just goes through the trees as though they aren't there.

Although trees can significantly improve the local climate, they do however take up a lot of space. There are root systems to consider and branches blocking windows and so on. It may therefore be difficult to fit trees into the local landscape. There is not a great deal you can do if you have what we call a street canyon – a whole set of high-rises enclosed in a narrow street. Trees need water to grow. They also need some sunlight to grow and you need room to put them. If you have the chance of knocking buildings down and replacing them, then suddenly you can start looking at different ways to design the streets and to introduce . . . (fade out)

TEXT B

[Test 4, Section 4, *Cambridge IELTS with Answers*, 4, 2005:151]

Today we're going to look at one of my favourite fish – the shark. As you know, sharks have a reputation for being very dangerous creatures capable of injuring or killing humans, and I'd like to talk about sharks in Australia.

Sharks are rather large fish, often growing to over ten metres, and the longest sharks caught in Australia have reached sixteen metres. Sharks vary in weight with size and breed, of course, but the heaviest shark caught in Australia was a White Pointer – that weighed seven hundred and ninety-five kilograms – quite a size! Sharks have a different structure to most fish: instead of a skeleton made of bone they have a tough elastic skeleton of cartilage. Unlike bone, this firm, pliable material is rather like your nose, and allows the shark to bend easily as it swims. The shark's skin isn't covered with scales, like other fish: instead, the skin's covered with barbs, giving it a rough texture like sandpaper. As you know, sharks are very quick swimmers. This is made possible by their fins, one set at the side and another set underneath the body, and the tail also helps the shark move forward quickly.

Unlike other fish, sharks have to keep swimming if they want to stay at a particular depth, and they rarely swim at the surface. Mostly, they swim at the bottom of the ocean, scavenging and picking up food that's lying on the ocean floor. While most other animals, including fish, hunt their prey by means of their eyesight, sharks hunt essentially by smell. They have a very acute sense of smell – and can sense the presence of food long before they can see it.

PAUSE INSERTED

In Australia, where people spend a lot of time at the beach, the government has realised that it must prevent sharks from swimming near its beaches. As a result, they've introduced a beach-netting programme. Beach-netting, or meshing, involves setting large nets parallel to the shore: this means that the nets on New South Wales beaches are set on one day and then lifted and taken out to sea on the next day. When shark meshing first began, in 1939, only the Sydney metropolitan beaches were meshed – these beaches were chosen because beaches near the city are usually the most crowded with swimmers. Ten years later, in 1949, systematic meshing was extended to include the beaches to the south of Sydney. As a result of the general success of the programme in Sydney, shark-meshing was introduced to the state of Queensland around 1970. The New Zealand authorities also looked at it, but considered meshing uneconomical – as did Tahiti in the Pacific. At around the same time, South Africa introduced meshing to some of its most popular swimming beaches.

When meshing began, approximately fifteen hundred sharks were caught in the first year. However, this declined in the years that followed, and since that time, the average annual catch has been only about a hundred and fifty a year. The majority of sharks are caught during the warmest months, from November to February, when sharks are most active and when both the air and ocean are at their maximum temperature.

PAUSE INSERTED

Despite quite large catches, some people believe that shark meshing is not the best way to catch sharks. It's not that they think sharks are afraid of nets, or because they eat holes in them, because neither of these is true. But meshing does appear to be less effective than some other methods, especially when there are big seas with high rolling waves and strong currents and anything that lets the sand move – the sand that's holding the nets down. When this moves, the nets will also become less effective.

Appendix 6.2
Tasks used in the study

TASK A

SECTION 4   *Questions 31–40*

Complete the notes below.

Write NO MORE THAN TWO WORDS for each answer.

THE URBAN LANDSCAPE

Two areas of focus:
• the effect of vegetation on the urban climate
• ways of planning our **31** .... better

Large-scale impact of trees:
• they can make cities more or less **32** ....
• in summer they can make cities cooler
• they can make inland cities more **33** ....

Local impact of trees:
• they can make local areas
    – more **34** ....
    – cooler
    – more humid
    – less windy
    – less **35** ....

Comparing trees and buildings

Temperature regulation:
• trees evaporate water through their **36** ....
• building surfaces may reach high temperatures

Wind force:
• tall buildings cause more wind at **37** .... level
• trees **38** .... the wind force

Noise:
• trees have small effect on traffic noise
• **39** .... frequency noise passes through trees

Important points to consider:
• trees require a lot of sunlight, water and **40** .... to grow

---

TASK B

SECTION 4   *Questions 31–40*

Questions 31–34

Complete the notes below.

Write NO MORE THAN THREE WORDS AND/OR A NUMBER for each answer.

Sharks in Australia

Length	largest caught: 16 metres
Weight	heaviest: **31** .... kg
Skeleton	cartilage
Skin texture	rough barbs
Swimming aids	fins and **32** ....
Food	gathered from the ocean **33** ....
	sharks locate food by using their **34** ....

Questions 35–38

Choose the correct letter, A, B or C.

35 Shark meshing uses nets laid

   A along the coastline.
   B at an angle to the beach.
   C from the beach to the sea.

36 Other places that have taken up shark meshing include

   A South Africa.
   B New Zealand.
   C Tahiti.

37 The average number of sharks caught in nets each year is

   A 15.
   B 150.
   C 1,500.

38 Most sharks are caught in

A spring.
B summer.
C winter.

Questions 39 and 40

Choose TWO letters A–G.

Which *TWO* factors reduce the benefits of shark nets?

A nets wrongly positioned
B strong waves and currents
C too many fish
D sharks eat holes in nets
E moving sands
F nets too short
G holes in nets scare sharks

Appendix 6.3
Sample transcriptions – Participant R

TEXT A (TEST CONDITION)

Italics indicate researcher's turns

1 *right + 31?*

2 er 31 ways to plan our cities' trees better.

3 *Sorry, what was the answer?*

4 'city'.

5 *'city' OK + why did you choose the word 'city'?*

6 um ++ I can hear the sentence.

7 *so you heard someone talking about cities?*

8 yeah.

9 *that's why you put 'city' in + OK fine + um number 32?*

10 er + sorry + I missed er the answer + the answer I think is wrong + I write here.

11 *OK that's OK + so you didn't hear something that would give you the answer?*

12 um I hear + I hear the er the sentence clearly but I I lost er + the the title + er + I

13 I missed the title + the recording is is er faster than I thought +

14 *so you heard the sentence but you didn't understand all the words?*

15 no I understand all the words but I I didn't er record down on the paper + I I

16 clearly know the the meaning of the recording.

17 *Yeah but you didn't why didn't you write it on the paper?*

18 Mhm + er + I + er + + er + sorry I er the time I just heard + er the the time gave

19 me to look out all that's all + the test is is short so I didn't think I'd finish all the

20 all the title so I + I missed the the key words.

21 *so you missed it because you were reading the sentence+*

22 Yeah.

23 *when when you were listening.*

24 yeah I just find the key words of the test.

25 *OK so what do you think the answer was for 32?*

26 32 ++ um 'comfortable' maybe.

27 *OK right + um right would you give me the answer for 33?*

28 um 'humid'.

29 *yeah + and why did you give that answer?*

30 mhm.

31 *what did you hear the speaker say?*

32 er the speaker say if er ++ plan er um plan more trees come makes inland city

33 more humid + I just caught the end + sentence.

34 *OK great + Um 34?*

35 um ++ I don't I don't have that that answer sorry.

36 *is that because you didn't understand everything or you didn't recognise a word.*

37 *or what?*

38 yeah.

39 *what, what was the problem there?*

40 er I can't understand er the recording + it it still talk about air but the record is

41 about air.

42 *you were looking at the wrong sentence*

43 yeah yeah.

44 *when the recording was talking about something else.*

45 yeah.

46 *OK. What about number 35?*

47 I just haven't found it. (laughs)

48 *so that was the same thing?*

49 yeah.

50 *looking at sentences at the beginning when you hadn't realised that it had it had*

51 *moved on?*

52 mhm.

53 *OK thanks for that + so now we're going to hear a little bit more, yeah.*

54 er again play again?

55 no no.

56 go on? OK.

57 *OK + have you answered some more? + right um + would you like to carry on?*

58 yeah yeah ++ er just give you the answer?

59 yeah + 36.

60 'leaves'

61 *'leaves' + why did you say 'leaves'?*

62 um ++ I got hear the sentence + the er this recording the second recording I I

63 thought I got be some um + I used to the recordings + and the + the voice, so I +

64 easier.

65 *easier + yeah.*

66 *and did you hear her say something about leaves?*

67 um.

68 *yeah + what did she say about leaves?*

69 er can ++ the building surface make +

70 *what did she say? + do you remember what she said about leaves?*

71 just this part this sentence.

72 *right + so the same thing.*

73 yeah yeah.

74 *OK + um now + what about 37?*

75 37 + um + I think maybe er maybe thirteen, thirty-eight level, or high level. I'm

76 not sure about this answer, but I . . .

77 *it's a high level +, or what was the other one?*

78 er + er + I just listen er 30 30 30 what I missed it.

79 *mhm.*

80 but the 38 is 'break'

81 *no hang on + you think it's um + you think it's a high level?*

82 yeah.

83 *why did you choose 'high'?*

84 um ++ er I hear I heard the the wind er + the wind go through the building can get

85 faster and faster er + particularly er in the tall buildings.

86 *mhm.*

87 so so + can cause more wind at a high level.

88 *OK so you heard the word 'high' did you?*

89 yeah.

90 yeah + OK + um 38?

91 38 + er 'trees break the wind force' + and er sentence is same as this the the

92 recording sentence.

93 *so you said the trees break the force of the wind?*

94 yeah.

95 *OK + so you actually heard that sentence?*

96 yeah.

97 *great + what about 39 and 40?*

98 'low' focusly for for frequently.

99 *low + low frequency?*

100 frequency ah.

101 *right right why did you say that?*

102 er I got the frequenc the frequency that word + because the word in this title is

104 unique + so I just hear er I just look er + where I listen the recording I look for the

105 frequency.

106 *frequency and you heard the word that came before it.*

107 yeah.

108 *OK great + and number 40?*

109 number 40 'room'.

110 *right.*

111 and he er + some the recording give some some interrupt er + because er + he she said

112 she water 'water' before 'the sunlight' + but at end is the room

113 *what does 'room' mean? Do you know?*

114 um space.

115 *right + great + well done ++ OK. I've got two questions about this then + and the first*

116 *one is were there parts of the recording that you found difficult to listen to?*

117 er you mean test + the +

118 *parts of the recording that you found difficult to understand.*

119 um I think all the all all the test all the test is not difficult.

120 *not the task the recording.*

121 the recording is not difficult to me.

122 *right.*

123 but bec because I missed the this this this answer + because I have lot of time to to

124 *because you're looking at the text yeah? + because you were reading.*

125 yeah yeah I + have a lot of a long time to to + have nice projects about about

126 listening um + especially this er professional listening so so I missed if give

127 some one some er just one week's I think I can get er better get better.

128 *now my um other question is what do you think the text is about? What were the*

129 *main points that the speaker was making?*

130 um the test was a recording + the recording talk about the er ++ talk about er the

131 tree grow tree in the city and er + I'm not sure the word + er some some some

132 good thing for grow tree in cities er can + can some in spite of the the weather +

133 not the weather the environment and the noise and the temperature and and +

TEXT B (NON-TEST CONDITION)

Italics indicate researcher's turns

1   OK um um the shark is actor's favourite fish + er it's very long + very long er

2   ten yard fish + they are they really kill humans + and the larger is the shark in

3   Australia named er + 'white + white shark' + and can er + sixteen metres long and er +

4   more than nine hundred kilo kilogram er + and the shark um can swim very quick +

5   and so they have good smelling to help them to find food + er it produce the smell

6   of bloody.

7   *mhm.*

8   at the beginning to er + the beginning maybe the shark attacked human in in 1939 +

9   1939 in beach + 19 + er some beach near the city + and then ten years later in 1949

10   in Sydney + and in 1970 in Queensland + and the shark eat the the food sign food

11   chain + food chain and er ++

12   *what you think the shark + you think that the speaker said that the shark + eats*

13   *everything that is smaller than the shark?*

14   um I I + think the meaning is um + like like er leo in the land + or like human in the

15   war is er + top list of eaten.

16   *so it's the top fish + so it eats all the fish that are smaller?*

17   yeah.

18   *OK*

19   um.

20   *anything else that they said about sharks?*

21   yeah er + um in in Australia there are some popular beach er to let people to to

22   play er + without er shark attack them + and the shark only live in the er warm

23   water um +

24   *mhm.*

25   I just got there.

26   *OK so why don't the sharks attack people on these beaches? + do you know?*

134   some some very important to human lives.

135   *mhm and the part at the end about trees + what did that say?*

136   pardon?

137   *there was something at the end the last part about trees + what did that say?*

138   and the (inaudible) is to grow trees.

139   *mhm.*

Appendix 6.4
Sample transcriptions – Participant V

TEXT B (TEST CONDITION)

Italics indicate researcher's turns

1 so first er 31 is seven hundred and ninety-five kilos + I've but I chose it because

2 I heard the the number + then +

3 *did you hear anything else + like the word 'kilo' or 'kilogram' or something like*

4 *that?*

5 I don't remember + I was really focusing on the number (laughs)

6 *but it seemed to be to do with weight?*

7 yeah.

8 yeah yeah + OK um + um + the second answer the 32 was 'tails' + um + I

9 heard this word because er + the the speaker said that + sharks um + swimming

10 with fin and tails and he I don't remember really why but I heard the word +

11 then . . .

12 *you understood 'fins' and 'tails'.*

13 yeah yeah + then the the the next one 33 I heard 'ocean floor' + and er I knew he

14 was talking about food the speaker +

15 *you heard 'ocean' and 'floor' together?*

16 yeah.

17 *had you ever heard the word 'floor' with the word 'ocean' before?*

18 No no.

19 *so you identified two separate words together.*

20 yeah.

21 *great.*

27 um + maybe they think that people interrupt them. (laughs)

28 *oh they're frightened of people +*

29 yeah.

30 *is that what you're saying? + on those beaches?*

31 yeah.

32 *so um what do you think the lecture was really about? + what were the important*

33 *points that the lecturer was making?*

34 um ++ I I don't think there there are some main idea in the + in the recording + and

35 the actor just er described er the shark + the kind of shark in Australia + and er tell

36 told some some + some truths er + for shark attack people um + but the people people

37 for the + of the recording um + don't have the I don't think it have a main body.

38 *OK um was there any part of the recording that you found very difficult to*

39 *understand? + the beginning or in the middle or at the end?*

40 the end.

41 *the end you found difficult to understand?*

42 yeah.

43 *um did you find this more difficult than the last one the one about the urban*

44 *landscape?*

45 yeah.

46 *why did you find it more difficult?*

47 um + if + er if I have this + something like this to ask me to do + some do some test

48 er maybe I can do it but +

49 *so if you have a sheet or an answer sheet it helps you.*

50 yeah yeah + er they can help me to um + to get some key words and I use the key

51 word to find the answer + but just listen and do some write + I I find I think is more

52 difficult.

22 um and the last one um + the 34 they used er the smell to find some to locate

23 some food + and well this this point I knew that they had a really good smell + so

24 er when I heard 'smell' I was sure it was the the answer.

25 *OK 35.*

26 yes OK + so first one the 35 + I'm not sure because er I didn't catch the um the

27 sentence + but I guess it's 'along the coastline' + but this +

28 *why did you guess that?*

29 because this is my this is my guess (laughs) + I mean um +

30 *did it seem +*

31 the second one + the second one is not logical at all + 'at an angle to the beach' +

32 it's quite strange + the second one 'from the beach to the sea' I don't really

33 understand how + how they could put a net from the beach to the sea + so 'along

34 the coastline' seems +

35 *that would be logical because you understood +*

36 yeah.

37 *it was to do with nets?*

38 yeah yeah + yes + um the the second one the 36 was a bit tricky because er he

39 mentioned all these places um + but I think it's South South Africa because um +

40 actually I know this but er + I know they use some some nets but I wasn't sure +

41 um +

42 *so basically you used your own knowledge?*

43 yeah. (laughs)

44 *any other reason for preferring South Africa?*

45 er because I'm um + I am a surfer + and I know that they are um + there are a lot
of

46 sharks in South Africa + and lots of um um + problems with with sharks and

47 South Africa + um the the answer for the 37 was 'one thousand and fifth

48 hundreds er + sharks caught' because I heard the answer.

49 *did you hear any other numbers at all?*

50 um I don't think so no.

51 *you just heard '1,500'?*

52 yes I guess + and the last one the 38 was the the + hottest er period + so it's the

53 summer even if it's November in the south part + it's it's the summer.

54 *39.*

55 OK so the 39 is B because um er + it reduce the benefits of shark nets when when the the

56 + waves and the currents are strong.

57 *did you hear them say something similar?*

58 um um not really + I heard about the strong waves and currents.

59 *so you heard him use the word 'waves' +*

60 yeah.

61 *and 'currents'.*

62 yeah + I heard these words.

63 *you didn't actually understand what he was saying about them + but . . . .*

64 well um + not really facts er yeah.

65 *logic again.*

66 excuse me?

67 *logic.*

68 yeah and um the second one the + the answer 40 um was E 'moving sands'.

69 *why?*

70 because um because I I guess again + but because I heard 'move moving

71 moving sands' + but I guess it's + it should be hard to fix some nets in the ground

72 um + which is too soft when the + when the the sand is moving yeah.

73 *OK thanks + now could you tell me what do you think the main topic or topics of*

74 *this um lecture is?*

75 the main topics is about er + how to keep er sharks away from the beach + to

76 avoid er injuries and accidents and +

TEXT B (NON-TEST CONDITION)

Italics indicate researcher's turns

1 OK. so this lecture's focused on the urban landscape and especially on one point

2 + was about the trees and + and see if trees er could provide any advantages in er

3 urban landscape in a urban area + and it revealed that it's er + very interesting to

4 have trees in cities + because the first example was that it reduce um + no the first

5 example was that it can regulate temp + the the the general temperature + er it can

6 + even a tree can even make it + make the temp + the the climate for example + a bit

7 more cooler or more humid it depends + and er the second point was that trees

8 um er can + how can I explain this? + um if you + if there are some trees in a city

9 um + the city is less windy + because er trees are able to absorb the um + the wind er +

10 whilst building are not able to do this + er it's with with the buildings + it's it is

11 even worse in fact because the the wind er hit the wall and then go down go

12 around buildings so it's really windy + and um the last point was er that it's quite

13 complicated to + to have trees in city because they use use a lot of a lot of space

14 a lot of room + so it's quite hard to find new places to + for trees + yes and I

15 think that's it.

16 *great + thanks for that + um so what do you think the main topic of this + or*

17 *topics of this um lecture were?*

18 it's um um + to analyse which are the advantages advantages to have trees in

19 cities and how which could be the solution er to to make this idea possible to + I

20 think.

21 *OK was there any part of the + of the lecture that you found particularly difficult*

22 *to understand? + the beginning or the middle or the end?*

23 no + no it was quite OK + it was OK.

24 *you found it quite OK?*

25 yeah, yeah, yeah + it was clear.

26 *OK + um compare this with the last one + the one about the sharks.*

27 yeah.

28 *which did you find more difficult?*

29 the first one + definitely.

77 *OK was there any part of the recording that you found difficult? + the beginning*

78 *or the middle or the end?*

79 the middle + um the points um 36 was quite + quite difficult yeah.

80 *why?*

81 because it's tricky when you have to find something but er the speaker men

82 mentions everything + it's really hard.

83 *for all those things?*

84 yeah + because you don't know if it's true if + or if it's not and yeah it's quite

85 hard.

The cognitive validity of the lecture-based question in IELTS Listening

30 *why?*

31 because um with this this tests + it it is um + how can I? + it's + I have I have a

32 lot of more stress with this sort of test + because you um you don't want to miss

33 any answer + but with this technique it's it is different + um even if you miss

34 something er + you you will understand the the general idea what is talking

35 about + but in this test + sort of test um you + when you miss + miss the point

36 then you you get stress and then for er + for for the following questions it's harder

37 + and so it's quite difficult.

38 *do you think you were behaving differently as a listener in the second one?*

39 *were you doing things that were different from the first one to the second?*

40 if if what? + I'm sorry.

41 *were you behaving differently as a listener when you did the first test to the way*

42 *you behaved in the second? + were you listening in a different way?*

43 um yes definitely + there's not the same way yeah + because in the first part

44 I'm just focusing on words not the general meaning + but in the second I focus

45 on the the the general ideas the most interesting points.

46 *OK + and did you find one of the recordings more difficult than the other?*

47 the the first one.

48 *you thought the first one?*

49 yeah.

50 *why was it more difficult?*

51 + I don't know really if it was the the speed um definitely again I think this is

52 + + the way how I + in the second one + it's really easy just to take notes to focus

53 on the main points + but there it's + no definitely I prefer the (unclear)

54 *you say + it's difficult to say if one recording is more difficult than the other +*

55 yeah really.

56 + *because it was the task +*

57 yeah because of the task.

58 + *you found*

59 exactly + yeah yeah yeah.

7 The use of tactics and strategies by Chinese students in the Listening component of IELTS

Richard Badger
University of Leeds
Xiaobiao Yan
Guangdong University of Foreign Studies (GDUFS)

Abstract

This study investigates whether there are differences between the strategies used by native speakers/expert users of English and those used by learners of English who are native speakers of Chinese when they take an IELTS Listening test. Twenty-four native speakers of Chinese (12 pre-undergraduate and 12 pre-postgraduate), at an IELTS level for the Listening paper of between 5.5 and 6.5 and eight native/expert speakers of English (three undergraduates, three master's level and two doctoral), took a sample Listening test (from McCarter and Ash 2003). Data was collected using a think-aloud protocol and then analysed using a framework based on Goh (2002) adapted to include particular features of the data sets based on a grounded approach (Glaser 1992, Glaser and Strauss 1967, Senior 2006). This produced a three-level system of coding, with an initial distinction between cognitive and meta-cognitive strategies, each of which was divided into sub-strategies and then again into the tactics used to carry out the strategies. The result of an independent samples 2-tailed t-test revealed there were no significant differences between the two groups in terms of strategy use. At the level of sub-strategy there were differences on two out of 13 meta-cognitive strategies. At the level of tactics there were significant differences for seven tactics (two cognitive and five meta-cognitive) out of 58 at $p \leq 0.005$. This suggests that the strategies and tactics adopted by native and non-native speakers of English in the IELTS Listening module are not significantly different. We also examined the differences between the 12 pre-undergraduate and 12 pre-postgraduate Chinese native participants but found no significant differences at strategy, sub-strategy or tactical levels. The paper then discusses possible reasons for the results.

1   Introduction

The IELTS test is a high-stakes test and relative success or failure can have a life-changing impact on candidates. The language use which the test attempts to measure is associated very closely with cultural patterns. Many commentators argue that the Confucian background of native speakers of Chinese (Gieve and Clark 2005, Scollon 1999, Yao 2000) is significantly different from the cultural background most common in Australia, Canada and the UK. It is important therefore that we have confidence that the IELTS test is proving an appropriate measure of the language ability of Chinese-speaking students. A related question concerns the level of education of candidates for IELTS and whether the intellectual development typically associated with the completion of a degree may have an impact on the way in which those preparing for undergraduate and graduate study take the IELTS examination. This study is an attempt to address these issues.

The focus of this research is on listening, a key skill in language use, but much harder to test and research than speaking and writing because, like reading, most of the processes involved in listening happen within the minds of language users. Testing these skills requires the creation of a construct to understand what happens when language users read or listen and the adoption of an indirect means of assessment for these skills. Even compared with reading, listening presents additional difficulties to the test writer and researcher because it is 'transient and occurs within limited capacity working memory' (Goh 2002:182).

IELTS is a test of communicative language use and, within the tradition of communicative language testing, the aim has generally been to evaluate whether candidates have the ability to communicate in the target-language use (TLU) domains (Bachman and Palmer 1996:18), that is 'the real world situation in which the language will be used' (Buck 2001:83). Many commentators use the term 'task' to describe the activities that are carried out by language users outside the test situation. Bachman and Palmer define a target language use domain as 'a set of specific language use tasks that the test taker is likely to encounter outside of the test itself' (Bachman and Palmer 1996:44). This notion means that one of the aims of test writers is to produce test tasks that are as similar as possible to TLU domain tasks. However, as Buck (2001:90) observes, 'test tasks can never be entirely authentic replications of target language use tasks'. For further discussion of the concept of 'authenticity', see Widdowson (2003).

Ellis (2003) addresses the impossibility of designing completely authentic test tasks by distinguishing between situational authenticity and interactional authenticity which may be taken as very similar to text and task authenticity (Guariento and Morley 2001, Skehan 1996). Situational authenticity is the extent to which the test task matches a real-life situation. It would provide a rationale, for example, for including a listening text related to the task of filling in a form where filling in forms was part of the TLU domain. Interactional authenticity reflects the extent to which the test task elicits language behaviour which 'corresponds to the kind of communicative behaviour that arises from performing real-world tasks' (Ellis 2003:6). For the form-filling task, this would be the way in which users would use the listening text in completing the form.

1.1 Situational authenticity

An examination of IELTS Listening test tasks shows that there is a plausible claim that they have some situational authenticity. For example, the test sample in *IELTS Testbuilder* (McCarter and Ash 2003), the commercial IELTS test practice book that we used in this research and which mirrors IELTS papers closely, included the following listening texts:

- a two-person conversation on the phone between a credit card holder and a call centre employee
- a radio show in which a speaker discusses his success in giving up smoking with the radio presenter
- a conversation between a tutor and two undergraduate students about what one of their coursemates is doing and the marks of the two undergraduate students
- an extract from an academic lecture on bullying in the workplace.

All of these could be seen as coming from the TLU domains that candidates who are going to study in higher education institutions in English-speaking countries might encounter. There are some issues, such as the intonation in the conversation between the tutor and the undergraduates, and the possibly inauthentic North American accent in the lecture on bullying. Nevertheless, it would be possible for test writers to use such listening texts as the basis for tasks with situational authenticity.

1.2 Interactional authenticity

Interactional authenticity is more problematic. The students have to complete a range of written multiple-choice questions and gap-filling exercises, neither of which are activities which would be carried out in relation to these kinds of listening texts outside an examination or language classroom and so do not have obvious interactional authenticity. However, it is possible to identify sufficiently strong links between non-examination and examination interactions to ground the validity of the examination. For example in the first section, candidates have to note down the postcode (Question 2) having heard the following extract:

Operator: And what's your postcode?
Customer: <u>SE1 8PB</u>
Operator: <u>SE1 8PB</u>
Customer: That's it. [our underlining]

Similarly, in Question 34 of Section 4 the candidates have to complete with not more than three words the gap in the following phrase.

Setting 34. _____ tasks.

The cue for this is:

The first item on the list: <u>giving people</u> tasks that managers themselves cannot do and which are therefore impossible to achieve. [our underlining]

This would seem to be fairly closely related to the task of taking notes in a pre-PowerPoint lecture and so to have interactional authenticity.

There are however several questions where the interactional authenticity is harder to justify. For example, in Task 2, which replicates an interview on the radio, candidates have to answer the following multiple-choice question:

11. Mr Gold had problems because he

    a. hated smoking
    b. smoked
    c. couldn't touch his toes
    d. was very lazy.

The relevant extract from the tapescript is:

Well I enrolled on a number of evening courses where I found I wasn't able to do the warm up sessions. Bending down to touch my toes made me breathless. Even though I hated to admit it <u>my problem was not so much my sitting around all the time but my fifteen to twenty a day smoking habit</u>. If I'd been able to limit myself to three or four cigarettes a day there would have been no problem but I was seriously addicted. And I'm talking about waking up at three a.m. and dying for a cigarette or in the days before twenty four hours shopping <u>driving across London to buy a packet of cigarettes when I ran out</u>. But above all my addiction meant making sure I never ran out at the expense of everything else including necessities. [our underlining]

It is quite difficult to see, first, what the interactionally authentic task would be for a radio interview, and, secondly, how the multiple-choice format would relate to such a task. Similar issues arise with the tutorial situation, where again it is not immediately obvious what the interactional task should be.

The weakness of arguments based on interactional or task authenticity mean that claims about the ability of the IELTS test to measure whether candidates can handle TLU tasks need support from elsewhere. In this paper, we explore the possibility that this may be found in the similarity of the behaviour of candidates taking IELTS to that of a group of people whose ability to handle the TLU can be assumed, that is native and expert users of English, and in particular we attempt to answer the following research questions:

• What are the similarities and differences in the mental processes of native speakers of English and native speakers of Chinese when taking the IELTS Listening test?

• To what extent do the mental processes of Chinese-speaking candidates preparing for undergraduate and postgraduate studies differ?

2 Background to the research

In the background literature section, we look at models of listening, the concept of strategies and talk aloud protocols.

2.1 Models of listening

Researchers such as Anderson and Lynch (1988), Buck (2001), Rost (2002) and White (1998) have offered a range of models of listening. Here we discuss firstly top-down, bottom-up and interactive models and then Anderson's (2000) perception, parsing and interpretation model. Flowerdew and Miller (2005:85) make a strong argument for saying that a model of listening should include a social element. However for the purposes of this piece of research and, in particular, the focus on listening within the socially constrained context of an examination, we have chosen to focus on psychological aspects of the listening process.

2.1.1 Top-down, bottom-up and interactive

A distinction is commonly made between top-down and bottom-up processes in listening. This is based on the view that there is a continuum of information that is needed for effective listening from phonetic and phonemic information at the bottom to schematic and world knowledge at the top. Buck (2001) argues that:

> Listening comprehension is the result of an interaction between a number of information sources, which include the acoustic input, different types of linguistic knowledge, details of the context, and general world knowledge and so forth (Buck 2001:3).

We regard this as an understatement of the degree of interaction required. Both top-down and bottom-up information require the interaction of listening text and the listener. To decode a series of sounds as being instances of particular phonemes, listeners need to have the raw data, that is, the listening text, but also need to bring to that data their knowledge of what counts as a phoneme in the language to which they are listening. The information that a particular sound represents, for example, /s/ in English, is not necessarily in the acoustic signal but in the acoustic signal as interpreted by listeners with the knowledge of what phones make up the /s/ phoneme in English.

Similarly, the relevant schemata that help listeners make sense of particular listening texts serve no purpose if they are simply stored in listeners' minds. The schemata need to be activated by the listening text. This is not to say that bottom and top information do not exist but that interaction is both between top and bottom information and between listener and listening text.

2.1.2 Perception, parsing, utilisation

Anderson (2000) argues for a three-stage view of comprehension: perception, parsing and utilisation. When applied to listening, this means that listeners first store the input as a sound string (Anderson 2000:388). They then parse the sounds into the combined meaning of the words (Nagle and Sanders 1986). The third stage is when the listeners use the mental representation of the message. This may be simply a question of storing the meaning in memory or listeners may combine it with other elements in memory or context to make inferences.

> While listening, listeners are not just involved in one of these stages:
> These three stages – perception, parsing and utilisation – are by necessity partly ordered in time; however, they also partly overlap. Listeners can be making inferences from the first part of a sentence while they are already perceiving a later part (Anderson 2000:388).

This also means that ambiguities at the perception stage may be resolved or rendered unimportant by information at the parsing or utilisation stages.

If listeners are able to carry out the three processes of perception, parsing and interpretation without any difficulty, listening should be a straightforward process. However, listening is often not straightforward and most language users experience problems with comprehension. To gain an insight into the difficulties that listeners, and in particular L2 listeners, face, we need a model of how people learn to carry out skills such as listening.

2.1.3 Learning to listen

Information processing models of learning see the development of skills as having at least three stages. The first is the cognitive stage during which learners acquire knowledge about listening, sometimes called declarative knowledge. This would include, for example, information about the grammatical structure of the target language.

Secondly, at the associative or controlled stage, declarative knowledge is gradually proceduralised (Anderson 2000:282). For example, knowledge about grammatical structure becomes an ability to parse a listening text. At this stage, listening is a demanding activity.

Learning of a skill initially demands learners' attention and thus involves controlled processing . . . Controlled processing requires considerable mental 'space' or attentional effort (Saville-Troike 2006:73). In the final stage, which Anderson terms 'autonomous' (2000:282), listeners carry out the listening in a more and more automatic fashion.

Learners go from controlled to automatic processing with practice. Automatic processing requires less mental 'space' and attentional effort (Saville-Troike 2006:73).

In this model, learning essentially involves development along a continuum from controlled to automatic use of the skills and sub-skills involved in listening, freeing learners' controlled capacity for new information and higher-order skills. We draw the implication from this that controlled processes are more likely to be conscious, and thus we interpret the term 'automatic' as meaning that the processes at this stage are not under conscious control.

If this model is correct, people who are learning to listen in a second language are at least partially at the controlled stage and so have limited capacity for perceiving, parsing or interpreting the listening texts to which they are exposed. In a test situation, such people need to come up with some way of dealing with the problems they face. These solutions are often labelled 'strategies' (Bialystok 1990, O'Malley and Chamot 1990, Oxford 1990).

2.2   Strategies and tactics

Strategies are frequently defined within a learning context. Oxford (1990:8) defines strategies as 'specific actions taken by learners to make learning easier, faster, more enjoyable, more self-directed, more effective, and more transferable to new situations'. Goh (2002:186) takes a broader view, saying strategies are 'mental steps or operations carried out to accomplish cognitive tasks such as map-reading, memorisation, processing information and problem solving'.

While there is extensive discussion of strategies in the literature on learning (e.g. O'Malley and Chamot 1990, Oxford 1990), here we are concerned with the processes that listeners go through in order to understand a listening text, and whether or not these lead to learning. Our concern is primarily with communication strategies but our understanding is informed by what people have written about learning strategies.

Although some writers suggest that strategies can be conscious or unconscious, for most authorities strategies are conscious steps taken by language users and this corresponds with the view of strategies being adopted to compensate for the fact that some part of the listening process has not become completely automatic. This is consistent with the research instrument we are using, think-aloud protocols, which assume that listeners can talk about the strategies they are using.

Goh (1998, 2002) makes a distinction between general and specific strategies. She describes tactics as 'individualised techniques through which a general strategy is operationalised' (Goh 2002:187). For example, a meta-cognitive sub-strategy such as directed attention can be operationalised through tactics, such as concentrating hard and identifying a failure in concentration.

2.3   A taxonomy for strategies and tactics

There is considerable disagreement about the best taxonomy for describing strategies and tactics in listening. For this study, we drew on Goh's (2002) taxonomy (see Appendix 7.3). This follows Purpura (1999) in identifying two broad strategies, cognitive and meta-cognitive, with cognitive strategies broadly covering the perception, parsing and interpreting process of listening, and meta-cognitive strategies covering problem-solving activities. These two broad strategies were divided into sub-strategies which were partly drawn from the literature and partly derived from Goh's data in line with a grounded theory approach to data analysis (e.g. Brown and Rodgers 2002, Glaser 1992, Glaser and Strauss 1967, Senior 2006). One of the most significant differences between our research and that of Goh is that ours related to an examination paper, and this raised the question of the extent to which the strategies, sub-strategies and tactics used in an examination would be found to differ from a non-examination context.

Goh identified eight cognitive and six meta-cognitive strategies. Each sub-strategy was realised in a set of tactics. For example, within the cognitive strategy, she identified a sub-strategy labelled fixation which could be realised by the following four tactics:

stop to think about the spelling of unfamiliar words

stop to think about the meaning of words

memorise/repeat the sounds of unfamiliar words

memorise words or phrases for later processing.

Again meta-cognitively, she labelled one sub-strategy, directed attention, which was realised through two tactics:

concentrate hard

continue to listen in spite of difficulty.

A complete list can be found in Appendix 7.3.

2.4 Think-aloud protocols

It is common to investigate strategies using questionnaires. Oxford's (1990) development of an inventory of learning strategies has produced a range of questionnaire-based studies (e.g. Phakiti 2003, Vanijdee 2003). However, we felt that this would not be appropriate with the kinds of learners we were investigating, particularly given the fact that we were not sure how accurately a questionnaire would capture strategy and tactic use. Instead, we drew on the research instrument of the think-aloud protocol (Brown and Rodgers 2002).

A verbal protocol is the data which is produced when a person 'is asked to either "talk aloud" or to "think aloud"' (Green 1998:1). It is made up of utterances made by an individual, either while or after the individual carries out a single task or a series of tasks; verbal protocols, thus, can be either concurrent or retrospective (Brown and Rodgers 2002). For listening, the technical problems that arise in recording what listeners are saying at the same time as they listen to a text and the difficulty that listeners have in talking aloud while trying to comprehend a text meant that we had to adopt a retrospective approach. However, the nearer the protocol is to the event that the listeners are talking about the greater the validity and so we divided the IELTS Listening test into sections at natural breaking points, and asked the listeners to think aloud about what they had just done.

Goh (2002:189) comments:

> Verbal data on listening processes are predominantly retrospective. Because of the rapid flow of information, the working memory has to be freed for processing continuous input. What listeners will typically do is to process the heeded input first before reporting through retrospective verbalisation.

Bearing in mind Anderson's (2000) model of learning above, we hypothesised that native speakers/expert speakers of English would report fewer cognitive strategies than learners of English because they would have been automatised and so no longer accessible to the think-aloud protocol.

2.5 Research questions

Having reviewed the literature we were in a position to pose more specific research questions:

1. What differences are there between native speakers of English and non-native speakers of English in terms of the strategies, sub-strategies and tactics they use when taking an IELTS Listening test?
2. What differences are there between Chinese-speaking candidates preparing for undergraduate and graduate studies in terms of the strategies, sub-strategies and tactics they use when taking an IELTS listening test?
3. To what extent are the strategies, sub-strategies and tactics used by native and non-native speakers of English in an IELTS Listening test different from those reported in Goh's studies of listening?

3 The study

The study was carried out in Guangdong University of Foreign Studies (GDUFS), Guangzhou, China and the University of Leeds (UOL), Leeds, UK.

3.1 The participants

We collected data from 24 volunteers on an IELTS preparation programme at GDUFS who had or were expected to obtain a score of between 5.5 and 6.5 on the Listening element. These bands were chosen because they are significant in deciding whether candidates are admitted to English-medium tertiary education.

Twelve of the students were preparing for undergraduate studies through the medium of English (four males and eight females) and 12 were preparing for postgraduate studies (four males and eight females). We collected information about the participants' disciplinary background. Eight different majors and four different majors were expected to study for pre-postgraduate and pre-undergraduate groups respectively. Subjects' previous IELTS scores were collected at the same time. Information on the subjects is presented in Tables 7.1 to 7.4.

Table 7.1 Subjects of pre-postgraduate study participants at GDUFS

Accounting	5
Human Resources	1
Fashion Design	1
Tourism Management	1
Hotel Management	1
Management for Information System	1
Culture and Translation	1
Finance	1

Table 7.2 IELTS scores of pre-postgraduate study participants at GDUFS

IELTS band scores	Number of students
5.5	3 (one score predicted by the teacher)
6.0	4
6.5	5

Table 7.3 Subject of pre-undergraduate study participants at GDUFS

International Relationships and English	1
International Trade and English	1
International Business	6
Accounting	4

Table 7.4 IELTS scores of pre-undergraduate study participants at GDUFS

IELTS band scores	Number of students
5.5	3
6.0	4
6.5	5

We had hoped to investigate the impact of disciplinary background and gender but the numbers of students from particular disciplines and the relatively small overall sample meant that this was not practicable. The fact that the levels of the students as measured by IELTS were comparable between the pre-postgraduate and pre-undergraduate course meant that we were able to explore the impact of educational level on strategies, sub-strategies and tactics.

In addition, we collected data from eight self-selecting participants with native levels of competence in Leeds (three undergraduates, three master's level and two doctoral). One of the doctoral students was not a native speaker of English but had a native-like command of the language. She had lived in the UK for over two years and prior to arrival had obtained a score of 8 on the IELTS Listening test.

3.2 Ethical issues

The participants were all volunteers and saw and signed the consent forms, the English version of which appears in Appendix 7.5. The institutions in which the research was carried out are identified in this paper. This meant that if we linked information about gender, level of study or discipline to a particular think-aloud protocol, it would be possible to identify particular participants and so we decided not to include this information, where it was linked to what participants said or did, to ensure anonymity as far as we could.

3.3   Data collection

The data was collected from participants individually. We first gave the participants training tasks to accustom them to producing a protocol. These involved two mental arithmetic calculations and two anagram puzzles. The participants then took the attached test and completed a blank version of the answer sheet. We had asked the Assistant Director in Cambridge ESOL's Research and Validation Group for permission to use an IELTS past paper in listening for this project but unfortunately this was not possible. Drawing on criteria proposed by Terry (2003:66–76) and Saville and Hawkey (2004:73–96), the sample test (McCarter and Ash 2003) was judged to be fairly close to an actual IELTS test. It was also appropriate because of the test paper's unfamiliarity for the research participants.

At naturally occurring stages in the test (e.g. between sections, between reading the questions and listening to the recording) we asked the participants to say what mental processes they had gone through in arriving at or failing to arrive at answers. The researchers limited their contribution once the participants had started doing the tests to the following utterances:

Keep talking

Comment on what you have just heard or read / question XX, section XX

If participants said they had nothing to say about a particular section we asked them once to comment and, if they did not say anything at that stage, we continued to the next section. In the transcription for data analysis we removed all utterances from the researchers for ease of coding.

GDUFS participants were able to respond in English or Chinese. The think-aloud protocols were recorded on a mini-disk recorder or else directly onto a laptop computer by Xiaobiao Yan in GDUFS and Richard Badger in Leeds.

The recordings were transcribed and, if the think-aloud had been carried out in Chinese, translated into English. A sample non-native speaker protocol is provided in Appendix 7.1 and a sample native speaker protocol appears in Appendix 7.2.

3.4   Data analysis

The data was first chunked into what appeared to be plausible units that corresponded to Goh's tactics. The following extract from one GDUFS participant's protocol was divided into two chunks:

A and C is much . . ., um, A is certainly not the answer, so I just choose between B and C (C-I). He said he is free in, in, um . . . I am not quite sure about this question, because in the last section, the woman said, she

will call. I don't remember what she said. She will call the man very soon
(M-CM).

In the first chunk (ending C-I), the participant was trying to process utterances directly in order to infer the answer, which we treat as a cognitive strategy. In the second chunk (ending M-CM), comprehension monitoring tactics were used to check, and confirm understanding during listening. We classified this as meta-cognitive.

Initially we separately chunked data from two participants, discussed differences and then coded a further data set from another participant. Our chunking on the third data set agreed in over 95% of cases. We did not compare chunking on later data sets but did check each other's view on problematic instances.

3.4.1 Revising Goh's taxonomy

The data was analysed using Goh's categories (see Appendix 7.3). However, we had to make some changes at the level of sub-strategy and tactic. Our final taxonomy is given in Appendix 4.

We reorganised Goh's strategies so that the cognitive sub-strategies corresponded to Anderson's stages of perception (fixation), parsing (reconstruction) and utilisation (inferencing). We also treated the tactics that Goh classified as realising the cognitive strategy of prediction as a realisation of the meta-cognitive strategy of pre-listening preparation. Further changes were made to render the taxonomy more consistent with our understanding model of listening. For the sub-strategy of fixation, Goh identified four tactics:

stop to think about the spelling of unfamiliar words

stop to think about the meaning of words

memorise/repeat the sounds of unfamiliar words

memorise words or phrases for later processing.

In our taxonomy, we added a further tactic to cover the situation where a listener focused on the sound of a phoneme (CFP in our taxonomy in Appendix 7.4), on the assumption that listeners would focus on the sounds in unknown words. This came up several times in our data for both UOL and GDUFS participants, not to do with individual phonemes, but related to the sounds of letters in a postcode:

The postcode, I suppose that's 8PB (UOL participant).

The nearest our participants came to commenting on the processing of phonemes was in the following data:

*I just heard the pronunciation, but . . . Wahace. I don't know what word
it is, may[be] it's a new word for me? Um 'Wahace' [Wales]* (GDUFS
participant).

This was treated as a fixation on a word rather than a phoneme (CFW –
see Appendix 7.4). Generally, both groups of listeners had automatised their
perception of individual sounds to the extent that they were no longer able to
report on them.

These changes related to our views of the listening process. Most of the
other changes related to the fact that we were working in an examination
context.

We eliminated the sub-strategy of elaboration because it did not appear
in our first three data sets and we did not require it in the remaining data
sets, presumably because elaboration is not a common tactic in examinations. The sub-strategy of visualisation also did not appear in these three
data sets although we had thought that learners might use visualisation in the
examination.

We also eliminated the sub-strategy of prediction because it overlapped
with the tactics under the sub-strategy of inferring answer. For instance, the
tactic 'anticipating details while listening' under the sub-strategy of prediction seemed very similar to 'using co-text' from the sub-strategy of inferring.

At the level of tactic, we made several changes which related to the fact
that our participants were taking an examination. So for example, under
the sub-strategy of 'reconstruction', we added the tactic of 'reconstructing
meaning from an examination question' and under the sub-strategy of 'inferring' added 'inferring the answer by using information from the text with the
examination question paper'. These are discussed in more detail below where
we address our third research question which relates to differences between
the ways people in Goh's study listened as compared to those in an IELTS
test.

Our taxonomy uses letter codes such as CRQ and CIQ to describe strategies, sub-strategies and tactics. The C in CRQ stands for 'cognitive', the R
for 'reconstruction' and the Q for 'examination question'. Similarly in CIQ,
the C stands for 'cognitive', the I for 'inferring' and the Q for 'examination
question'.

The changes in the meta-cognitive group were rather greater. First, we
introduced the new sub-strategy of real time assessment of output (MAO,
where M stands for 'meta-cognitive' and AO for 'assessment of output')
because participants referred quite extensively to tactics such as making sure
their answers had the right numbers of words.

We also made 11 changes at the tactical level, particularly realisations of
comprehension monitoring (while listening) and comprehension evaluation
(post listening).

3.4.2   Applying the new taxonomy

We jointly coded two data sets and discussed differences until we had reached agreement. We then coded a third data set independently and our coding agreed over 90% of the time.

3.5   Findings

In this section we address each of our research questions in turn.

3.5.1   Research Question 1

What differences are there between native speakers of English and non-native speakers of English in terms of the strategies, sub-strategies and tactics they use when taking an IELTS Listening test?

At the level of strategy, the UOL participants reported an average of just over 100 instances of strategy use compared to just below 80 for the GDUFS participants. This was almost all accounted for by differences in terms of cognitive strategies where the figures were just under 50 for the UOL participants and just over 20 for the GDUFS participants. We were surprised that the UOL participants were able to report this number of cognitive strategies. However, at the level of strategy, the differences were not significant at $p \leq 0.005$ (see Table 7.5).

Table 7.5 Descriptive statistics at the level of strategy

	NSS	N	Mean	Std. Deviation	Std. Error Mean
C	NESE	8	49.13	33.753	11.934
	NC	24	20.21	10.384	2.120
M	NESE	8	56.00	21.824	7.716
	NC	24	59.17	20.459	4.176
T	NESE	8	105.13	32.520	11.498
	NC	24	79.45	26.493	5.408

C=Cognitive; M=Meta-cognitive; T=total; NSS=Native speaker status; NESE=Native/ Expert speaker of English; NC=Native speaker of Chinese

At the level of sub-strategy, the differences between the groups were again largely not significant. However, there were significant differences at $p \leq 0.005$ for two meta-cognitive strategies, directed attention (i.e. monitoring attention and avoiding distraction) and comprehension monitoring (i.e. checking interpretation for accuracy while listening), as shown in Tables 7.6 and 7.7.

In both cases the GDUFS participants used these strategies more frequently than the UOL participants. The UOL participants were probably less likely to need to calm themselves down or perhaps they did not engage in as much comprehension monitoring after listening to the listening text given their reduced commitment to scoring well on the test. It was surprising that the number of reports of the assessment of output meta-cognitive sub-strategy was not significantly different between the two groups, perhaps indicating that the Leeds participants were less familiar with the IELTS question types and were likely to spend more time on the process of listening in order to answer the answers than expected.

Table 7.6 Descriptive statistics for significantly different sub-strategies

Sub-strategy	NSS	N	Mean	Std. Deviation	Std. Error Mean
Meta-cognitive: directed attention	NESE	8	0.75	1.39	0.49
	NC	24	4.13	2.42	0.49
Meta-cognitive: comprehension monitoring	NESE	8	6.88	4.58	1.62
	NC	24	20.63	6.16	1.26

NSS=Native speaker status; NESE=Native/Expert speaker of English; NC=Native speaker of Chinese

Table 7.7 Independent samples 2-tailed t-test for significantly different sub-strategies

Sub-strategy	t	df	Sig	Mean Difference	Std. Error Difference	95% Confidence Interval of the Difference	
						Lower	Upper
Meta-cognitive: directed attention	−3.720	30	.001	−3.375	.907	−5.228	−1.522
Meta-cognitive: comprehension monitoring	−5.780	30	.000	−13.750	2.379	−18.608	−8.892

At the level of tactics, there are significant differences at $p \le 0.005$ for two cognitive tactics ('fixation on spelling', 'inferring information using world knowledge') and five meta-cognitive tactics ('identifying a failure in concentration', 'identifying a problem with the amount of input', 'identifying a problem with the process of answering a question', 'confirming that comprehension has taken place', 'identifying partial understanding'), as shown in Tables 7.8 and 7.9. We discuss each of these briefly.

Table 7.8 Descriptive statistics for significantly different tactics

Tactic	Native speaker status	N	Mean	SD	SEM
Cognitive: fixation – spelling	NESE	8	0.00	0.00	0.00
	NC	24	1.58	1.79	0.37
Cognitive: Inferring answer – using world knowledge	NESE	8	5.63	3.96	1.40
	NC	24	0.71	1.12	0.23
Meta-cognitive: directed attention – failure of attention	NESE	8	0.38	0.74	0.26
	NC	24	3.38	2.06	0.42
Meta-cognitive: real-time assessment of input – problem with the amount	NESE	8	6.88	2.90	1.02
	NC	24	2.46	2.36	0.48
Meta-cognitive: real-time assessment of output – process	NESE	8	6.25	4.27	1.51
	NC	24	2.50	2.41	0.49
Meta-cognitive: comprehension monitoring – confirm comprehension has taken place	NESE	8	0.88	2.48	0.88
	NC	24	7.25	3.63	0.74
Meta-cognitive: comprehension monitoring – partial understanding	NESE	8	0.63	0.74	0.26
	NC	24	3.13	1.77	0.37

NESE=Native/Expert speaker of English; NC=Native speaker of Chinese; SD=Standard Deviation; SEM=Std. Error Mean

'Fixation on spelling' (CFSP) was not reported at all by the UOL participants but this tactic does seem to be reported by several of the GDUFS participants (1.58) as a way of fixing, or not, what they have heard:

> *I knew it was 'Wales', but I did not know how to spell it* (GDUFS participant).

Inferring information using world knowledge (CIW) was, rather surprisingly, used more by the UOL participants (5.63) than by GDUFS participants (0.71):

> *You actually have to use your own knowledge to think of the best answer, so it's different and strange in one set of questions, but I suppose that might be the object of it* (UOL participant).

Amongst meta-cognitive strategies, 'identification of a failure in concentration' (MDAF) was reported more by the GDUFS participants (3.38) than the UOL participants (0.38). Again this is probably related to the fact that the UOL participants were less concerned about their performance on the test:

Table 7.9 Independent samples 2-tailed t-test for significantly different tactics

Tactic	t	df	Sig	Mean Difference	Std. Error Diff	95% CI of the Difference	
						Lower	Upper
Cognitive: fixation – spelling*	−4.329	23	.000	−1.583	0.37	−2.340	−0.827
Cognitive: Inferring answer – using world knowledge	5.598	30	.000	4.917	0.88	3.123	6.710
Meta-cognitive: directed attention – failure of attention	−3.995	30	.000	−3.000	0.75	−4.534	−1.466
Meta-cognitive: real-time assessment of input – problem with the amount	4.335	30	.000	4.417	1.02	2.336	6.497
Meta-cognitive: real-time assessment of output – process	3.111	30	.004	3.750	1.21	1.288	6.212
Meta-cognitive: comprehension monitoring – confirm comprehension has taken place	−4.602	30	.000	−6.375	1.39	−9.204	−3.546
Meta-cognitive: comprehension monitoring – partial understanding	−3.861	29	.001	−2.505	0.65	−3.833	−1.178

*=Equal variance not assumed (Levene's test for equality of variance); CI=Confidence Interval. See Appendix 7.4 for an explanation of the tactic acronyms.

I was absentminded at that time (GDUFS participant).

'Identifying a problem with the amount of input' (MAIA) was rather surprisingly reported more by the UOL participants (6.88) than the GDUFS participants (2.46), perhaps because of the unfamiliarity with the exam format:

So I miss, I miss a lot of the blanks. Yeah. Yes, because I have to read and listen at the same time (GDUFS participant).

I mean because those two are quite close together at least that's what I thought, I thought those two [questions] were answered quite quickly (UOL participant).

This last comment reflected a common assumption among both UOL and GDUFS participants that the information needed for questions would be distributed relatively equally throughout the listening text.

'Assessment of output related to the process of answering a question' (MAOP) was reported an average of 6.25 times by UOL as opposed to 2.50 for GDUFS participants. The following comment from a UOL participant related to where the numbers appeared on the answer paper:

> *I mean I suppose in order to be able to fill it out in an official way you need some indication of where you have to write especially there, if someone wasn't confident about their own writing abilities in English it could make it difficult, could be confusing. It seems a bit needless because all the others are at the end of the sentence apart from that one* [Question 15].

Differences in the amount of experience of an IELTS-style examination paper resulted in the UOL group commenting more on the layout of paper or question than their more practiced GDUFS colleagues:

> *I wanted to write the first of July, but that's four words* (UOL participant).

> *Oh, I think in this [section], um, gap-filling, I think it is very difficult* (GDUFS participant).

'Confirming that comprehension has taken place' (MCMC) was reported 0.88 times by UOL and 7.25 by GDUFS participants. Again, this is likely to reflect both the higher confidence of the UOL participants about their ability to answer questions and the lack of a felt need to check what they had done:

> *The interest question was fairly straightforward* (UOL participant).

> *And the name, and the first name, he said that slowly, so I can hear very . . . very clear* (GDUFS participant).

For the tactic of 'identifying partial understanding' (MCMP), the UOL figure was 0.63 as against 3.13 for the GDUFS participants. This is in line with the view that GDUFS participants were less likely to feel they had completely understood what they had heard:

> *I didn't quite remember clearly, only that the man grunted that when he was handing in fees in the bank, he had given some extra money* (GDUFS participant).

The data from the native/expert users was related to more than one question as in the example below related to the final part of the test:

> *Again quite a lot of, quite difficult I thought. I didn't get it all* (UOL participant).

While the differences between the groups in tactics usage, where these are significant, do raise some interesting issues, such as why inferring information using general world knowledge was not more widely used by the GDUFS participants, most of the differences are easier to account for in terms of attitudes to the examination rather than an issue with the validity of the IELTS examination.

Generally, there do not seem to be any significant differences between native speakers of English and non-native speakers of English in terms of the strategies, sub-strategies and tactics they use when taking an IELTS Listening test.

3.5.2   Research Question 2

What differences are there between Chinese-speaking candidates preparing for undergraduate and graduate studies in terms of the strategies, sub-strategies and tactics they use when taking an IELTS Listening test?

The pre-undergraduate students reported over 160 strategies compared to just under 140 for pre-postgraduates with most of this difference accounted for by meta-cognitive strategies where the figures were about 120 as against about 100 respectively. However, the analysis of the protocols in terms of strategies, sub-strategies and tactics indicates that the difference between the means for undergraduate and postgraduate students were not significant.

3.5.3   Research Question 3

To what extent are the strategies, sub-strategies and tactics used by native and non-native speakers of English in an IELTS Listening test different from those reported in Goh's studies of listening?

We address this question using the data from the differences between Goh's taxonomy (Appendix 7.3) and the taxonomy we used on our data sets (Appendix 7.4). The process by which we altered Goh's taxonomy is described above in Section 3.4.1. As noted there, some of the changes relate to differences in our conception of listening rather than the IELTS context and so are not relevant here.

A second group of changes concerns tactics which are typical of examinations rather than listening beyond the exam hall but which would be extremely difficult to eliminate. The relevant tactics are listed below:

- Comprehension monitoring: confirm that an exam question has been answered (MCMQA)
- Comprehension monitoring: identify examination questions not answered (MCMQN)
- Comprehension monitoring: Identify examinations skills not applied (MCMS)
- Comprehension evaluation against examination questions (MCEQ)

- Comprehension evaluation against experience of examinations (MCEP).

A third group of changes related to the ways students used skills other than listening in the examination. Four relate to reading:

- Reconstruct meaning from examination question (CRQ)
- Inferring information from the listening text and exam question paper (CIQ)
- Prepare using exam paper questions (MPQ)
- Pay selective attention to exam questions (MSAQ)
- Assess input in terms of links between elements in listening text and examination questions (MAIQ).

Three relate to writing:

- Real-time assessment of output in terms of quantity required (e.g. one or two words) (MAOQ)
- Real-time assessment of output in terms of process required (e.g. multiple choice vs gap fill) (MAOP)
- Real-time assessment of output in terms of intermediate processes (e.g. note taking) (MAOI).

It would be hard to design a Listening examination which did not involve the use of other skills but it might be worth considering whether some of the reading could be replaced by further listening.

Finally at the level of sub-strategy we eliminated Goh's strategy of elaboration and, while we kept in the sub-strategy of visualisation, we found no instances of this in our data sets. The lack of elaboration reflects the fact that, unlike many other kinds of listening, exam listening rarely requires the listener to use the information obtained from a listening text in some other communicative activity. It is hard to see how this might be done if the focus is to remain on listening though a more holistic view of language use might permit this.

The absence of visualisation again seems to relate to the largely verbal nature of the examination paper. This may well be appropriate in a text which replicates a phone conversation, as in the first section on the examination paper we used, but seems less appropriate with the academic lecture in the final section. Academic lectures are increasingly multi-modal (O'Halloran 2004) and the test writers might consider whether this could be built into future tests.

While many of these changes raise issues related to the examination, they can also be interpreted in a way which relates to the role of native or expert users in research into the effectiveness of the IELTS examination. This is illustrated in differing frequencies of the use of what we term examination tactics by UOL and GDUFS participants (see Table 7.10).

The difference between the means for the tactics for UOL and GDUFS participants were not significantly different. However, we were surprised that native/expert users often made more use of the examination specific tactics than did the potential candidates. This may reflect the fact that the relative unfamiliarity of native/expert users with this examination leads them to rely on general examination-taking strategies and tactics.

Table 7.10 Descriptive statistics for 'examination' tactics

Tactic	Native speaker status	N	Mean	SD.	SEM
Meta-cognitive: comprehension monitoring: confirm that an exam question has been answered	NESE	8	0.63	0.92	0.32
	NC	24	1.75	2.21	0.45
Meta-cognitive: comprehension monitoring: identify examination questions not answered	NESE	8	3.38	3.78	1.34
	NC	24	4.75	2.36	0.48
Meta-cognitive: comprehension monitoring: identify examinations skills not applied	NESE	8	0.13	0.35	0.13
	NC	24	0.42	0.83	0.17
Meta-cognitive: comprehension evaluation against examination questions	NESE	8	5.63	5.40	1.91
	NC	24	2.54	2.25	0.46
Meta-cognitive: comprehension evaluation against experience of examinations	NESE	8	2.00	2.88	1.02
	NC	24	2.50	3.19	0.65
Cognitive: reconstruct meaning from examination question	NESE	8	1.86	2.61	0.99
	NC	24	0.08	0.28	0.06
Cognitive: inferring information from the listening text and exam question paper	NESE	8	3.88	6.14	2.17
	NC	24	2.50	2.41	0.49
Meta-cognitive: prepare using exam paper questions	NESE	8	11.88	11.28	3.99
	NC	24	1.58	2.13	0.43
Meta-cognitive: pay selective attention to exam questions	NESE	8	0.25	0.46	0.16
	NC	24	0.46	0.83	0.17
Meta-cognitive: real-time assessment of output in terms of quantity required(e.g. one or two words)	NESE	8	2.38	4.10	1.45
	NC	24	0.42	0.78	0.16
Meta-cognitive: real-time assessment of output in terms of process required e.g. multiple choice vs. gap fill	NESE	8	6.25	4.27	1.51
	NC	24	2.50	2.41	0.49
Meta-cognitive: real-time assessment of output in terms of intermediate processes e.g. note taking	NESE	8	0.25	0.71	0.25
	NC	24	2.42	2.48	0.51

None of the differences are significant at p<0.05. SD=Standard Deviation; SEM=Std. Error Mean; NESE=Native/Expert speaker of English; NC=Native speaker of Chinese

Whatever the reason, it does raise some quite difficult issues about how data from native/expert users can be used to inform test design. The native/expert users are treating IELTS as a specific kind of task in its own right, independent of the TLU tasks that test writers relate it to. In terms of the strategies and tactics, the test does not have task authenticity even for native speakers/expert users of English, though this may be seen less a critique of the IELTS test than of the use of task authenticity as a criterion for test evaluation. An exam is almost always perceived as an exam rather than as a replication of some other language task.

The aim of the IELTS test is in some sense to evaluate the relationship between the competence of those taking the examination and expert users of English in the TLU. However, how this relationship can be informed by the way expert users of English behave in an exam needs further exploration.

4 Discussion and conclusion

This study has shown that there are relatively few significant differences between the performances of native/expert users of English and potential IELTS candidates with Chinese as a mother tongue and the way in which they carry out the examination. This provides evidence for arguing that the IELTS Listening test does provide an accurate representation of candidates' language abilities.

The study found that there were no significant differences between pre-undergraduate and pre-postgraduate students taking the IELTS test. Again, this supports the validity of the IELTS test. However, this lack of significant differences may have been partially related to the small numbers of participants in this study and it would be worth investigating this issue with a larger number of participants.

The study found that the range of tactics reported by participants taking the IELTS Listening test differed somewhat from the strategies reported in a non-examination context. This raises at least two issues about the IELTS test which may need further investigation: firstly what texts are used in the IELTS test and, secondly, the use of native/expert users of English as one way of assessing the validity of the IELTS task.

4.1 Choice of texts

At the moment, students are exposed to a listening text and a written text comprising the test rubric and questions. The form of the examination requires that candidates make use of the written text to answer questions and it may be worth exploring whether some of the written texts may be replaced by additional listening texts.

For test-taking purposes, one advantage of written questions in a Listening examination is that it reduces reliance on memory. So, for example, in some sections of IELTS Listening, there may be 10 or more items and candidates would need to have a very good memory to answer all 10 items based on a single hearing of the text, particularly for questions where candidates have to fill in the blanks.

If a decision were made to have more spoken questions, this might be addressed by reducing the length of the sections, though this would reduce the text authenticity of what students hear. An alternative is to move to a system where the candidates hear the recording of both text and questions twice. This could be justified in terms of authenticity on the grounds that the second hearing compensates for the lack of contextual information that would be available to listeners outside a test or language learning situation.

However, our preferred solution is to maintain the convention that candidates only listen once to the spoken text but without seeing or hearing the questions. Although such a change would make the ability to take notes a more significant part of the listening construct, it would ensure that the listening was focused more directly on understanding spoken input rather than on combining more or less authentic spoken and more or less inauthentic written text.

Candidates might then listen to, or read, the questions in their current format. Providing a way of staging access to the written text might well be difficult and would also make it harder to separate out listening and reading abilities so we would favour the questions being spoken rather than written. This would involve a major change to the IELTS test and so would need to be trialled on native/expert speakers of English.

In addition, many of the TLU tasks on which the IELTS test is based, e.g. lectures, are now multi-modal events and it may be that test constructors need to consider the inclusion of other modalities such as still or moving visual images. There are clearly logistic issues for a paper-based testing system where replicating exposure to, for example, PowerPoint slides, is difficult but this would be less problematic for a computer-based testing system.

4.2 The use of native/expert users of English in test validation

The second issue relates to the use of native/expert users of English as one way of assessing the validity of the IELTS task. The data collected in this study suggests that native/expert users of English treat IELTS not as derived from the TLU tasks to which it relates but as a specific kind of task in its own right. This makes it difficult to evaluate the relevance of the native/expert user data collected in this study to the validation of the IELTS test.

One line of argument would be as follows: the IELTS examination is designed to judge to what extent candidates can perform as well as expert users of English in non-test contexts. At the moment, we have limited information about how expert users behave in these non-test contexts but we know how expert users behave in test contexts and this might be thought to relate in a systematic way to how they behave in non-test contexts. So, if candidates behave in a similar way to expert users in a test context, this is evidence for saying they will behave in a similar way to expert users in non-test contexts. At several points, this argument relies on plausibility rather than evidence. In particular, the claim that expert users' behaviour in test contexts relates to their behaviour in non-test contexts, though not unreasonable, is largely unsupported. Indeed, it is hard to see how we might collect evidence for such a link in most non-test contexts. How would one collect data about how someone processes and interacts with a credit card call centre, without the possibly distorting effects of setting up an experimental context?

However, in at least one context that is used in IELTS, the lecture, it would be possible to carry out research into how native speaker/expert users of English reach understandings of what is going on. When students attend lectures in higher education institutions, they are not provided with explicit questions to which they must find answers (Badger, Sutherland, White and Haggis 2001). Instead, they annotate handouts or write notes which then contribute to answers to examination question or assignment tasks. It would not be very difficult to research using interviews (Sutherland, Badger and White 2002) or stimulated recall (Hodgson 1997). This research could also link fairly directly to the design of tests of academic listening in IELTS.

References

Anderson, A and Lynch, A (1988) *Listening*, Oxford: Oxford University Press.

Anderson, J R (2000) *Cognitive Psychology and its Implications*, 5th ed, Basingstoke: Macmillan.

Bachman, L F and Palmer, A (1996) *Language Testing in Practice*, Oxford: Oxford University Press.

Badger, R, Sutherland, P, White, G and Haggis, T (2001) Note perfect: an investigation of how students view taking notes in lectures, *System* 29 (3), 405–417.

Bialystok, E (1990) *Communication Strategies: A Psychological Analysis of Second-language Use*, Oxford: Basil Blackwell.

Brown, J and Rodgers, T (2002) *Doing Second Language Research*, Oxford: Oxford University Press.

Buck, G (2001) *Assessing Listening*, Cambridge: Cambridge University Press.

Ellis, R (2003) *Task-based Language Learning and Teaching*, Oxford: Oxford University Press.

Flowerdew, J and Miller, L (2005) *Second Language Listening: theory and practice*, Cambridge: Cambridge University Press.

Gieve, S and Clark, R (2005) The Chinese approach to learning: Cultural trait or situated response? the case of a self-directed learning programme, *System* 33 (2), 261–276.

Glaser, B (1992) *Basics of Grounded Theory: Analysis Emergence vs Forcing*, Mill Valley, CA: Sociology Press.

Glaser, B and Strauss, A (1967) *The Discovery of Grounded Theory: Strategies for Qualitative Research*, New York: Aldine de Gruyter.

Goh, C (1998) How ESL learners with different listening abilities use comprehension strategies and tactics, *Language Teaching Research* 22, 124–147.

Goh, C (2002) Exploring listening comprehension tactics and their interaction patterns, *System* 30 (2), 185–206.

Green, A (1998) *Verbal Protocol Analysis in Language Testing Research: a handbook*, Studies in Language Testing volume 5, Cambridge: UCLES/ Cambridge University Press.

Guariento, W and Morley, J (2001) Text and task authenticity in the EFL classroom, *ELT Journal* 55 (4), 347–353.

Hodgson, V (1997) Lectures and the experience of relevance, in Marton, F, Hounsell, D and Entwistle, N (Eds) *The Experience of Learning: Implications for teaching and studying in Higher Education*, 2nd ed, Edinburgh: Scottish Academic Press, 159–171.

McCarter, S and Ash, J (2003) *IELTS Testbuilder,* Macmillan: Oxford.

Nagle, S and Sanders, S (1986) Comprehension theory and second language pedagogy, *TESOL Quarterly* 20 (1), 9–26.

O'Halloran, K (2004) *Multimodal Discourse Analysis: Systemic-functional perspectives*, London: Continuum.

O'Malley, J and Chamot, A (1990) *Learning Strategies in Second Language Acquisition*, Cambridge: Cambridge University Press.

Oxford, R (1990) *Language Learning Strategies: What every teacher should know*, Boston, Mass: Heinle.

Phakiti, A (2003) A closer look at gender and strategy use in L2 Reading, *Language Learning* 53 (4), 649–702.

Purpura, J (1999) *Learner Strategy Use and Performance on Language Tests: a structural equation modeling approach*, Studies in Language Testing volume 8, Cambridge: Cambridge University Press.

Rost, M (2002) *Teaching and Researching Listening*, Harlow: Longman.

Saville, N and Hawkey, R (2004) The IELTS impact study: investigating washback on teaching materials, in Cheng, L, Watanabe, Y and Curtis, A (Eds) *Washback in Language Testing*, New Jersey: Lawrence Erlbaum Associates, 73–96.

Saville-Troike, M (2006) *Introducing Second Language Acquisition*, Cambridge: Cambridge University Press.

Scollon, S (1999) Not to waste words or students; Confucian and Socratic discourse in the tertiary classroom, in Hinkel, E (Ed.) *Culture in Second Language Teaching and Learning*, Cambridge: Cambridge University Press, 13–27.

Senior, R (2006) *The Experience of Language Teaching*, Cambridge: Cambridge University Press.

Skehan, P (1996) A framework for the implementation of task-based instruction, *Applied Linguistics* 7 (1), 38–62.

Sutherland, P, Badger, R and White, G (2002) How new students take notes at lectures, *Journal for Further and Higher Education* 26 (4), 377–388.

Terry, M (2003) IELTS preparation materials, *ELT Journal* 51 (1), 66–76.

Vanijdee, A (2003) Thai distance English learners and learner autonomy, *Open Learning* 18 (1), 75–84.

White, G (1998) *Listening*, Oxford: Oxford University Press.

Widdowson, H G (2003) *Defining Issues in English Language Teaching*, Oxford Applied Linguistics, Oxford: Oxford University Press.

Yao, X (2000) *An Introduction to Confucianism*, Cambridge: Cambridge University Press.

Appendix 7.1
Non-native speaker protocol

The method I used to deal with the section 1 is to circle the key words while I was reading the introduction. And then I looked through the former questions roughly and judged the speaking speed and difficulty while he was reading the examples. Afterward I just did it according to the question order.

Shall I talk them one by one? You can make a brief analysis if you think there are some difficult questions.
I'm not very sure about the question 4 'day of birth' because I was a little bit absent-minded then.

And when it came to the tenth one, since I habitually do it according to the question order, he talked about the tenth one first during the ninth and tenth part which is different from my habit, therefore I just guessed it.

I've got some but they just flashed by.

Yes, I probably recalled a little and then I guessed them.

Section 2 is different from section 1 because of the faster speed and the gaping filling part. The fast speed is acceptable in the multiple choice part because I just circled the key words, but the gap-filling is relatively hard for it has word limit. Besides I think section 2 usually includes two parts and the second part is faster than the first part.

And question 17, he said 'he give up smoking' and another word which I can not catch, so I just guessed its meaning and filled in a familiar word.

And when it came to the eighteenth and the twentieth, I didn't catch them and do it orderly due to the faster speed. I just filled in a word probably because of my poor memory. So that's probably how I did them

Maybe I have more confidence in the nineteenth and the twentieth but little in the seventeenth and the eighteenth.

Oh, one by one? In the first question [question 11] he said that he did some exercises while he went to take part in a class. Since he felt painstaking if he smoked and he needed to 'touch his toes' when he did that exercise. Then, he couldn't do that. I was a little bit hesitant to choose B or C that is 'smoked' or 'couldn't touch his toes'. I had thought about it after the listening of this question and I finally chose C because his problem was always about the 'smoke'.

And question 12 I got it clearly in which he said 'he travel across London in order to get cigarette'. It mentioned about his fancy for cigarettes.

I also had hesitation in question 13 on whether he gets to sleep or get up early in the morning because the former section has mentioned that he gets up at 3 am. to smoke, so I chose D according to my former memory.

Um, I didn't hear question 14 clearly, 'stopped smoking', I just heard a date-July 1st and I filled in it.

The whole sentence has mentioned about it in question 15, but I was not familiar with that word, so I can just spell it based on my experience.

And question 16, what he said seemed not like the original words and he seemed not to mention about the whole sentence 'work side effect'. As for this question, I filled in the answer for question 16 after I heard the key word—'giving up smoking' of question 17.

Because it mentioned 'habit' during the process of 'cut down smoking and 'give up smoking' of Q 15. Then according to 'work side effect', I thought it should be 'habit'.

Just some words which I cannot spell out. Yes, spelling, especially in gap-filling.

Your attention will be distracted usually by two hesitating answers.

I think section 3 is a little bit simpler in content and slower in speed compared with section 2, maybe we were more familiar with its content, so we catch it easily.

I'm quite sure about the question 21 and 22, in which 21 is 'past three years' and 22 is 'got a job'. I can do questions like gap-filling more fluently because I know something about abbreviation.

When it came to question 23, the first time I heard … the Lorraine said that she would 'turn to exam week', so I wrote 'exam week' firstly.

But later I heard 'turn to Wales', in which I saw the preposition 'to' and so I filled in Wales. I guess it's a place name.

And then for question 24 since he didn't said clearly that he had 'any mistake in his project', I just guessed that it's probably because he was too 'easy to make mistake', so I chose A.

I think the answer for question 25 is B because he has mentioned that .... because I chose 'he has some mistake' as the answer for question I(Q24) and later I heard that there is something wrong with his end, so I chose B.

Besides I often made some written mistakes, like B and D. Since there is time for us to fill in the answer sheet in IELTS and I would look through that question again while I was writing, so it's not a big problem in this part.

Question 26, it seems that there is an 'end' to modify, so I chose C.

Question 27 is just a copy of the original sentences.

I was hesitant to choose the answer for question 28 because both B and D were mentioned and I had to choose a better answer—B.

About this? Since he has mentioned that Frances' project is better than before and 'you can get a PhD' in the last question, therefore I thought if he has mentioned that he did better than other classmates as he kept studying. I think it should be a summary because I didn't get it from the original text.

As for question 27, I just roughly heard a time and I filled it in the blank for there was little time to look through the former part.

In No. 39 .... based on my key word 'In groups ....' and it is 'tasks to .... make .... in groups or something else'. As for this question, I heard its text which is not always about this and he said 'other bullying strategies', so I wrote a very familiar word 'brainstorm'. At the first, I thought he would read the whole sentence directly but actually he divided it into two or three sentences. Afterwards I heard 'and way', since 'and ways in which' was directly mentioned in the latter part 'in which they can be counted', I just filled in 'counted'.

The major problem is the speed and the new words in section 4. Since the majority of the section 4 is gap-filling, the new words became a big obstacle. The only way is to spell them out according to their pronunciation even though they were still unknown.

Besides there are some traps in section 4 because of its requirement. Sometimes it requires 'no more than three words'. What I have met is 'no more than two words', so we have to pay attention to it or else you will fail.

In question 30, Steve has mentioned that not to 'go on his research' firstly because he had to 'turn to his work'. I was a little bit uncertain about answer D until he later mentioned that 'he didn't earn some money to do the things he would like to do'. So I finally chose C: 'He goes to earn some money'.

There is still the problem about spelling in question 21 and 23, because I forgot the spelling of some words and I just spelt them out according to the pronunciations. And next, there are also ambiguous choices in section 3, so I cannot fill it in the black successfully by getting it from the original text and I had to think it over like I did question 28.

Compared with question 29, I did question 25 and 26 sooner for I got the answer in the text and their answers are shorter. Actually I often spend some time on those equivocal answers.

Section 4 is a little bit difficult for its speed is faster than the former three sections. According to my experience of taking IELTS, section 4 usually refers to something about geography, biology and technology, so there will be some unfamiliar words in this section.

I missed question 35 while I was thinking question 34 because I felt puzzled about his former words.

Usually I would give it up usually in that case and turn to make sure the other questions. And the method is circling the key words as the former three questions. I heard 'technics and training' clearly in question 32 but I was not very sure about question 32, so I just wrote 'special economic'. What I heard was like 'ishal economic', and then I cannot catch it because it's a little bit fast.

Later, I circled 'experience, security and lack' in No. 33. According to the three key words I knew that its original text is based on this order, so I listened to it seriously when he mentioned 'insecurity' at the thought of the coming answer. Then I filled in 'a lack of awareness of the part of managers' for question 33

and 'set the management tasks' for question 34. Since he didn't read the whole sentence in No. 34, what I wrote is not the same as the original text, then . . .

probably, I missed No. 35 may be because the former two 'goalposts' are beyond my knowledge so that I could not catch the following part. Maybe it's related to my psychology to some extent. Speed is only one of the reasons but the unfamiliar words matters most. My mood will be influenced if I was not familiar with the word before the blank.

When it came to No. 36, I was slightly puzzled at first until I heard he 'replying to email" I recalled that the former part has mentioned that he 'mentioning the calling', so I wrote 'contact her' according to the text though I would change it a little while I wrote the answer on the answer sheet.

No. 37 I heard the answer directly from the text: 'you cannot expect your staff respect you'. Yes, I just very sure about this question.

I circled the key word for No. 38 which was 'technology'.

Soon in No. 37 I heard 'your staff respect you' and then 'technology' was mentioned later. And I wrote the answer for this question according to its text that is 'company's strategy or practice'.

Appendix 7.2
Native speaker protocol

Right so you want me to describe how I'm working it out ok,

well obviously it's an anagram,

so that one seems quite easy because instantly I'm seeing well I think it's table

and it's not that really separated it's just, they've just put the t in the middle rather than the a and the b.

I suppose because I've instantly seen those letters together and that's the most likely pattern, I've seen them before and instantly thought that

I'm having some trouble with the second one it seems a lot less immediate,

maybe they've scrambled the letters a lot more effectively,

possibly because it's, are there more vowels, yes I think there are, there's three vowels

Oh it's a mouse that's what it is. I just thought,

I started looking at it backwards then it becomes a lot easier

because I suppose the first bit which is O S U

if you look at that reading it backwards it becomes a lot easier,

I can't really describe it better than that.

It is important to blank temptation,

I would say shun because I suppose that just sounds like quite a formal sentence and shun possibly but I think shun would fit best in keeping with the character for that sentence

There is nothing so . . . practical

I suppose because possible doesn't make sense,

plausible makes sense very loosely but not really the correct use,

I think potential is a bit big, and doesn't make any sense

so I'm going to say practical.

Read the following text and choose the best answer, say why you reject the wrong answer,

right, what was the weather like?

I think brillig because, this is just a guess but I'm guessing that, I'm mean because it's not strictly a word obviously but um, I think he is sort of using that as a disambiguation to make that a word forming brilliant describing the weather, that's the best I can do,

I'll go down to six.

What came through the talgy woods,

um, the jabberwock, yes because it says the jabberwock with eyes aflame came wiffling through the talgy wood, yes so the jabberwock, so that's b for that question

Seven, the jabberwock is dangerous; because it says beware the jabberwock, the jaw that bites the claws that catch, which insinuates danger.

[subject listens to instructions for the test]

I thought the instructions were very clear,

I don't know I suppose it's one of those things where you are listening to it but sort of thinking more about what you are actually going to be doing

I mean it was very well phrased and everything and it seemed very clear

the only bit I don't really understand is why you have to transfer your answers at the end, that might be confusing.

So is that then the second I'm going to hear this conversation.

[subject listens to section one of the tapescript

Seemed quite complicated for a, I'm just imagining if I wasn't speaking English.

Yes I suppose it's fairly clear, so they want you to basically write what you hear down, yes that's fine.

It's quite fast;

it's good that obviously because I did not know how to spell Moore

yes it is quite fast.

There is potentially the bit where it says the 13th of 7th

but I mean probably most people would get that.

It's strange it's very different to any other speaking and listening tests I've ever done, because it's very specific about interest payments and banking, which is very strange,

but I mean the questions all seem fine they are all fairly self explanatory to me.

Once again I think it's quite fast, but I suppose if you where, oh I don't know. I mean I think there fine, they're fairly, well they say what you are suppose to do and they say it in simple language so yes.

It is another payment to another restaurant but that's not really the right answer because the thing that he is really worried about,

but I suppose that's just a bit of a tricky question, there's nothing wrong with it, it's just a bit mean, fair enough.

Once again, I suppose there's no ambiguity him saying the interest has gone up and she's saying it has gone down.

so that means C,

but I wouldn't be entirely sure if it's clear whether we are saying what the caller thinks what's happened to the interest or what has actually happened.

The only thing about that was, this might sound a little bit silly, if I had been learning say, if this was in German, you know this thing where they say 020 I don't know if people would understand that because surely they would have learnt zero, I mean maybe not I suppose it would be how colloquial their teaching had been, just a thought anyway

[time for checking answer]

Seems kind of pointless, because you wouldn't, I mean that half minute thing because you wouldn't really, I mean you can't hear it again and you are going to have been concentrating hard on each question so you're not really going to have anything more than just worrying about did I get that one right, you could check maybe having a summary of the conversation that might be more effective but I don't really see the point of that bit.

[subject listens to section 2]

Yes that looks fine simple.

I didn't get thirteen,

I think, I can't be sure that the mentioned all of those things actually

I mean because he did have trouble giving up smoking,

but obviously doing those things

so that didn't seem very clear.

I mean that one's more complicated than the previous one because it's sort of going through each section, bit by bit, it's giving you a whole conversation,

I mean because those two are quite close together at least that's what I thought, I thought those two [QUESTIONS] were answered quite quickly,

but that one I was sort of listening for, because in comprehensions like this you often find like there's the little bit saying, 'did you have trouble giving up smoking'? 'Yes I did have trouble giving up smoking' (time 8.38) and so you look out for that bit,

but I didn't, but that just might be a habit from doing this kind of thing,

but I didn't, well the answer certainly didn't leap out at me, I didn't get 13

I suppose if I was doing the test I would just go right, well he's given up smoking so I'll put that because, it's probably most likely to be correct,

but I didn't actually get it.

Sorry is this [subject looking at question 14–20] is there going to be more of him talking, or do we fill that out from what I've just heard.

[Subject listens to section 2b]

Oh better do all this quickly.

Well I didn't get the first one

it seemed very fast,

he just said a date

and it was like almost the first word he said and I was going, what was that?

But then he kept talking, so that was tricky apart from that as I was saying before he sort of, he says, it's basically paraphrasing the sentence, so that's quite easy,

but apart from that it seemed fairly . . .

apart from just because it's something people can panic about in exams because it's got a little line, I mean I suppose in order to be able to fill it out in an official way you need some indication of where you have to write especially there, if someone wasn't confident about their own writing abilities in English it could make it difficult, could be confusing. It seems a bit needless because all the others are at the end of the sentence apart from that one [question 15] . So it's not like testing really, I mean their ability in the middle of the sentence with only one, so it seems strangely done.

[30 second to check answers]

Once again I don't really see the point because you can't really check it unless you've got a really good memory or you hear it again, because, all you can do it brood on how well you think you did. I don't think that it's a good idea

that the question number is; I think that might be confusing because the question number is put immediately after the rest of the sentence.[in questions 21 to 23] so it seems very confusing. Just then I was looking at it and thinking have they tried to incorporate the question number into the question, it seems a bit strange. But then I realised it's just where they want you to write the answer, so I think it would be quite easy to just [question 21] on the left of the question like it is and all the others rather than on the right, it seems a bit strange and probably a bit confusing I would think.

Yes apart from the number thing it's very simple.

The only think I would say about that one is, it's all fine apart from, there's quite a lot at the beginning where they don't really answer any of the questions

and then it says 28, what the tutor thinks about Francis's chances of getting funding,

and it very quickly says

like well three years ago,

and at that point you have to be going very quickly, and so you would just lose is through no fault of your own,

just because you have to concentrate on that, and by the time that you got back to the tape it had gone onto the next one,

or so it says, I mean for question 30 it says return to his job

Appendix 7.3
Goh's 2002 taxonomy

S	Sub-strategy	Tactic
Cognitive	Inferencing	use contextual clues, use familiar content words, draw on knowledge of the world, apply knowledge about the target language
	Elaboration	draw on world knowledge, draw on knowledge about the target language
	Prediction	anticipate general contexts, anticipate details while listening
	Contextualisation	place input in a social or linguistic context, find related information on hearing a key word, relate one part of text to another
	Translation	find L1 equivalents for selected key words, translate a sequence or utterance
	Fixation	stop to think about the spelling of unfamiliar words, stop to think about the meaning of words, memorise/ repeat the sounds of unfamiliar words, memorise words or phrases for later processing
	Visualisation	imagine scenes events, objects etc being described, mentally display the shape of key words
	Reconstruction	reconstruct meaning from words heard, reconstruct meaning from notes taken
Meta-cognitive	Pre-listening	preview contents, rehearse sounds, encourage oneself to relax
	Selective attention	listen to words in groups, listen for gist, listen for content words, notice how information is structured pay attention to repetitions, notice intonation, listen to specific parts of the input, pay attention to visuals
	Directed attention	concentrate hard, continue to list in spite of difficulty
	Comprehension monitoring	confirm that Comp has taken place, identify words or ideas not understood, check current interpretation with content of the message, check current interpretation with prior knowledge
	Real-time assessment of input	assess the importance of problematic parts that are heard, determine the potential value of subsequent parts of input
	Comprehension evaluation	check interpretation against some external sources, check interpretation using prior knowledge, match interpretation with the context of the message

S=Strategy

I mean if you where just looking at it purely from a I suppose a tactical point of view he not really returning to a job, he's got a job, so that could be confusing.

Might make some think that it was C. but that's all I've got for that section.

Just because this one on each question you are getting more information than you are previously, I suppose the half minute could actually do a bit better because you are not having to rely on so much on your own memory you can think, well da, dum, da, dum, da, dum oh right, sorry that wasn't particularly well phrased.

Just because you get more information in the actual questions and in the answer you would stand a better chance of checking in that half minute

[subject reads questions 31–33]

Once again it's a bit confusing having the number, but not so much there because, having the number in the question it's not as confusing as it was previously there because it's, it seem more incongruous than it did before.

[subject lists to tape script for questions 31–33]

I don't need to say once again that could be confusing because I was starting to think, oh are we going straight on, because he kept talking. But no I suppose maybe if it was more clearly phrased it just the 31 to 33

Actually looking back it did but I suppose you could panic, I don't know that's ambiguous

. . . Once again it's one where the answers aren't necessarily in order

they're a conversation well not a conversation a speech

quite a realistic speech, not the most exiting one.

I think it says not blank or replying to e-mails,

and I thought that might be memoing

but I wasn't sure if that was a word, and obviously if I didn't know English that would be more of a problem.

Also with 35 it says stopping individuals blank to criticism

and for 34 and 38 and 37, I was waiting for the right word because I thought he would say it

but that one he didn't

so I put capacity because [that's the closest word I could think of]

from the gist of what he was saying that's the closest word I could think of

but it seems different to instead of picking out the word from a sentence which is what you do for most of the other questions, well 34, 37, 38, 39 and 40,

you actually have to use your own knowledge to think of the best answer, so it's different and strange in one set of questions, but I suppose that might be the object of it

that's all I've got for that section.

Appendix 7.4
Adapted taxonomy of strategies, sub-strategies and tactics

Cognitive strategies

Fixation (F) (Focusing attention on decoding a small part of a text)

- Spelling (Sp)
- Phonemes or sounds (P)
- Words or parts of input (W)
- Repeat/Memorise sounds (RS)
- Repeat/Memorise words phrases (RW)

Reconstruction answer from input (R) – using key words/phrase to recreate meaning including answering question (staying with literal meaning)

- Reconstruct meaning from word heard (W)
- Reconstruct meaning from phrase heard (P)
- Reconstruct meaning from notes taken (N)
- Reconstruct meaning from examination question (Q)

Inferring answer (I) by using information from the text plus one of the following (going beyond literal information)

- Co-text (C) – something from the listening text
- Familiar word (F)
- World knowledge (W)
- Knowledge of target language (L)
- Visual clues (V)
- Exam question paper (Q)

Contextualisation (C) (Relating new information to a wider familiar context)

- Social or linguistic context (SL)
- Find related information on hearing a key word (K)
- Relate one part of text to another (T)

Translation (T)

- Find L1 equivalents for key words (K)
- Translate a sequence of utterances (U)

Visualisation

- Imagine scenes being described (I)
- Mentally display the shape/sound of key words (K)

Meta-cognitive tactics

Pre-listening preparation (P)

- Preview contents (C)
- Rehearse sounds of potential key words (K)
- Encourage oneself to relax (R)
- Using exam paper questions to prepare (Q)

Selective attention (SA) (Decision to focus on specific aspects of input or identifying from something other than the listening text what to listen for)

- Listen to words in groups or phrases (P)
- Listen for gist or general meaning (G)
- Listen for key words/phrases (K)
- Listen for discourse markers (D)
- Listen for repetition (R)
- Intonation features (I)
- Pay attention to visuals and body language (V)
- Pay attention to exam questions (Q)

Directed attention (DA) (monitoring attention and avoiding distraction)

- Concentrate hard (C)
- Concentrate hard in spite of difficulty (D)
- Identify a failure in concentration (F)

Real-time assessment of input (AI) (determining the value of specific parts of the input)

- Assess the importance of problematic parts that are heard (P)
- Determine the potential value of later parts of the input (L)
- Determine links between elements in listening text and examination questions (Q)
- A problem with the speed/clarity of the input (S) e.g. the speaker speaks too fast or mumbles
- A problem with the amount of input (A) e.g. too much to read or listen to

Real-time assessment of output (AO)

- Quantity required (Q) (e.g. one or two words)
- Process required (P) (e.g. multiple choice vs., gap fill)
- Requirement for intermediate processes (I) (e.g. note taking)

Comprehension monitoring (CM) (Checking interpretation for accuracy while listening)

- Confirm that comprehension has taken place (C)
- Identify words or ideas not understood (N)
- Confirm that an exam question has been answered (QA)
- Identify examination questions not answered (QN)
- Check current interpretation with context of the message (M)
- Check current interpretation with world knowledge (W)
- Identify examinations skills not applied (S)
- Identify partial understanding (P)

Comprehension evaluation (CE) (Checking interpretation for accuracy after listening)

- Against examination questions (Q)
- Against world knowledge (W)
- Against context of message/rest of message (M)
- Against experience of examinations (P)
- Check interpretation using linguistic knowledge (L)

Appendix 7.5
Consent form for the research

Research background and aims

Thank you for agreeing to participate in this research, which focuses on investigation of how people do an IELTS listening test. Research findings will be used in the research project for the British Council.

As a researcher, I have an obligation to those taking part in the project to make sure that nothing negative arises from their involvement. The ethical principles governing my research are set out below.

Code of ethics

What participants tell me will be treated in the strictest confidence. No individual will be identified by name.

Any data which I might use when reporting the findings of this research will be anonymised.

Participation in the project is entirely voluntary.

Participants are under no pressure to answer any question they may feel uneasy about.

Consent

I would very much value your participation in this project and am happy to answer any further questions you may have about it. RMB 150 (£10) will be paid to each participant in this study.

If you would like to take part in the project, please sign below:

Signed_____ Date_____

8 Predictive validity of the IELTS Listening test as an indicator of student coping ability in English-medium undergraduate courses in Spain

Ruth Breeze and Paul Miller
University of Navarra, Spain

Abstract

In view of the enormous expansion of English-taught programmes at European universities over the last 10 years, it is imperative that appropriate tools for predicting student performance should be validated in this context, and apposite cut-off scores established for different subject areas. In this context, listening skills are particularly important, since the traditional form of instruction through lectures tends to predominate. This study investigates the issue of student listening skills from a variety of perspectives. Groups of students enrolled on bilingual programmes in Humanities, Law and Medicine took an IELTS Listening test at the beginning of their first semester. Questionnaires on student listening ability and coping skills and strategies were developed, and these were administered to the students at the end of the semester. Qualitative interviews were also carried out with a representative sample of students in each faculty, and the results of these were analysed in order to provide a richer, more detailed picture of the way that students face the challenge of taking academically demanding courses in English. Finally, statistical tests were performed to explore the relationship between students' numerical IELTS Listening scores and their final course grades, on the one hand, and their IELTS band scores and their self-report data, on the other. Small positive correlations were detected between students' numerical Listening scores and their final grades in the courses that were taught in English. Moderate to large correlations were found between the IELTS Listening band scores and self-report data obtained from the questionnaires. In parallel to this process, a modified Angoff procedure was performed with eight experienced teachers of English for academic purposes. A consensus cut-off score of 23 was obtained, which was consistent with the general practice of requiring a minimum band score of 6 at universities in English-speaking countries. Nonetheless, when the final course grades of students who had obtained 6 or more were compared with those of students who had obtained 5 or less, it was established that Listening scores less than 6 were not predictive of academic failure. The report concludes with a recommendation that the ideal cut-off score for Law, Medicine and Humanities should be Band 6, but that this may not prove feasible under current circumstances. Instead, it is suggested that students with band scores below 6 should be informed that the course will require them to invest more time than for an equivalent course in their native language, and that they should be offered language support.

1 Introduction

In the last 10 years, a large number of universities across continental Europe have introduced bachelor's and master's degree courses taught entirely or partly in English (Wächter and Maiworm 2008). In many of these universities, students are required to take English language tests before admission, or in the first year, either to determine whether or not their level of English is sufficient for them to succeed on their chosen course, or to plan provision for language back-up.

IELTS is commonly used as part of the university admissions criteria in the United Kingdom and Australia, mainly because it focuses on language skills in an academic context, and because it offers a very precise diagnosis of students' competences. However, there is some uncertainty as to whether it would be appropriate to transfer the use of IELTS examinations in general, and the cut-off scores in particular, to the European context, which is substantially different from the UK and Australian situation in various ways. First, it is unclear how the language requirements may be affected by the special situation in universities outside English-speaking countries. On the one hand, the students are not in an 'immersion' situation, and are unlikely to be exposed to a large amount of English outside their studies. This might mean that their initial level of English may actually need to be higher than in English-speaking countries, because of the lack of exposure to the language outside the classroom. On the other hand, in practice the opposite might also sometimes be true, because the teachers responsible for courses taught in English may adapt their style to a non-native audience, providing extra visual back-up, or integrating some language support into the course programme (Kurtán 2003, Panday, Hajer and Beijer 2007).

A second key issue is that of the relative importance of the different language skills, since the European situation may also differ in terms of the actual balance between reading, writing, listening and speaking. Even after the changes brought about as a result of the Bologna Process (EIAE 2010), the European university model tends to give priority to lectures rather than seminars or self-study (students may attend up to 8 hours of lectures every day), with a heavy emphasis on understanding and taking notes, rather than writing essays or participating in seminars. In such a context, students' listening comprehension ability is of paramount importance.

To date, the emerging panorama of bilingual universities in Europe has not been extensively researched in terms of the linguistic demands it makes on students or the competences students should have before admission to bilingual programmes. The aim of the present study was to explore the predictive validity of the IELTS Listening test as an entry test for students enrolled on three different bilingual degree programmes in a large Spanish university, and to propose appropriate cut-off scores for each course. This research was designed to provide greater insights into the appropriate use of IELTS Listening module scores for admission to degree courses taught partly in English within a European context, or for diagnostic purposes in that context.

2 Review of bibliography

Studies on the predictive validity of the IELTS test as an indicator of academic success have been carried out in various contexts, with diverse results. For example, Bellingham (1993), Ferguson and White (1998) and Allwright and Banerjee (1997) found that international students' overall IELTS band scores were positively correlated with academic success at universities in English-speaking countries, while Feast (2002) tracked international students from a variety of disciplines across five semesters and detected significant relations between their initial IELTS score and subsequent academic performance, which decreased over time.

However, other studies (Cotton and Conrow 1998, Fiocco 1992) found no such associations for the overall IELTS band score. After providing a comprehensive overview of previous studies, O'Loughlin (2008:6) concluded that IELTS generally has 'weak to moderate predictive power of academic success', and that IELTS band scores should not be used exclusively when considering the suitability of potential candidates in higher education. In particular, aspects such as the candidate's past academic record, their performance at interview, and their language learning aptitude, should also be taken into account when selecting students (Chalhoub-Deville and Turner 2000, O'Loughlin 2008, Rees 1999).

As far as the different components of the IELTS test are concerned, a considerable amount of attention has focused on the IELTS Reading examination, which was found to have small to moderate correlations with students' academic performance, particularly in the first year of study at an English-medium university. Studies by Hill, Storch, and Lynch (1999), Kerstjens and Nery (2000) and Dooey and Oliver (2002) suggest that the Reading component may correlate significantly with academic performance, measured as the first or second semester grade point average (GPA). Along similar lines, although Cotton and Conrow (1998) found no significant correlation with GPA, they were able to identify a positive association between students' reading and writing scores and staff ratings of academic performance. It has been suggested that the reason why reading is particularly important for international students' success is that the specific reading skills required for success in the examination model the type of reading needed for university study more exactly than the other competences tested in IELTS. It is therefore more easily transferred to actual study situations, thereby giving the student who is proficient in this area a head start over others (Picard 2007). This may hold true for students studying in English-speaking countries. However, in other situations, such as continental Europe where students are not expected to read widely or analytically, reading skills may be much less important.

Research into the predictive validity of the IELTS Listening tests has yielded somewhat inconclusive results (Lee and Greene 2007). In the studies listed above the students' Listening scores were not found to show any significant correlation with their GPA. Nonetheless, some research indicates that there may be a positive relationship between Listening scores and academic achievement, at least in the early years of study in English-medium universities. Elder (1993) found a correlation coefficient of 0.40 between students' IELTS scores and GPA in a small group of postgraduates in education (n=32). More recently, Woodrow (2006) found that Listening scores had a correlation of 0.35 with first semester GPA among international students in education and social work (n=82). In her study, IELTS Speaking scores also had moderate correlations with GPA, whereas Reading and Writing did not. She surmised that speaking and listening competences may be more important in her context because of the type of teaching and the nature of the assessment tasks in education, particularly at postgraduate level. Finally, a study by Huong (2001) brought to light significant correlations between IELTS Reading and Listening scores and GPA among groups of Vietnamese under- and postgraduate students at several Australian universities, across a range of disciplines. In this study, the correlation between IELTS Listening score and first semester GPA was 0.322, while in the second semester it had dropped to 0.309, presumably because the weaker students' listening ability had improved with practice. Although the positive relationship between listening and academic performance held for most of the groups of students in this study, it should be noted that one group actually had a negative correlation between the IELTS Listening score and academic results, a phenomenon which had previously been noted by Cotton and Conrow (1998). In this case, Huong (2001) suggested that the greater degree of social integration among students with good oral skills may actually have been detrimental to their academic performance in certain contexts.

Finally, approaching the question from a rather different angle, a study based on benchmarking and comparison with qualitative data about the tasks that students actually have to perform at a Canadian university suggested that listening was one of the least taxing aspects of the course for many overseas students, who agreed that listening was 'a fairly easy task' (Golder, Reeder and Fleming 2010:20). These authors came to the conclusion that candidates should have a Listening band score of 6.5, not on the grounds that this would reflect sufficient ability to follow lectures, but because it would show that they had good enough listening competence to 'understand complex and fast-paced conversations that take place among team-mates' (Golder et al 2010:2). By implication, the listening skills needed for lectures alone in this context would be represented by a somewhat lower band score.

The general picture is therefore uncertain regarding the relationship between IELTS Listening scores and overall academic achievement. A variety of factors, such as pedagogical approaches, assessment traditions, and the type of discipline being studied, play a part in determining the relative importance of the different skills, and the relationship between students' initial level and their subsequent performance. One major problem in previous studies is that most of them focus on the GPA as the point of comparison. The GPA measures academic success in general, and this is such a complex, multi-dimensional construct that student listening comprehension abilities are unlikely to influence the final outcome particularly heavily. Nonetheless, listening ability must have a considerable impact on the amount of benefit and satisfaction that students receive from attending lectures, and is therefore extremely important on balance.

This brings us to a slightly different issue, namely that of the general relationship between students' IELTS scores and their subjective coping ability in English-medium classes. In general, little information is available concerning what IELTS results may indicate about the more subjective aspects of the international students' experience. Fiocco (1992) reported that students' overall IELTS grades correlated with their self-perceived ability to manage in English in their university courses. More recently, Bayliss and Ingram (2006) studied a group of 28 international students at the University of Melbourne, and found that their self-perception of their language abilities was relatively close to their proficiency measured by IELTS scores. They emphasise the negative effects of low self-confidence among students with lower language levels, which may lead to a downward spiral of lack of integration and failure to meet course demands. However, the type of coping skills needed by international students in UK or Australian universities may differ radically from those required in European universities, where English is used only as a language of instruction, and possibly as a means of communicating with exchange students. It is therefore important to remember that results from English-speaking countries cannot simply be transferred to other situations where many of the parameters are utterly different.

3 Research design

Against the background described above, the primary aim of this project was to investigate the predictive validity of the IELTS Listening test in the context of a Spanish university in which specific content programmes are taught in English, and to determine the minimum Listening module band score that students should be recommended to attain before admission to bilingual degree courses in Law, Medicine and Humanities. At present, students are admitted to these bilingual programmes with a B1 certificate in English (Law), or with no specific qualification in English (Medicine and Humanities), and so this sample is likely to reflect a broad cross-section of the Spanish undergraduate population enrolled on degree courses in these areas. On the other hand, it should be borne in mind that there are several major differences between the three subgroups of students. The general entrance requirements for the degree in Medicine are more demanding than those for the degrees in Law and Humanities, which means that on average these students are likely to have higher academic qualifications. The students on the bilingual programme in Law constitute a subset of the students in the Law faculty who are particularly interested in gaining a qualification in Anglo-American Law or International Business Law to complement their Spanish Law degree, and they are likely to have a greater specific interest in English and the English-speaking world than other Law students. The students in Humanities are highly heterogeneous, but as such may be regarded as representative of students on non-vocational degrees in the Spanish context.

In the present study, the grade awarded in the courses taught entirely or partly in English is correlated with the students' IELTS Listening scores. However, since this grade is also inevitably influenced by factors other than listening ability, self-report data was also obtained from all the students in the study in order to fill in the broader picture of how listening ability may affect individual students in different aspects of their studies.

In summary, in order to obtain a broad view of this issue, we obtained three types of empirical data:

- IELTS Listening scores were obtained for first-year students registered for the bilingual programmes at the start of the course delivered in English. The Listening test was administered to all available students, most of whom continued on the bilingual programme and some of whom later dropped out. The function of the Listening test was diagnostic, and although the respective faculties were informed of the results, invidual students were not. The final grades for the courses taught in English were obtained at the end of the semester, and correlated with the individual students' IELTS Listening scores.

- A modified Angoff procedure was used with groups of teachers involved in teaching on bilingual programmes in order to establish a potential cut-off score.
- Self-report data was gathered from the same students at the end of the course, including their own impressions as to whether their level was sufficient to cope with the classes, and whether they had to resort to other means of understanding the course material. Qualitative, semi-structured interviews were held with students who had obtained different band scores, and were recorded and transcribed.

In short, the research questions addressed in this project were as follows:

- *Research Question 1*: What is the minimum IELTS Listening module band score that should be recommended for admission to bilingual degree courses in Law, Medicine and Humanities at a Spanish university?
- *Research Question 2*: How does student coping ability in English-taught courses map into their IELTS Listening band scores?

4   Listening scores

A full IELTS Listening test was administered to 289 students in January/February 2009. Scores were obtained for 202 students of Medicine, 74 students of Law and 13 Humanities students. The same test was administered to a further 42 Law students at the start of the first semester in September 2009, and the scores were recorded.

4.1   Reliability tests

To ensure that the Listening test was performing adequately in the context of this study, basic descriptive statistics and reliability coefficients were calculated for the test as a whole and for the different sections of the test, for the samples of students tested in January/February 2009. These calculations were subsequently repeated for each of the three student groups (Medicine, Law and Humanities). The full results are set out below in Tables 8.1 to 8.8.

Table 8.1 Full test reliability

N	Min	Max	Mean	SD	Cronbach's alpha
289	5	39	23.7	7.6	0.878

Table 8.2 Full test reliability by section

	N	Min	Max	Mean	SD	Cronbach's alpha
Section 1	289	0	10	6.1	2.2	0.665
Section 2	289	0	10	6.7	2.2	0.667
Section 3	289	0	10	4.8	2.7	0.742
Section 4	289	0	10	6.0	2.3	0.714

Table 8.3 Test reliability by group – Humanities

N	Min	Max	Mean	SD	Cronbach's alpha
13	5	37	21.3	9.5	0.926

Table 8.4 Test reliability (Humanities) by section

	N	Min	Max	Mean	SD	Cronbach's alpha
Section 1	13	1	10	5.7	2.7	0.774
Section 2	13	2	10	7.1	2.2	0.679
Section 3	13	1	10	4.2	2.9	0.789
Section 4	13	1	8	4.4	2.9	0.777

Table 8.5 Test reliability by group – Law

N	Min	Max	Mean	SD	Cronbach's alpha
74	13	36	25.6	6.1	0.806

Table 8.6 Test reliability (Law) by section

	N	Min	Max	Mean	SD	Cronbach's alpha
Section 1	74	1	10	6.6	2.2	0.503
Section 2	74	2	10	7.3	2.0	0.630
Section 3	74	1	10	5.7	2.5	0.70
Section 4	74	0	10	6.0	2.0	0.555

Table 8.7 Test reliability by group – Medicine

N	Min	Max	Mean	SD	Cronbach's alpha
202	6	39	23.1	7.9	0.889

Table 8.8 Test reliability (Medicine) by section

	N	Min	Max	Mean	SD	Cronbach's alpha
Section 1	202	0	10	6.0	2.2	0.698
Section 2	202	0	10	6.5	2.3	0.672
Section 3	202	0	10	4.6	2.7	0.750
Section 4	202	1	10	6.1	2.4	0.685

The Cronbach's alpha values indicate a good to high degree of reliability for this test across the samples studied. Overall, Parts 3 and 4 proved slightly more reliable than Parts 1 and 2, but the Cronbach's alpha values are within acceptable limits for all groups.

5 Angoff procedure

One significant question is that of establishing exactly what the minimum 'passing' score should be on the IELTS Listening test for students in this particular context. For the establishment of test cut-off points a wide range of methods are available (Measurement Research Associates 2004). Here, we used a variation of the Angoff method (1971), the so-called modified Angoff method or the Yes/No method. This procedure provides a systematic technique for eliciting judgements from groups of experts, discussing these judgements and then arriving at a reliable consensus. The modified method has been shown to produce results similar to those of the original procedure and also has the great advantage of being easier to administer and use (Impara and Plake 1997).

In our case eight teachers, all with substantial experience in the teaching of English for academic purposes to students such as those enrolled on the bilingual programmes in Law and Medicine, were asked to envision a student with the minimum linguistic ability to be able to successfully follow a lecture in their speciality in English. With this student in mind, and provided with the full text of the test, the teachers listened to the complete Listening module and decided for each item whether this minimally competent student would answer the question correctly or not. Teachers were asked to give the item a score of one if they considered that this hypothetical student would provide a correct answer and zero if not. The total scores were then summed and this represented the minimum 'passing' score as judged by each teacher. This first round was completed individually with no consultation between teachers. In round two, the procedure was repeated but after each section of the Listening test the teachers were asked to discuss their results in groups and come to a consensus score for each item and thus a 'passing' score for the whole subtest.

6   Questionnaires and interviews

6.1   Questionnaire development and administration

Two questionnaires were developed in order to obtain self-report data from students about their ability to cope with their English-medium courses. First, 10 semi-structured qualitative interviews with students were carried out to gain a rounded view of the English-taught courses for each degree programme, the difficulties that students have, and the strategies they adopt to overcome these. Each interview lasted around 20 minutes, and was recorded and transcribed. Following on from this, the construct of listening in the context of English-medium lectures was analysed (Buck 2001), and the information obtained from students was compared with the taxonomy of listening subskills devised by Richards (1987). A list of subskills was compiled, and a questionnaire was drafted. This was then piloted on a further set of five students for validation purposes: irrelevant items were eliminated, and confusing items were rephrased to ensure proper understanding. At the end of this process, two questionnaires were drawn up as set out below.

Questionnaire 1: The core of the questionnaire, to be used across all participants in the study, consisted of 15 questions focused on self-perception of listening ability, represented in one global question and 14 items dealing with subskills (Section 2). The other two sections of Questionnaire 1 contained further questions designed to provide a detailed picture of English-taught courses on the bilingual degree programmes in question, such as the self-help or survival strategies they had adopted, the degree of participation in lectures through asking and answering questions, and use of supplementary sources of information. All the responses in Section 2, and most of the responses in the other sections, were rated on a Likert scale from 1 to 5, although there were also four open-ended questions and three yes/no questions. This questionnaire was used with all the students in the Humanities course (n=13), and with a sample of students from each available IELTS Listening band score in Law and Medicine. The full questionnaire is provided in Appendix 8.2.

Questionnaire 2: The second questionnaire consisted of Section 2 of Questionnaire 1 (one global question and 14 questions designed to measure listening subskills, rated on a Likert scale from 1 to 5). Questionnaire 2 was used with all the participants in Law and Medicine. The full questionnaire is provided in Appendix 8.3.

6.2   Interview administration

Questionnaire 1 was used as a basis for semi-structured qualitative interviews with all available students on the obligatory English-taught first year subject of the degree in Humanities (13 students). Questionnaire 1 was also applied as the basis for semi-structured qualitative interviews with 11 Law students and six Medicine students in order to obtain descriptors of student self-evaluation at different band scores. These interviews were recorded and transcribed. The transcripts were then analysed by the principal researchers, and relevant information was extracted in order to complete the table of band score descriptors for each faculty. Where the interview data had been recorded in Spanish, the relevant parts of the transcripts were translated into English by the researchers.

7 Results

In this section, the results for the three bilingual degree programmes are reported separately.

7.1 Humanities

An IELTS Listening test was administered in February, at the beginning of the course *History of the English Language* (first year of degree in Humanities). The Listening test data was processed and band scores were calculated.

Towards the end of the course in May, interviews were carried out using questionnaire 1 (the full questionnaire) with all 13 students in order to obtain a thick description of students' coping skills and obtain students' responses to the open-ended questions in order to map them onto the IELTS band scores. The data from section 2 of questionnaire 1 (which is identical to questionnaire 2) was extracted for use in the statistical tests.

Basic statistical tests (scattergrams) were run to check for correlations between the IELTS Listening test raw scores and band scores, on the one hand, and the students' global self-assessment, the mean of the analytical self-assessment of Listening subskills, and the students' final course grade. Since the sample was very small (n=13), both Spearman's rank correlation coefficient and Pearson's correlation coefficient were used, as is standard practice in such cases. The results are displayed in Table 8.9 and in Figures 8.1 to 8.3 below.

Table 8.9 Correlations for Humanities sample

	Spearman's rho	Pearson's correlation coefficient
Correlation IELTS numerical score and final course grade	0.408	0.344
Correlation IELTS band score and global self-assessment	0.923**	0.914**
Correlation IELTS band score and analytical self-assessment	0.984**	0.921**

** *Correlation significant at 0.01 level.*

Figure 8.1 Scatterplot showing moderate correlations between IELTS Listening score and final course grade: Humanities

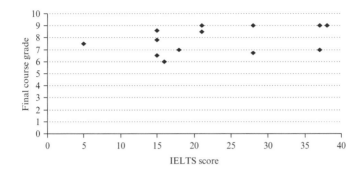

Figure 8.2 Graph showing correlations between IELTS Listening band score and students' global self-assessment: Humanities (numbers refer to bubble size)

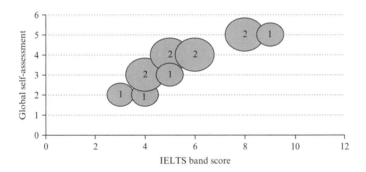

Figure 8.3 Scatterplot showing correlations between IELTS Listening band score and students' analytical self-assessment: Humanities

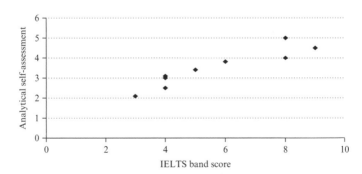

The IELTS scores show positive correlations with the final course grade, despite the fact that this is probably heavily influenced by each student's study skills and general academic ability. However, the correlations between IELTS band scores/numerical scores and their global and analytical self-assessments are very high (p<0.01) (Cohen 1988). This is a striking result, although it should be remembered that the sample of students in the Humanities sample was very small (n=13).

We matched the interview data with the IELTS band scores in order to obtain richer descriptions of what the different band scores appear to mean for this student population. Examples can be seen in Table 8.10 below.

Table 8.10 Band score descriptors for Humanities sample

IELTS Listening score	Descriptors obtained from interview transcripts
Band 8	I have no problems understanding the lecturer and taking notes.
Band 6	The course in English means more effort than the equivalent course in Spanish, but I can manage well if I consult outside sources to check my understanding of complex topics.
Band 5	I have to pay more attention than I would in Spanish. You have to concentrate more. I sometimes need to ask my fellow students if I don't understand a word or phrase.
	I need to use the dictionary frequently.
	Most of the time I can follow what the teacher says, but sometimes I lose the thread of what he is explaining. I often have to check whether my lecture notes are right by reading more.
Band 4	I can understand the lectures if I do extra reading before and after the class.
	I do not have a large enough vocabulary to follow the lectures easily.
	I can usually get the main points, but it is hard to concentrate for 50 minutes. I feel I miss the details.
	I need to look for extra information at home. I generally also have to put my notes together with a friend.
Band 3	The teacher speaks too fast for me to take notes effectively. It is particularly hard for me to concentrate over long periods of time.
	Because I don't understand everything, it is harder for me to integrate the new information given in the lecture with what I already know about the subject.
	It is very difficult for me to take notes because the lecture in English seems to go so fast. I have to ask my friends for their notes.
	Since I don't know all the words, I often miss important points in the lecture.

7.2   Law

The IELTS Listening test was administered to a sample of 74 students enrolled on the Anglo-American Law Programme and the International Business Law Programme (taught in English as part of the Spanish Law degree) in January/February 2009. The same test was administered to 42 new students enrolled on the Anglo-American Law Programme in September 2009. The Listening test data was processed and band scores were calculated. Questionnaire 2 was administered to both sets of students at the end of their respective English-medium courses (Criminal Law and Contract Law in May 2009, Introduction to Anglo-American Law in November 2009). After elimination of students who dropped out of the programme or who failed to complete the questionnaire, the total sample was reduced to 83 students (Table 8.11).

Table 8.11 Descriptive statistics for Law sample

	N	Min	Max	Mean	SD
IELTS score	83	4	39	26.08	7.310
Band score	83	3	9	6.097	6.096
Final course grade	83	3	9.5	6.7	1.738
Global self-assessment	83	2	5	3.904	0.906
Analytical self-assessment	83	2.14	5	3.661	0.654

As the Shapiro-Wilks test established that the data did not have normal distribution, Spearman's rho for non-parametric data was used to obtain the correlation coefficients between the different data sets (Table 8.12, Figures 8.4

Table 8.12 Correlations for Law sample (Spearman's rho)

	Spearman's rho
Correlation IELTS numerical score and final course grade	0.283**
Correlation IELTS band score and global self-assessment	0.453**
Correlation IELTS band score and analytical self-report data	0.546**

** *Correlation significant at 0.01 level.*

Figure 8.4 Scatterplot showing small correlations between IELTS Listening score and final course grade: Law

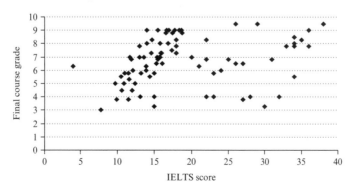

Figure 8.5 Graph showing moderate correlations between IELTS Listening band score and students' global self-assessment: Law (numbers refer to bubble size)

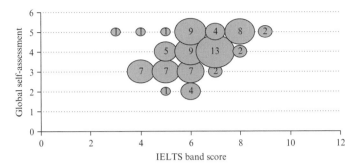

Figure 8.6 Scatterplot showing high correlations between IELTS Listening band score and students' analytical self-assessment: Law

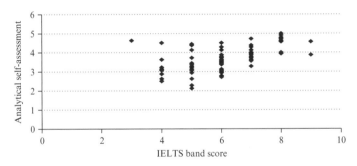

to 8.6). The IELTS scores for the Law students yielded positive correlations with the final course grade (rho of 0.283, p<0.01) that bordered on moderate, if Cohen's explanation of levels of significance for correlations is applied (Cohen 1988). Although course grades are heavily influenced by each student's study skills and general academic ability, the correlation detected here appears to indicate that listening comprehension ability does account for a small part of the differences in student performance. Moreover, the correlations between IELTS Listening band scores and global self-assessments are moderate, bordering on large, and the correlations between the IELTS Listening band scores and analytical self-report data are large (rho of 0.546, p<0.01).

On the other hand, if we take a cut-off score of 6 on the IELTS Listening test and compare the outcomes in terms of final course grade for students obtaining 6 or more, on the one hand, and 5 or less, on the other, the results appear to be less conclusive. In this sample, 47 students with a score of 6 or more passed the course, while 10 failed; of those with a score of 5 or less, 22 passed the course and four failed. Expressed in other words, the distribution

Table 8.13 Band score descriptors for Law sample

IELTS Listening score	Descriptors obtained from interview transcripts
Band 9	I have no problem at all understanding the lectures.
Band 8	In my case, I don't feel that I need help with the language, but I do think that the course in English requires more work than an equivalent course in Spanish.
Band 7	I understand most of what the lecturer says, but I really find it useful to complement the lectures and course notes with information from other sources. The schedule is very intensive, and although I understand most things, it is difficult to concentrate for such a long time without losing the thread of a complex argument.
Band 6	A law course taught in English definitely means more work than a law course taught in Spanish. We would benefit from more language support. It was essential for me to read through the material before the class.
	In my opinion, the lecturers speak too fast and try to cover too much material in one hour.
	They really don't try to adapt to a 'foreign' audience. It is sometimes hard for us even to understand what the lecture is really about. We get lost. The case study method is also quite strange for us. We are given the case to read before the class, but even if we read it, we don't really understand it, because we don't know what we are supposed to notice. In Spain, we learn the theory, and then we see a case and try to apply the theory. That is easier for me. Although we have the textbook in the exam, it doesn't help much. We need help with the language, but also with the contents.
	For me, the case-based method is frustrating. We want to know what the law is. There is too much material, and it is very difficult to concentrate on English for such a long time. Twenty minutes would be long enough for us. Since I don't understand everything, I feel insecure, especially since the legal system is so different and the way of explaining is quite strange for us.
Band 5	I think we have a lot of difficulties with the vocabulary. Sometimes we are not even sure what the lecturer is talking about, and we don't feel confident enough to ask questions.
	We would definitely benefit from more language support. The course in English was very hard work. In the end, an American student helped us by explaining the main ideas and words to us. It was particularly difficult to understand because the concepts are often different, for example in contract law, and you don't feel really sure that you have understood properly.
Band 4	I don't understand everything the lecturer says. I can manage in this course if I read the book and notes carefully and check all the things I don't understand using a dictionary. In law classes in general, I have to make my own 'picture' of what the teacher is saying. That is hard enough in my own language, but in English it is often quite confusing.

of pass/fail grades among students with IELTS scores over 6 and IELTS scores under 5 was close to the expected random distribution. The statistical analysis yielded a chi-square value of 0.055 (p=0.9966), which is not statistically significant.

7.3 Medicine

The IELTS Listening test was administered to a sample of 202 students enrolled on the Bilingual Degree in Medicine. After elimination of students who dropped out of the programme or who failed to complete the questionnaire, the total sample was reduced to 63 students (Table 8.14). Since the policy of the Medical School is not to teach entire courses in English, but to deliver 20–30% of the classes on specific compulsory courses in English, the course grade used as a reference point is an average of the marks obtained by these students in the two major courses with English-taught components given during the second semester of 2008–09 (Genetics and Immunology).

Table 8.14 Descriptive statistics for Medicine sample

	N	Min	Max	Mean	SD
IELTS score	63	12.00	38.00	27.159	6.533
IELTS band score	63	4.00	9.00	6.222	1.197
Final exam grade	63	3.30	9.50	6.706	1.506
Global self-assessment	63	2.00	5.00	4.032	.879
Analytical self-assessment	63	3.00	5.00	3.730	.515

Since the Shapiro-Wilks test showed non-normal distribution, Spearman's rho was used as above to obtain the correlation coefficients between the different data sets (Table 8.15; Figures 8.7 to 8.9). A small correlation was apparent between students' IELTS scores and final course grades (p<0.05), while there were moderate correlations between IELTS band scores and both types of self-assessment data.

Table 8.15 Correlations for Medicine sample (Spearman's rho)

	Spearman's rho
Correlation IELTS numerical score and final course grade	0.257*
Correlation IELTS band score and global self-assessment	0.346**
Correlation IELTS band score and analytical self-assessment	0.330**

*   *Correlation significant at 0.05 level*
** *Correlation significant at 0.01 level*

Figure 8.7 Scatterplot showing small correlations between IELTS Listening score and final course grade: Medicine

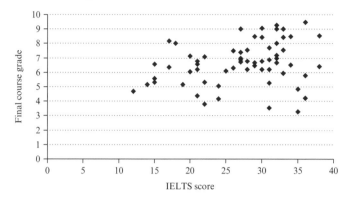

Figure 8.8 Graph showing moderate correlations between IELTS Listening band score and students' global self-assessment: Medicine (numbers refer to bubble size)

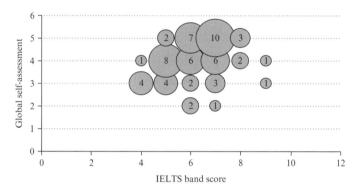

Figure 8.9 Scatterplot showing high correlations between IELTS Listening band score and students' analytical self-assessment: Medicine

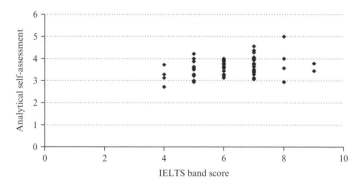

Table 8.16 Band score descriptors for Medicine sample

IELTS Listening score	Descriptors obtained from interview transcripts
Band 9	It is easy to understand the classes. For me, having a class in English is the same as having a class in Spanish.
Band 8	I have no problem following the lectures.
Band 7	It is not difficult to understand the lectures, but it may sometimes be hard to take notes when the lecturer speaks very fast. I sometimes need to spend time looking up new vocabulary.
Band 6	In general, it is easy for me to follow the lectures. I still have some difficulty integrating new information from the lecture with what I already know, and understanding what is important from the lectures. Some of the specialised vocabulary is new for me. I have no real problems understanding, but some of the scientific words are difficult.
Band 5	I can understand the lectures when the teacher speaks clearly and has a good accent. Sometimes the teachers speak too fast for me. I need to learn important words related to the topic.
Band 4	I find it hard to understand if the teacher does not pronounce the words clearly. I don't understand when the teacher speaks fast. It is definitely more work to take a class that is taught in English. I understand the subject better when I study the PowerPoint slides and textbooks after the class.

As far as the cut-off scores of 23 (Band 6) obtained by Angoff methodology were concerned, in the present study, the failure rate among students in Humanities, who had the lowest band scores, was 0%, the failure rate in Law was 17.5% among students with a band score of 6 or more, and 15.4% among students with 5 or less; and the failure rate in Medicine was 11.1% among students with scores of 6 or more, and 17% among students with scores of 5 or less.

The failure rate among the sample of students tested in Humanities, who had the lowest band scores (mean 5.5), was 0%. The failure rate in the Law sample was actually higher (17.5%) among students with a band score of 6 or higher, than among students with 5 or less (15.4%), although this difference was found not to be statistically significant when tested using Chi square. On the other hand, the failure rate in the sample from Medicine was 11.1% among students with scores of 6 or more, and 16.6% among students with scores of 5 or less, though this also lacked statistical significance.

7.4   Angoff results

Descriptive statistics for the individual Round 1 scores are shown in Table 8.17. As can be seen, a degree of variation existed between the different teachers. However, in Round 2 (Table 8.18) the discrepancies between the

Table 8.17 Individual Round 1 Angoff scores

Minimum score	Maximum score	Mean	SD
14	29	22	4.8

Table 8.18 Final (Round 2) group consensus scores

Minimum score	Maximum score	Mean	SD
22	24	23	1.0

three consensus group scores were much smaller with a real consensus being reached.

In conclusion, these results indicate that for these teachers, the cut-off score should be 23 points out of 40. This would correspond to Band 6 and would mean that of the 159 students who completed this study, 51 would have to be considered as not having a sufficient level of English language proficiency to successfully follow their lectures in English. The implications of the corresponding loss of one third of the students on the bilingual programme would have to be studied carefully before such a decision could be taken.

8 Discussion

The findings of the present study add important new information to the general picture concerning IELTS results and academic success, since they suggest that the relationship between students' IELTS Listening scores and academic performance in specific contexts may be more significant than has sometimes been supposed. This may be particularly relevant in the emerging panorama of English-taught programmes in non-English-speaking countries where lectures are the principal method of instruction. Moreover, the relationship found here between IELTS Listening scores and student self-assessments shows that IELTS Listening scores offer a reliable prediction of how well students will feel that they can manage on courses that are taught in English.

Previous research into the predictive validity of the IELTS Listening test for academic performance has yielded contradictory and somewhat inconclusive results. The consensus view appears to be that listening comprehension ability is just one variable among many that contribute to academic performance. The two recent exceptions to this general pattern are a study by Woodrow (2006), who found correlations between all the IELTS subcomponents and the first semester GPA of students, including a correlation of 0.35 between IELTS Listening scores and first semester GPA, and a study by Huong, in which there was a correlation of 0.32 between IELTS

Listening scores and first semester GPA. In the present study, the students' IELTS Listening scores were found to have small to moderate correlations (Spearman's rho of 0.408 in Humanities, 0.283 in Law and 0.257 in Medicine) with the final grades they were awarded in courses taught in English. In Law and Humanities, where the courses in question were given entirely in English, the correlation between IELTS Listening score and the final grade was significant at p<0.01, while in Medicine, where courses were taught only partly in English, the correlation was significant at p<0.05.

Our study also brought to light a significant relationship between IELTS band scores and students' perceptions of their own listening abilities. The correlation between IELTS band scores and global self-evaluation of listening abilities in English-medium courses was strong in Humanities courses (Spearman's rho of 0.947), and moderate in Law (0.453) and Medicine (0.346) (p<0.01 in all cases). Students' IELTS band scores also correlated significantly with their analytical self-evaluation scores (0.923 in Humanities and 0.546 in Law), and correlated moderately in Medicine (0.330) (p<0.01 in all cases). The students' own assessment of their listening ability and capacity to cope with lectures delivered in English thus tended to correlate strongly with their listening ability as assessed by their IELTS scores. This is the case despite the fact that the IELTS Listening test did not serve a high-stakes purpose, since the students had already been admitted to the university and met the minimum requirements for the bilingual programme, and some students may have underperformed. Moreover, since the students had not been informed of their IELTS scores, their self-perception cannot have been coloured by knowledge of their test results.

The fact that our results are not consistent with those of authors working in English-medium universities (Dooey 1999), which appeared to indicate that correlations between IELTS Listening scores and course grades were low or negligible, requires careful analysis. Several factors may account for these discrepancies. First, in the context of the present study, listening competence is arguably much more central to academic achievement than in English-speaking countries. In Spain, undergraduate courses are usually taught by formal lectures, with little opportunity for student participation. Examinations are based on the content of the lectures, and although further reading may be encouraged, students are generally not expected to read extensively. Moreover, examinations generally focus on short answers or problem-solving activities, so that there is less need for good writing skills and mastery of academic genres than there would be in a US, UK or Australian university where it is customary for students to write essays and term papers.

Secondly, the studies carried out at universities in English-speaking countries (Cotton and Conrow 1998, Dooey and Oliver 2002, Feast 2002) used the students' GPA as the measure of academic performance. The GPA is inevitably a composite grade which is influenced by many different aspects of the students' performance, including coursework and, in some cases, mathematical and other abilities, and it is therefore not surprising that GPA should not be strongly related to English listening ability. In any case, such a measure would not be relevant in our context, since only a few courses were being taught in English, and English proficiency would therefore be unlikely to affect students' overall grade to any significant extent. Nonetheless, the design of our study presents certain advantages in terms of clarity and simplicity. In the present case, by taking as a reference point the grades obtained in specific courses taught entirely (Humanities, Law) or partly (Medicine) in English, we obtained a clearer picture of the way that English listening proficiency might directly affect particular academic results.

Thirdly, our study included students with a wide range of IELTS scores, including many of Bands 4 and 5. Most of the studies conducted in the universities of English-speaking countries focus on groups of students who have scored at least 6 overall on the IELTS test, since this is the usual minimum requirement for university admission (Feast 2002). One exception to this, a study carried out in New Zealand across a sample of students with a wide range of IELTS scores including some below Band 5 (Bellingham 1993), reported a moderate association between language proficiency as measured by IELTS scores and academic success. In the present case, there 29% of Law and Medicine students and 62% of Humanities students had band scores of 5 or below. We may surmise that the wider range of scores (Bands 3 to 9) obtained by the students in our study may account for the higher correlations found between IELTS Listening scores and course grade. In most of the previous studies reviewed here, the nature of the sample meant that all students had obtained Band 6 or higher. In statistical terms, this would give rise to the phenomenon of range restriction, which would render it less likely that any strong correlations could be detected.

Finally, in addition to course grades, this study paid considerable attention to students' perception of their own coping abilities. IELTS band score correlated strongly with students' global self-assessment on all three bilingual programmes, and with their analytical self-assessment in Humanities and Law. This is an important consideration, since it provides an insight into the students' own feelings of satisfaction and achievement with the courses that are taught in English. A student who responds with less than 3 on a scale from 3 to 5, when asked how easy it is for them to understand lectures in English, is evidently experiencing a certain degree of real difficulty in understanding the course. Interview data revealed that many of the students who answered with 3 or less had to spend a considerable amount of time researching the subject outside the classroom, re-reading course notes obtained from other students, or working in study groups with students whose English level was better, in order to acquire the knowledge that they would usually have obtained from the lectures. It would be useful for universities to bear this in mind when setting the entry requirements for English-taught courses. This does not necessarily mean that universities should set a cut-off band of 6 on the IELTS Listening component for entry to the bilingual programmes, a move which would be unpopular with university admissions departments. Rather, it could be suggested that students with a lower IELTS score should be informed as to the amount of extra work they are likely to need to do in order to pass the course. If large numbers of students on a particular English-taught course fall into Band 5 or below, extra language support should be provided, if possible with an ESP focus, so that students can receive proper training in subject-related vocabulary, listening strategies and note-taking skills.

Regarding the cut-off score, the Angoff procedure carried out with staff members involved in the bilingual programmes produced a result that is completely consistent with university policies worldwide (Feast 2002, Woodrow 2006). The professionals who carried out the Angoff procedure item by item reached a raw score of 23 (beginning of Band 6) as the subjective cut-off point at which a student would probably be able to cope with courses taught in English. The current practice of requiring Band 6 or higher for study in an English-medium university has been shaped by research on the one hand, and market pressures on the other. However, there is a general consensus in the bibliography that 'Band 6 seems to represent some kind of cross-over line' (Ferguson and White 1998:34), since it appears to be a watershed below which the failure rates tend to escalate. The fact that the group of university teachers who participated in the Angoff study independently decided on a cut-off score of 23 on the Listening test would therefore seem to vindicate Angoff methodology as a procedure for determining cut-off scores for specific contexts.

Nonetheless, it should be emphasised that in the present study, students with Bands 6 or higher were not consistently more likely to pass the final examination than those with 5 or less. In fact, when the sample was divided at the cut-off point of 23, i.e. Band 6 or higher on the one hand, and Band 5 or lower on the other, the picture that emerged concerning pass and fail rates was unclear. The failure rate among the sample of students tested in Humanities, who had the lowest band scores (mean 5.5), was 0%, which would tend to suggest that the teacher responsible for the course makes adjustments for this type of student group. The situation in Law and Medicine, both high-profile degree courses with large student numbers, was rather different. The failure rate in the Law sample was actually higher (17.5%) among students with a band score of 6 or higher, than among students with 5 or less (15.4%), although this difference was found not to be statistically significant when tested using Chi square. On the other hand, the failure rate in the sample from Medicine was lower (11.1%) among students with scores of 6 or more, compared with 16.6% among students with scores of 5 or less, though this difference also lacked statistical significance. It is interesting to compare these findings with current practices in English-speaking countries, where IELTS scores of 7 or more are often required for degrees that are considered to be linguistically challenging, such as Law, while lower scores are needed for science-related courses (Hirsch 2007). What is clear here is that it is not easy to transfer results or recommendations from one context to another. The parameters in an English-taught course in a European university are not the same as those in Britain or Australia. Law students in Spain, even those studying areas of American law in English, are not likely to have to compete against native speakers in debates and class discussions, or in long written examinations based on the analysis of cases. The level of a particular course, and the demands placed on students, are inevitably conditioned by a multitude of factors which include the students' general level of English, as well as their educational background and culture.

On the basis of this evidence, we can conclude that although IELTS raw scores and band scores are correlated with academic performance in particular courses, this relationship does not determine success or failure in specific contexts. It should be stressed that some students who had obtained low IELTS scores managed to obtain good grades in the final exam, while other students with high scores failed the final exam. As in previous research, it is evident that aspects other than listening ability may condition students' success or failure on a particular course.

It could therefore be stated that IELTS band scores provide a reasonable indication of the way particular students will react to the experience of lectures delivered in English. Students with low Listening scores are likely to experience more anxiety and frustration than students with higher Listening scores. This may be reflected in a need to make a greater effort, to use more outside sources, and to bring a wider range of study skills to bear. English-medium courses will almost certainly prove to be more time-consuming and require more independent work than courses delivered in the students' native language, but this effect is likely to be less marked for students who have better listening skills in English from the outset.

In conclusion, a score of 6 or more on IELTS Listening may be proposed as desirable at admission, because this is the level at which students feel sufficiently comfortable in courses delivered in English and derive maximum benefit from such programmes. Students with lower IELTS Listening scores should be encouraged to bear in mind the following points before enrolling on bilingual degree programmes: they are likely to experience some degree of frustration in the lectures because they do not understand everything; they will probably need to complement their lecture notes with extra reading and research; and above all, the course taught in English will almost certainly mean more work than an equivalent course taught in their native language.

References

Allwright, J and Banerjee, J (1997) *Investigating the Accuracy of Admissions Criteria: A Case Study in a British University*, Lancaster: Centre for Research in Language Education, Lancaster University.

Angoff, WH (1971) Scales, norms and equivalent scores, in Thorndike R L (Ed.) *Educational Measurement*, American Council on Education, Washington DC, 508–600.

Bayliss, A and Ingram, D (2006) IELTS as a predictor of academic language performance, *Australian National Education Conference*, http://www.idp.com/aiec, accessed 15 February 2010.

Bellingham, L (1993) The relationship of language proficiency to academic success for international students, *New Zealand Journal of Educational Studies* 30 (2), 229–232.

Buck, G (2001) *Assessing Listening*, Cambridge: Cambridge University Press.

Chalhoub-Deville, M and Turner, C (2000) What to look for in ESL admission tests: Cambridge certificate exams, IELTS and TOEFL, *System* 28, 523–539.

Cohen, J (1988) *Statistical Power Analysis for the Behavioral Sciences*, Mahwah NJ: Lawrence Erlbaum.

Cotton, F and Conrow, F (1998) An investigation of the predictive validity of IELTS amongst a sample of international students studying at the University of Tasmania, in Tulloh, R (Ed.) *IELTS Research Reports, Volume 1*, Canberra: ELICOS/IELTS Australia Pty Limited 72–115.

Dooey, P (1999) An investigation into the predictive validity of the IELTS test as an indicator of future academic success, in Martin, K, Stanley, N and Davison, N (Eds) *Teaching in the Disciplines/Learning in Context, Proceedings of the 8th Annual Teaching Learning Forum*, The University of Western Australia, Perth, 114–118.

Dooey, P and Oliver, R (2002) An investigation into the predictive validity of the IELTS test as an indicator of future academic success, *Prospect* 17, 36–52.

EAIE (European Association for International Education) 'The Bologna Process', http://www.aic.lv/ace/ace_disk/Bologna/index.htm: accessed 15 February 2010.

Elder, C (1993) Language proficiency as a predictor of performance in teacher education, *Melbourne Papers in Language Testing* 2, 68–85.

Feast, V (2002) The impact of IELTS scores on performance at university, *International Education Journal* 3 (4), 70–85.

Ferguson, G and White, E (1998) A small-scale study of predictive validity, *Melbourne Papers in Language Testing* 7, 15–63.

Fiocco, M (1992) *English proficiency levels of students from a non-English speaking background: A study of IELTS as an indicator of tertiary success*, unpublished research report, Curtin University, Perth.

Golder, K, Reeder, K and Fleming, S (2010) Determination of appropriate IELTS band score for admission into a program at a Canadian post-secondary polytechnic institution, in Osborne, J (Ed.) *IELTS Research Reports, Volume 10*, Canberra: IELTS Australia Pty Ltd and London: British Council, 69–93.

Hill, K, Storch, N and Lynch, B (1999) *English Language Testing System Research Reports 1999, Volume 2*, 52–63.

Hirsch, D (2007) English language, academic support and academic outcomes: A discussion paper, *University of Sydney Papers in TESOL* 2 (2), 193–211.

Huong, T T T (2001) The predictive validity of the International English Language Testing System (IELTS) Test, *Post-Script* 2 (1), 66–96.

Impara, J C and Plake, B S (1997) Standard setting: An alternative approach, *Journal of Educational Measurement* 34, 353–366.

Kerstjens, M and Nery, C (2000) Predictive validity in the IELTS test, in *IELTS Research Reports, Volume 3*, Canberra: IELTS Australia Pty Limited, 85–108.

Kurtán, Z (2003) Teacher training for English-medium instruction, in van Leeuwen, C and Wilkinson, R (Eds) *Multilingual Approaches in University Education*, Maastricht: University of Maastricht, 145–161.

Lee, Y J and Greene, J (2007) The predictive validity of an ESL placement test: a mixed methods approach, *Journal of Mixed Methods Research* 1, 366–389.

Measurement Research Associates (2004) *Criterion Referenced Performance Standard Setting*, http://www.measurementresearch.com/media/standards.pdf accessed 15 February 2010.

O'Loughlin, K (2008) The use of IELTS for university selection in Australia: A case study, in Osborne, J (Ed.) *IELTS Research Reports, Volume 8*, Canberra: IELTS Australia Pty Ltd, 145–241.

Panday, R G, Hajer, M and Beijer, J (2007) Challenges in integrating academic and professional language competences in the curriculum in higher education, in Wilkinson, R and Zegers, V (Eds) *Researching Content and Language Integration in Higher Education*, Maastricht: University of Maastricht, 99–107.

Picard, M (2007) English entrance requirements and language support for international postgraduate students, in *Enhancing Higher Education: Proceedings of 30th HERDSA Conference*, Higher Education Research and Development Society of Australasia, Milperra, http://www.herdsa.org.au/wp-content/uploads/conference/2007/papers/p160.pdf, accessed 15 February 2010.

Rees, J (1999) Counting the cost of international assessment: why universities may need to get a second opinion, *Assessment and Evaluation in Higher Education* 24 (4), 427–438.

Richards, J C (1987) Listening comprehension: approach, design, procedure, in Long, M H and Richards, J C (Eds) *Methodology in TESOL: A Book of Readings*, Boston: Heinle and Heinle, 161–176.

Wächter, B and Maiworm, F (2008) *English- taught Programmes in European Higher Education: The Picture in 2007*, Bonn: Lemmens.

Woodrow, L (2006) Academic success of international postgraduate education students and the role of English proficiency, *University of Sydney Papers in TESOL* 1, 51–70.

Appendix 8.1
Calendar 2009–1010

2009

January	February	March	April	May	June
Listening tests administered	Listening tests administered	Interviews held and questionnaires developed	Questionnaires piloted. Angoff procedure (Humanities)	Questionnaires administered, interviews carried out	Listening test data processed and compared with questionnaire data

July	August	September	October	November	December
Angoff procedure (Law and Medicine)	Angoff procedure (Law and Medicine)	Further listening tests administered	Further questionnaires administered	Processing data and writing final report	Processing data and writing final report

2010

January	February
Processing data and writing final report	Submission of final report

Appendix 8.2
Questionnaire 1

Explanatory note

The questionnaire is intended to be administered through a structured interview which is recorded, and the transcript analysed. The questionnaire is in English, but the interview may be conducted in Spanish. The questionnaire is divided into three sections:

- Section 1: How do you see lectures and how do they fit in with the way you study your subjects?
- Section 2: Understanding lectures in English
- Section 3: Strategies and suggestions

Of these sections, 1 and 3 are designed to elicit the broader picture concerning English-taught courses in the Spanish university context. Section 2 is specifically useful for the Project, since it consists of one "global" question (A) and fourteen questions relating to listening subskills (C–P). It is proposed that the answers to question A and the mean of C–P should be added together to make a score out of 10 that constitutes the respondent's overall self-assessment of how easy it is to understand lectures delivered in English. This composite self-assessment score will be correlated with students' IELTS Listening scores.

IELTS Research Project

Follow-up Interviews

Name: _____

Course: _____

As we already have an idea of your general ability to listen to lectures in English (based on the results of the IELTS Listening exam you did) we would now like to analyse how easy or difficult it is for you to listen to real lectures in your subject area. Consequently we would be very grateful if you would answer the following questions. Obviously, all information given is confidential and has no connection with possible course grades.

Section 1: How do you see lectures and how do they fit in with the way you study your subjects?

A. How important do you consider understanding lectures to be?

Not important				Extremely important
1	2	3	4	5

B. How important is it to understand **all** the information given in a lecture?

Not important				Extremely important
1	2	3	4	5

C. What level of understanding do you think is necessary? _____ %

D. Do lecturers provide key lecture information as a back-up (eg notes/ slides in Copia/ADI?

E. Is it easy for you to find the information given in the lecture from other sources?

Not easy				Extremely easy
1	2	3	4	5

F. Do you normally supplement the information from lectures with information from other sources?

Never				Always
1	2	3	4	5

G. Do you take notes during the lectures?

Never				Always
1	2	3	4	5

H. In English or Spanish or both?

I. Do lecturers allow you to ask questions to clarify things you have not understood?

Never				Always
1	2	3	4	5

J. Are you expected in any way to actively participate in the lecture (eg by answering questions, giving opinions, etc)?

Never				Always
1	2	3	4	5

K. How frequently do you actively participate in the lecture (eg by answering questions, giving opinions, etc)?

Never				Always
1	2	3	4	5

L. In general, how difficult do you find it to participate in a lecture (by answering questions or giving opinions)?

Not difficult				Extremely difficult
1	2	3	4	5

M. To what extent do you feel that lecturers make a special effort to make themselves understood by students whose mother tongue is not English?

No effort				A lot of effort
1	2	3	4	5

N. Do you consider that a 3 credit course in English represents the same amount of student work as the equivalent 3 credit course given in Spanish?

O. If more, how much more?

Section 2: Understanding lectures in English

A. In general, how difficult is it for you to understand lectures in English?

Not easy				Extremely easy
1	2	3	4	5

B. What are the main problems you have found?

C. How easy is it for you to separate the sounds you hear into individual words you can recognise?

Not easy				Extremely easy
1	2	3	4	5

D. How easy is it for you to maintain your concentration over long stretches of talk?

Not easy				Extremely easy
1	2	3	4	5

E. How easy is it for you to deal with the more colloquial aspects of a lecture (false starts, irregular pausing, hesitations, etc)?

Not easy				Extremely easy
1	2	3	4	5

F. How easy is it for you to understand lecturers who speak fast or with particular accents?

Not easy				Extremely easy
1	2	3	4	5

G. How easy is it for you to identify the purpose and scope of the lecture?

Not easy				Extremely easy
1	2	3	4	5

H. How easy is it for you to identify the topic of the lecture and its development?

Not easy				Extremely easy
1	2	3	4	5

I. How easy is it for you to identify the main ideas (in contrast to supporting detail) of the lecture?

Not easy				Extremely easy
1	2	3	4	5

J. How easy is it for you to infer the relationships between different parts of the lecture (eg what causes what, what contrasts with what, what is an example, etc)?

Not easy				Extremely easy
1	2	3	4	5

K. How easy is it for you to identify irrelevant matter in the lecture (eg jokes, asides, digressions, etc)?

Not easy				Extremely easy
1	2	3	4	5

B. How often do you use the strategy of listening to the speaker's intonation as a way of helping you decide what is important and what is not?

Never				Always
1	2	3	4	5

C. How often do you use the strategy of listening for key words (*However/ although, Moreover/in addition, etc*) which clearly mark the relationship between specific concepts?

Never				Always
1	2	3	4	5

D. Can you name any specific strategies that you use to help you to "survive" on the courses that are taught in English (e.g. reading about the subject before the class, using a friend's lecture notes, etc.)?

E. Do you feel you would benefit/have benefited more from the course if you had received more **language** support? What kind of support (e.g. specific help on how to take notes, lists of key vocabulary, etc)?

L. How easy is it for you to identify key lexical items / terminology related to the subject of the lecture?

Not easy				Extremely easy
1	2	3	4	5

M. How easy is it for you to deduce the meaning of words that you do not know by using the context and what you know about the subject?

Not easy				Extremely easy
1	2	3	4	5

N. How easy is it for you to understand instructions given by lecturers?

Not easy				Extremely easy
1	2	3	4	5

O. How easy is it for you to understand chunks of language and remember them long enough so that you can take notes?

Not easy				Extremely easy
1	2	3	4	5

P. How easy is it for you to integrate the new information given in the lecture with what you already know about the topic?

Not easy				Extremely easy
1	2	3	4	5

Section 3: Strategies and suggestions

A. How often do you use the strategy of listening for key phrases (*Now I'm going to deal with, the main idea here is that, in other words, etc*) which clearly mark the general structure of the lecture?

Never				Always
1	2	3	4	5

Appendix 8.3
Questionnaire 2

Questionnaire on listening to lectures in English

Name: _____

Course: _____

As we already have an idea of your general ability to listen to lectures in English (based on the results of the IELTS Listening exam you did) we would now like to analyse how easy or difficult it is for you to listen to real lectures in your subject area. Consequently we would be very grateful if you would answer the following questions. Obviously, all information given is confidential and has no connection with possible course grades.

A. In general, how difficult is it for you to understand lectures in English?

Not easy				Extremely easy
1	2	3	4	5

B. What are the main problems you have found?

C. How easy is it for you to separate the sounds you hear into individual words you can recognise?

Not easy				Extremely easy
1	2	3	4	5

D. How easy is it for you to maintain your concentration over long stretches of talk?

Not easy				Extremely easy
1	2	3	4	5

E. How easy is it for you to deal with the more colloquial aspects of a lecture (false starts, irregular pausing, hesitations, etc)?

Not easy				Extremely easy
1	2	3	4	5

F. How easy is it for you to understand lecturers who speak fast or with particular accents?

Not easy				Extremely easy
1	2	3	4	5

G. How easy is it for you to identify the purpose and scope of the lecture?

Not easy				Extremely easy
1	2	3	4	5

H. How easy is it for you to identify the topic of the lecture and its development?

Not easy				Extremely easy
1	2	3	4	5

I. How easy is it for you to identify the main ideas (in contrast to supporting detail) of the lecture?

Not easy				Extremely easy
1	2	3	4	5

J. How easy is it for you to infer the relationships between different parts of the lecture (eg what causes what, what contrasts with what, what is an example, etc)?

Not easy				Extremely easy
1	2	3	4	5

K. How easy is it for you to identify irrelevant matter in the lecture (eg jokes, asides, digressions, etc)?

Not easy				Extremely easy
1	2	3	4	5

L. How easy is it for you to identify key lexical items / terminology related to the subject of the lecture?

Not easy				Extremely easy
1	2	3	4	5

M. How easy is it for you to deduce the meaning of words that you do not know by using the context and what you know about the subject?

Not easy				Extremely easy
1	2	3	4	5

N. How easy is it for you to understand instructions given by lecturers?

Not easy				Extremely easy
1	2	3	4	5

O. How easy is it for you to understand chunks of language and remember them long enough so that you can take notes?

Not easy				Extremely easy
1	2	3	4	5

P. How easy is it for you to integrate the new information given in the lecture with what you already know about the topic?

Not easy				Extremely easy
1	2	3	4	5

9 The relationship between test takers' listening proficiency and their performance on the IELTS Speaking test

Fumiyo Nakatsuhara
University of Bedfordshire, UK

Abstract

This study investigated the relationship between test takers' listening proficiency and their performance on Part 3 (discussion) of the IELTS Speaking test, as against that on Part 2 (individual long turn), in order to explore how communication problems associated with test takers' listening proficiency occurred and how these problems were dealt with. Data was collected from 36 pre-sessional course students at a UK university, who took both a Listening test and an IELTS Speaking test followed by a short semi-structured interview session. All Speaking test sessions were both audio and video recorded. The audio recordings were edited to separate the students' performances on Part 2 from those on Part 3, and each recording was rated by two out of the four trained IELTS examiners involved in this study. Examiners were also asked to write down reasons for awarding the scores that they did. Speaking test scores were analysed for any difference in difficulty between the two parts. Correlations between the Listening test scores and the Speaking test scores awarded on four analytical criteria were compared between the two parts. A Conversation Analysis (CA) methodology was utilised to illustrate salient occurrences of communication problems that were related to test takers' difficulties in hearing or understanding the examiner. The findings of this study highlighted the differences between Part 2 and Part 3 of the IELTS Speaking test in terms of the constructs they measure, showing that the latter format, at least to some extent, measures listening-into-speaking abilities. The interactional data also showed that the construct underlying Part 3 was not a purely productive speaking ability, especially for students at Band 5.0 and below who tended to encounter some difficulties in understanding the examiner.

1   Introduction

Since the IELTS Speaking test involves interactions between an examiner and a test taker, the interactive parts of the test inevitably require a degree of listening proficiency. Listening proficiency seems to have a role especially in Part 3 of the test, where the examiner invites a test taker to participate in discussion about more abstract topics than those in Part 2. In fact, recent research into the discourse of the IELTS Speaking test has identified examples of communication problems caused by the test takers' apparent failure to understand the questions (Seedhouse and Egbert 2006). It is also noteworthy that the majority of suggestions for changes in the rating scale and the interviewer frame made in recent IELTS studies relate either to test takers' listening problems and/or to the *Fluency and Coherence* component of the rating scale (Brown 2006a, 2006b, O'Sullivan and Lu 2006, Seedhouse and Egbert 2006).

Despite increasing interest in the relationship between listening proficiency and speaking performance in listening-into-speaking tests (Lee 2006, Sawaki, Stricker and Oranje 2009, Stricker, Rock and Lee 2005), no study has directly addressed this issue in Speaking test formats that include interaction between a test taker and an examiner. It is therefore important to investigate the impact of listening proficiency on IELTS Speaking test performance. The aims of this research are to investigate the relationship between test takers' listening proficiency and performance on Part 3 (discussion) of the IELTS Speaking test, as against that on Part 2 (individual long turn), and to explore how communication problems that are associated with test takers' listening proficiency occur and how these problems are dealt with.

2   Background to the research

2.1   Recent IELTS Speaking test studies

Four recent IELTS Speaking studies have identified potential concerns associated with test takers' listening proficiency and the *Fluency and Coherence* scale (Brown 2006a, 2006b, O'Sullivan and Lu 2006, Seedhouse and Egbert 2006).

Based on Conversation Analysis of 137 audio-recorded tests, Seedhouse and Egbert (2006) demonstrate that interactional problems can be caused by test takers' misunderstanding of what the examiner has said, although some communication breakdowns were also caused by the examiners' poor questioning. When test takers do not understand questions posed by examiners, they usually initiate repairs by requesting question repetition, and they may also occasionally ask for a re-formulation or explanation of the question. However, in Part 1 of the IELTS Speaking test, examiners are allowed to repeat the same question only once, and are not allowed to re-formulate questions. Thus, examiners usually reject the request for re-formulation. For Seedhouse and Egbert (2006:172), this highlights a discrepancy between IELTS test interactions and the kinds of interactions that students might expect to have in the university context. To avoid possible confusion to test takers, the researchers suggest that a statement on repair rules should be included in documentation for students. For a further research direction, they speculate that 'there does appear to be some kind of correlation between [the IELTS Speaking] test score and occurrence of other-initiated repair, i.e. trouble in hearing or understanding on the part of the candidate' (Seedhouse and Egbert 2006:193). In other words, it is important to explore the extent to which listening ability impacts on Speaking test performance.

The interlocutor frame is rather less rigid in Part 3 than in Part 1, and the examiner has greater discretion. In fact, using 85 audio-taped IELTS Speaking tests, O'Sullivan and Lu (2006) found that Part 3 involved a far greater number of examiner deviations from the interlocutor frame than Parts 1 and 2. The deviations particularly relate to the number of paraphrasing questions used by the examiner (91% of the paraphrasing questions occurred in Part 3). Paraphrasing is most likely to occur when the test taker has failed to understand the examiner's original question, pointing to difficulty with listening comprehension. Although Seedhouse and Egbert (2006) expressed concern that examiners' re-formulation and repetition of questions could be a potential source of unfairness as some exceeded the set rules for communication repair, O'Sullivan and Lu (2006) demonstrated that, among other types of deviations, paraphrasing resulted in only a minimal impact on test takers' performance as measured against criteria for *elaborating and expanding* in discourse, *linguistic accuracy, complexity* and *fluency*. On the basis of their findings, O'Sullivan and Lu (2006) suggest the possibility of allowing for some flexibility in examiners' use of paraphrasing questions. This issue of paraphrasing again indicates the need to investigate the relationship between test takers' listening proficiency and their performance in the interactive parts of the IELTS Speaking test.

Two recent studies on the validation of the analytical rating scales have investigated test takers' language and examiners' rating processes (Brown 2006a, 2006b). In order to validate descriptors for each of the four analytical rating scales (i.e. *Pronunciation, Grammatical Range and Accuracy, Lexical Resource* and *Fluency and Coherence*), Brown (2006a) analysed the IELTS Speaking test discourse of 20 test takers at different proficiency levels. She utilised a wide range of linguistic measures to evaluate key features described for each marking category. For example, in relation to the *Fluency and Coherence* scale, linguistic measures included the occurrence of restarts and repeats per 100 words, the ratio of pause time to speech time, the number of words per 60 seconds, the average length of responses, the total number of words etc. Although there was considerable variation in the size of the differences between other bands across measures, there was a clear step up from Band 5 to Band 6 for all of the measures relating to the *Fluency and Coherence* criterion. For the *Grammatical Range and Accuracy* measures, the greatest difference in grammatical complexity was also observed between Bands 5 and 6, while for the accuracy measures, the greatest difference lay between Bands 7 and 8. For the *Lexical Resources* measures, there was only small difference between means for all measures. Through detailed analysis of test taker language, the current study seeks a possible boundary in bands where the degree of impact of test takers' listening proficiency changes.

Brown (2006b) has also investigated how examiners interpret the analytical scales and what problems they identify when making rating decisions. Verbal reports from 12 IELTS examiners showed that the *Fluency and Coherence* scale was the most complex and difficult for them to interpret. One of the reasons for the problems seemed to be associated with the interpretation of hesitation. It did not always seem to be clear to the examiners whether test takers were hesitating because of a search for ideas or a search for language (Brown 2006b: 51). Furthermore, the examiners found *Fluency and Coherence* the most difficult to distinguish from the other scales. Investigating the role of listening ability may help to clarify the sources of test taker hesitation/pauses and so help to improve examiners' interpretation of the scale or suggest revisions in line with Brown's (2006b) intentions.

2.2 The impact of listening proficiency on Speaking test performance

Previous research into the impact of listening proficiency on Speaking test performance has yielded mixed results. This section will briefly describe previous research on this issue in a) *integrated tests of listening-into-speaking* and b) *paired and group oral tests*, while discussing a potential impact for listening proficiency on IELTS Speaking test performance.

Investigations of the impact of listening ability on scores on the integrated speaking tasks in the TOEFL iBT have found no impact for listening proficiency on listening-into-speaking scores (Lee 2006, Sawaki et al 2009). Two reasons have been put forward for this. Firstly, the listening texts employed in the integrated tasks were easier than those used in the Listening section (Sawaki et al 2009:26). Secondly and perhaps more importantly, the 5-level holistic rating scales used in these TOEFL iBT studies did not seem to be sensitive enough to tap the construct of listening-into-speaking. In contrast, the IELTS Speaking scale might have greater potential for detecting differences in test takers' listening proficiency. This is because, although the IELTS scale was not developed to reflect test takers' listening proficiency, the IELTS scale employs analytic scoring, and some phrases included in the *Fluency and Coherence* category in particular would seem to imply a role for listening proficiency (e.g. *cannot respond without noticeable pauses*).

The increasing use of paired and group oral tests has also attracted attention to the relationship between test takers' listening proficiency and their performance on these formats, and there is clear evidence here that listening ability does play a part in performance. In her analysis of group oral test discourse, Nakatsuhara (2009) reported that communication problems in group tests could be attributable in part to limited listening proficiency. Recent studies into paired tests also have pointed out the importance of listening as part of successful interaction (i.e., interactive listening) (e.g. Ducasse and Brown 2009, Galaczi 2010, May 2007). Ducasse and Brown (2009) illustrate two demonstrations of comprehension that contribute to successful interaction: 1) showing evidence of comprehension by the listener (e.g. filling in with a missing word to help the partner), and 2) showing supportive listening by providing audible support with sounds (e.g. back-channelling).

Although the IELTS Speaking test does not elicit as many interactional features as paired and group formats due to the nature of the one-to-one interview format (ffrench 2003), recent research, as reviewed in 2.1 above, has suggested that, even in this limited context, limitations in understanding the interviewer's questions could result in some difficulties for the test taker leading to less effective spoken responses (e.g. Mohammadi 2009, Seedhouse and Egbert 2006). Such problems are likely to be greater for test takers who have limited listening proficiency.

This section has reviewed recent research into IELTS and other Speaking tests which signals the importance of listening proficiency for the interactive parts, especially Part 3, of the IELTS Speaking test. It is fair to say that, while the interlocutors' input language in interactive spoken formats has been pointed out as one of the contextual parameters that could influence test takers' cognitive processes and therefore their output language (see Weir's (2005) socio-cognitive framework; further elaborated in Field, 2011), the relationship between their listening proficiency and their spoken performance has been under-researched. If the present investigation finds any impact of listening proficiency on test takers' performance on Part 3 of the IELTS Speaking test, this indicates that the part is at least to some extent tapping the construct of listening-into-speaking, and the literature reviewed above suggests that this could be reflected in scores on the *Fluency and Coherence* scale.

3 Research questions

This study considered three research questions concerning the relationship between test takers' listening proficiency and their scores on Part 3 of the IELTS Speaking test as against scores on Part 2, and explored how listening-related communication problems in Part 3 occurred and how these problems were dealt with.

> ***RQ 1:*** Is there evidence of any difference in difficulty between Part 2 (individual long turn) and Part 3 (discussion) of the IELTS Speaking test identified by overall scores and scores given to each analytical category?
> ***RQ 2:*** What are the relationships between test takers' listening proficiency and overall and analytical scores awarded on Part 2 and Part 3 respectively?
> ***RQ 3:*** How do communication problems in Part 3 that seem to be related to test takers' difficulties in understanding the examiner occur and how are they dealt with?
>
> - Are there any differences between different proficiency-level test takers in terms of the number and types of listening-related communication problems?
> - What are test takers' perceptions of difficulties encountered while communicating with the examiner?

4   Research design

4.1   Participants

The participants in this study were 36 pre-sessional course students at a UK university. Of the 36 participants, 17 were males (47.2%) and 19 were females (52.8%). They were all approximately 20 years old (mean: 19.34, SD: 1.31). Twenty-eight were from the People's Republic of China (L1: Chinese), and the rest included five participants from Hong Kong (L1: Cantonese), one from Kazakhstan (L1: Kazakh), one from Oman (L1: Arabic) and one from Kuwait (L1: Arabic).

Figure 9.1   Speaking English outside the class (%)

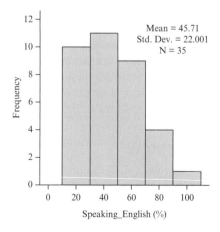

Figure 9.2 Listening to English outside the class (%)

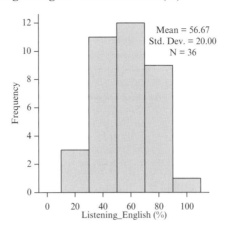

The length of stay in the UK ranged from one month to 24 months (mean: 7.72, SD: 4.88). Furthermore, as shown in Figures 9.1 and 9.2, after they arrived in the UK, the number of opportunities for speaking and listening to English outside the class also varied to a large extent; i.e., they reported that on average 46% of their speaking and 57% of their listening outside the class was in English and the standard deviations attached to these means were as large as 22 and 20. Therefore, it has to be acknowledged that the uneven mix of their first languages, the varied length of stay in the UK, and the varied amount of exposure to the English language outside the classroom could be potential uncontrolled test taker variables in this study.

To understand the participating students' profiles better, a self-assessment questionnaire about their capacity in coping with aural and oral communication inside and outside the classroom was administered, using Likert-scale questions and the Common European Framework of Reference (CEFR) self-assessment grid, which is referred to in Appendix 9.1 (see also Council of Europe 2001). Although it should be pointed out that their self-assessments may not be very accurate, the results indicated that their average listening ability assessment was between B1 and B2 according to the CEFR language proficiency levels and their average spoken interaction ability assessment was at B2 level. Thus, despite some uncontrolled test taker variables pointed out above, it seems that, considering most UK universities set the admission cut-off point of English proficiency around B2 and C1, these participating students are typical students on pre-sessional courses (who would also be preparing for IELTS) in terms of their capacity in coping with everyday English listening and speaking activities. Since this questionnaire is not central to this research, a summary of the findings is presented in Appendix 9.1.

Four trained IELTS examiners at an IELTS centre were also involved. Their IELTS examining experience ranged from 1½ to 12 years (see Table 9.1).

Table 9.1 IELTS examiners

Examiner ID	Gender	IELTS examining experience (years)
A	Female	12
B	Male	9
C	Female	5.5
D	Female	1.5

4.2 Data collection

All of the instruments described below were piloted with a small number of participants prior to the main experiment.

4.2.1 Listening test

To assess the test takers' listening abilities, the present study used a Listening component from the Cambridge Main Suite test instead of an IELTS Listening test. This was because the construct of the IELTS Listening test is the *academic* listening ability required for university study, and thus the test involves listening to lectures. However, the construct to be measured for the purpose of this study was a more *general* listening ability, and therefore, the content of the recordings in a Cambridge Main Suite test measuring general English proficiency is more akin to what IELTS test takers might listen to during the IELTS Speaking test. In order to reflect the range of abilities in the target group and so discriminate more effectively between participants in terms of their listening abilities, both *FCE* (B2) and *CAE* (C1) Listening test items were included in the test.

A Listening test that includes both *FCE* and *CAE* items was created using *FCE* and *CAE* practice materials published by University of Cambridge ESOL Examinations (Cambridge ESOL 2008a, 2008b, 2009a, 2009b). As shown in Table 9.2 below, 36 students took the 40-minute Listening test, with each of the 34 items being worth 1 mark.

4.2.2 Speaking test

Two sets of examiner prompts for the IELTS Speaking test were provided by Cambridge ESOL (Prompt 1: *Interest*, Prompt 2: *Parties*). These prompts were taken from the DVD, *IELTS Scores Explained* (IELTS Partners 2006). In the *interest* prompt, test takers are asked to describe an interest or hobby that they enjoy in the individual long turn part (Part 2) followed by a discussion with the examiner on more general themes such as the social benefits of hobbies and leisure time (Part 3). Under each theme, a number of questions are provided. In the *parties* prompt, they are asked to describe the best party they have ever been to, followed by a discussion on family parties in their

Table 9.2 Listening test (40 minutes) (taken from UCLES 2007a, UCLES 2007b)

Phase	Task type and focus	Format	No. of items
1 FCE Part 1	Multiple choice. General gist, detail, function, purpose, attitude, opinion, relationship, topic, place, situation, genre, agreement, etc.	A series of short unrelated extracts, of approximately 30 seconds each, from monologues or exchanges between interacting speakers. There is one multiple-choice question per text, each with three options.	8
2 FCE Part 2	Sentence completion. Detail, specific information, stated opinion.	A monologue or text involving interacting speakers and lasting approximately 3 minutes. Candidates are required to complete the sentences with information heard on the recording.	10
3 CAE Part 3	Multiple choice. Attitude and opinion.	A conversation between two or more speakers of approximately 4 minutes. There are six multiple-choice questions, each with four options.	6
4 CAE Part 4	Multiple matching. Gist, attitude, main points, interpreting context.	Five short themed monologues, of approximately 30 seconds each. Each multiple-matching task requires selection of the correct options from a list of eight.	10
		total 34	

countries, other parties and national celebrations. Instructions in both Part 2 and Part 3 and questions that the examiners ask in Part 3 are all scripted, and the examiners are required to follow the scripts word by word, though they can select one or two of the themes that are appropriate for developing discussion, depending on each test taker's response. Permission was granted for use of these prompts for the purpose of this study. Each prompt was used with 18 students.

Over two days of data collection, 36 students each took a 10-minute Speaking test. All the Speaking test sessions were both audio and video recorded. The test included three parts (see Table 9.3):

1. a very brief warm-up conversation (This was different from a usual IELTS Part 1)
2. Part 2 and
3. Part 3.

4.2.3 Audio-rating of the speaking performance

Non-live marking was conducted using audio-recordings of the test takers' performances. Since this study compares scores awarded on Part 2 and Part

Table 9.3 Speaking test structure and instructions for the examiner

1 **Warm-up** (30 sec–1 minute)	• Check the test taker's name & introduce yourself. • Ask the test taker about him/herself (e.g. home, work, studies).
2 **Part 2** **Individual long turn** (3–4 minutes)	• Using the two prompts: 1) Interest and 2) Parties in turn, carry out Part 2 and Part 3 as you would normally do in an IELTS Speaking test.
3 **Part 3** **Discussion** (4–5 minutes)	

3 separately, if examiners had assessed students' performances on Part 2 and on Part 3 during the same live session, the scores awarded on one part might have influenced those on the other part.

Therefore, in order to obtain more valid scores for each student on each test part, the audio-recordings were edited to separate the students' performances on Part 2 from those on Part 3, and a mixture of separate Part 2 and Part 3 recordings from different test takers were given to the examiners.

Each audio-recording was independently marked by two examiners out of the four examiners. The ratings followed a rating matrix to have all four raters overlap with one another, so that the FACETS program could calibrate speaking scores that take account of rater harshness levels.

The examiners were also asked to write down briefly why they awarded the scores that they did on each analytical category. This was thought to be useful when interpreting the score and interactional data. Compared with the verbal report methodology which has been employed in a number of recent Speaking test studies into examiners' scoring process (e.g. Brown, Iwashita and McNamara 2005, Brown 2006b, May 2007), a written description is likely to be less informative. However, considering the focus of this study, which was mainly on students' performance in the two parts of the test, it was decided to ask the examiners to provide brief notes on reasons for awarding each score.

4.2.4 A short interview concerning the students' Speaking test experience

Following each Speaking test, a short semi-structured interview was carried out, to elicit the participating students' perceptions of any communication problems encountered with the IELTS examiner. Although it was originally planned to give the students a short questionnaire on completion of the Speaking test, the pilot study demonstrated that a short interview would elicit richer responses. The short semi-structured interviews included the following scripted questions. These interviews were all audio-recorded.

1. I could <u>understand</u> the examiner's questions very well.

strongly disagree	disagree	neutral	agree	strongly agree

2. I could <u>answer</u> the examiner's questions very well.

strongly disagree	disagree	neutral	agree	strongly agree

3. What did you find difficult when you were communicating with the examiner?
   - Describe any difficulties/problems you had. (<u>Where? What?</u>)
   - Were the problems solved? How?

4.3 Data analysis

Listening and Speaking test scores were quantitatively analysed using SPSS and FACETS. After ensuring the quality of collected data by examining the reliability and fit statistics, overall and analytical Speaking scores awarded on Part 2 and Part 3 were firstly compared (*RQ 1*). Secondly, the strength of the correlations between the Listening scores and the overall and analytical Speaking scores awarded on Part 2 and Part 3 were compared (*RQ 2*).

Thirdly, to answer *RQ 3*, relevant parts of speaking video data were transcribed according to the Conversation Analysis (CA) conventions (Atkinson and Heritage 1984), and short interview data about the students' Speaking test experience was transcribed and coded. The examiners' notes on scoring were typed out and formatted in a table for easy comparisons. CA analysis was carried out to illustrate how communication problems in Part 3 that seemed to be related to test takers' difficulties in understanding the examiner occurred, and how these problems were dealt with by students and the examiners. A list of the transcription notations is provided in Appendix 9.3. Although detailed features of repair sequences have already been identified by Seedhouse and Egbert (2006), the present study has a slightly different perspective as it aims to identify sequences that involve listening-related communication problems which do not necessarily result in repairs. This study also aims at providing deeper insight into the interactional features including visual information (e.g. eye gaze and other forms of non-verbal communication), using video-recorded data.

Furthermore, to suggest a possible level boundary that differentiates the degree/types of communication problems related to test takers' listening proficiency on Part 3 speaking performance, the Speaking test transcripts and the coded interview data were qualitatively analysed. The qualitative data did not lend itself to statistical analysis due to the limited sample size and the limited number of communication breakdowns that it contained. However, it was hoped that the qualitative analyses of the Speaking test performance and short interview data could serve to suggest a possible boundary in IELTS Speaking band scores that differentiates the degree/types of impact of listening proficiency.

5 Results and discussion

5.1 Listening test scores

First of all, Listening test scores were pre-analysed. The reliability coefficient for the 34 listening items was .899 (Cronbach's Alpha). However, as shown in Table 9.4 below, seven items were not functioning adequately: their item-total correlation values being lower than .25. These seven items were therefore excluded from further analysis.

Table 9.4 Item-total statistics of the deleted items

	Mean	Corrected item-total correlation	Cronbach's Alpha if item deleted
q08	.50	.179	.901
q19	.33	.197	.900
q20	.36	.186	.901
q23	.47	−.149	.906
q24	.47	.199	.901
q25	.28	.160	.901
q32	.22	.175	.900

After deleting these seven items, Cronbach's Alpha improved to .918. Descriptive statistics are shown in Table 9.5, and are represented visually in Figure 9.3.

Table 9.5 Descriptive statistics of 27 item Listening test scores (N=36)

	Min	Max	Mean	SD
Listening test (27 items)	2	27	12.03	7.45

5.2 Speaking test scores (RQ 1)

5.2.1 Overview of Speaking test scores and comparing Part 2 and Part 3 overall scores

Here, overall scores in Part 2 and Part 3 mean aggregated scores obtained from the four analytical scales in each part (i.e. *Pronunciation, Grammatical Range and Accuracy, Lexical Resource* and *Fluency and Coherence*).

Figure 9.3 Listening test score histogram

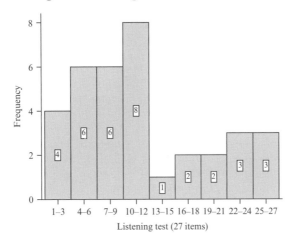

Listening test (27 items)

Figure 9.4 on page 532 shows the overview, plotting estimates of *examinee ability, examiner harshness, prompt difficulty, part difficulty* and *rating category difficulty*, which are the five main sources (i.e. facets) for the test score variance. They were all measured by the uniform unit (logits) shown on the left side of the map called 'measure', making it possible to directly compare all the facets. The more able examinees are placed towards the top (e.g., *S10* is the most able) and the less able towards the bottom (e.g., *S18* is the least able). The more lenient examiners and the easier prompt, part and categories appear towards the bottom, and the harsher examiners and the more difficult prompt, part and rating categories towards the top (e.g. *C* is the harshest examiner). The right-hand column, 'scale', refers to the IELTS Speaking band scale.

Concerning the examinee facet, while most students were plotted around Band 4 and Band 5, examinees' ability measures ranged from –6.34 logits (ID: *S18*) to 7.23 logits (ID: *S10*). As shown in Table 9.6 on page 532, examinee separation value was 5.35, meaning that about five statistically distinct levels can be identified in this sample. The person reliability showed .97, which is the Rasch reliability equivalent to the Cronbach Alpha statistics.

This study employed a formula for calculating fit value ranges provided by McNamara (1996:181); a good range of fit values is within the mean ± twice the SD of the mean square statistics. One misfitting student was identified as shown in Table 9.6, *S17*. The percentage of misfitting student(s) in the given data was 2.78%, and seemed fairly reasonable, although the figure was a little greater than the 2% that any test development should aim at (McNamara 1996:178).

Tables 9.7–10 show measurement reports of *1) examiner, 2) prompt, 3) part* and *4) rating category* facets. All elements of the four facets showed

Figure 9.4 Overall Facet map

```
+------------+------------------------+----------+----------+----------+--------------------+--------+
|Measr|+Examinee                     |-Rater    |-Prompt   |-Part     |-Category           |Scale|
+------------+------------------------+----------+----------+----------+--------------------+--------+
|  8 +                               +          +          +          +                    +  (9) |
|    |  S10                          |          |          |          |                    |      |
|  7 +                               +          +          +          +                    +      |
|    |                               |          |          |          |                    |      |
|  6 +                               +          +          +          +                    +  --- |
|    |                               |          |          |          |                    |      |
|  5 +                               +          +          +          +                    +      |
|    |                               |          |          |          |                    |    7 |
|  4 +                               +          +          +          +                    +      |
|    |                               |          |          |          |                    |      |
|  3 + S13                           +          +          +          +                    +      |
|    |                               |          |          |          |                    |  --- |
|  2 + S05                           +          +          +          +                    +      |
|    |  S33                          |          |          |          |                    |    6 |
|  1 +                               + C        +          +          +                    +      |
|    |  S06                          |          |          |          |                    |      |
|    |                               |          |  Parties |          |  gram              |      |
|* 0 *                               * D        *          * Part 2  Part 3 * lex          *  ---  *
|    |  S16                          |  B       |  Interest|          |  flu      pron     |      |
|    |  S20                          |  A       |          |          |                    |      |
| -1 + S22                           +          +          +          +                    +      |
|    |  S31                          |          |          |          |                    |      |
|    |  S02   S15   S24              |          |          |          |                    |    5 |
| -2 + S36                           +          +          +          +                    +      |
|    |  S04   S21   S32   S35        |          |          |          |                    |      |
|    |  S08   S25                    |          |          |          |                    |      |
| -3 + S14   S34                     +          +          +          +                    +      |
|    |  S03   S07   S23   S28        |          |          |          |                    |  --- |
|    |  S01   S26   S29              |          |          |          |                    |      |
| -4 + S27                           +          +          +          +                    +      |
|    |  S30                          |          |          |          |                    |      |
| -5 + S11   S19                     +          +          +          +                    +    4 |
|    |  S12                          |          |          |          |                    |      |
|    |  S09   S17                    |          |          |          |                    |      |
| -6 +                               +          +          +          +                    +      |
|    |  S18                          |          |          |          |                    |  --- |
| -7 +                               +          +          +          +                    +  (2) |
+------------+------------------------+----------+----------+----------+--------------------+--------+
|Measr|+Examinee                     |-Rater    |-Prompt   |-Part     |-Category           |Scale|
+------------+------------------------+----------+----------+----------+--------------------+--------+
```

Table 9.6 Examinee measurement report

	Fair average	Measure	Real SE	Infit MnSq
S17 (Misfitting)	3.82	−5.61	.76	3.47
Mean	4.81	−2.29	.48	.97
SD	.84	2.63	.07	.55
Separation 5.35 Reliability .97				

Table 9.7 Rater measurement report

	Fair average	Measure	Real SE	Infit MnSq
Examiner A	5.00	−.69	.27	.93
Examiner B	4.89	−.35	.30	1.36
Examiner C	4.76	.08	.13	.99
Examiner D	4.48	.96	.10	.90
Mean	4.78	.00	.20	1.04
SD	.19	.62	.08	.18
Fixed (all same) chi-square: 57.4 d.f.: 3 significance: p<.005 (sig.)				

Table 9.8 Prompt measurement report

	Fair average	Measure	Real SE	Infit MnSq
Interest	4.85	−.21	.11	.83
Parties	4.72	.21	.11	1.11
Mean	4.78	.00	.11	.97
SD	.03	.21	.00	.14
Fixed (all same) chi-square: 7.3 d.f.: 1 significance: p=.01 (sig.)				

Table 9.9 Part measurement report

	Fair average	Measure	Real SE	Infit MnSq
Part 2	4.82	−.10	.10	.96
Part 3	4.75	.10	.11	.98
Mean	4.79	.00	.11	.97
SD	.03	.10	.00	.01
Fixed (all same) chi-square: 2.0 d.f.: 1 significance: p=.16 (non sig.)				

Table 9.10 Rating category measurement report

	Fair average	Measure	Real SE	Infit MnSq
Fluency	4.86	−.25	.15	.95
Pronunciation	4.84	−.18	.16	1.17
Lexis	4.75	.13	.15	.91
Grammar	4.69	.30	.15	.86
Mean	4.78	.00	.15	.97
SD	.07	.23	.01	.12
Fixed (all same) chi-square: 9.0 d.f.: 3 significance: p=.03 (sig.)				

acceptable fit values, suggesting all examiners, prompts, parts and rating categories were not unsystematically inconsistent or unsystematically difficult.

The FACETS program yields the fixed (all same) chi-square, which tests the null hypothesis that all elements of the facet are equal (Linacre 2006). The analysis of each facet revealed that the *part* facet (χ^2=2.0, p=.16) did not show a significant difference between the two parts, while all the other four facets showed a statistically significant difference among elements.

Among these facets, the *examiner* facet showed the largest impact on scores (χ^2=57.4, p<.005). The difference in raw scores (see Fair averages, which indicate expected average raw score values transformed from the Rasch measure) between the most lenient (Examiner *A*: 5.00) and harshest rater (Examiner *C*: 4.48) was as large as 0.52 of a band on the IELTS Speaking test scale. The level of discrepancy between the most lenient and harshest raters was similar to the level reported in Brown and Hill's (1997) study where they found a difference corresponding to 0.6 of a band among six examiners.

5.2.2 Comparing Part 2 and Part 3 analytical scores

Following the overall score analysis that did not show a statistically significant difference between Part 2 and Part 3 scores, further analyses were conducted for each of the four rating categories. Tables 9.11–14 show part measurement reports of the four rating categories.

Chi-square statistics of each category revealed that the *part* facet had a statistically significant impact only on the *Fluency and Coherence* category (χ^2=7.4, p=.01, see Table 9.11 below). For *Fluency and Coherence*, Part 3 (Fair average: 4.88) was significantly more difficult than Part 2 (Fair average: 4.99), although the actual difference was rather small.

Table 9.11 Fluency and Coherence – Part measurement report

	Fair average	Measure	Real SE	Infit MnSq
Part 2	4.99	−.49	.27	1.11
Part 3	4.88	.49	.24	.79
Mean	4.94	.00	.26	.95
SD	.05	.49	.01	.16
Fixed (all same) chi-square: 7.4 df.: 1 significance: p=.01 (sig.)				

Table 9.12 Lexical Resources – Part measurement report

	Fair average	Measure	Real SE	Infit MnSq
Part 2	4.88	−.21	.26	.94
Part 3	4.78	.21	.25	.90
Mean	4.83	.00	.26	.92
SD	.05	.21	.00	.02
Fixed (all same) chi-square: 1.4 df.: 1 significance: p=.24 (non sig.)				

Table 9.13 Grammatical Range and Accuracy – Part measurement report

	Fair average	Measure	Real SE	Infit MnSq
Part 2	4.64	−.07	.25	1.06
Part 3	4.60	.07	.25	.78
Mean	4.62	.00	.25	.92
SD	.02	.07	.00	.14
Fixed (all same) chi-square: .2 df.: 1 significance: p=.68 (non sig.)				

Table 9.14 Pronunciation – Part measurement report

	Fair average	Measure	Real SE	Infit MnSq
Part 2	4.78	−.19	.23	.87
Part 3	4.69	.19	.24	1.06
Mean	4.74	.00	.24	.96
SD	.05	.19	.00	.09
Fixed (all same) chi-square: 1.2 df.: 1 significance: p=.27 (non sig.)				

5.3 Relationship between Listening and Speaking scores (RQ 2)

Having examined the Listening and Speaking scores separately in 5.1 and 5.2, the correlations between the Listening and the Speaking scores (both overall and analytical scores) were investigated.

For the Listening test scores, 27 items selected in 5.1 were used. For the Speaking test scores, fair average scores produced by the FACETS program were used, as fair average scores are adjusted ratings in a standardised environment in which all other elements interacting with the Speaking test scores have the mean measure of all elements in their facets, for example, adjusting raw ratings for lenient and harsh examiners (Linacre 2006).

As indicated in Tables 9.5 and 9.15 and Figures 9.3, 9.5 and 9.6, neither Listening scores nor Speaking fair average scores were normally distributed. Therefore, non-parametric correlation coefficients (Spearman's rho) were used in the following correlation analyses.

Table 9.16 on page 537 summarises Spearman's rho tests for correlations between Listening test scores and Speaking test scores in Part 2 and Part 3, and Figures 9.7 and 9.8 on page 538 visualise the relationship between Listening test scores and overall Speaking scores in Part 2 and Part 3.

There are three main findings related to the second research question of this study; that is, the relationships between Listening and Speaking test scores. Firstly, except for the pronunciation scores in Part 2, scores in all categories showed statistically significant correlations with Listening scores at the .05 or the .01 level. The correlation coefficient values ranged from .411 to .643, and therefore the strength of correlations were medium to large, according

Table 9.15 Descriptive statistics of Speaking fair average scores (N=36)

		Mean	SD	Min	Max	Skewness	Kurtosis
Part 2	Overall	4.92	.84	3.69	7.73	1.38	2.59
	Fluency and Coherence	5.01	.87	3.58	7.64	.85	1.27
	Lexical Resource	4.90	.88	3.35	7.85	.99	2.19
	Grammatical Range & Accuracy	4.80	.91	3.76	7.76	1.62	2.55
	Pronunciation	4.90	.99	3.33	7.89	1.13	1.47
Part 3	Overall	4.71	.98	2.75	8.08	1.23	3.41
	Fluency and Coherence	4.69	1.05	2.00	8.00	.62	2.88
	Lexical Resource	4.69	1.02	2.85	8.00	.81	1.91
	Grammatical Range & Accuracy	4.69	1.02	2.85	8.00	.81	1.91
	Pronunciation	4.77	1.00	3.06	8.41	1.77	4.75

Figure 9.5 Speaking fair average scores in Part 2 (overall)

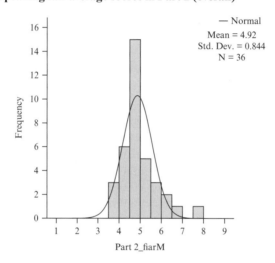

to Cohen's (1998) definition (small: $\rho = \pm.10$ to $\rho = \pm.29$, medium: $\rho = \pm.30$ to $\rho = \pm.49$, large: $\rho = \pm.50$ to $\rho \pm 1.0$). One might find it surprising that Part 2 of the Speaking tests which does not involve any listening had some significant, medium-strength correlations with Listening scores. This finding, however, is not unexpected, considering its consistency with the current multi-componential view of language ability in the literature, language ability being accounted for by both underlying general trait and local skill-specific factors (e.g. Bachman, Davidson, Ryan and Choi 1995, Shin 2005, Sawaki et al 2009).

Secondly, it was interesting that throughout all rating categories, stronger correlations with Listening scores were observed for Speaking scores in Part 3 than those in Part 2. While most correlations in Part 2 showed medium

Figure 9.6 Speaking fair average scores in Part 3 (overall)

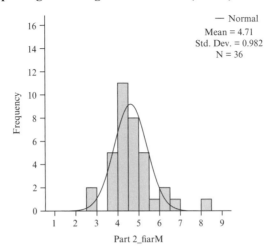

— Normal
Mean = 4.71
Std. Dev. = 0.982
N = 36

Part 2_fiarM

Table 9.16 Correlation between Listening scores and Speaking scores (N=36)

Speaking in Part 2	Overall	Flu	Lex	Gram	Pron
Spearman's rho	.418*	.471**	.490**	.481**	.294
Sig. (2-tailed)	.011	.004	.002	.003	.082

Speaking in Part 3	Overall	Flu	Lex	Gram	Pron
Spearman's rho	.597**	.522**	.643**	.643**	.411*
Sig. (2-tailed)	.000	.001	.000	.000	.013

** *Correlation is significant at the 0.01 level (2-tailed).*
* *Correlation is significant at the 0.05 level (2-tailed).*

strength (ρ.294 to ρ = .490), most correlations in Part 3 showed large strength (ρ = .411 to ρ = .643). The statistical significance in the differences in the rho between Parts 2 and 3 was tested, using the Hotelling-Williams test (Howell 2002:281). Although the sample size of the present study was rather small (N=36), *p* values of the correlational differences in *Overall* and *Lexical Resource* scores approached significance (*Overall*: t(33)=−1.604, *p*=.059 ; *Lexical Resource*: t(33)=−1.543, *p*=.066). This finding suggests that it is worth examining the interactional data qualitatively for a possible impact of test takers' listening proficiency on their performance on Part 3, and that further investigations with a larger sample size should be undertaken to confirm the statistical significance of the differences.

Thirdly, for both Part 2 and Part 3, *Lexical Resource* and *Grammatical Range and Accuracy* scores showed the strongest correlation with Listening

Figure 9.7 Listening test scores and Speaking test scores in Part 2 (overall)

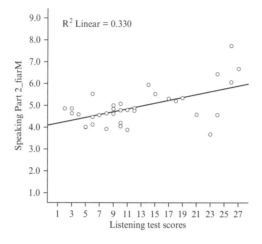

Figure 9.8 Listening test scores and speaking test scores in Part 3 (overall)

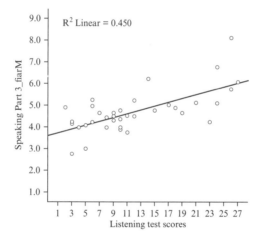

scores, followed by *Fluency and Coherence*. *Pronunciation* had the weakest correlation. This finding is in accordance with previous studies that showed lexico-grammatical elements usually contribute to a significant amount of the total variance in test takers' scores on skills-based tests (e.g. Geranpayeh 2007, Green 2007, Hawkey 2009, Joyce 2008, Shiotsu and Weir 2007, Weir 1983). For example, based on his Structural Equation Modelling (SEM) analyses of two large sets of CAE test takers' scores on all five papers, Geranpayeh (2007) demonstrated that the Use of English paper correlated with the other four papers better than any of the other papers did, and the correlation with the Listening paper was especially high (.805 in one of the analyses). Joyce

(2008) also found that, based on his SEM study taking syntactic knowledge, vocabulary breadth, phonological knowledge, phonological awareness, sentence stress awareness, metacognitive strategy use, working memory and the overlap between these different sub-skills into account, syntactic knowledge was the strongest and most consistent predictor of L2 listening comprehension. However, we also need to bear in mind that even if syntactic knowledge is the best predictor of the L2 Listening test scores, it does not necessarily mean that syntactic knowledge holds the key to listening, since parsing (i.e. the phase of listening that involves syntactic analysis) is critically dependent upon earlier decoding at phoneme and word levels as well as on working memory capacity and the ability to retain words in L2 in mind.

5.4 Communication problems related to test takers' limited listening proficiency (RQ 3)

Conversation Analysis of the Part 3 speaking interactions identified 22 instances of communication problems by 17 test takers that seemed to be associated with their difficulties in understanding the examiner. The communication problems identified here are limited to those involving obvious troubles in hearing or understanding on the part of the test takers. Thus, the instances do not include test takers' hesitations where it was not clear whether these were caused by speaking problems (e.g. searching for ideas and language) or listening problems (e.g. taking some time to retrieve the meaning of words in the examiner's questions).

The listening-related communication problems varied in terms of how the problems occurred and how they were dealt with by test takers and the examiner, and could be categorised into the following five patterns:

a) A test taker asked the examiner to repeat or to rephrase a question, and after the question was repeated or rephrased, they responded to the question relevantly.

b) A test taker asked the examiner to repeat or to rephrase a question, and after the question was repeated or rephrased, they responded irrelevantly to the question.

c) A test taker misunderstood a question and 1) responded very irrelevantly to the question or 2) gave a somewhat related but mostly irrelevant response.

d) A test taker echoed a part that they did not understand to signal their comprehension difficulty, sometimes with notable facial expressions or gestures.

e) A test taker answered 'no' to a question they did not understand.

Table 9.17 summarises the number of instances categorised into the five communication problem patterns, Listening test scores and overall Speaking scores on Part 2 and Part 3 of those students who encountered the problems, and differences between Part 3 and Part 2 scores. In this table, test takers are ordered according to their Part 3 scores in each communication problem pattern. For a complete list of all test takers' Listening scores and analytical Speaking scores, see Appendix 9.2.

Table 9.17 The number of instances of each communication problem pattern and students' Listening and Speaking test scores

Type of communication problems	Number of instances	ID	Listening test score	Speaking test score		
				Part 2	Part 3	Part 3–Part 2
Type a) asking a question and then responding relevantly	7	S11	10	4.02	3.87	−0.15
		S12	8	3.93	3.98	0.06
		S30	5	4.07	4.06	−0.01
		S14	12	4.70	4.49	−0.21
		S04	24	4.47	5.16	0.69
		S24	21	4.63	5.37	0.74
		S06	26	5.99	5.67	−0.32
Type b) asking a question and then responding irrelevantly	2	S09	11	3.84	3.47	−0.37
		S07	10	5.05	3.96	−1.09
Type c) misunderstanding a question, and 1) responding very irrelevantly (S17, S18) or 2) giving a somewhat related but mostly irrelevant response (S32, S36, S02)	5	S17	3	4.88	2.80	−2.09
		S18	5	3.96	3.05	−0.91
		S32	9	4.88	4.87	−0.02
		S36	2	4.64	4.92	0.27
		S02	12	4.74	5.03	0.29
Type d) echoing uncomprehended parts	7	S17	3	4.88	2.80	−2.09
	(3 instances)	S11	10	4.02	3.87	−0.15
		S28	3	4.63	4.13	−0.51
		S03	8	4.62	4.55	−0.07
		S15	19	5.36	4.67	−0.69
Type e) saying 'no' to an uncomprehended question	1	S09	11	3.84	3.47	−0.36

Table 9.17 illustrates that a certain type of listening-related communication problem could be associated with a certain level of listening and speaking proficiency. For example, among the 17 test takers who encountered listening-related communication problems, *S06*, *S24* and *S04* who scored the highest both in the Listening test and Part 3 of the Speaking test had Type a) problem. Test takers who encountered Type a) problem also seemed to get

Part 3 scores either similar to their Part 2 scores or, in some cases, higher than their Part 2 scores. It is also important to note that except for the three students who encountered Type a) problem, all of them scored 5.0 or below in Part 3 of the test, indicating that 5.0 could be a possible level boundary where the degree of impact of test takers' listening proficiency changes.

In order to gain further insights into the relationship between types of listening-related communication problems in Part 3 and the scores awarded by examiners, this section describes each of the five patterns with transcription excerpts from a few test takers, together with their Listening scores and analytical Speaking test scores awarded on Part 2 and Part 3. The descriptions are also elaborated on, wherever possible, by some data obtained from 1) short semi-structured interviews with the participating students regarding their perceptions of any communication problems encountered with the examiner in Part 3, and 2) examiners' comments on awarding the scores that they did. Findings of the semi-structured interviews will be again summarised in 5.5.

a) A test taker asked the examiner to repeat or to rephrase a question, and after the question was repeated or rephrased, they responded to the question relevantly

Excerpts 1–3 below illustrate how students asked the examiner to repeat a question. It seemed common for students with Part 3 Speaking analytical scores around 4.0–5.0 to ask the examiner to repeat a question by simply saying 'sorry?' (see Excerpts 1 and 3), often together with a gesture of sitting forward or moving forward towards the examiner. Most times, such requests were made rather naturally. Table 9.18 shows Student S30's Listening score and Speaking analytical scores in Part 2 and Part 3.

Table 9.18 Student S30's Listening and Speaking scores

Listening	Speaking	Flu	Lex	Gram	Pron
5	Part 2	4.02	3.62	4.02	4.62
	Part 3	4.03	3.85	3.85	4.49

Excerpt 1. Topic: Parties (E: Examiner, S: Student S30)

1   E: *What makes a good family party?*

2 → S: *Sorry? ((moving forward))*

3   E: *What makes a good family party?*

4   S: *Uh:: uh Maybe just ah food. (1.0) uh:: (.5) uh in China, family party sometimes*

5   *lot beer. Although I don't like beer, my friend like beer.*

In Excerpt 1, immediately after the examiner's question in line 1, S30 said 'Sorry?' while moving her upper body forward to be closer to the examiner. There was no gap between the two turns. Following S30's question in line 2, the examiner repeated the question in the same manner as he did in line 1. Then, S30 started responding to the question relevantly in line 4. In the interview session after the Speaking test, S30 reported that she had a listening problem; 'Sometime I don't understand questions. About parties, family party, friends party, I don't understand questions' (S30). Nevertheless, it did not seem to have affected the examiners' impression of the candidate's performance, as examiners' comments between Parts 2 and 3 were highly consistent (see Appendix 9.4).

Compared with the above question that was rather naturally and appropriately produced, one student with Part 3 analytical scores ranging from 3.5 to 4.5 (see Table 9.19) asked a question rather abruptly using an informal register ('Wha-?') as in Excerpt 2, line 2, which was not suitable in the formal interview situation. The examiner rephrased the original question, altering 'the work life balance' into 'the balance between work and leisure activity', while gesturing balancing by her hands. S12 showed his understanding by giving two response tokens 'Yeah' (lines 4 and 6), and responded to the question relevantly from line 6.

Table 9.19 Student S12's Listening and Speaking scores

Listening	Speaking	Flu	Lex	Gram	Pron
8	Part 2	4.02	4.03	3.76	3.89
	Part 3	3.43	4.01	4.01	4.47

Excerpt 2. Topic: Interest (E: Examiner, S: Student S12)

1		*E: So do you think the work life balance is good?*
2	→	*S: Wha-?*
3		*E: The the balance between work and leisure [activity,*
4		*S: [Yeah*
5		*E: this is good? ((gesturing balancing by hands))*
6		*S: Yeah actually, but sometimes have more homework and class and uh*

Judging from examiners' comments, the reasons why S12 had the *Fluency and Coherence* score half a band lower in Part 3 did not seem to be due to listening problems. Indications from examiner comments suggest that it was occasioned by speaking difficulties rather than listening difficulties:

Fluency and Coherence

- *Part 2: noticeable pauses with some repetition (Examiner C, Band 4); appears able to maintain flow of speech but without being able to communicate a sufficiently clear message (Examiner D, Band 4)*
- *Part 3: frequent repetition and self correction, linked some sentences (Examiner A, Band 4); simple responses, frequently unable to convey basic message (Examiner C: Band 3)*

When test takers did not understand the examiner even after one repetition or rephrasing of the question, they tended to request the examiner to repeat or rephrase the question by using a different phrase (e.g. questions such as 'Can you repeat it again?' or statements like 'I didn't understand it.'). Excerpt 3 is one of these cases. However, S11's question was unusual as he asked the examiner to show him the interlocutor script in line 5, having noticed that the examiner had been following a scripted list of questions. The surprised examiner, hiding the script from the student, started rephrasing the question in line 6. This example highlighted the discourse asymmetry between the examiner and test taker in interview test events where the examiner is solely a goal-oriented party by following their plan of introducing a new topic (van Lier 1989).

Table 9.20 Student S11's Listening and Speaking scores

Listening	Speaking	Flu	Lex	Gram	Pron
10	Part 2	4.04	4.04	4.12	3.88
	Part 3	3.79	4.01	4.01	3.66

Excerpt 3. Topic: Parties (E: Examiner, S: Student S11)

1		E: .hh Ah:, how do families celebrate birthdays in your country?
2	→	S: Uh Sorry? ((moving forward))
3		E: How do families celebrate <birthdays> in your country?
4		S: uh:: cel- (.5) uh actually this is (.) uh I am not sure, everybody is different. Uh:
5	→	(1.5) ah: uh (1.5) I Can I look at your and ah ((pointing at the interviewer's script))
6		E: Uh, Birthday parties= ((showing surprised face, hiding the script))
7		S: =Yes
8		E: Uh huh, uh Can you describe birthday parties in China, [what people do?
9		S: [Uh Ah OK
10		E: uh [huh
11		S: [In China, ah:: (1.0) uh for me, I want- my birthday, I just I with my friend
12		and ah eat some food, that's OK.

It seems that students with Speaking scores around 5.5 and above hardly encountered listening difficulties. Among the 17 test takers who encountered listening-related communication problems in this study, there were only three students who scored around 5.5 and above in some of the analytical criteria in Part 3 (S06, S26 and S04, see Tables 9.21, 9.22 and 9.23; the overall scores of S26 and S04 did not reach 5.5, but their analytical scores on *Lexical Resource* and *Grammatical Range and Accuracy* criteria in Part 3 were around or above 5.5).

These test takers seemed to know the nature of their listening problems more specifically, and asked a specific question rather than simply asking for a repetition. Two of them explicitly asked for a re-formulation or explanation of a question. This could suggest that they did not have a problem in decoding sound information at the phoneme, syllable, word, syntax and intonation levels (see Field 2008:114–115, for a model of decoding processes). Rather, they might have had a problem or lacked confidence in relating a proposition to its wider context or co-text. Thus, the problem was more related to the stage of 'meaning building' (adding to the literal meaning provided by decoding and relating it to what has been said before and the listener's background knowledge). Their spoken proficiency was also high enough to express their need for a re-formulation or explanation of the question rather than simply making one-word requests such as 'Sorry?'.

Excerpt 4 below shows how naturally S06 asked the examiner to rephrase the question in line 4. As shown in Table 9.21 below, S06's Listening score was 26 out of 27, indicating her high proficiency in listening (around the C1 level). Her Speaking scores in all analytical criteria but pronunciation were around Band 6.0 or above. In line 6, following some hesitation devices, she uttered 'What do you mean by', and the examiner re-formulated the question in a latching manner (i.e., the two turns were not overlapping but there was no gap at all between them). After the re-formulation, she understood the question and provided the answer in lines 6–9. In the short interview after this test session, she remembered this interaction and mentioned that she knew the meaning of *originated* but could not retrieve the meaning on the spot; 'I forgot the meaning of *originated*. I was thinking "how can I forget it?" and I asked the meaning of *originated* and I understood it.' (S06). She was one of the few students who actually remembered their own communication problem well and who could explain the problem in detail.

Table 9.21 Student S06's Listening and Speaking scores

Listening	Speaking	Flu	Lex	Gram	Pron
26	Part 2	6.30	6.08	6.21	5.36
	Part 3	6.00	5.97	5.97	4.74

Excerpt 4. Topic: Parties (E: Examiner, S: Student S06)

1	*E: Is this a national celebration?=*
2	*S: = a- Yeah*
3	*E: Uh, How do you think it's originated?*
4 →	*S: (.5) Uh:: (.5) what do you mean by=*
5	*E: = How do you think it's started?*
6	*S: Start, uh >( )< international places and people came here for investment or to*
7	*find a job, and they want places to get themselves together,*
8	*E: Uh huh*
9	*S: to maybe uh enjoy, to find relax places for them.*

Excerpt 5 is another example of asking the examiner to re-formulate a question. S24 scored 21 in the Listening test and his analytical Speaking scores in Part 3 were around Band 5.5. While the examiner repeated the same question rather than rephrasing it as requested, S24 immediately got the meaning as shown by his latching utterance in responding to the question in line 4. In the following interview session, he mentioned that he did not find understanding the examiner difficult at all. This could mean that he perhaps did not have any decoding difficulty, but instead he might have been taking some time in processing the meaning in the specific context.

Table 9.22 Student S24's Listening and Speaking scores

Listening	Speaking	Flu	Lex	Gram	Pron
21	Part 2	4.77	4.86	4.67	4.22
	Part 3	4.81	5.83	5.83	5.00

Excerpt 5. Topic: Parties (E: Examiner, S: Student S24)

1	*E: So what what needs to be planned when you are organising a formal party?*
2 →	*S: What do you mean, to be [planned?*
3	*E: [What needs to be planned?=*
4 →	*S: =Ah:: firstly uh time, venue, venue the(h)re ((scratching his head)) ah places*
5	*places, and uh:: hhh (1.0) and you should consider the: the: budget*

The other test taker, S04, who scored a little lower than the above two test takers, seemed to have just missed hearing a word, 'celebrations'. In Excerpt 6 below, S04 prolonged the final vowel of the preceding word 'family:::' to invite the examiner to repeat the following word in line 2. Immediately after the examiner repeated the word, she responded to the question overlapping to the examiner's utterance.

Table 9.23 Student S04's Listening and Speaking scores

Listening	Speaking	Flu	Lex	Gram	Pron
24	Part 2	4.82	4.87	4.12	4.06
	Part 3	5.00	5.44	5.44	4.74

Excerpt 6. Topic: Parties (E: Examiner, S: Student S04)

1   E: Have ah family celebrations changed in your lifetime?

2 → S: (1.0) family::= ((puzzled face, moving forward))

3   E: =celebrations a[h

4   S: [ah: I guess it didn't very, ah it didn't ah change

5   ah (.) much. This huh (.5) Usually, ah du- you celebrate it with

6   your relatives and family members.

In the short interview session, although S04 did not exactly remember any particular communication problems, she reported, 'I had to listen to her, her accent carefully and when I couldn't understand, I asked her to repeat it again'. This could explain this instance.

In general, examiners' comments on these candidates who encountered Type a) problem tended to be consistent between Part 2 and Part 3, and these comments did not seem to reflect listening problems.

b) A test taker asked the examiner to repeat or to rephrase a question, and after the question was repeated or rephrased, they responded irrelevantly to the question

Some test takers asked the examiner to repeat or to rephrase a question, and after the question was repeated, they misunderstood the question and responded irrelevantly. Two of such communication problems were observed as described in Excerpts 7 and 8. In the interview session, both S07 and S09 reported that they encountered difficulties in understanding the examiner due to unknown vocabulary.

It is noteworthy that both S07 and S09 who encountered this problem got much lower scores in Part 3 than in Part 2 (see Tables 9.24 and 9.25).

Table 9.24 Student S07's Listening and Speaking scores

Listening	Speaking	Flu	Lex	Gram	Pron
10	Part 2	5.05	4.87	4.92	5.36
	Part 3	3.79	4.01	4.01	4.04

Excerpt 7. Topic: Parties (E: Examiner, S: Student S07)

1   *E: What about, ah how do family parties compare to more formal parties?*

2 →   *S: Uh::::::: (.5) uh:: ((smiling)) ca(h)n you repeat uh ( ) your question?*

3   *E: Family parties, how do they compare with more formal parties, such as parties in*

4   *schools or universities or in a work place?*

5 →   *S: Uh: So compare uh the uh party from home [and another ah: place.*

6   *E: [Uh huh yes*

7 →   *S: uh (.5) uh: more relax, I think, because ah ( ) your closest, uh closest friend.*

8 →   *Ah a(h)nd a(h)h if you go: to: the party, ah with your how to say, classmates or*

9   *others, you may be able to some some place, ah: suitable for the young people,*

10   *like clu:b, pu:b, but with your: family, you should consider your parents, so you*

11   *should go to the (.) have have ( ) or shopping yeah, in supermarket.*

12 → *E: Uh huh ah do you think social events are important for schools or work places?*

13   *S: Uh, of course.*

In line 2, following a long filled pause and a smile, S07 asked the examiner to repeat a question provided in line 1. The examiner repeated the question, while adding some examples of formal parties ('such as parties in schools or universities or in a work place'). However, S07 interpreted that she would need to compare parties at home and at different places without understanding the contrast between informal and formal parties. This misunderstanding was somehow accepted by the examiner in line 6. Then, from line 7, she started a long turn which was not responding relevantly to the examiner's question. When she completed the turn, the examiner gave a brief response token (Uh huh) and moved on to another question.

In Excerpt 7, it seems that the long filled pause in line 2 and two more filled pauses in lines 5 and 7 were associated with her listening difficulties. The pauses could partially explain why her *Fluency and Coherence* score was around Band 4.0, as the descriptors at Band 4 include 'cannot respond without noticeable pauses'. It is worth noting that S07's *Fluency and Coherence* score in Part 2 was about 5.0. This speculation seems to be supported by examiners' comments, as their comments on S07's *Fluency and Coherence* in Part 3 included 'cannot speak without noticeable pauses', while they thought that S07 was able to 'maintain flow of speech' with 'some hesitation' in Part 2 (see Appendix 9.4). Hence, this part of the descriptor seems particularly related to the fluency construct in Part 3, which involves a role for listening proficiency. Such discrepancy in the fluency construct between Part 2 and Part 3 might account for Brown's (2006b) finding that the examiners found the interpretation of the *Fluency and Coherence* scale the most difficult among the four analytical scales.

Excerpt 8 shows a similar example to Excerpt 7. S09 asked the examiner the meaning of 'national celebration' in lines 3 and 5. After the examiner rephrased it to 'national party', S09 misunderstood it, and started talking about parties with international people in line 7. This was the final question in the Speaking test, and the examiner closed the conversation in line 12.

Table 9.25 Student S09's Listening and Speaking scores

Listening	Speaking	Flu	Lex	Gram	Pron
11	Part 2	3.82	3.35	4.12	4.06
	Part 3	3.79	3.03	3.03	4.04

Excerpt 8. Topic: Parties (E: Examiner, S: Student S09)

1   *E: Uh and can you tell me about (.) national celebrations in your country?*

2   *Can you describe a national celebration?*

3 → *S: Uh: national celebration?*

4   *E: Uh huh*

5 → *S: (2.0) Uh I don't understand what this mean.*

6   *E: OK, ah like a national (.) party=*

7 → *S: =Ah year, ah uh ah before come here before, my English is very very bad, [so*

8   *E: [huh*

9   *S: I- I am afraid to meet uh national people, so I think I can't come here.*

10   *E: Uh huh.*

11   *S: Uh*

12 → *E: OK. Thank you very much. This is the end of the speaking test.*

Like S07 above, examiners also commented on S09's pauses for their judgement of the *Fluency and Coherence* scores in Part 3 (e.g. noticeable pauses (Examiner A, Band 4)), although their comments on Part 2 were more related to coherence features (e.g., gives a short, simple response, repeats ideas, overuses 'but', and the coherence of the speech flow breaks down on two occasions (Examiner D, Band 4)).

c) A test taker misunderstood a question and 1) responded very irrelevantly to the question or 2) gave a somewhat related but mostly irrelevant response

Test takers did not always notice a problem related to their listening difficulties. Sometimes they misunderstood a question without realising the difficulties that they encountered and responded very irrelevantly to the question. This tended to happen with test takers at a lower level of listening and speaking proficiency, and it seems that these test takers tended to get considerably lower scores in Part 3 than in Part 2 (see Tables 9.26 and 9.27). When this type of miscommunication occurred, the examiner tended to ask a question to change the deviated topic back to the originally intended topic, but the miscommunication tended to be solved much later or not solved at all.

Table 9.26 Student S17's Listening and Speaking scores

Listening	Speaking	Flu	Lex	Gram	Pron
3	Part 2	4.82	4.87	4.92	4.92
	Part 3	2.00	2.85	2.85	3.49

Excerpt 9. Topic: Parties (E: Examiner, S: Student S17)

1   *E: How do families celebrate birthdays in your country?*

2 → *S: uh birthday is the ah first (.5) ah October.*

3   *E: Uh huh*

4   *S: yeah.*

5   *E: How how do they celebrate birthdays?*

6 → *S: (2.5) Ah (.5) I don't know how to call this (.5) ah (1.0)*

7   *E: Do families have parties for a birthday?*

8 → *S: Uh:: (.5) No, just together have a dinner.*

9   *E: Alright.*

In Excerpt 9, S17 told the examiner his birthday in line 2, instead of describing how families would celebrate birthdays in his country. This miscommunication implies that S17 must have understood the keyword 'birthday' only and guessed the meaning of the question. The examiner repeated the question in line 5, which S17 again failed to understand. Then, the question was rephrased in line 7, which seemed to be understood as shown in S17's response in line 8. Considerably lower scores were given to his performance in Part 3 compared to Part 2. His analytical scores in Part 3 were 1.5 to 2.5 bands lower than those in Part 2. While S17 had three more communication problems that were categorised into Type d), this serious miscommunication must have helped to make the examiner match his performance to 'little communication possible' at Band 2 of the *Fluency and Coherence* scale and 'has insufficient vocabulary for less familiar topics' at Band 3 of the *Lexical Resources* scale. This seems to be supported by the examiners' comments on S17's performance shown below (comments on the other two criteria are also shown in Appendix 9.4).

Fluency and Coherence

- *Part 2: was slow speech to keep going (Examiner C, Band 5); maintains flow of speech but does not use connectors to organise the response (Examiner D, Band 4)*
- *Part 3: long pauses, frequently unable to convey basic message, little communication possible (Examiner C, Band 2); the candidate speaks with very long pauses (Examiner D, Band 2)*

Lexical Resource

- *Part 2: limited flexibility (Examiner C, Band 5); limited resource, covering familiar topics only; word choice error ('I think the party is very well') (Examiner D, Band 4)*
- *Part 3: has insufficient vocabulary, very little production, just repetition of test questions (Examiner C, Band 2); uses simple vocabulary to convey personal information (Examiner D, Band 3)*

Excerpt 10 shows another test taker's serious misunderstanding of the examiner's question. It seemed that S18 interpreted 'hobby' as 'habit'. Perhaps due to the limited intelligibility of her pronunciation of 'eat', it appeared that the examiner did not realise that S18 was talking about her habit, but assumed that she was talking about 'meeting' people through her hobby (instead of 'eating' an apple a day as a habit). The examiner asked, 'Is it a good way to meet new people?' in line 5. From this point, the misunderstanding continued for a while, till this topic ended in line 16. As shown in Table 9.27, this test taker's scores in Part 3 were almost one band lower than those in Part 2.

Table 9.27 Student S18's Listening and Speaking scores

Listening	Speaking	Flu	Lex	Gram	Pron
5	Part 2	3.66	4.03	4.07	4.07
	Part 3	3.00	3.06	3.06	3.06

Excerpt 10. Topic: Interest (E: Examiner, S: Student S18)

1   *E: Do you think having a hobby is good for people's social life?*

2 → *S: Yeah, I think it's good to people. Ah: (.5) uh example, for example*

3   *uh I like ah to (eat) apple everyday. I my ( ) tell me uh ah:: one day one people,*

4   *people have.*

5 → *E: Is it a good way to meet new people?*

6   *S: Yeah*

7   *(1.0)*

8   *E: Is it a good way to meet ((moving her right hand forward)) [other people?*

9   *S: [((imitating the*

10	*examiner's gesture)) it's good to new, it's uh: good to*
11	*(.5) uh it's (.5) I don't kno(h)w.*
12	*E: Can you make <new friends> [with your hobby?*
13	*S: [Yeah, yeah I meet my new friends with uh,*
14	*when I ru I ru ra because I feed you oh no no no I meet you and uh: he and she*
15	*and she and she ((gesture of running)), she is brand-new so I with you together.*
16	*E: OK.*

In the short interview session, both S17 and S18 reported that it was difficult to understand the examiner's question, though they could not elaborate on the problems they had encountered.

On the other hand, even when a test taker misunderstood the question and responded irrelevantly, if the response was relatively related to the questioned topic, he or she did not tend to get lower scores in Part 3 than in Part 2. Unlike the above two examples where the test takers' Listening and Speaking scores were quite low (Listening score: 3–5, Speaking score in Part 3: 2.0–3.5), occurrences of slight misunderstanding were observed with students who had a little higher proficiency-level of listening (scores at 9–12) and speaking (around Band 5.0). Furthermore, when the response was mostly irrelevant but still related, it seemed that the examiner tended to amend the deviated topic back to the original track in the course of topic development (see Excerpt 11) or just let it pass (see Excerpt 12).

Table 9.28 Student S02's Listening and Speaking scores

Listening	Speaking	Flu	Lex	Gram	Pron
12	Part 2	5.05	4.87	4.12	4.92
	Part 3	5.00	5.00	5.00	5.13

Excerpt 11. Topic: Parties (E: Examiner, S: Student S02)

1	*E: Uh what do you think family celebrations may have changed in any way*
2	*in your lifetime?*
3 →	*S: Yeah yes might be (1.0) but parents are the most important people for me.*
4	*E: Uh In what way?*
5	*S: Uh: some- sometimes my teacher to teach me how to do something, and*
6	*sometimes it could be my ah little brother just the: share fashion information,*
7	*and the sometime the- my parents they told me ( ) dangerous things dra(h)gs*
8	*or something else.*
9	*(.5)*
10	*E: Uh, what about other parties? How do family parties compare to more formal*

11   *parties, like at school or in the work place?*

12 →   *S: Ah: I think family member can't be changed, but uh school colleague uh*

13   *membership can be changed. If I don't like this school, or you don't like this*

14   *company, you can change another one. But if you don't like your parents,*

15   *can't be cha(h)nged. So (.5)*

16   *E: Ah and family parties (.5) ah are they different from or similar to parties*

17   *in a school, for example?*

18 →   *S: Uh:: uh Some parties are similar. Because we are ah so- uh together every*

19   *time, sometime we: call each other, each other with small things, but most*

20   *times, uh: we can (.) stay well, I think.*

21   *E: Uh huh*

In Excerpt 11, while the examiner asked about any changes in family celebrations in the test taker's lifetime, S02 started talking about the importance of her parents to her. However, since this was followed by 'Yeah yes might be (1.0) but' (line 3), her response, '<u>parents</u> are the most important people for me', sounded related to the topic, contrasting what has been changed and what has not been changed in her lifetime within a broader topic of families. Then, in line 10, the examiner returned to the original topic of parties, and asked another question about any differences between family parties and more formal parties. Again, S02's response from line 12 was slightly off topic, although she was talking about people who would be involved in family parties and more formal parties. In line 16, the examiner made another attempt to change the topic back to parties, emphasising '<u>family parties</u>', and rephrased the question that was raised in line 10. At that point, it seemed that S02 got the meaning of the question and said, 'Uh:: uh Some parties are similar' in line 18, although she failed to justify the opinion.

Excerpt 12 below shows another example of a test taker's misunderstanding of the examiner's question. Instead of providing a response regarding the importance of national celebrations for a country, S32 talked about international celebrations and communication between different countries. In this example, the examiner did not make any attempt to obtain an answer to the original question, and closed the topic by saying 'OK'.

Table 9.29 Student S32's Listening and Speaking scores

Listening	Speaking	Flu	Lex	Gram	Pron
9	Part 2	4.82	4.87	4.92	4.92
	Part 3	4.81	4.83	4.83	5.00

Excerpt 12. Topic: Parties (E: Examiner, S: Student S32)

1   E: *How important are national celebrations for a country, do you think?*

2 → S: *Uh: I think it's communication which uh con- the uh among countries*

3   *they should uh: talk to each other and how to protect our (rules) and how to*

4   *uh (contend) between the countries.*

5   E: *OK.*

Both S02 and S32 did not report any listening problems in the short interview sessions, suggesting that they did not notice the mismatch between the examiner's questions and their responses. Examiners' comments between Parts 2 and 3 on S02's and S32's performances were also relatively consistent.

d) A test taker echoed a part that they did not understand to signal their comprehension difficulty, sometimes with notable facial expressions or gestures

Test takers' listening problems were also signalled without an explicit question to repeat or rephrase a question. Some test takers simply echoed the part that they did not understand. This was often accompanied with notable facial expressions or gestures. This echoing strategy was utilised by test takers with their Listening scores from 3 to 10 and Speaking scores from 2.0 to 4.5.

As shown in Excerpts 13 and 14, some test takers utilised such echoing as the first question, followed by an explicit request to repeat the question, which confirmed that they echoed to signal their problems in understanding the examiner.

Table 9.30 Student S03's Listening and Speaking scores

Listening	Speaking	Flu	Lex	Gram	Pron
8	Part 2	4.65	4.83	4.07	4.94
	Part 3	4.32	4.43	4.43	5.03

Excerpt 13. Topic: Interest (E: Examiner, S: Student S03)

1   E: *Do you think they <u>will</u> get more free time?*

2 → S: *Uh: (.5) I think, uh more free time ((unfocused eyes, stroking his chin))*

3   E: *Will they, will they get more free time?*

4   *(.5)*

5   S: *uh I don't understand your questi(h)on. ((stroking his chin))*

6   E: *Do you think in the future, the job people do, ah will be uh will take up a lot*

7   *of their time, or they will work less and have more free time?*

8   S: *(.5) Yes, I I think that people work less and you can more free time to relax,*

9   *but (.) but they have no mon-, only a little money.*

In Excerpt 13, after the examiner's question in line 1, S03 murmured "more free time" with his eyes unfocused and while stroking his chin, which triggered the examiner to repeat the question. Looking at the discourse only by this point, it may not be certain if the murmur was indicating a listening-related difficulty (i.e. this might also be signalling a problem in generating an idea to answer the question). However, after half a second of silence, he explicitly stated that he did not understand the question, again while stroking his chin, indicating that the echoing was actually signalling his difficulty in understanding the question.

The following example is similar to Excerpt 14. S11 echoed 'changed' in line 2 while pinching his cheek. Following the utterance and gesture, the examiner rephrased the question in line 3. Then, S11 made an explicit request for the examiner to repeat the question, indicating that the echoing was signalling his comprehension problem.

Table 9.31 Student S11's Listening and Speaking scores

Listening	Speaking	Flu	Lex	Gram	Pron
10	Part 2	4.04	4.04	4.12	3.88
	Part 3	3.79	4.01	4.01	3.66

Excerpt 14. Topic: Parties (E: Examiner, S: Student S11)

1 E: Have ah celebrations changed in your life time?

2 → S: ah:: Changed ((pinching his cheek))

3 E: Have have they changed? Are they different?

4 → S: (.5) Uh: (1.0) Can you repeat it again?

5 E: Uh huh. for example, when you were younger or when you were a child,

6 did you have the same kind of birthday party you have now?

7 S: No I haven't.

8 E: Can you tell me the differences?

9 S: OK

In the short interview after each Speaking test session, both S03 and S11 reported that they had difficulties in understanding the examiner, saying 'One time, I didn't understand a question, it was about my interest in the future' (S03) and 'Some words I cannot understand' (S11).

For S11's performance, Examiner C wrote down 'frequently fails to understand the question, simple responses, limited ability to link sentences' as her reason for awarding Band 3 for the *Fluency and Coherence* scale. Among all examiners' comments, this was the only one comment explicitly referring to the candidate's understanding of questions paused by the examiner. Although no generalisation can be made based on one instance, it is still interesting to note that the only one comment on the candidate's difficulty in understanding the examiner was made for the *Fluency and Coherence* scale.

e) A test taker answered 'no' to a question they did not understand

Finally, there were two instances of a test taker saying 'no' to a question that she did not understand. This test taker exemplified in Excerpt 15 is the same test taker shown in Table 9.25 above (also presented again below).

Table 9.25 Student S09's Listening and Speaking scores

Listening	Speaking	Flu	Lex	Gram	Pron
11	Part 2	3.82	3.35	4.12	4.06
	Part 3	3.79	3.03	3.03	4.04

Excerpt 15. Topic: Parties (E: Examiner, S: Student S09)

1		E: *Ah, Have family celebrations changed in your lifetime?*
2		*(2.5)*
3	→	S: *No no uh*
4		E: *Have they, they have always been the same?*
5		*(2.0)*
6	→	S: *N(h)o*
7		E: *Uh, can you tell me more about this?*
8	→	S: *(1.0) Uh .hh can repeat the question, sorry?*
9		E: *Uh huh when you were younger, [did you have the same birthday party as you have now,*
10		S: *[uh*
11		E: *when you are a bit older?*
12		S: *Uh when I was a child, uh I my grandmother don't like me,*

In Excerpt 15, for a question regarding any changes in family celebrations in the test taker's lifetime, after 2.5 seconds of silence, S09 responded negatively in line 3, by simply uttering 'No no uh'. However, in line 4, when the examiner confirmed her answer by rephrasing the question, S09 said 'N(h)o' after 2 seconds of silence. This response was actually contradictory to her first response due to the way the examiner re-formulated the question. Then, the examiner requested S09 to elaborate on her contradictory responses. Only at that time did she express that she in fact had not understood the preceding questions, and she asked the examiner to repeat the question in line 8.

Although this was the only example of this type of communication problem occurrence among the 36 test takers in the main study, a similar example was also observed in the pilot stage of this study. When the researcher asked the student why he said 'no' for what he did not actually understand, he mentioned that it was a test-taking strategy, as examiners are likely to move on to the next question if he gives a negative answer. While it is not certain whether or not S09 in the main study also said 'no' for the same reason, it is worth noting that this could be a test-taking strategy that some test takers might utilise when encountering a comprehension problem in Speaking tests.

This section has illustrated how communication problems in Part 3 that seemed to be related to test takers' difficulties in understanding the examiner occurred and how they were dealt with, and categorised these occurrences into five types. It has been suggested that a certain type of listening-related communication problem could be linked to a certain level of listening and speaking proficiency. Each pattern of communication problems and test takers' listening scores and Part 3 Speaking analytical scores can be summarised as follows:

- *Type a)* asking a question and then responding relevantly [Listening scores: 5–12, Part 3 Speaking analytical scores: 4.0–5.0 (occasionally those with higher listening (21–26) and spoken proficiency at 5.5 and above)]
- *Type b)* asking a question and then responding irrelevantly [Listening scores: 10–11, Part 3 Speaking analytical scores: 3.0–4.0]
- *Type c1)* misunderstanding a question and responding very irrelevantly [Listening scores: 10–11, Part 3 Speaking analytical scores: 2.0–3.0]
- *Type c2)* misunderstanding a question and giving a somewhat related but mostly irrelevant response [Listening scores: 2–12, Part 3 Speaking analytical scores: 5.0]
- *Type d)* echoing uncomprehended parts [Listening scores: 3–19, Part 3 Speaking analytical scores: 2.0–4.5]
- *Type e)* saying 'no' to an uncomprehended question [Listening score: 11, Part 3 Speaking analytical scores: 3.0–4.0]

It has also been suggested that a certain type of breakdown could be contributing more to lowering test takers' Part 3 scores than their Part 2 scores. Among these patterns of listening-related communication problems, some test takers who had Type *b)*, Type *c1)* and Type *d)* problems received considerably lower scores in Part 2 than in Part 3. However, Speaking scores in Part 2 and Part 3 did not differ for test takers with Type *a)* and Type *c2)* problems, and some of them even received higher scores in Part 3 than in Part 2. Such interpretations of the interactional data were, whenever possible, elaborated on or supported by the candidates' interview data and examiners' comments for awarding scores that they did.

Test takers who had some of the Part 3 analytical scores at 5.5 and above did not tend to encounter listening-related problems during Part 3, and even when it happened, they solved the problem naturally with an appropriate request. It demonstrates their understandings of the nature of the problems that they encountered, and their listening problems in the processing model seemed to be associated with the higher, meaning-building level, or indicated that they had just missed hearing a particular word. Therefore, the results suggest that a possible boundary in bands where the degree of impact of test takers' listening proficiency changes might be Band 5.0.

5.5 Test takers' perceptions of communication problems

Immediately after each Speaking test session, a short semi-structured interview was carried out on the participating students' perceptions of any communication problems encountered with the examiner in Part 3 of the test (some of the short interview data has already been briefly referred to in 5.4 for illustrative purposes). The interviews followed three scripted questions. The researcher took notes during the interview and these interviews were also audio-recorded. The first two questions were to be answered with 5-point Likert scales (1. Strongly disagree 2. Disagree 3. Neutral 4. Agree 5. Strongly agree). Figures 9.9 and 9.10 show the visual representations of responses to these two questions.

For Question 1, '*I could understand the examiner's questions very well*', 22 students out of the 36 students (61.1%) strongly agreed and 12 students (33.3%) agreed with the statement, while only two students (5.6%) disagreed. Thus, approximately 95% of the students indicated that they could understand the examiner's questions without major problems.

Figure 9.9 Understanding the examiner

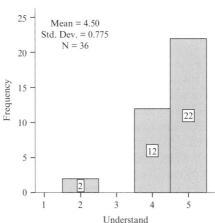

Figure 9.10 Answering the examiner

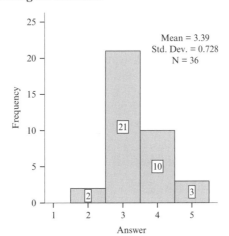

For Question 2, '*I could answer the examiner's questions very well*', the responses were more varied. Three students (8.3%) strongly agreed, 10 students (27.8%) agreed, 21 students (58.3%) showed a neutral view to the statement, and two students (5.6%) disagreed. Therefore, students were less positive about their perception towards their performances of answering the examiner's questions, and more than half of the students showed a neutral view.

The two students who disagreed with both statements were S17 and S18. Both of their communication problems were illustrated in Excerpts 9 and 10 above. Interestingly, both of them experienced a similar listening-related miscommunication situation, where they misunderstood the examiner and responded very irrelevantly and the examiner tried to change the misunderstood topic back to the original track, which turned out to be unsuccessful.

Following these questions, they were asked to describe *what they found difficult when they were communicating with the examiner and if/how these difficulties were solved*. Students could mention more than one difficulty. Their responses can be generally broken down as in Table 9.32.

More difficulties in speaking (N=23) were reported than those in listening (N=7). These difficulties were further classified according to the nature of the problems that students reported (see the third and fourth columns of Table 9.32). Vocabulary-related difficulties were most frequently reported both for listening and speaking.

Out of the seven listening problems reported, five responses were related to vocabulary. As shown in example responses below, when students encountered listening problems, three of them reported that they asked the examiner to repeat or rephrase the questions and they were able to solve the problems.

Table 9.32 Difficulties encountered while communicating with the examiner in Part 3

Problems in:	Number of responses	Related to:	Number of responses
Listening	7*	Vocabulary	5
		Pronunciation	1
Speaking	23	Vocabulary	15
		Topics	7
		Grammar	7
		Pronunciation	4
		Fluency	1
		Organisation	1
Others	7	Nervous	6
		Lack of experience	1
No problems	4		

* *One response did not elaborate about the nature of the difficulty.*

Listening (vocabulary)

- *Sometime I don't understand questions. About parties, family party, friends party, I don't understand questions (S30).*
- *One time, I didn't understand a question. About my interest in the future. I asked the examiner to repeat the question and understood the question (S03).*
- *Some questions I can't understand the meaning, because it's not very large. It wasn't solved. I skipped the vocabulary (S08).*
- *Some words I cannot understand. If I cannot understand the words meaning, I asked the questions to be repeated (S11).*
- *I forgot the meaning of 'originated'. I was thinking 'how can I forget it?' and I asked the meaning of 'originated' and I understood it (S06).*

Listening (pronunciation)

- *I had to listen to her, her accent carefully and when I couldn't understand, I asked her to repeat it again (S04).*

Hence, to summarise test takers' own perceptions towards their communication problems with the examiner in Part 3 of the test, almost 60% of the students neither agreed nor disagreed with the statement that they could answer the examiner's questions very well. This result seems reasonable, considering the spoken proficiency level of the participating students and the target level of the IELTS Speaking test. On the other hand, about 95% of the students thought that they could understand the examiner's questions fairly well, and even when they encountered some listening problems, most of them reported that they could solve their problems. Therefore, most students did not feel that their listening proficiency caused a major problem in communicating with the examiner in Part 3 of the Speaking test.

However, it is also worth noting that Section 5.4 showed 17 out of the 36 participating students in fact encountered listening-related communication problems, whether the problem was serious or not. It also illustrated some examples of misunderstanding on the part of the test taker, without realising their misunderstanding of the examiner's questions. In particular, such incidences that were categorised in Type *b) asking a question and then responding irrelevantly*, and Type *c1) misunderstanding a question and responding very irrelevantly*, were those which might have led the examiner to make a harsher judgement on Part 3 scores.

6   Conclusion

This study has investigated the relationship between test takers' listening proficiency and their performance on Part 3 (discussion) of the IELTS Speaking test, as against that on Part 2 (individual long turn). It has explored how communication problems associated with test takers' listening proficiency arose and how these problems were dealt with by the test takers and the examiners.

Overall performance, as captured by aggregated scores, did not show any significant difference between Part 2 and Part 3. However, in some cases, as shown in Appendix 9.2, there were noticeable differences in the band scores obtained by individual test takers on these two parts of the test. The difference in the scores awarded to some test takers' performances on Part 2 and Part 3 was greater than 1.0 band (for example, see *S07, S17, S18, S21* and *S26* in Appendix 9.2). This suggests that awarding separate scores for test takers' performances on monologic and interactional tasks might provide a clearer picture of test takers' differential abilities across these different modes of speaking. However, it should be noted that I am not recommending that separate scores should be reported to the end-users, who would probably prefer the simpler option of a single Speaking band score. This recommendation applies to the rating system, or how the final Speaking band scores should be reached. O'Sullivan (2007) and O'Sullivan and Nakatsuhara (2011) advocate separate scores for different test tasks, arguing that a single score for performances on a number of tasks will not provide a clear reflection of a test taker's speaking proficiency. O'Sullivan's (2007) argument was based on the impact on performance of variables associated with a test taker's interlocutor in paired tests. O'Sullivan and Nakatsuhara (2011) refer to the effects of the nature of the tasks used in group oral tests on test taker conversational style (measured by topic initiation, topic ratification and the amount of talk). They express their concerns that when a single score is awarded for performance on a set of tasks, the examiner's decision on the overall score might be overly influenced by either good or poor performance on a particular task.

The findings of this study support their arguments, providing empirical evidence that, for some test takers, scores on different tasks, when rated separately, can vary to a noticeable extent. In order to ensure that differential abilities displayed in different tasks all feed into the final scores to reflect the construct of the test as a whole, separate ratings on different tasks are preferable. Set against this are the practical constraints all examining boards have to work under. There would be an increased burden on the examiners, especially as they are acting both as an interlocutor and an examiner. It might be worth considering the possibility of introducing a non-live second marking system where the separate scoring method is employed using test takers' recorded performance. This could be a relatively cost-effective solution for generating more reliable scores without placing any additional burden on the examiners in the live tests.

Furthermore, the data confirmed that the level of language produced by test takers was significantly higher in Part 2 than in Part 3 for the *Fluency and Coherence* category. The interactional data also indicated that it could be those aspects of fluency which relate to interaction that contributed to the differences (e.g. filled and unfilled pauses before responding to the examiner), serving to depress performance on this criterion. This suggests that, in order to offer a true reflection of a candidate's true ability required in the two tasks, it might be worth considering using different formulations of the *Fluency and Coherence* descriptors in rating performance on Part 3 from those used in rating Part 2, explicitly making the Part 3 descriptors reflect the construct of listening-into-speaking. For instance, since some listening-related problems tend to be realised at turn-initial parts of test takers' utterances, descriptors for Part 3 could include graded (dis)fluency elements associated with turn-initial parts of test takers' utterances, such as hesitations, false starts, repetition and reformulation. Descriptors about how naturally they request the examiner to repeat, rephrase or explain a question, when they have listening-related difficulties, and how they fill a gap in their turn-initial parts to gain some time to formulate ideas and utterances will also be useful, taking into consideration the cognitive processing demands of interactional communication that take place under time pressure. It is also important that the examiner training should make examiners more aware of the role of listening in Part 3 of the test. On the other hand, descriptors for Part 2 could expect fewer hesitation markers and less repetition and a greater extent of coherence in utterances from test takers at the same proficiency level, considering the nature of monologic speech and also the 1-minute planning time prior to the monologue (Field 2011).

The discrepancies in the fluency construct between Part 2 and Part 3 may also help to explain Brown's (2006b) finding that the examiners found the *Fluency and Coherence* scale the most difficult to interpret. In addition to the ambiguity in test takers' hesitations whether they are caused by a search for ideas or a search for language (Brown, 2006b:51), this study highlights another level of complexity in interpreting the cause of hesitations, which is whether test takers are hesitating because of their speaking-related limitations or listening-related limitations. Formulating separate sets of descriptors for monologic and interactional tasks, reflecting a clearer operationalisation of the *Fluency and Coherence* construct, and providing separate scores on each part could be a key to solving this issue.

The results of this study have also suggested that the Part 3 interactive task assesses a more integrated listening-into-speaking construct as distinct from the more purely speaking construct measured in the Part 2 monologic task. Correlations between listening and speaking scores were higher in Part 3 (discussion) than in Part 2 (individual long turn), and some of the differences approached significance even with the small sample size of this study. There was additional evidence in the interactional data presented in the study that the construct underlying Part 3 of the IELTS Speaking test was not a purely productive speaking ability, especially for those at Band 5.0 (in Part 3) and below who tended to have some difficulties in understanding the examiner. In contrast, test takers at Band 5.5 and above did not tend to encounter listening-related problems, and even when they did, they solved the problem naturally with an appropriate, specific request, demonstrating their understandings of the nature of listening problems, or they have just missed hearing a particular word. This finding would seem to support Seedhouse and Egbert's (2006) supposition that there would be a correlation between the IELTS Speaking test scores and difficulty in hearing or understanding on the part of test takers. It may be that for students at Band 5.0 and below, their deficits in listening affected attention or working memory capacity, which might have impaired speech planning. The importance of listening ability to the discussion task is also reflected in the stronger correlation between the Listening test scores and scores awarded to Part 3 discussion tasks as against Part 2 monologue tasks. Additionally, in case the weight of listening seems larger than it should be (e.g. S17 who had difficulties in understanding almost all questions posed by the examiner), it might also be worth considering using easier question scripts for low-level test takers so they can follow the examiner and provide ratable speech samples in Part 3. This would improve the scoring validity of the IELTS Speaking tests for candidates with Band 5.0 and below. However, great caution may be required if easier question scripts are to be introduced, because it could compromise comparability and fairness. If this recommendation is pursued, rules on the use of graded cues should be clearly established, integrated into the interlocutor frame and examiner training.

In conclusion, the findings of this study have highlighted the differences between monologue and interactional tasks in terms of the constructs they measure, showing that the latter format, at least to some extent, measures listening-into-speaking abilities. This has broader implications for the relationship between test takers' listening proficiency and performance on other more interactive Speaking test formats such as paired and group oral tests. However, in these peer–peer formats, since all test takers are supposed to have an equal level of goal-orientation and they can manage the interaction as they wish, they could more freely use avoidance strategies to cover their listening limitations (e.g. Excerpt 15). Test takers in these formats are also expected to support each other to be fluent and create a 'confluence' in the conversation (McCarthy 2005), and thus the listening deficits might not be as noticeable as an examiner–examinee format. Future studies comparing monologue, examiner–examinee discussion and peer–peer discussion tasks will be useful to gain further insights into this issue.

7 Limitations of the study and future research

This study has shortcomings to be acknowledged in terms of its methodological design and its scope. Based on these limitations, some directions for future research will be proposed in order to confirm and extend the findings of the present study.

As described in Section 4.1, 28 out of the total 36 participants shared the same first language, Mandarin Chinese. Therefore, it should be noted that the uneven mix of participants' first languages may restrict the generalisability of the results obtained in this study. Additionally, the length of stay in the UK and the amount of exposure to English outside the class also varied to a large extent. These differences could be potential uncontrolled variables, as learners might listen in a different way once they have integrated into the L2 environment. Hence, it will be necessary to replicate this study with different test taker populations to confirm the findings of this study.

In this study, the Speaking test transcripts and the coded interview data were qualitatively analysed to suggest a possible level boundary that differentiates the degree/types of communication problems related to test takers' listening proficiency on Part 3 speaking performance. However, due to the limited sample sizes, no statistical analysis was utilised for this part. It will be useful to replicate this study with a larger sample size and carry out inferential statistics on the data, to confirm the boundary suggested in this study. Replicating this study with a larger sample size is also necessary to carry out more reliable inferential statistics on the differences in correlations between listening scores and Parts 2 and 3 scores of the Speaking test.

Due to practical constraints, it was not possible to interview students for longer than 5 minutes following each Speaking test session. In future research, it might be more informative if retrospective interviews could be carried out with test takers after each test session while showing a video of their performance. Additionally, more detailed information could probably be obtained if these retrospective interviews could be conducted in the test taker's L1, since it seemed too demanding for some students at the lower proficiency levels to explain what problems they had encountered while communicating with the examiner.

Finally, to sum up, three key recommendations arise from this study to be considered by the producers of the IELTS Speaking test; they are to:

- score Part 2 and Part 3 of the Speaking test separately
- formulate different descriptors for the *Fluency and Coherence* scale reflecting a clearer operationalisation of the *Fluency and Coherence* construct in Part 2 and Part 3
- grade the language of the interviewer cues, and use easier question scripts for test takers with low-level listening proficiency to help them follow the examiner, in case the weight of listening seems larger than it should be.

Each of these points needs to be further investigated and followed up, in order to confirm and extend the findings of the study and to provide recommendations in fine detail.

Acknowledgements

I am very grateful to Shaida Mohammadi, Head of English at the International Study Centre, Leicester University for allowing me access to students and facilities at the centre and for assisting me with various aspects of the speaking and listening data collection. I am also grateful to Prof Liz Hamp-Lyons for helping me to find IELTS examiners for this study. I am indebted to the students and IELTS examiners who participated in the data collection. I would also like to express my appreciation to Prof Cyril J Weir, Dr Tony Green, Dr Stephen Bax and Dr John Field for their valuable suggestions and comments on earlier versions of this report.

References

Atkinson, J M and Heritage, J (1984) *Structures of social action,* Cambridge, New York: Cambridge University Press.

Bachman, L F, Davidson, F G, Ryan, K and Choi, I- C (1995) *An Investigation into the Comparability of Two Tests of English as a Foreign Language: the Cambridge – TOEFL Comparability Study*, Studies in Language Testing volume 1, Cambridge: UCLES/Cambridge University Press.

Brown, A (2006a) Candidate discourse in the revised IELTS Speaking Test, in McGovern, P and Walsh, S (Eds) *IELTS Research Reports, Volume 6*, Canberra: British Council & IDP Australia, 71–89.

Brown, A (2006b) An examination of the rating process in the revised IELTS Speaking Test, in McGovern, P and Walsh, S (Eds) *IELTS Research Reports, Volume 6*, Canberra: British Council & IDP Australia, 41–69.

Brown, A and Hill, K (1997) Interviewer style and candidate performance in the

IELTS oral interview, in Woods, S (Ed.) *IELTS Research Reports, Volume 1*, Sydney: ELICOS, 1–19.

Brown, A, Iwashita, N and McNamara, T (2005) *An examination of rater orientations and test-taker performance on English-for-Academic-Purposes speaking tests*, TOEFL Monograph Series MS-29, available online at http://www.ets.org/Media/Research/pdf/RR-05-05.pdf.

Cambridge ESOL (2008a) *Cambridge Certificate in Advanced English 2*, Cambridge: Cambridge University Press.

Cambridge ESOL (2008b) *Cambridge First Certificate in English 2*, Cambridge: Cambridge University Press.

Cambridge ESOL (2009a) *Cambridge Certificate in Advanced English 3*, Cambridge: Cambridge University Press:

Cambridge ESOL (2009b) *Cambridge First Certificate in English 3*, Cambridge: Cambridge University Press.

Cohen, J (1998) *Statistical Power Analysis for the Behavioural Sciences*, Hillsdale, NJ: Erlbaum.

Council of Europe (2001) *Common European Framework of Reference for Languages: Learning, teaching, assessment*, Cambridge: Cambridge University Press.

Ducasse, A M and Brown, A (2009) Assessing paired orals: Raters' orientation to interaction, *Language Testing* 26 (3), 423–443.

ffrench, A (2003) The change process at the paper level – Paper 5, Speaking, in Weir, C J and Milanovic, M (Eds) *Continuity and Innovation: Revising the Cambridge Proficiency in English Examination 1913–2002*, Cambridge: UCLES/Cambridge University Press, 367–471.

Field, J (2008) *Listening in the Language Classroom*, Cambridge: Cambridge University Press.

Field, J (2011) Cognitive validity, in Taylor, L (Ed.) *Examining Speaking: Research and Practice in Assessing Second Language Speaking*, Studies in Language Testing 30, Cambridge: UCLES/Cambridge University Press, 65–111.

Galaczi, E D (2010) *Interactional competence across proficiency levels*, oral presentation at the 32nd Language Testing Research Colloquium, University of Cambridge, UK, April 2010.

Geranpayeh, A (2007) Using Structural Equation Modelling to facilitate the revision of high stakes testing: the case of CAE, *Research Notes* 30, 8–12.

Green, A (2007) *IELTS Washback in Context: Preparation for Academic Writing in Higher Education*, Studies in Language Testing volume 25, Cambridge: UCLES/Cambridge University Press.

Hawkey, R (2009) *Examining FCE and CAE: Key Issues and Recurring Themes in Developing the First Certificate in English and Certificate in Advanced English Exams*, Studies in Language Testing volume 28, Cambridge: UCLES/Cambridge University Press.

Howell, D (2002) *Statistical Methods for Psychology*, Pacific Grove, CA: Duxbury.

Hutchby, I and Wooffitt, R (1998) *Conversation Analysis*, Cambridge: Cambridge University Press.

IELTS Partners (2006) *IELTS scores explained* (DVD).

Joyce, P (2008) *Linguistic knowledge and psycholinguistic processing skills as components of L2 listening comprehension*, unpublished PhD thesis, Roehampton University.

Lee, Y-W (2006) Dependability of scores for a new ESL speaking assessment consisting of integrated and independent tasks, *Language Testing* 23 (2), 131–166.

Linacre, M (2006) *A User's Guide to FACETS: Rasch- model Computer Programs,* Chicago, IL: MESA Press.

May, L (2007) *Interaction in a paired speaking test: the rater's perspective,* unpublished PhD thesis, the University of Melbourne, Australia.

McCarthy, M (2005) Fluency and confluence: What fluent speakers do, *The Language Teacher* 29 (6), 26–28.

McNamara, T F (1996) *Measuring Second Language Performance,* Harlow: Longman.

Mohammadi, S (2009) *Assessing spoken language: Validity in the language proficiency interview,* unpublished MPhil thesis, University of Nottingham, UK.

Nakatsuhara, F (2009) *Conversational styles in group oral tests: How is the conversation co-constructed?* unpublished PhD thesis, the University of Essex, UK.

O'Sullivan, B (2007) *Modelling Performance in Tests of Spoken Language,* Frankfurt: Peter Lang.

O'Sullivan, B and Lu, Y (2006) The impact on candidate language of examiner deviation from a set interlocutor frame in the IELTS Speaking Test, in McGovern, P and Walsh, S (Eds) *IELTS Research Report Volume 6*, Canberra: British Council and IDP Australia, 91–117.

O'Sullivan, B and Nakatsuhara, F (2011) Quantifying conversational styles in group oral test discourse, in O'Sullivan, B (Ed.) *Language Testing: Theories and Practices,* London: Palgrave, 164–185.

Sawaki, Y, Stricker, L J and Oranje, A H (2009) Factor structure of the TOEFL Internet-based test, *Language Testing* 26 (1), 5–30.

Seedhouse, P and Egbert, M (2006) The interactional organisation of the IELTS Speaking Test in McGovern, P and Walsh, S (Eds) *IELTS Research Report Volume 6*, Canberra: British Council and IDP Australia, 161–205.

Shin, K (2005) Did they take the same test? Examinee language proficiency and the structure of language tests, *Language Testing* 22 (1), 31–57.

Shiotsu, T and Weir, C J (2007) The relative significance of syntactic knowledge and vocabulary breadth in the prediction of reading comprehension test performance, *Language Testing* 24 (1), 99–128.

Stricker, L J, Rock, D A and Lee, Y-W (2005) *Factor structure of the LanguEdge test across language groups (TOEFL Monograph Series MS-32),* Princeton, NJ: Educational Testing Service.

UCLES (2007a) *Certificate in Advanced English: Handbook for teachers,* available online at https://www.teachers.cambridgeesol.org/ts/digitalAssets/109740_cae_hb_dec08.pdf

UCLES (2007b) *First Certificate in English: Handbook for teachers,* available online at: http://www.cambridgeesol.org/assets/pdf/resources/teacher/fce_hb_dec08.pdf

van Lier, L (1989) Reeling, writhing, drawing, stretching, and fainting in coils: Oral proficiency interviews as conversation, *TESOL Quarterly*, 23 (3), 489–508.

Weir, C J (1983) *Identifying the language problems of the overseas students in tertiary education in the UK,* unpublished PhD dissertation, University of London.

Weir, C J (2005) *Language Testing and validation: An Evidence-based Approach*, Basingstoke: Palgrave Macmillan.

Appendix 9.1
Self-assessment questionnaire

To gain information about the participating students' capacity in coping with aural communication as well as oral communication inside and outside the classroom, students were asked to assess their listening and speaking ability, by answering six questions about their everyday English activities and by rating their abilities against two self-assessment grids of the CEFR (COE 2001:27).

The six questions about their everyday English listening and speaking activities were answered with 5-point Likert scales (1. Strongly disagree 2. Disagree 3. Neutral 4. Agree, 5. Strongly agree). The first two questions were about their listening and speaking activities in lectures, the next two questions were about their listening and speaking activities in classes, and the last two questions are about their listening and speaking activities outside the class. Results are shown in Table 9.33 and Figures 9.11–9.16.

Table 9.33 Self-assessment questionnaire results

Questions (N=35)	Mean	SD
a) I find it easy to understand teachers in class.	3.94	.838
b) I find it easy to ask questions in class.	3.63	.808
c) I find it easy to understand discussion in class.	3.94	.802
d) I find it easy to talk in class.	3.91	.781
e) I find it easy to understand English spoken outside the class.	3.49	.742
f) I find it easy to easy to speak English outside the class.	3.51	.781

Firstly, 74.3% of the students agreed or strongly agreed with statement *a) I find it easy to understand teachers in class*, only 48.1% agreed or strongly agreed with *b) I find it easy to ask questions in class*. Wilcoxon Signed Rank test (non-parametric alternative of Paired Samples T-test) showed that the difference between the two sets of ratings was statistically significant ($Z=-2.4$, p=.016).

Secondly, 71.4% of the students agreed or strongly agreed with statement *c) I find it easy to understand discussion in class*, and 71.5% agreed or strongly agreed with *d) I find it easy to talk in class*. The difference between the two sets of ratings was not statistically significant ($Z=-.232$, p=.817).

Figure 9.11 a) easy to understand teachers in class

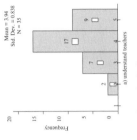

Mean = 3.94
Std. Dev = 0.838
N = 35

a) understand teachers

Figure 9.12 b) easy to ask questions in class

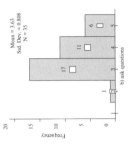

Mean = 3.63
Std. Dev. = 0.808
N = 35

b) ask questions

Finally, 45.7% of the students agreed or strongly agreed with both *e) I find it easy to understand English spoken outside the class* and *f) I find it easy to speak English outside the class*, and the difference between the two sets of ratings was not statistically significant ($Z=-.206$, p=.837).

Therefore, more than 70% of the students reported finding it easy to understand teachers in class and to understand discussion in class and talk in class, while less than half of them found it easy to ask questions in class and to understand or speak English outside the class.

567

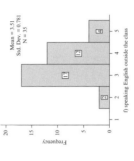

Figure 9.15 e) easy to understand English spoken outside the class

Mean = 3.49
Std. Dev. = 0.742
N = 35

e) understand English outside the class

Figure 9.16 f) easy to speak English outside the class

Mean = 3.51
Std. Dev. = 0.781
N = 35

f) speaking English outside the class

Figure 9.13 c) easy to understand discussion in class

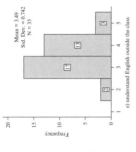

Mean = 3.94
Std. Dev. = 0.802
N = 35

c) understand discussion

Figure 9.14 d) easy to talk in class

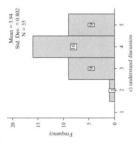

Mean = 3.91
Std. Dev. = 0.781
N = 35

d) talk in class

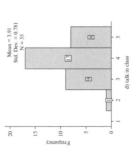

Furthermore, a Friedman test (non-parametric alternative to one-way repeated ANOVA) showed that, among three questions on listening and speaking activities respectively, there were statistically significant differences for both listening (χ^2=10.051, p=.007) and speaking activities (χ^2=10.174, p=.006). As illustrated in Figures 9.17 and 9.18 below, the significant difference among listening activities occurred between a) understanding teachers in class and e) understanding English spoken outside the class (Z=−2.826, p=.005) and between c) understanding discussion in class and e) understanding English spoken outside the class (Z=−2.683, p=.007). The significant difference among speaking activities occurred between

b) asking questions in class and d) talking in class (Z=−2.500, p=.012), and between d) talking in class and f) speaking English outside the class (Z=−2.401, p=.016).

For the CEFR self-assessment grid, two grids were chosen: listening and spoken interaction ability (Council of Europe 2001:27). As illustrated in Figures 9.19 and 9.20 below, students' self-assessments varied from A1 to C2, and their average listening ability assessment was between B1 and B2 (mean: 3.76, SD: 1.30) and their average spoken interaction ability assessment was at B2 level (mean: 4.00, SD: 1.52).

The results from the two CEFR self-assessment grids are in accordance

Figure 9.20 CEFR spoken interaction

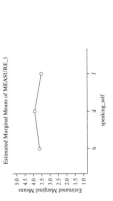

with those from the six questions presented above, since **B1** in listening is the level where students 'can understand the main points of clear standard speech on familiar matters regularly encountered in work, school, leisure, etc.' and B2 is the level where they 'can understand extended speech and lectures and follow even complex lines of argument provided the topic is reasonably familiar'. For spoken interaction, students at B2 'can interact with a degree of fluency and spontaneity that makes regular interaction with native speakers quite possible' and 'can take an active part in discussion in familiar contexts, accounting for and sustaining my views' (Council of Europe 2001: 27). Therefore, considering most UK universities set the admission cut-off point of English proficiency around B2 and C1, it seems that these participating students are typical students at pre-sessional courses (who would also be preparing for IELTS) in terms of their capacity in coping with their everyday English listening and speaking activities.

Figure 9.17 Self-assessment on three listening activities

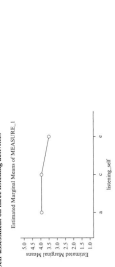

Figure 9.18 Self-assessment on three speaking activities

Figure 9.19 CEFR listening (N=29) (N=28)

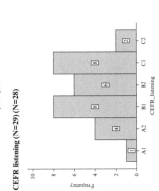

Appendix 9.2
Test takers' Listening and Speaking scores and self-assessment ratings

ID	Listening score	Speaking score (fluency & coherence)		Speaking score (lexical resources)		Speaking score (grammatical range & accuracy)		Speaking score (pronunciation)		Self-assessment (everyday activities)						Self-assessment (CEFR)	
		Part 2	Part 3	Part 2	Part 3	Part 2	Part 3	Part 2	Part 3	a	b	c	d	e	f	Listening	Spoken interaction
S01	9	4.65	4.32	4.83	4.00	4.80	4.00	4.07	4.55	5	4	4	5	4	4	C1	C1
S02	12	5.05	5.00	4.87	5.00	4.12	5.00	4.92	5.13	3	3	3	3	3	3	B2	B2
S03	8	4.65	4.32	4.83	4.43	4.07	4.43	4.94	5.03								
S04	24	4.82	5.00	4.87	5.44	4.12	5.44	4.06	4.74	4	3	4	4	4	3	B1	B1
S05	27	6.65	5.99	6.06	5.96	6.84	5.96	6.97	6.07	5	5	5	5	4	4	B2	B2
S06	26	6.30	6.00	6.08	5.97	6.21	5.97	5.36	4.74	4	4	5	4	3	4	B1	B1
S07	10	5.05	3.79	4.87	4.01	4.92	4.01	5.36	4.04	4	3	4	2	2	3		
S08	6	4.65	5.00	4.83	5.71	4.07	5.71	4.07	4.47	2	2	3	3	3	3	C1	
S09	11	3.82	3.79	3.35	3.03	4.12	3.03	4.06	4.04	2	3	2	3	3	3		
S10	26	7.64	8.00	7.85	8.00	7.76	8.00	7.89	8.41	5	5	5	5	5	5	C2	C2
S11	10	4.04	3.79	4.04	4.01	4.12	4.01	3.88	3.66	4	3	3	4	4	3		
S12	8	4.02	3.43	4.03	4.01	3.76	4.01	3.89	4.47	4	4	4	5	3	3	C1	C2

ID	No.																
S13	24	6.30	7.00	5.86	5.98	6.66	5.98	6.95	6.97	5	5	5	5	5	5	C2	C2
S14	12	5.02	5.00	4.03	4.02	4.80	4.02	4.94	4.91	3	4	4	3	4	5	B2	C2
S15	19	4.82	4.03	5.15	4.83	5.47	4.83	5.99	5.00	4	4	3	4	4	3	A2	A2
S16	6	5.62	5.15	5.11	5.00	5.30	5.00	6.01	4.91	3	4	4	4	3	3	A1	A1
S17	3	4.82	2.00	4.87	2.85	4.92	2.85	4.92	3.49	4	3	4	3	4	4	A2	A1
S18	5	3.66	3.00	4.03	3.06	4.07	3.06	4.07	3.06	4	4	4	4	4	4	B2	B2
S19	23	3.58	4.47	3.81	4.82	4.02	4.82	3.33	4.00	2	3	4	4	4	4	C1	C1
S20	17	5.74	5.47	5.84	5.00	5.17	5.00	4.86	4.49	5	4	5	5	5	5	C1	C2
S21	10	5.52	4.47	4.81	4.82	4.54	4.82	4.24	4.91	4	5	4	4	3	4	B2	C2
S22	18	5.74	4.81	5.84	5.00	4.67	5.00	4.86	5.00	3	3	3	3	3	3	A2	B2
S23	3	4.58	4.47	5.80	4.02	4.54	4.02	3.99	4.30	3	3	4	4	2	3	B1	B1
S24	21	4.77	4.81	4.86	5.83	4.67	5.83	4.22	5.00	5	3	5	5	4	5	B1	B1
S25	11	5.00	4.47	4.47	4.82	4.41	4.82	5.09	4.30	5	3	3	5	5	3		
S26	4	4.75	3.60	4.55	3.85	4.54	3.85	4.62	4.49	4	4	3	4	3	4	B1	C2
S27	6	4.02	4.03	4.00	3.85	4.02	3.85	4.62	5.00	4	3	4	3	3	3	C1	
S28	3	5.00	4.47	4.47	4.02	4.41	4.02	4.65	4.00	3	3	3	4	3	4	B2	B2
S29	10	4.55	5.00	4.47	4.02	4.41	4.02	3.66	4.00	4	3	5	3	4	3	B1	B2
S30	5	4.02	4.03	3.62	3.85	4.02	3.85	4.62	4.49	3	4	3	4	3	4	C1	C1
S31	15	5.62	5.00	5.82	5.00	5.30	5.00	5.39	4.30	5	5	4	4	5	4	C1	B1
S32	9	4.82	4.81	4.87	4.83	4.92	4.83	4.92	5.00	4	4	4	5	4	3	A2	B1
S33	14	6.10	5.15	5.82	5.97	5.98	5.97	6.01	6.78	5	4	5	5	4	4	B1	B1
S34	7	4.82	5.00	4.87	5.00	4.12	5.00	4.06	4.01	4	3	4	4	3	3	B1	B1
S35	9	5.02	5.00	4.83	4.02	4.80	4.02	5.39	4.91	4	3	3	3	3	3	C1	C2
S36	2	5.05	5.00	4.04	4.83	4.12	4.83	5.36	5.00	3	4	4	4	4	4	B1	B1

Appendix 9.3
Transcription notation

(based on Atkinson and Heritage 1984, Hutchby and Wooffitt 1998)

Unfilled pauses or gaps	Periods of silence; micro-pauses (less than 0.2 seconds) are shown as (.); longer pauses appear as a time within parentheses.
Colon (:)	A lengthened sound or syllable; more colons prolong the stretch
Dash (-)	A cut off
.hhh	Inhalation
hhh	Exhalation
hah, huh, heh	Laughter
(h)	Breathiness within a word
Punctuation	Intonation rather than clausal structure; a full stop (.) is falling intonation, a question mark (?) is rising intonation, a comma (,) is continuing intonation
Equal sign (=)	A latched utterance
Open bracket ([)	Beginning of overlapping utterances
Percent signs (% %)	Quiet talk
Empty parentheses ( )	Words within parentheses are doubtful or uncertain
Double parentheses (( ))	Non-vocal action, details of scene
Arrows (><)	The talk speeds up
Arrows (<>)	The talk slows down
Underlining	A word or sound is emphasised
Arrow (→)	A feature of interest to the analyst

Appendix 9.4
Examples of examiners' comments

[S30, who encountered Type a) communication problem]

Fluency and Coherence

- Part 2: slow speech, noticeable pauses, self correction (Examiner A, Band 4); noticeable pauses but acceptable range of linkers (Examiner C, Band 4)
- Part 3: slow with noticeable pauses (Examiner C, Band 4), speaks slowly, frequently hesitates, repeats information and does not use enough connectors to signal logical relationships between ideas (Examiner D, Band 4)

Lexical Resource

- Part 2: conveys basic meaning, rarely attempts paraphrase (Examiner A, Band 4); has insufficient vocabulary for the topic (Examiner C, Band 3)
- Part 3: can only convey basic meaning (Examiner C, Band 4); uses only simple vocabulary to convey personal information (Examiner D, Band 3)

Grammatical Range and Accuracy

- Part 2: basic forms, some correct simple sentences, subordinate clauses rare (Examiner A, Band 4); relies mostly on present tense and basic sentence forms (Examiner C, Band 4)
- Part 3: produces basic sentence forms, over reliance on present tense (Examiner C, Band 4); produces mainly basic sentence forms ('sometimes I will go to a friend at home', 'I eat some food and best wishes for my friend', 'in China too many course need the study') (Examiner D, Band 4)

Pronunciation

- Part 2: generally understood throughout, limited range of pronunciation features (Examiner A, Band 5); mispronunciation can cause difficulty (Examiner C, Band 4)
- Part 3: limited range of pronunciation (Examiner C, Band 4); the candidate uses a limited range of pronunciation features but the level of difficulty caused to a listener is not high enough for Band 4 (Examiner D, Band 5)

[S07, who encountered [Type b] communication problem]

Fluency and Coherence

- Part 2: some hesitation but does use connector 'cos' (Examiner C, Band 5); a strong 5, maintains flow of speech and uses simple connectives effectively (Examiner D, Band 5)
- Part 3: cannot speak without noticeable pauses, little linking (Examiner A, Band 4); short responses, frequently unable to convey basic meaning (Examiner C, Band 3)

Lexical Resource

- Part 2: basic vocabulary to convey meaning (Examiner C, Band 4); uses vocabulary with limited flexibility and makes word form errors ('I like to make some friends from foreign') (Examiner D, Band 5)
- Part 3: could only convey basic meaning on unfamiliar topics (Examiner A, Band 4); can only convey basic meaning (Examiner C, Band 4)

Grammatical Range and Accuracy

- Part 2: simple sentences predominate, occasionally past tense but unable to use present perfect (Examiner C, Band 4); uses a limited range of more complex structures; simple structures are not sufficiently well-controlled for accuracy (Examiner D, Band 5)
- Part 3: subordinate structures rare – one 'if' clause (Examiner A, Band 4); subordinate clauses rare, some simple sentences correct (Examiner C, Band 4)

Pronunciation

- Part 2: a little robotic but some evidence of chunking (Examiner C, Band 5); limited control over pronunciation features, appears to confuse pleasure and price at one point (Examiner D, Band 5)
- Part 3: limited range, mispronunciation causes difficulty (Examiner A, Band 4); patches that are unclear (Examiner C, Band 4)

[S17, who encountered [Type c) and d)] communication problems]

Fluency and Coherence

- Part 2: was slow speech to keep going (Examiner C, Band 5); maintains flow of speech but does not use connectors to organise the response (Examiner D, Band 4)
- Part 3: long pauses, frequently unable to convey basic message, little communication possible (Examiner C, Band 2); the candidate speaks with very long pauses (Examiner D, Band 2)

Lexical Resource

- Part 2: limited flexibility (Examiner C, Band 5); limited resource, covering familiar topics only. Word choice error ('I think the party is very well') (Examiner D, Band 4)
- Part 3: has insufficient vocabulary, very little production, just repetition of test questions (Examiner C, Band 2); uses simple vocabulary to convey personal information (Examiner D, Band 3)

Grammatical Range and Accuracy

- Part 2: basic forms are correct (reasonably accurate) (Examiner C, Band 5); frequent errors occur in simple structures; unable to produce accurate simple sentences (Examiner D, Band 4)
- Part 3: attempts basic sentence forms with little success (Examiner C, Band 3); does not succeed in producing full sentences (Examiner D, Band 2)

Pronunciation

- Part 2: some disappearing final consonants/syllables (Examiner C, Band 5); mispronounces individual phonemes and causes substantial strain for the listener (Examiner D, Band 4)
- Part 3: limited range (Examiner C, Band 4); the language produced and the rate of speech does not allow the candidate to display sufficient control over pronunciation features (Examiner D, Band 3)

10 Impact of the joint-funded research studies on the IELTS Listening test

Lynda Taylor
Consultant to Cambridge ESOL

The four funded research studies reported in Part 2 of this volume focused primarily on the IELTS Listening test and were conducted between 2005 and 2011 (under Rounds 11–15 of the IELTS Joint-funded Research Program). The studies provided the IELTS partners with valuable insights into the construct validity of the Listening test, as well as into the nature of test takers' listening performance and the relationship between test takers' listening and speaking skills. Research findings offered useful evidence in support of claims about test usefulness, while at the same time helping to highlight specific aspects needing closer review and possible future revision. In combination with outcomes from other commissioned studies and internal validation investigations, they feed into the ongoing process of IELTS Listening test development and validation. The specific contribution of each of the four studies is reviewed and evaluated in the sections that follow.

Chapter 6: The cognitive validity of the lecture-based question in the IELTS Listening paper (Field)

John Field investigated the cognitive validity of one part of the IELTS Listening test (Part 4) by comparing the performance and experience of subjects when completing a sample IELTS task with their performance and experience when doing a similar task that closely replicated the demands of an actual academic context but was not constrained by the conditions of test administration. Field drew on the theoretical framework for test validation offered by Weir (2005), in particular the cognitive validity component of Weir's socio-cognitive framework, to analyse and evaluate the extent to which the cognitive demands of a test task reflect those of the target study context. This is a critical issue in the design of language proficiency tests touching directly upon matters of construct validity and requiring *a priori* as well as *a posteriori* evidence.

Using verbal report methodology within a case study approach, Field gathered process data from 29 second language users preparing for university entrance. Two IELTS Listening tasks were used – one conducted under test conditions and the other under non-test conditions. Following each task, subjects were invited to describe and reflect on their experience of completing the test task answers, and of extracting information and building meaning from the non-test listening task. The process data was then examined in relation to established models of listening drawn from cognitive psychology and underpinned by empirical evidence.

The findings from Field's study provide a number of useful insights into the ways candidates responded to the two types of test method used in the experimental design – gap-filling and multiple choice; both methods are employed in IELTS Listening Part 4. The study's findings shed light on how far the cognitive processes adopted resemble those that listeners would employ in a real-life lecture-listening situation. Clear use of test-wise strategies was evident, though these often varied from one participant to another, perhaps due to variation in training for the test. In some cases, however, it was questionable whether the training strategies adopted actually aided understanding, or whether they encouraged an over-dependence on the content and layout of the written text on the answer sheet.

Field comments on differences between the listening input-task sheet relationship in the test, and the relationship of a university lecture to an accompanying handout or set of PowerPoint slides. He suggests that these differences may result in differential cognitive processing across the two conditions, thus raising issues for cognitive validity claims. A second observation concerns the relative shallowness or depth of processing across the test and non-test conditions respectively. A third observation highlights the possible role of cognitive complexity and/or cognitive load imposed by the test tasks due to test conditions such as time constraints and correct spelling requirements.

Field sensibly acknowledges that it is of course impossible for any test to replicate all the processes that a real-life listening event demands, and that test producers need to balance a range of considerations, including factors such as administrative efficiency and marker reliability in large-scale proficiency assessment. Nevertheless, his study usefully highlights ways in which a test format may risk being more cognitively demanding than an actual lecture-listening task, or may fail to embrace certain aspects of the construct of interest (e.g. the need to build a macro-comprehension structure). These are issues that test designers constantly grapple with when seeking to operationalise the assessment of the construct in an achievable and sustainable way. There is undoubtedly scope for further research into appropriate Listening test methods that limit the listener's tendency to focus heavily at the word level, or to become over-dependent on the written structure of the task sheet. Field's practical suggestions for re-engineering listening tasks to resolve these issues are useful and relevant for test designers, and can certainly inform the test writing process. However, they are rather more difficult to operationalise successfully in large-scale contexts than in smaller scale testing enterprises.

His additional discussion and recommendations about playing listening texts more than once is convincing in some respects but this too is difficult to implement in the context of a test like IELTS, where once-only listening has been the default since the earliest days of ELTS in the 1980s. To some degree the once-only listening approach reflects the heritage of ELTS/IELTS with its roots in the needs analysis and ESP movement of the 1970s where authenticity was a strong design feature.

Moving beyond the purely ecological argument, however, it is important to realise once-only listening also permits a larger number of texts and types of listening activity to be sampled within the test administration time available, and this in turn allows for a larger number of test items and more response data to be gathered. Sampling and test length, in terms of range and number of items, are understandably constrained if all the listening input has to be repeated. Breadth of content sampling and quantity of response data are important considerations for IELTS because the test reports a modular Listening band score as well as an overall band score, and since IELTS test scores are used in high-stakes decision-making they need to be as valid and reliable as possible.

Furthermore, it is important to note that IELTS is not a level-based language test (like the *First Certificate in English* or the *Certificate of Proficiency in English*) but instead measures across a fairly broad proficiency continuum. The 40 test items in the IELTS Listening module are thus written with the aim of ranging and discriminating across a relatively wide range of proficiency levels. Pretesting and calibration are used to confirm the statistical characteristics of the test items and to determine those selected for the test. Double play of each listening passage would require a reduction in the number of test items which would in turn impact on test sampling and reliability. An alternative would be to double the length of the Listening test but this too would entail significant practical difficulties and risk increasing the fatigue effect for test takers.

Field's point about the multi-modal nature of lecture-listening is well taken and it may well be that in a future incarnation the IELTS Listening test will be able to benefit from enhanced visual as well as auditory input through computer- or internet-based technology. Technological solutions and innovations may also help to address some of the test method issues highlighted by Field in his study, though test method effects are unlikely to be mitigated entirely, however the test is delivered. There are potential logistical problems in ensuring that all test takers have equal access to the accompanying visual information.

In the final sections of his report, Field is realistic about the limitations and disadvantages of retrospective verbal report methodology, despite the rich insights it can bring. He identifies the potential for further replication studies exploring variables in greater depth, e.g. the impact on cognitive processes of L1, cultural/educational background, IELTS preparation, etc. Field's study is a first step in developing our current understanding of the cognitive processing that takes place in the IELTS Listening test and it provides the IELTS test producers with some useful evidence to support preliminary claims about the cognitive validity of the test.

Chapter 7: The use of tactics and strategies by Chinese students in the Listening component of IELTS (Badger and Yan)

Richard Badger and **Xiaobiao Yan**'s study on the IELTS Listening test echoes some of the themes previously traced in Field's study. Like Field, Badger and Yan are also interested in issues of situational and interactional authenticity in second language listening assessment. The main focus of their study was a comparative analysis of the strategies used in an IELTS Listening test by L1 users of English and by Chinese learners of English.

Given the rapid growth in recent years in the take-up of IELTS within China and among Chinese L1 speakers in other parts of the world, the IELTS partners regard research conducted among Chinese test takers as an important strand within the overall research agenda for the IELTS test. This study therefore adds to insights gained from earlier studies among Chinese test takers and test users undertaken by Mayor, Hewings, North, Swann and Coffin (2007), Banerjee, Franceschina and Smith (2007), and Coleman, Starfield and Hagan (2003). It also complements a study by Wray and Pegg (2009) which examined the performance of Chinese test takers in the IELTS Academic Writing test. When any test is taken by major stakeholder groups, it is important to explore perceptions of and performance in the test and to develop awareness of the potential for test bias arising from nationality, L1, socio-educational, cultural or other factors. One distinct advantage of the IELTS Joint-funded Research Program is that it can encourage this sort of research to be conducted in the local context by those who are well qualified and well positioned to undertake studies of this kind, not least because they have a sound understanding of the cross-linguistic or cross-cultural issues involved, and because they have direct access to the participants and resources needed.

Badger and Yan gave a sample IELTS Listening test to 24 native speakers of Chinese, 12 pre-undergraduate and 12 pre-postgraduate, as well as to eight English L1 speakers at undergraduate, master's and doctoral levels. They selected a think-aloud protocol methodology to gather data on strategy use. A coding framework, adopting a grounded approach, was then used to analyse the protocol transcript data into categories of cognitive and meta-cognitive strategies, each with their own sub-strategies and tactics. Subsequent statistical analyses identified no significant differences in terms of strategy, and only small differences in some of the sub-strategies and tactics used, suggesting that the strategies and tactics adopted by the Chinese and English speakers in the IELTS Listening test tasks were broadly similar in nature. This finding, admittedly based upon a relatively small sample, provides limited but encouraging support for claims about the construct validity of the Listening test in terms of the match between the processing engaged in by native/expert users and by second language users in the test.

However, Badger and Yan also noted that the range of tactics reported by participants differed somewhat from those that are typically reported in a non-examination context. In light of this, the researchers raise issues about the nature of the task materials used in the Listening test, specifically the task rubric (i.e. the instructions) and the response format, both of which are presented in written form. Badger and Yan echo Field's concern about the potential impact on test taker cognitive processing when using a test method or response format that involves some reading and writing in what is primarily intended as a test of listening ability. As discussed above, these are challenging questions for the test designer who must design a test method that will faithfully and accurately measure the ability construct of interest (i.e. listening), ideally without confounding it with other ability traits (i.e. reading and writing). The problem of mitigating the potential interference of the test method is not easily resolved without incurring other problems, such as potential threats to test reliability. In reality, of course, any test will to some degree be a pragmatic compromise, involving the balancing up of a number of competing considerations and constraints. Not surprisingly, perhaps, testing is sometimes described as 'the art of the possible'!

Like Field, Badger and Yan also comment on the multi-modal nature of listening activities in contemporary academic education and they recommend the inclusion of other modalities in a Listening test such as still or moving visual images. Advances in computer-based testing technology mean that academic Listening tests sometimes do now include visual input such as a still photo or short video clip, on the grounds that it offers a more authentic experience and provides relevant support, i.e. it facilitates listening comprehension. The use of video in Listening tests remains controversial, however, as it can risk introducing construct-irrelevant aspects (see Taylor and Geranpayeh 2011).

Contemporary academic study typically requires students to manipulate information from multiple sources (print and multimedia) and real-life lecture listening today is routinely multi-modal in nature. Though there may be a strong ecological argument in favour of using modern technology in our tests to simulate real-life lecture listening, there are obvious constraints on how far this reality can be achieved. One the one hand, visual cues (e.g. facial expression, gesture and PowerPoint slides) might be seen as supplying information not present in an audio recording. On the other hand, the requirement to heed those cues and also to note-take might be seen as imposing a heavier cognitive load than a straightforward audio test. As computer- and web-delivered testing becomes more widely available for IELTS, consideration can be given to incorporating a multi-modal approach into the test's design, though attempts to replicate real-life language use in any test will always need to be balanced against other essential qualities of the test.

The researchers conclude with some interesting observations on the use of L1 English speakers as a source of insight and evidence for validating a test of second language ability. They comment on the perception among their native/ expert user group that IELTS Listening test tasks possess some sort of intrinsic task status in their own right, rather than being tasks derived from the target language use context to which the test relates. This raises an interesting question over the perceived and actual relationship of any language test to the world beyond itself. Perhaps it challenges the traditional view in language testing over how far tests and test tasks can be considered as instances of 'real life' language use in their own right compared to existing as some sort of proxy for real-life situations. Given the increasingly central role played by testing and assessment in education and society today, including the way in which technology is allowing testing and assessment to be dynamically embedded within day-to-day human activities, we might speculate whether the traditional distinction between the 'artificial' world of a language test and the 'authentic' world of real-life language use needs re-conceptualising. The recent growth of interest in alternative paradigms such as 'dynamic assessment' and 'assessment for learning' are perhaps a step in this direction.

Chapter 8: Predictive validity of the IELTS Listening test as an indicator of student coping ability in English-medium undergraduate courses in Spain (Breeze and Miller)

Ruth Breeze and **Paul Miller**'s study investigates the issue of student listening skills against the wider background of a huge expansion over the past decade in English-taught programmes at European universities. The researchers explain how, in many of these universities, students are required to take English language tests before admission or in the first year to determine whether or not their level of English is sufficient for them to succeed on their chosen course, or to plan provision for language back-up during their studies. Although IELTS has long been used as a language proficiency measure for entry to higher education in English-speaking countries such as the UK, Australia and New Zealand, the authors sensibly ask how far it is appropriate to transfer the use of IELTS and the recommended cut-off scores into other European countries where the social and educational contexts may be rather different, i.e. students are not facing an 'immersion' situation and exposure to English outside their studies may well be limited in nature. They also question the potentially different balance of language skills needed in the universities of continental Europe, where good listening comprehension skills may be a high priority due to the volume of lectures attended, while extensive reading and writing may be less of a priority. Thus the aim of the study was to explore the predictive validity of the IELTS Listening test as an entry test for students enrolled on three different bilingual degree programmes in which English is used at a large Spanish university, and to propose appropriate cut-off scores for each course. Specific research questions sought to identify the minimum IELTS Listening module band score to be recommended for admission to bilingual degree courses in Law, Medicine and Humanities, and the relationship between IELTS Listening band scores and coping ability in English-taught courses. The study builds upon a variety of other predictive validity studies conducted on IELTS over 20 years, including studies carried out under the IELTS Joint-funded Research Program (e.g. Cotton and Conrow 1998, Ingram and Bayliss 2007, Kerstjens and Nery 2000).

Over 300 students enrolled on bilingual programmes in Humanities, Law and Medicine took an IELTS Listening test at the beginning of their first semester. Breeze and Miller also developed questionnaires on student listening ability and coping skills and strategies, and administered these to their sample population at the end of the semester. They carried out qualitative interviews with a representative sample of students in each faculty and analysed the results of these to provide a detailed picture of how students deal with the challenge of taking academically demanding courses in English. Finally, statistical tests were performed to explore the relationship between students' numerical IELTS Listening scores and their final course grades, on the one hand, and their IELTS band scores and their self-report data, on the other.

The researchers detected small positive correlations between students' numerical listening scores and their final grades in the courses taught in English. Moderate to large correlations were found between the IELTS Listening band scores and self-report data obtained from the questionnaires. In parallel to this process, a modified Angoff procedure was performed with eight experienced teachers of English for academic purposes. A consensus cut-off score of 23 (out of 40) was obtained, which the researchers considered as consistent with the general practice of requiring a minimum band score of 6 at universities in English-speaking countries. Nonetheless, when the final course grades of students who had obtained 6 or more were compared with those of students who had obtained 5 or less, it was established that Listening scores less than 6 were not necessarily predictive of academic failure. The report concludes with a recommendation that the ideal cut-off score for Law, Medicine and Humanities should be Band 6, but that this may not prove feasible under current circumstances. Instead, the researchers suggest that students with band scores below 6 should be informed that the course will require them to invest more time than for an equivalent course in their native language, and that they should be offered appropriate language support to assist with this.

Breeze and Miller's research provides us with some useful insights into the relationships between performance on the IELTS Listening component, student self-assessments and likely academic success within a given context. It also highlights the importance of acknowledging the likely variation between students studying in full-immersion, English-medium universities within English-speaking countries as compared with students following bilingual courses with an English-medium element in other countries, especially where such courses are typically taught through formal lectures requiring good listening skills along with the ability to engage in spoken (as opposed to written) examinations on the course content. From a methodological perspective, Breeze and Miller also point to the complexities involved in identifying and selecting an appropriate measure of academic performance in a context such as theirs, since the contribution of English listening proficiency to subsequent academic outcomes is also likely to be affected by the nature of the surrounding educational ecology.

Their study is also interesting in that it includes students with a wide range of band scores, including those at bands lower than IELTS Band 6 which is sometimes used as a cut-off score for university admissions. With many more bilingual and English-medium higher education courses on offer throughout continental Europe and elsewhere, we surely need to understand more about the level of English language support which both national and international students are likely to need in order to achieve their academic goals, particularly those who enter with lower levels of English language proficiency. The study's findings regarding students' perceptions of their own coping abilities and their need for a variety of additional support outside the course are especially insightful in this regard.

Breeze and Miller's study provides further empirical evidence in support of the long-established view that an overall Band 6.5 in IELTS constitutes a reasonable cut-off score for admission to university studies. They reinforce the idea that below that level, students risk struggling in their studies because of their limited language proficiency and thus should be made aware in advance of the extra 'investment' they will have to make to keep up with their studies and achieve their objectives. This diagnostic function may also inform decisions about specialist ESP provision in some departments with large numbers of lower-level students.

Finally, this study points once again to the reality that a good level of English language proficiency cannot necessarily guarantee academic success, since the level of a course and the demands facing students are conditioned by a multitude of factors relating to educational background and culture, as well as language. Furthermore, we must always remember that academic outcomes are invariably shaped by a complex interaction among individual characteristics, including personality and motivation.

Chapter 9: The relationship between test takers' listening proficiency and their performance on the IELTS Speaking test (Nakatsuhara)

Although **Fumiyo Nakatsuhara**'s study does not primarily focus on the IELTS Listening test component, as was the case for the three previous studies in Part 2, it does have direct relevance for the assessment of listening ability across the IELTS test as a whole. Her research neatly highlights the extent to which the subdivision of language proficiency into separate skills, each with their own appropriately labelled test component, is to some degree a matter of convenience and practical expediency.

As a direct test of speaking, the IELTS Speaking test entails a 15-minute face-to-face interaction between an examiner and a test taker. The test format is designed to afford opportunities for the candidate to engage in both monologic and dialogic talk across three different phases and task types. Parts 1 and 3 are more interactive, involving question and answer and discussion, while Part 2 takes the form of a long turn in which the test taker responds to a prompt from the examiner but is then given the floor to speak at length without interruption. The interactive parts of the test inevitably require a degree of listening proficiency, and this is particularly true in Part 3 of the test, where the examiner invites the candidate to take part in a discussion about more abstract topics than those in Part 2. This study set out to investigate the relationship between test takers' listening proficiency and their performance on Part 3 (discussion) of the IELTS Speaking test, as compared with their performance on Part 2 (individual long turn). The motivation for the study was to explore the nature of any communication problems likely to be associated with test takers' listening proficiency and the way in which such problems were dealt with.

Data was collected from 36 pre-sessional course students at a UK university, who took both a Listening test (specially constructed for the study using listening passages and items from Cambridge's General English Listening practice tests for *FCE* and *CAE*) and an IELTS Speaking test followed by a short semi-structured interview session. All Speaking test sessions were both audio and video recorded. The audio-recordings were then edited to separate the students' performances on Part 2 from those on Part 3. Each recording was rated by two out of four trained IELTS examiners who also wrote down reasons for awarding their scores. Speaking test scores were analysed for any difference in difficulty between the two parts. Correlations between the Listening test scores and the Speaking test scores awarded on four analytical criteria were compared between the two parts. Conversation Analysis (CA) methodology was employed to highlight salient occurrences of communication problems related to test takers' difficulties in hearing or understanding the examiner.

Nakatsuhara's findings highlight some noticeable differences between Part 2 and Part 3 of the IELTS Speaking test in terms of the constructs they appear to measure, suggesting that the latter format, at least to some extent, measures listening-into-speaking ability. The interactional data seems to suggest that the construct underlying Part 3 is thus not a purely productive speaking ability, especially for students at Band 5.0 and below who tended to encounter greater difficulty in understanding the examiner. In one sense, this can be seen as welcome news for the test developers who specifically designed the IELTS Speaking test to elicit, through its separate parts and differing tasks, different types of talk from the candidate and thus provide a broad sample of oral communication skills for the purposes of evaluation. Furthermore, the fact that Nakatsuhara found evidence of a significantly higher level of language in Part 2 than in Part 3 might be viewed as evidence of the test developers' intention that the demands of the test should vary across the different parts and thus make it suitable for use with a broad proficiency range.

Nakatsuhara's study usefully builds on some of the earlier funded projects that closely analysed the discourse of the IELTS Speaking test (e.g. Brown 2006a, Brown 2006b, O'Sullivan and Lu 2006, Seedhouse and Egbert 2006). The outcomes of these studies have informed revisions to the IELTS interlocutor frame and examiner training programme as well as to the assessment criteria and rating scales.

In terms of the specific recommendations made at the end of this latest study, there are a number of points worthy of discussion. First of all, Nakatsuhara recommends that Parts 2 and 3 of the IELTS Speaking test should be scored separately, arguing that to award separate scores for test takers' performances on monologic and interactional tasks might provide a clearer picture of test takers' differential abilities across these different speaking modes. An associated recommendation is that different descriptors might be developed for the *Fluency and Coherence* scale in Part 2 and for the same scale in Part 3 which reflect the differing features of the construct as operationalised through the two tasks. Such a move, it is claimed, might help to ensure that differential abilities displayed across different tasks will all feed into the final score to reflect the overall construct (see O'Sullivan and Nakatsuhara 2011 for more discussion on this point). The study's observations on the location and nature of listening-related problems have the potential to inform future revisions of the rating descriptors and could also feed into elements of the examiner training programme. However, as Nakatsuhara rightly points out, there are several practical and operational matters to consider here. In the current IELTS Speaking test, the IELTS examiner assumes the role of both interlocutor/facilitator <u>and</u> examiner/rater – managing the test input, controlling the timing and awarding the scores across four separate assessment criteria, each one with a nine-point scale. Increasing the number of criteria and scales, together with the number of online decisions to be made by the rater during the test clearly increases both the cognitive and administrative burden of the IELTS examiner and risks negatively impacting on examiner behaviour. For a fuller discussion of how many scales and criteria examiners can realistically manage and how many judgements they can reliably make during a timed Speaking test, see Taylor and Galaczi (2011). These issues also have clear implications for examiner training, standardisation and monitoring. Nakatsuhara speculates on whether a non-live second marking system could be employed in the test, whereby the test taker's recoded performance could be marked using the separate scoring method. She suggests this as a cost-effective solution for generating more reliable scores without placing any additional burden on the examiners in the live tests. The IELTS partners have for some time been researching the benefits and challenges of a part-scoring approach in the IELTS Speaking test, though its implications for costs in terms of additional administration and examiner training should not be underestimated.

Interestingly, Nakatsuhara does not extend her recommendation on separate test part scores to include the reporting of these to score users, despite the potential diagnostic value which might come with such an approach. A mitigating factor against this step may be the question of whether the sample obtained in one (relatively short) test part is sufficiently rich to justify a reported subscore from which appropriate inferences can be made to the world beyond the test.

The final recommendation made in Nakatsuhara's report concerns the possibility of grading the language of the interviewer cues, i.e. using easier question prompts for test takers with low-level listening proficiency so they can follow the examiner. This would seem to avoid the weight of listening being greater than it should be but it is not straightforward to implement, especially in a test which is designed to be accessible and to function effectively across a fairly broad proficiency continuum, e.g. from Band 3/4 to Band 7/8. Carefully graded cues are already used in Parts 1 and 2 of the IELTS Speaking test for purposes of standardisation and fairness, to ensure that all lower level test takers can fully access the test tasks and optimise their performance. In Part 3, however, the prompts are specifically designed to offer the examiner greater flexibility in choosing and phrasing their questions and comments, matching them as far as possible to the level of the test taker so that each candidate has maximum opportunity to display their speaking proficiency. Despite that, it may be worth exploring further how best to grade the Part 3 cues for use with lower-level test takers and to incorporate this into the interlocutor frame and into examiner training, without necessarily reducing the level of linguistic challenge that is needed for reliably assessing the more proficient candidates.

Thus far, the potential impact of Nakatsuhara's study findings has, not surprisingly, been discussed with regard to the IELTS Speaking test. In terms of the relevance of her findings for the IELTS Listening test, perhaps there is a case for a more explicit articulation on the part of the test developers concerning how the assessment of listening ability is distributed across more than one component of the IELTS test. While the Listening component of IELTS clearly focuses on the assessment of receptive listening comprehension ability, it is the IELTS Speaking component which seems to address the more interactive dimension of listening ability, i.e. listening-into-speaking skills.

References

Banerjee, J, Franceschina, F and Smith, A M (2007) Documenting features of written language production typical at different IELTS band score levels, in McGovern, P and Walsh, S (Eds) *IELTS Research Reports, Volume 7*, Canberra: IELTS Australia and London: The British Council, 241–309.

Brown, A (2006a) Candidate discourse in the revised IELTS Speaking Test, in McGovern, P and Walsh, S (Eds) *IELTS Research Reports, Volume 6*, Canberra: IELTS Australia and London: British Council, 71–89.

Brown, A (2006b) An examination of the rating process in the revised IELTS Speaking Test, in McGovern, P and Walsh, S (Eds) *IELTS Research Reports, Volume 6*, Canberra: IELTS Australia and London: British Council, 41–69.

Coleman, D, Starfield, S and Hagan, A (2003) Stakeholder perceptions of the IELTS test in three countries, in *IELTS Research Reports, Volume 5*, Canberra: IELTS Australia Pty Limited, 156–235.

Cotton, F and Conrow, F (1998) An investigation of the predictive validity of IELTS amongst a sample of international students studying at the University of Tasmania, in Tulloh, R (Ed.), *IELTS Research Reports, Volume 1*, Canberra: ELICOS/IELTS Australia Pty Limited, 72–115.

Ingram, D and Bayliss, A (2007) IELTS as a predictor of academic language performance, in McGovern, P and Walsh, S (Eds) *IELTS Research Reports, Volume 7*, Canberra: IELTS Australia and London: British Council, 137–204.

Kerstjens, M and Nery, C (2000) Predictive validity in the IELTS test, in *IELTS Research Reports, Volume 3*, Canberra: IELTS Australia Pty Limited, 85–108.

Mayor, B, Hewings, A, North, S, Swann, J and Coffin C (2007) A linguistic analysis of Chinese and Greek L1 scripts for IELTS Academic Writing Task 2, in Taylor, L and Falvey, P (Eds) *IELTS Collected Papers: Research in Speaking and Writing Assessment,* Studies in Language Testing volume 19, Cambridge: UCLES/Cambridge University Press, 250–313.

O'Sullivan, B and Lu, Y (2006) The impact on candidate language of examiner deviation from a set interlocutor frame in the IELTS Speaking Test, in McGovern, P and Walsh, S (Eds) *IELTS Research Report Volume 6*, Canberra: British Council and IDP Australia, 91–117.

O'Sullivan, B and Nakatsuhara, F (2011) Quantifying conversational styles in group oral test discourse, in O'Sullivan, B (Ed.) *Language Testing: Theories and Practices,* London: Palgrave, 164–185.

Seedhouse, P and Egbert, M (2006) The interactional organisation of the IELTS

Speaking Test, in McGovern, P and Walsh, S (Eds) *IELTS Research Report Volume 6*, Canberra: British Council and IELTS Australia, 161–205.

Taylor, L and Galaczi, E (2011) Scoring validity, in Taylor, L (Ed.) *Examining Speaking: Research and Practice in Assessing Second Language Speaking,* Studies in Language Testing volume 30, Cambridge: UCLES/Cambridge University Press, 171–233.

Taylor, L and Geranpayeh, A (2011) Assessing listening for academic purposes:
‘ defining and operationalising the test construct, in *Journal of English for Academic Purposes* 10 (2), 89–101.

Weir, C J (2005) *Language Testing and Validation: An Evidence-Based Approach*, Basingstoke: Palgrave Macmillan.

Wray, A and Pegg, C (2009) The effect of memorised learning on the writing scores of Chinese IELTS test takers, in Thompson, P (Ed.) *IELTS Research Reports, Volume 9*, Canberra: IELTS Australia and London: The British Council, 191–216.